CRAVING
FOR
ECSTASY
AND NATURAL HIGHS

To those who seek understanding as the pathway to purpose and freedom.

—H. B. M. & S. G. S.

CRAVING
FOR
ECSTASY
AND NATURAL HIGHS
A Positive Approach to Mood Alteration

Harvey B. Milkman
Metropolitan State College of Denver

Stanley G. Sunderwirth
Indiana University-Purdue University Columbus

⑤SAGE

Los Angeles • London • New Delhi • Singapore • Washington DC

For information:

SAGE Publications, Inc.
2455 Teller Road
Thousand Oaks, California 91320
E-mail: order@sagepub.com

SAGE Publications India Pvt. Ltd.
B 1/I 1 Mohan Cooperative
  Industrial Area
Mathura Road, New Delhi 110 044
India

SAGE Publications Ltd.
1 Oliver's Yard
55 City Road
London EC1Y 1SP
United Kingdom

SAGE Publications Asia-Pacific
  Pte. Ltd.
33 Pekin Street #02-01
Far East Square
Singapore 048763

Printed in the United States of America.

Library of Congress Cataloging-in-Publication Data

Milkman, Harvey B.
Craving for ecstasy and natural highs: A positive approach to mood alteration/Harvey B. Milkman, Stanley G. Sunderwirth.
  p. cm.
Includes bibliographical references and index.
ISBN 978-1-4129-5673-4 (pbk.)
  1. Adjustment (Psychology) 2. Compulsive behavior. 3. Mood (Psychology) I. Sunderwirth, Stanley G. II. Title.

BF335.M53 2009
616.85′84—dc22   2008051983

Printed on acid-free paper.

09   10   11   12   13   10   9   8   7   6   5   4   3   2   1

Acquiring Editor:	Kassie Graves
Editorial Assistant:	Veronica Novak
Production Editor:	Sarah K. Quesenberry
Copy Editor:	Teresa Herlinger
Proofreader:	Scott Oney
Indexer:	Will Ragsdale
Typesetter:	C&M Digitals (P) Ltd.
Cover Designer:	Arup Giri
Marketing Manager:	Carmel Schrire

Contents

List of Figures _____

List of Tables _____

Prologue _____

Look to this day!

For it is life, the very life of life.

For yesterday is but a dream

And tomorrow is only a vision

But today well lived makes

every yesterday a dream of happiness

And tomorrow a vision of hope.

Look well, therefore, to this day!

Such is the salutation of the dawn.

—*Kalidasa, 3rd century* AD
Sanskrit poem

Preface _____

The explosion of Internet technology, international terrorism, and economic instability have altered the landscape of human experience. How are people coping with such dramatic change? Some are using drugs and alcohol—old standbys when times get rough. Others take refuge in a gamut of tension-relieving pursuits, including unhealthy eating, online pornography, promiscuity, gambling, or joining fundamentalist cults. Some simply live out their days in quiet desperation.

This book is designed to provide insight into how ordinary people, from all walks of life, somehow fall off track and lose themselves in a web of counterfeit pleasures. Almost everyone has experienced cravings or urges that he or she couldn't or wouldn't control. If we are not personally affected, someone that we deeply care about is entrenched in a cycle of unhealthy mood control. Many of us have watched the lives of loved ones unravel to the point of utter despair, or even death. Our aim is to provide readers with the understandings, skills, and attitudes to take a positive approach to mood alteration and the pursuit of pleasure. Through understanding the fundamental principles of mood alteration, readers will not only improve their capacity to manage stress and live more fully; they can also serve as strong allies to those who would benefit from an educated perspective.

Craving for Ecstasy and Natural Highs: A Positive Approach to Mood Alteration is aimed at all those who seek science-based answers to two basic questions: (1) How is the mind so easily corrupted by unhealthy pleasures? and (2) How can we take charge, to increase the likelihood of lasting happiness and fulfillment? Our approach brings together state-of-the-art theory and research from brain science, human development, and the new and exciting field of positive psychology. We hope to present a cogent picture of how to orchestrate positive feeling states, conducive to improved physical and mental well-being.

After exploring biological, psychological, and social pathways to pleasure, need gratification, and dependence—on food, sex, drugs, the Internet, gambling . . . or whatever—readers discover healthy means for feeling good (i.e., natural highs), favorable to achieving happiness throughout the life span. The following discussion outlines our systematic examination of these topics.

The Plan of This Book

Section I. The Universal Desire to Feel Good

Mood alteration is mediated by the human capacity to alter consciousness via self-induced changes in brain chemistry. Throughout time, and across place and culture, people have developed ways to relieve suffering and to enhance pleasure by either ingesting drugs or having experiences that change their perceptions and moods (e.g., fasting, stimulus isolation, religious ceremonies). The need for intimacy is both the source of resilience and comfort and the wellspring of desperate, pleasure-seeking pursuits. Unsatisfied needs for safety and belonging (i.e., to feel nurtured and protected) result in over-attachment to specific objects or activities (e.g., drugs, sex, food). These provide "false refuge" from loneliness, anxiety, and fear. Addiction results from failed attempts to achieve extended ecstasy (extreme and prolonged pleasure) from experiences that are, by their very nature, impermanent and short-lived.

In *Chapter 1, Addiction to Experience,* the pursuit of pleasure is associated with three primary states of being: arousal, satiation, and fantasy—the beacons of human compulsion. Within each domain, we discover specific means to manage stress through self-induced changes in the chemistry of our brain (e.g., taking risks, using sedative drugs, seeking magical solutions to real problems). Humans alter their brain chemistry using means that are in accord with their genetic template and learned patterns for inducing pleasure. These include, but are not limited to, alcohol, electronic media, sex, gambling, and eating. Certain personality characteristics such as sensation seeking and rebelliousness are favorable to addictive styles of coping. A multidisciplinary (bio/psycho/social) model is used to explain how hedonic dependencies (addictions) first gain a foothold within the personality, later becoming firmly ingrained as repetitive problem behaviors.

Chapter 2, Pleasure and the Brain, describes the brain as designed to manage emotions through an ebb and flow of neurochemical reactions. Psychoactive drugs and certain behaviors have powerful effects on the brain's reward centers, which have evolved to enable survival. This chapter lays the groundwork for understanding how dopamine in the nucleus accumbens is the common neurochemical factor that unites all pleasure-seeking actions. The *reward cascade* is presented as a unified model to explain how a panoply of activities—as different as automobile racing and gorging yourself on chocolate pie—can trigger a common, intense, and highly pleasurable biochemical response within the limbic system of the brain.

Section II. Finding Relief and Letting Go

This section examines the neurochemical and psychosocial similarities between a range of stress-dampening activities, including excessive drinking, unhealthy eating, smoking cigarettes, and injecting heroin. In *Chapter 3, Hey, What's in This Stuff, Anyway?* the question of how alcohol can trigger addiction is followed by a discussion of possible health benefits (cardiovascular) and potential risks (cancer) from moderate drinking. *Chapter 4, The Great Psychiatric Tavern,* examines the barroom setting metaphorically, whereby a host of psychological and social needs are managed by a surrogate "mental health treatment" team. *Chapter 5, Self-Medication,* discusses how a variety of licit and illicit psychoactive chemicals—including inhalants, stimulants, cigarettes, and heroin—are used to "self-medicate." Nicotine is examined as the world's most prolific antidepressant. The chapter goes on to discuss how oftentimes women who become alcohol or drug dependent use these substances in an attempt to control psychological pain. The chapter goes on to examine how self-medication is a useful model to explain the actions of individuals who court street drugs or illegally obtained pharmaceuticals. *Chapter 6, Eating for a Change,* analyzes how food may serve as a drug to alter mood.

Section III. The Thrill of Excitement and Risk

This section on the allure of sensation and excitement begins with three examples of thrill-seeking behavior: having sex on an airplane, base-jumping from a skyscraper, and gambling at the expense of job and family security. As disparate as these actions appear, they share similar biological and psychological threads. In *Chapter 7, Stress Hormone Highs,* we describe neurochemical mechanisms common to the array of thrill-seeing activities. *Chapter 8, Rock Around the Clock,* presents an interdisciplinary analysis of the wild stimulation produced by methamphetamine and cocaine, and how "club drugs" have become part of a fast-paced, roller-coaster scene that combines extreme brain stimulation with intense human contact.

Section IV. Mental Excursions

The purpose of this section is to explore the gift of fantasy as an essential means for experiencing pleasure, deriving meaning, and enhancing survival. The development of our personality, including how we view ourselves in relation to others and the outside world, is to a great extent determined by fantasy images and imaginative thought. Exploration of the child's use of fantasy in fairy tales and storybooks sets the stage for understanding the adaptive function of imagination. Religion and myth play similar roles in providing guidelines for ethical and responsible living within a context of family, community, and culture. The function of dreams is explored in terms of enhancing one's capacity to solve problems and to reduce stress. Each of the three chapters of this section is predicated on the adaptive, survival nature of fantasy, as it is thereby endowed with high potential for pleasure and abuse.

Chapter 9, Virtual Reality and Electronic Bogeymen, focuses on the emergence of virtual reality as an important element of the media age. Synthetic online worlds such as *World of Warcraft* are examined in terms of how players escape into imagination to combat their enemies. The virtual world *Second Life* is discussed as an "engine of creativity" where residents own the intellectual property inherent in their creations. *Chapter 10, Fantasy and the Drug Experience,* examines how certain drugs, particularly the hallucinogens, may be used to activate the imagination, and to create alternative states of awareness, for better or worse. *Chapter 11, Compelled by Fantasy,* explores how the boundaries between fantasy and reality may become blurred and cross over into destructive action. Born from intense psychological need, destructive fantasy fuels a host of compulsive problem behaviors ranging from wanton sexual acts to terrorism on a world scale. Fanaticism in belief and behavior is examined as a primary human response to unfulfilled psychological need. Variations of the widespread apocalyptic fantasy (world destruction followed by heaven on earth) are examined as misguided and highly dangerous manifestations of the basic human capacity for wish-fulfilling fantasy.

Section V. Craving for Intimacy

Social connectedness is vital to physical and mental health. Inadequate bonding with other human beings affects blood pressure, the incidence of heart disease, and the immune system. It has also been shown that quality time spent in meaningful relationships is a factor that enhances the brain's healing process, which leads to a greater life expectancy. This section explores the basic struggle for human relatedness, which too often morphs into complex patterns of compulsive problem behaviors. At some level, craving for intimacy is at the core of our reliance on the counterfeit pleasures evoked by drugs, promiscuity, ideological fanaticism, and other forms of unhealthy attachment.

Chapter 12, Love or Addiction? examines the agony and ecstasy of romance. By nature, we become impassioned by elements that create or sustain life. But all too often the delicate process goes awry. The nightmare of tormenting love is a miscarriage of our natural attraction toward people who evoke feelings of safety and pleasure. The psychology of love is explored in terms of a dynamic interplay of arousal, satiation, and fantasy. Underlying neurochemical processes are explained in terms of how sexual contact triggers brain chemicals that enhance feelings of closeness and decrease the perception of stress. Romantic attachment also produces a surge in excitatory neurotransmission resulting in feelings of optimism, increased energy, and euphoria. The popular club drug *Ecstasy* is examined as a form of "synthetic love," whereby advocates claim to experience a 2- to 4-hour high that dissolves anxiety, makes people less defensive, enhances communication and insight, and leaves people more emotionally open.

Chapter 13, Marijuana—Reefer Madness Revisited, discusses the disconnect between health science and popular culture with respect to marijuana, the most widely used illicit drug in the United States. The user's experiences of enhanced intimacy and heightened relaxation alongside pleasurable cognitive and perceptual shifts are alluring aspects of cannabis. However, tidal social forces (e.g., popular music, movies, and concerts) constitute even more powerful determinants of contemporary pot culture. Given all the media propaganda for the "pot scene" and testimonials from the drug users themselves, why would anyone *not* want to use marijuana? Potential adverse health effects are summarized, including short-term cognitive impairment, panic attacks, withdrawal symptoms, negative effects on the immune system, respiratory disease, and the possibility of increased risk for psychosis.

Chapter 14, Romantic Sex Fantasy, examines the monumental demand for novel, no-strings-attached sexual stimulation. Nearly every major city in the free world has its share of erotic venues where men and women interact with alcohol and fantasy lovers. According to Schlosser (2004), Americans spend $8 to $10 billion per year on adult entertainment (p. 113) with about 2,300 strip clubs nationwide (p. 284). The euphemistic "Gentlemen's Club" is by far the most prevalent type of sex bar facility. Needs for sensation seeking, sexual arousal, and intimacy are routinely handled by a cadre of fantasy lovers. "Lap dances" are often the prelude to more isolated settings where the level of touch and intimacy is further advanced. Activities such as these allow for limited sexual pleasure; they conjure up feelings of intimacy and romance, without the interpersonal demands, anxiety, guilt, and fear that often accompany sexual encounters in the "real world." The impacts of strip clubs and prostitution are examined in terms of potential hazards to patrons, their families, and female service providers.

Section VI. Journey to Oblivion

Chapter 15, The Voyage of Hardship and Suffering, examines addiction as a progressive, chronic, and relapsing brain disease. Historically, this perspective originates from a series of lectures presented in the early 1950s by E. M. Jellinek in which he formulated a four-phase model of addictive disease. Since Jellinek's early formulation, the disease model for alcoholism has been embraced by Alcoholics Anonymous, the National Council on Alcoholism, the National Institute on Alcohol Abuse and Alcoholism, and the American Medical Association. The pros and cons of this formulation are discussed relative to the entire range of behavioral addictions. The disease model has the potential for co-opting social and personal responsibility through the connotation that uncontrollable biological influences are at the root of antisocial patterns of behavior.

Section VII. Natural Highs:
The Cutting Edge of Mood Alteration

Culture, social learning, brain chemistry, and genetics all conspire toward the relentless quest for exalted delight. It can be excruciatingly difficult to overcome renegade biological processes that are further encouraged by powerful social and psychological influences. Yet, it can be done. Biologically, the question is this: Can the human brain gain control over inherited impulses that were appropriate for prehistoric man but are inappropriate in the modern age? We are currently in the midst of a revolution in how humans manage stress. The old standbys of being angry, depressed, anxious, drunk, or otherwise misbehaving are no longer acceptable. We have reached an evolutionary juncture in self-regulation. Culture now calls upon humans to take charge of their emotions and actions by changing or managing the dysfunctional thoughts from which negative feelings and problem behaviors arise. We refer to this perspective as the *cognitive-behavioral revolution*.

Chapter 16, The Cognitive-Behavioral Revolution, explains how cognitive-behavioral therapy (CBT) has become the predominant treatment modality for the three pillars of maladaptive functioning: addiction, crime, and mental disorder. However, the value of CBT extends far beyond treating the broad spectrum of social problem behaviors; it has also become the predominant means for better managing the ups and downs of everyday life. Cognitive-behavioral restructuring (CBR) can improve the lives of everyone who develops the skills to better manage thoughts and actions, resulting in positive effects on mood, behavior, and overall quality of life.

After learning the principles and skill sets enveloped by CBR, and incorporating the CBR model into daily life, readers are ready to engage in the process of attaining natural highs: "self-induced changes in brain chemistry that result in positive feeling states, health, and well-being for the individual and society"—in other words, feeling good and creating win–win, long-term outcomes for ourselves and those around us. The final chapters of this book explore the five remaining tenets of the natural highs perspective: maintaining close and intimate relationships; relaxation, mindfulness, and meditation; healthy eating; exercising; and meaningful engagement of talents.

Chapter 17, Maintaining Close and Intimate Relationships, examines early attachments with parents and caregivers as the foundation for trusting and intimate relationships. The experience of love is explored in terms of its three components: passion, commitment, and intimacy. The chapter discusses how healthy relationships allow for the expression of individual interests and talents in an atmosphere of mutual respect and appreciation. Suggestions are provided for improving sexual and emotional intimacy.

Chapter 18, Relaxation, Mindfulness, and Meditation, discusses meditation and other self-calming techniques as positive means for stress reduction and improved quality of life. By learning techniques for being "in the present," we gain the invaluable opportunity to live life more fully and with increased novelty; diminished stress; greater empathy; fewer value judgments; and a deeper sense of beauty, contentment, and meaning. Today there is an abundance of scientific research on how meditative, self-calming skills can improve physical and mental health. Strategies are presented for including relaxation, mindfulness, and meditation into one's daily routine.

Chapter 19, Eating Yourself Fit, explores dieting as a viable option for the huge proportion of adults who qualify as overweight or obese. Although many diets will facilitate short-term weight loss, those who sustain control over their body mass include a healthy quantum of exercise in their daily and weekly schedules. The principles of cognitive-behavioral restructuring create the mental set for including goals, values, and rational thinking in any program for weight control.

Chapter 20, Exercise: The Magic Bullet, is designed to develop a better understanding of the whole-life benefits of a sensible exercise program. Physical fitness is not just for those who wish to lose weight. It is also a prescription for participating in the fullness of life. Exercise can enhance self-esteem, social interaction, motivation, and self-image as well as decrease stress levels, anxiety, and depression. For those who enjoy sensation seeking and excitement, exercise (and competitive sport) can offer natural highs alternatives to risk-taking activities such as gambling, promiscuity, and the abuse of stimulant drugs. To top it off, the biological health of regular exercisers is that of someone 10 years younger than their sedentary counterparts!

Chapter 21, Meaningful Engagement of Talents, concludes the book. With the goal of facilitating natural highs as positive means for mood alteration, Gardner's theory of *multiple intelligences* is integrated with Csikszentmihalyi's conceptualization of *flow.* Gardner discovered that humans are gifted with multiple forms of innate talents, well beyond the traditional mathematical and verbal abilities stressed in school. People show different degrees of ability in artistic, musical, kinesthetic, interpersonal, and intrapersonal domains. Intrigued by the stories of artists who lose themselves in the passion for their work, Csikszentmihalyi found that they share a sense of profound pleasure in their chosen activity, an intense and focused concentration on what they are doing in that present moment, and a loss of self-consciousness. Whatever the type of intelligence employed (e.g., music, art, writing, mathematics, sports), the desired state of flow requires pushing the envelope beyond one's comfort zone. The chapter explores two paths to achieving natural highs throughout the life span: (1) identifying and shaping environments conducive to flow experiences, and (2) identifying personal characteristics and attentional skills that can be honed to make the experience of flow more likely.

Acknowledgments _____

Many individuals have contributed to the development of this book. Kenneth Axen's artistic, graphic, and academic contributions added scientific clarity, humor, and aesthetic appeal to our work. Kenneth Wanberg is treasured for decades of friendship, scholarly example, and collaboration in developing cognitive-behavioral alternatives to an array of social problem behaviors. Alex Hunter, while serving as district attorney for the City and County of Boulder, Colorado, is deeply appreciated for his crucial role in furthering the concept of *natural highs*. Cleo Parker Robinson is cherished for her partnership in providing a decade of artistic alternatives to teenagers who struggled with drug abuse, crime, and emotional distress.

Karen Storck is commended for her editorial assistance and research support, without which the academic rigor of this volume could not have been achieved. We are grateful to Vicki Carter for her encouragement and tireless work as a research assistant during the final months of manuscript preparation. Tyghe Boone-Worthman is appreciated for his topical research support, and we are thankful to Heather Smith for her research assistance and conceptual contributions. We appreciate the fine work of Teresa Herlinger in her steadfast and rigorous copyediting of the final manuscript.

Our heartfelt gratitude is extended to Kassie Graves, acquisitions editor, SAGE Publications, for patience, guidance, and personal attention in bringing this volume to life.

SECTION I

The Universal Desire to Feel Good

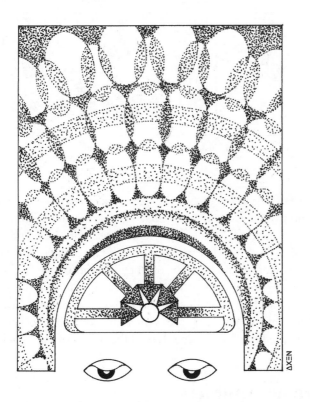

The experience of pleasure is derived from stimuli, originating outside or inside the body, that increase the concentration of dopamine in the nucleus accumbens, the primary reward center of the human brain.

Introduction

Our discussion begins with a fundamental source of human unrest: the relentless urge to feel wonderful. Consider a conversation between the legendary cartoon characters Calvin and Hobbes:

SOURCE: Calvin and Hobbes © 1990 Watterson. Dist. By Universal Press Syndicate. Reprinted with permission. All rights reserved.

The desire to have *more* of everything, to "experience only peaks," is basic to the human psyche. *Craving for ecstasy*—the root cause of compulsive pleasure seeking—springs from one's early encounters with pleasurable activities. Just as a toddler discovers that spinning oneself into a dizzy heap can ramp up feelings of intoxication and bliss, the older child or adolescent seeks out a drug knowing that he or she can produce an altered state. It's the sensation of altered mood, the effect it produces—*not* the substance itself—that we crave. This fundamental verity of drug use is often overlooked as society's attention remains fixated on the drugs themselves as the source of our problems.

Addiction Syndrome Disorders

It is common to describe specific drugs, activities, or objects as addictive (e.g., alcohol, gambling, and the Internet). This view implies that the cause of each problem is different (H. J. Shaffer, LaPlante, et al., 2004). Specific measures for prevention and treatment are therefore designed for particular forms of behavioral excess. Today, a commonalities approach to addictive disorders, the signature of our earlier work (Milkman, 2001; Milkman & Sunderwirth, 1987, 1998), is supported by research from both biological and social sciences.

There is an accruing body of biological research that points to common genetic underpinnings for a variety of addictive behaviors (e.g., Betz, Milhalic, Pinto, & Raffa, 2000; Potenza, 2001; Wise, 1996). Evidence from longitudinal twin studies shows a common *externalizing factor* underlying symptoms of impulsivity, sociability, and rebelliousness (Blonigen et al., 2005; Burt, McGue, Krueger, & Iacono, 2005; King, Iacono, & McGue, 2004). The disruptive or *externalizing disorders* consist of attention deficit hyperactivity disorder (ADHD), conduct disorder, and oppositional defiant disorder. When an identical twin is affected with an externalizing disorder, the other twin has a very high probability of manifesting a disorder from the same category. Also, genetics and environment have been shown to mediate the relationship between a particular pattern of brain wave activity (slower P300 brain waves) and a range of externalizing disorders (e.g., see Hicks et al., 2007; Iacono, Malone, & McGue, 2003; Kendler, Prescott, Myers, & Neale, 2003; Patrick et al., 2006). Alcohol dependence, drug dependence, nicotine dependence, conduct disorder, and adult antisocial behavior are rampant in these diagnostic categories.

From a psychosocial perspective, personality and environmental risk factors are common across both chemical and behavioral expressions of addiction. Impulsivity, poor parental supervision, and delinquency, as well as various demographic risk factors such as poverty, geography, and peer groups, can influence the onset and course of both drug use and other risk-taking activities, such as gambling. Furthermore, when those in treatment for diverse substance abuse problems (e.g., drug dependence or driving under the influence) are studied for co-occurring disorders there are commonalities in other forms of psychopathology such as increased rates of anxiety and depressive disorders (H. J. Shaffer, LaPlante, et al., 2004).

Other similarities across the range of hedonic dependencies (e.g., gambling, sex, eating, drugs, and alcohol) include

- Common milestones in the progression of behavioral dysfunction (e.g., relationship, work, and economic problems);
- Dopamine malfunction, which plays a primary role in both drug and behavioral addictions;
- Parallel neurobiological consequences across addictive behaviors (e.g., neuroadaptation resulting in tolerance and withdrawal);
- Nonspecificity of object choice (i.e., it is common for people who are recovering from one pattern of addiction to "hop" to another); and
- Comparable patterns of emotional distress.

The upshot of these explicit commonalities is the emergence of a syndrome approach to addictive disorders. Although the specific objects of addiction show considerable variability, they share a cluster of signs and symptoms related to a common underlying condition.

> The current view of separate addictions is similar to the view espoused during the early days of AIDS diagnosis, when rare diseases were not yet recognized as opportunistic infections of an underlying immune deficiency syndrome. Our analysis of the extant literature reveals that the specific objects of addiction play a less central role in the development of addiction than previously thought, and it identifies the need for a more comprehensive philosophy of addiction. (H. J. Shaffer, LaPlante, et al., 2004, p. 367)

The foundational premise of this book is that our understanding of a broad array of hedonic activities is dramatically improved through a commonalities approach. Those who are concerned about the prevention, treatment, and aftercare for addictive disorders will benefit from this perspective. The information contained herein may be compared to a broad-spectrum vaccine, effective across a range of disease agents. By way of analogy, in 2007 the World Health Organization (WHO) convened the third meeting on "Influenza vaccines that induce broad spectrum and long-lasting immune responses." The objectives of the meeting were to review the current status of research in the area of influenza vaccine strategies targeting vaccines that are able to induce broad-spectrum or long-lasting immune responses and to provide cross-protection against divergent influenza virus strains (WHO, 2007).

Extent of the Problem

> *First, we have to be courageous enough to say, "it's in my living room."*
>
> —Hoffman & Froemke, 2007, p. 33

The statistics on compulsive pleasure seeking are astounding. The phenomenon of alcohol or drug dependence is so pervasive that addiction impacts 1 in every 4 families (Hoffman & Froemke, 2007). Table I.1 shows prevalence data on just a few of the most common hedonic dependencies: alcohol, cigarettes, marijuana, the Internet, online pornography, gambling, and obesity.

Table I.1   Prevalence and Severity of Common Hedonic Dependencies

Drug or Activity	Prevalence and Severity of Outcomes
Alcohol	The prevalence of lifetime and 12-month alcohol abuse is 17.8% and 4.7%, respectively; the prevalence of lifetime and 12-month alcohol dependence is 12.5% and 3.8% (Hasin, Stinson, Ogburn, & Grant, 2007).
Alcohol and Other Drugs (AOD)	An estimated 19.5% of the U.S. population experiences some substance use disorder during their lifetime (Kessler, Berglund, Demler, Jin, & Walters, 2005). A total of 22.2 million Americans age 12 and older currently suffer from dependence on or abuse of drugs and alcohol (National Survey on Drug Use and Health [NSDUH], 2005).
Cigarettes	The lifetime prevalence of nicotine dependence is 24% (Breslau, Johnson, Hiripi, & Kessler, 2001). Cigarette smoking is the most preventable cause of premature death in the United States, accounting for nearly 440,000 of the more than 2.4 million annual deaths (American Heart Association, 2008).
Marijuana	Marijuana is the most commonly used illicit drug in the United States. According to the 2006 National Survey on Drug Use and Health, an estimated 97.8 million Americans age 12 or older (or 39.8% of the U.S. population of that age-group) have tried marijuana at least once in their lifetime.
The Internet	A 2006 telephone study of 2,500 adults (Stanford University School of Medicine, 2006) showed that the average number of hours spent online is 3.5 per day, per person.
Online Pornography	Sex is reported to be the topic researched most frequently on the Internet (Carroll et al., 2008), comprising 25% of all search engine requests, which total about 68 million per day (A. Cooper, Delmonico, & Burg, 2000). An estimated 40 million adults in the United States regularly visit Internet pornography sites. The porn industry annually generates about $100 billion worldwide and $13 billion in the United States (Ropelato, 2007).
Gambling	The lifetime prevalence of problem gambling is 4% (H. J. Shaffer, Hall, & Vander Bilt, 1999; H. J. Shaffer & Korn, 2002). "Governments around the world have legalized lotteries, casinos and sports betting as well as machine-based gambling, such as slots and video lottery terminals (VLTs) as sources of vast profit for both state and commercial enterprise" (Reith, 2007, p. 35).
Obesity	It is estimated that between a quarter and a third of all adults in the United States are clinically obese. For most developing nations, obesity is a more serious health threat than hunger. Worldwide, more than 1.3 billion people are overweight, possessing a body mass index (BMI) of 25 or higher, or obese (BMI of 30 or higher), whereas about 800 million people are underweight (Popkin, 2007).

Positive Psychology and Natural Highs _____

When spider webs unite, they can tie up a lion.

—Ethiopian proverb

By approaching the age-old search for pleasure from an addiction syndrome perspective, we develop a more complete and helpful understanding of human compulsion and loss of control. Sound principles from psychology and sociology are integrated with emerging discoveries in brain science to present a positive approach to self-regulation of the need to feel good.

Since the discovery of endorphins (Hughes, 1975; Kosterlitz & Hughes, 1975), neuroscience has amassed conclusive evidence that the brain is a giant pharmaceutical factory that manufactures its own mind-altering chemicals. During the past decade, positive psychologists (those working in the field of positive psychology, defined below) have actively addressed the fundamental need to achieve pleasure and well-being without the debilitating fallout from "excessive dopamine backlash" (e.g., Cloninger, 2004; Milkman, 2001; Milkman & Sunderwirth, 1993; Peterson & Seligman, 2004; Seligman, 2002).

Based on a commonalities model, whereby hedonic pursuits are linked by altered brain chemistry, we developed a multidisciplinary definition of addiction inclusive of both drug and behavioral dependencies.

> *Addiction:* "Self-induced changes (psychology) in neurotransmission (biology) that result in problem behaviors (sociology)." (Milkman & Sunderwirth, 1983)

In light of the seemingly universal need to seek out altered states, it behooves researchers, educators, parents, politicians, public health administrators, and treatment practitioners to promote healthy means to alter brain chemistry. We have posited the concept of "natural highs" in order to promote awareness of the need to actively pursue changes in brain chemistry that lead to health and well-being (Milkman, 2001; Milkman & Hunter, 1987, 1988; Milkman & Sunderwirth, 1993).

> *Natural highs:* "Self-induced changes in brain chemistry that result in positive feeling states, health, and well-being for the individual and society." (Milkman & Sunderwirth, 1993)

Consistent with our definition, health practitioners and researchers agree that there is more to optimal living than freedom from biological aberration. The World Health Organization (1948) has defined health as "a state of complete physical, mental and social well-being and not merely the absence of disease or infirmity." This definition has not been amended since its origination more than 60 years ago. Realization of optimal health is the implicit goal of the burgeoning field of *positive psychology,* "the scientific and applied approach to uncovering people's strengths and promoting their positive functioning" (Snyder & Lopez, 2007, p. 3). Positive psychology embodies principles for cultivating strength of character (e.g., authenticity, persistence, kindness, gratitude, hope, and humor) and virtues (wisdom, courage, humanity, justice, temperance, and transcendence) as indispensable means for achieving happiness throughout the life span (Peterson & Seligman, 2004).

Our approach to hedonic dependencies seeks to create a more balanced view of human functioning. We examine both the positive and negative sides of pleasure. After exploring a broad range of destructive strategies to achieve feelings of well-being and wholeness, we present positive approaches to mood alteration and lasting happiness. The matrix of cognitive, emotional, and behavioral skills enveloped by the construct of natural highs include the ability to manage thoughts in the service of generating positive feelings and actions; the use of mindfulness skills to achieve peace of mind and connection with others; a positive program of nutrition and physical activity; and the realization of our individual areas of interest, passion, and ability.

Across the broad spectrum of society's efforts to prevent, intervene in, and treat hedonic dependency, the single most important remedial factor is the experience of intimacy characterized by a deep-seated sense of nurturance, trust, and support.

Critical Study: Resilience on the Garden Island of Kauai

Indeed, human connectedness—so difficult to measure—has been documented as the foundation for health and well-being. In her groundbreaking work, Werner (1989) published the findings of her 30-year study that underscore the vital importance of nurture and support. In 1955, all 698 children who were born on the Hawaiian island of Kauai participated in Werner's study, which followed their development at 1, 2, 10, 18, 31, and 32 years of age. While 422 were judged to have a supportive environment, 201 were considered at risk for developing some form of emotional or behavioral disorder later in life. These vulnerable youth had four of the following risk factors prior to their second birthday: perinatal stress, chronic poverty, parents' education level less than the eighth grade, family discord, or divorce. They constituted 30% of the surviving children on the island. Two-thirds of these children (129) did develop serious learning or behavioral problems by age 10 or had delinquency records, mental health problems, or pregnancies by the time they were 18.

More important, 1 of 3 did not! Seventy-two of these high-risk children grew into competent young adults who loved, worked, and played well. The research team was able to identify a number of factors that seemed to protect vulnerable children from poor adjustment. Their temperaments were characterized by high activity, low excitability and distress, and high sociability.

Their social circumstances were perhaps even more revealing. Kids who remained healthy had four or fewer children in their immediate family. Also, there were at least 2 years between the births of siblings. The at-risk children who succeeded had emotional support outside of their immediate family. They participated in extracurricular activities and had formed a close bond with one or more caretakers during the first years of life. Of paramount importance was the establishment of at least one genuine, caring relationship. Werner (1989) found that "the resilient children . . . had at least one person in their lives who accepted them unconditionally regardless of temperamental idiosyncrasies or physical or mental handicaps." She concluded that "all children can be helped to become more resilient if adults in their lives encourage independence, teach them appropriate communication and self-help skills and model, as well as reward acts of helpfulness and caring" (p. 106).

Nurturing healthy children by guiding them through critical phases of development has benefits throughout their lives. Natural highs depend on the positive resolution of specific psychological conflicts through caring, nurturing, and intimate human relationships. Otherwise, energy is directed to problems that were not effectively handled during childhood, often resulting in misguided attempts to reduce suffering.

From the perspective of object relations theory, addiction results from a failure in the separation-individuation process (e.g., Baker & Baker, 1987; Kohut, 1977). Due to the lack of reliable caretakers and the incapacity to make "transmuting internalizations" (incorporating a solid sense of self through exposure to and nurturance from genuine and caring others), the addict remains dependent upon external sources of tension reduction. Because comfort provided by external addictive agents cannot be internalized into the self, the process inevitably fails (Graham & Glickauf-Hughes, 1992). Treatment involves providing opportunity for healthy resolution of the need for separation-individuation through internalizing the soothing and resilient characteristics of the therapist or fellow group members.

During his ninth decade of life, Erik Erikson (1982) expanded upon the template he and his wife, Joan, had developed 40 years earlier for understanding how lessons from each of life's stages mature into multiple facets of wisdom that blossom during old age. As shown in Table I.2, positive attributes (e.g., hope, will, purpose) generated from the resolution of specific psychological conflicts culminate in a strong sense of purpose and meaning, even in the face of death.

Throughout the remainder of this book, after exploring the nature and causes (biological, psychological, and social) of the three basic patterns of behavioral excess: *arousal, satiation,* and *fantasy,* along with basic human needs for *intimacy, love, and belonging,* we delineate *natural highs* as positive means to cope with the inevitable *sturm und drang* (storm and stress) of being alive. Personal accounts highlight our vulnerability to cravings and addictions and how natural highs can become powerful allies for establishing enduring health and well-being.

Table I.2   The Completed Life Cycle of Natural Highs

Conflict and Resolution	Attribute	Attainment in Old Age
Old Age Integrity vs. Despair	Wisdom	Existential identity; a sense of identity strong enough to withstand physical disintegration
Adulthood Generativity vs. Stagnation	Care	Caritas, caring for others; and agape, empathy and concern
Early Adulthood Intimacy vs. Isolation	Love	Sense of the complexity of relationships; value of tenderness and loving freely
Adolescence Identity vs. Confusion	Fidelity	Sense of complexity of life; merger of sensory, logical, and aesthetic perceptions
School Age Industry vs. Inferiority	Competence	Humility; acceptance of the course of one's life and unfulfilled hopes
Play Age Initiative vs. Guilt	Purpose	Humor; empathy; resilience
Early Childhood Autonomy vs. Shame	Will	Acceptance of the cycle of life, from integration to disintegration
Infancy Basic Trust vs. Mistrust	Hope	Appreciation of interdependence and relatedness

SOURCE: Adapted from "Erikson in his old age expands his view of life" by D. Goleman, 1988, June 14, *New York Times*, pp. 13–14.

We conclude our introduction to natural highs with some thoughts of Albert Hofmann, who is viewed by many as the father of the modern drug age. In April 2008, Hofmann, known for his discovery of LSD-25, died at the age of 102. Hofmann discovered the world's most famous hallucinogen on April 16, 1943, at the Sandoz research laboratory in Basel, Switzerland. He was isolating and synthesizing the unstable alkaloids of the ergot fungus and inadvertently ingested the drug. Hofmann viewed LSD as a sacrament for the modern age. He perceived that it had given him a sense of union with nature and of the spiritual basis of creation. Throughout the 60-plus years after his mind-shattering discovery, Hofmann believed that he had unveiled the potential antidote to the problems associated with consumerism, industrialization, and the vanishing sense of the divine. Although he remained saddened by the misuse of and consequent ban on LSD in most countries, he believed that the power of LSD is based on access to the radiance and sense of oneness with creation that could be accessed naturally, often during childhood, through communion with nature. His advice to those seeking a powerful altered state was simple: "Go to the meadow, go to the garden, go to the woods. Open your eyes!" ("Obituary: Albert Hofmann," 2008).

1 Addiction to Experience

Some to dance, some to make bonfires, each man to what sport and revels his addiction leads him.

—*Othello*, Act II, Scene 2

The Broad Scope of Addiction

In the drama of human excess, experience is the protagonist, and drugs or activities are merely supporting actors. We are compelled by repetitious urges to *become energized*, to *relax*, to *imagine*. These three citadels of consciousness are the beacons of compulsive behavior.

Recognition that the term *addiction* should transcend drug abuse emerged from the problem of categorizing so-called nonaddictive and addictive drugs. By the late 1960s, it became clear that some people could become compulsively involved with marijuana and LSD, substances that seemed to have a relatively low potential for physical dependency. Meanwhile, some users could maintain relatively casual relationships with opium derivatives such as heroin or codeine, customarily associated with rapidly increased tolerance and severe discomfort upon discontinuance. Scientific research during the past 20 years had shown that focusing on a physical versus psychological distinction is a distraction from the real issues.

> From both clinical and policy perspectives, it actually does not matter very much what physical withdrawal symptoms occur. Physical dependence is not that important, because even the dramatic withdrawal symptoms of heroin and alcohol addiction can now be easily managed with appropriate medications. Even more important, many of the most dangerous and addicting drugs, including methamphetamine and crack cocaine, do not produce very severe physical dependence symptoms upon withdrawal. (Leshner, 2007, p. 43)

Today, more than 11 million people in the United States have tried MDMA (Ecstasy) at least once (NSDUH, 2005). Although nearly 60% of those who reported use acknowledge symptoms of withdrawal (i.e., fatigue, loss of appetite, depression, and trouble concentrating), about 23% do not meet the diagnostic criteria for abuse or dependence (National Institute on Drug Abuse [NIDA], 2007e).

Behavioral Addictions

Behavioral science research has developed the scientific underpinning for a syndrome approach to addictive behaviors (e.g., Cloninger, Svrakic, & Przybeck, 1993; Iacono et al., 2003; Krueger et al., 2002; Legrand, Iacono, & McGue, 2005; Milkman & Sunderwirth, 1983, 1987, 1993, 1998; H. J. Shaffer, LaPlante, et al., 2004). Parallels have been drawn between traditionally held ideas about drug involvement and a host of pleasure-fueled activities far removed from the compulsive intake of food or drugs (Figure 1.1). People regularly describe themselves as "addicted" to seemingly harmless activities like aerobics or watching MTV. Media-coined disorders such as "chocoholism" (Ozelli, 2007) or "workaholism" are widely acknowledged by scientists with an abundance of biological explanations. Phenethylamine, found in chocolate, is said to be the chemical of love (Liebowitz, 1983; Parker, Parker, & Brotchie, 2006), and endorphins, our internal opiates, are proposed as the "keys to paradise" for runners who push beyond "the wall."

Television, magazines, and newspapers have all jumped on the bandwagon of a commonalities approach to habitual behaviors. Of current notoriety is addiction to computer games such as *World of Warcraft* or *Second Life*. During the past two decades, the worldwide population of online users grew from 500,000 to over 700 million, with an estimated 5.9% to 13% exhibiting some form of disturbed behavior related to online pursuits (Morahan-Martin, 2001). Fifteen percent of university students in the United States and Europe reported that they knew someone who is addicted to the Internet (K. Anderson, 1999).

The Addictive Personality

The addictive personality is described in various scientific reports as impulsive, rule breaking, deviant, nonconformist, and depressed (e.g., Iacono et al., 2003; Jessor, 1998; Krueger et al., 2002; Legrand et al., 2005). Youngsters who later develop compulsive problem behaviors often experience difficulty in school and in their family relationships. Auto accidents, fighting, truancy, delinquency, and vicious struggles with parents are common. Perhaps the entire spectrum of antisocial behavior patterns provides some relief to youth who encounter genetic predisposition, familial inadequacy, poverty, bereavement, or geographic instability. Figure 1.2 shows the composite of risk factors that contribute to addictive patterns of behavior.

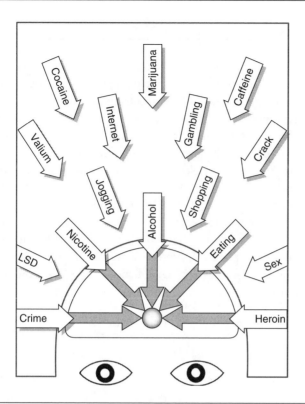

Figure 1.1   **The broad scope of addiction.** Brain science provides scientific underpinning for a syndrome approach to addictive behaviors. The nucleus accumbens and pathways connected to it mediate natural rewards and are affected by mood-altering drugs.

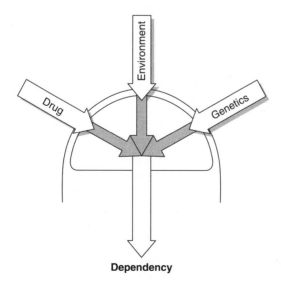

Figure 1.2   **Risk factors for dependency.** Genetic factors, including the effects of environment and gene expression, account for between 40% and 60% of a person's vulnerability to addiction.

Who Is Most at Risk?

Scientists estimate that genetic factors account for between 40% and 60% of a person's vulnerability to addiction, including the effects of environment and gene expression and functions. Adolescents and other individuals with mental disorders are at greater risk of drug abuse and addictive behavior than the general population. Of course, parents and other family members who abuse alcohol or other drugs or engage in criminal activity increase children's risks of developing addictive problems. And during adolescence, friends and acquaintances appear to have the greatest impact on the development of social problem behaviors. As with other mental or physical disorders, vulnerability varies from person to person. Generally, the more risk factors an individual has, the greater chance that partaking of risky behavior will lead to compulsion and loss of control. Protective factors (the other side of the coin) reduce a person's risk for developing addiction. Table 1.1 shows examples of both risk and protective factors.

Table 1.1   Examples of Risk and Protective Factors

Risk Factors	Domain	Protective Factors
Early aggressive behavior	Individual	Self-control
Poor social skills	Individual	Positive relationships
Lack of parental supervision	Family	Parental monitoring and support
Substance abuse	Peer	Academic competence
Drug availability	School	Anti-drug use policies
Poverty	Community	Strong neighborhood attachment

SOURCE: From "The science of addiction" by *National Institute on Drug Abuse,* 2008, NIH Pub. No. 07-5605, p. 7.

Acquisition and Maintenance of Reward-Dependent Behavior

It is unnecessary to develop separate sets of principles to explain how drug use and other compulsive behaviors gain control over human life. Drugs, food, sex, gambling, and aggressive outbursts all give prompt, salient, and short-lasting relief to the people who indulge in them due to dopamine being released in the brain's reward center. In addition to sharing pleasure-inducing properties, both substance use and other mood-altering activities tend to produce an initial state of euphoria, which is then followed by a negative emotional state—that is, a high followed by a low. This post-euphoric discomfort gives further impetus to repetition of the rewarding activity. The old "hair of the dog" remedy of drinking to restore "normal" brain chemistry and relieve hangover symptoms is consistent with this idea.

As illustrated in Figure 1.3, Wikler (1973) developed a two-phase model for the origins and progression of narcotics addiction that is applicable to other compulsions as well. In the *acquisition phase,* the novice begins and continues a potentially compulsive activity because of pleasurable sensations brought about through the experience. We now know that this is the result of an increased concentration of dopamine in the reward centers of the brain (e.g., Milkman & Sunderwirth, 1998; NIDA, 2007a; Ozelli, 2007). The environment in which the desired feeling occurs becomes associated with a "rush" or sense of well-being. Thus the pleasure setting becomes a composite of cues that stimulate craving for the need-satisfying activity. The alcoholic, for example, who has previously enjoyed the euphoria brought on by drink, cannot resist temptation when fate (usually self-orchestrated) delivers him or her to the neighborhood bar or an old friend's New Year's Eve party. This phenomenon is known as *conditioned desire* (Heinz, 2006). The human body eventually adapts to most novel stimulation by reducing the potency of its effect. The user soon needs more of the mood-altering activity in order to experience similar alterations in feeling. The addicted climber must increasingly seek out more difficult cliffs; the hooked skydiver compulsively finds more challenging and frightening drops.

In the *maintenance phase* of addiction, a person is no longer motivated by any sense of pleasure from the drug or other need-gratifying behavior. Rather, the repetitive activity now serves only to relieve the sense of despair

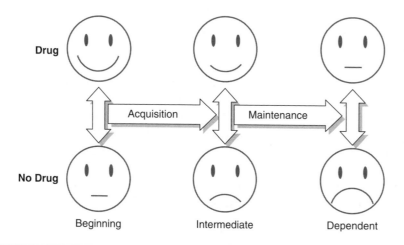

Drug		
	Acquisition	Maintenance
No Drug		
Beginning	Intermediate	Dependent

Figure 1.3   **The addictive progression.** In the *acquisition phase,* the individual experiences pleasure as the result of hedonic (drug or behavior) activity. Without the activity, he or she experiences the "normal" state of mood. In the *intermediate state,* tolerance results in the need for more of the hedonic activity in order to achieve positive effects. In the *dependence state,* hedonic activity no longer evokes pleasure, only relief from the suffering brought on by withdrawal.

and physical discomfort that is felt when the mood-altering action or substance is not present. The user can only "break even" by performing his or her tension-relieving activity. Without it, the addicted person suffers from a devastating combination of physical dependence and an even more complicated and stressful environment. The compulsive meditator, for example, increasingly seeks out quiescent relaxation to escape from stress that builds from increasing social isolation and decreased productivity at home and at work.

Figure 1.4 shows how an initially rewarding or need-gratifying activity can progress into a persistent problem of substance abuse or other reward-seeking behavior. Life situations at point A lead to a need or desire to modify mood through drugs or other mind-altering behavior. At point B, the participant experiences pleasure or decreases discomfort as the result of mood alteration. Hence, at point C the user's thoughts (positive outcome expectations) and mood-altering behaviors are strengthened (reinforced) as the result of successful changes in mental state. Points A, B, and C constitute the mental and behavioral correlates of the acquisition phase of a problem dependency. At point D, the individual begins to experience negative consequences from the activity, such as getting fired, relationship problems, and so forth. If the person does not intervene on his or her own behalf, at point E he or she may increasingly rely on the temporary need-gratifying behavior to counter the increased stress brought on by the "rewarding" behavior pattern. At point F, there is an even further negative consequence from use, resulting in another escalation of stress and discomfort. At point G, the individual is faced with having to deal with the original life problems now compounded by overreliance on the addictive activity. Points D through G correspond to Wikler's maintenance stage, as shown in Figure 1.3 (Wanberg & Milkman, 2006).

As shown in Figure 1.4, an addictive pattern is evident when one becomes progressively less able to control the beginning or end of a need-fulfilling activity. As reward-dependent behavior increasingly leads to harmful outcomes, the maintenance cycle is initiated with increasingly devastating consequences. Yet below the surface are more profound explanatory links. The spectrum of addictive behaviors is connected by a biochemical thread. Advances in scientific understanding of the reward centers of the brain (discussed in detail in Chapter 2) depart from moralistic explanations of addiction, that is, "lack of motivation, poor character." Science increasingly views the problem as rooted in aberrations of the brain (e.g., Leshner, 2007). It has become obvious that individuals can change their brain chemistry through immersion in salient mood-altering activities as well as through ingesting intoxicating substances. As earlier stated, addiction is best defined as *self-induced changes in neurotransmission that*

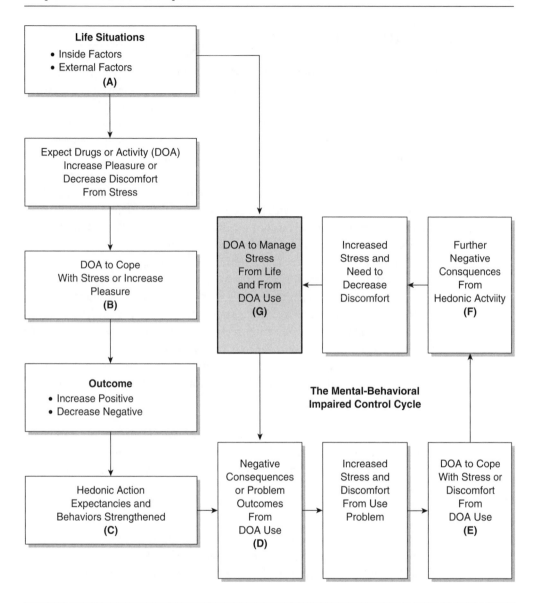

Figure 1.4   The mental-behavioral impaired control cycle.

SOURCE: Adapted from *Criminal conduct and substance abuse treatment: The participant's workbook* by K. Wanberg & H. Milkman, 2006, Thousand Oaks, CA: Sage Publications.

result in problem behaviors. Our discussion now turns to exploring each component of this definition: self-induced (psychology) changes in brain chemistry (neuroscience) that lead to problem behaviors (sociology).

Drugs and Activities of Choice

Given that we may voluntarily alter our neurotransmission to achieve a desired feeling, why do only some of us become compulsively involved in this pursuit? After all, most people can safely become disinhibited by having a few drinks or occasionally experience some degree of mania at the race-track without going off the deep end. Exposure to sexual imagery is rampant, yet most people do not squander their money and success on pros-titution or pornographic pursuits. Along with genetic factors that predispose individuals to particular behavioral styles (e.g., Cloninger et al., 1993), learned patterns of coping with stress (internal and external) are common to most forms of addiction. The chronic absence of good feelings about the self provokes a dependence on mood-changing activity.

Whether internal or external in origin, a powerful way of coping with dis-tress is to immerse oneself in an activity—a tension-relieving behavior—that provides psychological respite (Briere & Rickards, 2007). The climber, cling-ing to a mountain face with only a rope, pitons, and a tenuous foothold, while satisfying a primary sensation-seeking drive, has few moments to spare on self-derogation. The risk taker may figuratively bridge the crevasse of his or her inner turmoil by temporary surrender to something outside the self. Brian, a 32-year-old cocaine user, reported a particularly vivid dream that illustrates this point:

> I recall seeing my personality as a huge concave surface. It looked like a great ceramic bowl with irregularly spaced craters on an otherwise smooth surface. Somehow I could patch the holes with ultra-fine putty made of cocaine paste. The new shimmering surface appeared nearly unmarred. (Personal communication, December 2008)

The user's drug or activity of choice often depends on his or her style of coping with stress. In a research study at Bellevue Psychiatric Hospital in New York, Milkman and Frosch (1973) found a striking relationship between per-sonality and drug of choice. Those who preferred heroin (or other narcotics) used passive withdrawal and reduced sensory stimulation as primary coping devices. In sharp contrast, amphetamine users were apt to confront a hostile or threatening environment with physical or intellectual activity. People who used hallucinogens such as LSD reported that they characteristically relied on imagery, daydreaming, and altered thought processes to reduce tension. The examples shown in Table 1.2 illustrate differences among compulsive users of heroin, amphetamine, and LSD in their management of self-esteem.

The key that opens the doorway to excess for the pre-addict is the good feeling that he or she learns to create, and repeatedly re-create, through self-determined activity. Unaccustomed to the wine of success, the novice experi-ences as a godsend any involvement that provides escape from the increasing sense of despair born of inner turmoil experienced in the "straight world." He or she not only delights in a reprieve from tension, but also experiences elevated feelings of self-worth for having discovered the ability to produce a pleasurable sensation. In "The Road to H: Narcotics, Delinquency, and Social Policy," Chein, Gerard, Lee, and Rosenfeld (1981) describe the addict's infatuation with self-determined mood change as a consequence of having achieved a strong state of tension reduction and pleasure at his or her own doing.

> In [heroin] addicts with strong craving . . . it is in large measure a psychic consequence of achieving a state of relaxation and relief from tension or distress through one's own activities, not through a physician's recommendation or prescription, but through an esoteric, illegal, and dangerous nostrum. We can observe an analogous phenomenon in people who win the Irish Sweepstakes; win on dice, cards, horses or numbers; or even in persons who park in no-parking zones without getting a traffic ticket. They feel important, worthwhile, and interesting; they feel a sense of pride and accomplishment. Such an illusory achievement is an important psychic phenomenon, particularly important when it stands out by contrast with the remainder of a person's life. (p. 111)

Beacons of Compulsion

After studying the life histories of drug abusers, we have seen that drugs of choice are harmonious with an individual's usual means of coping with stress. The discovery of a need-fulfilling drug is usually a serendipitous event; the novice becomes infatuated because of the immediate reduction of stress achieved through the experience. Incipient addicts usually experience behavioral compulsion and loss of control before ever ingesting a psychoactive substance. Juvenile delinquency, persistent and vicious family struggles, and inability to adequately cope with everyday demands are common childhood precursors to drug abuse. Heroin users often show histories of passivity alternating with uncontrolled rage; stimulant users describe multiple episodes of life-threatening impulsiveness; those who rely on hallucinogens report that they regularly avoided problems through fantasy during prolonged periods of their childhood.

We repeatedly pursue three avenues of experience as antidotes for psychic pain. These preferred styles of coping—*satiation, arousal,* and *fantasy*—may have their origins in the first years of life. Childhood experiences combined with genetic predisposition are the foundations of adult compulsion. The drug group of choice—depressants, stimulants, or hallucinogens—is the one that best fits the individual's characteristic way of coping with stress or feelings of unworthiness. People do not become addicted to drugs or mood-altering activities as such, but rather to the satiation, arousal, or fantasy experiences that can be achieved through them.

Table 1.2   Use of Various Drugs to Regulate Self-Esteem

Heroin	Amphetamine	LSD
How do you feel about yourself generally?		
Lousy. I don't like myself.	I think I'm all right, ya know.	I feel like a voyager in an awesome adventure.
What about your looks? Do you think you're good-looking?		
I don't like them and I don't know why.	I think they're all right. I'm satisfied. Yeah, I think I'm good-looking.	Sometimes I feel like an alien, like I'm a gorgeous being from another planet.
How do you compare with others your age?		
Right now I know I don't compare well. I can't control my desire for drugs. I can't do what I want to do . . . I can't be a man. I am not doing anything.	I don't think I'm as mature, serious, or business-minded as a 25-year-old should be. As a man, I'm all right. I'm big and strong and I try to be kind. I love women and I dig kids.	I don't compare myself to others. I just think about how I'm dealing with my own Karma so I can improve my chances now and in a future life.
What do you believe that other people think of you?		
That I'm a cop-out; some people would say degenerate.	I think others like me—some people would say they like me a great deal. They really do not say it, but I know they do. I make friends easily and people smile and they embrace me and make me feel like I'm not rejected.	They think I'm on a path of spiritual discovery. That I am in touch with some cosmic force that they would like to understand.
What kind of person would you like to be?		
I'd just be average and get along, say middle class. I want to be able to work and be middle class. I don't have goals of making a million or anything, just make a living.	I would like to be free of drugs. I would like to not even have to put a grape pop in my mouth if I didn't want to. Right now I'm taking vitamin D and taking grape ice pops. I'm playing with kids. I bought a yo-yo yesterday. I'm laughing a lot and enjoying life.	I would like to be in flow with the forces of the universe . . . to experience oneness with people and nature . . . to merge with the cosmos.

SOURCE: Adapted from "On the preferential abuse of heroin and amphetamines," H. Milkman & W. Frosch, 1973, *Journal of Nervous and Mental Disease, 156*(4), 242–248.

For example, addicts whose basic motivation is satiation are likely to binge on food or television watching or to choose depressant drugs such as the benzodiazepines (e.g., Xanax). Psychologically, they are trying to shut down negative feelings by reducing stimulation from the internal or external world. The life of the satiation type of addict bears striking similarity to that of a child during the first year of life. The mouth and skin are the primary receptors of experience, and feelings of well-being depend almost completely on food and warmth. Khantzian (1997) explains how narcotics provide a pharmacologic defense against the user's own aggressive drives. Binge eating or excessive television watching may fulfill the same adaptive role by helping people quiet strong hostile impulses. On a biochemical level, the effect of satiation activities may be similar to that of opiates. Growing dependence on behaviors such as overeating and watching television may be analogous, though more subtle, versions of opiate addiction.

While satiation addicts try to avoid stimulation and confrontation, others actively seek it. The behaviors associated with the arousal mode of gratification include crime, gambling, risk taking, and use of stimulant drugs such as amphetamines or cocaine. These addicts seek to feel active and potent in relationship to their environment and people in their midst. They are often boastful about their artistic talent, intellectual skill, and sexual or physical prowess. Their vast expenditures of mental and physical energy are designed to deny underlying fears of helplessness. This posture is reminiscent of 2- and 3-year-olds coping with the world of giants in which they live. Asked, "Who is biggest or toughest?" they often reply, "I can beat up Daddy." They protect themselves through the defense of magical denial: "I am really not helpless and vulnerable; I am powerful and feared."

The third type of addict, the one who uses fantasy as the preferred way of dealing with the world, favors repetitive activation of right-hemisphere thinking (Pink, 2005). Thoughts become dreamlike with rapidly shifting imagery and illogical relations between time and space. This style of coping often includes preoccupation with day or night dreams; compulsive artistic expression; or various forms of mystical experience, sometimes expressed as a quest for the feeling of oneness or cosmic unity. People who rely on this style partially overcome their fears by creating fantasies in which they are effective and important. They may travel with extraterrestrials, encounter the "Grim Reaper," or have their body entered by a supernatural entity. Religious fanaticism is another manifestation of this coping mode.

These addicts favor hallucinogens (such as LSD), mushrooms containing psilocybin, or peyote. Interestingly, the two basic types of chemical molecules present in nearly all hallucinogens—variations of indole and phenethylamine—are also found in many compounds that occur naturally as neurotransmitters. For example, dopamine and norepinephrine have the basic phenethylamine structure, whereas serotonin has the indole structure. The fantasy aspects of some artistic, romantic, or spiritual activities may be brought about by conversion of the brain's own indole or phenethylamine compounds into hallucinogenic variations of these chemicals.

Behavioral Excess and the Brain

Addiction covers a broad spectrum of compulsive pleasure-seeking activities with common neurochemical underpinnings. The root of craving lies in the brain's reward system, a network of neurons that become activated when we perform functions that help us to survive, such as eating or sex. The reward network includes a set of neurons found in the ventral tegmental area (VTA) of the brain, which connects to the nucleus accumbens and other areas such as the prefrontal cortex. Reward payoffs create conditioned responses (i.e., reward-seeking behaviors) that are subsequently evoked at the mere sight of food or a sexual object, or by the environment in which these activities occurred. Illicit drugs stimulate this pleasure circuit and can induce even greater feelings of pleasure than natural functions. Compulsive eaters, gamblers, and drug addicts may be unwittingly trying to compensate for an abnormal response to dopamine, the neurotransmitter that regulates reward-seeking activity. An irregularity or an inability to achieve satisfaction from "normal" amounts of dopamine may cause them to continuously dose themselves with a broad spectrum of pleasure-inducing acts (Delgado, 2007; Ozelli, 2007; Reuter et al., 2005). Here is our own take on how food may be used to satisfy an underlying craving for dopamine:

> You rummage through the kitchen cupboard, frantically seeking remaining squares of the Hershey bar that you started last night.... Damn ... someone else must have eaten it.... What about the M&M's? ... No luck either ... so you desperately hoe into a few tablespoons of peanut butter followed by a marshmallow chaser (finally, a dopamine rush).

Compounds that block opioid receptors can reduce the intake of sweets. Foods high in sugar are thought to stimulate the release of internal opioids, which create a pleasurable response. When opioid receptors are blocked, there is a corresponding reduction in the urge to consume sweets. It is known that some addictive drugs like heroin or morphine directly target these opioid receptors. Although addictive drugs undoubtedly cause much more powerful reactions in the brain, it is likely that there are neurochemical parallels between drugs and sweets (Society for Neuroscience, 2003).

In contrast to their commonality of depositing dopamine in the nucleus accumbens, the three types of addiction seem to involve different parts of the brain. Mood shifts are influenced by excitatory and inhibitory pathways in the limbic system, located near the middle of the brain. This system is associated with emotions and with sexual, feeding, and aggressive responses. As arousal decreases, moods may downshift from relaxation to tranquility and finally to a state of blissful satiation. Conversely, increases in arousal are accompanied by changes in experience that range from ordinary alertness to creativity, and ultimately to manic states.

While the limbic system appears to play a major role in pleasurable sensations connected with altered levels of arousal, the convoluted outer brain known as the cerebral cortex is an important determinant of mental content. Excessive activity in the cortex of the right hemisphere may help explain the uncontrolled imagery found in the fantasies of heroin users, mystics, and schizophrenics. Increased activity in the left cortical hemisphere may intensify sensations of perceptual clarity and mental alertness reported during high-risk activities that require an accurate and logical appraisal of one's options, such as rock climbing and skydiving.

As shown in Figure 1.5, the objects of addiction, whether substances (e.g., depressants) or behaviors (e.g., risk taking), are fueled by combined activation of limbic and cortical systems. The "sphere of ordinary experience," in the center of the illustration, pertains to lower-intensity (healthful) activities (e.g., tennis) or substance use (e.g., drinking black tea) that also alter mood, albeit safely.

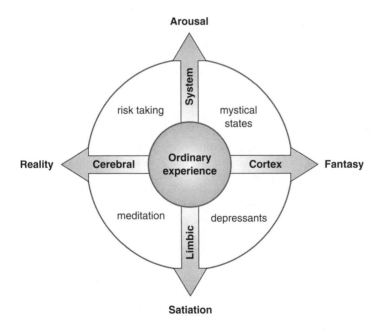

Figure 1.5 **Addictive states.** While the brain's limbic system appears to play a major role in the pleasurable sensations of addiction, the cerebral cortex influences mental content. Its right hemisphere may be involved in fantasy experiences such as those achieved through LSD or other imagination-oriented activities. The heightened sense of reality experienced during compulsive risk taking or work may be linked to activity in the left hemisphere.

Mismanaging the Brain

The case of New York governor Eliot Spitzer (Hakim & Rashbaum, 2008), who resigned from office after being discovered as "Client 9" of a prostitution ring, exemplifies how a "limbic hijacking" can achieve governance over the cerebral cortex, which is designed to inhibit wayward aggressive, sexual, or other hedonic impulses (e.g., gambling, food, or drugs). Rather than attributing Spitzer's behavior exclusively to a "sexual addiction," a more sophisticated explanation would include lifelong patterns of narcissistic self-inflation, sensation seeking, and extreme needs for power and control. Of course, these characteristics are the very ones that elevated Mr. Spitzer to the pinnacle of political success. An old proverb captures the biological determinants of Spitzer's situation: "When the penis goes to the sky, the brain falls to the ground" (source unknown).

While Spitzer may have fallen prey to the complications of extreme need for arousal, others may be waylaid by needs for satiation or fantasy. Advocates for mind-altering substances, for example, may rationalize drug use in terms of "mind expansion" or "spiritual discovery." When taken out of context (e.g., fasting or use of psychedelic plants during religious ceremonies), attempts to induce spiritual awakenings may lead to gross misunderstandings and perceptual inaccuracies. Consider the case of Pat, a college student who earnestly believed that her use of LSD would catalyze a spiritual bond with a complete stranger.

Case Example: User–Observer Discord

It was 1969 and I was in Philadelphia and I was in art school. It was an incredibly interesting time. The war was going on and there was a whole group of people that were being very experimental with some sort of light, sound and electronic equipment—experiential kinds of things that are especially designed for drug taking.

So anyway, I got involved with these people. They called themselves "the group." We were just friends. And they were smart and really hip and for some reason I got in with these people and I didn't really have to do anything. I just kind of hung around. But for one of the gigs they were brought in by various colleges to put on these environmental kind of music light shows. So they brought me in because it became more and more holistic and experiential. I helped them design this one little tunnel of plastic that you go through where you get to feel everything. There are no visuals and all you do is feel various things.

Then there was this one experience that they wanted me to kind of get involved in, in the massage room. I think they only did this at one college. I don't think it was part of their normal thing. This was a Catholic college that hired them and I came with them on this one. It was wonderful. We set up and the whole gym was given over to a huge screen with this pulsing light show and music that went with it and this huge experiential sort of large snake that people went through. And then on the side in one of the classrooms we set up candles and all these mattresses on the floor and dropped acid [laugh]. So, all kinds of people started to come in. They came in one by one and the idea was that I would massage one person and that they would feel this, this inspiration, and basically—the whole notion was I felt, was that I was channeling the cosmic, loving, healing, energy of the universe. So, I came in and I was given a massage and I was on acid already. So . . .

Then I had my massage and I was very impressed and I felt very connected with all of the energy in the universe. So, I massaged numerous people as they came in. And then, a nun came in, one of the sisters. She was in full habit. She lay down on the mat and I was just, at that point—I was just feeling—oh this is just so beautiful. It's just all about love, basically, and God, and I just want to be nothing but the hands of God and the loving touch of the cosmos. So I just began, you know, with her neck. She was lying down. There was lovely music, our own lovely sort of music playing— candle light. I was very near her neck going down her shoulders and her arms and her fingers and down into her back. And then I kept going—it took me awhile—finally I got down to her low, low back and then just started without even thinking about it, just thinking and knowing and feeling that the entire human organism was just nothing but sacred.

So I was just beginning to massage her butt and really into it and tripping [laugh] and all of a sudden, all I know is she just got up and flew out of the room and I just didn't know what was going on, it was a real shock. She came back in very quickly, flipped on all of the fluorescent lights, and got out a razor blade, and started scraping up the wax that had hit the floor. At that point, everything was shut down. The whole experience came to a screeching halt [laugh] and we all basically had to pack up and go home.

But, my experience wasn't her experience of the whole thing [laugh]. It was, in retrospect, very funny, but it was very upsetting at the time. On the way back, we just kind of couldn't quite get it, but these are Catholics, after all [laugh].

Anyway, that's the whole story as I remember it. Basically, we were all tripping. . . . All of the people, you know, who put on the event. It was very cosmic. Really, my intentions were only of the purist nature, although it was quite naïve of me, I have to say.

Society and the Deviant Career

Differences in neurotransmission, influences from the limbic and cortical systems, and the effects of various brain enzymes all interact with powerful social forces that can push susceptible individuals toward activities that have a high dependency potential. Computer games, public lotteries, and telephone escorts are just a few examples of widely available escapes from routine existence. Advertising plays on the human quest for effortless, impersonal reduction of stress. There is an implicit promise that participation in activities with high dependency potential will diminish the discrepancy between actual self-concept and ideal self-concept. Tobacco and alcohol propaganda provide the most blatant examples of this phenomenon. A visual, ego-ideal fantasy is provided in association with the product, often accompanied by a verbal suggestion for indulgence: "Come to X-Brand country." In this context of promoted immediacy, the individual moves through a network of social interactions that may influence his or her reliance on particular channels of behavioral excess.

As illustrated in Figure 1.7, in the earliest phase of deviant identity, a child may possess a subtle yet identifiable characteristic that steers him or her in the direction of behavior outside the norms of mainstream culture. Consider the 2-year-old who enjoys his or her first taste of beer or the young boy whose nickname is "Lucky" or "Romeo" (i.e., who displays early characteristics). The young person may be valued conditionally so that parental affection depends on performance of expected behaviors (i.e., channelization). Further socially driven behavior occurs when an early sense of low self-worth is relieved through rewards associated with a specific activity. The dejected young person may begin to feel potent as a result of attaining external reinforcers such as drugs, money, or sex.

Although parental role models and styles of child rearing are viewed as important contributors to future coping patterns, adolescent adjustment is inextricably bound to peer influence. According to Kandel and Maloff (1983), the most reliable finding in drug research is the strong relation between one person's drug use and concurrent use by friends. The strength of peer conformity is symbolized by the varied dress rituals among subculture groups. Although members of a particular subculture (e.g., rockabilly, hip hop, punk, Goth, stoner) differentiate themselves by style of dress, taste in music, choice of drugs, types of crime, and so forth, there is a high level of horizontal conformity within each group. Ironically, strong needs for nonconformity result in more parochial and rigid adherence to the norms of a particular subculture (Figure 1.6).

If a person's channelization toward problem behaviors continues into early adulthood, opportunities for success diminish as he or she is increasingly imprisoned, both socially and personally, within a deviant role. The adolescent reaches a point of no return when the social and personal costs of changing lifestyles seem to outweigh the benefits. Imagine the difficulty of a 17-year-old high school dropout and long-standing street gang member suddenly attempting to become an athlete or college student. Eventually, the emerging deviant is labeled by those around him or her as a member of a deviant subgroup such as alcoholic, obese, or criminal. This stigmatization tends to further decrease the addict's sense of self-worth. The youngster may begin to enact socially expected roles such as being irresponsible, nonconforming, or impulse-ridden. The stereotyped individual thus becomes further engulfed in a pattern that restricts his or her life opportunities. As the addict now drifts from stable family and love relationships, social settings are increasingly selected because of their potential for immediate gratification. The bar, sex parlor, discotheque, or video arcade may become important islands of alienated comfort.

The progression of deviance can result in dramatic conflict with the environment. Heightened environmental demands and repeated personal failures require increasingly severe efforts to recoup self-esteem through excessive pleasure-seeking activity. The downward spiral of functioning may lead to a variety of social service interventions including hospitalization, incarceration, or both, often occurring on a cyclical basis. What social scientists have labeled as relapse may simply reflect another episode in the naturally oscillating course of the person's futile struggle to regain control. As shown in Figure 1.7 the "deviant career" is characterized by a progression of stages from childhood to old age.

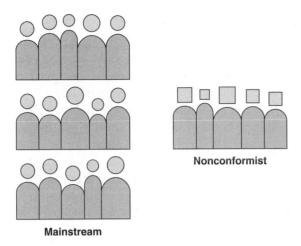

Figure 1.6   **Horizontal conformity.** While mainstream conformity involves adherence to the norms of society at large, "nonconformist" subgroups also adhere to the standards of their group by conforming to the patterns of thought and action of the subculture to which they belong.

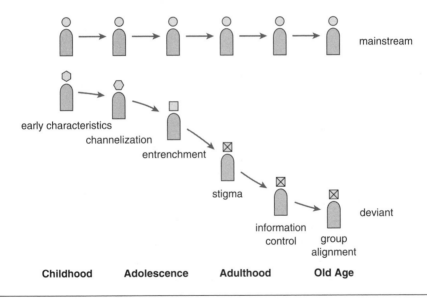

Figure 1.7   **The deviant career.** The process of becoming dependent on a hedonic activity may be conceptualized as a "deviant career." Novices advance through a series of socially influenced stages as they progress to full status in their offbeat professions. The negative effects from being marked or stigmatized (i.e., x, as shown in the figure) as an "addict" or otherwise deviant personality—fatty, junkie, criminal, alcoholic, and so on—may last throughout a person's lifetime.

SOURCE: Based on Goffman, E. (1963). *Stigma: Notes on the management of spoiled identity.* Englewood Cliffs, NJ: Prentice Hall.

Chapter Summary

This chapter sets the groundwork for understanding addiction as a broad spectrum of hedonic dependencies including overindulgence in food, sex, drugs, and risk-taking activity. A multidisciplinary definition of addiction, *self-induced changes in brain chemistry that lead to problem behaviors,* highlights the need to integrate information from psychology, neuroscience, and sociology to arrive at a deeper understanding of the ubiquitous craving for ecstasy. We attempt to manage life's inevitable storm and stress through activation of three primary experiential modes: arousal, satiation, and fantasy. Psychologically, one's chosen drug or pleasure-producing activity is harmonious with his or her characteristic style of coping with stress. The biological underpinnings of compulsive pleasure seeking reside in genetic predispositions that manifest in differential neurologic patterns within the brain. Sociologically, subculture provides the normative structure through which individuals can develop "careers" in a broad array of tension-reducing styles such as alcoholism, promiscuous sexual behavior, and compulsive gambling.

2 Pleasure and the Brain

[W]hen each minute brain component has been located, its function identified and its interactions with each other component made clear—the resulting description will contain all there is to know about human nature and experience.

—R. Carter, 1998, p. 8

Before discussing the powerful effects of drugs or activities on the mind, we will take some time to explain the basic design of the brain, which has been described as more complex than the entire known universe. First, it should be clear that the language of the brain is chemistry. Indeed, the brain is a giant pharmaceutical factory constantly manufacturing chemicals that result in moods such as fear, anger, shame, despair, joy, depression, mania, and any other mood to which the human species is subjected. However, in this chapter we are interested in how drugs manufactured *outside the brain* (possibly in your neighbor's SUV) affect mood and behavior. To comprehend how these external chemicals affect the internal chemistry of the brain, we need to understand how the brain itself works. So prepare yourself for Neurochemistry 101.

Neurochemistry 101

Although the metaphor is not perfect, it is helpful to consider the brain as an electrochemical computer as well as a chemical factory (Milkman & Sunderwirth, 1993). Its 100 billion or so nerve cells, which constitute the brain's hardware, are able to store more information than all the libraries in the world combined. Each of these nerve cells (neurons) is in turn composed of three basic elements (Figure 2.1). The nucleus of the cell body (soma) constitutes a miniature brain within a larger brain. It is the soma that "decides" to transmit a message (an electrical impulse) from one nerve cell to the next, that is, to "fire." Or the soma may decide to ignore a message, that is, to "not fire." This is the only decision the soma needs to make, but it needs to make that decision very quickly. For example, you don't want to wait 5 minutes to remove the hand you unknowingly placed on a hot stove while the soma takes its time deciding to transmit the message to the next neuron and ultimately on to the brain. Like a computer, the soma is a "fast idiot." It has to make one of only two possible decisions, that is, to fire or not to fire. Connected to the soma is a long fiber, the *axon,* through which the message must travel on its way to the next neuron. The message is transferred from one of the many branches at the end of the axon of the sending neuron to one of a number of branches on the receiving cell. These branches on the receiving cell are called *dendrites;* each neuron may have up to 10,000 dendrites. If we consider the possibilities of interaction among the 100 billion neurons found in the human brain with 10,000 dendrites per neuron, we have the possibility of quadrillions of connections—different ways to send messages to different "receivers," with different results. Clearly, as we have said, the brain is the most complex entity in this universe.

Incredibly, this process of communication between neuron and neuron is carried out without any direct physical contact between the two cells—as if this were all taking place in a city of trillions of people, all talking to each other on cellular telephones! Neurons are separated by a gap known as the synapse or synaptic junction. The message is carried from one neuron to the next by molecules known as neurotransmitters, which in our computer analogy may be considered as the software of the brain. Chemical changes

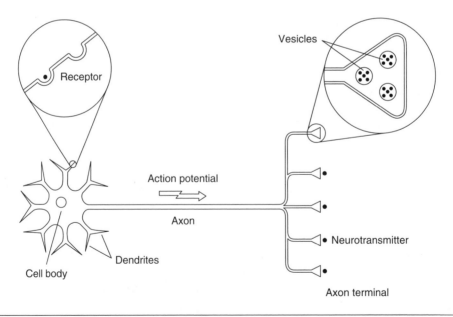

Figure 2.1   **The neuron.** Neurons are made up of a cell body, an axon that transmits electrical impulses called action potentials, dendrites with receptors that respond to chemical signals (neurotransmitters, left blowup), and axon terminals that store neurotransmitter molecules of in vesicles (membrane-enclosed sacs, right blowup).

that occur in these neuronal spaces determine how we respond to each "message." This process of communication between neurons, known as neurotransmission, is largely responsible for the brain functions that determine what we are as individuals including our personalities, intellect, and character. It is precisely because the neurons are separated by a synapse—in other words, they are not "hardwired"—that the brain ends up with nearly limitless options for neurotransmission, which results in the limitless complexity of the human species, with its limitless ability to "screw up."

We are our neurotransmission. What we are as human beings is reflected in the way our neurons communicate and form new pathways as well as utilize old ones. Crick (1995) summarizes the relationship between self and neurotransmission as follows:

> The astonishing hypothesis is that you, your joys, and your sorrows, your memories and ambitions, your sense of personal identity and free will, are in fact no more than the behavior of a vast assembly of nerve cells and their associated molecules. As Lewis Carroll's Alice might have phrased it, "You're nothing but a pack of neurons." (p. 3)

In order for us to understand the effect of drugs on the brain, we need to know how the brain works, and especially the role of neurotransmitters. Let us consider a very important neurotransmitter, norepinephrine (NE), which is found in a part of the brain known as the locus coeruleus (Figure 2.2). One of NE's primary functions is to produce arousal and excitability, including

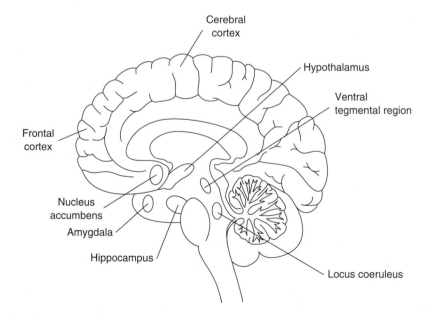

Figure 2.2 **Cross section of the human brain.** The frontal cortex, major components of the limbic system, and locus coeruleus are shown.

the "fight or flight" phenomenon associated with the release of adrenaline. The ability of NE to stimulate the fight or flight response is an evolutionary survival mechanism. The rise in NE levels in times of danger or stress results in an increase in adrenaline, which raises blood pressure and increases heart rate. This forces more oxygen-carrying blood into the muscles, which in turn enabled our prehistoric ancestors to fight if the attacker was a small bear or "run like hell" if it was a saber-toothed tiger. Sapolsky (1994), in his book *Why Zebras Don't Get Ulcers,* explains that zebras, unlike humans, don't activate their stress response, that is, release NE, until a lion (or your boss) actually appears. The rest of the time, they are munching grass on the savanna unconcerned that a lion, or an angry boss, may attack. Many of the illnesses present in modern society are due to the release of stress hormones and NE with the accompanying increase in blood pressure and blood glucose (among other effects), which over time may result in cardiovascular disease and diabetes. But let's leave these side issues and get back to brain chemistry.

To understand how NE, as well as other neurotransmitters, is involved in communication between neurons, let us continue in Neurochemistry 101.

As we have said, the language of the brain is chemistry, and therefore the flow of information (impulse) from one neuron to the next must be chemical. This action is illustrated in Figure 2.3, indicating what occurs at a single synaptic junction between two neurons during the saber-toothed tiger episode. Chemical messages flow from the axon on the top (presynaptic) neuron across the synapse to the dendrite of the postsynaptic neuron on the bottom, and then on to the soma of the postsynaptic neuron. As the impulse reaches the presynaptic terminal, specific channels open in the membrane of this neuron, which allows doubly charged calcium atoms (ions) to enter the cell. This in turn stimulates the release of the neurotransmitter—in this case, NE (illustrated by round dark molecules)—into the synapse. NE moves across the synapse, carrying the message to the postsynaptic neuron. Embedded in the outer membrane of this neuron are hundreds of complex chemicals (proteins) that act as receptors for NE. These receptors have specific shapes that exactly complement the shape of NE. This enables the molecules of NE to attach themselves to these receptors in much the same way that a key fits into a lock. In fact, the key must not only fit the lock perfectly but must also open the door. Just as many Cadillac keys will fit the ignition of Buicks but will not start the engines, the same is true of neurotransmitters and receptors.

Norepinephrine not only fits the locks but also opens the doors (ion channels) of the postsynaptic cell. Opening these cell doors allows certain ions (potassium, sodium, and chloride) to go in and out of this cell. If enough channels (doors) are opened and enough ions go in and out, the electrical nature of the receiving cell's outer membrane is altered (depolarized). This enables the message to be sent to the cell body (soma) of the postsynaptic cell, where it is processed with input from thousands of other cells, all undergoing the same process.

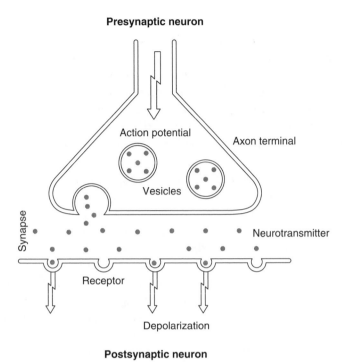

Presynaptic neuron

Action potential

Axon terminal

Vesicles

Synapse

Neurotransmitter

Receptor

Depolarization

Postsynaptic neuron

Figure 2.3   **Mechanism of neurotransmission.** Signals are transmitted from presynaptic to postsynaptic neurons by neurotransmitters. An action potential in the presynaptic neuron causes vesicles to migrate to the cell membrane and release their neurotransmitter into the synapse (the space between adjacent neurons). The neurotransmitters diffuse across the synapse and combine with receptors on the postsynaptic membrane; this can open channels that permit ions (charged particles) to flow across the membrane. The postsynaptic neuron is said to be depolarized when positive ions enter the cell, and it will generate an action potential if a sufficient amount of depolarization occurs (see Figure 2.1).

Before the membrane of the postsynaptic cell can fire (become depolarized and send its impulse to the soma), a critical number of the many receptor sites must be occupied by NE. The more molecules of this neurotransmitter (NE) that we can shove into the synapse, the quicker this critical number of sites will be occupied. Imagine trying to fill the holes of an egg carton by dropping ping-pong balls from 10 feet above. Many of the balls will not land in the holes of the egg carton. If we want to fill the carton quickly, we need to drop more ping-pong balls in a given period of time. In the case of neurotransmission, the more molecules of NE released into the synapse, the sooner these receptor sites are occupied—and the more rapidly the neurons will fire, and the more aroused you will be and able to run from the saber-toothed tiger or your abusive boss. Just exactly how does this increase in NE neurotransmission bring this about?

Stimulant drugs can increase the number of neurotransmitter molecules in the synapse, and therefore increase the rate of neurotransmission (changing your emotional state) by two different methods. Some drugs (amphetamine) increase the rate of release of neurotransmitters from the presynaptic terminal, while others (cocaine) prevent the reuptake of the neurotransmitter from the synapse back into the presynaptic terminal, thereby expanding the amount of available dopamine (Floresco, 2007). Either way, the increase in synaptic neurotransmitters increases the rate of neurotransmission with a resulting change in mood.

The increased level of NE signals a region of the brain known as the *hypothalamus* to send messages to another region, the pituitary gland, which in turn causes the adrenal glands (adrenal cortex) sitting on top of the kidneys to produce *cortisol*, known as the stress hormone. Cortisol enhances memory and immunity and decreases sensitivity to pain. For example, when meeting the tiger, you don't want to try to remember if he or she is "really bad," or begin to worry about catching a cold or suffering from a sore tooth.

Activation of this system, known as the hypothalamic-pituitary-adrenal (HPA) axis (Figure 2.4), accelerates the heart rate, which brings oxygen and other nutrients to the various parts of the body, increasing strength, and decreasing reaction time. Following the escape from the tiger, or your boss, you will be unable to sleep for many hours because the chemicals (NE) produced by this episode cascade back and forth across the synapse, keeping the rate of neurotransmission high, your eyes wide awake, and your brain pulsating.

What makes neurotransmission so remarkable is the speed with which this seemingly very cumbersome and complex process occurs. It is like running a marathon race in which there are a thousand streams to cross. At each stream, the runner must gather rocks (neurotransmitters) from the first shore (presynaptic terminal) to build stepping stones to the next shore (postsynaptic terminal). The encounter with the tiger (boss) increases the number of "neuronal" rocks that are available on the shore where the runner arrives (presynaptic neuron); the more rocks available, the more rapidly will the runner be able to build a path to cross over the stream.

Of course, most activities in which we engage do not alter our consciousness to the level of arousal brought on by the attack of the tiger or serious confrontation with our boss. The tiger scenario should, however, give you some idea of how the mind and body can be energized, how mood can dramatically shift, and how the moment can be seized—all through the power of brain chemistry. It should be noted that this elevation of neurotransmission (i.e., mood) is brought about without resorting to stimulant drugs such as cocaine or methamphetamine. In today's society, we are often tempted to alter our mood by the use of drugs, which, as we shall see, can increase neurotransmission in certain parts of the brain that result in pleasurable experiences. Let us now turn our attention to the effect of drugs on the brain (Neurochemistry 102). It turns out that most of the mood alterations brought about by drugs are due to the role of a neurotransmitter known as dopamine (DA).

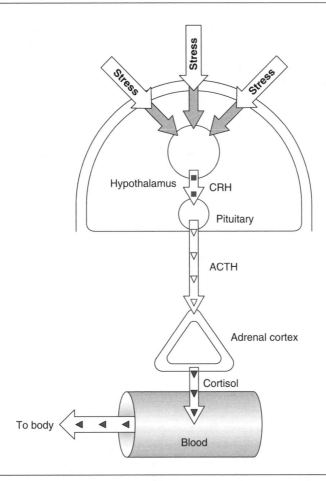

Figure 2.4 **Hypothalamic-pituitary-adrenal (HPA) axis.** In response to stress, the hypothalamus secretes corticotrophin-releasing hormone (CRH) into a specialized blood supply that transports it to the pituitary gland where it stimulates the release of adrenocorticotropic hormone (ACTH) into the general circulation. ACTH, in turn, stimulates the adrenal cortex to release cortisol into the general circulation. Cortisol is a steroid hormone that decreases inflammation and mobilizes fuels.

_____ The Joy of Dopamine and the Reward Cascade

The most pleasure that life has to offer is an adequate flow of dopamine into the nucleus accumbens.
—S. G. Sunderwirth

Understanding the joyful feelings evoked by brain chemistry begins with a search for a site in the brain responsible for this pleasure. The presence of a _pleasure center_ in the brain was demonstrated by Olds and Milner (1954) at McGill

University. They found that a rat with an electrode implanted into a certain region of the brain would continually press a lever in order to receive electrical stimulation. Routtenberg (1978) of Northwestern University later showed that, given a choice between a lever that delivered food for survival and one delivering brain stimulation, rats would forgo food in favor of the "reward" of brain stimulation. In other words, they chose ecstasy over survival. Rats, it seems, may become as addicted to an artificial (and ultimately fatal) paradise as humans.

In these experiments, the preference for "prolonged ecstasy" occurred only if the electrode was placed in a very small part of the brain, which Routtenberg (1978) referred to as the *reward center*. In recent years, the search for the specific site in the brain that regulates mood has led scientists to a complex array of neuronal clusters known as the *limbic system* (Figure 2.2). This region of the brain is believed to control emotions and is often referred to as the "reptilian brain," since we share this primordial brain with other living creatures.

Blum (1991) has proposed a model for reward (pleasure) involving the interaction of several neurotransmitters with the various parts of the limbic system that compose the reward center. The release of dopamine into the nucleus accumbens, an important reward site, plays a major role in mediating our moods (Carelli, 2002). Although there are other reward sites in the limbic system, for simplicity we will limit our discussion to the action of dopamine on the nucleus accumbens. In Blum's model, which he calls the *reward cascade,* feelings of well-being, as well as the absence of craving and anxiety, depend on an *adequate supply of dopamine* flowing into the nucleus accumbens. Dopamine mediates the rewarding properties of both natural and drug-induced pleasures (Carelli, 2002). In humans, any imbalance that would lead to a deficit of dopamine would produce anxiety and a craving for substances (alcohol, cocaine, heroin, amphetamine, etc.) or activities (e.g., gambling, crime, promiscuous sex, hang gliding) that would temporarily restore this deficit. The levels of dopamine in the nucleus accumbens are increased with virtually every drug of abuse (Carelli, 2002).

A modified version of the reward cascade (Figure 2.5) helps us to understand this complex interaction of neurotransmitters. Let's start with serotonin, that ubiquitous neurotransmitter about which thousands of articles have been written. The introduction of Prozac and other selective serotonin reuptake inhibitors (SSRIs) has made serotonin (5-HT) a household word. In the hypothalamus, serotonin neurons stimulate the release of methionine enkephalin (or simply enkephalin), which in turn inhibits the release of GABA (gamma-aminobutyric acid) in the limbic system. (It seems that we have one more chemical to consider.) What is GABA? The brain must have synapses that retard neurotransmission as well as increase it; otherwise we would be in a constant state of emotional turmoil even more than we are now. GABA is the neurotransmitter utilized by these inhibitory synapses; it's our own internal "Valium," regulating our mood through inhibition of the release of neurotransmitters such as dopamine and norepinephrine. "GABA is the major inhibitory neurotransmitter in the mammalian nervous system" (Hu & Quick, 2008, p. 309).

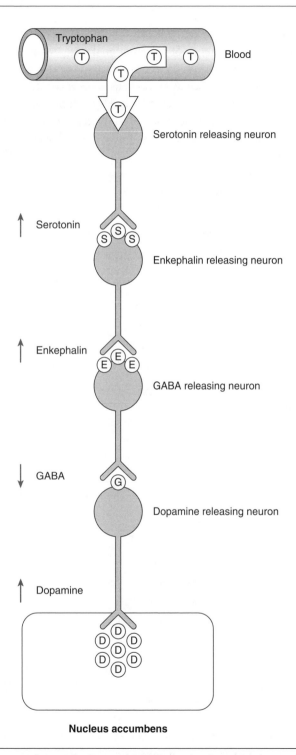

Figure 2.5   **The reward cascade.** Serotonin neurons stimulate the release of enkephalin, which in turn inhibits the release of GABA (gamma-aminobutyric acid) in the limbic system. As GABA decreases, we can expect the release of dopamine to increase. In other words, the enkephalin has inhibited the inhibitor (GABA).

Now that we have struggled through these technical terms, let's see what they really mean in terms of our emotional state. As we follow the reward cascade, the most important concept to keep in mind is that an adequate supply of dopamine in the nucleus accumbens is necessary for feelings of well-being. Studies have shown that increased levels of dopamine in the nucleus accumbens can lead to increased pleasure and reward as well as decreased anxiety. As earlier stated, most drugs of abuse as well as certain activities increase the supply of DA in the nucleus accumbens (Blum, 1991; Carelli, 2002). Tables 2.1 and 2.2 summarize these effects. Figure 2.6 highlights common effects of drugs and certain activities on dopamine in the nucleus accumbens.

Table 2.1   Effect of Various Drugs on Dopamine Levels in the Nucleus Accumbens

Drug	Effect on Dopamine Level in the Nucleus Accumbens
Alcohol ⟶	Increase
Amphetamine ⟶	Increase
Cocaine ⟶	Increase
Heroin ⟶	Increase
Marijuana ⟶	Increase
Nicotine ⟶	Increase

Table 2.2   Effect of Various Activities on Dopamine Levels in the Nucleus Accumbens

Activity	Effect on Dopamine Level in the Nucleus Accumbens
Crime ⟶	Increase
Eating ⟶	Increase
Gambling ⟶	Increase
Hugs ⟶	Increase
Risk taking ⟶	Increase
Sex ⟶	Increase

Figure 2.7 illustrates where various drugs act on the brain to increase DA in the nucleus accumbens. It is now generally accepted that DA is the master chemical of pleasure and that the "high" from drugs is caused by this increase in DA.

How does the reward cascade work to produce this flow of DA into the nucleus accumbens? As we have said, the process is initiated by the neurotransmitter serotonin (5-hydroxytryptamine, or 5-HT), which is produced in the brain from the amino acid tryptophan and is enhanced by antidepressants such as Prozac. Once we have a supply of serotonin, what does this do for us? How does it help us not only to sleep but in general to reduce

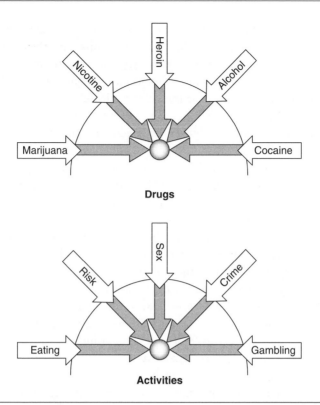

Figure 2.6 **Effects of drugs and activities on the nucleus accumbens.** Addictive drugs and compulsive problem behaviors share the common effect of increasing levels of dopamine in the nucleus accumbens.

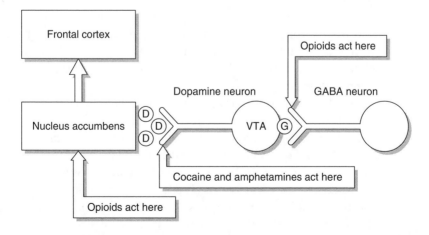

Figure 2.7 **Action of various drugs on the brain to increase dopamine.** Addictive drugs act on different sites in the brain with the common effect of increasing dopamine in the nucleus accumbens.

feelings of anxiety and craving? In the hypothalamus, serotonin-releasing neurons impinge on enkephalin neurons, enhancing the release of enkephalin. In Figure 2.5, the up and down arrows indicate an increase or decrease, respectively, of the appropriate molecules. The primary function of enkephalin neurons in the brain is to inhibit the release of neurotransmitters from any neuron with which they interact; the more enkephalin released from these neurons, the more inhibition they exert on neurons on which they impinge (Figure 2.5).

Now, how does GABA fit into this neurochemical puzzle? Conveniently, GABA-releasing neurons, as well as other neurons, have receptor sites for enkephalin molecules. As the number of these receptor sites occupied with enkephalin molecules increases, the release of GABA decreases. But GABA keeps the release of dopamine in check through another inhibitory synapse. Therefore, as GABA decreases due to either enkephalin increase or opiate ingestion, we can expect the release of dopamine to increase. In other words, the enkephalin has inhibited the inhibitor (GABA). This process works with the logic of a double negative and results in a positive increase in dopamine at the nucleus accumbens, which brings about a decrease in feelings of restlessness and anxiety as well as a general increase in feelings of well-being. Serotonin is the battery that starts the engine (reward cascade) that brings about enhanced dopaminergic neurotransmission.

Although serotonin starts the reward cascade engine, the real power behind the pleasure pathway is enkephalin, that internal opiate produced by our brains in response to both internal and external stimuli. It is this euphoric effect that has resulted in enkephalins and their cousins, the *endorphins*, being referred to as "the keys to paradise." Enkephalins and endorphins, although structurally different, are often grouped together under the generic name *endogenous* or *internal opiates*. These self-produced opiates are involved in the reward system, the regulation of mood, and the stress response (Nikoshkov et al., 2008).

Much to our credit—and eternal regret—humankind has been able to find drugs (morphine) and even manufacture drugs (heroin) that have chemical structures similar to our own enkephalins (and endorphins) and, as we shall see later, can produce the feelings of euphoria even more intensely than our internal opiates.

For a drug to produce reward or pleasure, that is, to increase levels of dopamine, it must attach itself to receptor sites that are present in the brain. In other words, the drug just mimics compounds for which the brain already has receptors. For example, opiates can occupy the receptor sites for enkephalins, which are in the brain, and therefore activate the reward cascade. Milkman and Sunderwirth (1982, 1987, 1998) proposed that people could become addicted to activities as well to drugs and that the brain chemistry associated with these activities was similar to that of drugs. We now know that many rewarding activities do increase the level of dopamine.

Even the anticipation of reward increases the level of dopamine in animals. For example, Phillips, Stuber, Heien, Wightman, and Carelli (2003) at the University of North Carolina have shown that when rats encounter anything that they associate with past drug taking (cocaine), dopamine levels "surge," which pushes the rats to seek more of the drug. In humans, similar encounters with drug contexts also produce dopamine surges and push the addict toward further drug-seeking activity.

The concept of conditioned craving has been picked up by the popular press. A *Newsweek* article entitled "Electronic Morphine" (Will, 2002) dealt with the problem of compulsive gambling by citing the case of an individual earning $35,000 a year who lost $175,000 during several years of gambling. This behavioral compulsion has become a serious problem with the increase in gambling opportunities that include online poker, other video games, service station pull tabs, and riverboat casinos. A recent automobile advertisement for the Lincoln LS had the following heading: "The Pleasure Neuron: Luxury May Be Habit-Forming, and We Have the MRIs to Prove It." This was followed by "I love this car." Dopamine is released, producing a feeling of well-being.

Clearly, the concept of the relationship between pleasure and dopamine release has reached the general public. The fundamental concept is that drugs or behaviors that elicit pleasure or reward are accompanied by an increase of dopamine in the nucleus accumbens. Table 2.1 shows the wide variety of drugs that cause an increase in dopamine in the nucleus accumbens, ultimately interpreted by the user as rewarding. Extra activity in the nucleus accumbens occurs when the person is involved in rewarding activities (Floresco, 2007). Activities or certain behaviors can mimic the neurochemistry of drugs of abuse. Activities as different as crime and eating have been shown to increase the level of dopamine in the nucleus accumbens. Table 2.2 shows the various activities that also bring about this increase. Obviously, hugging your child will not give you the same sensation as a line of cocaine. Although both are accompanied by an increase in dopamine in the nucleus accumbens, other pathways in the brain are also involved. To be sure, nothing in brain chemistry is simple. But in this chapter, let's stick to the effect of drugs of abuse on the brain and the *dopaminergic reward system.*

Table 2.3, adapted from the work of Di Chiara and Imperto (1988); Tanda, Pontieri, and Di Chiara (1997); and Joseph, Young, and Gray (1998), indicates the sites of action and the percentage increase in dopamine compared with controls (absence of drugs). It is clear that *amphetamine has the greatest influence* (900+%), followed by cocaine, heroin, and marijuana. Methamphetamine has an even greater effect than amphetamine. Although alcohol is not as powerful as a stimulant for DA release, as we shall see, the amount in which it is consumed in this country makes its use the second most serious drug problem in the United States, after nicotine.

Table 2.3   Site of Action of Drugs in the Reward Cascade and Percentage Increase in Dopamine in the Nucleus Accumbens

DRUGS AND DOPAMINE

Control: (Absence of Drugs)

Serotonin ↑ → Enkephalin*↑ → GABA ↓ → DA ↑

Amphetamine: Enhances release and blocks reabsorption of DA

Serotonin ↑ → Enkephalin*↑ → GABA ↓ → DA ↑↑ (900+%)[2]

Cocaine: Prevents reuptake of DA

Serotonin ↑ → Enkephalin*↑ → GABA ↓ → DA[1] ↑↑ (200+%)[2]

Nicotine: Stimulation of exicitatory ACH receptors on DA cell bodies

Serotonin ↑ → Enkephalin*↑ → GABA ↓ → DA[1] ↑↑ (100%)[2]

Heroin: Increases DA through opioid receptors

Serotonin ↑ → Heroin (Enkephalin*)[1] ↑↑ → GABA ↓↓→ DA ↑↑ (160%)[2]

Marijuana:

Serotonin ↑ → THC (Enkephalin*)[1] ↑↑ → GABA ↓↓→ DA ↑↑ (130%)[2]

Prozac: Inhibits reuptake of serotonin

Serotonin[1] ↑↑ Enkephalin* ↓↓ → GABA ↓↓ → DA ↑↑

Morphine: Inhibits the inhibitor (GABA), therefore increasing DA

Serotonin ↑ → Mor (Enkephalin*)[1] ↓↓ → GABA ↓↓ → DA ↑↑ (60+%)[2]

Alcohol: Increases serotonin

Serotonin ↑ → THIQ (Enkephalin*)[1] ↑↑ GABA ↓↓ → DA ↑↑ (100%)[2]

* an opioid   [1]site of action   [2]% increase over control

SOURCE: Di Chara, G. et al. Proceedings of the National Academy of Science, USA, 85, 5274–5278 (1988). Joseph, M. H. et al. Human Psychopharmacology. Vol. II S55–S63 (1996); and Tanada, G. et al. Science. Vol. 276, 2048–2050 (1997).

Genes and Drug Abuse— Choose Your Parents Carefully

Not everyone responds equally to the same drug. There is considerable variation in the drug-induced pleasure of dopamine from one individual to another. Why is this true?

Studies of twins (e.g., Ferguson & Goldberg,1997; Legrand et al., 2005) point to genes as the basis for the variance in the vulnerability of individuals to alcohol and drug abuse and dependence. Nikoshkov et al. (2008) assert that addiction has been shown to be linked to the reward sensitivity of the individual, and more specifically, that opioid abuse is correlated to some variability in the endogenous opioid systems mentioned earlier (enkephalins), which have a profound effect on pleasure. According to Uhl, Liu, and Naiman (2002), genes in the dopamine circuit are "likely candidates" for the variation in the susceptibility of individuals to drug abuse and addiction. To understand the genetic contribution to dopamine-seeking behaviors, let's continue in Neurochemistry 101 and see how dopamine is produced in the brain. Dopamine is produced from phenylalanine, which is present in foods such as meat. Phenylalanine is converted into dopamine by a series of reactions, each of which requires a special enzyme. Should any of these enzymes be deficient, the production of dopamine would be decreased. This would result in a decreased ability to experience pleasure. Individuals with this enzyme deficiency may be more prone to compensate for the resulting decrease in dopamine by choosing dopamine-enhancing drugs such as opiates, cocaine, or methamphetamine. Before leaving this section on dopamine, it is important to note that imbalances in dopamine have been implicated in disorders such as Parkinson's disease, schizophrenia, and even anorexia.

Another example of the role of genes in substance abuse can be seen in the reward cascade (Figure 2.5). Tryptophan, found in many foods, is converted into serotonin (5-HT) by a series of reactions, each of which is catalyzed by an enzyme. An enzyme deficiency would result in a decrease in the production of serotonin. You will recall that serotonin starts the reward cascade, which results in the flow of dopamine into the nucleus accumbens. Therefore, any decrease in serotonin would result in a decrease of dopamine, with the resulting craving for drugs or hedonic activity to make up for this deficiency. Enzymes are proteins that are formed by the following scheme:

Parents → DNA → RNA → Proteins (enzymes)

Since DNA is genetically determined by your parents, it is important to *choose your parents carefully!*

Drugs to Fight Drugs

The history of using medication to combat drug abuse is not rosy. Aside from the traditional wariness from 12-step programs that pharmaceutical patches will likely result in substitute addictions, anti-addiction medication (although bursting with promise) does not have a great track record. Dating back to the late 1800s, both opium and cocaine were introduced as cures for alcoholism. Followed by the introduction of heroin as a safe replacement for morphine, methadone to treat heroin addiction turned out to be highly addictive itself. The effects of Antabuse, highly touted for its ability to cause illness and vomiting after ingestion of just a small amount of alcohol, can be sidestepped by skipping the dose. Despite these problems and disappointing outcomes, there are currently more than 200 compounds being developed or tested by the National Institute on Drug Abuse to suppress the impulse, block the intoxication, or manage the withdrawal from psychoactive drugs (Interlandi, 2008).

Table 2.4 summarizes promising research on some of the medications that may be effective in combating drug dependence.

Table 2.4   Promising Pharmacologic Adjuncts for Substance Abuse Treatment

Drug Name	Mechanism of Action	Research Findings
Vigabatrin	Gamma-aminobutyric acid, or GABA, exerts an inhibitory effect on neurons, instructing the body to stop potentially dangerous actions. Addicts' brains are deficient in GABA, so researchers are conducting trials with Vigabatrin, which stimulates its production.	Thirty percent of patients who took Vigabatrin stayed off cocaine during the 9-week study, compared with 5% of the controls.
Campral	Already available as a treatment for alcoholism, Campral works on the brain chemical glutamate. While the early stages of addiction are driven by pleasure seeking—hence the importance of dopamine—the motive eventually shifts to avoiding the pain of withdrawal; at that point, drug-seeking behavior is fueled by glutamate.	By suppressing glutamate, Campral can reduce craving during recovery.
D-Cycloserine (DCS)	Helps erase learned fear responses. DCS makes this happen faster. Successfully tested in people as a treatment for acrophobia (fear of heights).	Research explores if DCS can eliminate the association between visual cues and the impulse to relapse into drug or alcohol addiction. Presently, testing is only on cocaine, but if it works there, it might work for other addictions as well.
Naltrexone	This pill has been around for a decade and blocks the intoxicating effects of alcohol, but an addict driven to get high can just skip his or her dose.	Short acting. Blocks the action of alcohol.
Vivitrol	Longer-lasting, injectable form of Naltrexone, available since 2006. Does not enhance self-control or stop the craving for liquor, but it blocks its effects. Injected once per month.	Can have severe side effects along with alcohol withdrawal, including sweating, shaking, vomiting.

SOURCE: From "What addicts need" by J. Interlandi, 2008, February 23, *Newsweek*. Available at http://www.newsweek.com/id/114716.

In addition to a growing arsenal of pharmaceutical devices to treat drug addiction, researchers are focused on developing vaccines that will prevent intoxicants from affecting the brain. As described earlier, cocaine and most other drugs of abuse use the dopamine reward pathway in the brain.

> Drugs of abuse activate pathways to a 20-fold extent greater than the usual pleasures of life; good food, sex, music, etc. When you are doing that repeatedly, the whole system down-regulates, meaning that it simply doesn't respond to the usual rewards in life anymore, because they are below the threshold. (Kosten, 2007, cited by Madden-Fuentes, 2007)

As described by Madden-Fuentes (2007), the brain of a 22-year-old cocaine abuser can deteriorate enough to look like that of a 60-year-old Parkinson's patient. Given that this type of damage can permanently alter the quality of life for millions of stimulant abusers, a vaccine that could inoculate certain people from contracting brain disease could be of enormous value. In fact, an anti-cocaine vaccine is being seriously studied at Baylor University. The new vaccine has been scheduled to undergo large-scale human trials (Madden-Fuentes, 2007). The vaccine's preventive action is predicated on "tricking" the body into creating antibodies normally used by the immune system to identify and neutralize foreign particles, usually bacteria or viruses. Cocaine is attached to the outside of inactivated cholera toxin proteins. By inactivating the cholera proteins, they are prevented from causing disease, but when injected they are still recognized by the immune system, which makes antibodies to cholera and cocaine at the same time. Hence, the same injection vaccinates against both cholera and cocaine.

> Blood vessels are distributed all over the brain, but the cocaine does not get into the brain because when it is bound to the antibodies, which are fairly large proteins, it cannot get through the blood-brain barrier (a natural formation that prevents foreign substances from going into the brain). . . . It's just like a big sponge for cocaine in the bloodstream. The function of the vaccine is to "soak up" enough cocaine that addicts cannot get high, which will soon extinguish desire for the drug. The vaccine would be given three or four times a year but not likely to be needed for one's entire life. (Kosten, 2007, cited in Madden-Fuentes, 2007)

Anti-psychoactive vaccination is potentially the pièce de résistance of weapons against addiction. In addition to the cocaine vaccination, inoculations against nicotine, heroin, and methamphetamine are also in development. Although appealing on a number of levels to law enforcement officials, parents, and pediatricians, the uncharted territory of *addiction vaccination* will likely face many civil liberties challenges (Interlandi, 2008). For instance, how about vaccinating high-risk teenagers (Who would decide the criteria for "high risk"?) until they are old enough to make better use of their prefrontal cortex?

Chapter Summary

This chapter lays the groundwork for understanding how drugs and activities modify mood by affecting changes in the reward centers of the brain. Beginning with an overview of how neurotransmission is the biological substratum for all aspects of our awareness including thought, perception, and emotion, the chapter moves to a discussion of how the HPA axis mediates the interaction between neurotransmission and the body's global response to stress. This provides a template for understanding how an emergency situation (or a perceived emergency situation) can release powerful chemicals throughout the brain and body, similar to the powerful effects of stimulant drugs. The reward cascade is then discussed as the unifying mechanism for a range of drugs and behaviors, through which dopamine arrives at the nucleus accumbens, thereby resulting in the subjective experience of pleasure. Genetics are then discussed in terms of individual differences in reward sensitivity, which may contribute to an individual's compulsion toward pleasure-seeking activity. The chapter concludes with a discussion of how pharmacological research is engaged in developing new compounds to stave off craving, reward activation, and withdrawal associated with various agents of addiction.

SECTION II

Finding Relief and Letting Go

I do not think that anyone completely understands its mechanism, but it is a fact that there are foreign substances which, when present in the blood or tissues, directly cause us pleasurable sensations; and they also so alter the conditions governing our sensibility that we become incapable of receiving unpleasurable impulses.

—Sigmund Freud (1929/2005, p. 27)

Overview: Seeking Safety and Comfort

The goals of this section are to first illuminate neurochemical similarities between a range of satiating activities, including excessive drinking, unhealthy eating, smoking cigarettes, and injecting heroin. The question of how alcohol can trigger addiction is followed by a discussion of health benefits (cardiovascular) and potential risks (cancer) from moderate drinking. In Chapter 4, we examine the barroom setting, which we have dubbed "The Great Psychiatric Tavern," whereby a host of psychological and social needs are managed by a surrogate "mental health treatment" team. Discussion in Chapter 5 of how some women misuse alcohol or other sedatives to control psychological pain is followed by an examination of how a variety of licit and illicit psychoactive chemicals—including inhalants, cigarettes, and heroin—are used to "self-medicate." Nicotine is examined as the world's most prolific antidepressant drug. Chapter 6, Eating for a Change, analyzes how food may serve as a drug to alter mood.

Metaphorically, growing up consists of finding the right substitutes for your thumb. From the cradle to the crypt, we discover various means—some socially approved, others highly disdained—for coping with the inevitable stress of walking through life's corridor. As infants, we have limited resources for dealing with repetitive swells of physical or emotional discomfort. Whether we survive depends on adult caretakers. We require proper nourishment, safety, and love. From the newborn's perspective, the universe is benign or malevolent depending on his or her experience with feeding and forming intimate emotional bonds. The nursling's knowledge that he or she will be lovingly fed allows baby to develop a basic trust in other human beings. As earlier stated in the Introduction, this perspective is embodied by *object relations theory* (e.g., Baker & Baker, 1987; Graham & Glickauf-Hughes, 1992; Kohut, 1977).

An infant's tension is reduced through the kind deliverance of food and touch. Misery and despair soon fade into gurgles and coos as the baby swoons in a state of blissful delight. Food, touch, and novelty become associated with love and the pleasures of being unshackled from disquieting physical sensations. A soothing influence appears from the outside world and suddenly baby feels better. A flailing state of alarm melts into passive euphoria. Like Sinbad on his magic carpet, the newborn simply forms a whimper and a wish and "zam-zam alacazam," a Shangri-La of nurturance and affection quickly unfolds: mother's breast, mommy and daddy's bed, a kiss, a caress, sumptuous creamy food. Behold, the Garden of Eden. All this for some rapid breathing, a few tears, and several whining screams. The infant soon discovers that a measure of tension can also be regulated through self-stimulation. Syllabic babbling, masturbation, and thumb sucking become important means for reducing stress. As Freud stated in *Three Essays on the Theory of Sexuality* (1905/1962),

It is impossible to describe what a lovely feeling goes through your whole body when you suck; you are right away from this world. You are absolutely satisfied and happy beyond desire. It is a wonderful feeling; you long for nothing but peace—uninterrupted peace. It is unspeakably lovely: you feel no pain and no sorrow, and ah! you are carried into another world. (p. 47)

As adults, we repeatedly seek passage to the infant's heavenly retreat. Wistfully lamented by folk singers Peter, Paul, and Mary, "A million dollars at the drop of a hat/ I'd give it all gladly if life could be like that." Life's stressful and perilous journey is made more bearable by brief excursions into pleasurable moments that we have dubbed "substitutes for your thumb." Yet, as the poet John Milton sagely advised, "The mind is its own place. . . . It can make a heaven of hell or a hell of heaven." The same stimulus—whether a mood-altering drug or an activity like sex—can evoke paradise for one person and a fiery inferno for another.

An individual's unique combination of genetic characteristics and early childhood experiences determines his or her specific inclinations toward pleasurable activities. Some patterns emerge as early as the first year of life, while others are spawned during critical periods after many years of social learning and personal development. Quite naturally, need-gratifying behavior of any kind tends to be repeated because it continues to reduce conflict and tension. However, it is our biological adaptation to repeated mind-affecting stimuli—whether food, activities, or drugs—that requires increasing levels of exposure to achieve comparable feelings of pleasure. Any activity that produces salient alterations in mood (which are always accompanied by changes in neurotransmission) can lead to compulsion, loss of control, and progressively disturbed functioning.

Although the consequences of compulsive eating, TV watching, and repetitively abusing alcohol or other sedative drugs are obviously not the same, several commonalities exist. Subjectively, there develops an irresistible craving for food, drink, or activities that appear to lessen the impact of physically or psychologically arousing stimuli. Behaviorally, there are recurrent action patterns designed to re-create placid emotional states. Psychologically, satiation seekers reduce stress by adopting a stance of passive withdrawal from internal or external conflict.

Many today find soothing relief through electronic parent surrogates, for example, the Internet, DVDs, and TV. Parents enjoy hours of relative calm as their children remain fixated on a plethora of computer-generated images, interactive games, chat rooms, text messages, and iPod music. For adults, soap operas, reality shows, and sitcoms provide temporary relief from unpleasant emotions, thoughts, or circumstances in daily life. Compulsive viewers eagerly await the times of day when they can watch the tormented lives of television characters who, in fantasy, become substitute members of their own family. Between episodes, reality show junkies, on some levels of consciousness, remain focused on an artificial, pre-scripted crisis. These agencies of tension reduction are examined in Section IV of this book, Mental Excursions.

A humorous example of how media can become addictive is taken from one of Greg Howard's "Sally Forth" cartoons:

> Listen Carol, just don't get yourself into the kind of trouble I did when I was on maternity leave. One day when I was nursing Hilary I turned on a soap opera just for fun. Within a week I was mainlining. I was doing four hours of soaps a day. Then I really flipped out and started to mix soaps and game shows. Finally I had to quit cold turkey. It was awful! Do you know I still get occasional flashbacks from *General Hospital?*

The Chemistry of Calm

The heroin rush is said to be king of the opiate-mediated sensations. Indeed, the quiet lethargy induced by heroin is reminiscent of the infant's calm, sleepy satisfaction after being breastfed. Are we then to assume that the world's most infamous narcotic and mother's milk have a chemical similarity? Is there an underlying biochemical thread that can explain the common reaction to these very disparate yet similarly satisfying substances? At first, even the suggestion of some commonality between milk and heroin seems ridiculous, even disrespectful. Yet these seemingly diverse substitutes for your thumb trigger similar changes in the brain's reward system. Similar biochemical principles may be used to account for progressive dependence on a wide spectrum of mood-calming activities—taking sedative drugs, listening to music, watching television, undergoing massage, or eating your grandmother's chicken soup— and yes, it is possible to develop a growing dependence on these chemically similar though more subtle versions of opiate addiction.

Enkephalins and related compounds, the endorphins, occur naturally in the brain and mimic the effect of morphine. They decrease the number of neurotransmitter molecules released into the synapse, or the space between neurons, which ironically increases dopamine in the nucleus accumbens, the brain's reward center, with a resulting decrease in the rate of neurotransmission in the pain pathways of the central nervous system (refer back to Chapter 2).

Unfortunately, too many people seek substitutes for their thumbs (ecstasy) through use of alcohol or other drugs. According to the Substance Abuse and Mental Health Services Administration (SAMHSA), in 2006 an estimated 9.2% (or 22.6 million) of the population aged 12 and older in the United States had a substance abuse or dependence problem. Of these, 3.2 million were dependent on or abused both alcohol and illicit drugs, 3.8 million were dependent on or abused illicit drugs but not alcohol, and 15.6 million were dependent on or abused alcohol but not illicit drugs (SAMHSA, 2007b).

It is estimated that by 2012 there will be a potential alcohol-medication market of 30 million people in the United States, Europe, and Japan. This does not include the 71.5 million people in the United States who presently use tobacco, which is the greatest killer of all the drugs—nearly half a million per year die from tobacco use in the United States alone. This death rate is followed by the rate of deaths due to consumption of alcohol, whose excessive use causes more deaths than all illegal drugs combined (Thayer, 2006).

Both internally produced endorphins and ingested opiates occupy neuronal receptor sites that regulate neurotransmitter release. The greater the number of occupied sites, the fewer the neurotransmitters that are released into the synapse. When there is a dramatic decrease in the number of neurotransmitter molecules released into the synapse, neuronal impulses become insufficient to support vital functions such as breathing, heartbeat, and blood pressure. Fatal heroin overdoses are the result of exceeding the body's capacity for occupation of opiate receptor sites in the central nervous system. Fortunately, the probability of overdosing on endorphins as a result of non-drug-induced ecstasy is very remote.

Endorphins and enkephalins are opiates produced by the body to control pain. Without them, we would constantly suffer from the slightest injury. The Spanish conquest of Mexico, as recorded by Bernal Diaz del Castillo, provides an excellent example of the body's ability to carry on in spite of serious and painful injuries. In the attack by Hernán Cortés on the Aztec capital of Tenochtitlán, Diaz records that there were no noncombative casualties as a result of injuries to the often-outnumbered conquistadors. The Spanish were either fighting or dead, even if the injuries were of such a serious nature that death ultimately followed.

Not only do the endorphins and enkephalins reduce pain, they also produce euphoria much like that of opiates. It is known that neuronal pathways associated with pain pass through that portion of the brain known as the limbic system (see Chapter 2, Figure 2.2), which is also the seat of emotion and feeling. Therefore, any substance that tends to reduce pain has a soothing effect on our emotions. Mood-calming activities also have the effect of releasing endorphins, which in turn decreases the number of neurotransmitter molecules released into the synapse. This results in the feeling of well-being experienced during and immediately following these activities. For this reason, opiates, as well as our own endorphins, produce both analgesia and euphoria. One well-known endorphin-releasing activity is eating warm and pleasant-tasting food. The relief from a cold, sore throat, or other minor pain upon eating warm soup (chicken or otherwise) is familiar to us all. It is the body's own endorphins that mimic the effect of opiates and bring about the desired satiation effect. Since pain relief and emotional soothing are both mediated by the occupation of opiate receptor sites on certain neurons of the brain, we have coined the term *opmex* (opiate-mediated experience) to refer to the set of behaviors that include the ingestion of opiate drugs and also non-drug activities that release the body's internal opiates, the endorphins.

Before proceeding too far into a discussion of the chemistry of contentment, we should remember that the brain also has neuronal connections that decrease, rather than increase, neurotransmission in nerve pathways associated with emotions, feelings, and pain. These synaptic connections are referred to as *inhibitory,* whereas those that are associated with an increase in neurotransmission are called *excitatory.* Under normal conditions, the brain maintains a fairly constant rate of neurotransmission through the combined effort of the inhibitory and excitatory neurons.

The importance of the regulation of neurotransmission can be seen in those neuronal disturbances that often result in bizarre behavioral changes. Most people are familiar with the late folk singer Woody Guthrie, who developed a disorder known as Huntington's chorea in the prime of his life. This disease is caused by a deterioration of inhibitory synapses with the resultant loss of control of neurotransmission. Another disorder known as Parkinson's disease is caused by a deterioration of those cells in the brain that produce dopamine, a neurotransmitter in the excitatory pathways. The well-known photographer Margaret Bourke-White suffered from this disorder. On another level, psychotic disorders such as mania, depression, and schizophrenia are the result of an imbalance between inhibition and excitation in the brain. In addition to these internal factors, we have seen that drugs and activities can create aberrant neurotransmission with resulting abnormal behavior.

This brings us back to the baby's warm milk opmex. The act of eating or drinking pleasant-tasting food, such as warm milk, releases endorphins, which decreases the release of excitatory neurotransmitters. This results in a decreased rate of neurotransmission in the excitatory pathways, which soothes and calms the infant. Warm milk also contains another ingredient that brings about a soothing effect on the central nervous system. This substance is the amino acid tryptophan, which enters the brain through the blood–brain barrier. Once inside the brain, tryptophan is converted to serotonin, which also decreases excitatory neurotransmission. This contributes to the overall relaxing effect of the warm milk and helps the baby to sleep. Hence the old folklore of drinking warm milk to aid sleep is valid in terms of modern brain chemistry.

An empirical relationship between eating and endorphins has been demonstrated by Woods et al. (1981). These researchers showed that in some cases, giving endorphins to laboratory animals caused them to eat uncontrollably. In an experiment at the National Institute of Mental Health, Martin Cohen (Cohen, Cohen, Pickar, & Murphy, 1985) showed that administration of naloxone, a drug that blocks endorphin action, caused a

28% decrease in the amount of food consumed by volunteers who were furnished with ample amounts of their favorite foods.

As noted earlier, endorphins and enkephalins have been referred to as the "keys to paradise." However, many people who seek paradise through drugs or activities soon find that heaven transforms into a living hell of uncontrolled craving. How can the pleasures associated with eating, opiates, or smoking cigarettes turn into such a Dr. Jekyll and Mr. Hyde experience?

We have briefly described how the brain contains regulatory mechanisms that maintain a relatively constant level of neurotransmission. Externally induced variations in this level, which account for our mood swings, bring about a counterreaction as the brain attempts to return neurotransmission to a normal level. This regulatory mechanism is essential for general health maintenance and is, in fact, necessary for our very survival. An overproduction of endorphins or excessive opiate ingestion would lower neurotransmission and pain perception to the point at which slowed physical reactions could endanger our lives. Placing your hand on a hot stove, for example, would result in serious injury were it not for the phenomenon of pain. Therefore, it is essential that the brain have a mechanism to maintain a "normal" level of neurotransmission. This natural, life-sustaining, internal regulatory mechanism accounts for dependence, tolerance, and addiction.

Dependence means that after repeated exposure to an event that decreases neuronal activity in the brain, a person leans on that experience in order to feel adjusted or normal. The rate at which one becomes dependent is variable, depending upon the type of experience, amount of exposure, and individual differences among users. All things being equal, a user can become dependent on morphine in about a week by using a typical dose once daily. With heroin, on the other hand, typical doses must be taken about twice daily for dependence to occur. At present, the parameters of dependence for activities such as watching media, playing video or Internet games, and eating mood-modifying foods are not known. When prolonged participation in behaviors associated with the ingestion of opiates or release of endorphins is abruptly discontinued, a characteristic disturbance known as withdrawal or abstinence syndrome begins to occur. The phenomenon of dependence is fundamentally a biochemical process. Even addicted animals that have had the thinking portions of their brains removed, and babies who have inherited opiate dependence from their mothers, will experience acute physical withdrawal symptoms, without conscious awareness.

The amount of subjective distress that occurs during withdrawal, however, is very much a function of the user's expectations, beliefs, and life circumstance. Those who insist, for example, that they will endure incredible torment if they discontinue heroin will undoubtedly report acute psychological and physical suffering. Part of being "hooked" on a satiation experience—whether shooting heroin or excessive alcohol consumption—is the phenomenon of self-identification as an addict. The belief that "I need to have . . . [x, y, or z]" is no doubt influenced by the biological fact of dependence, but the intensity of subjectively perceived pain is very much influenced by psychology and circumstance.

Tolerance of the opiate-mediated experience develops much more slowly than dependence. The tolerant heroin addict can safely ingest a far greater amount of opium than the nonaddict, for whom a large dose might cause coma or death from respiratory inhibition. Tolerant satiation addicts can avoid becoming ill or physically distressed by maintaining a constant dose of their preferred drug or activity. Feeling high is a different story. To achieve pleasurable sensations, the addict constantly must increase the frequency or amount of opmex. In the lingo of the street, "He can stay normal, but he can't get high." Some addicts continue their habits for months or years, resigned to the fact that they will no longer get high. As soon as withdrawal symptoms begin, they will administer an accustomed dose and take pleasure in simply having achieved relief from the sufferings of abstinence. The primary allure of smoking the next cigarette is apparently the temporary quelling of craving, rather than any experience of pleasure (DiFranza, 2008).

Under increased internal or external stress, however, staying normal is not enough; the addict once again craves the feeling of getting high. At this point, he or she must again increase the opmex, either in frequency or in quantity. A common experience among addicts when they can do nothing more than stay normal is to construct their lives around "getting straight." They self-impose a period of abstinence, which usually involves an initial period of acute withdrawal and at least a few weeks of recuperative discomfort. Tolerance is lowered, and the satiation addict may once again experience the precious high, which for many stands out as the most salient experience of their lives.

3

Hey, What's in This Stuff, Anyway?

Alcohol and not the dog is man's best friend.

—W. C. Fields

There are many admonitions about the dangers of drink across time, place, and culture.

Proverbs 23:29–35 in the Old Testament, for example, presents an insightful description of the progressive effects of alcohol, including those on the central nervous system:

Who has woe? Who has sorrow? Who has strife? Who has complaining? Who has wounds without cause? Who has redness of eyes? Those who tarry long over wine, those who go to try mixed wine. Do not look at wine when it is red, when it sparkles in the cup and goes down smoothly. At the last it bites like a serpent, and stings like an adder. . . . You will be like one who lies down in the midst of the sea, like one who lies on the top of a mast. "They struck me," you will say, "but I was not hurt; they beat me, but I did not feel it. When shall I awake? I will seek another drink."

The Old Testament also describes pleasure associated with alcohol: "Shall I leave my wine which cheers gods and men?" (Judges 9:13); "Mark when Amnon's heart is merry with wine" (2 Samuel 13:28).

This dichotomy was also prevalent in the Aztec city of Tenochtitlán, where drinking *pulque* (a very strong alcoholic beverage) was common practice, but public drunkenness was punishable by death.

The dual message of condemning excess while condoning moderation is at the heart of contemporary science and continued debate on this subject. In moderation, alcohol appears to have a beneficial effect, not only on the emotions but arguably on health as well (Klatsky, 2006). It is crossing that fine line, when use turns to abuse, that devastation begins to occur.

Everyone has heard the statement, "Alcohol is a depressant." Why then would anyone drink? Most people drink to feel better, to be more sociable and less depressed, not more so. Indeed, as we watch people who come to a cocktail party, we observe that after the first several drinks they seem to loosen up and become more relaxed. Rather than depressed, they appear to be more enthusiastic, animated, and expressive. As the party continues, and some guests are putting away their fifth or sixth drink, we notice a change in their behavior. Their speech becomes slurred, and they seem unable to comprehend simple concepts. If they drive, they are more likely to become involved in accidents because of delayed reaction time. Continued drinking may result in loss of consciousness.

How can we explain this apparent contradictory effect: initial excitation followed by sedation? As mentioned earlier, the central nervous system has many checks and balances to prevent either chronic overstimulation or understimulation. One mechanism for maintaining a baseline level of neurotransmission is the existence of the two types of synaptic connections mentioned earlier in this chapter. One is the excitatory pathway, which is responsible for increasing the state of arousal. Obviously there must be some means to regulate these excitatory connections, or everyone would be in a chronic state of hyperactivity. The second is inhibitory, serving as a check on neuronal over-excitation. When alcohol is ingested, the inhibitory synapses are depressed first. Excitation momentarily predominates, and the drinker feels exhilaration rather than sedation. As drinking continues, however, the excitatory pathway is also depressed. The stupor and slowed reaction time of excessive drinking set in.

How does this seemingly benign beverage become the self-inflicted poison par excellence? In some ways, the answer may lie in the fact that not everyone who drinks, even excessively, becomes addicted. Historically, alcoholism was regarded as a sign of a weak or vicious personality. Consider these words from an 1897 temperance lecture, describing the behavior of someone under the influence of alcohol: "But see that fiend incarnate with loathsome breath and oath-stained lips as he stumbles across the room to drag the dying wife from her last repose!" (Craig, 1897, p. 446).

Inheriting Alcoholism

The contemporary perspective held by the National Council on Alcoholism, Alcoholics Anonymous, and the American Medical Association is quite different from the moral depravity explanation above. Alcoholism is regarded as a chronic and potentially fatal disease that pays little respect to strength or weakness of character. The disease concept, which has been invoked for other addictions as well, holds that addicts have inherited maladaptive bio-chemical responses to certain chemicals. Faulty genes lead to the production of faulty enzymes that disturb the normal metabolism of alcohol. This in turn results in a pathological response to the drug.

Studies from the field of behavioral genetics have confirmed a heritable aspect of alcoholism. Identical twins, who share the same genes, are about twice as likely as fraternal twins, who share on average 50% of their genes, to resemble each other in terms of the presence of alcoholism. It has also been shown that 50% to 60% of the risk for alcoholism is genetically determined, for both men and women. Genes alone do not preordain that someone will be alcoholic; features in the environment along with gene–environment interactions account for the remainder of the risk (Crabbe, 2002; Heath et al., 1997; Heath & Martin, 1994; Kendler, Neal, Heath, Kessler, & Eaves, 1994; Prescott & Kendler, 1999).

To understand the theory of inherited alcoholism, consider the pathway by which alcohol is metabolized in the liver (Figure 3.1). In the first step, alcohol (ethanol) is converted to acetaldehyde using an enzyme called alco-hol dehydrogenase (ADH). This conversion requires a coenzyme, nicotin-amide adenine dinucleotide (NAD+), which will be important to remember when we discuss the addictive nature of alcohol. In the second step, acetaldehyde is then changed to acetate and finally to carbon dioxide and water. The conversion of acetaldehyde to acetate requires another enzyme known as aldehyde dehydrogenase (ALDH), as well as the same coenzyme (NAD+) used in the initial conversion of alcohol to acetaldehyde.

Since enzymes (in this case ADH and ALDH) are involved in the metab-olism of alcohol, alterations in their level would change the rate at which alcohol is processed. Further, since the formation of enzymes ultimately depends on our genetic makeup, inappropriate drinking behavior may be partly explained by inherited irregularities of ADH, ALDH, or both. A number of studies show that certain individuals are at genetic risk for alco-holism because they metabolize alcohol differently from others.

For example, Schuckit (1984) has shown that the blood acetaldehyde level is higher in those with a family history of alcoholism. He has further shown that acetaldehyde is converted into acetate at about half the rate in confirmed alcoholics as in nonalcoholics. This explains the established fact that acetaldehyde accumulates in alcoholics. Schuckit also demon-strated that this metabolic irregularity may exist even before heavy drink-ing. That is, the children of alcoholics, who before the experiment had never ingested alcohol, were unable to convert acetaldehyde to acetate at the normal rate.

On a behavioral level, Schuckit (1984) observed that novice drinkers with family histories of alcoholism sway less after three or four drinks than those without familial alcoholism. This may be a simple test to detect a genetic pre-disposition to alcoholism (Heinz, 2006). One of the best protections against excessive drinking (perhaps excessive anything, for that matter) is nausea (Schuckit, cited in Heinz, 2006). For people who get sick from drinking too

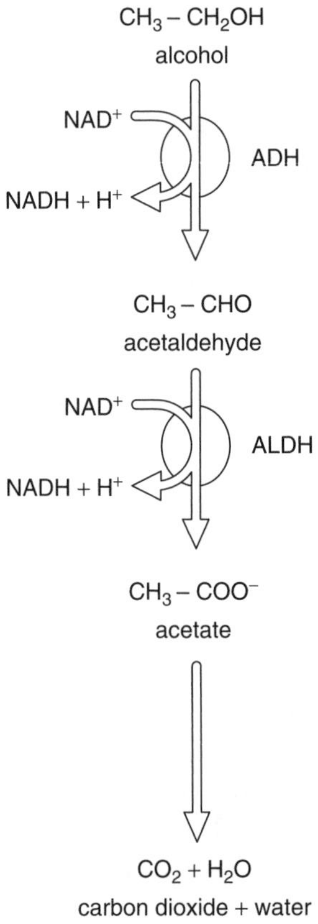

$$CH_3 - CH_2OH$$
alcohol

NAD$^+$

NADH + H$^+$

ADH

$$CH_3 - CHO$$
acetaldehyde

NAD$^+$

NADH + H$^+$

ALDH

$$CH_3 - COO^-$$
acetate

$$CO_2 + H_2O$$
carbon dioxide + water

Figure 3.1   **Metabolism of alcohol.** In the first step, alcohol (ethanol) is converted to acetaldehyde using the enzyme alcohol dehydrogenase (ADH) and the coenzyme nicotinamide adenine dinucleotide (NAD+). In the second step, acetaldehyde is changed to acetate and finally to carbon dioxide and water. The conversion of acetaldehyde to acetate requires aldehyde dehydrogenase (ALDH), as well as (NAD+).

much (most of the population), this is a protective factor. The problem is that those who can drink us under the table are at especially high risk. People who can drink more send more alcohol to the brain, increasing the chance that a neurochemical imbalance will occur.

Besides genes, there are experiential factors that increase one's ability to handle large amounts of alcohol. Before we blame our parents for all of our drug and alcohol problems, let us consider other factors besides "faulty" genes. The most obvious one is that addiction may be caused by the altered brain functioning resulting from excessive abuse of a substance (or behavior). Begley (2007) found that the brain exhibits plasticity and will rewire itself in response to challenges in normal neurochemistry caused by drugs or mind-altering activities. Even our thoughts, either positive or negative, can create changes in the brain.

According to Higley (cited by Heinz, 2006), a research scientist at the National Institute on Alcohol Abuse and Alcoholism, motherless rhesus monkeys (who grew up in the wild or in the lab) reacted less to drinks of high proof alcohol and other substances that affect the impact of the neurotransmitter GABA. As a result of stress-induced reduced sensitivity, these monkeys could drink huge quantities of alcohol, which they did when provided free access. Although genes play a decidedly important role in decreased sensitivity to the effects of alcohol, human studies have shown similar changes in people's brain chemistry as the result of loss and deprivation.

There is reason to believe that genetic influences, similar to the ones identified for alcoholism, may be found for other compulsive behaviors as well. Many years of twin and adoption studies have demonstrated that the heritability of liability for nicotine dependence (ND) is at least 50% (Ball, 2008; Li, 2006).

The Addictive Quality of Alcohol

Chronic ingestion of alcohol can cause neurochemical imbalances that are characteristic of alcoholism. This does not negate the concept of addictive disease, since many illnesses related to a genetic predisposition can also be worsened by environmental and behavioral factors. Diabetes, for example, is a disease whether it is inherited or environmentally induced. When the alcoholic faces potentially fatal consequences because of his or her uncontrolled behavior, altered biochemical processes may require the problem to be treated as a disease. The individual who alters his or her brain chemistry by excessive drinking is just as addicted as the person who happened to have "faulty" parents.

The concept of alcoholism as a disease, whether environmentally or genetically induced, encourages us to examine the nature of alcohol's addicting power. Often we hear the comment that something (drug or other) is psychologically and not physiologically addicting. Such a distinction is artificial and has no place in a sophisticated discussion on addiction. The distinction implies that the central nervous system (psychological addiction) is somehow separate from the rest of the body's functions (physiological addiction). This is not a useful distinction.

Many theories attempt to explain the addictive quality of alcohol. A cursory look at the molecular structures of the substances that are most addicting leaves one with the feeling that alcohol does not belong in this group. As seen in Figure 3.2, alcohol is the only substance that does not contain the element nitrogen (indicated as N in the formulas). In addition, alcohol is by far the smallest of the molecules in Figure 3.2. Generally, one thinks of addicting molecules as those of moderate size (for example, cocaine) that

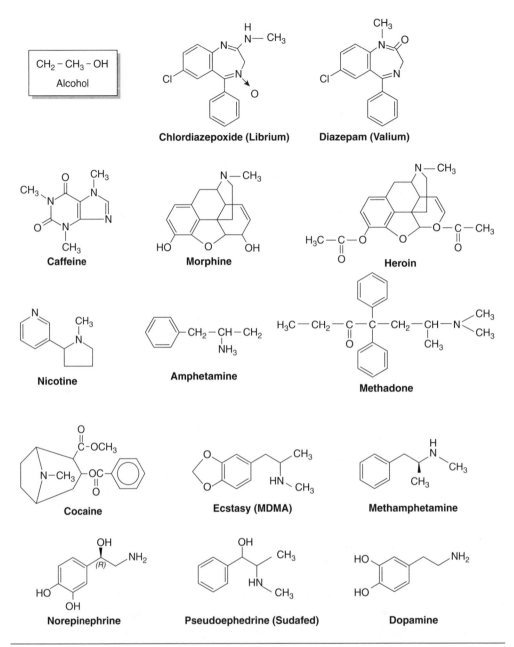

Figure 3.2   **Chemical structures of the mind benders.** Since alcohol is much smaller than the other addicting molecules and contains no nitrogen, scientists have looked to other factors that contribute to its addictive nature.

contain nitrogen. Since alcohol is much smaller than the other addicting molecules and contains no nitrogen, scientists have looked to other factors that contribute to its addictive nature.

One of the earlier theories of alcohol addiction (R. D. Meyers, 1989) involves synthesizing opiates in the central nervous system. To understand this model, consider the fate of the neurotransmitter dopamine. The level of neurotransmitters is regulated by their composition and degradation within the central nervous system. This process is necessary to maintain a balanced level of dopamine. Figure 3.3 illustrates the usual metabolic degradation of dopamine, with and without alcohol.

In the first step of degradation, dopamine (I) is converted to 3,4-dihydroxyphenylacetaldehyde (II). Normally, this substance is then converted to 3,4-dihydroxyphenylacetate (III). Note that this last step requires the same coenzyme (NAD+) that is required to convert alcohol to acetaldehyde (see Figure 3.1). Consider the person who is a heavy drinker. To metabolize large quantities of alcohol, that person requires large quantities of NAD+. Since NAD+ is not present in unlimited amounts in the body, it is possible that the heavy drinker may not have enough NAD+ to convert alcohol to acetaldehyde and also to convert dopamine to compound II (Figure 3.3). If this is the case, the body must choose at which metabolic site to use the limited amount of NAD+. The choice is easy: alcohol is very toxic. To live, the body of a heavy drinker must metabolize and eliminate the alcohol as quickly as possible. Therefore, the available NAD+ is used in the removal of alcohol from the system. This could deplete the limited supply of NAD+ to the point at which compound II is not converted to compound III. When this occurs, the normal reaction flow is blocked. Just as water backs up behind a dam, compound II backs up and becomes present in excess. This excess of compound II then begins to react with unconverted dopamine (I) to form another compound (IV), which has a structure similar to opiate narcotics (see morphine in Figure 3.2).

According to R. D. Meyers (1989), this compound (IV), which is an example of a class of chemicals known as tetrahydroisoquinolines (THIQ), is believed to behave much as opiates or our own internal endorphins. We would expect the THIQs to occupy the same neuronal receptor sites as those occupied by opiates. If this occurs, then the same addictive processes for opiates would be operative for THIQs. In support of the THIQ theory, Meyers created alcoholic rats by injecting THIQ into their brains.

It should be noted that, as with most scientific theories, the THIQ model is by no means the only explanation of alcohol addiction. Certainly alcohol dependence is not identical to opiate addiction. One of many reasons for this difference is the powerful effect that alcohol and its first metabolic product, acetaldehyde, has on many cells in the body, including brain cells. Chronic alcohol ingestion is believed to permanently alter the membranes of nerve cells. This alteration itself could contribute to the addictive nature of alcohol.

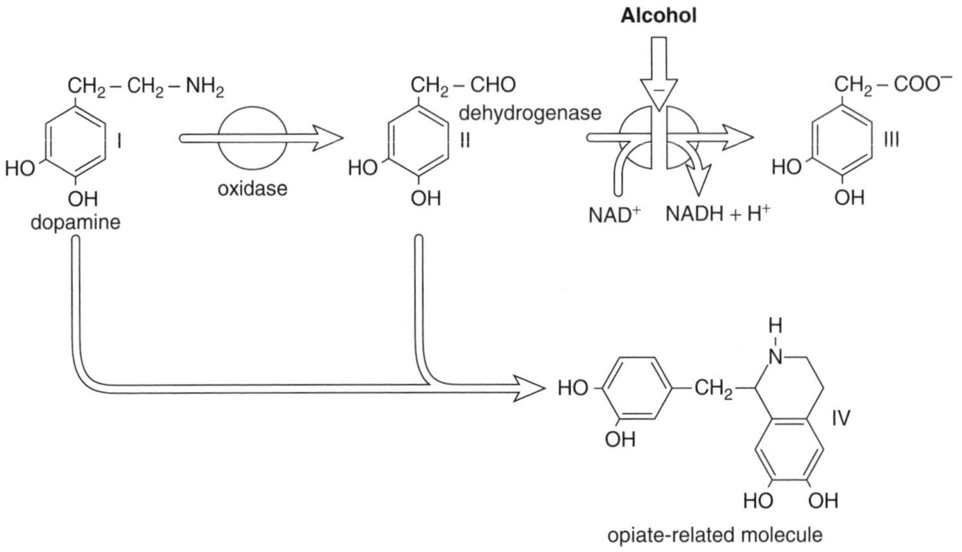

Figure 3.3   Effect of alcohol on dopamine metabolism. Dopamine (I) is converted to 3,4-dihydroxyphenylacetaldehyde (II). Normally, this substance is then converted to 3,4-dihydroxyphenylacetate (III), requiring the same coenzyme (NAD+) needed to convert alcohol to acetaldehyde. Because of the limited supply of NAD+, compound II is not converted to compound III. Compound II backs up and becomes present in excess. This excess of compound II then begins to react with unconverted dopamine (I) to form another compound (IV), similar in structure to opiate narcotics.

Neurotransmitter Regulation and Dysfunction _____

Heinz (2006) considers the effects of other neurochemicals involved in chronic alcohol ingestion—glutamate and GABA (gamma aminobutyric acid). These molecules influence our moods as well the uncomfortable and sometimes dangerous symptoms of withdrawal. Glutamate is an excitatory neurotransmitter that enhances or speeds up neurotransmission along the neuronal pathways. Any substance that enhances glutamate release from the presynaptic neuron will increase the rate of neurotransmission, which may result in arousal, depending on the neuronal pathways involved. GABA is an inhibitory neurotransmitter that slows down neurotransmission. The effect of alcohol on these two neurotransmitters is shown in Figure 3.4.

Alcohol blocks glutamate from binding to its NMDA (N-methyl-D-aspartic acid, a type of glutamate) receptors. This creates a decrease in glutamate-induced neurotransmission resulting in relaxation, such as sleep or even passing out. This is one of the reasons alcohol is often used for its calming effect in stressful situations. Alcohol also enhances the effect of GABA, resulting in a further decrease in neurotransmission (remember, GABA is an inhibitory neurotransmitter). So the effect of decreased glutamate and increased

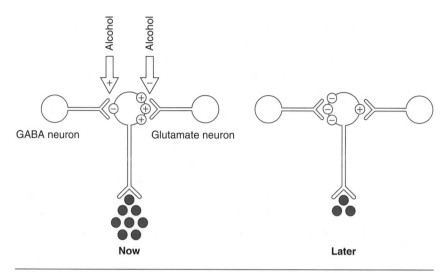

Figure 3.4   **Effect of alcohol on neurotransmission.** Alcohol excites inhibitory
GABA neurons but inhibits excitatory glutamate neurons
(left panel). Increased inhibition coupled with decreased
excitation reduces neurotransmitter release (right panel).

GABA may be the drunken stupor, slurred speech, instability, impairment, and sleepiness characteristic of excessive alcohol consumption.

So we see how alcohol produces powerful states of sedation, but the human brain is not to be trifled with. The phrase "synaptic homeostasis" describes the brain's reaction to sustained attempts to achieve ecstasy by altering our "normal" neurotransmission. Consider the attempt, using alcohol, to achieve relaxation by blocking the binding of glutamate to NMDA receptors. For most moderate alcohol consumers, this works well. However, sustained heavy drinking alters the brain in a way that decreases the effect of the amount of alcohol that initially increased positive feelings. In order to counter this blocking of glutamate to NMDA receptors, the postsynaptic membrane creates more NMDA receptors. More alcohol must be consumed to achieve the desired pleasure. After a while, alcohol is consumed mostly to not feel "crappy," and the hope of experiencing ecstasy is long gone.

_____ Harmful Effects on the Mind, Body, and Brain

Aside from understanding alcohol's relatively transient effects on excitatory and inhibitory neurotransmission and potential health benefits from drinking in moderation (discussed below), a thorough risk–benefit analysis must also consider the dark side. One obvious problem with moderate drinking (e.g., 1–2 drinks per day), as attested to by legions of neurologists, cardiologists, liver specialists, and mental health professionals, is that not everyone who attempts to have only one or two can actually do so. In addition to the severe brain damage and associated dementia related to chronic and heavy alcohol consumption, one must also consider its effects on other systems of the body. The liver, for example, finds alcohol extremely alarming. Inflammation of the liver (hepatitis) can lead to scarring (cirrhosis) and eventual death. Heavy drinking can increase blood pressure and damage the heart muscle (cardiomyopathy). Alcohol has also been linked to cancers of the mouth, throat, esophagus, colon, and breast. Even moderate drinking carries health risks. Alcohol can disrupt sleep, and it can interact adversely with acetaminophen (Tylenol), antidepressants, painkillers, sedatives, and anticonvulsants. Its harmful effect on judgment is legendary, as evidenced by frequent connections with crime and violence. De Bellis and colleagues (2000) have related use of alcohol by adolescents with decreased size of the hippocampus, the part of the brain associated with conversion of short-term to long-term memory.

Do I Have a Drinking Problem?

Surely, multiple biological events, as well as powerful psychological and social factors (discussed below), are related to alcohol's addictive properties. Whatever the constellation of causes (which may be different in each person), alcohol addiction remains the world's most serious drug problem. To complicate matters further, most people who abuse alcohol have difficulty in admitting that it presents a serious problem in their lives. The questions in Table 3.1 are suggested for people who want to take an honest inventory of their current relationship with alcohol. They are designed to enhance self-awareness, with the objectives of improved levels of personal and social responsibility. "Thus, a series of questions that circumvent denial have been devised that can identify most people with alcoholism. The list of questions in Table 3.1 provides the most useful single guide I know to the clinical interview" (Vaillant, 1983, p. 296).

Sobriety and the Brain: What If I Quit?

Let's suppose that you or someone you are trying to help wants to quit drinking. In addition to being mindful of all the psychological booby traps en route to health and well-being, we shall now examine the brain's reactions to getting sober. Case examples of Regis and Mike illustrate two primary neurobiological challenges to sobriety: *conditioned desire* and *conditioned withdrawal;* however, new medications are proving helpful.

Regis stopped drinking about 2 years ago with the help of a buddy who turned him on to AA. His girlfriend works as a waitress in the neighborhood bar and Regis picks her up after work on Saturday nights to spend some time together and to give her a ride home. He doesn't go inside the bar; rather, he waits in the car until the customers begin to leave. Once, after watching patrons becoming energized at the proverbial "last call for alcohol," Regis began to leap from his car, reacting to heavy sensations of scotch in his nostrils and throat.

Table 3.1   Questions That Circumvent Denial

1. Do you occasionally drink heavily after a disappointment or a quarrel, or when the boss gives you a hard time?

2. When you have trouble or feel under pressure, do you always drink more heavily than usual?

3. Have you noticed that you are able to handle more liquor than you did when you were first drinking?

4. Do you ever wake up the "morning after" and discover that you could not remember part of the evening before, even though your friends tell you that you did not pass out?

5. When drinking with other people, do you try to have a few extra drinks when others will not know it?

6. Are there certain occasions when you feel uncomfortable if alcohol is not available?

7. Have you recently noticed that when you begin drinking you are in more of a hurry to get the first drink than you used to be?

8. Do you sometimes feel a little guilty about your drinking?

9. Are you secretly irritated when your family or friends discuss your drinking?

10. Have you recently noticed an increase in the frequency of your memory "blackouts"?

11. Do you often find that you wish to continue drinking after your friends say that they have had enough?

12. Do you usually have a reason for the occasions when you drink heavily?

13. When you are sober, do you often regret things you have done or said while drinking?

14. Have you tried switching brands or following different plans for controlling your drinking?

15. Have you often failed to keep promises you have made to yourself about controlling or cutting down on your drinking?

16. Have you tried to control your drinking by making a change in jobs, or moving to a new location?

17. Do you try to avoid family and close friends when you are drinking?

18. Are you having an increasing number of financial or work problems?

19. Do more people seem to be treating you unfairly without good reason?

20. Do you eat very little or irregularly when you are drinking?

21. Do you sometimes have the "shakes" in the morning and find that it helps to have a little drink?

22. Have you recently noticed that you cannot drink as much as you once did?

SOURCE: Reprinted by permission of the publisher from *The Natural History of Alcoholism* by George E. Vaillant, pp. 296–297, Cambridge, MA: Harvard University Press. Copyright © 1983 by the President and Fellows of Harvard College.

Regis was experiencing *conditioned desire.* When in situations similar to the ones in which the person had always consumed alcohol, the "feeling of the need for alcohol becomes almost irresistible. Then, even after years of abstinence, consuming a single drink can set off a powerful longing to imbibe more and more" (Heinz, 2006, p. 57).

A related phenomenon is *conditioned withdrawal.*

> Mike had been sober for the past 5 years. He had reestablished good relationships with his two children and his wife who had threatened to leave if he didn't "clean up his act." He worked as manager of several commercial buildings. Suddenly, when the buildings were purchased by another corporation, Mike found himself out of a job. His initial response was to seek assistance from an employment agency. As time went on, the agency couldn't open any doors for interviews and Mike started to feel desperate. Tension in his primary relationship began to build as his wife complained about finances and her fears that Mike would fall back into old habits. Just after his older daughter blurted out that he was "becoming a bum," Mike started to think about running down to the pub and downing a few beers. Suddenly, he began to sweat profusely and his hands began to shake. Although he hadn't drank in years, he felt similar withdrawal effects as after months of binge drinking.

Neuroscience can explain conditioned desire and conditioned withdrawal by tracking the brain's reactions to prolonged and excessive use of alcohol. Although high tolerance to alcohol seems like a beneficial adaptation, it functions more like a curse. As shown in Figure 3.4, alcohol affects neural mechanisms that regulate GABA and glutamate. Figure 3.5 provides an illustration for our discussion of why withdrawal occurs.

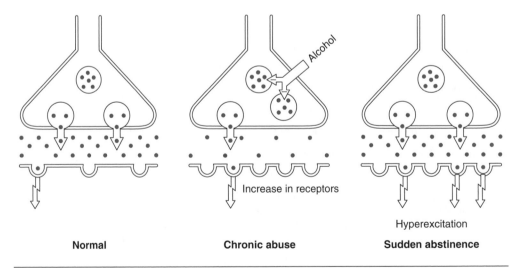

Figure 3.5   **Mechanism of alcohol withdrawal.** The low level of neurotransmitters in chronic alcohol abuse (Figure 3.4) leads to a compensatory increase in the number of postsynaptic receptors (middle panel of Figure 3.5). Under these conditions, a normal amount of neurotransmitters (left panel), as would occur when alcohol is not present, stimulates more receptors and thereby causes hyperexcitation (right panel).

Regis's and Mike's symptoms are related to the brain's adaptation to chronic alcohol abuse. As shown in Figures 3.4 and 3.5, alcohol blocks the binding of glutamate to NMDA receptors. To increase the probability of capturing glutamate, the brain compensates by increasing or sensitizing the number of NMDA receptors in the brains of those who chronically consume alcohol (Figure 3.5, middle). When alcohol use is suddenly interrupted (either through forced abstinence—e.g., jail—or voluntarily, by "going on the wagon"), the receptors continue to be more sensitive (Figure 3.5, right). This hyperactivity results in an overreaction to glutamate (no longer blocked by alcohol), which causes symptoms of withdrawal such as cramps, unstable blood circulation, and anxiety. These symptoms may occur when alcohol is withdrawn for a few days or even overnight. In addition, the excessive neural activity can destroy large numbers of neurons, causing dementia or long-term damage to the neuronal system (Heinz, 2006).

NMDA receptors remain hypersensitive while GABA receptors continue to be undersensitive, resulting from the overactivity of GABA induced by alcohol ingestion (see Figure 3.4). These withdrawal symptoms can be treated with drugs such as chlormethiazole or benzodiazepine, which restore the sensitivity of GABA receptors. Another medication, acamprosate, is effective in suppressing the hyperexcitability of NMDA receptors and seems especially helpful for people like Mike, who suffers from conditioned withdrawal. Heinz (2006) reports that that 30% to 40% of patients who take acamprosate during the first few months of abstinence remain dry for the first year after detoxification. Of course, this leaves a great deal of work for counselors and mentors who are vitally needed to transcend the limits of medical intervention (see Coping With Cravings and Urges, p. 68).

Now back to Regis and his apparently conditioned desire. Just as in the case of compensating for excess activity of GABA and decreased activity of glutamate, the brain deals with another major factor in addiction—overstimulation of the reward center. To compensate for what it interprets as excessive bombardment from dopamine, the brain reduces the number of binding sites (called D2 receptors) on neurons that process dopamine. MRI studies show that when people with a history of alcohol dependence, like Regis, look at photographs of beer and wine, the regions of the brain that control attention are aroused more than in nonalcoholics (Heinz, 2006). The fewer D2 receptors available, the more attention is aroused by the sight of an alcohol-related image, and the more difficult it is for the individual to find satisfaction from anything besides alcohol, be it relationships, hobbies, or food. Some may desperately seek dopamine by switching to another drug or a behavioral addiction such as gambling or sex.

Although dopamine directs attention and desire, other neurochemicals—the endorphins—are intimately involved in the experience of pleasure. As discussed above, repeated overstimulation alters the system. Because alcoholics develop an increased number of binding sites for the endorphins, when they consume alcohol their neurons bind more endorphins, resulting in increased pleasure from drinking. Naltrexone is a drug that can considerably reduce the risk of relapse by blocking the receptor sites for the endorphins and causing a taste that ranges in quality from foreign to terrible. However, the need for psychosocial intervention is highlighted by the fact that by the second or third dose, the drink begins to taste good. Naltrexone might help to avert the first sip, but after the gate is open, all hell can break loose.

Coping With Cravings and Urges

It is obvious that pharmaceutical supports like acamprosate and naltrexone are insufficient by themselves to prevent cravings and urges from triggering old patterns of abuse and dependence. Marlatt's (1985) relapse prevention model, shown in Figure 3.6, has been the foundational tool used by cognitive-behavioral therapists during the past 20 years to provide substance abuse clients with an understanding of how high-risk situations (e.g., negative feelings, peer influence, stimulus cues, interpersonal conflict, change in self-image) can evoke a progression of thoughts and actions that can lead to full-blown relapse. The usual thinking response to a high-risk situation is loss of confidence in one's ability to cope (decreased self-efficacy) coupled with an expectation that a tension-reducing drug or action will bring relief (positive outcome expectancies). The next stage of relapse is acting out the impulse to use by indulging in the perceived tension-relieving behavior (e.g., ingesting alcohol, taking drugs, eating) in some intended measured and controlled manner (lapse). The cognitive dissonance (tension evoked by having overthrown a primary rule of conduct, e.g., abstinence) leads to the co-occurring process of self-justification (e.g., Who wants to be sober anyway?) and the perception that the drug or behavior is in fact working as intended (perceived effects). Further, the individual is likely to attribute his or her "fall" to personal weakness (self-attribution). Marlatt has used the term *rule violation effect* to describe the combined influences of cognitive dissonance, self-attribution, and perceived effects, as they set the stage for return to earlier patterns of abuse and dependence (full relapse). Individuals who are interested in quitting are well-advised to give serious consideration to this model by developing and rehearsing alternative patterns of thoughts and actions at each stage of a potential relapse process.

In addition to in-depth reflection on the progression of relapse and alternative patterns of thoughts and action as indicated above, Table 3.2 presents viable strategies for coping with cravings and urges that may threaten our resolve to achieve freedom from any hedonic dependency.

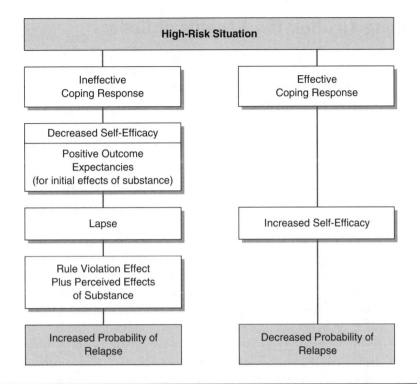

Figure 3.6 **Marlatt's model for relapse prevention.** By understanding the sequence of thoughts prior to violating a self-defined rule for maintaining personal responsibility in regard to substance abuse or other potentially harmful behavior (e.g., binge drinking, promiscuity, overeating), a person can learn to restructure his or her dysfunctional thoughts, feelings, and actions in response to high-risk situations.

Table 3.2   Strategies for Managing Cravings and Urges

Sharing	Talk to family, friends, or someone you trust and ask for their support.
Toughing It Out	Get control over the craving by accepting the discomfort and implementing the following:
	Notice how you experience the craving. What are your thoughts and feelings about the craving? Where does it occur in your body?
	Is it still a craving, or has it become an urge (when your physical body becomes activated and you take steps to fulfill the craving such as searching out a friend you can get high with)?
Talk Yourself Down	When the craving becomes an urge, focus on your body where you feel the urge. Talk to yourself and take control of your actions, figuring out alternative ways to feel comfortable.
Urge Surfing	Ride out the wave, and visualize relaxing at the shore.
Alternatives	Find another activity that will distract you from the craving or urge.

Redeeming Alcohol: The Benefits of Booze _____

> *[N]one seemed to think the injury arose from the use of a bad thing but from the abuse of a good thing.*
>
> —Abraham Lincoln, addressing the
> Illinois Temperance Society, 1842

> *I have taken more out of alcohol than alcohol has taken out of me.*
>
> —Winston Churchill

One of the authors (Milkman) has an ongoing argument with his daughter about the concept of *natural highs*. She claims that there is no such thing as "unnatural" because everything that exists, including plastics, cocaine, atomic bombs, marijuana, and cigarettes, is derived from substances that exist here on earth. From her point of view, there is no valid distinction between "natural" and "unnatural" highs. Even synthesized drugs are "natural" because they are made from chemical elements, which are natural. Can one say, without being moralistic, that moderate consumption of alcohol, even to the point of feeling somewhat euphoric (without risk of harm), is not a natural high?

Following from our definition, that "natural highs are self-induced changes in brain chemistry that result in positive feeling states, health, and well-being for the individual and society," does moderate consumption of beer, wine, or spirits constitute an alcohol-mediated natural high? To be sure, there are vested interests in showing the bright or dark side of drinking. Presently, however, a preponderance of evidence accrued over the past 30 years (not without controversy) shows substantial health benefits from moderate consumption. Despite centuries of biblical, religious, moral, and medical objections to alcohol, what new evidence supports the proclamation of "health benefits"?

We shall begin our discussion of healthy drinking by defining what qualifies as reasonable or "moderate" consumption. First of all, what actually constitutes a drink? In the United States, "one drink" is usually defined as 12 ounces of beer, 5 ounces of wine, or 1.5 ounces of spirits. Each delivers about 12 to 14 grams of alcohol. Check your bartender's skills—he or she might pour a shot twice that amount—no doubt doing you a "big favor." The concept of moderation is even more slippery. In some studies, less than one drink per day is considered moderate, and in others, daily consumption of as much as three to four drinks qualifies (Dufour, 1999). The current consensus, in accordance with the U.S. Department of Agriculture and the Dietary Guidelines for Americans, is no more than one to two drinks per day for men and no more than one drink per day for women (U.S. Department of Health and Human Services [USDHHS], 2004).

Linking Alcohol and Health

Pathologists first discovered hints of the link between alcohol consumption and cardiovascular health about 100 years ago, noting that the large arteries of people who died of alcohol-related liver disease were remarkably "clean"—that is, free of arteriosclerosis (fatty plaque). According to Klatsky (2006), senior consultant in cardiology at the Kaiser Permanente Medical Center, a meta-analysis of 28 previously published studies on the relationship between alcohol intake and cardiovascular disease (CVD) showed that the risk of acquiring CVD went down as the daily amount of alcohol consumed went up from 0 to 25 grams (about 2 standard drinks). At 2 drinks, an individual's risk of a major coronary heart disease (CHD) "event"—either heart attack or death—"was 20 percent lower than for someone who did not drink at all" (p. 76). Furthermore, at a meeting of the American Heart Association in 2002, Klatsky and colleagues reviewed an updated analysis of 128,934 patients who had checkups between 1978 and 1985. They found that "those who had one or two alcoholic beverages a day had a 32 percent lower risk of dying from CHD than abstainers did" (p. 77).

Further, as presented in an article published by the Harvard School of Public Health (2008) entitled "The Nutrition Source: Alcohol and Heart Disease," it was discovered that "[m]ore than 100 prospective studies show an inverse association between moderate drinking and risk of heart attack, ischemic (clot-caused) stroke, peripheral vascular disease, sudden cardiac death, and death from all cardiovascular causes" (p. 2). Table 3.3 summarizes the results of some of the largest studies.

Is Red Wine Better for You?

Nearly 200 years ago, an Irish physician made the observation that angina (chest pain) was less frequent among the French than the Irish and attributed the difference to the "French habits and mode of living" (Black, 1819). The comparatively low rate of cardiovascular disease in France, despite their reputed diet as rich in butter and cheese, has become known as the "French paradox." The view that health benefits derive from the chemistry of red wine is challenged by the fact that there are many other aspects of French lifestyle that may influence health outcomes. For example, the French diet, particularly for those who live in southern France, is similar to those of other Mediterranean cultures, which are also lower in heart disease.

Some studies suggest that red wine, especially when drunk with a meal, offers more health benefits than beer or spirits, that is, wine-drinking cultures fare better in terms of health (e.g., Rimm, Klatsky, Grobbee, & Stampfer, 1996; St. Leger, Cochrane, & Moore, 1979). Although it has been speculated that besides alcohol, red wine may contain health-augmenting substances, a

Table 3.3   Results of Some Large Prospective Studies of Alcohol Consumption and
Cardiovascular Disease

Participants	Duration	Association With Moderate Alcohol Consumption
Japan Collaborative Cohort Study for Evaluation of Cancer Risk cohort: 97,432 men and women aged 40 to 79 (Lin et al., 2005)	10 years	12–20% decreased risk of all-cause mortality in men and women who consumed less than 23 grams per day of alcohol; heavy drinking increased the risk of all-cause mortality
Kaiser Permanente cohort: 123,840 men and women aged 30+ (Klatsky, Armstrong, & Friedman, 1990)	10 years	40% reduction in fatal myocardial infarction; 20% reduction in cardiovascular mortality; 80% increase in fatal hemorrhagic stroke
Nurses' Health Study: 85,709 female nurses aged 34–59 (Stampfer, Colditz, Willett, Speizer, & Hennekens, 1988)	12 years	17% lower risk of all-cause mortality; an earlier report showed a 40% reduction in risk of CHD and 70% reduction in risk of ischemic stroke
Physicians' Health Study: 22,071 male physicians aged 40–84 (Camargo et al., 1997)	11 years	30–35% reduced risk of angina and myocardial infarction; 20–30% reduced risk of cardiovascular death
Cancer Prevention Study II: 489,626 men and women aged 30–104 (Thun et al., 1997)	9 years	30–40% reduced risk of cardiovascular death; mortality from all causes increased with heavier drinking, particularly among adults under age 60
Eastern France cohort: 34,014 men and women (Renaud, Gueguen, Siest, & Salamon, 1999)	10–15 years	25–30% reduced risk of cardiovascular death
Health Professionals Follow-up Study: 38,077 male health professionals aged 40–75 (Mukamal et al., 2003)	12 years	35% reduced risk of myocardial infarction

SOURCE: Reprinted from *The Nutrition Source,* Department of Nutrition, Harvard School of Public Health, "Alcohol and Heart Disease," http://www.hsph.harvard.edu/nutritionsource/what-should-you-eat/alcohol-and-heart-disease/index.html. Copyright © 2008 by the President and Fellows of Harvard College.

Health Professionals Follow-up Study of 38,000 men carried out over a 12-year period showed that, independent of type of beverage (i.e., wine, beer, or spirits) or whether it was drunk with or without food, moderate drinkers were 30% to 35% less likely to have heart attacks than nondrinkers. Men who drank every day were at lower risk than those who drank once or twice per week (Mukamal et al., 2003). As in many aspects of health and nutrition, it appears that the jury is still out regarding red wine.

Hold the Press, What About Cancer?

So you no longer smoke, you eat fruits and veggies, exercise robustly, and gracefully pour one or two glasses of red wine each night. Just when drinkers were clapping their hands about how alcohol lowers the risk of heart disease, a major study conducted by the International Agency for Research on Cancer (IARC-WHO; Baan et al., 2007) throws a cat among the pigeons.

Although moderate drinking may improve coronary health, drinking even a small amount of alcohol daily could increase the risk of colon and breast cancer—two of the four major cancer killers. Based on findings from the European Prospective Investigation into Cancer and Nutrition (EPIC), which asked more than 480,000 Europeans about their drinking, those who drank over one drink a day (100 grams in a week) increase their chances of developing colon cancer by about 15%. For those who consume about four drinks daily, the risk is 40% higher. Apparently, the risk is dose dependent—the more you drink, the more your risk goes up (Baan et al., 2007). Regular consumption of more than one drink per day has been associated with an increased risk of breast cancer in women (Hamajima et al., 2002).

To Quit or Not to Quit?

How does an ordinary person sensibly decide about how to manage alcohol, truly one of the world's amazing chemicals? Drinking small amounts of alcohol—a shot of hard liquor or a glass of beer or wine daily—does have proven health benefits, that is, heart attacks and strokes caused by blocked arteries are reduced by 10% to 15% (probably because alcohol increases good cholesterol—HDL—and prevents blood platelets from clumping together). On the other hand, according to Rehm, head of public health and regulatory policies at the Ontario Center for Addiction and Mental Health, and his colleagues (Rehm, Patra, & Popova, 2007), alcohol is detrimental for more than 60 diagnoses. After smoking and obesity, alcohol consumption is the third-biggest cause of preventable death in the United States (R. N. Anderson, 2002). In 2002, the most recent year for which data is available, drinking caused 100,000 deaths—including more than 12,000 cancer deaths, comparable to the 13,674 killed in alcohol-related traffic accidents. The same data show that about 30,000 fatal heart attacks were prevented by moderate alcohol consumption. However, the evidence for alcohol preventing heart attacks is less reliable. Compared with teetotalers, those who drink moderately tend to exercise more, have better medical insurance, and have lower fat-to-muscle ratios, that is, they probably have had fewer heart attacks because of factors other than alcohol intake.

At present, we don't know exactly how alcohol affects cancer. Science is pursuing several promising leads: the influence of alcohol on estrogen levels, which can affect the risk of breast cancer; and how alcohol challenges liver function, which could impair the body's ability to get rid of potential cancer-causing agents.

Inevitably, some who are now considering abstinence are thinking that if they have already caused the damage, why not have some fun? To help you decide, there is additional data. Quitting seems to eventually reverse the added risk. In a study published in the *International Journal of Cancer,* Rehm et al. (2007) showed that the risk of head and neck and esophageal cancer decreased significantly within 10 years of giving up booze and was the same as that for nondrinkers after 20 years. Although even one or two drinks a day raised a woman's breast cancer risk, there was no increased risk for those who reported having a few drinks a week. So where is the tipping point, or put another way, what is the threshold for abuse?

Like many short-term pleasure/long-term pain puzzles, risk–benefit analysis will be different for each person. A person in his or her late teens or early twenties with very low risk of heart disease will probably suffer more damage from loss of judgment associated with drinking than gain any long-term cardiovascular benefits. On the other hand, a 50-year-old man with neither a personal history of alcohol abuse nor family history of colon cancer may enjoy distinct cardiovascular benefits from moderate consumption. Correspondingly, a younger woman with no cardiac risk and a family history of breast cancer would probably do better not to drink. Finally, in deciding whether to drink, you may want to ask, how important is alcohol to your lifestyle and how much benefit do you personally derive in terms of pleasure, anxiety management, and connections with others?

Chapter Summary

Beginning with a short discourse on biblical admonitions about the abuse of alcohol, we move to a science-based discussion of why some people seem to be more vulnerable to alcohol than others. Aside from cultural and environmental influences, genetics are implicated because they bring about individual differences (metabolic and neurochemical) in how people react to the same drug. The addictive qualities of alcohol are discussed in terms of the drug's effects on glutamate, GABA, and the brain's internal opiates. A brief discussion of the many organ systems that are harmfully affected by alcohol is followed by an inventory designed to help the reader assess whether he or she is actually at risk for abuse or dependence (see Table 3.1). The chapter moves to a discussion of the psychobiological factors involved in drinking cessation, including conditioned desire and conditioned withdrawal. Marlatt's relapse prevention model is presented as a cognitive-behavioral tool for self-regulation during high-risk situations. Specific strategies are offered as allies in one's resolve to resist potentially harmful cravings and urges. Although alcohol is clearly implicated in premature death, massive harm to communities and families, and a host of disease states, research during the past 30 years shows cardiovascular benefits for those who consume in moderation. However, recent studies point to increased risk for certain types of cancer, even when drinking is done in moderation. A risk–benefit analysis is suggested for each person in consideration of age, sex, family disease history, and alcohol's perceived contribution (or lack thereof) to quality of life.

4 The Great Psychiatric Tavern

Figure 4.1 Psychiatry in the barroom setting.

A magical movement of the hand introduces a magical substance, and behold, pain and suffering are exorcised, the sense of misery disappears and the body is suffused by waves of pleasure. . . . [T]he ego is, after all, the omnipotent giant it had always fundamentally thought it was.

—Sandor Rado, "The Psychoanalysis of Pharmacothymia"

A Stage for Letting Go

Throughout most of the world, there is an abundance of public and private settings in which the use and abuse of alcohol are fundamental to the needs and expectations of participants. A description of a brewery on an Egyptian papyrus dating back to 3500 BC provides the earliest record of alcohol production (Fort, 1969). The first evidence of prohibitionist teaching (2000 BC) is found in the writings of an Egyptian priest: "I thy superior forbid you [his student] to go to the taverns: Thou art degraded like the beasts" (King County Bar Association Drug Policy Project, 2005, p. 3). Today, taverns of varied design and diverse clientele exist in most societies, cutting across racial, ethnic, gender, social, religious, and geographic lines. Historically, the bar has been frequented mostly by men, but over the past 50 years female attendance has increased dramatically. Considering that an estimated 90% of college-age women drink (K. A. Parks, Miller, Collins, & Zetes-Zanatta, 1998), it is reasonable to assume that many of these women are also going to bars.

Although the typical bar or tavern serves as a center for relaxation, interpersonal encounters, and casual business negotiations, it is also a venue to observe and express deviant behavior. Throughout Western society, small neighborhood bars cater to otherwise unmet needs of local residents. Metropolitan centers additionally supply a plethora of "clubs" where there is an expectation of meeting strangers who may become friends, lovers, or objects of brief sexual liaison. In a quasi-controlled environment (the bar), both men and women may sidestep ordinary social norms. They are free to become more aggressive or sexually disinhibited (Garland, Hughes, & Marquart, 2004). Men can tell dirty jokes, churn out lewd comments, and make sexual propositions. Women may dress and act provocatively or allow themselves to be touched sexually (K. A. Parks et al., 1998). Essentially, the bar is a place of *license,* that is, acceptable deviance, where "out of line" behaviors are permitted and even encouraged. For those who play within the rules, there is ample opportunity for unleashing libido and partially satisfying a host of unmet needs. Not only can patrons shirk their ordinary social roles, they can also dissociate from "being naughty" once they leave the barroom setting (Goffman, 1963).

There are many types of bar settings in contemporary society. Trendy places feature hip music, fusion food, and a mélange of artistic devices ranging from exotic wood-sculpted backdrops to open-air cityscapes. Encounters with strangers are encouraged by adjacent, knee-level tables with complementary cushioned seating. However, the basic small-town, belly-up bar with café seating and standard recreational ploys (e.g., pool or shuffleboard) is where most people go to drink. Although atmospheres vary widely, fundamental patterns of human behavior remain the same.

By way of analogy, the bar serves as a type of mental health center where people can explore relationships, release tension, and act out impulses, the expression of which is unacceptable in ordinary social discourse. People can also discuss everyday problems, forbidden fantasies, and deep-seated emotional conflicts. Indeed, a striking parallel exists between the psychiatrist and the bartender, each of whom, with a range of pharmacologic supports, ministers to an unsettled clientele—"Doctor, may I please have a beer?"

In a typical neighborhood bar, the tavern "doctor" conducts individual and group treatments, assisted by a team of "nurses" (waitresses) and other support (e.g., bouncer = orderly; taxi cab = ambulance). Recreational devices include live music, dancing, darts, billiards, TV, and computerized games, all geared toward a broad spectrum of consumer interests and needs.

"Therapeutic décor" is choreographed to elicit emotional arousal, thereby stimulating increased alcohol consumption. Rock and country music are appealing to those with depression, anxiety, and sensation-seeking needs (Stratton & Zalanowski, 1999). Environmental cues for erotic mood activation derive from combining dim light, increased noise, and crowding. Ordinary boundaries for space and touch are short-circuited. Alcohol may be used to "speed" mood, increasing either depression or euphoria, depending on current life circumstance or preexisting personality (Zinberg, 1984). The "well-medicated" patron reaches an optimal state of emotional reactivity, which furthers attraction to, interest in, and attachment to the barroom setting.

To continue with our analogy, for the more affluent, "therapy" venues are aesthetically designed and immaculately maintained. "Medicines" are fashionably delivered, meeting rooms are filled with artistic splendor, and meals are served with elegance and charm. In more pedestrian locations, "bar-patients" are coaxed to heighten dose levels through seductive devices such as "Happy Hour" and "buybacks" (a drink "on the house" for every few the patient buys). "Prescriptions" are self-selected on the basis of the customer's perceived state of psychological need. Provocatively named concoctions like the screaming orgasm, zombie, or B-52 invigorate erotic, masochistic, or power fantasies.

_____ Who Shows Up and What Do They Do?

Legions of bar-patients discuss forbidden desires in a highly permissive environment that encourages childish fantasy and adolescent bravado. Garland et al. (2004) described patterns of behavior in a small-town bar patronized by college students and locals. Male students were classified as jocks, frat boys, and wolves; females were divided into Madonnas and sheep.[1] Locals were identified as professionals or blue collar. Whereas jocks mostly huddled in all-male groups, mulling over this or that sporting escapade, frat boys (recognizable by their style of dress, e.g., T-shirts and baseball caps with fraternity logos) became increasingly loud and aggressive toward females as the evening progressed and more alcohol was consumed. Wolves (a.k.a. "the wolf pack") were particularly aggressive in targeting women (e.g., grabbing females around the waist or smacking their buttocks with the group egging them on).

Madonnas conformed to the stereotype of talking only to the man they were with, never ordering drinks for themselves. Usually, they did not come of their own accord, but because of a desire to please the man who brought them. In contrast, sheep were distinguished by their good looks and provocative dress, showing up in groups, rarely before 10 PM. They were scantily attired in midriff shirts, revealingly short dresses, and 3-inch heels. Instantly barraged by male attention, their residence at the bar is short-lived.

After drinking small amounts of alcohol, they often leave as a group after only about 20 minutes.

Like the mental hospital depicted in *One Flew Over the Cuckoo's Nest* (Kesey, 1962), the bar often features a comingling of needy personalities, poor impulse control, and abuse of power.

> These women bask in the attention they receive from the male patrons and often participate in their own sexualization. For instance, during one observation period, a sheep [lay] on the pool table while a male patron straddled her body. (Garland et al., 2004, p. 24)

Flack and colleagues (2007) conducted a study of unwanted sexual experiences in a collegiate "hookup" culture. One-off, casual encounters known as "hooking up," sometimes involving intercourse with no expectation of a continued relationship, appear to be increasing in the college population. "Hooking up is typically although not always unplanned, with the often implicit assumption of physical but not necessarily emotional intimacy and with no sense of commitment over time" (p. 153). The phenomenon of hooking up has been reported in numerous research studies (e.g., Lampert, Kahn, & Apple, 2003; Paul & Hayes, 2002).

In a representative sample of 178 students at a small liberal arts university, 23% of women and 7% of men reported one or more episodes of unwanted sexual intercourse. Seventy-eight percent of unwanted oral, vaginal, or anal intercourse took place while "hooking up," and 78% of unwanted fondling incidents took place at parties or bars. The most common reason for unwanted sexual intercourse was "impaired judgment due to alcohol" (Flack et al., 2007).

Hooking up may originate in bars or in the hypermasculine atmospheres encouraged by fraternities (Boeringer, 1999). Women may be invited through perusal of high school "mug shots" (sometimes dubbed "pig books") or the campus computer system (sometimes dubbed "the stalker net"). Upon gaining entrance to the frat, bar, or club scene, "women may be plied with sweet-tasting drinks that mask high alcohol content or with other date rape drugs, substantially increasing the odds of overconsumption, intoxication, and amenability to intimate advances" (Flack et al., 2007, p. 155). Some college men encourage use of their bedrooms as "hookup rooms."

The bar attracts a much larger clientele than the 4 million or so college students who engage in excessive alcohol consumption. Cloyd (1976) described the "marketplace bar" as a business establishment that "caters to young and usually single persons interested in meeting and possibly having sexual intercourse with persons of a similar orientation" (p. 293). On the basis of observations conducted in 11 bars in a Midwest metropolitan area, he identified a 3-phase "pairing ritual" in the barroom setting:

1. *Initiation*—Interpersonal encounters are usually predicated upon approach-oriented body language and eye contact. Women may raise

their negotiating "ante" by presenting themselves with more provocative clothing and body language. Males size up their possibilities and assess whether or not this is something they "can handle."

2. *Squaring Off and Negotiations*—Of paramount importance is an individual's projected self-confidence as being someone who can fulfill the needs and interests of his or her alter ego.

3. *Disclosures and Settlements*—Members disclose their ultimate intentions, and the settlement of gains and losses occurs. For example, a female may unfold her commitment to a boyfriend or mate or require a higher level of dating before having sex. From a male perspective, this is the time when he either "gets lucky" or gets "shut down."

In some of the rougher settings, tempers may flare and fights may break out. Observers have reported holes punched in bathroom walls, particularly over the urinals around closing time. If the support of friends, for example, "she's not worth it anyway," is not sufficient, in the vernacular of the bar, the bouncer's job becomes "cooling the mark" (Goffman, 1967).

With so much sexual innuendo and opportunity for alcohol-lubricated aggression, how can the bar function with any semblance of comfort and safety? As in most high-population psychiatric settings, this cannot always be guaranteed. Leonard, Quigley, and Collins (2002) found that in a randomly selected community sample, 25% of men and 12% of women had exposure to barroom aggression. In their study of bar aggression toward women, Buddie and Parks (2003) found that among females, more severe bar-related aggression was associated with heavier drinking, which correspondingly was related to "going to and leaving the bar with less known individuals and with talking to more people in the bar" (p. 1389).

In large measure, however, order in the "psychiatric tavern" is maintained by shared understanding of informal rules, enforced by a team of "mental health" specialists (i.e., bartenders, waitresses, and bouncers). In cases of serious or persistent infringement, violators are ostracized and forced to find a new subculture where they can try to belong (Garland et al., 2004).

Surrogate Family Atmosphere

An intriguing similarity between the mental hospital and the tavern is the illusion of a familiar family setting. In atmospheres such as these, where childlike behavior is expected, staff become symbols of parental authority. The alluring waitress delivers the "milk of human kindness" in an atmosphere of heightened stimulation and increased vulnerability. Like the oedipal boy, the incipient "bar-patient" naturally develops amorous feelings toward the seductive beauty who triggers his sexual fantasies. He harbors secret wishes that the barman—who symbolizes his father—would either cease to exist or at least temporarily disappear. Yet sexual intimacy is forbidden. When the mixture of intoxication and libido erode his dignity, the love-struck patron is doomed to rejection. A hassled waitress will first avoid personal contact, and then she will limit service availability. Disorderly conduct may ultimately be reported to that awesome symbol of patriarchal (or matriarchal) authority, the bartender. Anxiety caused by the fear of being rejected is conveniently blunted through increasing doses of alcohol. When sex or aggression becomes seriously unbridled, the waitress, on orders from the chief, may deliver the humiliating sentence, "You're cut off!" At this point, the emasculated patron is denied service for the duration of the evening. More reprehensible behavior, sometimes based on a cumulative record of misconduct, will ultimately result in the penalty of being "eighty-sixed," or thrown out. Customers such as these unwittingly re-create their own oedipal disappointment: they experience unrequited love and reprisal at the hands of a surrogate mother and father.

Full-time inhabitants of the local pub learn to repress their sexual impulses while forming amicable relationships with the barman and staff. Day into night, the "revolving door" tavernite looks toward the barkeeper for his or her attention and counsel. Increasingly, alcohol releases private fantasies of power and control; these serve in the struggle against deep-seated feelings of inadequacy and sexual unfulfillment. The bartender performs a dual role: providing psychoactive medicine, enabling partial relief from suffering and rage; he or she also functions as a limited yet reliable source of human relatedness. The bartender becomes a kind of adjunct personality or alter ego through which the patron, bearing the load of clouded consciousness, maintains some contact with the real world. The situation is described by Paul, a bartender employed by day as a psychiatric nurse:

> They could be looking directly at a mirror. Most bars have mirrors so you can look at your own reflection. . . . I do it myself. I've sat down in bars when I'm by myself and I don't know the clientele or the barman, so I will stick to him—probably in fleeting moments—exactly as they do. And I can sit at the bar and look in the mirror, and let my mind wander . . . what they do when I'm on the other side of the bar. And of course when you walk past there's an exchange of conversation, which can be short, depending on the business at the bar. When I walk away, you can see the customer drift off into fantasy. When I return, it gives him the opportunity to respond to his own thoughts. You might be a Christmas tree but he thinks that you are listening.

When a customer telegraphs potential danger, the bartender becomes a crucial source of control. He signals the inebriated patron to regain composure using facial expressions, direct commands, or outright discontinuance of service. Paul recounts his experience as a bar disciplinarian:

> There's the younger ones and the older ones. Some will tap on the bar.
> . . . One thing I can't stand is whistling. If someone whistles, I just say,
> "I'm not going to serve you—I'm not a dog." So I wait. . . . [I]f they whistle twice, I won't serve them for a little longer. And so there you see.
> They've got to behave or leave it as you please. You train the client to
> your own pace because you're in control. . . . You can always turn
> around and say, "You're the drunk and I'm sober."

As a last resort, the barman may discontinue service and defer "treatment" until the following day. Like the hostage who develops the so-called Stockholm syndrome (feeling affection for one's captor), tavern regulars eventually feel gratitude and devotion toward the bartender. They murmur platitudes of respect, tipping lavishly, existing in drugged anticipation of a few sporadic moments with a longed-for confidant. Taxis run ambulance from mental hospital to home.

Despite the watchful eyes of saloon personnel, some patrons have a repeated history of acting out bizarre impulses while intoxicated.

Case Example: Disinhibition in the Bar

Roger is a successful young lawyer with a boyish face and contagious smile. He enjoys a lucrative corporate practice in a large metropolitan area. His favorite tavern is designed for the more impulse-ridden patron—waitresses allow physical contact, and the floor manager has been known to drink and share drugs with customers. One evening when Roger was feeling particularly alone—and very intoxicated—he quietly stood on the bar stool and urinated on the counter. He was immediately "cut off" and "eighty-sixed" from the premises.

Prior to the incident, Roger had a history of being unable to form intimate relationships with anyone but his mother. He was an only son, and when he was 6 years old his father died suddenly. Roger's mother assuaged her intense mourning by encouraging undue physical contact and a deepening emotional dependence. The actualization of oedipal conquest left the young boy with a great sense of guilt. He had unconscious wishes for male domination, paternal reprisal, and ultimate forgiveness.

As a young lawyer, Roger symbolically performed penance by impressing the judge with his sincerity and hard work; as an intoxicated tavernite, he yearned for punishment and pardon from a substitute father—the bartender. His wish-fulfilling choreography was so adept that the sympathetic manager, who had been abandoned by his father early in life, reinstated Roger with full "treatment" privileges within 6 months of the dramatic incident.

The "Regulars"

But what of the multitude of alcoholic patrons who establish unwrinkled residence in the mainstay of the great psychiatric tavern, the neighborhood bar? Eventually, "regulars" understand that continued attempts to seduce female employees are destined for failure and possible reprisal. Erotic or hostile impulses toward parental figures gradually fade into feelings of affection and respect. Interpersonal relationships become increasingly centered on daily encounters between regulars and staff. The function of the tavern begins to merge with that of a traditional family unit. Cohorts of alcoholics develop tight sibling bonds, while humor and wit become the currency for fraternal affection and staff approval.

Below the surface image of happy-go-lucky rogue, the chronic alcoholic suffers from deeper feelings of worthlessness and despair. His equilibrium and composure depend on the firm guidance and external support of a professional team of tavern personnel. The bouncer (or hospital guard), who represents a visible extension of paternal authority, must be vigilant and instantly available to quell primitive expressions of lust or rage that may surface during the intoxicated state. Because machismo and stupor barely soften the bludgeons of self-perceived failure and ineptness, minor interpersonal confrontations can acquire the intensity of powerful sibling rivalries— rivalries that may even explode into fits of rage.

Research shows that drinking games increase the per capita blood alcohol level (Clapp, 2008). Correspondingly, it is expected that drinking games increase the risk of dangerous driving, unwanted sexual activity, and aggressive breakthroughs (i.e., verbal abuse or actual fights).

Case Example: The Drinking Game of Spoons

"Spoons" is a bar game that exemplifies the breakthrough of aggression in the absence of adequate external controls. A naive customer enters a tavern patronized by a cohort of well-established chronics. The newcomer becomes chatty, has a few drinks, and begins to enjoy a sparring camaraderie with several regular group members. Under the pretense of "fair game," the initiate is invited to partake in a unique sporting competition known as "spoons." The newcomer is cajoled into watching a round and then having a go. Two of the regulars pull their bar stools to within a foot of one another. Each places the handle of a tablespoon solidly between his teeth with the ladle turned upright. To the crowd's seeming delight, one bows his head forward, inviting the other to serve him a crown (i.e., bop him on the head with the mouth-held spoon). Amidst great oohs and hollers, the attacker twists his head up, musters maximum torque, and delivers the first blow. Players alternate between banger and taker while the crowd roots them on. After several exchanges, the novice is invited to give it a try. "No harm can be done with a slight knock on the head. . . . The spoon is so close. . . . Go on, give it a try. . . . See who hits harder." Aiming to please, to be a good sport, to belong to the group, the novice takes up the dare. What he doesn't suspect is that when he courageously lowers his head, a conspiring group member—who has concealed his own spoon— will blast him unmercifully.

The scheme is unraveled as a member of the group mischievously directs the "pigeon" or "chump" to the sight of three spoons placed on the bar. "Now how many spoons do ya see there?" Amidst the cackles and squeals of an ecstatic crowd, it dawns on the victim that he has been duped. The newcomer's ability to handle humiliation and deceit will ultimately determine whether he is permitted to join the fellowship of regulars.

Figure 4.2   **"Spoons."** Drinking games increase the per capita blood alcohol level along with the risk of dangerous driving, unwanted sexual activity, and aggressive breakthroughs (i.e., verbal abuse or actual fights).

In a properly managed tavern, primitive expressions of anger or uncontrolled sexual breakthroughs rarely occur. The well-behaved chronic accepts medication beyond the point of disinhibition and impulsive acts; he welcomes sedation and stupor. Like the overmedicated mental patient pacing the hospital ward in a daze, the heavily intoxicated regular staggers from bar stool to toilet, and eventually goes home. The abrupt declaration of "Last call for alcohol" pierces through ethanol's cushion of befogged escape. The noise level soars as drunken conversations become louder and more intense. The vociferous flurry, just before closing, represents an emergent awareness that the sleep that follows will be on a pallet of loneliness, discomfort, and desperation. At a notorious bar in Philadelphia, the announcement of last call is, "If you're not fucking the help, please leave."

The past decade has borne witness to a shift in the management policy of the great psychiatric tavern. Traditionally, residents have been mostly male, skillfully maintained on massive doses of psychoactive substances (i.e., various concoctions of alcohol). Women were sporadic visitors who, by and large, have had only limited access to the tavern as a means of coping with stress. Increasingly, however, women have come to rely on the tavern as a socially approved means of coping. The "white wine syndrome" has become an occupational hazard for executive females, particularly those between

21 and 24 years of age. Young professional women have discovered the "businessman's lunch," which may continue after work, through dinner, and on into the evening.

Meanwhile, fraternal excess, which has been encouraged for decades, may have reached a point of social disfavor. It appears that the alcohol industry has taken an "If you can't beat 'em, join 'em" stand on the issue of health promotion. It is common knowledge that heavy drinking can lead to liver, heart, and kidney problems and increase the risk of cancer (see Chapter 3, Hey, What's in This Stuff, Anyway?). Increasingly, wine and beer are marketed as better choices than hard liquor, and moderate, relaxed drinking is in vogue as a constructive means of reducing stress. The wine cooler, a low-alcohol mixture of wine, fruit juice, and carbonated water, is consumed by a growing number of female tavernites.

Chapter Summary

The "great psychiatric tavern" remains a bastion of male camaraderie and psychological support. Many thousands of neighborhood saloons continue to function as informal mental health centers that provide short-term relief for a vast clientele of lonely and emotionally troubled patrons. In the long run, multitudes of "regulars" find only temporary refuge as they undergo progressive deterioration through hopeless entrenchment in a miscarried form of self-repair. Caring communities are challenged to develop alternative means for gratifying the needs that have been previously met through tavern life. Atmospheres must be created in which surrogate family networks promote constructive measures for coping with internal conflict and social stress. The sense of adventure, spontaneity, relaxation, and human relatedness, all within reach at the pub, must somehow be preserved, without the unwanted consequences of repetitive intoxication and loss of impulse control.

Note

1. The authors view the use of denigrating terms such as "wolves" (predatory) and "sheep" (passive) to depict certain character types at the bar as a form of negative stereotyping that would insult, rather than educate, the many readers who might identify with observed patterns of social interaction in certain bars. However, the study by Garland et al. (2004) is one of the few published accounts of the matrix of interactions in the heterogeneously populated tavern setting.

5

Self-Medication

This chapter posits that a critical facet of addictive behavior is that people use drugs to deal with discomfort and lack of meaning. Our discussion begins with cigarettes, perhaps the most widely used and most damaging drug the world has ever seen. By increasing the availability of dopamine (evoking pleasure) and acetylcholine (enhancing memory and mental alertness), nicotine and other ingredients in tobacco set the stage for rapid onset and extremely high rates of dependency. Given that there is almost universal awareness of the hazards associated with the myriad drugs available on the licit and illicit market, why does such a high percentage of humanity knowingly place themselves in harm's way?

Are drug and alcohol abusers dyed-in-the-wool hedonists? Are they covertly suicidal? Most likely, neither is true. After having personally been involved in the treatment of more than 1,000 patients with substance abuse problems, Khantzian (1997, 2001), at the Department of Psychiatry, Harvard Medical School, has developed the "self-medication" model of addiction. According to Khantzian, an individual's vulnerability to substances is founded on what Carl Jung famously referred to as *spiritum contra spiritus*, figuratively translated as "spirituality can overcome spirits (alcohol)." This formulation implies that harmful involvement with mind-altering chemicals is related to our drive for comfort, connection, and wholeness. Drugs push aside suffering. The following quote from German poet Rainer Maria Rilke (1954) captures the essence of this perspective:

> How should we be able to forget those ancient myths . . . about dragons that at the last minute turn into princesses who are only waiting to see us once beautiful and brave? . . . [P]erhaps everything terrible is in its deepest being something helpless that wants help. (p. 69)

The propensity for self-medication is particularly evident in those who suffer traumatic life events. Sharp (2003) calls substance use and abuse "almost inevitable" for women and girls coping with abusive experiences.

Although the co-occurrence of posttraumatic stress disorder (PTSD) and substance abuse is more common in females, a significant proportion of the male population is seen as abusing substances to cope with suffering resulting from traumatic life events.

Whether the focus of self-repair is a drug or an activity, understanding and compassion require consideration of the internal struggle from which hedonic dependency derives. In this chapter, we explore biological, psychological, and social mechanisms that underlie self-medication through the abuse of tobacco, alcohol, heroin, and inhalants. Obviously, our list could include all of the misguided avenues to comfort and survival, which constitute the entirety of this book, and topics too numerous to discuss or as yet unforeseen. Perhaps the underlying issue is unfulfilled needs for intimacy (personal and spiritual), a topic that is covered at length in Section V, Craving for Intimacy.

Nicotine: The World's Antidepressant

Tobacco is the crème de la crème of addictive drugs. In the United States, cigarette smoking causes an estimated 438,000 deaths, or about 1 of every 5 deaths, each year (an estimated 259,500 men and 178,000 women). This estimate includes approximately 38,000 deaths from secondhand smoke exposure (Centers for Disease Control and Prevention [CDC], 2005). More deaths are caused each year by tobacco use than by human immunodeficiency virus (HIV), illegal drug use, alcohol use, motor vehicle injuries, suicides, and murders combined (McGinnis & Foege, 1993).

Worldwide, about 80% of deaths among the 2.7 billion adults over age 30 involve vascular, respiratory, or neoplastic (cancer-related) disease. Smoking is associated with an increase in the frequency of many of these diseases. Estimates of global tobacco mortality indicate that in 2000, about 5 million premature deaths were caused by tobacco. About half (2.6 million) of those deaths were in low-income countries. Males accounted for 3.7 million deaths, or 72% of all tobacco deaths. Approximately 60% of male and 40% of female tobacco deaths were of middle-aged persons (ages 35 to 69). Future increases in tobacco deaths worldwide are expected to arise from increased smoking by males in developing countries and by women worldwide. If we conservatively assume that "only" about one-third of smokers die as a result of smoking, then smoking will eventually kill about 10 million people a year. Thus, for the 25-year period from 2000 to 2025, there would be about 150 million tobacco deaths, or about 6 million deaths per year on average; from 2025 to 2050, there would be about 300 million tobacco deaths, or about 12 million deaths per year (Jha et al., 2006).

Effects on the Brain

Nicotine is one of the active ingredients in cigarette smoke that partially accounts for the addicting power of cigarettes. As we covered in Neurochemistry 101

(Chapter 2), the addicting power of tobacco is due to an increase of dopamine (DA) in the nucleus accumbens (NAc). Nicotine directly stimulates the flow of DA into the NAc (Figure 5.1). Nicotine also stimulates the release of the excitatory neurotransmitter glutamate, which triggers additional release of DA. But as we have seen, GABA (produced by the ventral tegmental area—VTA) moderates DA release. The VTA initially enhances GABA release (producing calming effect) to moderate the increase of DA produced by nicotine. However, within a few minutes nicotine kicks in to inhibit the release of GABA (Mansvelder & McGehee, 2002). Inhibiting the DA-releasing inhibitor results in high DA levels in the NAc. The combination of these effects, that is, (1) direct stimulation of DA release and (2) inhibiting the inhibitory effects of GABA on DA, results in an increase in DA in the NAc and an amplification of the rewarding properties of nicotine (Mansvelder & McGehee, 2002). It should be of no surprise that the Japanese name for a type of cigarette translates to "Short Hope."

It gets even worse. There appears to be an unknown substance in cigarette smoke that blocks the action of monoamine oxidase (MAO), which is responsible for breaking down (destroying) DA in order to maintain a balance of this neurotransmitter. So now it seems that smoking is a *triple-sided sword:* one to directly enhance DA, one to inhibit the DA inhibitor, and the third to block the DA destroyer (MAO). It would not be possible for the best pharmaceutical company in the world to design a more potent combination of drugs (nicotine and the unknown MAO inhibitor) to produce addiction.

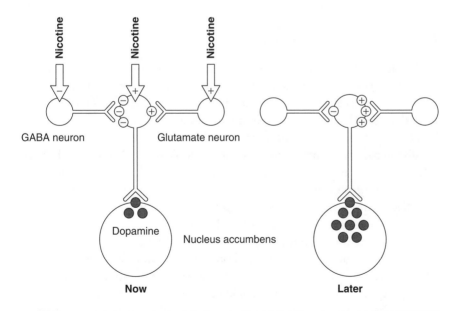

Figure 5.1   **Neurochemical effects of nicotine.** Nicotine inhibits inhibitory GABA neurons, stimulates dopamine-releasing neurons, and stimulates excitatory glutamate neurons (left panel). Each of these effects increases the amount of dopamine released in the nucleus accumbens (right panel).

Even this is not the end of the nicotine story with its multitude of effects on the brain. Many smokers, quite aware that smoking is really stupid, will claim that smoking makes them temporarily smarter and more alert. Actually, this is probably true. It is known that the chemical structure of nicotine is similar to that of the neurotransmitter acetylcholine, which is involved in many brain functions including memory and mental alertness. Because of the similarity in chemical structure, nicotine is able to attach itself to and activate acetylcholine (cholinergic) receptor sites.

On the other hand, Ott and his colleagues (2004) have shown that mental functioning degrades 5 times faster in elderly smokers than in elderly nonsmokers. They also observed that those who smoked more declined faster (showed more cognitive deficits) than those who smoked less. This is especially significant as we observe an increase in the average age of the population in the United States and around the world.

As is the case with all addicting drugs, continued activation of either the DA-enhancing neurons or the cholinergic receptors changes the sensitivity of these neurons to nicotine, which results in tolerance, dependence, and addiction. Nicotine seems to be one of the most addicting of all drugs of abuse. More than one-third of the 46 million adult smokers in the United States attempt to quit each year, but less than 10% succeed (American Heart Association, cited in *Quit Smoking Hub*, n.d.). As we have indicated, nicotine has receptors in many sites of the brain, which contributes to this powerful addiction.

How Fast Can I Get Hooked?

DiFranza (2008) explored how nicotine addiction develops in novice smokers. He developed a stunning hypothesis: limited exposure to nicotine—as little as one cigarette—can change the brain, causing neuronal modifications that stimulate the craving to smoke. He considered the defining feature of addiction to be *loss of autonomy,* that is, that quitting requires an effort or discomfort. DiFranza developed the Hooked on Nicotine Checklist (HONC), now available in 13 languages (see Table 5.1), to operationally define symptoms of nicotine addiction. The HONC, which could easily be modified to fit most other hedonic dependencies, is currently the most thoroughly validated measure of nicotine addiction.

The HONC was administered to hundreds of teenagers repeatedly over 3 years, and it turned out that rapid onset of addiction was very common. The most likely time for addiction to begin was the month after having the first cigarette. HONC symptoms could occur within the first weeks of smoking onset. "On average, the adolescents were smoking only two cigarettes a week when the first symptoms appeared. . . . A dozen studies have now established that nicotine withdrawal is common among novice smokers"—10% within 2 days and 25% to 35% within a month of having their first cigarette. In a large study of New Zealand youth, 25% had withdrawal effects after smoking one to four cigarettes (DiFranza, 2008, p. 84).

Table 5.1   The Hooked On Nicotine Checklist (HONC)

An answer of "yes" to any one of the questions indicates that addiction has begun:

Have you ever tried to quit smoking but couldn't?

Do you smoke now because it is really hard to quit?

Have you ever felt like you were addicted to tobacco?

Do you ever have strong cravings to smoke?

Have you ever felt like you really needed a cigarette?

Is it hard to keep from smoking in places where you are not supposed to, like school?

When you tried to stop smoking (or when you haven't used tobacco for a while):

- Did you find it hard to concentrate because you couldn't smoke?
- Did you feel a strong need or urge to smoke?
- Do you feel nervous, restless, or anxious because you couldn't smoke?

SOURCE: DiFranza et al., 2002.

A New Theory of Nicotine Addiction

The drug nicotine appears to create craving and to suppress it: "[T]he direct immediate action of nicotine is to suppress craving and this action is magnified to an extreme because subsequent doses of nicotine provoke greater responses than the first dose" (DiFranza, 2008, p. 85). This phenomenon (sensitization), common to all addictive drugs, suggests that nicotine is addictive, not because it causes pleasure but rather because it suppresses craving. Apparently, nicotine, from the first cigarette, is sufficient to trigger a remodeling of the brain (DiFranza, 2008). This finding highlights the importance of anti-smoking campaigns.

Studies that show images comparing brain responses to the first dose of nicotine through the fifth dose given 4 days later, illustrate dramatic changes in brain function in areas such as the anterior cingulate gyrus and the hippocampus. The response to the first dose is relatively limited, but brain activity is far more intense and widespread after the fifth dose. These findings indicate that the brain quickly becomes sensitized to nicotine, enabling addiction to begin after just a few doses (DiFranza, 2008).

Other Health Effects of Smoking

The truly devastating effects of smoking are not the multifaceted action of nicotine in the brain. Figure 5.2 (from the CDC) shows serious effects on the health of smokers in the United States. Obviously, lung cancer is the greatest hitter, followed by heart disease. In terms of health effects and deaths, cigarette smoking is the most serious drug problem in the United States today.

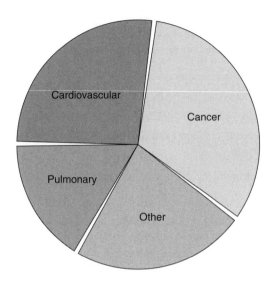

Figure 5.2   Smoking-related deaths. According to the CDC (2005), based
on statistics from 1997–2001, of an approximate 430,000 annual
deaths in the United States attributable to cigarette smoking,
35% were due to lung cancer (125,000) and other (30,000)
cancers, 28% were due to cardiovascular disease (coronary heart
disease [100,000] and stroke [25,000]), and 17% were due to
pulmonary disease (75,000).

Summary of Tobacco Effects

Tobacco is the most widely used drug of abuse and is responsible for more
deaths and more financial expenditures due to health problems and lost productivity than all other legal and illegal drugs combined. Smoking is also the
most preventable cause of death in the United States today. The deaths from
cigarette smoking are not due to the nicotine, but to the 200 known poisons,
including 50 carcinogens, in the smoke. However, it is the nicotine that is
addicting and keeps the addict smoking. Nicotine is a drug that activates the
dopamine reward system by direct stimulation of dopamine release as well as
release of glutamate and inhibition of the inhibitory neurotransmitter GABA.
In addition, there is a component of cigarette smoke that inhibits monoamine
oxidase from destroying dopamine. These combined effects make nicotine
one of the most addicting drugs, legal or illegal, in our society. The major negative health effects of tobacco are due to smoking (and chewing) and not to
the nicotine. In fact, some evidence indicates that nicotine may increase cognition. Smoking is responsible for most of the lung cancer in the world as well
as cancer of the larynx, esophagus, bladder, kidney, pancreas, stomach, and
uterine cavity. It is also the major cause of chronic bronchitis and emphysema, and a major cause of heart disease.

_____ Alcohol and Drug Use Among Women

Gender Differences in Patterns of Abuse

Several large-scale studies have shown that the prevalence rates of drug and alcohol use disorders are higher among men than women (Kessler et al., 1994; Regier et al., 1990). The National Institute on Alcohol Abuse and Alcoholism's National Epidemiologic Survey on Alcohol and Related Conditions (NESARC), surveyed more than 40,000 adults (Conway, Compton, Stinson, & Grant, 2006). The study showed that men are twice as likely as women to meet lifetime *DSM-IV* criteria for any drug use disorder—13.8% of men versus 7.1% of women. Twelve-month prevalence rates of alcohol abuse are almost 3 times as high among men as they are among women—6.9% of men versus 2.6% of women (Grant, Dawson, et al., 2004).

These findings are congruent with earlier studies that show gender differences for alcohol use disorders to be greater than for drug use disorders (Grant & Harford, 1995; Kessler et al., 1994). In contrast to alcohol disorders, for example, prescription drug abuse is similar across gender. The National Survey on Drug Use and Health reported 12-month prevalence rates of abuse or dependence for nonmedical use of pain relievers to be 1.4% for men and 1.1% for women 18 to 25 years old, and 0.5% for men and 0.4% for women 26 years and older (SAMHSA, 2005).

About 60% of U.S. women have at least one drink per week, and among women who drink, 13% have more than seven drinks per week. Although fewer women than men drink, among the heaviest drinkers, women equal or surpass men in alcohol-related problems. Female alcoholics have death rates that are 50% to 100% higher than male alcoholics, including deaths from suicide, alcohol-related accidents, heart disease and stroke, and cirrhosis of the liver (National Institute on Alcohol Abuse and Alcoholism [NIAAA], 2005).

In terms of cigarette smoking, the overall prevalence among U.S. adults during the 30 days before being surveyed was 26.9%, and the prevalence rate for adult women was 24.9%. In all racial or ethnic groups and subgroups, men had significantly higher prevalences of tobacco use than did women. For some subgroups (e.g., many Asian subgroups), the difference in tobacco use between men and women was substantial (Caraballo, Yee, Gfroerer, & Mirza, 2008).

Co-occurring Disorders

The presence of mental health problems co-occurring with alcohol or drug abuse disorders highlights the importance of the self-medication hypothesis. Women are more likely to meet criteria for anxiety, depression, eating disorders, and borderline personality disorder, and men are more likely to meet criteria for antisocial personality disorder (Brady, Grice, Dustan, & Randall, 1993; Sinha & Rounsaville, 2002). For women, the onset of a psychiatric disorder is more likely to antedate the onset of the substance use disorder. This suggests that women are more likely to abuse substances as a form of self-medication (Kessler, 2004). In fact, using data from the Epidemiologic Catchment Area Study, Gilman and Abraham (2001) found that after a 2-year follow-up period, women with a major depressive episode (MDE) were more than 7 times as likely as women without an MDE to have alcohol dependence. However, men with an MDE were not at higher risk for the development of alcohol dependence.

Females also use cigarettes as a form of self-medication. Research has shown that across gender, individuals with depression are more likely to smoke cigarettes and are less successful in smoking cessation attempts. This relationship appears to be particularly strong for women. Oncken, Cooney, Feinn, Lando, and Kranzler (2007) found that women with a history of MDEs were twice as likely to relapse to smoking at a 1-year follow-up as women without an MDE.

Multiple studies show that relationships among trauma, posttraumatic stress disorder, and substance use disorders are highly important for women. Sexual abuse in particular and early life stress in general appear to be more common in girls than in boys (Kendler et al., 2000). Also, women who were exposed to violence in adulthood tend to use substances to self-medicate their feelings of anger, guilt, anxiety, fear, and shame, which places them at increased risk for repeated victimization, thus perpetuating the cycle of victimization and substance use (Kilpatrick, Resnick, Saunder, & Best, 1998). In animal studies, uncontrollable stress mediated by neurobiological reactions has been found to increase drug self-administration (Jacobsen, Southwick, & Kosten, 2001).

Understanding gender differences in the neurobiological response to stress may shed light on the relationship between trauma and substance use disorders for women (Stewart, 2000). In short, women's substance-using careers are far different from men's.

Biological Differences

Women also differ in the way in which they metabolize alcohol: females are more vulnerable to organ damage, notably liver disease, and brain damage, which has been attributed to having a lower volume of body fluid in which to distribute alcohol. In addition, because women metabolize alcohol more slowly, they experience higher blood alcohol concentrations with similar drinking amounts (Lieber, 2001). Thus, lower levels of drinking are recommended for women than for men. According to the NIAAA (2005), drinking more than seven drinks per week increases a woman's chances of abusing or becoming dependent upon alcohol; also, women who drink fewer than seven drinks per week but have four or more on any given day are more likely to develop alcohol abuse or alcohol dependence.

There is also mounting evidence that hormonal fluctuation during the menstrual cycle can impact response to and craving for drugs. It has been shown that estrogen augments behavioral responses to cocaine in female rats (Lynch, Roth, & Carroll, 2002). In human females, this may explain increased responsiveness to cocaine cues at the beginning (follicular phase) of menstruation (Robbins, Ehrman, Childress, & O'Brien, 1999). Evans and Foltin (2006) showed that administration of progesterone during the follicular phase of the menstrual cycle attenuated the positive subjective effects of cocaine, indicating that progesterone may reduce the response to cocaine in women.

The case history of Bernice (below) is illustrative of a woman whose life has been fraught with guilt, depression, anger, and hostility in regard to current and past relationships. Her problems with alcohol are inextricably connected with a deep sense of disappointment regarding her feminine role. From a research perspective, women who have difficulty with their intimate relationships tend to drink more than others. Heavy drinking is more common among women who have never been married, are unmarried and living with a partner, or are divorced or separated. Also, a woman whose husband is a heavy drinker is more likely than other women to drink excessively (NIAAA, 2005).

Case Example: Female Alcohol Abuse

Bernice is a middle-aged housewife who lives with her husband and 23-year-old son in the suburbs of a relatively large metropolitan area. Many years of hidden drinking eventually became visible through a series of emergency hospitalizations. During the past decade, she has been hospitalized numerous times for alcoholism. When asked to describe the reasons for her recent relapse, Bernice began to reminisce about her daughter, who suffered from cerebral palsy and died more than 10 years ago. She explained that the present hospitalization was precipitated by a full night of solitary drinking after she felt rejected and insulted by a female friend. Bernice called her psychiatrist and asked to be treated for alcohol withdrawal symptoms. She said that she was frightened by the illusion of a young, dark-haired girl who appeared at the side of her bed. Bernice denied any connection between her vision of the young girl and her daughter. She felt that the underlying reason for her hospitalization was to escape from her husband's and son's anger and the feelings of loneliness she experienced at home.

Bernice was raised in a Midwestern city along with her sister, who is 5 years older. At the time of this writing, her mother and father were still alive and were in their seventies. In her early childhood, Bernice remembered feeling coerced to conform to what she regarded as unreasonable parental expectations. Her earliest memory, for example, involves a trip to Baltimore, where she was required to change clothes in the woods in order to appear neat and tidy while visiting her grandmother. Her early relationship with her mother is described as "OK," but as she grew older, the situation deteriorated dramatically. Bernice believes that her mother lived vicariously through her children. "She wanted me to do what *she* wanted to do." Her memory of her father is somewhat more pleasant. She describes him as an "intelligent, ingenious, fun-loving person . . . whose idealism causes him to be disappointed in people who don't live up to his standards." She also remembers being pressured by her father into living up to unreasonable expectations. "He wished more from me than could be expected of a young child."

During early childhood, Bernice had only one female friend, a mentally ill foster child. Bernice was looked after by her sister, who resented having to take care of a child 5 years younger. Until Bernice was 15 years old, they occupied the same bed. Bernice recalls the physical closeness that

(Continued)

(Continued)

she and her sister shared with displeasure, and describes resentment at being ordered about. Her teenage years are described as "ghastly," and most of her adolescent friendships were with boys. During this period, her sister joined the military, and Bernice was left to care for her mother who suffered from epilepsy. She has horrible memories of her mother being stricken with grand mal seizures, sometimes becoming injured from losing consciousness, often screaming from lack of oxygen. During this time, the relationship between Bernice and her mother was most stressed. Bernice felt the brunt of her mother's frustrations. She remembers being told, "You're cold, abrupt, unaffectionate . . . contemptuous," and often being confronted with her unattractiveness to men.

Bernice studied psychology in college, where she met her husband. Their courtship lasted about 2 years and was for the most part asexual. Her first sexual encounter occurred at about 17 years of age, although she did not have intercourse until sometime after. She had intercourse with her husband and one other man prior to marriage, and in 1950 became pregnant with her first child—out of wedlock. She and her husband went to great lengths to conceal the pregnancy from her parents until after they were married. The child was born brain-injured with a diagnosis of cerebral palsy.

At the time of the most recent hospitalization, Bernice associated her problem drinking with the agony of caring for her daughter, who developed allergies and asthma for which she required medication to be administered in the early hours of the morning. Bernice would remain awake reading and drinking vodka until her daughter was sedated. She continued drinking after her daughter's death and believes that she had been alcoholic about 3 years prior to that.

Bernice became very disturbed at the thought of divorce. She recalled her doctor's warning that "he may have to divorce you in order to get you to stop drinking." She expressed the belief that her husband and son were angry at her for her drinking. She believed that she could use alcohol in order to avoid their anger. Her marriage was further complicated by Bernice's concern about not having reached orgasm for the past year. She wondered whether this was alcohol related. Another aspect of her problem was the loneliness that she experienced during her husband's absence from home. She resented his travel as a salesman: "I'd like to get a map of the U.S. someday and the first big black thumbtack would go into Chicago because that is where he goes most . . . then Santa Fe, Albuquerque, and El Paso."

At the onset of psychotherapy, Bernice had neither a strong sense of femininity nor a sufficient degree of positive self-regard. Early experiences with females were unusually stressful. One friend was mentally ill, her mother was epileptic, and her sister appears to have been overly aggressive and demanding. Having internalized a rather strict set of parental expectations, Bernice was critical of others and of herself. The guilt engendered by a premarital pregnancy was considerable, but the feelings of worthlessness surrounding the mothering of her severely afflicted daughter were enormous. Bernice felt victimized, viewing herself as being at the mercy of circumstances and people—her parents, sister, and daughter in the past, and her friends, husband, and son in the present. Drinking was the vehicle through which she had been able to cope with her surroundings. She became as helpless as the people to whom she dedicated much of her life. At the same time, she could use alcohol to escape from the guilt, loneliness, and anger that she was continuously plagued by. Like her mother, she was able to command assistance from those who cared about her.

In the course of psychotherapy, Bernice began to assume personal responsibility for alcoholism, while she gradually revised the deep-seated view of herself as a victim. In-depth explorations of her feelings about femininity and motherhood were beneficial. In the context of a safe and caring relationship with a female therapist, she was able to disclose feelings of guilt, inadequacy, and failure. After one year of individual therapy, her husband participated with Bernice in the counseling process. The couple was helped to understand the relationship between Bernice's drinking and her husband's moods and absence. Although Bernice was the "identified patient," her husband also benefited from treatment. They made a commitment to spend more time together in mutually satisfying activities. Bernice and her therapist explored her relationship with her son, specifically how she would cope with separating—if and when he left home. She began to realize that her intellectual skills were sufficient to qualify her for interesting and rewarding employment; she set a long-term goal to transform from a woman feeling inadequate and victimized to one who accepts the challenge of having a comfortable and responsible life without the use of substances.

Of particular benefit to Bernice was her therapist's use of Marlatt's (e.g., Marlatt & Gordon, 1985; Marlatt & Witkiewitz, 2005) relapse prevention strategy (see Figure 3.6 in Chapter 3). By systematically reviewing and exploring her typical thoughts and actions just before she began drinking, Bernice was able to understand the mental precipitants of previous relapses and to remain sober.

After summarizing the literature on gender-focused treatment, the next section of this chapter, Posttraumatic Stress Disorder and Self-Medication, details self-medication with alcohol, drugs, or other tension-reducing behaviors (e.g., sex, gambling, eating) as a misguided form of self-repair for both men and women. A broad spectrum of external props are used to cope with traumatic life events beyond the range of ordinary human suffering.

Gender-Focused Treatment

Women generally begin substance abuse later than men, and there is some evidence that they respond better to treatment. In an 8-year follow-up, Timko, Moos, Finney, and Connell (2002) found that the outcomes for women were somewhat better than for men using the same services. Jarvis (1992) found that women are likely to do less well in mixed-sex group therapy because of the overrepresentation of men and unfavorable sexual dynamics. Furthermore, women who report sexual or physical abuse tend to prefer a female therapist, while others do equally well with male or female therapists (Connors, Carroll, DiClemente, Longabaugh, & Donovan, 1997).

As summarized by Back, Brady, Jaanimagi, and Jackson (2006), women are less likely to enter substance abuse treatment because of sociocultural factors (e.g., stigma, lack of partner/family support to enter treatment), socioeconomic factors (e.g., child care), pregnancy, fears concerning child custody issues, and complexities associated with increased rates of co-occurring psychiatric disorders. Furthermore, many women seek treatment at other settings (e.g., primary care, mental health). However, once women do enter treatment, they are at least as likely as men to complete therapy and have positive outcomes. Programs that address barriers to treatment that are specific to women (e.g., child care) and provide careful psychiatric assessment and treatment are likely to be the most effective.

The cognitive-behavioral approach (see Chapter 16) is a breakthrough for examining the relapse process and teaching relapse prevention skills for both men and women (Marlatt & Witkiewitz, 2005). However, for women with addictive disorders, *gender-focused* treatment is strongly indicated (Milkman, Wanberg, & Gagliardi, 2008). Table 5.2 presents general principles for treating women in counseling settings (Williams-Quinlan, 2004).

Women-focused treatment may produce improved outcomes because women perceive the same-sex treatment environment as one in which it is easier to disclose information about themselves such as issues with children,

Table 5.2   Guidelines for Treating Women in Counseling Settings

- Effective treatment with women should be free of restrictions based on narrowly defined gender stereotypes.
- The empowerment process involves recognition that women are able to accomplish what they make a commitment to and that the female substance abuse clients are no different from other women.
- Women should not be expected to act in stereotypical ways, and nontraditional role choices should be respected.
- Marriage should not be encouraged as a solution to women's problems.
- Women should be helped to recognize that the "socially appropriate" ways they have been taught are not ideal for mental health and adjustment (Crawford & Unger, 2000; Gergen & Davis, 1997; Matlin, 1996).
- Women should be treated and addressed with respectful language that communicates their equal status to men (Covington, 2000; Matlin, 1996; McMahon, 2000; Pollock, 1998).
- Service providers should help women recognize the realities of sexism, racism, and economic discrimination and develop effective means of coping with these issues (Matlin, 1996).

SOURCE: Williams-Quinlan, 2004.

sexuality, prostitution, sexual abuse, and physical abuse (e.g., Milkman et al., 2008; Sun, 2006). In addition, women-only settings eliminate the possibility of negative stereotyping and sexual harassment from their male counterparts (Weisner, 2005).

Perhaps the most important key to empowerment and strengthening women's resiliency lies in provision of a safe and reliable environment for trust, bonding, and intimacy. A typical component of substance abuse is violence in the female's domestic setting (Velez et al., 2006). Treatment that places the source of a woman's problems solely within herself can actually do damage to the recovery process by exacerbating already existing tendencies toward self-blame and feelings of powerlessness (Covington, 2000; Crawford & Unger, 2000; Matlin, 1996; Pollock, 1998). Equally important is helping women to see that assuming a victim stance in response to social realities is not an excuse to avoid personal responsibility for their actions.

The bottom line is that treatment outcomes are enhanced through gender-specific programs. Multiple treatment benefits are realized by empowering women to become self-sufficient and take personal responsibly for their own recovery (Milkman et al., 2008). These include

- Lower rates of relapse and recidivism;
- Lower rates of inpatient care;
- Greater job constancy; and
- Better parenting relationships resulting in higher rates of child custody.

"Protector (NOT!)," written by a woman with firsthand experience in the treatment system, addresses a woman's journey from abusive relationships and codependence to self-awareness and personal empowerment.

Protector (NOT!)

When I was a child

She taught me to fear the wild . . .

You need a protector . . .

Need a protector . . .

You need a protector

From the BIG BAD WOLF.

And when I was bad (or not)

I was punished by the dad (or what) . . .

He's our protector . . .

He's our protector . . .

But he's also the BIG BAD WOLF.

And when I was grown

I wanted out on my own.

Not without a protector . . .

You need a protector . . .

Need a protector

From the BIG BAD WOLF.

And so I was married

And tradition carried . . .

I had a protector . . .

Had a protector . . .

I had a protector

Who turned into the BIG BAD WOLF.

LEARN TO PROTECT YOURSELF.

—LaRee Herod

SOURCE: Reprinted with permission of LaRee Herod.

Posttraumatic Stress Disorder and Self-Medication[1]

Earnest research concerning PTSD began after the Vietnam War due to the profound psychological problems experienced by its veterans, both men and women. However, it has been reported that PTSD-like symptoms have been observed in all veteran populations, including those of the World Wars, the

Korean conflict, and United Nations peacekeeping forces deployed to other war zones. Similar symptoms also occur in veterans from countries outside the United States including Australia and Israel (Beall, 1997). Written accounts of PTSD symptoms are documented from the U.S. Civil War, when it was known as "Da Costa's Syndrome," based on a paper written by Da Costa in 1871 (cited in Beall, 1997), which described it as "soldier's heart" or "irritable heart." Holocaust survivors are also discussed in medical literature as having similar symptoms, as are survivors of railway disasters and of the atom bombs dropped on Hiroshima and Nagasaki. Most recently, PTSD has come to the forefront of psychological interest as the survivors of the September 11, 2001, terrorist attacks in New York City exhibit symptoms of this disorder; survivors of the 2004 tsunami in southeastern Asia and eastern India, and survivors of the 2005 earthquake in Pakistan and hurricanes in the southeastern United States will undoubtedly suffer PTSD as well.

Today, PTSD is no longer considered a disorder only of war veterans, as it occurs in both men and women, adults and children, Western and non-Western groups, and at all socioeconomic levels. Only a small minority of people appear to be invulnerable to extreme trauma. These stress-resistant individuals appear to be those with high sociability; a thoughtful coping style; and a strong perception of their ability to control their own destiny, or possessing an "internal locus of control" (Herman, 1997).

At the core of PTSD diagnosis is an etiological agent (i.e., a traumatic event) that is outside the individual, as opposed to a weakness or flaw within the individual (Bayse, 1998). The traumatic event was described in the *DSM-III* as a catastrophic stressor that was outside the range of usual human experience. At that time, reactions to such events as divorce, failure, rejection, and so forth would have been diagnosed as adjustment disorders rather than PTSD. As Herman (1997) points out, however, rape, battery, and sexual and domestic abuse are so common that they can hardly be described as outside the range of ordinary experience. Military trauma, too, affects millions; thus, she asserts that traumatic events are extraordinary not because they are rare, but because of the way in which they affect human life.

Included in the *DSM-IV* as categories of traumatic events are those *within* the range of usual human experience such as automobile accidents and deaths. The *DSM-IV* specifies that the individual must have an intense emotional reaction to the traumatic event, such as panic, terror, grief, or disgust (Bayse, 1998). Herman (1997) uses the *Comprehensive Textbook of Psychiatry*'s description of trauma: "intense fear, helplessness, loss of control, and threat of annihilation" (p. 33).

PTSD Population Statistics

The National Center for Posttraumatic Stress Disorder (NCPTSD; 2007) reports that about 8% of the population will have PTSD symptoms at some time in their lives. Approximately 5.2 million adults have PTSD during a given year; however, this is only a small portion of those who have experienced a traumatic event. About 60% of men and 50% of women experience a traumatic event at some time in their lives.

Women are more likely to experience sexual assault and child sexual abuse. Men are more likely to experience accidents, physical assault, combat, or disaster, or to witness death or injury. About 8% of men and 20% of women who experience a traumatic event will develop PTSD (NCPTSD, 2007). Sexual assault is more likely than other events to cause PTSD (Vogt, 2007).

Approximately 30% of men and women who served in war zones experience PTSD symptoms. An additional 20% to 25% have had some symptoms. Specific to the Vietnam War, research shows that of those who served, over 30% of men and 26% of women experienced PTSD symptoms at some time during their lives (Beall, 1997). As many as 10% of Gulf War (Desert Storm) veterans, 6% to 11% of Afghanistan (Enduring Freedom) veterans, and 12% to 20% of Iraq (Iraqi Freedom) veterans are estimated to have experienced, or be likely to experience, PTSD (NCPTSD, 2007).

According to the NCPTSD (2007), those most likely to develop PTSD

- Were directly exposed to a traumatic event as the victim or as a witness;
- Were seriously injured during the event;
- Experienced a trauma that was long lasting or very severe;
- Believed their lives were in danger;
- Believed that a family member was in danger;
- Had a severe reaction during the event such as crying, shaking, vomiting, or feeling separated from their surroundings;
- Felt helpless during the trauma, not being able to help themselves or family member(s);
- Had an earlier life-threatening event, such as being abused as a child;
- Had another mental health problem;
- Had family members with mental health problems;
- Had minimal support from family and friends;
- Recently lost a loved one, particularly if it was unexpected;
- Had recent, stressful life changes;
- Drank alcohol in excess; or
- Were women, poorly educated, or relatively young.

The NCPTSD (2007) also reported that African Americans and Hispanics may be at higher risk than Whites to develop PTSD, and that one's culture or ethnic group may affect how one reacts to PTSD symptoms; people from groups that are open and willing to talk about problems may be more likely to seek help.

While some people may have few problems adjusting and returning to a normal state after a traumatic event, others may be debilitated for years; two people exposed to the same event will have different levels of reaction. Behavioral scientists are unable to predict or measure the potential effect of a traumatic event on different people, but certain variables seem to have the most impact, including

- The extent to which the event was unexpected, uncontrollable, and inescapable;
- The level of perceived extent of threat or danger, suffering, upset, terror, or fear;
- The source of the trauma: human-caused is generally more difficult than an event of nature;
- Sexual victimization, especially when betrayal is involved;
- An actual or perceived responsibility for the event; and
- Prior vulnerability factors including genetics or early onset as in childhood trauma.

Symptoms of PTSD

Chronic PTSD typically involves periods of increase in symptoms, followed by a remission. Some individuals experience symptoms that are unremitting and severe, while others report a lifetime of mild symptoms, with significant increases in symptoms following major life events such as retirement, medical illness, or reminders of military service such as reunions or media attention to anniversaries of events. Table 5.3 shows the symptoms of PTSD.

Table 5.3   Symptoms of PTSD

Reexperiencing the trauma

- Flashbacks
- Nightmares
- Intrusive memories and exaggerated emotional and physical reactions to triggers that remind the person of the trauma

Emotional numbing

- Feeling detached
- Lack of emotions, especially positive ones
- Loss of interest in activities

Avoidance

- Avoiding activities, people, or places that are reminders of the trauma

Increased arousal

- Difficulty sleeping and concentrating
- Irritability
- Hypervigilance
- Exaggerated startle response

PTSD also creates physiological changes in the body including:

Neurobiological changes

- Alterations in brainwave activity
- Changes in the size of brain structures including decreased size of the hippocampus and abnormal activation of the amygdala
- Changes in functioning such as memory and fear responses

Psychophysiological changes

- Hyperarousal of the sympathetic nervous system
- Increased startle reaction
- Sleep disturbances
- Increased neurohormonal changes resulting in heightened stress and increased depression

Physical manifestations

- Headaches
- Stomach or digestive problems
- Immune system problems
- Asthma or breathing problems
- Dizziness
- Chest pain
- Chronic pain or fibromyalgia

Psychological outcomes can include the following:

Depression, major or pervasive

Anxiety disorders such as phobias, panic, and social anxiety

Conduct disorders

Dissociation

Eating disorders

Social manifestations include

Interpersonal problems

Low self-esteem

Alcohol and substance use

Employment problems

Homelessness

Trouble with the law

Self-destructive behaviors

- Substance abuse
- Suicidal attempts
- Risky sexual behaviors
- Reckless driving
- Self-injury

SOURCES: Dryden-Edwards & Stopler, 2007; Kinchin, 2005; M. Smith, Jaffe, & Segal, 2008.

To be diagnosed with PTSD, according to the DMS-IV, the stressor must be of an extreme nature, as in something life-threatening; however, in adjustment disorder (AD), the stressor can be of any severity, including divorce or job loss. Symptoms of avoidance, numbing, and increased arousal that are present before exposure to the stressor do not meet the criteria for PTSD diagnosis and should be considered as a mood disorder or another anxiety disorder.

Physiological Diseases and Disorders

Bender (2004) reports that women with PTSD experience more adverse medical conditions such as arthritis, lower back pain, obesity, emphysema, and hypertension than women in general or those with depression only. Depression has long been known to be associated with poor physical health, but women with PTSD exhibit even worse health, based on a 1999 survey of 30,000 female veterans. Almost 90% of women with a diagnosis of PTSD experienced at least one medical condition, which, in addition to the above-mentioned conditions, included low energy, chronic pain, and poor physical functioning. According to this study, women with PTSD also experienced more physical pain than women with depression or with neither diagnosis. Bender states that the study suggests that trauma may be linked to "chronic neuroendocrine dysregulation" as well as to poor personal habits such as smoking, drinking, or drug use, and cautions those in the mental health care field to be aware of the need for additional treatment for comorbid medical conditions.

Kimerling, Prins, Westrup, and Lee (2004) concur that both men and women with PTSD have a greater incidence of functional impairment as well as a poorer course of disease. These include cardiovascular disorders (a significant finding, since heart disease remains the leading cause of death among women in the United States) and gastrointestinal disorders including liver disease, viral hepatitis, irritable bowel syndrome, and gastro-esophageal reflux disease (commonly known as chronic heartburn).

Women with PTSD who experienced childhood sexual trauma are also commonly found to have sexually transmitted diseases, suggesting that trauma exposure serves as a risk factor for infection, particularly HIV. Sexual trauma exposure is a direct risk factor for sexually transmitted diseases. Kimerling et al. (2004) reported that a 1996 study of HIV-infected women showed that 43% had been sexually assaulted at some time in their life. It was also reported that the disease progresses more rapidly among women with PTSD than among those without.

Studies also show that, in victims of trauma, there are physical changes, specifically volume reduction in the hippocampus, the learning and memory center of the brain. The hippocampus works in tandem with the medial prefrontal cortex, the area that regulates emotional response to fear and stress, thus indicating a physiological relationship to PTSD symptoms (Bremner, 2002). Combat veterans were found to have an 8% reduction in hippocampal volume, yet no differences were found in other parts of the brain. Interestingly, Bremner also reported that the hippocampal volume reduction is specific to those with PTSD, not being associated with closely related disorders such as anxiety or panic disorder. Further, the hippocampus has the ability to regenerate neurons; however, stress has been found to stop or slow neuron regeneration. Bremner suggested that this change in size of the learning and memory center of the brain among PTSD sufferers may explain the delayed recall or "recovered memories" that many victims of childhood abuse experience. He explains that the abuse caused damage to the hippocampus, leading to a distortion or fragmentation of memories.

The changes in the function of the prefrontal regions of the brain may explain the pathological emotional responses in those with PTSD (Bremner, 2002). Bremner reported that studies of veterans with PTSD showed a decreased blood flow to this area when viewing combat-related scenes and sounds. This did not occur in veterans without PTSD. Similar results were found when comparing women who experienced childhood sexual abuse and suffer PTSD with those with childhood sexual abuse and no PTSD symptoms. However, a more recent controlled study indicated that twins not exposed to emotional trauma showed the same amount of "shrinkage" in their hippocampus, suggesting that a small hippocampal volume may be a pre-incident risk factor rather than brain damage from the emotional trauma (Herbert & Sageman, 2004).

Depressive Disorders

As noted above, major depressive disorder (MDD) is a frequent partner of PTSD, with studies showing similar rates of occurrence in both genders. As Kimerling et al. (2004) point out, this is an interesting phenomenon since women's risk for MDD in the absence of PTSD is greater than men's. Their explanation is that PTSD "may create a vulnerability toward depression in men that suppresses the protective effect of male gender" (p. 579).

Due to the overlap of MDD and PTSD symptoms (diminished interest in activities, sleep and concentration disturbances), assessment and diagnosis can be difficult. Kimerling et al. (2004) report that clinicians have outlined several methods of distinguishing between the two disorders. Diminished interest in activities in PTSD is specific to cues of past trauma exposure; MDD, on the other hand, is characterized by loss of energy and hopelessness. PTSD sleep difficulties are characterized by nightmares and hypervigilance that occur only after the traumatic event. Difficulties in concentration with MDD are more global, whereas with PTSD they are dissociative and result from trauma-related memories.

Substance Abuse

A 1990 study found that approximately 74% of men and 29% of women with PTSD had a lifetime diagnosis of alcohol abuse (Ouimette, Wolfe, & Chrestman, 1996). Kimerling et al. (2004) report that approximately 30% to 50% of men and 25% to 30% of women with lifetime PTSD also are substance abusers. It has been shown that a comorbid diagnosis of PTSD and SUD (substance use disorder) is associated with poorer substance use outcomes: Those with PTSD relapse more quickly, drink more on days when they do drink, have a greater percentage of heavy drinking days, and suffer greater negative consequences due to their substance abuse than do non-PTSD abusers (P. J. Brown, 2000).

Interestingly, women are more likely than men to develop substance use disorders after exposure to a traumatic event and symptoms of PTSD, with approximately 65% to 84% of women experiencing PTSD before developing substance use disorders. This points toward the "self-medication" hypothesis for PTSD/SUD comorbidity among women, where women use alcohol or drugs to cope with trauma-related symptoms. Sharp (2003) calls substance use and abuse "almost inevitable" for women and girls coping with abusive experiences. In contrast, men are more likely to experience trauma due to their behaviors linked to substance use, which then results in PTSD symptoms (Kimerling et al., 2004). Kimerling et al. strongly suggest that clinicians routinely screen clients for SUD when PTSD is suspected.

Recovery From Trauma

Recovery from traumatic events is described by Herman (1997) as unfolding in three stages, the first being that of *establishing safety*. The second stage includes the tasks of *remembrance and mourning*, while the third stage encompasses *reconnection with ordinary life*. As with any abstract concept, the stages are not followed exactly nor are they linear. Herman describes traumatic syndromes as "oscillating and dialectical in nature . . . defy[ing] any attempt to impose such simpleminded order" (p. 155). These stages are defined here in an attempt to assist clients and clinicians alike in simplifying and gaining control of a seemingly uncontrollable process.

Safety

Survivors of victimization must shift their surroundings from that of unpredictable danger to reliable safety. This includes recognizing and naming the demon. As Herman (1997) discusses, some may feel relieved to learn that there is a name for their problems. Others, however, resist the diagnosis out of fear of the stigma associated with any psychiatric diagnosis; some may deny the condition out of a sense of pride. Many survivors of physical or sexual abuse do not make the connection that their experience of abuse is directly related to their symptoms or behaviors. Herman goes on to emphasize that the process of developing a framework that relates the client's problems to the traumatic history is beneficial, as it assists in developing a therapeutic alliance.

Establishing safety includes allowing the victim to regain control. While those who become dependent on drugs or other tension-reducing behaviors may have attempted to regain control through external stimulation, true control is accomplished when victims feel safe in relation to others, as well as with their own thinking and feeling. As Herman (1997) suggests, gradually developing a safe and trusting therapeutic relationship is key. In addition, family, friends, and lovers who were *not* involved in abuse of the victim should be mobilized to act as a support system. Further, any attachment to those involved in the victimization must be disconnected, as must use of illicit drugs or alcohol (assumed, in the case of incarcerated victims).

Remembrance and Mourning

After having regained a sense of control, developed a feeling of safety within the self and among others, and discontinuing self-destructive behaviors, trauma victims can gradually move on to stage two: *remembrance and mourning*. This is the phase where victims verbally tell the whole in-depth, sordid story. As Herman (1997) notes, the difference between remembering the trauma and retelling the trauma is likened to a series of still snapshots as opposed to full cinematic movies with the inclusion of words and music.

Retelling the story must be repetitive; eventually, the story no longer will arouse such intense feelings (Herman, 1997). Ultimately, it becomes only a part of the survivor's experience rather than the focus of it. The memory fades, and grief loses its strength. The victim's life story begins to take on other aspects rather than only one. This, indeed, is a simple explanation of a complex process, but one that can be accomplished with a knowledgeable and trained clinician who can look past the anger and hatred that may accompany PTSD and its symptoms.

Reconnection

After mourning the loss of the person they were before the trauma, victims must create a new self and a new future. As quoted by Herman (1997), psychiatrist Michael Stone describes this task (specific to his work with incest survivors) thusly:

> All victims . . . have, by definition, been taught that the strong can do as they please, without regard for convention. . . . *Re-education* is often indicated, pertaining to what is typical, average, wholesome, and "normal" in the intimate life of ordinary people. Victims . . . tend to be woefully ignorant of these matters, owing to their skewed and secretive early environments. Although victims in their original homes, they are like strangers in a foreign country, once "safely" outside. (p. 198)

Herman (1997) believes the statement "I know I have myself" is the anchor of the third stage. No longer possessed by past trauma, the survivor now understands the results of the damage done and becomes the person he or she wants to be. Imagination and fantasy, desire and initiative are at the core of this stage, where hopes and dreams are weaved into reality.

Herman (1997) emphasizes that resolution of the trauma is never final, and recovery is never complete; the impact of trauma will "reverberate throughout the survivor's lifecycle" (p. 211). While incomplete, recovery will allow the survivor to return to the normal tasks of life. Becoming more interested in the present and future than the past, a survivor of trauma overcomes fear and opposition and gradually engages in new and healthy relationships.

In summary, there are seven criteria for the resolution of trauma (Herman, 1997):

- The physiological symptoms of PTSD have been brought within manageable limits;
- The survivor is able to bear the feelings associated with traumatic memories;
- The person has authority over the memories; for example, he or she can either remember the event or put it aside;
- The memory is coherent and linked with feeling;
- The survivor's self-esteem has been restored;
- Important relationships have been reestablished; and
- A coherent system of meaning and belief concerning the trauma has been constructed. (p. 213)

Patients in the Street

A complicating feature of the drug scene is that addicts often appear to have more practical information about the effects of mind-altering drugs than the physicians who prescribe them. An old adage is, "The doctor who treats himself has a fool for a patient." Deep in the gutter of the treatment community, a group of patients prescribe and administer their own medications. Through rumor and experimentation, they discover illegal, mood-affecting drugs, which appear to magically induce enormous pleasure and also subdue undesired emotions. Through trial and error and various social influences, the novice learns to procure a host of substances that are known among street users to influence or improve painful emotions. Illicit drugs serve as prosthetic devices that temporarily reduce discomfort from feelings such as anxiety, rage, hurt, shame, and loneliness. Addicts select their drugs of choice based on an interaction among street mythology, the chemical action of the drug, and the nature of their particular cognitive and emotional state.

On the basis of observations and interviews with hundreds of addicts, Khantzian (1997, 2001) found that opiate users are particularly compelled by the anti-aggression and anti-rage action of narcotic drugs. Addicts' life histories reveal prolonged periods of uncontrolled rage and anger, replete with horrifying accounts of violent episodes that predate their drug experiences. The addicts themselves were often victims of unusual levels of aggression in their family, their community, or both. During treatment, opiate-dependent patients repeatedly explained their compulsion for narcotics on the basis of how it made them feel in relation to their anger. They frequently use such terms as mellow, soothed, normal, calm, and relaxed. Khantzian also found that patients who often appear hyperaggressive, restless, or even assaultive in group therapy become more relaxed as they adjust to a therapeutic dose of methadone. Many patients who started their drug abuse with another type of drug switch to heroin as their drug of choice when they repeatedly experience uncontrolled fits of violence or rage under the influence of alcohol, sedatives, amphetamines, or cocaine.

In his 14-year history of experimentation, abuse, addiction, and drug-related crime, Philip became extremely knowledgeable about the commodities and characters in the drug world. In the following case study, we shall "inject" Philip's understanding of his progression from heroin use to addiction with an explanation of the biochemical substratum of his progressively disturbed functioning. His case illustrates how an addict learns to regulate his physiology through a well-planned self-medication schedule. His skill reflects a high level of street knowledge of how to cope with the medical issues of dependence, tolerance, and withdrawal.

Case Example: Self-Medication and Recovery

Philip switched his drug of choice from cocaine to heroin after discovering heroin's soothing and anti-aggressive effects. When interviewed, he was 29 years old and had been in drug-free treatment for nearly 14 months. He had begun smoking pot and using amphetamines at 13 years of age and maintained a $100 to $200 per day heroin habit for 5 years, prior to his conviction and mandatory treatment. He supported his addiction primarily through the sale of marijuana and cocaine. In lieu of prison, Philip opted for placement at a residential drug treatment center after having been arrested for possession and attempted sale of 10 grams of cocaine.

Philip is the only male in a family of eight children. He felt "robbed" at the age of 9 when his father suddenly died of a heart attack while serving in the military. During adolescence, in the mid-1960s, he lived in a large metropolitan area where illicit drugs were readily available. He started experimenting with marijuana and amphetamines at the age of 13. At 15, he began to sniff cocaine and would sell grams of coke to his friends and school contacts. He first sniffed heroin at 17, recalling that he was tricked by a friend who told him it was cocaine. He was initially angry because he had heard about the perils of heroin on the street. He ignored the warnings, however, as he enjoyed the soothing sensations brought on by the drug. He continued to use heroin, blocking from his mind any thoughts of becoming "strung out."

Through sniffing heroin, Philip brought about a temporary decrease in the rate of neurotransmission in his central nervous system, which was precisely the effect that he enjoyed. However, in a few hours the drug sensations wore off, and his level of neurotransmission returned to normal. Subjectively, he experienced a return to his customary state of loneliness and tense depression. He continued to episodically sniff heroin for the next 6 months when the drug was available and when inner distress and anxiety seemed unbearable. Although filling opiate receptor sites in the brain by the ingestion of heroin caused a corresponding decrease in neurotransmission, the brain would automatically initiate a self-regulatory process to reinstate normal neuronal activity. Enzymatic changes occurred in an attempt to accelerate neurotransmission to offset the decrease brought about by heroin.

When he first began to use heroin, Philip could be satisfied with an amount about the size of one match head. It would "nod him out" for about 6 hours. Between irregularly timed doses, which he ingested two to three times weekly, his functioning seemed unimpaired. In only a few hours, the drug sensations seemed to wear off and Philip could conduct his business as usual. He was able to eat and

(Continued)

(Continued)

sleep regularly. Yet the immediate soothing effects that he derived from ingesting heroin were slowly being challenged by longer-lasting changes in brain chemistry. Although he continued to use heroin at the initial match-head level, the intensity of his feeling was being eroded constantly by these insidious chemical changes that attempted to return his neurotransmission to a "normal" level.

After several weeks, Philip noticed that he needed an increased amount of heroin to feel high. His required dose began to swell to two, three, four, and still more match heads. Even at higher doses, however, he began to recognize that he wasn't getting the same feeling of pleasure. He recalled that after about 6 months of frequent and escalating use, he woke up one morning "feeling shitty." Philip had become physically dependent on heroin and required it regularly just to feel normal. He was getting strung out.

About 2 months later, he allowed a crony to "geez" him with a hypodermic syringe. "Hitting up" was like nothing he had ever experienced before. It was "heaven . . . like everything in the world had just been taken care of." He quickly learned to self-administer the drug and began to use it on a daily basis. Without heroin, he would anticipate becoming sick. His thoughts became obsessed with when and how he was going to "do some stuff." He would attribute all unpleasant bodily sensations, even hunger, to the absence of heroin in his system. His body weight decreased from 150 to 118 pounds. When heroin wasn't readily available, Philip would use prescription narcotics. He knew a physician who, in exchange for cocaine, would allow him to browse through the PDR *(Physician's Desk Reference)* and pick out any drug he wanted. He would select Dilaudid to avoid being sick, but always preferred heroin, which didn't seem to have negative side effects like headaches or ringing in his ears. At this point in his addictive "career," his entire life began to revolve around not being sick. His dependence was so great that he could get "normal," but he couldn't get high. Philip was deeply entrenched in the maintenance phase of his habit. The enzyme levels in his brain had changed so drastically that even large doses could not re-create the feelings of pleasure and calm, hallmarks of his initial use.

After 2 to 3 years of regular use, Philip recalls having to wake up every 3 to 5 hours to inject himself with heroin. When he was without the drug for more than 8 hours, his withdrawal symptoms would become very severe. He remembers his skin becoming blotchy; breaking out in cold sweats; shaking all over; getting cramps in his legs, back, and stomach; and sometimes vomiting. In the absence of the drug, his neurotransmission did not return to normal; rather, it became accelerated because of his chronic drug abuse. Somehow he would manage to get some heroin from a spoon into a syringe, then into a vein. Within about 30 seconds, he felt as if heroin were "filling all the gaps" in his body. Sometimes he would "jack off" with the needle by pulling up blood into the syringe and then injecting it back into his vein. For the most part, Philip found this practice repulsive and he did it infrequently. He remembered a female addict, however, who would sit, sometimes for 20 minutes, "pulling it up in the syringe . . . in and out."

During the lengthy maintenance period, Philip was nearly always obsessed with the functioning of his body. He recalls being regularly constipated from the effect of heroin on his digestive system. When several days passed without a bowel movement, Philip would interpret being constipated as "something wrong." His remedy was based on practical experience with a range of pharmacological effects. He would sit on the toilet, get some cocaine, and then "hit it up." By repeating this procedure at least twice per week, Philip was able to "clean himself out." After 5 years of living in this hellish state, Philip was ordered by the court to choose between jail and treatment for his drug problem at a therapeutic community (TC).

In this setting, drug addiction is traditionally viewed as a symptom of weakness in character, usually associated with alienating childhood circumstances. The addict chronically avoids dealing with conflict by withdrawing into a protective shell. This self-destructive pattern is interpreted as a response to feelings of incompetence and inadequacy. While using drugs to escape from stress, the addict denies personal problems and hides behind a criminal mask of toughness and superiority. Under the guise of sincere friendship and urgent need, addicts manipulate others to assist them in gratifying their infantile wishes.

The therapeutic community strives to provide a positive family atmosphere in which self-realization can occur. In a setting where drug inaccessibility is strictly enforced, addicts are given the opportunity to clarify their values and goals in life. They are expected to move toward the development of a greater sense of moral responsibility. These opportunities are possible largely because the addict has been removed from the environmental stimuli—drug access, recurrent stress, and drug-using friends—that have surrounded and fostered his compulsive drug-using behavior. Correspondingly, TC graduates are expected to eliminate drug use, learn adaptive responses to stress, and readjust to the outside world as comfortable and responsible citizens.

The new resident's involvement in the TC program is strongly influenced by his or her experience during the initial or "prospect" phase of treatment. Philip was tempted to "jump" several times, but each time a senior resident talked to him, and he decided to stay. He remembers feeling completely disoriented during the beginning of treatment when he was required to wear pajamas, work at menial chores, and sit in groups with fellow residents who "confronted each other whenever someone would hide out in their druggie attitude."

A hierarchical arrangement of leadership roles within the resident group is an integral part of the TC treatment approach. Residents take on increasing responsibility for operating the facility as they earn status as reliable and trustworthy members of the community. Conversely, verbal reprimands, role demotions, and increased work assignments are directed toward shaping and directing clients who have been observed to "slip."

As time went on, Philip began to realize the importance of being in treatment. In the beginning, he remembers feeling that it didn't matter how he acted; he would get accused, insulted, and questioned anyway. He felt "damned if you do, damned if you don't." He later understood that the purpose of frequent personal confrontations was to promote healthy responses to stress. "No matter what situation you were in, no matter what you tried to work out, you could always do it without stickin' a fucking needle in your arm." He remembers always being scrutinized and challenged by other members of the group about minute details of his demeanor. After several months of being constantly and thoroughly checked for his motives and attitudes, he noticed that he began checking himself. "All of a sudden you caught yourself like, I'm doing something wrong. I shouldn't be doing this. . . . [Y]ou started to feel guilt. For once you started feeling happy. You noticed the birds singing and the sun's shining, and they're gonna let us out in the park to throw the football around."

When positive experiences such as these occur, the result is often enhanced self-esteem and a corresponding reduction in alienated-alienating behaviors. Philip now regards having "stuck out" the therapeutic community as the best decision of his life. He views the TC as the only place where a hard-core drug abuser can have a chance at getting his life together. He feels that in the course of treatment, he came across many people who helped him to "clean up," but the person he thanks most is himself. After 14 months of complete abstinence, Philip reported that he reached a point where he made the decision to stay clean permanently. He realized that there was no way that he could continue doing heroin and be a normal human being, "and what I want to be is a normal human being, so I decided never to do it again."

Philip was hired as a counselor in the therapeutic community. He has been able to use his drug abuse and treatment experiences to guide others through the recovery process. At the time of this writing, he has been entirely drug-free for 16 years.

Prescription Drug Abuse

McCabe (2008) reported increases in the prescription rates of potentially addictive medications in the United States, including stimulants, opioids, and benzodiazepines. These increases are likely the result of many factors, including improved awareness regarding the usefulness of drugs in the treatment of mental disorder, increased duration of treatment, availability of new medications, and increased marketing. The public has become alert to the abuse potential of these medications and high prevalence rates of nonmedical use, especially among young adults 18 to 24 years of age.

McCabe (2008) used questionnaire data to study prescription drug use and potential drug abuse among 3,639 college students (average age, 19.9 years). Students were asked if they had been prescribed or had used without a prescription four classes of prescription drugs—opioids, stimulants, sleeping aids, and sedative or anxiety medications. In addition, they were asked if they had experienced drug-related problems (e.g., performed illegal activities to obtain drugs, had withdrawal symptoms, or experienced medical problems as a result of drug use).

Fifty-nine percent reported having used at least one of the drugs with a prescription for medical reasons, while approximately one in five reportedly took them without a prescription for nonmedical reasons. Those who had reported that they used drugs without a prescription—whether or not they had also used them for medical reasons—were more likely to screen positive for drug abuse than those who had used the drugs only for medical reasons or had never used them at all.

Inhalants: How Stupid Can You Get?

Inhalants, which are volatile substances that produce breathable vapors, include paint sprays, paint thinners and removers, spray paints, deodorant, vegetable oil, gasoline, glues, and other aerosols. In addition, certain medical anesthetics found in commercial and household uses are abused. These include chloroform, ether, nitrous oxide (laughing gas), and aliphatic nitrites (NIDA, 2005a).

Nitrites, which include cyclohexyl, amyl, and butyl nitrite, are often used to enhance sexual performance. Nitrites act much like Viagra by dilating blood vessels and relaxing muscles. Cyclohexyl nitrite is found in room deodorizers, while amyl nitrite is sometimes prescribed by doctors for heart pain. Both amyl and butyl nitrites are packaged in small bottles, and are referred to as "poppers."

Inhalants and the Brain

One of the most dangerous as well as widely used inhalants is the organic aromatic compound toluene (found in gasoline, paint thinner, and correction fluid). It is used commercially to make TNT (trinitrotoluene), an explosive used in military bombs. Although quite different from TNT, toluene does a number on the brain not unlike that of TNT on a city. But first, let's see if we can explain why anyone would use inhalants such as toluene. Toluene and most other inhalants (except nitrites) activate the brain's dopamine reward system. That should not come as any surprise at this point. The rapid high produced by inhalants resembles that of alcohol intoxication. This high is followed by drowsiness, lightheadedness, apathy, impaired functioning and judgment, disinhibition, and belligerence. The other short-term effects of inhalant abuse are too numerous to mention here, but include dizziness, slurred speech, increased lethargy, muscle weakness, and stupor. Heart failure and death can occur within minutes after a prolonged "sniffing." While long-term effects include weight loss, irritability, decreased coordination, depression, and withdrawal, the real bomb—figuratively speaking—is the damage to the brain. Much of it is damage to the myelin sheath, which insulates the neurons and significantly speeds neurotransmission. This insulating sheath is soluble in many organic solvents including toluene, which literally dissolves this protective layer.

Toluene's effects on the brain are shown in Figure 5.3. The brain actually shrinks in size with chronic toluene abuse. The neurons are destroyed in a manner similar to that of buildings in a city being destroyed by TNT. Since toluene affects nearly all areas of the brain, it is like a "dumb bomb," indiscriminately destroying everything it hits. This is really bad news, since the two areas we need to preserve are the hippocampus, for memory, and the frontal cortex, for cognition. Rosenberg, Grigsby, Dreisbach, Busenbark, and Grigsby (2002) have shown that inhalant abusers suffer more brain abnormalities and cognitive deficits than cocaine users. It is also believed that much of this damage by inhalants is irreversible.

Summary of Inhalant Effects

Inhalants exert their effect on the brain by activating the dopamine reward system. In many ways, the high produced by inhalants resembles that produced by alcohol, but is much more damaging to the neurons in the brain. As noted above, this is due to the damage to the protective myelin sheath, which surrounds nerve fibers in the brain and other parts of the nervous system.

National surveys (e.g., NIDA, 2005a) indicated that nearly 23 million Americans have abused inhalants at least once. Even a single session of inhalant abuse can cause death from cardiac arrest or asphyxiation. Regular abuse can result in serious harm to the brain, heart, kidneys, and liver.

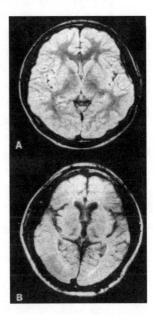

Figure 5.3 Toluene's effect on the brain.
The brain shrinks in size. Brain images show marked shrinkage of brain tissue in a toluene abuser (B) compared to a nonabusing individual (A). Note the smaller size and the larger (empty) dark space within the toluene abuser's brain.

Chapter Summary

Khantzian's (2001) self-medication model of addictive behavior views the use of mind-altering chemicals as misguided attempts to cope with feelings of discomfort, lack of meaning, and a fragmented sense of self. An underlying theme in many substance abusers' lives is unfulfilled longings for intimacy.

The widespread abuse of tobacco is viewed as a worldwide system of self-medication that serves to improve attention and concentration and to relieve symptoms of depression. Upon ingestion of nicotine, immediate sensations of relaxation, produced by increased availability of the inhibitory neurotransmitter GABA, are quickly followed by a surge of dopamine in the nucleus accumbens. Further, nicotine activates acetylcholine receptor sites resulting in the perception of improved memory and concentration. Nicotine addiction occurs rapidly—as little as one cigarette can change the brain—causing neuronal modifications that stimulate the craving to smoke. The neurobiological effects of nicotine and tobacco on the brain are far overshadowed by the devastating effects of cigarette smoking in terms of lung cancer, coronary heart disease, stroke, and chronic lung disease.

The section on substance abuse among women begins with comparing prevalence rates for alcohol and drug abuse between men and women. Although men have higher prevalence rates for alcohol and drug abuse disorders, the rates of prescription drug abuse and nicotine dependence are similar across gender. Among female substance abuse clients, the presence of mental health problems co-occurring with alcohol or drug abuse disorders highlights the importance of the self-medication hypothesis. Women are more likely to meet criteria for anxiety, depression, eating disorders, and borderline personality disorder. Gender differences in biology and social learning experiences (often trauma associated with childhood and adult sexual abuse) highlight the need for women-focused models of treatment. The case study of female alcohol abuse is illustrative of a woman's struggle with female role expectations, unpleasant feeling states, and unfulfilled longings for intimacy.

The section on posttraumatic stress disorder explains how conceptualizations of causality are grounded in psychobiological responses to such horrific events as natural disasters, rape, or exposure to war. Approximately 60.7% of men and 51.2% of women report at least one traumatic event in their lives. Only a small portion of those who have experienced at least one traumatic event actually develop PTSD. The symptoms of PTSD include re-experiencing the trauma, emotional numbing, avoidance, increased arousal, neurobiological changes, physiological changes, physical manifestations, and disturbances in psychological and social functioning. In addition to being twice as likely to suffer from PTSD as men, women experience more chronic forms of the disorder with some differences in the appearance of co-occurring disorders: Men are more likely to manifest alcohol dependence and antisocial personality disorder, and women are more likely to experience depression, phobias, and more adverse medical conditions. Recovery from trauma is discussed in terms of three interrelated stages: (1) establishing safety, (2) remembrance and mourning, and (3) reconnection with ordinary life. Becoming more interested in the present and future than the past, a survivor of trauma overcomes her fear and opposition and gradually engages in new and healthy relationships.

The section called Patients in the Street explores how heroin may initially serve as a means of achieving a sense of comfort and relaxation with reprieve from feelings of anger and desperation. As compelling biological forces combat the changes brought on by chronic abuse, the addict becomes "expert" at prescribing means to maintain his or her involvement with the drug. The case of Philip illustrates an addict's progression into deeper and deeper levels of despair. The therapeutic community is discussed as a means to promote recovery and a responsible relationship to society.

Finally, inhalant abuse is shown as one of the gravest drug threats to the integrity of the brain—a classic example of how misguided attempts at self-repair can morph into permanent patterns of self-destruction.

Note

1. This section is derived from the chapter "Understanding Posttraumatic Stress Disorder," by Karen Storck, in *Criminal Conduct and Substance Abuse Treatment for Women in Correctional Settings: Female Focused Strategies for Women in Correctional Settings,* by Milkman, Wanberg, and Gagliardi (Sage, 2008).

6

Eating for a Change

It is health which is real wealth and not pieces of gold and silver.

—M. K. Gandhi

People are bent out of shape about their weight! Nearly 90% of Americans believe that they are overweight and more than 35% say they want to lose at least 15 pounds. In the U.S. alone, dieting is a $46-billion-a-year industry (*U.S. Weight Loss & Diet Control Market*, 2005), and an estimated $92.6 billion dollars—9.1% of the country's health expenditures—are spent on overweight and obese patients (Grimm, 2007). Although being svelte is undoubtedly in vogue, and many who diet are actually quite healthy, much of the world is, in fact, dangerously overweight. Obesity is generally defined as exceeding the average weight for one's height and age by 20%. It is estimated that in the United States, somewhere between a quarter and a third of all adults fall into this category. For most developing nations, obesity is a more serious health threat than hunger. Worldwide, more than 1.3 billion people are *overweight,* possessing a body mass index (BMI) of 25 or higher, or *obese* (BMI of 30 or higher). Comparatively, about 800 million people are underweight (Popkin, 2007). As shown in Figure 6.1, there is a direct relationship between body mass and risk of disease.

Whether medically indicated or not, hundreds of millions of dollars are spent on appetite-suppressing drugs containing caffeine and amphetamine-related compounds. The diet-conscious purchase weight control and fitness guides with such regularity that at least one appears on the bestseller list each week; they maintain a torrid love affair with low-calorie foods; and join health spas and self-help groups like Weight Watchers or TOPS (Take Off Pounds Sensibly) by the millions. An amalgam of nutrition gurus including doctors, psychotherapists, and religious fanatics are enlisted to coach self-denial and impulse control.

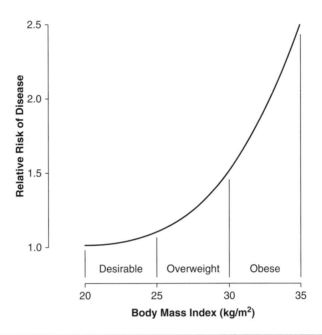

Figure 6.1 **Body mass index and risk of disease.** Relative risk of disease plotted against body mass index (BMI), calculated as (body mass in kg)/(height in meters)^2 or, alternatively, as (body mass in lbs × 703.1)/(height in inches)^2. BMI values in the 20–25 range are considered desirable, those 25–30 are classified as overweight, and values over 30 are classified as obese. The relative risk of disease compares an individual's probability (corrected for age) of having a disease with that of the general population. The curvilinear relationship indicates that obesity markedly increases disease risk.

Fortunately (or unfortunately, depending on your viewpoint), there is a tailor-made diet for every taste. Eating fads range from high-protein to high-carbohydrate diets, with obligatory emphasis on vegetables, fruits, and high-fiber foods. Some regimens emphasize eating certain foods at fixed times of the day; others stress not mixing particular foods. Recommendations and admonitions are often contradictory and sometimes bizarre: no salt, no milk products, lots of milk products, fasting, eating as much as you like, fruit juice only, no fruit juice, no meat, all meat, drinking vinegar or even your own urine (e.g., Christy, 1994)—you name it. A popular women's magazine published a feature article extolling the practice of an exclusive rice diet. Devotees are promised weight loss of 15 to 25 pounds within 2 weeks. It is apparent to most people who have traveled in the Third World and observed the effects of rice-rich regimens, that this diet does indeed have the ability to produce skinny, even emaciated people.

To be sure, the contemporary obsession with weight control—the svelte craze—is influenced by the whims of Hollywood and Madison Avenue.

Among movie stars and models, thinness is not only fashionable but an occupational necessity. Since *Playboy* began publishing in 1953, centerfold models have become progressively slimmer.

Social class seems to play a role. Women from lower-class backgrounds, whose diets are more likely to be higher in fats and carbohydrates, are 6 times more likely to be obese than upper-class women. Studies of immigrants and their descendants show that as new generations move up the socioeconomic scale, obesity, especially among females, declines. A simple extrapolation from the body measurements of a child's Barbie doll reveals the tremendous social pressure toward slimness and form. As a symbol of femininity, Barbie is not a harmless toy—not with a physique that when translated into human terms measures 33–18–28½.

As in other compulsive disorders, overeating usually leads to progressively impaired functioning. While the psychological and social complications are severe—interpersonal anxiety, job discrimination, sexual and social limitations—the physical dangers are even more frightening. Obese people are at increased risk for high blood pressure, heart disease, diabetes, back and joint problems, and respiratory disorders. Fat men have a higher incidence of certain cancers, including those of the colon, rectum, and prostate. Overweight women are at a greater risk for developing malignant tumors of the ovaries and uterine lining, and after menopause, of the breasts. With stereotypic joviality, an obese woman whose blood pressure began to soar as her weight reached nearly 300 pounds recalls her doctor's warning: "If you don't lose weight, I'll put you in a coffin with a shoehorn."

On counterpoint, there is an alarmingly high incidence of dangerously underweight individuals in today's "slimness generation." In some cases, dramatic weight loss may be attributed to a brain tumor, bowel disease, or glandular dysfunction. Recent studies, however, have identified figures as high as 1% of selected populations, primarily females, who for no known biological reason appear to be starving themselves—sometimes to death.

_____ Anorexia, Bulimia, and Binge Eating Disorder

Anorexia nervosa and bulimia are closely related eating disorders primarily found among middle- and upper-middle-class women who appear to be victims of fad and fashion. The core symptom of anorexia nervosa is a relentless pursuit of excessive thinness. Diagnostic criteria include self-imposed dieting; weight loss of at least 25% of the person's usual body weight; distorted perception of the body; cessation of menstruation; and no known medical illness to account for the weight loss. Approximately 50% of anorexics are also diagnosed as bulimic (M. J. Cooper, 2005; Hoek, 2006). Family and twin studies show that genetic factors contribute about 50% to the development of an eating disorder (Klump, Kaye, & Strober, 2001) and that anorexia shares a genetic risk with clinical depression (Wade,

Bulik, Neale, & Kendler, 2000). It appears that genes influencing both eating regulation and emotion may be important contributing factors.

Research on the epidemiology of anorexia suggests an average prevalence of 0.3% (3 out of 1,000), with a much higher rate (up to 10%) in selected populations (e.g., achievement-oriented female high school or college students). Studies show that the condition largely affects adolescent females, with teens between 15 and 19 years of age making up 40% of all cases (Bulik, Reba, Siega-Riz, & Reichborn-Kjennerud, 2005; Hoek, 2006). About 10% of people with anorexia are male, and about 90% are female (Lask & Bryant-Waugh, 2000). However, anorexia is not limited to any particular demographic. In March 2008, Rosemary Pope, a 49-year-old British senior university lecturer with a PhD in psychology and a professional background in health, died from anorexia ("Professor, 49, Died From Anorexia," 2008).

Bulimia is a chronic dieting disorder usually associated with binge eating. Bulimics may be emaciated, of average weight, grossly obese, or anywhere in between. Experts disagree as to whether bulimia and anorexia are part of the same disorder. Characteristically, an individual with bulimia consumes an excessive amount of food in a short period of time. Binges are usually planned and may last from several hours to several days. Food tends to be eaten very rapidly, gobbled rather than chewed. It is often very sweet and high in calories. Eating usually occurs in a clandestine manner, in which the eater experiences a sense of loss of control and an inability to stop. Binging varies in frequency between individuals, from several times a month to several times a day. Many people who suffer from bulimia, which literally means pathologically insatiable hunger, begin to induce vomiting to prevent weight gain and to decrease sensations of physical discomfort. The binge-purge cycle often includes the use of such cathartic devices as laxatives, suppositories, or enemas for rapid evacuation of the bowels. This pattern of dietary chaos is often accompanied by periods of intense and sometimes excessive exercise, which may be interpreted as a form of penance for partaking of forbidden fruit (American Psychiatric Association, 1994).

Just as the overeater seeks ecstasy through food, the person with anorexia seeks ecstasy through not eating. It is estimated that 1 in 100 females will develop anorexia sometime in her life, and 10% of these will die of it (Tyre, 2005). In terms of brain chemistry, anorexics are shown to have abnormally high levels of serotonin. Serotonin at normal levels is associated with feelings of well-being. However, excessive levels may be associated with anxiety and obsessive thinking. By limiting food intake, the anorexic reduces the amount of tryptophan entering the brain where it forms serotonin (Tyre, 2005). While this decrease in serotonin caused by food deprivation may not be ecstasy, it is perceived by the sufferer as being better than the alternative (anxiety and obsession).

Harvard researchers found binge eating disorder (BED) to be the most common eating disorder in the United States, even more prevalent than anorexia and bulimia combined (Hudson et al., 2007). Obviously, the problem is associated with the health hazards of obesity, a natural consequence of the disorder. Even when not gorging themselves, binge eaters are thinking about food, easily succumbing to their craving—a heavy price to pay for momentary ecstasy. In some very fundamental ways, compulsive eating is akin to addictions of all stripes, including gambling, sex, and drugs.

According to Leutwyler (2006), most people will over- or undereat when confronted with stress. However, biology and personality types push some to the extremes. Anorexics tend to be "good students, dedicated athletes and perfectionists. . . . In contrast, bulimics and binge eaters are typically outgoing and adventurous, prone to impulsive behaviors" (p. 86). Depression, anxiety, and obsessive compulsive disorder often co-occur in each of these disorders. Each disorder is linked genetically and related to malfunction of the serotonin regulation system.

Regarding treatment, because of their normal weight, and their secretive and strange eating rituals, bulimics can be very difficult to identify. Anorexics, however, present the most obstacles to treatment because they view dramatic weight loss as positive, indicative of control over their life. When family, friends, or ill health directs a person with an eating disorder to seek help, cognitive-behavioral treatment (CBT), sometimes combined with medication, shows promise (M. J. Cooper, 2005). The three main components of the CBT approach are the following: (1) Patients keep diaries of what, how, and when they eat and what prompted them to eat as they did; (2) flawed perceptions about food and body image are identified (e.g., "I'm fat"), and with the help of the therapist, evidence against these ideas is listed and they are corrected; and (3) strategies are developed to eliminate cues that reinforce abnormal perceptions (e.g., eliminating scales and mirrors). Treatment outcomes for both anorexia and bulimia may improve when CBT is combined with Prozac, a serotonin reuptake inhibitor (Leutwyler, 2006).

Eating and the Brain

According to Nora Volkow (interviewed in Ozelli, 2007), director of the National Institute on Drug Abuse, food, sex, and drugs activate the same brain circuitry that evolved to ensure our survival. However, natural reinforcers, such as food and sex, take longer than drugs to activate the reward centers. Through the process known as classical conditioning, memory forges a link, not only between pleasure and the rewarding stimulus (in this case, food), but also with the surrounding environmental cues. Just like Pavlov's conditioned dogs that salivate to a sound (after repeating pairings of the sound and presentation of food), compulsive eaters (and drug addicts) develop a reflex to overindulge. In the case of eating, high-calorie foods, especially those high in fat or sugar, are more apt to trigger compulsive eating. In terms of evolution, the human hunter did not always have access to a ready food supply, so foods that stored a lot of energy (i.e., those that are high in calories) boosted survival. So today—whether trolling the supermarket or scanning our own fridge—we are magnetized by high-fat, high-sugar foods. Genetically, we are the same; however, environmentally, there is an abundance of rich food. In the case of eating, a genotype mismatch with our environment makes for a culture of obesity.

Had Pavlov been able to peer inside his dogs' brains when they salivated (conditioned response) to the sound (conditioned stimulus), he would have observed an increase in dopamine. This neurochemical messenger serves to alert us to information that will increase survival. It is activated by any promise of food, sex, and pleasure, as well as danger and pain. When people are shown foods to which they have been conditioned, there is a documented increase of dopamine in the striatum, which is the region of the brain involved in reward and motivation. The increase of dopamine occurs from just smelling or looking at food, the same type of neurochemical response that occurs when a drug addict sees a video of people engaging in any activity reminiscent of his or her drug of choice. The dopamine messenger impels the organism to action, an impulse that sheer willpower cannot easily overcome.

Volkow (quoted in Ozelli, 2007) further explains that in the brains of both drug addicts and the obese, there is typically a reduced number of D2 dopamine receptors. This may be either the result of compensation from overstimulation by dopamine (the brain's compensatory response to repetitive overeating or drug taking) or because these individuals have a lower number of dopamine receptors at birth, leading to an addictive predisposition (i.e., predisposed to seek dopamine). Volkow found an inverse relationship between obesity and D2 receptors (i.e., the more obese a person was, the fewer D2 receptors he or she had). Obviously, the genes that control dopamine receptors are not the only biological mechanisms involved in obesity. Twin studies show that genetics plays a significant role in the risk of both addiction and obesity. However, manifestations of genetic influence range from differences in the efficiency of metabolizing certain foods (or drugs) to differences in our likelihood to participate in behaviors that are high in sensation or risk. In the case of obesity, some people may be inherently more sensitive to the neurochemical rewards associated with food.

Why Chocolate?

Chocolate is the most commonly craved food. According Parker et al. (2006), the sight and smell of chocolate and the desire for sensory gratification are sufficient to trigger cravings. There is a distinction between craving chocolate and sweets versus the more general craving for carbohydrates. Chocolate also contains fat, as do ice cream, doughnuts, and cakes, whereas bread and pasta do not. Psychoactive ingredients in chocolate include amines (organic derivatives of ammonia): caffeine, theobromine, tyramine, and phenethylamine. However, their concentrations are so low, they would not have a significant psychoactive effect in human consumption. In addition, when comparing milk chocolate, dark chocolate, white chocolate, and cocoa powder, milk chocolate is preferred by the most people. According to Parker et al., if psychoactive substances were involved, then cocoa powder would satisfy craving and dark chocolate would be the most preferred.

Some obese people have increased brain activity in response to mouth, tongue, and lip sensations—*orosensory pathways* to addiction. Similarly, some have lower sensitivity to cues of satiety (knowing that they have had enough), thereby rendering them more vulnerable to cravings triggered by environmental food cues. Orosensory effects provide positive feedback; ingestion causes negative feedback, with eating typically stopping when the negative effects (fullness in the stomach or satiety) outweigh the positive orosensory effects. The satiety mechanism is not always effective, however, as is evidenced by a "moreishness" factor (i.e., you want more) among chocolate cravers attempting self-restraint; craving is experienced during abstinence, and moreishness is experienced while eating (Parker et al., 2006). The effects of carbohydrates on the brain are discussed in the section on biology versus psychology further below.

Obesity Around the Globe

According to Popkin (2007), for most developing nations, obesity, leading to an explosive epidemic of diabetes and heart disease, has become a more serious health hazard than hunger. Much of this upsurge is attributed to the fact that corporate empires (e.g., Coca-Cola and Pepsi) are flooding the Third World with cheap sweeteners, oils, and meat while doing nothing to promote healthy consumption of fruits and vegetables. Mexico is a prime example of a developing nation in the throws of an obesity epidemic. In 1989, less than 10% of the Mexican population was overweight. National surveys conducted in 2006 showed that 71% of Mexican women and 66% of Mexican men were overweight or obese. As people migrate from rural to urban areas, obesity rates tend to increase, but the prevalence of obesity has grown in rural areas as well. In Mexico, Turkey, South Africa, and Jordan, more than half the rural women are overweight (Popkin, 2007).

The connection between poverty and obesity seems to provide the best explanation for these findings. Just as it is in the United States, obesity seems to be largely a problem of the poor. In all countries with a gross domestic product in excess of $2,500 per capita (which includes most of the developing nations excluding sub-Saharan Africa), obesity rates are higher for poor women. With increasing income, farm laborers and the urban poor tend to adopt habits associated with obesity (e.g., television watching and shopping in supermarkets), without educational and recreational counterpoints to control their weight. Compounding the problem is that inhabitants of the Third World (Latin America, Africa, South America, and South Asia) may carry a disproportionate amount of "thrifty genes" that evolved to help them survive famine by enabling more efficient storage of fat. The problem is that for people with these genes, body fat tends to accumulate around the heart and liver, increasing the risk of heart disease and diabetes. In China, for example, nearly one-third of the population suffers from high blood pressure (Popkin, 2007).

Obesity in America

According to the *Harvard Health Letter* ("Is Overweight Okay?," 2006), over 30% of the U.S. population is considered to be obese; that is, their body mass index is equal to or greater than 30 kg/m². Obesity is clearly one of the most serious health problems in the United States today. Stand in any public place, especially an "All You Can Eat" buffet, and observe people, and you will be astonished at the number of overweight and obese men, women, and even children. Obesity is the major cause of many health-related disorders, especially diabetes and heart disease. It is also implicated in certain cancers, cardiovascular disease, osteoarthritis, gall bladder disease, hypertension, and even dementia.

Obesity in America began to rise precipitously in the 1980s (Figure 6.2). The "calories in" phenomenon is explained by sociologists as being the result of increasing demands of an overworked population for convenience foods (i.e., prepared, packaged products, and meals served in restaurants), usually higher in calories than home-cooked meals. Other forces include the Reagan administration's deregulation of controls on the agriculture industry and encouragement of farmers to increase production, consequently increasing calories available in the national food supply from 3,200 a day in 1980 to 3,900 per day in the year 2000 (Nestle, 2007). Furthermore, stockholder demands for higher short-term dividends on Wall Street pushed the food industry to expand sales by changing social norms such as increasing frequency of between-meal snacking, encouraging eating in bookstores, and serving larger portions.

According to Nestle (2007), a substantial rise in U.S. obesity rates during the past few decades was paralleled by increases in the availability of larger portion sizes, total calories, caloric sweeteners, and sugary soft drinks in the food supply. The apparent dip in three of these measures (calories, sugars, and sugary soft drinks) after 1998 may be explained by greater use of artificial sweeteners and the partial replacement of sugary soft drinks with beverages that are not sweetened with sugars.

Overeating and Psychoanalysis

A popular belief is that people become compulsive eaters because of unresolved childhood problems. Bruch (1961) explored this notion in her study of New York families during the Depression years. She observed that many

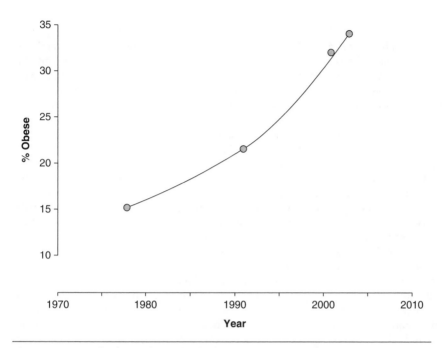

Figure 6.2   Obesity in the United States. The percentage of the U.S. population classified as obese plotted against year. The curvilinear relationship indicates that obesity rates are on the rise.

mothers seemed to offer food to their children as a way of showing affection and devotion. Food became a means of appeasing the anxiety and guilt that these mothers felt about the material impoverishment that was imposed upon their children. The youngsters appeared to increase their demands for food as needs for gratification and security in other areas remained unfulfilled. Bruch reported that obese patients suffered from "conceptual confusion," which she could trace to early childhood experiences. They seemed to have difficulty in perceiving and forming appropriate responses to their emotional needs. A desire to be with another person, for example, might be confused with a desire to eat with another person (see Section V of this book). In the case study below, we summarize Rowland's (1980) psychoanalytic treatment of a 39-year-old obese woman.

Case Example: A Psychoanalytic Perspective on an Eating Disorder

Joan sought help for severe depression after the disintegration of her 5-year marriage. Since childhood, her eating disorder was characterized by bouts of yo-yo dieting. She experienced cycles of weight increase from 20 to 50 pounds, followed by lengthy periods of strenuous dieting, then losing control and regaining the lost weight. During her life, she could truthfully say that she had lost hundreds of pounds.

Joan is a physician who married another physician during medical school. Her father was also a physician, obsessed with the fear that he would die, as his father did, from a weight-related disorder.

(Continued)

(Continued)

He managed to contain his death anxiety by placing himself and all other members of the family on a strict, low-cholesterol diet. Everyone became weight conscious and was fearful of his authority. He showed favoritism toward Joan's younger brother, and he often promised Joan rewards that were soon forgotten or somehow spoiled. On her graduation from college, for example, he gave Joan a sports car that wouldn't run. Her mother was unable to provide adequate emotional support to help Joan with her father's irrational and unfair behavior. In some ways, Joan's husband behaved as her father did; he was extremely critical at home and openly had affairs, blatantly violating Joan's understanding of the promise and commitment of marriage.

As a child, Joan sneaked forbidden foods as a way of mothering herself and rebelling against her tyrannical father. When she became fat, at least her father was interested enough to harass her about her appearance. He would offer her dollar rewards of so much per pound for losing weight. He also showed interest when she received good grades in school or accomplished projects at home. Beginning in the first grade, Joan compulsively reached for her father's approval through an endless stream of academic achievements. She used food as a means of rewarding herself for overwork, ensuring her father's attention while continuously expressing her outrage toward his domination and control.

The breakup of Joan's marriage symbolized the loss of the battle for her father's attention and approval. Upon entering treatment, she felt unable to control an overwhelming sadness that began when she and her husband first separated. After more than 3 years of psychoanalysis, Joan began to focus on her problems with weight and food intake. As she became aware of angry feelings toward her parents and husband, she became less obsessed with food. At the end of treatment, although her weight was still high, she appeared to be moving in a more self-assertive, independent direction. During the following year, she lost 40 pounds due to her own incentive.

Biology Versus Psychology

Psychotherapists report numerous case studies like Joan's, in which food is interpreted as a symbol of parental affection, a means of reducing internal conflict, or a passive expression of anger toward family members who are perceived as hostile and controlling. The obese person is trapped in a vicious circle: Overeating originally relieves feelings of low self-regard, loneliness, and tension; however, the consequences of becoming overweight are even more intense feelings of low self-esteem, anxiety, and lack of belonging. In response, the person eats even more and becomes even more overweight. Undoubtedly, many people suffer from obesity as a consequence of psychological distress. Research studies, however, do not support blanket acceptance of this interpretation for the vast majority of overweight people. Actually, the backgrounds of people challenged by obesity are no more psychologically disturbed than those of normal-weight people. More evidence appears to point to biological causes for obesity rather than psychological ones. Although overweight people are often depressed, it may well be that their suffering is the *result* of being overweight, rather than the *cause*.

J. J. Wurtman and Marquis (2006) describe a biological link between depression and obesity. Some depressed people who are also obese have a low level of the neurotransmitter serotonin. It is known that serotonin is manufactured in the brain from its chemical precursor, tryptophan, an amino acid that is found as a component of many foods such as milk. Consumption of foods rich in carbohydrates favors the transport of tryptophan over other amino acids from the blood into the brain. R. J. Wurtman and Wurtman (1989, 1995), and more recently J. J. Wurtman and Marquis (2006) and Parker et al. (2006), have made a strong case for people craving foods like spaghetti or cupcakes, rich in carbohydrates, to compensate for their brain serotonin deficiency. Since many carbohydrate snacks are high in calories and loaded with fat, obesity can easily result. Obese patients tend to overeat carbohydrates (especially snack foods like potato chips or cakes that are high in carbohydrates) in order to feel better. Interestingly, when opiates are not available, heroin addicts experience cravings for sweets. The release of B-endorphins in the hypothalamus may increase the pleasure of eating through an analgesic effect, which is reversible through administration of the narcotic antagonist naltrexone. In addition, sucrose has been shown to reduce crying in infants during hospital procedures, suggesting the release of endorphins (Parker et al., 2006).

R. J. Wurtman and Wurtman (1995) discovered that at meals, obese subjects consumed an average amount, about 1,900 calories per day with proteins and carbohydrates in balance. But for snacks, these carbohydrate cravers consumed an additional 1,000 calories per day in foods rich in carbohydrates. When asked to describe their mental state before eating, the subjects reported feeling anxious, tense, and unhappy. After snacking, they often reported feeling less tense and sometimes even relaxed. According to Wurtman and Wurtman, carbohydrates serve the same function for these people as antidepressant drugs: By increasing serotonin and thereby subduing depression, not only do they improve mood and diminish sensitivity to negative stimuli, they also ease the way to sleep. There is also the strong possibility that the act of eating releases endorphins, which further the sense of well-being and relaxation (Parker et al., 2006).

> Hence many patients learn to overeat carbohydrates (particularly snack foods, like potato chips or pastries, which are rich in carbohydrates and fats) to make themselves feel better. This tendency to use certain foods as though they were drugs is a frequent cause of weight gain, and can also be seen in patients who become fat when exposed to stress, or in women with premenstrual syndrome, or in patients with "winter depression," or in people who are attempting to give up smoking. (R. J. Wurtman & Wurtman, 1995, p. 477S)

Another biological factor contributing to obesity is the number of fat cells within one's body. Normal adults have anywhere from 30 billion to 40 billion fat, or adipose, cells. These cells swell or shrink like sponges to accommodate the amount of fat that is stored inside them. Fat cells appear in early childhood, but more develop later, especially during adolescence. In overweight people, the cells expand to hold more fat. Extra fat cells have been found only when a person is at least 60% above the ideal weight for his or her height and age. In obese adults, the amount of adipose tissue is often 3 times greater than what is found in people of normal weight. If an obese person diets, the fat cells will shrink in size, but their total number remains unchanged.

It has been posited that this adipose albatross manages to fix a "set point" for obesity (Paradis & Cabanac, 2008). The brain's hypothalamus is thought to receive signals that urge further eating until shrunken fat cells are once again refilled. The person who manipulates his or her own weight to fall below the set point may feel irritable or depressed as a consequence of unanswered brain signals. The dieter often feels out of sorts until he or she regains every bit of missing cellular baggage. When a person uses an appetite-suppressant drug to lose weight, he or she may be artificially low-ering the set point and briefly suppressing appetite. Once the diet medication is stopped, the person usually gains weight rapidly because the brain is once again receiving set-point messages in accord with a permanent repository of adipose tissue. What has been jokingly referred to as "the rhythm method of girth control" may very well have an underlying biological substratum.

A related handicap for overweight people is their relatively low rate of energy expenditure. How the body uses food as energy depends on two inter-related factors: (1) physical activity and (2) basal metabolic rate, or the energy required to maintain minimal body functions. In people of normal weight, basal metabolism accounts for roughly two-thirds of their energy expendi-ture. Because the metabolic rate is lower in fat tissue than lean tissue, the obese person's basal metabolic rate decreases as lean tissue is replaced by fat. To make matters even worse, basal metabolic rate further decreases when a person starts to diet. These factors work against the efforts of an overweight person to reduce and also to maintain enduring weight loss. It may be the case that the formerly obese person can maintain a reduced level of body weight only if he or she consumes about 25% fewer calories than people who are normally at that level. The "used-to-be-overweight" people may never be able to return to a "normal" eating pattern.

While this chapter examines many of the factors that underlie the unhealthy use of food as a drug, Chapter 19, Eating Yourself Fit, in the final section on natural highs presents healthy strategies for taking charge of—while deriving pleasure from—one of the most enjoyable aspects of life besides sex: eating. Both activities ensure survival of the species.

Chapter Summary

Weight management is a multibillion-dollar business—understandably so, when one considers that more than 1.3 billion people in the world are either overweight (BMI 25 or higher) or obese (BMI 30 or higher). Anorexia nervosa and bulimia, closely related eating disorders, appear to be highly influenced by media portrayals of feminine beauty. However, family and twin studies show that genetic factors contribute about 50% to the development of an eating disorder. In addition, anorexia shares a genetic risk with clinical depression. Genes influencing both eating regulation and emotion may be important contributing factors. Binge eating disorder (BED) is reported to be the most common eating disorder in the United States, even more prevalent than anorexia and bulimia combined.

Food, sex, and drugs activate the same brain circuitry that evolved to ensure our survival. Natural reinforcers such as food and sex, however, take longer than drugs to activate the reward centers. With regard to craving, chocolate is the most commonly craved food. This may be in part attributed to mouth feel (pleasurable mouth and tongue sensations), but also to the general phenomenon of carbohydrate craving, which among obese people appears to be neurochemically related to the same deficit found in compulsive drug users—a reduced number of dopamine (D2) receptors.

For most developing nations, obesity, leading to an explosive epidemic of diabetes and heart disease, has become a more serious health hazard than hunger. National surveys conducted in 2006 show that the majority of Mexican men and women are either overweight or obese. The connection between poverty and obesity seems to provide the best explanation for these findings. With increasing income, farm laborers and the urban poor tend to adopt habits associated with obesity (e.g., television watching and shopping in supermarkets), without educational and recreational counterpoints to control their weight. In the United States, over 30% of the population is considered to be obese.

While psychological theories have traditionally considered the role of food in coping with stress, there is currently more evidence pointing to biological causes for obesity than psychological ones. Some researchers have made a strong case that overweight people crave foods like spaghetti or cupcakes, rich in carbohydrates, to compensate for their brain serotonin deficiency. Since many carbohydrate snacks are high in calories and loaded with fat, obesity can easily result. Another biological factor contributing to obesity is the number of fat cells within one's body. In overweight people, the cells expand and increase in number to hold more fat. Extra fat cells have been found only when a person is at least 60% above the ideal weight for his or her height and age. In obese adults, the amount of adipose tissue is frequently 3 times greater than in people of normal weight. If an overweight person diets, the fat cells will shrink in size, but their total number remains unchanged. This creates a "set point" for obesity in that the person experiences strong cravings until the fat cells are once again expanded. The "used-to-be-overweight" person may never be able to return to a "normal" eating pattern.

SECTION III

The Thrill of
Excitement and Risk

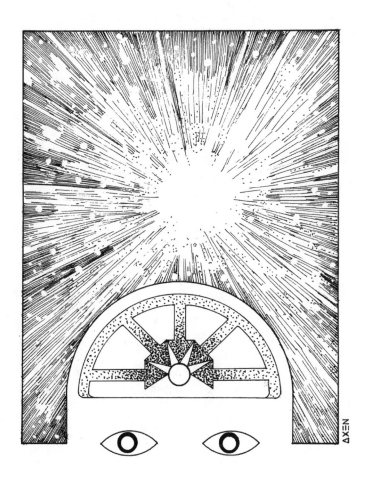

Security is mostly a superstition. It does not exist in nature, nor do the children of men as a whole experience it. Avoiding danger is no safer in the long run than outright exposure. Life is either a daring adventure or nothing.

—Helen Keller

Overview: What a Rush!

Our discussion of excitement and risk begins with three examples of thrill-seeking behavior: sex in an airplane, base-jumping from a tall building, and gambling to the point of losing job and freedom. As disparate as these actions appear, they share similar biological and psychological threads. In Chapter 7, Stress Hormone Highs, we describe neurochemical mechanisms common to the array of thrill-seeking activities. The trend to amp up on an increasing array of heavily caffeinated power drinks is explored in terms of the abuse potential of coffee, soft drinks, and newer beverages explicitly marketed as energy supplements. Chapter 8, Rock Around the Clock, examines the wild stimulation produced by stimulant drugs and how "club drugs" have become part of a fast-paced, roller-coaster scene that combines extreme mind alteration with intense human contact.

Sex in an Airplane

Paul, a 58-year-old accountant, was returning home on a 12-hour flight from Singapore to Los Angeles after a 2-week vacation in Fiji with his wife and two children. He obtained a prescription of Ambien from his primary care physician to promote sleep on the long flight. He intended to combat the inevitable boredom and fatigue of the trip by downing two glasses of wine and taking the 10-milligram dose of Ambien about 7 hours prior to landing. His plan was to pass time more quickly and get sufficient rest to start work upon arriving home in Los Angeles.

About 10 minutes after swallowing the Ambien, he got up (he was sitting in the row directly in front of his wife and two children) and walked to the flight attendant station intending to ask for his second glass of red wine. Upon peering behind the curtain of the attendants' quarters he spotted a woman who appeared sexy, a bit tipsy, and older than her prime. Disinhibition quickly came upon him, and he struck up a conversation about her tattoos. She confided that before her current career as a forest ranger, she was a dancer at gentlemen's clubs.

Both ripe for sexual adventure, the hitherto strangers began to touch erotically in the aisle behind the serving section. Consumed by the thrill, Paul invited her to join him in the bathroom, intending to escalate their sexual tryst. The two snuck into the flight restroom, undressed and carried out a variety of sexual acts, culminating in Paul reaching orgasm. He carried out this scheme without concern about the multiple risks of being discovered by his wife, his children, the flight staff, fellow passengers, or possible legal and health ramifications of having sex with a stranger in the bathroom of a commercial airline.

Jumping Off a Building

Robin and Brian ascend the 700-foot United Bank of Denver building, eager to jump off. Upon reaching the top, both fastidiously check their parachutes, making sure that everything is correctly rigged. Robin's father, who accompanies the duo, comments, "I'll bet you boys are feeling some butterflies now." His son replies, "We were scared yesterday and the day before . . . We're just in the groove . . . We're ready to go for it."

Robin steps out on the end of a scaffold that is being used to finish the building's construction. He begins the countdown—"Okay—four . . . two . . . three . . ." He turns to Brian and both begin to laugh. Robin continues, "Boy that was great, wasn't it?" Then he resumes concentration, makes the proper countdown, and delicately steps off the edge. Time seems to stand still as Robin savors a sense of weightlessness and the dual feelings of fragility and power in the same instant. Exhilarated by the experience of total control, his life seems at once supreme and valueless.

When the chute opens, he is pleased. He gracefully navigates his floating assemblage through a half circle, deliberately drifting to an urban clearing, descending on a stunned pair of middle-aged passersby. Wide-eyed, smiling, and invigorated with curiosity, one excitedly blurts out, "Jesus, what planet did you come from?" Robin's nonchalant reply: "Oh, you liked it, huh?"

Brian jumps. As soon as he lands, the two hop in the getaway car, driven by Robin's mother. The police arrive 4 minutes after the daring fait accompli.

In the aftermath, Brian and Robin become intoxicated by the wine of success. The pristine ecstasy of free fall is replaced by group celebration, euphoria, and bliss.

Gambling-Addicted Casino President

In March of 2001, the highest-ranking casino executive ever to confess to being a compulsive gambler was banned from New Jersey casinos for 5 years. New Jersey gaming regulators voted unanimously to strip the casino key license of Gary DiBartolomeo, 46, for lying about his gambling activities to his employers and licensing authorities. DiBartolomeo, by establishing himself as a player development executive who could charm high rollers, ultimately landed a $362,000-a-year job as president of Caesars Atlantic City. He ultimately succumbed to the lure of the blackjack tables and roulette games that he so skillfully managed.

As a condition of his license renewal, he was warned by regulators to quit gambling, but on dozens of occasions he violated the restrictions. While playing in casinos in Nevada, Connecticut, Mississippi, the Bahamas, and Monte Carlo, he bet up to $1,500 per hand and lost $389,000 in an 18-month period. One time he recruited a fellow Caesars worker to act as his "alter ego" to play blackjack with DiBartolomeo's money as DiBartolomeo supervised the bets. Tearfully, DiBartolomeo described himself before the gaming commission as "the David Copperfield of deception." He called compulsive gambling the demon inside of him.

Throughout the remainder of this section, we examine the psychological, biological, and social underpinnings of the pursuit of pleasure through deliberate participation in energizing, potentially dangerous, and sometimes even life-threatening activity.

7 Stress Hormone Highs

Psychologists have long known that people perform most effectively when under some degree of stress. A moderate level of arousal tends to produce alertness and enthusiasm for the task at hand. When emotional excitement exceeds an optimal point, however, whether the evoked feelings are positive or negative, the result is progressive impairment of one's ability to function. Figure 7.1 shows the basic relationship between arousal and performance.

What is it about people like Robin and Brian that enables them to remain composed while most of us would literally become scared stiff under similarly arousing circumstances? In William James's classic, *The Varieties of Religious Experience* (1902), the author quotes Lutfullah, describing his

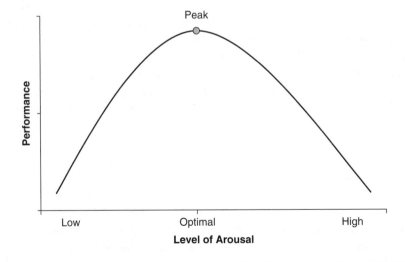

Figure 7.1   **Relationship between arousal and performance: Yerkes-Dodson law.** Performance increases with physiological or mental arousal, but only up to a point. When levels of arousal become too high, performance decreases.

experience when arousal becomes too intense, and adaptive coping is no longer an option.

> It was about eleven o'clock at night . . . but I strolled on still with two people . . . Suddenly upon the left side of our road, a crackling was heard among the bushes; all of us were alarmed, and in an instant a tiger, rushing out of the jungle, pounced upon the one of the party that was foremost, and carried him off in the twinkling of an eye. The rush of the animal, and the crush of the poor victim's bones in his mouth, and his last cry of distress, "Ho hail" involuntarily re-echoed by all of us, was over in three seconds; and then I know not what happened till I returned to my senses, when I found myself and companions lying down on the ground as if prepared to be devoured by our enemy, the sovereign of the forest. I find my pen incapable of describing the terror of that dreadful moment. Our limbs stiffened, our power of speech ceased, and our hearts beat violently, and only a whisper of the same "Ho hail" was heard from us. In this state we crept on all fours for some distance back, and then ran for life with the speed of an Arab horse for about half an hour, and fortunately happened to come to a small village . . . After this every one of us was attacked with fever, attended with shivering, in which deplorable state we remained till morning. (Lutfullah, 1857, quoted in James, 1902)

Selye (1956, 1971, 1974) introduced the concept of getting high on our own stress hormones. When we become excited, through either anger or fear, the brain signals hormone-producing glands to release chemicals that prepare us for fight or flight. The adrenal glands produce cortisol, a chemical that increases blood sugar and speeds up the body's metabolism. Other messages to the adrenal glands result in the release of the amphetamine-like stimulant epinephrine (adrenaline), which helps supply glucose to the muscles and brain, and norepinephrine, which speeds up the heart rate and elevates blood pressure. Figure 7.2 illustrates the body's chemical response to stress.

The psychological by-products of a moderate biochemical emergency are noticeable increments in one's feelings of physical prowess and personal competence, often associated with strong sensations of pleasure. In many ways, the state of biological and psychological "readiness" produced by stress is mimicked by the effects of stimulant drugs. People may self-induce similar alterations of consciousness with amphetamine, methamphetamine, cocaine, or caffeine (two-and-a-half cups of coffee will double the level of epinephrine in the blood), or by engaging in activities that appear to be life threatening. Positive experiences—falling in love, riding a roller-coaster, or watching a thrilling movie—can evoke the same stress hormones as more troublesome flirtations with danger or drugs (Manhart, 2005). Apparently, our brains will not distinguish between a real and a manufactured dose of dopamine, so the stimulant seeker may quell his or her need for dopamine through high-risk activity or stimulant drugs—often both.

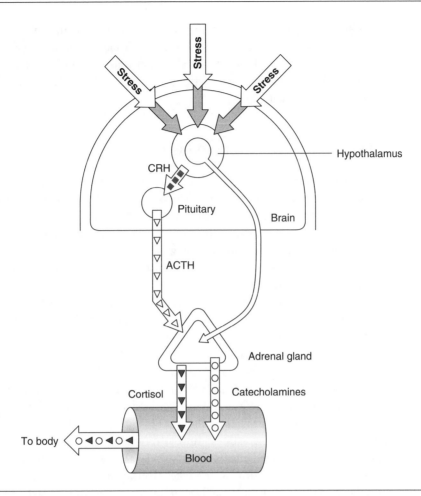

Figure 7.2   **Stress response.** In response to stress, the hypothalamus secretes corticotropin-releasing hormone (CRH), which stimulates the pituitary gland to release adrenocorticotropic hormone ACTH into the general circulation. ACTH stimulates the adrenal cortex to release cortisol (see Figure 2.4). The hypothalamus also stimulates the adrenal medulla to release the catecholamines, epinephrine and norepinephrine, into the general circulation. Catecholamines mobilize stored fat and make the heart beat faster and stronger.

Wake Me Up! Caffeine Buzz

Caffeine is the most popular psychoactive substance in the world with approximately 80% of the population in the United States, including children, consuming it each day (Reissig, Strain, & Griffiths, 2008). And coffee is just the beginning. With enticing names like Jolt, AMP, Monster, and Rockstar, what teenager or young adult wouldn't be tempted to "hit the can"? In fact, that is a slogan of some "energy drinks" proudly displayed in grocery stores, gas stations, and even drink dispensers on college campuses.

Brands have even begun to mimic "the illicits" with names like XTC and Cocaine. First introduced in 1997, energy drinks are immensely popular. From June 2006 to June 2007, U.S. consumers gulped to the tune of $744 million (Consumer Reports, 2007, as cited in International Food Information Council, 2008).

Do Energy Drinks Really Work?

A large percentage of the products contain caffeine and sugar along with other herbal ingredients that marketers claim will naturally boost energy (Scholey & Kennedy, 2004; Reissig et al., 2008). Actually, there are few if any studies on the energizing effects of the extra ingredients usually consisting of guarana, taurine, ginseng, or ginkgo biloba. Caffeine, however, has been amply studied, as coffee is a mainstay of societies around the globe (Scholey & Kennedy, 2004).

Ingestion of either caffeine or glucose (sugar) causes a brief increase in cognitive performance (Reissig et al., 2008; Scholey & Kennedy, 2004). The effects are especially apparent when it is used in situations of fatigue or boredom. However, much of caffeine's effects are due to consumer expectations and psychological effects related to the setting in which consumption occurs (Childs & de Wit, 2008). Childs and de Wit studied whether the energizing effects of coffee and energy drinks are exclusively due to caffeine, or if one's sense of increased vigor is also related to taste and expected outcomes. They found that indeed caffeine does improve mood and mental energy (e.g., reaction time), but expected effects also play a large role in subjective experience. Decaffeinated energy drinks enhance arousal and cognitive performance similarly to those with caffeine. Decaffeinated coffee also caused an increase in subjective alertness in people when they were made to believe they had consumed the caffeinated counterpart. Although caffeine is a mild psycho-stimulant, consuming it daily, even in low doses, can produce dependence. Withdrawal symptoms of caffeine include headache, fatigue, increased tension, and decreased alertness.

A study by Scholey and Kennedy (2004) looked at the effects of caffeine and glucose in a created "energy drink" along with three comparison beverages: (1) only the caffeine, (2) only glucose, and (3) only the herbal flavorings (ginkgo biloba and ginseng). They found that the drink they had concocted with both the caffeine and sugar produced the most cognitive improvements and mood changes. When a beverage has a high content of glucose but a modest amount of caffeine, it will actually worsen fatigue due to the fact that glucose immediately takes effect, increasing alertness, but that effect only lasts 10 to 15 minutes, while caffeine takes 30 minutes to activate the alerting effect but lasts an hour or more (C. Anderson & Horne, 2006). This information leads researchers to theorize that energizing effects are due to a combination of glucose and caffeine working together, but the drinks require a goodly amount of caffeine in order to bring about the changes in performance.

One fad that has spread across America along with the burgeoning hype of the energy drink is the combination of energy drinks with alcohol. Anyone who has been to a bar in the past 5 years has surely seen or even tasted a Red Bull and vodka or a Jägerbomb (Jägermeister and energy drink). These beverages are particularly dangerous in that the caffeinated beverages are stimulants and the alcoholic beverages are depressants. The stimulant effects of the energy drinks mask the intoxication effects of the alcohol and can prevent a person from realizing how drunk he or she really is. The energy drink may also falsely imply to the person that he or she really is not impaired, but once the stimulating effects wear off, the depressant effects of the alcohol remain and could possibly cause vomiting or respiratory depression. Finally, both alcohol and caffeine are very dehydrating, as they are diuretics. The body's ability to metabolize alcohol is disturbed when dehydrated, increasing toxicity and the severity of a hangover the following day (Brown University Health Education, 2008).

Stress Intoxication

Selye, who is regarded by many as the grandfather of all modern stress researchers, was acutely aware of the intoxicating correlates of fight-or-flight reactions. He pointed to "stress-drunkenness" (i.e., loss of judgment and decreased impulse control) as causing more overall harm to society than the universally acclaimed demon of demons, alcohol, and all other psychoactive drugs combined.

What is even more incredible than this seemingly outrageous claim by Selye (1956, 1971, 1974) is that much of the stress-drunkenness is deliberately self-induced. "Skydiving is the most fun you can have with your clothes on," proclaims Robin Held (personal communication, June 1986), who dives not only from buildings but also from smokestacks, mountain cliffs, airplanes, and bridges. "The greatest joy is being in such a dangerous situation that you nearly wet your pants," says a private detective who purposely seeks out dangerous assignments for thrills. Eric, a young man in his early twenties, goes to the most savage, bloodthirsty movies in town because he "loves to be scared." These seemingly outrageous utterances can be repeated many times over by "adrenaline junkies" who are addicted to a wide variety of risk-taking activities.

What is so attractive about risk taking and fear-inducing situations? These dopamine-triggering activities give our brain a dopamine-mediated high, and the individual wants that feeling to remain (Manhart, 2005). In terms of brain chemistry, risk taking produces the same mind-altering escape from depression, stress, or fear of nonbeing as the use of powerful stimulant drugs. Whether through skydiving, gambling, or cocaine, self-induced changes in neurotransmission may well lead to the familiar path of compulsion, loss of control, and continuation in spite of harmful consequences.

Figure 7.3 is a simplified representation of the neurochemical pathways associated with the brain's reward (extreme reward = ecstasy). As previously discussed (see Chapter 2), in order to produce drug-like feelings of pleasure and euphoria, the activity, drug, or behavior must have the ability to increase dopamine in the nucleus accumbens, a major reward center. In addition to increasing the levels of cortisol and norepinephrine, stress hormone highs, such as from gambling, dangerous sexual liaisons, and skydiving, increase the level of dopamine in the nucleus accumbens.

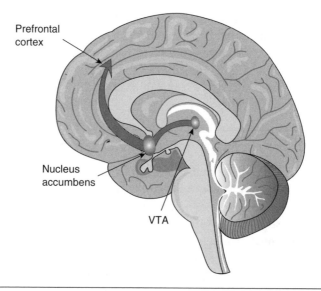

Figure 7.3   Neurotransmission and the experience of ecstasy. In order to produce drug-like feelings of pleasure and euphoria, the substance or behavior must have the ability to increase dopamine in the nucleus accumbens.

Addiction: The Curse of Ecstasy

Let us now turn our attention to the role that pleasure can play in the addictive process. Addiction is a by-product of the brain's ability to restore neurotransmission to a baseline level (homeostasis) following "self-induced changes." Consider the person who engages in either cocaine ingestion or a risk-taking behavior (skydiving). As the self-induced level of dopaminergic neurotransmission shifts into overdrive, the brain's homeostatic restoring mechanism prepares for action. Continued cocaine or behavior-induced alteration of dopamine levels brings about changes in enzyme (adenylate cyclase) levels, which decrease the effectiveness of dopamine neurotransmission by lowering the number of three-way combinations of neurotransmitter, receptor, and enzymes (see Chapters 2 and 9).

As the abuse continues, the brain begins to decrease production of both adenylate cyclase and dopamine. Because the dopamine remains in the synapse, there is no reason to make more. Adenylate cyclase decreases in order to restore baseline neurotransmission, which is being upset by an increase in the three-way combination of dopamine, receptor, and adenylate cyclase. The abuser then experiences an escalating need for increased activity, drug dose, or behavior. At some point, the person becomes dependent on the activity or drug just to feel normal. The earlier dose of cocaine no longer excites. To experience an elevated mood, he must use more of the drug or an even more potent type of drug such as crack cocaine. Removal of the drug or cessation of the behavior produces a feeling of dysphoria from a deficiency of dopamine in the nucleus accumbens. This deficiency results from a decrease in the adenylate cyclase needed for neurotransmission as well as the dwindling supply of dopamine. Also, the number of dopamine receptors and their sensitivity have become altered during the time of substance abuse.

In a similar manner, the abuser of opiates experiences alterations in brain chemistry that have the potential to produce addiction. Interestingly, not everyone who uses drugs or engages in mood-altering behavior becomes addicted. It is believed that those who do become addicted may be attempting to compensate for a genetic or environmentally induced deficiency of dopamine in the nucleus accumbens. It is important to keep in mind that any drug or activity repeated specifically for pleasure has the potential to become addicting.

The following activity may be used to illustrate the principles of neurotransmission that underlie the brain's (and consequently the mind's and body's) dysfunctional response to cocaine.

Activity: Cocaine in the Brain

There are eight volunteers. One person represents cocaine, three represent the presynaptic neuron, three represent the postsynaptic neuron, and one person represents a beautiful sunrise. A container (clear bowl or glass) of small packages of sugar symbolizes the synaptic vesicle, which contains many molecules (the sugar packets) of the neurotransmitter dopamine. The six people who represent the neurons arrange themselves in two lines of three with a 3-foot space between them (the synapse). The perception is a beautiful sunrise.

	Beautiful Sunrise					Cocaine			
pre	1	2	3	synapse	post	4	5	6	synapse

At one end (presynaptic terminal)—triggered by sensations from the sunrise—person #1 makes a motion and taps person #2 on the shoulder, who taps #3, who is standing at the synapse. Then #3 reaches into the synaptic vesicle and takes out one of the sugar packets (dopamine) and moves it across the synapse, giving it to person #4 who then taps #5 who taps #6 who exclaims, "Whoa!"—waving his or her hand in ecstatic delight (showing a natural sense of joy that might come from seeing a beautiful sunrise).

When #4 sends the message on, he or she hands the neurotransmitter (sugar packet) back to #3, who replaces it in the synaptic vesicle. Then #1 at the presynaptic neuron starts the process again. Practice this one to two times until it runs smoothly.

In comes cocaine . . . The message comes in normal fashion; that is, #1 taps #2 and so on. The dopamine (sugar packet) crosses the synapse; however, this time when #4 attempts to give it back to #3, cocaine steals the sugar and hands it back to #4 (blocks the reuptake of the dopamine), and #4 sends the message in the usual fashion by tapping #5. As soon as #4 taps #5, #4 *attempts* to return the sugar packet to #3 but *again cocaine takes it and hands it straight back.* At this point, #6 is saying, *"Whoa! Whoa! Whoa!"* very fast (excess dopamine).

Person #3 is just sitting there with the remaining sugar packets in the synaptic vesicle (the container), and *he or she doesn't need them anymore.* So #3 *empties the cylinder* and dumps the sugar packets (dopamine) on the floor. The police officer (person who facilitates the exercise) then removes the cocaine, and the neurotransmitter (sugar packets) can no longer be accessed from the cylinder. Withdrawal comes when the cocaine is no longer available, and the pleasure derived from the excess dopamine is absent because the supply of dopamine has been depleted. This leads to *cocaine withdrawal.*

With some slight modifications, the same model could be used to explain withdrawal from other drugs like caffeine, methamphetamine, Ecstasy, or nicotine. Now let's do one more exercise, this time showing the various ways that people deal with the crash or withdrawal effects of various drugs.

The Up and Down Game

The repeated pairing of opposite emotional experiences, and their underlying physiological counterparts, may be the sustaining force behind many forms of human compulsion. According to R. L. Solomon (1980), the same principle that produces alcoholics and drug addicts can be used to account for chronic daredevils, Coca-Cola addicts, and compulsive sexual activity.

R. L. Solomon's (1980) opponent-process theory of motivation posits that every event in life that exerts a potent effect on mood or feeling also triggers an oppositional biochemical process. When first attracted to a pleasurable experience induced through drugs or activities, people are motivated by the dominant sensations of euphoria or well-being. Mood-altering behavior is often sustained, however, because people seek to avoid the unpleasant effects that have been set in motion by the opponent process. In some addictions—for example, running—the initial experience of pain is followed by a highly pleasurable reaction, probably related to the release of pain-relieving endorphins. As shown in Figure 7.4, the opponent process leads to a waving pattern of mood alterations, which varies among people in terms of frequency and intensity. Some people seem to exist on a constant roller-coaster of mood change, seeking pleasure and avoiding pain, while others remain emotionally bland with only minor ripples in how they feel.

In some patterns of behavioral excess, a person may continue an experience that is no longer pleasurable because of a growing aversion to the sensations brought about through stopping it (i.e., opponent unpleasant state).

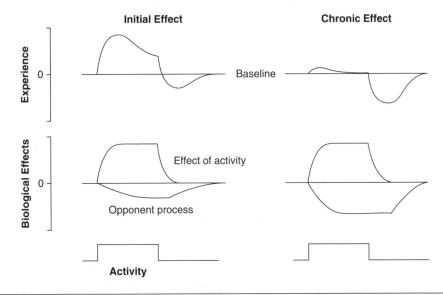

Figure 7.4 **Opponent-process model of addiction.** This figure shows the standard pattern of mood alteration based on opponent-process theory. The upper graphs (experience) depict an individual's subjective experience of pleasure in the initial and chronic phases of drug use or other mood-altering activity. The initial experience is the algebraic sum of the immediate biological effects of the mood-altering activity and the body's homeostatic response to neurochemical changes. Since the brain has not yet adapted to the neurochemically mediated high, a heightened sense of pleasure is experienced. After chronic mood alteration, homeostatic effects become so large that the pleasure-oriented activity can only return the user to his or her baseline state (before the beginning of chronic use). In the absence of mood-altering activity, the individual's subjective experience is significantly below baseline (i.e., withdrawal or suffering).

In the case of extended risk taking, for example, chronic thrill seekers may increasingly seek to avoid the unpleasant feelings associated with lowered enzyme and neurotransmitter levels by seeking out new and more dangerous activities. In the case of satiation activities (e.g., opiates, TV addiction), euphoria is soon replaced by the anticipation of suffering and pain from withdrawal. Thrill seekers often exhibit more drug and alcohol abuse, and more gambling and risky behaviors such as drinking and driving, than the average person (Gupta, Derevensky, & Ellenbogen, 2006).

Although there are obvious differences in withdrawal symptoms from the diverse array of pleasure-inducing activities, Glassman, Jackson, Walsh, Roose, and Rosenfeld (1984) proposed that the same brain mechanism may account for the experience of craving, which is common to all addictions. Whether people are trying to kick alcohol, cigarette, or opiate addiction, they experience similar changes in brain chemistry, which create craving for drug use. According to Glassman et al., all these addictions are characterized by an excess of norepinephrine, which is concentrated in a small area of the brain called the locus coeruleus. A person may subdue biochemical excitation in this area of the brain by using cigarettes, alcohol, or opiates. During withdrawal, however, the locus over-fires, producing too much norepinephrine, which results in the common experience of craving.

The fact that stress elevates the level of norepinephrine in the brain may account for the increased craving and frequency of addiction relapse during periods of duress or conflict. Glassman's model may also help to explain the high frequency of dual addictions, as in the upper-downer cycle of cocaine-heroin dependence, and the various combinations or switches among risk taking and alcohol, cigarette, and opiate abuse.

Problem and Pathological Gambling

Pathological gambling is considered an impulse control disorder characterized by persistent and recurrent gambling behavior; preoccupation with gambling; loss of control; "chasing" losses; and continued gambling despite problems in personal, family, or vocational pursuits, that worsens over time (American Psychiatric Association, 1994, 2000). Gambling is readily available almost anywhere, with lotteries, casinos, sports betting, slot and poker machines, and especially the online casinos that are overwhelming the Internet (Gupta et al., 2006).

Personality characteristics common in problem gamblers include competitiveness, disinhibition, impulsivity, above-average intelligence, and high energy. Adolescents show a higher rate of problem gambling than do adults, and adults that do have severe gambling problems often begin their gambling as adolescents (Gupta et al., 2006). Adolescents and adults with gambling issues specifically deviate from normative samples in impulsivity, distractibility, overactivity, self-indulgence, and difficulty adapting to group norms (Gupta et al., 2006). Compulsive gamblers often find themselves in financial distress, emotional and physical demise, and dealing with impaired interpersonal relationships (LaPlante & Shaffer, 2007).

Problem gambling is more prevalent in persons seeking treatment for addictions and other psychiatric issues (Nelson & Oehlert, 2008). In a large epidemiologic study ($N = 43,093$), Morasco et al. (2006) examined medical disorders and health service utilization associated with problem and pathologic gambling. They assessed self-reported medical diagnoses and past-year medical services used. Their research showed that compulsive gambling is associated with many adverse health consequences. Pathologic gamblers were more likely to have been diagnosed with tachycardia, angina, and cirrhosis and other liver disease. Gambling severity was also associated with higher rates of medical utilization, with pathologic gamblers more likely than low-risk individuals to have been treated in the emergency room in the year before the survey. The authors conclude that "a lifetime diagnosis of pathologic gambling is associated with several medical disorders and increased medical utilization, perhaps leading to a burden on healthcare costs in the United States" (p. 976).

Gambling is thought to activate the same neurochemicals that drugs and other risky behaviors do, causing excitement and physiological arousal (Wexler & Wexler, 1992). Depending on timing, venue, and win-or-lose outcomes, gambling can be stimulating, tranquilizing, or pain-relieving, sometimes all experienced during one episode. The withdrawal symptoms from pathological gambling are similar to drug withdrawals, following the opponent-process model as presented above. Because compulsive gambling can be assumed to entail a high degree of ongoing stress over time, overstimulation of the hypothalamic-pituitary-adrenal (HPA) axis would be expected to increase vulnerability to a host of medical and psychiatric conditions including damage to the reproductive organs, disordered menstrual cycles, suppression of growth hormone, irritable bowel syndrome, diabetes, depression, phobias, and panic attacks (Englert, 2003).

Research shows that as exposure to gambling increases in the community, so does the rate of pathological gamblers and also the availability of self-help groups. More chapters of Gambler's Anonymous can be found in areas where gambling is legal and therefore more accessible and socially encouraged (e.g., where the ads read, "Buy a lottery ticket for the one you love"). Individuals of lower socioeconomic standing tend to spend greater proportions of their income on gambling (Shaffer, LaBrie, LaPlante, Nelson, & Stanton, 2004).

Shop 'Til You Drop

Shopping, a seemingly benign arousal activity, may achieve the status of a mood-altering addiction, characterized by powerful mood swings from intense arousal to blissful satiation, often followed by depression and remorse. In the case study below, Karen, a Los Angeles–based writer and single mother of two school-aged children, reminisces about her uncontrolled passion for clothes.

Case Example: Compulsive Shopping

Sometimes I go for months without buying anything; however, I recently went through a major binge in which I bought a Dior suit (at half price, $130), a dress and suit ($268), and ski pants and a parka ($240). All in about one week. I had some extra money because my father sent me some, but I should have used it to pay off part of my credit card debt. So I started thinking about this behavior and my inability to control it. I know the experience—when I see something I like, and I try it on, and it looks good on me, I get a euphoria that I love. It's seeing myself in the mirror looking good; there's also an aspect of costume to it—wearing many different kinds of clothes is like playing lots of different roles, being different people. I began my clothing fascination with the images of women in comic books when I was 8–10 years old. There was a comic series about Katy Keene the Pinup Queen; these comics were full of pictures of clothes. I cut them out and filled two large scrapbooks with the pictures. When I woke up in the morning and it was time to get dressed, I would look in the scrapbook and try to put together an outfit from my own clothes that resembled something in the book. It usually meant wearing a red blouse to try to copy a red strapless evening gown. I wished I could have all those numberless outfits for every kind of fantasy occasion. And in fact, one of Katy's two boyfriends (the other was a tall, rich blond) was K. O. Kelly, a red-headed freckle-faced boxer who looked a lot like my last boyfriend, John.

For 3 years, a friend and I owned and ran a small dress shop. There, I was able to buy clothes on a grand scale for the shop, and we had a rule that whenever we marked anything down, one of us could take it for herself if she wanted. Every Saturday when I worked in the shop, after I closed up, I pulled everything I liked off the sale rack and tried it on—everything I liked, I took home. I built an enormous wardrobe that way. When we sold the shop, for months afterward, I dreamed of being in the shop and being able to have all the clothes I wanted. And it was after we sold the shop that I started to go on clothes-buying binges. Before having the shop, I had always been very frugal about buying clothes, as about everything.

The first time John and I broke up, I was devastated. I couldn't sleep properly for months, and for the first few weeks I went 2 nights out of 3 hardly sleeping at all, and then the third night I would fall into a sort of coma from sheer exhaustion. Getting through every day was a struggle, trying to keep my feelings under control and maintain an appropriate demeanor at work. One day, about 4 or 5 weeks after we broke up, I dropped the kids off to see a movie at a shopping center. I was going to kill time till the movie was over, browsing. I saw some wonderful clothes in a store window; I went in and started trying things on, and in 20 minutes I had picked out $500 worth of clothes and shoes. I put a deposit on them and came back the next day and paid for them all. After trying them all on and picking them out, I floated out of the store on a cloud. It was my first happy moment after breaking up with John, and it was a heady, euphoric high.

Unfortunately, the initial high experienced in connection with the newly acquired symbols of self-love soon fades into what has become known to psychologists as "buyer's remorse." Shopping euphoria turns to depression and feelings of unworthiness. After the binge, buyers confess that they didn't discriminate among purchases. They find that they bought clothes that are all the same, or that don't seem to match at all. In either case, they do not seem to use what they buy; sometimes they return all the purchases, only to go off on another binge. Some addicts fear embarrassment that they will be recognized by shopkeepers as "binge-purge" shoppers. They maintain their composure simply by keeping the items around, much as a young child clings to a security blanket.

Autoerotic Fatalities

Perhaps the most extreme and bizarre example of the relationship between opponent processes and human compulsion is drawn from a growing body of literature on autoerotic fatalities. Each year, an unknown yet substantial number of people, primarily males, accidentally die in the course of voluntary participation in dangerous sexual practices.

For certain individuals, the preferred or exclusive mode of producing sexual excitement is to be mechanically or chemically asphyxiated to or beyond the point at which consciousness or perception is altered by cerebral hypoxia (diminished availability of oxygen to the brain). Nevertheless, other individuals for whom this is not the preferred means for enhancing sexual arousal repeatedly self-induce a state of cerebral hypoxia to the degree where consciousness or perception is sufficiently altered so as to produce sexual excitement (Dietz, 1983).

In a more or less typical case (e.g., Sheehan & Garfinkel, 1987; Uva, 1995), a 15-year-old boy was referred for psychiatric care after he told the police of his practice of suspending himself from a door with a rope and ejaculating while hanging. The boy would repeatedly hang himself from the clothes rod in his closet by lifting his feet from the ground, and he learned to place a towel around his neck, under the rope, to prevent marks or bruises. He reported that he would hang for one-half to 2 minutes and nearly always ejaculated while suspended. The frequency of self-hangings increased from once every 2 weeks to four times a week. The boy said that he repeatedly engaged in this bizarre practice because he wanted to anger his mother and because it relieved his depression and temporarily made him feel good.

Of people who describe themselves as "bondage practitioners," many use hanging or strangulation in their sexual practices. Sexual excitement is apparently heightened for some people when they engage in sexual acts in which they might be caught breaking a social custom or religious taboo. For such people, risk taking is more than simply spicing an already tasty dish; it can be the major component of the entire sexual act, as in widely practiced sadomasochistic sex rituals, with or without the aid of mechanical props or psychoactive drugs. Rupp (1973) concluded that autoerotic asphyxia is carried out by large numbers of individuals who arrive at this practice independently of one another.

Am I a Speed Demon?

To be sure, a thrilling adventure such as skydiving, mountaineering, or white-water rafting would elicit squeals of delight from some and shrieks of horror from others. According to Manhart (2005), the difference in the reactions may be explained by individual differences between people's dopamine systems (i.e., how much dopamine people have access to and how readily it can be used to transmit messages between neurons). When we consider that (1) a mild to moderate level of arousal tends to help people perform at their maximum effectiveness, (2) people are aroused to different degrees by the same stimuli, and (3) optimal performance is usually accompanied by enhanced self-esteem, then it becomes readily apparent that some people thrive on excitement while others become disoriented and emotionally disturbed by it. When skydivers—who may represent a broad spectrum of high-risk adventurers—are interviewed about the thrill of free falling, the common response is, "Skydiving is the most enjoyable sport imaginable," with nearly universal agreement that the greatest feelings of excitement and pleasure are experienced during free fall.

The subjective experience of boredom has been linked to the need for excess excitement (Gosline, 2007). Boredom, however, is not a one-dimensional concept; it is derived many things including level of attention and emotional factors. A person more susceptible to this trait has a higher need for excitement, variety, and novelty and usually requires a constant and changing supply of stimulation to achieve his or her optimal level of arousal (Gosline, 2007). Stimulants such as caffeine and amphetamines reduce fatigue and inattention during monotonous tasks as well as decrease reported boredom. Those who are predisposed to boredom have a higher rate of depression and drug addiction, as well as decreased performance in school and work. They are also at increased risk for anxiety, anger, aggressive behavior, and lack of interpersonal skills. Risky behaviors may be used to provide "false refuge" from these negative experiences. But thrill chasing often leads to self-destructive behaviors like gambling, drugs, and crime. Better ways to achieve optimal dopamine levels include: a challenging job or course of study, or finding new interests, skills, and hobbies could satisfy some of the need for thrills. In Chapter 20, we examine exercise as an important means to achieve stimulation and arousal in the service of improved mental and physical health outcomes. Chapter 21 explores meaningful engagement of talents as a primary means to sidestep boredom and wasted energy.

Consistent with our discussion on the factor of boredom, Farley (1986) identified a "type T" or thrill-seeking personality. According to Farley, thrill seekers opt for excitement and stimulation whenever they can find it, through intense physical or mental activity, or both. Farley postulates that a combination of genetics, early childhood experience, and nutrition contribute to the development of a thrill-seeking disposition. Under positive environmental conditions, a type T might channel his or her propensity for risk to the benefit of society, as exemplified by heroes such as Charles

Lindbergh or Martin Luther King. In the negative case, however, a type T predisposition may lead to pointless self-destruction or even the bizarre criminal behavior of a serial killer like the infamous Ted Bundy.

Farley (as cited in Rouvalis, 2006) divided his type T individuals into two categories, positive and negative. A positive risk taker will use the need for the rush to create, invent new things, explore new places, or start his or her own businesses. A negative thrill seeker will use the rush in unfavorable ways such as compulsive gambling or criminal activity. Often, a person with a type T personality will fall into both categories; the person will have aspects of each element in his or her personality. Risk takers often deny that they are participating in risky behavior, as they often see their fate as in their control.

In terms of general characteristics, Farley (1986) describes type T people as creative, risk-taking extroverts who prefer more sexual variety than average. Their artistic preferences tend to be experimental; they are more likely to be juvenile delinquents and reckless drivers. In the mental arena, type Ts are creative thinkers who have a talent for transforming one type of mental representation into another. They may shift from abstract to concrete thinking and tend to form images into words more easily than other people. Farley finds that biology is the major determinant of the type T personality, but socialization decides whether the individual will become a preserver or destroyer. Underlying the constitutional predisposition for the thrill-seeking personality may be a low level of physiological arousability.

According to Zuckerman's (2007) research on the biological basis of sensation seeking, numerous studies point to low levels of monoamine oxidase (MAO) as a biochemical determinant of the risk-taking personality. As mentioned in Chapter 5, this enzyme plays a vital role in the regulation of excitatory neurotransmission in the brain. The less of this enzyme a person has, the more dopamine flows into the nucleus accumbens and the more likely the individual is to seek out exciting, daring pastimes (Manhart, 2005). Perhaps sensation seekers require higher levels of external stimulation to evoke a substantial change in their already high rate of excitatory neurotransmission.

From 1969 to 1972 at Bellevue Psychiatric Hospital in New York City, Milkman and Frosch (1973) conducted a study of the relationship between personality and drug preference. Subjects who preferred amphetamine as their drug of choice were similar in many respects to both Zuckerman's biologically based sensation seekers and Farley's type T thrill seekers. When rated according to their responsiveness to external stimuli, which included noise, light, sound, and pain, amphetamine users appeared to be less responsive than normal and significantly less sensitive than those who preferred narcotics as their drug of choice. The "speed freaks" observed by Milkman and Frosch appeared to use stimulant drugs as a means of putting themselves in closer touch with environmental stimuli—stimuli that they would ordinarily find dull or uninteresting because of their "thick-skinned" reactions to sensory cues. In terms of personality characteristics, Milkman and Frosch found that amphetamine users fit Farley's description to a "T."

The amphetamine user is characterized by active confrontation with his environment. While the heroin user feels overwhelmed by low self-esteem, the amphetamine user utilizes a variety of compensatory maneuvers. He reassures and arms himself against a world perceived as hostile and threatening via physical exhibition of alienated symbols of power and strength. Identification with radical political groups further serves the need for active expression of hostility. Promiscuity and prolonged sexual activity may be the behavioral expression of needs to demonstrate adequacy and potency. High-level artistic and creative aspirations are usually unrealized self-expectations, bordering on delusional grandiosity. Such beliefs often lead to compulsive and unproductive behavior. Active participation in hand crafts, music, drawing, or physical labor is striking in nearly all of the amphetamine users studied. To maintain his tenuous sense of self as a potentially productive individual, the amphetamine user deploys many defenses. Denial, projection, rationalization, and intellectualization are characteristically observed. Equilibrium is maintained at the cost of great expenditures of psychic and physical energy. (p. 244)

More recently, personality traits of internalizing and externalizing behaviors (keeping emotions in or expressing them in negative ways) have been associated with the user's drug of choice (Hopwood, Baker, & Morey, 2008). Those who prefer psychostimulants tend to have higher tendencies for sensation seeking and disinhibition. Those addicted to stimulant drugs tend to behave more impulsively and take more risks (White, Lejuez, & de Wit, 2007).

After more than a decade of clinical observations on the personality characteristics of cocaine and more recently methamphetamine users (see Chapter 8), it appears that they are much like their predecessors, the sensation-seeking amphetamine users of the late 60s and 70s. Each generation of speed demons seems to cope with underlying feelings of helplessness via the energizing effects of stimulant drugs. The arousing qualities of stimulants serve the users' needs to feel active and potent in the face of an environment perceived as hostile and threatening. Massive expenditures of psychic and physical energy are geared to defend against underlying fears of vulnerability, passivity, and inadequacy.

The style of coping is reminiscent of a phase of early childhood development that culminates around the middle of the second year of life. During this stage, described by Mahler (1967) as the practicing period, "the freely walking toddler seems to feel at the height of his mood of elation. He appears to be at the peak of his belief in his own magical omnipotence which is still to a considerable extent derived from his sense of sharing in his mother's magic powers" (p. 749). The child seems to delight in flooding his or her senses while moving with reckless abandon through an environment fraught with diversity, difficulty, and danger. The fearless conduct is of course little more than a behavioral facade to compensate for continuous threats to a sense of self-importance or personal safety. As Reich (1960) explains, "The need for narcissistic inflation arises from a striving to overcome threats to one's bodily intactness." If early traumatizations are too frequent, the primitive ego defends itself via magical denial: "It is not so, I am not helpless, bleeding, destroyed. On the contrary, I am bigger and better than anyone else" (p. 220).

Those who thrive on courting danger appear to have carried this primitive style of coping into the adult realm. They win admiration and approval from witnesses by appearing to be tougher and more daring than everyone else. As described by Tom Wolfe in *The Right Stuff* (1980), both heroes and psychopaths have the uncanny ability to tread on the brink of disaster while maintaining their calm; they can function with wit and poise even when confronted with gargantuan distress. Brigadier General Chuck Yeager, one of America's original astronauts, appears to fit Wolfe's criteria for a fearless person. He is said to have hidden the fact that he had broken several ribs during a reckless midnight horseback ride so that he could crawl into a tiny X-1 rocket and allow himself to be ejected from the belly of a B-29, flying at 26,000 feet, to become the first man to travel faster than the speed of sound.

Other far less esteemed yet equally fearless members of our society attain the ignoble title of psychopath. As originally described in psychiatrist Cleckley's classic work, *The Mask of Sanity* (1941), psychopaths are generally quite intelligent. Their charm is undoubtedly more compelling because they lack visible tension or anxiety. Yet they are basically incapable of genuine affection or love and have no respect for the truth. They are characteristically unreliable, taking senseless risks even after having been punished for similar acts. The psychopath does not seem to learn from unpleasant past experiences and lacks the capacity for genuine remorse or shame. He is usually male—in three cases out of four—and has great facility for blaming others for his inappropriate or criminal actions. He seems unable to appreciate or foresee how others will react to his behavior. Cleckley portrays the psychopath not as deeply vicious, but as unable to take seriously the threat of disaster or harm and respond accordingly.

Following Farley's (1986) concept of the type T personality, psychopaths may be viewed as the black-sheep cousins of respectable adventurers. Both may be cut from the same biological cloth; they differ primarily in their early childhood experiences with parents and other socializing influences.

At the time of the following case example (Milkman, 1987), Detective Daril Cinquanta had been with the Denver Police Department for 17 years. He had been involved in more than 3,000 felon arrests without ever shooting a suspect. Detective Cinquanta is regarded by both criminals and responsible citizens as a law enforcement hero and champion of justice. He attributes much of his success as a crime fighter to his ability to understand the mentality of the people that he arrests. Coming from a lower-class background himself, Cinquanta is known among criminal adversaries for his cunning and fearlessness. He purposely cultivates the image of a maniacal daredevil to inspire as much fear as possible in his foes.

In the following case example, Cinquanta communicates the deep sense of pleasure and mental exhilaration that he derives from the excitement and risk of being a professional crime fighter.

Case Example: Officer Cinquanta—Type T Hero

We had a series of armed robberies in north Denver where somebody was robbing fast food restaurants with a sawed-off shotgun. We didn't have anything on this until one robbery when we got a surveillance photograph and it shows this Chicano male with a mask on. The only thing you can see is the shave line on his neck, that his wrists are hairy and his eyebrow . . . and he's got a sawed-off shotgun. . . . One morning during this rash of robberies, a little girl gets killed at McDonald's at 38th and Irving. . . . [G]uy comes in, hits the place and shotguns this little girl—kills her in the robbery.

Well, I knew this guy. I just *had* to know him. I developed a suspect from his eyebrow. I went through my pictures and I figured out who it was . . . and then I directed an informant of mine who had done time with him—who was a friend of his—to make contact with him . . . and one day [the suspect] admitted to him that he killed the girl in McDonald's. . . . So then my informant corroborates. He says, "God damned, he admitted it; said he shot her because she was ugly!" I go, "Jesus Christ!" He [informant] says he's [suspect] all strung out, doing dope and paranoid. So I figured the only way I'm going to do this guy is to follow him to his next robbery. I need to get some physical evidence; we need to make him surface that shotgun or the shoes he wore because we had a shoe print from the counter he jumped over at McDonald's. . . . I convinced Command to let me follow this guy 24 hours a day and live with him.

And we did. . . . On the 14th day he, guess what? He commits an armed robbery. . . . Well, he tried to hit a Pizza Hut first, and we were moving in on him when he abandoned it because he saw a police car go by. . . . [H]e had the mask down and he was just getting ready to pull the gun and go in the back door. . . . He went back to the car. So then he cruised around. . . . This is after 8 hours— we followed him 8 hours the last day until he picked his target. So he picks this gas station and he got down by a dumpster, his partner parked about 100 feet away . . . and he pulled the mask down and got his gun out of his sock. He had a .25 and put the gloves on and then went around to the gas station.

As he was going around, I ordered that we move in. We had two teams coming around from opposite directions. Well, I was right behind him when they confronted him. He panicked . . . he had the gun . . . he turned around and I was going to do him and said "drop it!" He leaped between two fences, between a lumber yard and the back of the station . . . and he raised the gun . . . and one of the detectives shot him.

[I]t was exciting . . . it was wonderful . . . I loved it. . . . [I]t's just unbelievable . . . the exhilaration.

Some of the same qualities that distinguish Detective Cinquanta as a successful crime fighter have apparently gone astray in the people that he apprehends. Whether the game is "cops and robbers" or the Web-based *World of Warcraft*, children derive primal pleasure from both sides of the chase. The thrill of conquest or danger is undoubtedly connected with the excitement that one experiences when the senses become flooded by survival cues. Sensation seeking appears to be a trait common to the entire spectrum of adventurous personalities—cops, criminals, coke addicts, and Casanovas included. Zuckerman (1994, 2007) developed the Sensation-Seeking Scale (SSS) to measure an individual's desire to engage in risky or adventurous activities, seek new kinds of sensory experiences, enjoy the excitement of social stimulation, and avoid boredom. Table 7.1 offers a sample of items from the SSS and a scoring procedure.

The people who score high on the SSS are more likely than others to enjoy risk in their work and play. High-sensation types are more probable candidates for variation and experimentation in their patterns of drug use and sexual practices; they tend to behave more fearlessly when confronted with such common phobic situations as heights, snakes, or darkness; they take more risks when gambling; and they report driving at higher speeds than low-sensation seekers. They are more likely to engage in such dangerous sports as parachuting, motorcycle riding, or scuba diving. Zuckerman and his colleagues have found that compatibility in sensation seeking is also a meaningful predictor of marital adjustment. According to one happily married team of underwater adventurers, "The couple that dives together, thrives together."

Chapter Summary

This chapter begins with a description of the relationship between arousal and performance. People perform most effectively when under some degree of stress. A moderate level of arousal tends to produce alertness and enthusiasm for the task at hand. This may account for the universal use of the stimulant caffeine, found in coffee, and increasingly used as an ingredient in a slew of "energy drinks." When emotional excitement exceeds an optimal point, even when the evoked feelings are positive, the result is progressive impairment of one's ability to function.

Selye introduced the idea that people could alter consciousness though chemical changes associated with stress. The psychological by-products of a moderate biochemical emergency are noticeable increments in one's feelings of physical prowess and personal competence, often associated with strong sensations of pleasure. In many ways, the state of biological and psychological "readiness" produced by stress is mimicked by the effects of stimulant drugs. In addition to increasing the levels of cortisol and norepinephrine, pleasure derived from fear-inducing activities, such as gambling, dangerous sexual liaisons, and skydiving, increases the level of dopamine in the nucleus accumbens. However, to maintain the intensity of an elevated mood, the sensation seeker must escalate his or her use of the drug or activity. Cessation of the drug or behavior produces a feeling of dysphoria mediated by neurochemical changes in the brain.

The repeated pairing of opposite emotional experiences, and their underlying physiological counterparts, may be the sustaining force behind all forms of human compulsion. According to R. L. Solomon's opponent-process model of mood oscillation, the same principle that produces alcoholics and drug

Table 7.1   Am I a Speed Demon?

Each item contains two choices. Choose the one that best describes your likes or feelings. If you do not like either choice, mark the choice you dislike the least. Do not leave any items blank.

1. A. I have no patience with dull or boring persons.
   B. I find something interesting in almost every person I talk to.

2. A. A good painting should shock or jolt the senses.
   B. A good painting should provide a feeling of peace and security.

3. A. People who ride motorcycles must have some kind of unconscious need to hurt themselves.
   B. I would like to drive or ride a motorcycle.

4. A. I would prefer living in an ideal society in which everyone is safe, secure, and happy.
   B. I would have preferred living in the unsettled days of history.

5. A. I sometimes like to do things that are a little frightening.
   B. A sensible person avoids dangerous activities.

6. A. I would not like to be hypnotized.
   B. I would like to be hypnotized.

7. A. The most important goal of life is to live to the fullest and experience as much as possible.
   B. The most important goal of life is to find peace and happiness.

8. A. I would like to try parachute jumping.
   B. I would never want to try jumping from a plane, with or without a parachute.

9. A. I enter cold water gradually, giving myself time to get used to it.
   B. I like to dive or jump right into the ocean or a cold pool.

10. A. When I go on a vacation, I prefer the comfort of a good room and bed.
    B. When I go on a vacation, I prefer the change of camping out.

11. A. I prefer people who are emotionally expressive, even if they are a bit unstable.
    B. I prefer people who are calm and even-tempered.

12. A. I would prefer a job in one location.
    B. I would like a job that requires traveling.

13. A. I can't wait to get indoors on a cold day.
    B. I am invigorated by a brisk, cold day.

14. A. I get bored seeing the same faces.
    B. I like the comfortable familiarity of everyday friends.

Scoring: Count one point for each of the following items that you have circled: 1A, 2A, 3B, 4B, 5A, 6B, 7A, 8A, 9B, 10B, 11A, 12B, 13B, 14A. Add your total for sensation seeking and compare it with the norms below:

0–3 Very low
4–5 Low
6–9 Average
10–11 High
12–14 Very high

SOURCE: This is an arbitrary sampling of items and not the full Sensation-Seeking Scale, which can be found in M. Zuckerman (1994), *Behavioral expressions and biosocial bases of sensation seeking.* New York: Cambridge University Press. Also see M. Zuckerman (2007), *Sensation seeking and risky behavior.* Washington, DC: American Psychological Association.

addicts can be used to account for daredevils, coca-cola addicts, and promiscuous sex junkies. Mood-altering behavior is often sustained because people seek to avoid the unpleasant effects that have been set in motion by the opponent process. Compulsive shopping and autoerotic fatalities are presented as examples—one relatively benign (shopping), and the other lethal—of opponent-process dynamics.

Pathological gambling exemplifies a mood-altering activity that triggers neurochemical messages similar to those induced by stimulant drugs. Personality characteristics of gamblers parallel those of other sensation-seeking types (e.g., competitiveness, disinhibition, impulsivity, above-average intelligence, and high energy). Because compulsive gambling often entails a high degree of ongoing stress over time, overstimulation of the HPA axis is likely to increase vulnerability to a host of medical and psychiatric conditions. In fact, research shows that compulsive gambling is associated with many adverse health consequences.

The chapter concludes with a discussion of the psychological and neurochemical characteristics of sensation seekers and the related factor of propensity toward boredom. A person more susceptible to becoming bored has a higher need for excitement, variety, and novelty and usually requires a constant and changing supply of stimulation to achieve his or her optimal level of arousal. By themselves, sensation seeking and escape from boredom are neither positive nor negative. The important question is how these fundamental human needs may be channeled and developed for the mutual benefit of the individual and society. Finally, readers are invited to examine their own sensation-seeking needs through a self-assessment instrument, Zuckerman's Sensation-Seeking Scale (Table 7.1).

8 Rock Around the Clock

Methamphetamine, Cocaine, and the Club Scene

Now I'm losing touch with reality and I'm almost out of blow

It's such a fine line; I hate to see it go

Cocaine, runnin' all around my brain

> —"Cocaine," by Gary Davis; additional lyrics
> by Glenn Frey and Jackson Browne

Introduction

This chapter explores the psychosocial underpinnings and neurochemical effects of two illegal stimulants, methamphetamine and cocaine. Although each has limited medical use, the psychological, social, economic, and health damage associated with illegal use of these drugs is enormous. Our discussion begins with methamphetamine, a powerful stimulant that has moved from biker gangs and all-night raves to just about every nook and cranny of society. Then we explore the popular "club drugs" including Ecstasy, GHB, ketamine, and Rohypnol.

Methamphetamine—A Dopamine Blast

Methamphetamine (ice, meth, speed, crystal, and scores of other slang names ranging from dummy dust to zoom) has seeped into commonplace venues across the United States. Meth users can be found in dingy basements, prisons, middle-class suburbs, million-dollar homes, urban gay communities, on the job, and at all-night raves (Jefferson, 2005; Moore & Miller, 2005; Owen, 2007). The drug affects all levels of society, from the homeless to professionals such as doctors, lawyers, accountants, and designers (Jefferson, 2005; Ladika, 2005; Owen, 2007). Often linked with sex, the drug produces a feeling that the user can last longer and longer. It is also linked with risky sex practices in both the straight and gay communities (Halliburton, 2005). During the early phases of use, there is a sense of enhanced concentration and alertness, personal empowerment, and increased capacity for work or criminal activity.

Identity theft is generally considered a relatively low-risk crime with light penalties for first-time offenders. Using the Internet, it remains quick, anonymous, and nonviolent. So meth addicts turn up as suspects in Internet crime rings across the country. After stealing bank account and credit card information, cybercriminals send in meth-addicted cronies to extract the stolen money from accounts (Acohido & Swartz, 2005).

Meth is easily manufactured in homes, barns, pickups, and SUVs using a common cold remedy, Sudafed (pseudoephedrine), and easily available chemicals such as anhydrous ammonia and lithium batteries. The manufacturers of homemade meth are not professional chemists (not even close), and with highly flammable substances, explosions and flash fires are rampant (Falkowski, 2003). The Patriot Act, signed in 2006, attempted to reduce the availability of over-the-counter cold medicines that contain pseudoephedrine (the active ingredient in Sudafed used to manufacture meth) by requiring them to be placed behind the pharmacy counter and only sold in limited amounts to people after identification is shown. A log is kept of the amount and date they were purchased (Bren, 2006). The restrictions on readily available components of the drug have made a huge impact on the amount of "mom-and-pop" labs, resulting in a drastic decrease in the number of labs seized in the United States (Zernike, 2006). But the demand for the drug remained unchanged, so the supply started coming in from Mexico. "Mexican ice" is crystallized and more potent than the product manufactured in the mom-and-pop labs, increasing probabilities for addiction and overdose.

Whether used to party, or to enhance capacity for sex, work, or crime, the usual aftermath of abusing methamphetamine is incredible hardship and suffering. Consider Haley's description of how her experience with methamphetamine became so degrading that it is a wonder she is alive and capable of functioning as a college student.

Case Example: Haley's Meth Run

I found myself sitting in a dirty hotel room, and my friend was clearing a spot off the night stand to do a line. The drug in front of me is not what made me nervous but how to actually snort the line without a bill or straw and not look like a fool. I was so nervous of being judged by my new "hardcore" friends; all I wanted was for them to like me. I was a college student in my sophomore year, [I had a] full-ride scholarship, volunteered at a hospital, coached volleyball, and got good grades; I did not fit in with them. After a few more lines, we were off on our way to a party, but I was the only one with a license and a clean record and don't forget, the nice car, so I was going to be the driver. A few more nights like this soon led to partying on the weekends—Friday through Sunday, not just one night. During all this, I tried to keep a job, managed to get through the semester with only a couple bad grades, but I figured I had the time to waste.

Meth is a dirty and disgusting drug, but for some reason it had an appeal to me. Basically, getting high consisted of sitting around on couches and passing the pipe around all night long. One person played video games all night and his girlfriend cleaned; I did not know what to do, so I just sat there and clenched my jaw. The high lasted all night no matter what I did; I was not able to get to sleep until the next night. This habit turned into an every-other-weekend thing and quickly progressed into every weekend. I actually had a group of friends now for the first time that were like big brothers, or so I thought. So I continued to party with them and felt special that I was always with the main man, the dealer. Looking back, I know I was mistaken. I was the one with the car, the money that I saved up from scholarships, and the fact that I was a girl [fed their] hopes they could persuade me to have sex with them or do other things for them.

I ended up finding another meth dealer through someone else that was supposed to have better stuff. I hung out with this dealer one night and his friends, got high on meth, and it was the night before college was starting for the semester. I allowed a guy to sleep on my couch for only one night because he was about to get evicted, but he didn't leave for a year. I continued to hang out with this boy because his friend was a dealer and he knew plenty of others. My meth use then quickly progressed from 2 or 3 days in a row to pretty much every other day and sleeping only every third day. I began to lose so much weight and I loved it! Losing the weight almost became a motivator to keep using. At the depths of my addiction, I was snorting a gram in one line multiple times a day as well as smoking it and swallowing it in toilet paper or empty vitamin capsules. My $10,000 savings account was diminishing faster than I could even find my next bag, even though it was everywhere at all times of the day and night.

I had to move out from where I was living so that I could smoke freely in my own apartment and stay up all night every night without anyone saying anything. After a couple more moves and apartment deposits later, I was running out of money, but still managed to find meth. I saved money by going to the food bank to get food instead of spending it on groceries. At this point I had to drop out of school for the semester and had lost 35 pounds in just a couple months. It was hard enough to do simple tasks like driving a car when you have not slept for 4 days, let alone try to go to school and maintain a 3.5 average; I was in big trouble.

I decided to tell my mom in hopes I could clean up for a while, but in all actuality I was not ready to stop. I looked good, I was skinny and attractive and having so much fun living the life of the drugs and partying, but I gave recovery a try. I had no idea how hard it was going to be to come off of meth. My body craved food so much, things like sweets and junk food. I was basically living off of Gatorade because I knew I needed something in my body so I could at least function. Nighttime was the worst, horrible nightmares all night long, and I was always so tired. I had to take a nap after breakfast, get up and eat lunch, then go back to sleep and do it again for dinner and go back to sleep. The thing was, though, that even being so tired, when you fall asleep you feel like you are dying. It's hard to describe because I have never felt anything like it before, but you dream that something is on top of you like a huge brick and you can't move or breathe. Sometimes you don't even dream it but it wakes you up and you actually can't move and it happens multiple times throughout the night. It was so scary to wake up and feel suffocated and stuck to the ground. I would have to force my arm to twitch to pull out of it, and it was so hard to get a body part to move.

This sucked so badly and I was putting back on all the weight I had just lost so I started to use again, figuring all I had to do was hide it. The thing was that this time meth was not as available, only crack. I hated crack. It was only a 30-second intense high, but it was more intense than anything I had ever felt. It numbed my throat and made me gag every time and the comedown starts in 2 minutes. The comedown honestly makes you want to scream and pull your hair out or even kill yourself. The only way around it is to do more, which just starts the cycle over. I hated this drug so much but did it multiple times.

When I finally got back to meth, I wanted to try shooting it up. It was a whole new feeling, different than snorting or smoking either of the two drugs. With coke you get an intense rush that makes your head buzz and ring; you can barely see or stand up for a good 2 minutes. With meth it sends a hot rush through your chest that feels like fire is oozing from your lungs, throat, and whole body. It made my chest get all red and my body shake, making it hard to walk. You are almost too high, so all you can do is just sit there and feel the effects until it calms down a little. That night or the next, I don't remember, I ended up in the emergency room and I thought meth was to blame. Going into the hospital and having them draw blood from an arm with bruised veins due to the drug sent a rush of guilt, anxiety, fear, and shame. I didn't know what they would do to me, knowing I am a drug user. It ended up being related to other health causes from prolonged use of meth and on top of it I was pregnant. Now I really needed to clean up. My boyfriend went to jail to help himself, and I was all alone on the journey to get clean and raise a healthy baby. I managed to stay clean for 4 months until I lost the baby as my body was not healthy enough to support another life,

(Continued)

(Continued)

barely my own. It was tough to get through the loss of my child and more so to realize I had to move on with my life, get away from the scene. To this day, it is still hard to think about, to write about, and to stay away from.

Methamphetamine and the Brain

As a close relative of amphetamine, we would expect meth to have many negative effects on the body, especially the brain and the cardiovascular system. Besides addiction, serious effects from meth usage include rapid and irregular heartbeat and increased blood pressure resulting in irreversible damage to small blood vessels in the brain, which in turn may result in strokes. Other effects include increased wakefulness; insomnia; convulsions; tremors; confusion; anxiety; aggressiveness; hyperactivity; heart palpitations; delusions of grandeur; kidney, lung, and liver disorders; and paranoia. Possibly the most serious health problem from chronic methamphetamine abuse is damage to the neurons of the brain. Previous studies have shown that meth causes damage to neurons in several parts of the brain, including the frontal cortex, which is responsible for cognitive functioning and decision-making capacity. It also is known to damage cells in the striatum. Damage to these cells could lead to movement disorders resembling Huntington's chorea and tardive dyskinesia. Cadet, Ordonez, and Ordonez (1997) have shown that methamphetamine not only damages neurons but actually destroys them through a process called *apoptosis* (Figure 8.1).

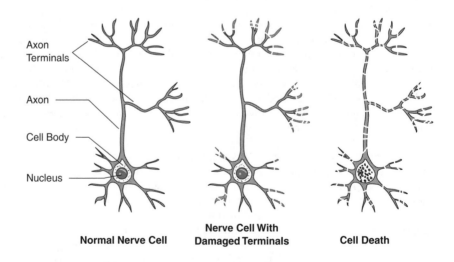

Figure 8.1   **Neurotoxic effects of methamphetamine.** Possibly the most serious health problem from chronic methamphetamine abuse is damage to the neurons of the brain.

SOURCE: From *NIDA Notes, 15*(4).

In experiments using rodents (mice), Cadet et al. (1997) showed that neuronal death was also prominent in the frontal cortex and hippocampus, which is utilized in the formation of long-term memory. There is also extensive damage in the striatum (Figure 8.2).

Cell death in the frontal cortex, which is involved in cognition and reasoning, is especially troublesome for young adults since during adolescence this area is still undergoing rapid change. Immature development makes this part of the brain especially vulnerable to apoptosis. It is obvious that this combination of damage to cell terminals and death of neurons in the young adult would result in permanent brain damage.

Another serious consequence of meth usage is damage to the nerve endings of dopamine-producing cells due to overstimulation. This injury persists for at least 3 years after drug intake has ceased. This damage to dopamine-producing cells is similar to that caused by Parkinson's disease and may be responsible for the addicting aspects of methamphetamine usage. These earlier claims regarding the effects of methamphetamine on the brain have been confirmed by Chang et al. (2002) using a technique called perfusion nuclear magnetic imaging (pNMI), which measures blood flow into important brain regions.

If meth is so harmful, then why is it so popular? If you don't know the answer to this, go back and review Neurochemistry 101 (Chapter 2). It is

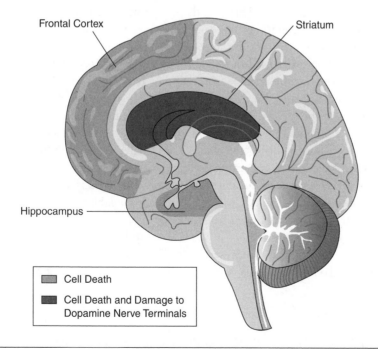

Figure 8.2   Human brain areas corresponding to the mouse brain areas damaged by methamphetamine. The figure shows that neuronal death is prominent in the frontal cortex and hippocampus.

SOURCE: From *NIDA Notes, 15*(4).

no surprise that meth produces its "special high" through a very rapid and prolific release of dopamine (DA) from the presynaptic terminal. In addition, it also blocks the reuptake of DA from the synapse, which adds an additional boost to the overall effect. It also releases norepinephrine (NE) and possibly serotonin. The release of NE would account for the wakefulness and hyperactivity associated with meth usage. The resulting euphoria lasts from 8 to 24 hours, unlike that associated with cocaine, which lasts 20 to 30 minutes (NIDA, 2007f). These chemical disruptions in the brain cause an initial rush of euphoria followed by increased concentration, alertness, and energy, and a decrease in appetite and need for sleep (Falkowski, 2003).

In January of 2005, Pfizer, the manufacturer of Sudafed, substituted another chemical, phenylephrine, for the pseudoephedrine present in the drug. According to Pfizer, it is impossible to convert this new compound (Sudafed PE) into methamphetamine (Butterfield, 2005). The original formula, however, remains on the market.

Cocaine: "Gift of the Gods"

In the early 16th century, when Francisco Pizarro encountered the Quechua (usually referred to as the Inca) people of present-day Peru, he found that royalty used the extract of a local shrub known today as Erythroxylon coca, or simply the coca plant. This was the first contact of Europeans with this drug, which was soon to become one of the most widely abused drugs in the world. In Peru, the extract of the coca plant was considered to be "the gift of the gods" and was used in religious ceremonies as well as for medicinal purposes. The use of cocaine was initially banned by the Spanish conquerors, but they soon learned that the enslaved natives could not work the gold mines in the rarified air of Peru without the stimulation of coca leaves that were distributed several times a day to the workers. The returning conquistadors called the drug "the elixir of life." They introduced the coca leaf to Europe, where it soon became used in a fashionable social beverage.

Sherlock Holmes used cocaine, and doctors even prescribed it as an antidote to morphine addiction. Cocaine was readily available in the late 19th and early 20th centuries either over the counter or in beverages such as Coca-Cola, which was introduced in 1886. It was claimed to be a brain tonic and a cure for nervous affliction. A typical serving of Coca-Cola contained about 60 mg of cocaine. Today Coca-Cola contains only the name "coca," not the drug.

Crack Is Wack[1]

Crack is cocaine base that has not been neutralized by an acid to make the hydrochloride salt. This form of cocaine comes in a rock crystal that can be heated and its vapors smoked. The term "crack" refers to the crackling sound heard when it is heated.

—NIDA (2008) *InfoFacts: Crack and Cocaine*

Cocaine is found in the coca plant as the freebase form where it constitutes less than 1% of the leaf. After being extracted, the paste is treated with hydrochloric acid. This forms cocaine hydrochloride, an organic salt. This is the form in which it arrives in the United States, as a white powder. Cocaine can be extracted from the leaves in hot water to make coca tea, a popular beverage in Peru. Cocaine becomes dangerous when extracted and concentrated to form pure cocaine hydrochloride. This form is usually snorted since it is not sufficiently volatile to smoke. The hydrochloride salt may be converted to "crack" by a general chemical reaction (acid plus base) learned by every beginning student of chemistry. Treatment of the acid salt with any household base, such as ammonia or sodium bicarbonate, releases the hydrochloric acid to form the volatile "freebase," known as crack, which, once extracted with ether and dried, can be smoked to give a much faster high than can be obtained by snorting. Sounds easy, right? Actually, it is very easy for anyone in a chemistry laboratory equipped with an exhaust hood. The problem arises when inexperienced "chemists" evaporate the ether extract to get the pure cocaine. Ether is very volatile and flammable, and many serious accidents have resulted from igniting the ether during extraction. The comedian Richard Pryor suffered severe burns while attempting to evaporate the ether extract with a flame. The Inca of Peru were also able to "freebase" cocaine by using calcium oxide as the base to remove the hydrochloric acid.

Cocaine and the Brain

How does cocaine react in the brain to give such an immediate and intense high? Let's return to Neurochemistry 101 for an answer. Briefly stated, cocaine obtains its high by increasing the availability of guess what, our good friend, dopamine. No surprise there. When dopamine is released from the presynaptic neurons (Figure 8.3) of the dopamine-producing nerve cells in an area of the brain known as the ventral tegmental area (VTA), it causes a flow of dopamine into the reward center, the nucleus accumbens, where it produces the expected high (Ikegami, Olsen, D'Souza, & Duvauchelle, 2007). After activating the cells of the nucleus accumbens, dopamine is transported back into the presynaptic VTA cells by transporter receptors. Cocaine blocks these transporter receptors (Figure 8.3), which prevents dopamine from being reabsorbed. Since it stays in the synapse, it is able to be used over and over again and to continually activate the neurons of the nucleus accumbens, giving the user the intense high characteristic of cocaine use.

Obviously, cocaine, like most drugs of abuse—even caffeine—exerts its major effect on the brain. Because of the intense high associated with the drug, addiction can occur during a single binge episode. It has been shown by Ciccocioppo et al. (2004) that a single cocaine binge can establish cue-induced, long-term drug-seeking behavior in rats. Once addicted, the user

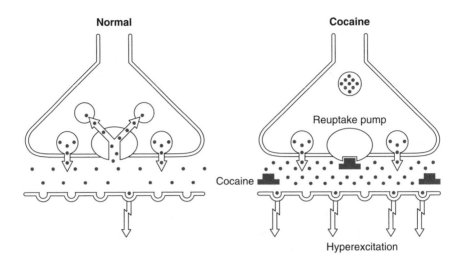

Figure 8.3   **Cocaine in the brain.** The amount of neurotransmitters in a synapse depends on the balance between the rate at which neurotransmitters are released into the synapse (from vesicles) and the rate at which they are removed from the synapse by the reuptake pump (left panel). By blocking the reuptake pump, cocaine increases the concentration of neurotransmitters, which in turn occupy more receptors and cause hyperexcitation (right panel).

finds him- or herself in a continuing spiral of increased usage to reach the previously obtained high and especially to avoid the effects of withdrawal. These effects include severe depression, with the resulting intense craving to resume using. Prolonged usage can produce paranoia, especially among crack users, who may become aggressively paranoid. Dopamine activity in the brain of people expecting a cocaine high is stimulated when they see a conditioned stimulus, meaning if they see a place where they used the drug, their dopamine levels will surge in their reward center and they will expect the cocaine or crack rush (Ikegami et al., 2007).

A. J. Siegel et al. (1999) at the Alcohol and Drug Abuse Research Center at McLean Hospital in Belmont, Massachusetts, have shown that cocaine use increases the risk of sudden heart attack and stroke. Also, according to Satran et al. (2005) at the Minneapolis Heart Institute, another negative health effect of cocaine is the increased risk of fatal coronary aneurysms. The prefrontal cortex, in control of long-term memory and higher-level thinking, has been shown to be affected by the continued use of cocaine (Ikegami et al., 2007), especially when the use starts in adolescence (Santucci, 2008). The disruption in the cortex could explain the errors in judgment frequently displayed by addicts (Ikegami et al., 2007). The use of cocaine in adolescence, a developmentally critical period for the cortical areas of the brain, is especially detrimental, as research has shown that it can be more addicting than if it was started in adulthood (Brenhouse & Anderson, 2008;

Santucci, 2008). The effects of dependence on a still-maturing brain can cause many different psychosocial dysfunctions. Even if an individual gets into recovery, clear of the behavioral problems attributed to cocaine addiction, the person may still have subtle neuronal impairments, specifically in his or her neurotransmitters. A study by Santucci provided data to "imply that drug use in adolescent humans may have long-lasting consequences on cognitive and emotional functioning" (p. 83). According to Brenhouse and Anderson, changes in the brain put teenagers at a higher risk for cue-associated and drug-seeking behaviors.

Crack Babies Revisited

Not only does cocaine have profound effects on the adolescent and adult brain, but pregnant women who use cocaine (crack) may cause serious damage to the fetus. In the 1980s, scary reports about the effects of cocaine on the brains of the developing fetus were widespread. Women whose fetuses were allegedly damaged by cocaine use during pregnancy were subject to criminal prosecution. Then in the 1990s, research began to soften regarding brain damage suffered by the fetuses of women who used cocaine. It is now clear that cocaine may not be a "sledge hammer" for the developing brain, but it clearly does have serious negative effects on the brain later on in the life of the exposed child. These include behavioral problems such as aggression, inability to stay focused, and impulsivity. In addition, crack-exposed children were more anxious and depressed (Chasnoff, 1997). Mayes (1995) reported that "crack babies" at 3 to 6 months of age showed more signs of irritability than those in the control group whose mothers were exposed to alcohol, nicotine, and drugs other than cocaine. At 12 to 18 months, the crack babies were having more trouble focusing their attention than the control group. Preschool children born of crack-addicted mothers are reported by their teachers to be more disruptive, are less inhibited, and are more impulsive (Dennis, Bendersky, Ramsay, & Lewis, 2006). Older children may take more time to solve problems and be slower mentally. Although children are very resilient, a study by Dennis et al. showed that "prenatal exposure to cocaine increases the risk for problems related to frustration reactivity and regulation of problem-solving behavior in early childhood" (p. 693). The study showed delays in problem solving with children exposed to cocaine, as it took them longer to process the problem and they were less engaged in it.

Cocaine and Neuronal Growth

As we have seen, cocaine acts by increasing the supply of dopamine in the synaptic junction of neurons. This enables more dopamine receptors to be activated, which in turn brings about the "high" characteristic of cocaine. In research on animals, the number of dopamine receptors designated as D1 were normal in rabbits exposed to cocaine, but the exposed receptors did not transmit their signal as efficiently as those in normal brains. According to Levitt, Harvey, Friedman, Simansky, and Murphy (1997), this may result in the abnormal growth of the dendrites, which causes them to weave around each other to accommodate this abnormal growth. This is believed to have a significant effect on their circuitry. Abnormal growth of the dendrites was found in the anterior cingulated cortex, which is the area of the brain involved in learning and attention. This abnormal growth and interweaving of neurons would be especially significant for young adults. As we have seen, the cortex of these young adults is still undergoing changes. Any alteration in the normal growth patterns could have significant effects on cognition.

Compulsion to Use

Women living in inner cities tend to show more dependence on crack (smokable) cocaine than any other illegal drug (Lejuez, Bornovalova, Reynolds, Daughters, & Curtin, 2007). When one thinks of the crack environment, images of dirty run-down houses, prostitution, or homelessness come to mind. These stereotypes are in part due to the fact that there is more research on crack use in the inner cities (i.e., lower-income areas). Impoverished settings and cocaine abuse have been associated with other high-risk behaviors such as nonuse of condoms, trading sex or sexual acts for drugs, crime, homelessness, and the contraction of HIV through unprotected sex or the sharing of needles (Lejuez et al., 2007). However, the use of crack extends well beyond the lower socioeconomic bracket.

As described below, Vivian's struggle began when she was 17 and had graduated high school, while she was living with her parents in a middle-class neighborhood; she began with a strong appetite for powdered cocaine.

Case Example: Vivian's Cocaine Nightmare

For over 4 years, I lived deep in the darkness of cocaine and crack. I started getting deep into powdered cocaine at age 17 when I still lived at my parents' house, right after I graduated high school. I would stay awake all night drawing twisted demons and demented aliens. I would do it in the bathrooms everywhere, including gas stations I would stop off at on the road to a party. I often missed out on the socializing and brawls at parties because I was holed up in the bathroom or a back room all night snorting a teener [1.75 grams of cocaine] with a couple other people. I ended up getting kicked out of my house and living in my car for a month, all the while scraping up change for gas because all my money I made at work went to purchasing the drug. After losing my home and then my job, I ended up attempting rehab and got clean for a few months. I was not yet ready to quit though, and soon found a new group of people who enjoyed the drug.

With my compulsive need to have some coke in my pocket and share with everyone else (that way I was the "cool" one, the life of the party), I soon became a fixture in a dingy apartment on the rough side of town. I would spend days, sometimes even weeks at a time awake on the drug, rarely seeing the light of day. We would go through 8-balls [3.5 grams of cocaine, or 1/8 of an ounce] like there was no tomorrow. If I was sick of sharing with other people, I would get in my car, snorting a line drawing some messed up stuff, then getting paranoid and driving to a new spot, doing a line, drawing macabre things, getting paranoid, and the cycle would continue for 14 to 16 hours. I would be missing for weeks at a time, only because I was in the apartment and no one that really loved me knew where I was or how to get ahold of me. Pretty soon my dealer ran out of supply and we needed to find a new one quick.

This is when I met up with a hard-core, New York–raised crack pusher that knew how to run the game and was not the least bit apprehensive to put someone in their place. I ran with this crowd for about 10 months, hanging out in more dingy apartments, snorting while driving my car, and isolating myself from everyone I knew before this crowd. It was at this time that I got introduced to smoking crack. I had always passed up crack, preferring the powdered coke and the rush I got from it. That was, until I tried crack. I had been up for 16 days straight off cocaine at that point, and the dealers had run out of powdered and were passing around three crack pipes filled to the max. In my desperation of coming off my powdered high, I went ahead and started hitting up the pipes. Talk about a crack high. I still believe if you looked up crackhead in the dictionary you would see a picture of me that night. It was a whole new rush.

From the next day on, I was chasing that dragon, trying my hardest to get to that insane, discombobulated, euphoric state that I was in that night. I kept smoking crack after that. I would stay in dark, dirty apartments for days and weeks at a time still, but now I would be peeking under doors while my pal was checking out the blinds. I would be tweaking, or searching the floors and couches and any place I could possibly think of to find a piece of crack I just knew I had dropped. I would pride myself on showering every day, but I wore the same clothes over and over, only washing my undies in sinks and blow-drying them or wearing them soaking wet. I thought I was so great because I still kept up my hygiene (or so I thought), but my clothes were always dirty, my teeth were half-assed brushed, and all I did all day was sit in smoke-filled cracked-out spaces, searching for, begging for, and needing more. I cringe to think about how disgusting some of the places were that I was spending my time, and even more when I think about what I had become. I would smoke it everywhere, even in the car while driving; I just needed the rush so bad.

I remember on one New Year's Eve I was speeding, trying to get back to "home base" to pick up the main guy for a kilo run, and I lit up the crack pipe in my car. Glancing over, I saw that I was staring in the eyes of the police officer driving next to me. He slowed down, got behind me and I knew I was toast. The ironic thing was that I was not scared about getting busted by the cops, not scared about the paraphernalia and drugs in my car. I was terrified that if I got sent to jail and this huge drug deal did not go through because my car was not there, then I would be dead by the main guy. He would take me out in the blink of an eye for messing up the transaction.

The Club Scene

Over the last few decades, a new trend in drug use has emerged with the rising popularity of dance clubs and raves (all-night electronica music and dancing events complete with neon lights, friendly strangers, and usually plenty of club drugs) (Office of National Drug Control Policy [ONDCP], 2008). In these settings, some drugs have surpassed the demand of the rest of the illicit drugs and are currently considered "club drugs." The most popular drugs in a club or rave setting include MDMA (Ecstasy), ketamine, GHB, and Rohypnol. Raves got their start in Europe in the 1980s as secret parties for members of a youth subculture (McCaughan, Carlson, Falck, & Siegal, 2005), and they soon spread to the United States through such ports as Chicago, New York, and Detroit (Ter Bogt & Engels, 2005). The popularity and availability of these parties expanded in the last two decades of the 20th century (McCaughan et al., 2005).

The widespread sponsorship and advertising of these raves led to an increase in attendance and drug consumption. In the 1980s, raves were underground, with venues kept secret until hours before the start in order to keep the police at bay. The organizers behind the scenes would have backups, places where the rave could be held if the venue was discovered by the police. In the 1990s, different areas in the United States would have different numbers to call, and directions to the parties would come on an answering machine (Carter, personal communication, 2008). Often would-be rave attendees would be following the directions to find a big empty field, and so would call the number back to find it had been moved to a different space. Since the late 1990s and early 2000s, advertising has moved to fliers for clubs, the Internet via chat rooms or e-mail, and sponsorship by multinational corporations like energy drink companies. Raves are usually overcrowded and held in sites that are not adequate for the number of people attending. Often these settings are poorly ventilated, and with all of the bodies, dancing, and drugs, this can lead to deadly combinations (Rivas-Vasquez & Delgado, 2002).

Raves are typically held in old warehouses, clubs, open fields, and airport hangars, on beaches, and even at concert venues and sports arenas ("The History of Rave Culture," n.d.)—anywhere the organizers can find space or sponsorship for a loud speaker system and thousands of people. Today, raves are attended by counterculture "ravers" as well as more mainstream youth. Raves are now seen as a place to gather together, listen to music, and do drugs. Since their origination in the 1980s, they have gone from secret, hush-hush events to "highly organized, commercialized, worldwide party culture[s]" (National Drug Intelligence Center [NDIC], cited in McCaughan et al., 2005). Teenagers and young adults are especially drawn to these settings, as raves are now advertised on college campuses, at night clubs, and even on the radio. Attendees are more likely to be introduced to the genre of club drugs because of the myths and beliefs held about their effects. For instance, Ecstasy is commonly promoted as a love drug as well as a dance and sex enhancer.

Club Drugs (Ecstasy, Ketamine, GHB, and Rohypnol)

Ecstasy (MDMA)

Ecstasy is judged as the most popular club drug among youth at this time. When all-night dance festivals, or raves, became popular in the mid-1980s, countries around the world saw a dramatic increase in Ecstasy's use (Diamond, Bermudez, & Schensul, 2006). Although extremely popular in club settings, the use of Ecstasy is much more widespread (Rivas-Vasquez & Delgado, 2002). In the 1990s, as raves moved to mainstream bars, clubs, and other venues, the use of MDMA began to seep into well-trafficked urban venues frequented by more mainstream and minority clientele.

In a study focusing on the effects of rap music and the rise in mainstream Ecstasy use, Diamond et al. (2006) found that the number of songs promoting MDMA use increased as it was finding popularity in urban areas throughout the United States. Of the 69 songs they studied, the most common scene described was the use of MDMA at a club or party. Ecstasy was also largely promoted as a sex-enhancing love drug. Many of the songs focused on men giving women the drug, making them less inhibited and more willing to perform risky sexual practices. Interestingly, the rise of Ecstasy as a sexual enhancer coincided with the introduction of Viagra, both of which make it more feasible to maintain sexual arousal.

Ecstasy produces euphoria, increased energy and happiness, heightened sensations and sexual desire, and emotional openness (Diamond et al., 2006). On the romantic plane, advocates for Ecstasy believe that the drug promotes feelings of closeness and intimacy. We will further discuss the common perception of enhanced intimacy and the psychological draw of Ecstasy in Chapter 12.

Extent of Use

A large proportion of youth have tried Ecstasy at least once in their lifetime. According to the 2006 National Survey on Drug Use and Health (NSDUH), an estimated 12.3 million Americans aged 12 or older tried MDMA at least once, representing 5% of the U.S. population in that age group. The number of past-year MDMA users in 2006 was approximately 2.1 million (nearly 1% of the population aged 12 or older), and the number of past-month MDMA users was 528,000. Results of the 2007 Monitoring the Future survey indicate that 2.3% of eighth graders, 5.2% of tenth graders, and 6.5% of twelfth graders reported use of MDMA in their lifetime.

Negative Effects

Ecstasy has many negative psychological effects including depression, sleep difficulties, anxiety, agitation, drug cravings, and impulsiveness (NSDUH, 2006; Rivas-Vasquez & Delgado, 2002; Ter Bogt & Engels, 2005). As the amount of ingested MDMA increases, so do the adverse physical effects, including hyperthermia, or increased body temperature, which can lead to failure of bodily organs such as the kidney and liver. If the damage is bad enough, this can cause a fatality. Other unfriendly physical side effects of the drug include muscle tension, nausea, stiff jaw, teeth grinding and clenching, hypertension, perspiration, loss of appetite, headache, and heart palpitations (Ter Bogt & Engels, 2005). The combination of increasing body heat and low air flow often found in clubs and raves while people are dancing can cause a person using Ecstasy to overheat, sometimes drinking too much water, which disturbs the body's sodium balance causing organs to swell. Since the brain cannot expand inside the skull, the resultant compression puts pressure on the brain stem, which controls heart and breathing functions. In extreme cases, this can lead to coma and death (Rivas-Vasquez & Delgado, 2002). Liechti and Vollenweider (2001) reported that women seem to be *more susceptible* than men to the subjective effects of Ecstasy, including perceptual changes, thought disturbances, and fear of loss of body control.

Neurotoxic Effects

Chemically, Ecstasy is 3,4-methylenedioxymethamphetamine (MDMA). The significant part of the name is *methamphetamine,* which should be a red flag. As a derivative of "meth," it would be expected to exhibit many of the deleterious effects of that drug, which were discussed earlier. This it does well, with a few added zingers of its own. Some studies (e.g., Colado, O'Shea, & Green, 2004; Escobedo et al., 2005; D. C. Jones et al., 2005) have shown MDMA to be *neurotoxic* in rats and primates. The process of neuron degeneration is thought to be exacerbated by high ambient temperatures (e.g., being overheated at raves) and mainly occurs in serotonin-producing neurons (Saldaña & Barker, 2004). Low levels of serotonin have been associated with depression and violence.

Since any drug that causes the type of mood swings attributed to Ecstasy obviously has a strong effect on the brain, let's examine these effects first. It is believed that the major contributor to the euphoria experienced by MDMA users is our familiar neurotransmitter, serotonin. The euphoria brought about by Ecstasy is due, at least in part, to the *rapid release of serotonin* from nerve endings. Overstimulation of these nerves may cause irreversible damage to the nerve endings (U. D. McCann, Szabo, Scheffel, Dannals, & Ricaurte, 1998). Even if the serotonin neurons do regrow, they won't grow back normally and in the right location in the brain. Some studies in monkeys have shown that after only 4 days of exposure to Ecstasy, brain damage was apparent 6 to 7 years later (NIDA, 2001). This points to the possibility of permanent brain damage in humans. Cowan et al. (2003) have shown that Ecstasy users have a decrease in the concentration of *gray matter* in several brain regions when compared with nonusers.

Ricaurte and colleagues (Ricaurte, Yuan, Hatzidimitriou, Cord, & McCann, 2002) reported that in monkeys exposed to Ecstasy, the area of the brain that produces serotonin was badly damaged. They also reported that Ecstasy kills dopamine-producing cells after only one night's dose. Damage to these cells would put users at risk for Parkinson's disease, which is characterized by non- or poorly functioning dopamine-producing neurons. In general, dopamine deficiency is associated with cognitive deficiency as well as psychiatric problems. However, it should be noted that Ricaurte's work has been widely criticized. Apparently, the primates used in the study were injected with methamphetamine and not Ecstasy. The original article was retracted and the entire episode reported in the *Chronicle of Higher Education* (Bartlett, 2004).

It has also been shown that unborn rats exposed to MDMA during what corresponds to the third trimester of human pregnancy suffered memory and learning deficiencies throughout their adult lives (Broening, Morford, Inman-Wood, Fukumura, & Vorhees, 2001). Rodgers et al. (2001) have shown that regular users of Ecstasy report experiencing long-term memory difficulties and are significantly more likely to report problems with remembering things than nonusers. Even after at least 2 weeks of abstinence, users have significant memory problems. An added health risk for Ecstasy users is the fact that the drug is often *consumed with other drugs,* especially marijuana or alcohol, seemingly a deadly combination for damaging the brain.

Even with all of the negative consequences known to result from MDMA use, only 38% of youth surveyed in the 2000 Monitoring the Future Survey considered it to be a harmful drug (as cited in Diamond et al., 2006).

GHB, Ketamine, and Rohypnol

These are considered "newer" club drugs and are often used in "clubbing settings" (preclub bars, in-club spaces, dance music festivals, after-parties) (Moore & Miller, 2005, p. 5). According to users' self-reports, they are effective as tools to enhance sociability, dancing, and good times (Moore & Miller, 2005; G. A. Parks, 2005). Many claim to use only a few times per month, returning to "real life" during the weekdays and feeling secure in their knowledge and capacity to manage possible dangers. (Ketamine is further discussed as a dissociative drug in Chapter 10.)

Gamma hydroxybutyrate (GHB) is a depressant drug that comes in liquid or powder form (ONDCP, 2008). The liquid form has been used as a "date rape drug" by offenders slipping the colorless, odorless liquid into unaware victims' drinks. Weightlifters sometimes use this drug for its supposed muscle-building effects. GHB was originally investigated in the 1960s for potential anesthetic use and was used for sleep disorders, depression, anxiety, and symptom relief of alcohol and opiate withdrawal (Sumnall et al., 2008). It has only recently become self-administered for nonmedicinal purposes. Euphoria, relaxation, disinhibition, and increased sensuality are some of the attractive effects of the drug. Individuals taking the drug to enhance a club experience will attend to the effects of the drug that are compatible with this. On the negative and extremely dangerous side, GHB has been shown to produce drowsiness, nausea, unconsciousness, seizures, severe respiratory depression, and coma. In addition, GHB has increasingly become involved in poisonings, overdoses, date rapes, and fatalities.

Ketamine is an animal tranquilizer that became a popular drug to misuse in the 1980s due to its effects (ONDCP, 2008). Large doses of this drug tend to cause dissociative states and hallucinations, much like the effects of PCP (discussed in Chapter 10). Users may perceive sights and sounds differently from when in a sober state, and they often feel as if they are disconnected from their bodies and uncoordinated. The effects tend to last for an hour or less and can cause respiratory depression and irregular heartbeats. Ketamine comes in both liquid and powder form, and it is often injected, taken orally (i.e., in drinks), smoked, or snorted.

Rohypnol is a tranquilizer that is a legal prescription drug in numerous countries outside of the United States (ONDCP, 2008). This depressant drug is often consumed orally or snorted after the pill form has been crushed down to a powder. It has sometimes been used in sexual assaults because it has a sedating effect.

Rohypnol, GHB, and ketamine are all central nervous system depressants. Lower doses of Rohypnol can cause muscle relaxation and can produce general sedative and hypnotic effects. In higher doses, Rohypnol causes a loss of muscle control, loss of consciousness, and partial amnesia. When combined with alcohol, the toxic effects of Rohypnol can be aggravated. Of an estimated 106 million emergency department (ED) visits in the United States during 2004, the Drug Abuse Warning Network (DAWN) estimates that 1,997,993 were drug-related. DAWN data indicate that MDMA was involved in 8,621 ED visits, GHB was involved in 2,340 visits, Rohypnol was involved in 473 visits, and ketamine was involved in 227 visits (SAMHSA, 2008).

Combining Drugs

Most club drugs (including MDMA) are used in combination with other drugs, be it more club drugs, alcohol, or marijuana (Sumnall et al., 2008). G. A. Parks (2005) found that ketamine was used most often for stress reduction, relaxation and escape, at home, with others, or at raves. GHB has a popular reputation as a club drug consumed with the intent to enhance sociability, dancing, and the overall clubbing experience. However, Sumnall et al. (2008) found that GHB was primarily used in the privacy of homes, rather than at clubs. Sumnall's group found that GHB was typically used along with alcohol to settle down from the negative feelings brought on by uppers (e.g., insomnia), or to enhance sex. GHB has been reported to produce heightened touch and sensory experiences as well as less inhibition around sexual contact.

Chapter Summary

Methamphetamine has seeped into commonplace venues all across the United States. Whether used to party or to enhance one's capacity for sex, work, or crime, the usual aftermath of abusing methamphetamine is incredible hardship and suffering. Besides addiction, serious effects from meth usage include rapid and irregular heartbeat and increased blood pressure resulting in irreversible damage to small blood vessels in the brain—which in turn may result in strokes. Possibly the most serious health problem from chronic methamphetamine abuse is damage to the neurons of the brain.

The intense and long-lasting euphoria (8–24 hours) produced by methamphetamine results from profuse release of dopamine from the presynaptic neuron in combination with meth's ability to block reuptake of DA from the synapse, thereby strengthening the overall effect. In addition, meth facilitates the release of norepinephrine, which accounts for the sleeplessness and hyperactivity experienced during the high.

Cocaine exerts its effects on the brain by increasing the amount of dopamine flowing into the nucleus accumbens. There is general agreement that maturing "crack" babies exhibit attention deficits, irritability, and aggression. Cocaine interferes with the normal growth of dendrites, especially in the area of the brain involved in learning and attention. This is especially troubling for young adults whose brains are not completely developed. Other health effects include brain damage, addiction, euphoria followed by depression, increased blood pressure, increased risk of heart attack, coronary aneurysms, and compromised immune systems.

The cocaine scene is still going strong, despite the efforts in the 1980s and 1990s to reduce the use of powdered cocaine and crack by increased international surveillance, police work, and criminal sanctions (Gips, 2006). Cocaine is regularly referred to as a club drug because of the heightened activity and energy one gets from using it at bars, clubs, parties, and raves. Cocaine is also used in private residences and even in cars on the street. Some people use the drug to enhance their dancing and socializing while others use it to stay awake on the job. Gips (2006) reported that cocaine use is still rampant in the workplace, with over 23% of positive tests in early 2005 resulting from cocaine use.

A new trend in drug use has emerged with the rising popularity of dance clubs and raves. The most popular "club drugs" include MDMA (Ecstasy), ketamine, GHB, and Rohypnol. Raves got their start in Europe in the 1980s as secret parties in youth subcultures, and they soon spread to the United States. The popularity and availability of these parties expanded in the last two decades of the twentieth century. Along with the increase in these club and rave atmospheres came increased availability and use of the club drugs. Each of them has its own negative effects and perceived benefits. But as with all of the mind-altering drugs and activities discussed so far, the risks far outweigh the wished-for "benefits."

Note

1. From the New York City "Crack Is Wack" mural by artist Keith Haring.

SECTION IV

Mental Excursions

When I examine myself and my methods of thought, I come to the conclusion that the gift of fantasy has meant more to me than my talent for absorbing positive knowledge.

—Albert Einstein

Overview: Imagination—The Quintessential Human Trait

Fantasy may be described as the ability to reproduce elements from prior experience (e.g., faces of persons, snatches of dialogue, objects in the universe) presently unavailable to our senses, and to reshape these into new and complex forms (J. L. Singer, 1976). The purpose of this section is to explore the gift of fantasy as an essential means for experiencing pleasure, understanding the world, and enhancing survival. The human proclivity for imagination, however, carries the same abuse liability as our needs for arousal and satiation.

Our ability to create mental events, which stand as intermediaries between biological impulse and instinctual reactions, may be the single most important difference between humans and all other life on earth. We not only forecast the weather and visualize tomorrow's clothing, but we can also imagine our own death. The ability to project ourselves into future environments and to appreciate the likely consequences of intended actions has undoubtedly enabled the prolific survival of the human species. However idyllic, bizarre, improbable, or grotesque, imagination usually reflects a response to psychological need. Fantasies are spoken about, privately savored, or preserved as forms of art.

The interplay between our internal mental experience and information from outside sets the stage for individualized representations and interpretations of the world. The development of self-concept, cognitive styles, emotional reactivity, and behavioral responses are, in part, determined by fantasy and imaginative thought.

Without actually forming fantasy images of our own, we may be engaged in attending to others' fantasy expressions. *Receptive fantasy* is the concentration on thoughts or pictures that have been produced from outside ourselves—for example, watching television, reading a novel, being at a concert, or going to an art gallery. *Active fantasy* is the production of images and thoughts that emerge spontaneously from one's own psyche. These may be highly representational and reality oriented, such as a person visualizing how to approach his or her employer, or they may be abstract and unrealistic, such as imagining the creation or destruction of the universe. Figure IV.1 illustrates the distinction among three different categories of visual fantasy: realistic, unrealistic, and abstract.

Exploration of the child's use of fantasy in fairy tales and storybooks sets the stage for understanding the adaptive function of imagination. Religion and myth play similar roles in providing guidelines for ethical and responsible living within a context of family, community, and culture. The function of dreams is explored in terms of enhancing one's capacity to solve

REALISTIC   UNREALISTIC   ABSTRACT

Figure IV.1   Continuum of fantasy images. Fantasies range from representational and reality oriented to unrealistic and abstract.

problems and to reduce stress. Each of the three chapters in this section is predicated on the adaptive, survival nature of fantasy, thereby associating it with both pleasure and high potential for abuse.

Chapter 9, Virtual Reality and Electronic Bogeymen, focuses on the emergence of virtual reality as an important element of the media age. Synthetic online worlds such as *World of Warcraft,* prolific in the genre of "massively multiplayer online role-playing games," or MMORPGs (pronounced "morepegs"), are examined in terms of how players escape into imagination to combat their enemies. *Second Life* (whose membership exceeded 10,000,000 residents as of September 2007) is discussed as an "engine of creativity" where residents own the intellectual property inherent in their creations ("Virtual Online Worlds," 2006). These "pixelated worlds" have brought countless hours of excitement, creativity, and peace of mind to millions of players. Unfortunately, some have become entrapped in a web of compulsion, loss of control, and continuation despite harmful consequences (i.e., they have become addicted).

Chapter 10, Fantasy and the Drug Experience, examines how certain drugs may be used to activate the imagination, for better or worse. In particular, lysergic acid diethylamide, LSD-25, is discussed as a pharmaceutical wonder, first synthesized on April 16, 1943, by Albert Hofmann, a chemist working for Sandoz Labs in Basel, Switzerland. In the 65 years following his discovery, Hofmann took a lot of LSD. He credited the drug with providing him with a sense of "union with nature and the spiritual basis of all creation" ("Obituary: Albert Hofmann," 2008). Many others, some creative geniuses, have held similar opinions. Hofmann died on April 29, 2008, at the age of 102, still mourning the unfulfilled promise of his "problem child," which he regarded as "a sacrament for the modern age: the antidote to the ennui caused by consumerism, industrialization, and the vanishing of the divine from human life"

("Obituary: Albert Hofmann," 2008). In the past 15 years, brain science has reopened the doors for exploring the use of psychedelics (e.g., LSD, psilocybin, DMT, MDMA) as tools for unraveling the stranglehold of mental disorders (e.g., obsessive compulsive disorder [OCD], severe anxiety in terminal cancer patients, posttraumatic stress disorder) (D. J. Brown, 2007).

Chapter 11, Compelled by Fantasy, explores how the boundaries between fantasy and reality may become blurred and cross over into destructive action. Born from intense psychological need, destructive fantasy fuels a host of compulsive problem behaviors ranging from wanton sexual acts to terrorism on a global scale. Fanaticism in belief and behavior is examined as a primary human response to unfulfilled psychological and social needs. Many researchers now believe that terrorism is not a manifestation of mental illness but rather a "rational choice" to meet political and religious objectives (Schaefer-Jones, 2007). Variations of the widespread apocalyptic fantasy (world destruction followed by heaven on earth) are examined as misguided and highly dangerous manifestations of the basic human capacity for wish-fulfilling fantasy.

Electronic Media Everywhere

Images and ideas from our surroundings are the psychic nutrients for our fantasies. There is a constant interplay between a person's spontaneous production of thoughts and images and the incredible array of external stimuli to which we are exposed. Television, which dominated the world of electronic media until the 1990s, has been joined by a vast array of information delivery systems: video players, audio media (such as compact disc players), video games (both console-based and handheld), computers, cell phones, personal digital media players (PDMPs), personal digital assistants (PDAs), and handheld Internet devices (Brooks-Gunn & Donahue, 2008).

A typical 8- to 18-year-old in the United States lives in a home with three TVs, three video players, three PDMPs (e.g., iPods or other MP3 devices), two video game consoles, and a personal computer (Roberts, Foehr, & Rideout, 2005). Shocking as it may seem, the average 8- to 18-year-old in the United States reports more than 6 hours of daily media use. When we include the phenomenon of "media multitasking" (using several media at the same time), which most teenagers do, the figure expands to an average of 8.5 hours of media exposure daily (Roberts & Foehr, 2008). Many teenagers spend more time engaged with electronic media than with any other element of life, including sleep.

Electronic media devices coexist with basic print (e.g., magazines, paperbacks, and newspapers) and other informational devices (e.g., billboards, graffiti, shopping mall displays, and movies). Together, they bombard the public with information ranging from intellectually stimulating, practical, and aesthetically pleasing, to whimsical, violent, horrifying, and obscene.

The content of visual productions (e.g., YouTube, virtual reality, tattoos, pornography) and acoustic presentations (e.g., songs, slam poetry, religious propaganda) exists on a continuum, from representational and easily understood, to highly abstract (see Figure IV.1).

The Child's Use of Fantasy

The basic function of fantasy is to explore our relationship to the world. As children we begin to develop specific mental pictures of who we are, which become a kind of personal identity uniting our past experiences to our intended actions. By imagining, we can work through painful memories and sufferings or formulate models of enchantment through which we will soar to blissful heights with our lovers, family, or friends. The emergence of new ideas from the reshaping of a multiplicity of past events, in a sense, becomes a vast additional source of knowledge.

According to Greenspan (1985), between the ages of 18 and 38 months, the child begins to create an internal world of ideas, symbols, and representations. He or she learns to abstract the functional properties of objects and form mental representations of the outside world. These are not only visual, but also multisensory and interactive images. For example, if a 2½-year-old thinks of "mother," the internal image is of smell, touch, voice, actions, feelings, and interactions, as well as past and present subjective experiences.

From 2 to 4.5 years, single repetitive play (e.g., doll drinks from a cup) evolves into "the grand epic drama." For example, "the doll drinks from the cup, goes to sleep, is awakened, spanked for spilling the milk and then spanks the mommy doll back, and finally is in love and cuddling" (Greenspan, 1985, p. 151). Thus, fantasy is used to internalize a template for managing the emotional themes of life, that is, "dependency, pleasure, curiosity, assertiveness, aggression, protest, anger, self-limit setting and by age 3–4 empathy and consistent love" (p. 151).

If for any reason the child is not sufficiently practiced in the use of fantasy and pretend play (parents may be made anxious by the use of fantasy in emotionally relevant contexts, e.g., separation or divorce), deficits or constriction in representational capacity can occur. As a result, the child (and later the adult) may become limited to a pattern of restricted and concrete thought. "Many adults are more frightened by the representation of a theme, such as sexuality or aggression, than the behaving or acting out of the same theme" (Greenspan, 1985, p. 151). Drug abuse and other forms of hedonic escape may serve the purpose of providing "false refuge" for those who lack internal means for managing the "emotional themes of life" (i.e., those who have a poorly developed capacity for fantasy). According to Singer and Kolligian (1987), moderate use of imagination is necessary for adaptive living. Singer's research with overeaters and drug abusers reveals their impoverished fantasy lives. These individuals may react by responding primarily to external stimulation. The outside world seems to cry out for sensory encounters, namely food, sex, or drugs. Similarly, children who do not partake of imaginative play tend more toward fighting, delinquency, and antisocial acts.

Whereas fairy tales largely provide guideposts for children to master the tasks of growing up, religion and myths provide ethical prescriptions for conduct in the adult world. The adaptive function of imagination, however, far exceeds that of helping to establish meaning, purpose, and patterns of conduct in an often confusing existence. Fantasy affords us an internal system for reducing stress. We can diminish tension through the imagined gratification of physical or psychological cravings or needs. By creating alternative mental environments, we are temporarily released from internal conflict or from tension in the outside world. Parents longing for the return of their college-bound children may find solace in their fantasy of having a joyous Thanksgiving reunion. By virtue of these intense reward capabilities, we regularly rely on fantasy solutions to everyday problems in living.

The interplay of *receptive* and *active* forms of fantasy is best understood by examining imagination in one of its simplest forms: the child's experience with the fairy tale. In its pure form, the fairy tale helps children to understand the inner pressures and concerns entailed in growing up. It offers both temporary and permanent solutions to pressing difficulties. Bettelheim (1976), renowned for his expertise on the meaning and importance of fairy tales, describes how children may benefit from enchanting stories:

> In order to master the psychological problems of growing up—overcoming narcissistic disappointments, oedipal dilemmas, sibling rivalries, becoming able to relinquish childhood dependencies, gaining a feeling of selfhood and self-worth, and a sense of moral obligation—a child needs to understand what is going on within his conscious self so that he can also cope with that which goes on in his unconscious. He can achieve this understanding, and with it the ability to cope, not through rational comprehension of the nature and content of his unconscious but by becoming familiar with it through spinning out daydreams—ruminating, rearranging and fantasizing about suitable strong elements in response to unconscious pressures. . . . Fairytales have unequaled value because they offer new dimensions to the child's imagination which would be impossible for him to discover as truly on his own. Even more important, the form and structure of a fairy tale suggests images to the child by which he can structure his daydreams and then give better direction to his life. (p. 7)

Examination of the tale of Peter Rabbit (Potter, 1902/1991) sheds light on youngsters' use of fairy tales to cope better with the fears and impulses of childhood. To date, the story has sold more than 40 million copies worldwide. Beatrix Potter's now-classic story begins,

> Once upon a time there were four little Rabbits and their names were Flopsy, Mopsy, Cottontail and Peter. . . . "Now my dears," said old Mrs. Rabbit

one morning, "you may go into the fields or down the lane, but don't go into Mr. McGregor's garden. Your father had an accident there; he was put in a pie by Mrs. McGregor. . . .

Flopsy, Mopsy and Cottontail, who were good little bunnies, went down the lane to gather blackberries. But Peter, who was very naughty, ran straight away to Mr. McGregor's garden and squeezed under the gate! (pp. 5–6)

Peter did not understand the value of portion control and was beginning to learn a lesson about giving carte blanche to wayward impulses.

But round the end of a cucumber frame, who should he meet but Mr. McGregor! . . . Peter got frightened and ran but got caught by the large buttons on his jacket in a gooseberry net. . . . Peter gave himself up for lost and shed big tears; but his sobs were overheard by some friendly sparrows who flew to him in great excitement and implored him to exert himself. (Potter, 1902/1991, p. 10)

Freud believed that only by struggling courageously against what seems like overwhelming odds can one succeed in wringing meaning out of life. This is an essential message of most fairy tales.

Peter had a very bad time running away from Mr. McGregor. He was frightened and cried, lost his clothes, and became wet and cold before he ran into a white cat who was staring at some goldfish. "Peter thought it best to go away without speaking to her; he had heard about cats from his cousin, Little Benjamin Bunny" (Potter, 1902/1991, p. 19). This is perhaps the most moving and essential part of the story. Young Peter must learn to take the advice of others—vicarious learning—in order to avoid making similar mistakes. Recall his father who was turned into rabbit pie.

Finally, Peter slips by Mr. McGregor, but not before he has a peek at what happened to his clothes: "Mr. McGregor hung up the little jacket and the shoes for a scarecrow to frighten the blackbirds" (Potter, 1902/1991, p. 23). Perhaps this is a symbol of crucifixion and a last reminder that death may be a penalty for impulsive behaviors.

When Peter got home, he was not feeling well. His mother put him to bed and gave Peter a dose of chamomile tea, one tablespoonful to be taken at bedtime. But Flopsy, Mopsy, and Cottontail had bread and milk and blackberries for supper. The good children were rewarded for their good behavior. Peter, on the other hand—whose nerves were undoubtedly shot—was mildly "medicated" and ordered to rest.

It is self-evident that when a young child becomes riveted by this enthralling tale, he or she inadvertently internalizes schemas (scripts) for impulse control and vicarious learning. The next time you have the chance to read *The Tale of Peter Rabbit* to a young child, notice how seriously he or she attends to every detail.

Religion and Myth

Be it Buddhism, Christianity, Hinduism, Islam, or Judaism, modern religion provides allegorical counsel for child, adolescent, and adult questions about life and death. Throughout the world, groups of people accept as truth ideas, concepts, or images that appear to violate the laws of nature. Beliefs in the supernatural are generally accepted as truths within a practicing group and regarded as myths or false beliefs by outsiders. These shared stories and legends become so ingrained that entire cultures may be guided by their meaning.

The organization of beliefs, rituals, and images that collectively purport to explain the meaning of life for a specific group may be considered a religion. For example, a large segment of the people in India share a set of beliefs, rich in imagery, depicting incredible supernatural events. To a Westerner, the stories enveloped by the religion of Hinduism are understood as fascinating myths. To the Hindu, the causes of the fantastic events in these widely shared stories are attributed to gods.

Religion and myth, fairy tale and fable, folklore and legend collaborate to form intricate systems of informal social controls over human impulse and action. Whereas the law provides direct mandates for correct action, shared parables usually enhance survival by providing internalized road maps for correct action. In the story of Abraham and Isaac (common to Judaism, Christianity, and Islam), Abraham subjugates himself to a power (God) that supersedes individual will or self-love. Clearly, Abraham's willingness to sacrifice his only son promotes respect for a force mightier than personal volition. A group's survival is enhanced if its members can be guided by symbols that encourage cohesiveness and allegiance to a shared set of values and leaders.

Even atheist communism uses symbolism to instill shared cultural beliefs. During a trip to mainland China, one of the authors (Milkman, 1981) asked his tour guide to explain China's position if Russia and the United States were at war. The guide offered the following parable:

> It is for you to decide who is China, Russia, or the U.S.
>
> There sits a large clam on the beach with its shell wide open.
>
> A seagull moves in to devour the flesh.
>
> Now the clam closes its shell on the seagull's beak.
>
> The seagull cannot escape and the clam cannot release its grip.
>
> A fisherman comes by and takes them both.

When one considers the audacious awakening of China (a.k.a. "the sleeping giant") during the early part of the 21st century, the guide's parable seems prophetic. Culturally shared parables like "the seagull and the clam" have great psychological impact, with the power to influence the course of human life. In effect, symbols become the "social transmitters" of cultural understanding.

Hindu stories are probably the richest in imagery of all living religions. The Hindu religion has survived for thousands of years in spite of repeated conquests from foreign powers who brought with them different religious beliefs. According to the Hindu faith, men are often unable to combat the powers of evil. In situations such as these, the Hindu god Vishnu temporarily returns to help the people on earth in their struggle against the evil person or situation. Thus through symbol, there develops a mental preparedness, or cognitive schema, to emulate Vishnu in the struggle for group cohesiveness and survival.

One of Vishnu's more interesting reincarnations is as Narasinha, who comes to the earth to free the world from the powers of a demon king who had obtained a promise from the god Brahma. The promise consisted of an immunity that would prevent the demon king from being killed by man or beast, by day or by night, inside or outside his house, in heaven or on earth. Instead of using this miraculous safeguard from death to help the people, the demon king became so depraved that he forbade worship of all other gods and demanded the worship of himself in their place. He even attempted to kill his own son, whom he found doing obeisance to Vishnu. The demon king finally created so much misery for the people on earth that Vishnu returned in the form of Narasinha, the man-lion. He immediately attacked the demon king, took him to a doorway of a house at twilight, held him on his knees, and tore out his heart.

The story of Narasinha illustrates the concept that good will triumph over evil in spite of all odds to the contrary (i.e., through perseverance, success will follow—recall the sparrows' message to Peter Rabbit). Also, consider the power of visual imagery in this story. Narasinha is usually pictured as the half-man, half-lion hybrid holding the demon king on his knees. Combination creatures are not only found in other avatars of Vishnu, but are also common in mythology throughout the world. For example, the Olmec people, who lived in the land occupied by present-day Veracruz in Mexico, believed that they were descendants of a mating between a jaguar and a goddess. Much of the art of the Olmecs depicts people as werejaguars, hybrids of men and jaguars. The centaur of ancient Greek mythology is a hybrid of a man and a horse, while the Roman griffin has the head and wings of an eagle and the body of a lion.

As depicted in "Reflections on an Indian Train" and the illustration that follows (Figure IV.2), fantasy is a powerful wish-fulfilling device for easing life's heavy burdens.

Reflections on an Indian Train

(Where the solution is the problem and its genesis)

The people are so poor and so many

Only fantasy can fulfill their desire

Where there is little to possess

Detachment becomes a virtue

When horror is normal

Shock abounds

If the self is so neglected

The gods are even more mighty

When the senses are so assaulted

Pleasure becomes a vice

Where life is chaotic

Ritual provides relief

Where death lurks in each corner

Preservation of life becomes a fetish

Where substance is remote

The gimmick is fascination

Where nurturance is so sparse

The feminine is worshipped

When life is compensation

Rationalization is a savior

—H. Milkman (1980)

Figure IV.2   Fantasy and reality. Symbols are the "social transmitters" of cultural understanding.

In the folklore of seafarers, mermaids symbolize the sailor's ultimate dichotomy: rescue by a gorgeous companion (wish) from the nightmare death at sea (fear). The last stanza of an old English sea shanty, "Married to a Mermaid," supports this view:

We lowered a boat to find him; we thought to see his corpse,

When up to the top, he came with a shock, and said in a voice so hoarse,

"My ship mates and my mess mates, oh, do not weep for me,

For I'm married to a mermaid at the bottom of the deep blue sea."

Science and Religion

Whether called hybrid creatures, omnipotent deities, or just plain superstition, there appears to be a basic human drive to believe in something transcendent, incomprehensible, and otherworldly, beyond the reach of scientific explanation. Even people who claim to be atheists are prone to magical thinking. Scott Atran (2002), an anthropologist at the National Center for Scientific Research in Paris, presented college students with a wooden box that he said was an African relic. He told them that if they had negative sentiments toward religion, the box would destroy whatever they placed inside. When instructed to put their pencil in the box, the nonbelievers had no problem. Next came their driver's license—most did, but with considerable hesitation. When he told them to put their hand in, however, few complied.

Why do we believe in the supernatural beyond all reason? According to anthropologists, religion exists in virtually every culture on earth, with common notions of an afterlife and belief in the power of prayer to change the course of human events (Henig, 2007). This is certainly true in the United States, where about 60% of the population report that they believe in the devil and hell, 70% believe in angels, and 92% believe in a personal God (Henig, 2007).

Atran (2002) posits a biological explanation for the belief in God. He regards the god concept as an evolutionary by-product of a complex neurological matrix for survival, yet with no functional value of its own. In architecture, this may be compared to the V-shaped structure formed between two adjacent rounded arches, or the empty triangular space beneath a staircase. Stephen Jay Gould (1997, 2002), the famed evolutionary biologist at Harvard, coined the term "spandrel," borrowed from architecture to describe a human trait that has no adaptive value—like the triangular space beneath a staircase that could remain neutral or be made functional by using the area for a closet or storage cabinet. So, if God is a spandrel, what is the evolutionary value of the neurologically mediated cognitive structures from which it derives?

The hardships facing early humans favored the development of certain cognitive tools that increased the probability of survival: (1) the ability to recognize creatures that might cause harm, (2) the capacity to develop causal explanations for natural events, and (3) recognition that there are other beings that have minds of their own. Anthropologists refer to these propensities respectively as "agent detection," "causal reasoning," and "theory of mind" (a.k.a. folk psychology), respectively. From an evolutionary perspective, one need only to fill in the blanks or connect the dots across time, place, and culture to show how religion is a universal by-product of these protective neuropsychological devices.

Elkind (1970) noted some remarkable parallels between four basic elements of religion and four stages of a child's intellectual growth. First, every religion has a concept of a god, a deity that is permanent and immortal across all time and space. This parallels the child's understanding of the *permanent object* by the end of the first year of life. There develops the belief that people or things no longer available to the senses will remain present.

Second, by the age of 2 the child attains the ability to create, comprehend, and employ symbols. For example, anything that floats can become a toy boat. This is paralleled by the presence of *religious symbols* that stand for elements of pious belief (e.g., wine and bread in Christianity, the Torah in Judaism, and head coverings in Islam).

Third, religion carries a set of *rituals,* whether kneeling, standing, or rocking during prayer, or taking Holy Communion. This is paralleled by the development of rules that children adopt at about the age of 6 or 7 when they enter the "age of reason." Children can play scripted games or create structures and rules to play by on their own.

Finally, during adolescence there is a propensity to consider ideal life circumstances and fact-challenging propositions (e.g., a world without poverty or war). Similarly, all theologies provide *idealistic visions* and urge their adherents to live according to the highest standards of conduct (e.g., compassion and right actions in Buddhism; the Ten Commandments in Judaism, Islam, and Christianity).

The implication of these parallels is that our developmental modes of thought provide a predisposition for comprehending the primary elements of religion, which also parallel the four basic elements of science: conservation, symbolism, ritual or experimentation, and theory. From this perspective, religion and science represent alternative means of applying our four basic modes of thought, neither one right or wrong.

Einstein (1937/1956) had a similar idea (Figure IV.3):

All religions, arts and sciences are branches of the same tree. All these aspirations are directed toward ennobling man's life, lifting it from the sphere of mere physical existence and leading the individual towards freedom. (p. 7)

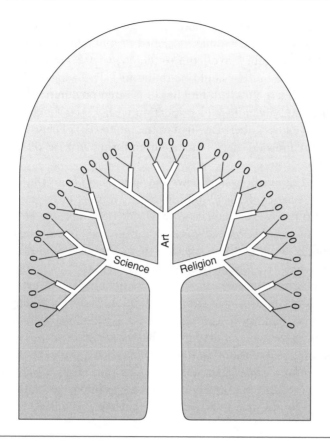

Figure IV.3   **Branches of the same tree.** All these aspirations are directed toward ennobling man's life.

Personal Fantasy

On an individual level, the images of politicians, deities, prophets, or movie stars become internalized as guiding factors in personal life. We identify or put ourselves in the place of the darlings of our time and shape our behavior through vicarious experience of their lives. Idolizing, or overidentification with highly visible members of a community, is yet another vehicle for patching the self from without. In some cases, the fantasy of being *like* one's chosen idol unconsciously ensures the wish to be *liked by* that idol and to experience some measure of the idol's success. How many articles of clothing are sold every day carrying the logo of a famous sports figure or team? It is not at all unusual for members of a social group to mimic the dress and look of their media heroes. Scarlett Johansson, Angelina Jolie, Jessica Simpson, Brad Pitt, Matt Damon, and George Clooney each has his or her share of look-alikes, not to even mention the millions of sports fans who walk around with T-shirts or hats symbolizing their athlete heroes.

Some individuals form pathological identifications with their heroes and antiheroes. Mark Chapman reasoned that he murdered John Lennon "because he loved him." In a letter to the *New York Times,* he wrote that the answer to the murder could be found in J. D. Salinger's *The Catcher in the Rye* (Holden, 2008). John Hinkley's attempted murder of President Reagan involved his fantasy identification with Travis Bickle, a psychotic assassin (played by Robert DeNiro) in the movie *Taxi Driver.* Columbine-style copycat murders may remain an enduring feature of U.S. culture (Nizza, 2007).

Based on 132 five-hour interviews and survey data from 18,000 people in Britain and America, Kahr (2008) unveils the results of his comprehensive research into their sexual fantasies. In *Who's Been Sleeping in Your Head: The Secret World of Sexual Fantasies,* Kahr not only reveals the ubiquity of sexual fantasy (9 out of 10 people have them), but also reports on the common occurrence of people having such lurid fantasies as doing disgusting things in front of strangers, or relaxing by thinking about extreme sexual violence toward unsuspecting strangers. Kahr explains his findings to mean that people use fantasy to rewrite unpleasant childhood memories, sometimes to wreak revenge on absent or abusive adults or to redress harm by sanitizing unpleasant memories. Rather than viewing sexual fantasy as a sign of troubled relationships, Kahr sees them as a kind of safety valve for blowing off dangerous steam. As shown in the case example below, the benefit of wish fulfillment is a strong element of the fantasy experience.

Case Example: Wish-Fulfilling Dream

Dr. Saul's (not his real name) dream illustrates how a powerful fantasy, accessed after awakening from sleep, can be an effective tool for coping with stress. Prior to the dream, Dr. Saul was engaged in a fierce bureaucratic struggle at work. He perceived institutional attempts to crush a professional goal of his that symbolized 15 years of research and academic concentration. He was considering abandoning his project and resigning from work. The dream began with the visualization of a theater marquee that featured the film *Holocaust From the Side of the Germans.* Dr. Saul awakened with full recollection of his dream and wrote the following verbatim report:

Last night before I went to sleep I was feeling persecuted by a number of people, primarily faculty and other associates with whom I've recently had some rather unpleasant business dealings. I had a vivid dream of Nazi persecution in which I saw a billboard that read, "Holocaust From the Side of the Germans, shown in cinema vérité."

The dream was extremely lucid and portrayed huge German armies engulfing relatively small groups of Jews who were armed with primitive jousting instruments: long sticks with hatchets tied on the ends. The weapons were modifications of the stickball bats I used as a child in the Bronx. In my adolescent bursts of power I reveled in the thrill of hitting a rubber ball a distance of more than three sewers.

I recall the feeling of becoming so irate about having to defend my right to exist as a free human being that I, along with hundreds of others, lunged into ferocious battle with the German tormentors. My whole being shrieked in an exhilarated frenzy as I maimed and killed German soldiers, helter-skelter, all the time thinking that I would most probably die.

Miraculously, I survived the episode and was amazed at how nicely the Germans behaved toward the Jews the following day. Suddenly the Jewish people were walking in peace among Nazis, albeit a temporary state of tranquility.

I awakened with a distinct feeling of rejuvenation along with the conscious thought that I had acted heroically. I was true to myself and my people by successfully opposing the sadistic tormentors. As soon as I woke up, I pondered how I could create this wonderful dream again. That morning I met with the college president, who gave me complete freedom to carry on with my project.

Clearly the dream fantasy was a symbolic representation of what the dreamer was experiencing in waking life. He was of Jewish descent and felt exposed to hatred similar to what he had learned about the Jewish experience in Nazi Germany. Upon waking, he reported a sense of increased vigor, optimism, and heightened commitment to pursue his academic goals. The tension of the past week had suddenly dissipated. The vivid dream fantasy served to channel an aggressive impulse that might otherwise have been expressed through self-punishment (e.g., alcohol abuse) or self-defeating hostility toward his employers. Instead, he would stand up to his opponents and ask the college president to intervene.

Daydreams or night dreams are augmented by fantasy objects in our midst. In *The Movies on Your Mind* (H. R. Greenberg, 1975), psychoanalyst Greenberg shows how cinema preferences may be used as diagnostic interviews, much like the Rorschach inkblot test. In analyzing his patients, Greenberg discovered that most were at least "moderately addicted" to the cinema and that movie associations were an effective route to the unconscious. A patient's ruminations about a particular movie may give invaluable insight into his or her childhood conflicts, troubled present, or anxious premonitions about the future. Greenberg cites the example of an adolescent with a school phobia who reported that his favorite film was *King of Kings*.

> He especially enjoyed the part where the Roman soldiers pounded the nails into Jesus' hands. I discovered that his cranium was jammed with homosexual and masochistic fantasies: he avoided school because of a tremendous fear—and hidden wish—that a gang of local bullies would beat and rape him. In his daydreams, he would show a Christ-like forbearance and pity for his tormentors, so that they would give up their evil ways and worship, rather than despise him. (p. 4)

Certainly, *King of Kings* helped this young man to validate his persecutory beliefs and to organize his underlying fears and wishes. Greenberg finds that those most prone to movie mania are rigid, inhibited types who characteristically avoid any close interpersonal contact. Individuals such as these become intolerably anxious when faced with the spontaneity of a personal encounter and only feel alive as vicarious participants in adventures of their movie heroes.

Overview Summary

Our ability to create mental events that stand as intermediaries between biological impulse and instinctual reactions may be the single most important difference between humans and all other life on earth. This overview examines the gift of fantasy as an essential means for experiencing pleasure, deriving meaning, and enhancing survival. The human proclivity for imagination, however, carries the same abuse liability as our needs for arousal and satiation.

The interplay between our internal mental experience and information from outside sets the stage for individualized representations and interpretations of the world. The development of self-concept, cognitive styles, emotional reactivity, and behavioral responses are all, in part, determined by fantasy images and imaginative thought. The typical U.S. 8- to 18-year-old spends an average of 6 hours per day on electronic media. When we include the phenomenon of "media multitasking," the figure expands to 8.5 hours. Many teenagers spend more time with electronic media than they do participating in any other element of life, including sleep.

If the child is not sufficiently practiced in the use of fantasy and pretend play, deficits or constriction in representational capacity can occur. The child, and later the adult, may become limited to a pattern of restricted and concrete thought. Drug abuse, delinquency, and various forms of hedonic escape may provide "false refuge" for those who lack internal means for managing the "emotional themes of life."

Whereas fairy tales largely provide guideposts for children to master the tasks of growing up, religion and myths provide people with ethical prescriptions for how to conduct themselves within the boundaries of cultural norms. The adaptive function of imagination, however, far exceeds that of helping to establish meaning, purpose, and patterns of conduct in an often confusing existence. Dreams and reverie are examined as adaptive means to reduce tension and to channel impulses that might otherwise result in stress, emotional discomfort, and negative behavioral outcomes. Although fantasy affords us an internal system for reducing stress, when imagination is more satisfactory than direct action, we begin to tread on the road to harmful consequences. With each experience of pleasure or removal from pain, the probability of seeking out an imaginary solution increases. Our work, love, and play may progressively falter as the result of an increasing reliance on imaginary pleasures.

9

Virtual Reality and Electronic Bogeymen

Bogeyman: *An imaginary person or monster that causes fear or is invoked to cause fear, especially in children*

—Encarta (online dictionary)

Introduction: The Evolution of Electronic Media

In Western culture, the gods of science and technology have developed synthetic tools for fulfilling wishes and satisfying unmet needs. The 21st century has seen the emergence of electronic media beyond our wildest dreams. Television, which dominated the "pixilated world" through the mid-1990s, has been assailed by a throng of electronic media devices including cell phones, iPods, video games, instant messaging, interactive multiplayer video games, virtual reality sites, Web social networks, and e-mail (Brooks-Gunn & Donahue, 2008). The impact of massively multiplayer online role-playing games (MMORPGs) is of particular significance during adolescence, when one considers that the primary developmental task is to form a coherent sense of self. The possibility of substituting cyberspace personas for face-to-face interaction may facilitate peer group interactions, yet some players may suffer the aftershock of failure to develop the capacity for genuine closeness. "In other words, he could put on a new identity like a new suit of clothes, becoming someone who walked on water, healed others, and cast lightning bolts, in stark contrast to his daily experience of himself as inadequate" (Allison, von Wahlde, Shockley, & Gabbard, 2006, p. 381).

As examined in the next section, *craving for intimacy* is a root cause of suffering and addictive behavior. If fantasy relationships take precedence over direct human contact for some people, how does this phenomenon affect primary needs for love and belonging? Our discussion of virtual reality begins with the evolution of three great waves of electronic media: television, video games, and MMORPGs.

In *Four Arguments for the Elimination of Television,* Mander (1978) presented the most scathing indictment of Filo Farnsworth's monumental 1927 invention: TV.

- *First,* TV is limited as a source for gathering information, compromising other, more vital forms of human interaction and experience (Figure 9.1).
- *Second,* TV is foremost a political device. By regulating the information that people receive and therefore what they think, TV is used for social control and human domination. The enormous human capacity for identification and modeling has been a means of steering human actions in every civilization. A cogent example was the Soviet satellite system until the 1990s. It spanned ten time zones with high priority given to the broadcast of socialist achievement and the rhetoric of Soviet philosophy.
- *Third,* TV produces a hypnotic-addictive effect because of the neurophysiologic responses of human beings to the television signal. By introducing a device that renders viewers passive they become unable or unwilling to attend to many of their own best interests and needs of society.
- *Fourth,* TV has only a very limited capacity to improve one's understanding of life. It characteristically reduces complex issues into overly simplistic representations of reality. The mentality derived from TV programming tends to be materialistic, devoid of meaning, and lacking in real-life experience.

By the early 1980s, we progressed to the second level of the media revolution. Rossel Waugh (2006) describes video games as a new and more advanced stage in our addiction to media. Scripts were parallel to the basic dramatic

Figure 9.1   **Information at the expense of experience.** TV viewing compromises more direct forms of interaction and human experience.

themes of cartoons, Westerns, space fantasies, or murder mysteries. However, whereas television requires passive observation with occasional lapses in concentration, video games require full attention and active participation. The games graphically play out fantasy confrontations with fundamental anxieties of life: conquest and defeat, pursuit and flight, heroic struggle, envelopment and escape. Participants enjoy fantasy experiments with anxiety-provoking or life-threatening situations in a limited and safe way.

The vast majority of people who play video games use them for enjoyment and relaxation, with no problems of compulsion or loss of control. Yet, for some, the use of interactive video technology is dangerously enthralling because it provides fantasy reprieve from problems in living. The bizarre, yet true, case example below illustrates how a young man improvised a scheme for using video images and cocaine, combined with biofeedback, to inundate his nucleus accumbens with giant spurts of dopamine.

Case Example: Virtual Sex

A 30-year-old Los Angeles cocaine user reported that he was no longer satisfied having sexual intercourse with "biological units." A career musician, familiar with electronics, he was able to develop a biofeedback contrivance that could register changes in penile erection and transmit the information to an Apple computer. He would mechanically masturbate via an automatic vacuum device, developed to provide sexual stimulation for people who could not masturbate because of spinal injury. The penile biofeedback would program the computer to project increasingly explicit pornographic footage, excerpted from a database of 400 films. The whole experience was augmented by repeated and heavy use of cocaine.

Through this synthetic orgy, he was able to manifest ecstatic states that corresponded to the great surges of dopamine delivered to the pleasure centers of his brain.

SOURCE: David Smith, MD, June 1992, personal communication.

In the more mundane world of basic video game attraction, the desire (for some, the compulsion) to play can be explained from a cognitive-behavioral perspective. In terms of operant conditioning (behavioral component), when an action is followed by reward, the probability of that behavior recurring will increase. Video games provide a series of intermittent (variably timed) prizes that are contingent upon positive outcomes (i.e., successful maneuvers are registered via points, lights, noises, and free replays). In terms of addiction, if using an intoxicant results in a deposit of dopamine in the nucleus accumbens (the reward), the behavior will increase in frequency.

In the cognitive domain, fantasies of empowerment are even more compelling than the rewards associated with skill development and competitive success. The pre-scripted drama of escaping danger and conquering hostile or alien forces is both exciting and compelling. Fears associated with technology, natural disasters, and wars diminish through the fantasy of controlling negative, potentially tragic situations. For example, the wish-fulfilling fantasy of surviving a military invasion or even a nuclear holocaust contributes to the compulsion to play. The 1980s produced such prolific games as *Missile*

Command (civilization is defended by using an antiballistic missile system to protect six major cities), *Space Invaders* (where the object is to attack aliens—strange creatures from outer space that threaten our moon base), and *SCRAM* (in which players use their home computers to build and control a nuclear power plant and control a meltdown).

Although there is much pleasure in the fantasy of vanquishing evil, a major disadvantage of video games is that they constrain imagination. Like other "pre-scripted toys," the player is restricted by limited play options. In the simplest form of pre-scripted devices, dolls have been programmed to shoot, cry, burp, or wet (or even talk like George W. Bush), making it difficult for the child to invent alternatives. Nonetheless, the pre-scripting ploy is beneficial for manufacturers. The initial appeal of the game is high, but boredom and abandonment quickly set in. In short measure, players look for a similar play object, only with a slightly modified script. So at the onset of the 21st century, we have progressed to the third level of human–media interaction: massively multiplayer online role-playing games.

Massively Multiplayer Online Role-Playing Games

Massively multiplayer online role-playing games are developed worlds with intense visual and auditory components (Cole & Griffiths, 2007). Players have the capacity to control the movement of their characters, engage with the environment, network with fellow gamers around the world, and experience new situations that are not possible in real life (Calleja, 2007). Millions of people are attracted to the fulfilling rise of status and power for their character and the authority to create their character or avatar by themselves.

Thanks to the progress of third-generation games such as *Second Life* and *World of Warcraft (WoW),* video and online gamers are increasingly moving from single- and dual-player games to "massively multiplayer" systems where thousands of players can interact simultaneously—just as the acronym says (Bainbridge, 2007).

The increasing popularity of these online games has exceeded the motion picture industry in terms of dollars spent. In 2006, "gamers" forked out $2.1 billion on virtual goods and services (Greenemeier, 2007). People are spending and making real-life money in accordance with their characters' role. According to Greenemeier, hard-core gamers tend to see their virtual property and goods as status symbols; some report feeling social pressure to have a significant amount of money put into these alternative lives. Unlike the popular view, research has shown that most players are not adolescents, but adults (Bainbridge, 2007; Cole & Griffiths, 2007).

Players use online games to create characters through which they feel free to explore new people, objects, and surroundings. The resounding themes of social interaction, working on a team, mastery and manipulation of characters, status building, and exploration are common. According to Bainbridge (2007), "Virtual worlds are creating a very new context in which young people are socialized to group norms, learn intellectual skills, and express their individuality" (p. 475). Not only are these games entertaining, but they are also used for escape and opportunities not found in everyday life (Bessiere, Seay, & Kiesler, 2007). Players may use their avatars (movable three-dimensional images used to represent humans or other conscious beings in cyberspace) to express their ideal selves, or aspects thereof. This enhances a sense of personal power by creating a representation of who they see themselves as or who they would like to be. Gamers are connected to their online persona psychologically, socially, and emotionally. They can use the anonymity of the Internet to manifest wish-fulfilling fantasies and to explore aspects of themselves not available in the real world (Bessiere et al., 2007).

Virtual-world gamers tend to find emotional satisfaction by being able to select environments and life events compatible with desired moods. If a player is missing excitement, the games will create it for him or her. If the player is experiencing too much excitement, the game can be used to calm the self with peaceful imagery and friendly interactions. If a player feels intellectually understimulated, he or she can find interest in a game's strategic challenges. Similar to addicts who choose drugs that coincide with their natural means of coping (Milkman & Frosch, 1973; Milkman & Sunderwirth, 1983, 1987, 1998), players choose games that correspond with their attitudes and emotional states (Calleja, 2007). Thrill seekers will likely seek out exciting, arousing, action-packed games, while those who relish shutting down may select calming or stress-reducing scenarios.

As evidence of the breakthrough of virtual reality into the mainstream culture, high-profile adult cartoons such as *The Simpsons* and *South Park* have begun to caricature MMORPG influence. In episode 1817, Lisa Simpson tells her mother, Marge, who has become consumed with a game very similar to *WoW*, "You're like Christopher Columbus. You discovered something millions of people already knew about." Marge finds the online game *Earthland Realms* and spends every waking minute playing it, even staying up all night the first time she is introduced to it.

South Park, on the other hand, really likes to push buttons as it depicts the four main characters, Cartman, Stan, Kyle, and Kenny, becoming so immersed in *WoW* that they stop taking care of themselves. The boys become extremely overweight and full of pimples as they no longer feel the need to do anything but play; they eat, consume high-sugar energy drinks, and stay inside on the computer rather than going outside to play with their other school friends. In an ironic twist, the show depicts the "creators" of *WoW* sitting in a meeting room, astonished at four newer players who have increased 50 levels in 3 weeks. One exclaims, "Oh my God, they must have no lives at all." And indeed these four boys have given up everything in order to band together and destroy the man behind the powerful character they are trying to get rid of because he keeps killing everyone. When they succeed, after spending weeks of nonstop playing, by killing the evil character, they wonder what they are to do next. An obese, zit-filled Cartman replies that they can finally play outside because that guy's character will no longer kill them. Some of the top online games include *World of Warcraft, Second Life, Starcraft, Runescape, Halo,* and *Lord of the Rings Online.* Our focus here is on *WoW* and *Second Life* because they are two of the most popular MMORPGs.

Second Life and *World of Warcraft* have different underlying purposes. *Second Life* avatars are usually depicted as the identities of the humans behind the game, while *WoW* refers to the people playing as surreal warring characters, so the players are slightly more distanced from the game than their *Second Life* counterparts (Bainbridge, 2007).

World of Warcraft

As of 2008, *World of Warcraft* was reported to have 9.3 million users that spent up to $14.99 per month to play (Melby, 2008). *WoW* is a game that allows a person to take his or her virtual character on quests, fight monsters, build skills, and interact with other players as well as computer-controlled characters. The rewards from successful quests include in-game money, items, status, and increased levels, which in turn allow the player to become more skilled and powerful. The character can develop noncombat skills in what are known as *professions*. Professions allow the character to create or enhance items such as weapons. The quests in the game get more complex as the player moves up through the levels, and it takes an increasing number of people teaming up to succeed. By triumphing in a quest, a player is rewarded with goods, gold, experience, or reputation. Reputation, or status as it is called in other areas, is a very important and complex part of the game. Increased reputation allows for price reduction from in-game merchandise vendors, more access to restricted parts of the world, and the ability to purchase special items.

One die-hard *WoW* aficionado explains his attraction to the game this way:

World of Warcraft offers a sort of second reality for me to dwell in. I can band together with others and accomplish great and daring missions, gain friendships, and feel more powerful than I do in everyday life. I think I am so hooked on cyber games because they give me an escape from the lonely aspect of life and I have a place where I can feel welcome no matter what, even wanted, and in this other reality I am powerful. It's great to have a way to unwind at the end of the day and get my mind off whatever is bothering me. I get excited if I know the workday is almost done and I can go home and play for an hour, to settle down. If it's a bad day at work, I might play longer, just to make sure I don't bring the rotten feelings into my relationship.

Second Life

As of 2007, Linden Labs, owner and creator of *Second Life*, reported 9.8 million users, although some were no longer active (Melby, 2008). One of the main points of attraction is that this online world is created by the residents. Everything in the *Second Life* "metaverse" is constructed by its inhabitants, and there is always plenty to find and do. A person can shop, play, eat, party, gamble, have sex, and even wed in *Second Life*. There are nightclubs and strip clubs, and many people profit by working in or selling these services such as escorting, prostituting, and stripping. Not only do the residents create the world, but they also create the character they want to be. They can make their avatars realistic and similar to themselves, or they can make them fanciful, changing their gender, ethnicity, and the like. Although most people feel they have found a place that is more accepting and tolerant than in "real life," people still bring their real-life attitudes and biases to the game.

Residents of *Second Life* own the intellectual property inherent in their creations. Players can determine whether the inventions, architecture, or other materials that they conceive of can be copied, modified, or transferred. In accordance with these property rights, residents actively buy, sell, and trade their creations in Linden dollars (the in-world currency), which can be exchanged for real money, that is, real-life currency ("Virtual Online Worlds," 2006).

Boellstorff (2008), an anthropologist, used an ethnographic approach in studying the virtual world of *Second Life*. For 2 years he lived among the residents, participated in everyday activities, and spoke with avatars about their experiences. He found this virtual reality to have subcultures, its own economy, and even its own celebrities. A virtual newspaper would often report on real-life events, or real-life musicians holding virtual concerts. He saw that many people found relationships, friendships, family, and sexual experiences. They were able to experiment with their creativity, sexuality, gender fantasies, and social well-being. Boellstorff found both kindness and cruelty, just as one would find in the real world. He speaks of "griefers," or people who deliberately set out to annoy or harm others. Conversely, altruism was also generously displayed, as he witnessed many acts of sharing or giving away items as well as avatars helping one another with explanatory texts.

Second Life is not merely a game. Its seemingly unlimited capacity engulfs participants in different realities and has enormous potential as an educative tool. Peter Yellowlees (cited in "Virtual Online Worlds," 2006), a professor of psychiatry at the University of California, Davis, has used *Second Life* to create a virtual mental hospital. Psychiatric residents walk through a hospital ward. Suddenly, a picture on the wall flashes the word "shitface." Unexpectedly, the floor morphs into a path of stones above the clouds, and the screen on an in-ward TV changes from a normal political speech to a prominent politician shouting, "Go ahead and kill yourself, you wretch!"

Yellowlees was able to create a window into the mind of a person suffering with schizophrenia, exemplifying the versatility of virtual reality in the realm of education. He leases an island in *Second Life,* for $300 per month, where he built a clinic that is a virtual replica of the one in Sacramento where his students practice. Yellowlees's students are given avatars so they can attend his lectures in *Second Life* and experience the psychiatric symptoms of the disorder that he is presenting ("Virtual Online Worlds," 2006).

Online Game Addiction

As with any substance or action that produces a change in the neurochemistry of the brain, the Internet can become addicting. Research has shown that people can lose control of their lives after becoming involved so deeply with games, chat rooms, or even online shopping (Young, 2004). Many online players will skip basic needs such as sleeping and eating, even ignoring work and school so that they can keep playing these games. Young reported that nearly 6% of Internet users have symptoms of addiction, while many more fit the category of abuse.

What distinguishes Internet addiction from drug addiction? If, unrelated to school or work, a person experiences one or more of the following patterns, he or she may be suffering from abuse of or dependence on the Internet, just as if the object were alcohol or any other intoxicant:

- Preoccupied with the Internet
- Using the Internet for increasing periods of time
- Tried unsuccessfully to control or cut back use
- Feel irritable and depressed when attempting to control use
- Staying online longer than planned
- Lying to close people about use
- Using the Internet to escape or cope with problems
- Continuation despite harmful consequences

According to Young (2004), Internet addicts can indulge themselves for 40 to 80 hours per week with sessions running up to 20 hours. Thus, the compulsion to use tends to disrupt sleep, adversely affect work, and impair school performance. Other problems involve lack of proper exercise, poor eating habits, and weakening of the immune system. Some addicts also suffer physical disability due to carpal tunnel syndrome.

Perhaps the most damaging aspect of Internet addiction, however, is the impact it has on relationships (Young, 2004). Long-term relationships can be harmed or even destroyed when a person becomes compulsively involved in a cyber affair. Why would a person go online and cheat on his or her real-life partner with someone the person has never met and most likely never will? It appears that in the virtual world, people can interact with less inhibition and more honesty, revealing themselves more fully and quickly, which in turn leads to an intimacy that might not be achieved for months or years in a real-life relationship. Some indications that a significant other may be pursuing a cyber affair include a change in sleep patterns, the need for privacy with the computer, responsibilities being ignored, getting caught in lies, changes in personality, a loss of interest in sex, and decreased interest in maintaining the relationship.

Internet abuse and addiction is an area of concern across high schools and colleges throughout the United States (Young, 2004). According to Young, approximately 58% of the student population may be experiencing some compromise of their school performance due to their use of the Internet. They report poor study habits, failed classes, and lower grades. It is not surprising that a youthful college student can get entrapped, as free and unlimited access to the Internet and computers is the status quo. With students often leaving home for the first time, the newfound freedom can result in excessive online gaming, shopping, and dating.

A third crisis in Internet abuse is related to employees abusing the Internet while at work. According to Young (2004), "employee abuse of the Internet during work hours results in lost productivity, negative publicity, and possible legal liability" (p. 410). About 70% of companies provide access to the Internet, and while 64% of these have taken corrective action against Internet abuse, 30% have actually fired employees for their online activities (Young, 2004). Employers lose billions of dollars annually from online misuse. In addition to loss of productivity, companies lose revenue from negative publicity. When a company receives bad press from employee Internet abuse, consumers lose confidence. Finally, under the Americans with Disabilities Act it is illegal to terminate employment when the company itself provides the user with a "virtual intoxicant." Wrongful termination lawsuits are increasingly filed under this pretense as companies are attempting to crack down on the unproductive surfing of the Net during paid time.

According to Cole and Griffiths (2007), excessive online interaction negatively affects social development, lowers self-esteem, makes for social inadequacy, and often creates more social anxiety. The games are socially interactive, but this is at the expense of creating and maintaining social interaction with other real-life humans. Although computer games are available to a great number of players at any one time, only one person needs to be at an isolated computer to partake. Individuals often become obsessed with their virtual selves, seeing them as a true part of themselves at the expense of responsibilities such as school, work, and relationships. People go to *Second Life* and *World of Warcraft* to create an ideal self, to experiment, to sell their creations, even to seek social and emotional interaction (Melby, 2008). Some may believe they are more social than usual because they talk to many people online and reveal more personal things to the other avatars. In reality, being excessively online takes away from face-to-face contact. Gamers often consider their online friends to be better than or as good as their real-life friends.

While men tend to engage in virtual reality to improve their self-perception of higher status and success, women are more apt to prefer the social aspects of these games. More research on pathological computer use is taking place, and such use is now being seen as a problem. In South Korea, for example, there are nearly 50 treatment centers specializing in this area (C. Mears, 2007).

Is the Internet Good or Bad?

Internet activity reflects the profound drive toward survival and self-realization present in all humankind. Through identification, imitation, and observational learning, young people are gaining the skills to manage the technology of the future. In response to the criticism of the computer's limited interactional capabilities, as evidenced by such innovations as *World of Warcraft* and *Second Life,* we are witnessing an increased development of software that provides opportunities for chance, paradox, ambiguity, intimacy, and humor. There appears to be no turning back. The line between virtual and actual reality has become so blurred that a clear distinction is no longer possible.

In a special issue of *The Future of Children*[1] entitled *Children and Electronic Media,* Subrahmanyam and Greenfield (2008) explore the question of whether online communication has made teenagers more isolated and emotionally damaged or whether it actually strengthens their social connections. The authors conclude that although we are just in the early days of this type of research positive effects overshadow the negatives. They find that children and youth primarily use Internet tools to enhance communication with people they already know. In the past few years, even though some children and youth have continued to interact with people that they don't know—in chat rooms, bulletin boards, or online multiplayer games—communication with strangers has declined. Such communication tools, however, should not necessarily be construed as negative. Although the new means for social interaction can provide a platform for bullying and predation, Subrahmanyam and Greenfield dispute the notion that the Internet is the cause of the problem. Rather, the negative behavior is simply being transferred to a new context—from offline to online. In an important sense, the Internet may have become the latest scapegoat for more basic problems in Western culture. As we are so immersed in the new digital age, it is not surprising that juvenescence zealously embraces a symbol that distinguishes it from earlier times. The key challenge is for parents to be knowledgeable and aware of inappropriate Internet involvement and to provide guidance for their children.

Heavily influenced by science, perhaps the most eagerly anticipated video game of all time has come of age. *Spore,* which first appeared on the commercial market in September 2008, was developed by Will Wright, best known as the creator of *The Sims* ("Will Wright on Creating 'The Sims' and 'SimCity,'" 2000), in which players run the lives of a virtual family. *The*

Sims is the best-selling video game franchise in history, with sales exceeding $100 million. *Spore* is designed to simulate the process of evolution. Players start with single-cell microbes that can evolve into intelligent, multicellular creatures capable of building civilizations, colonizing the galaxy, and populating new planets (Zimmer, 2008). *Spore,* possibly the mother of all future video games, may symbolically point to a new branch of the evolutionary tree. In terms of human evolution, it is entirely conceivable that natural selection and mutation may favor humans with the kind of neural networking (i.e., computer-friendly brains) that can thrive in the computer age.

Chapter Summary

This chapter traces the evolution of electronic media from the invention of TV in 1927 through the emergence of interactive video games to the development of massively multiplayer online role playing games at the onset of the 21st century.

In MMORPGs, players create three-dimensional online characters (avatars) with whom they explore new people, objects, and environments. The themes of social interaction, working in a team, mastery and manipulation of characters, status building, and exploration are common. *Second Life* and *World of Warcraft* are examined as preeminent examples of online role-playing games with somewhat different agendas. While *Second Life* avatars are usually fairly realistic manifestations of the humans behind the game, *WoW* involves surrealistic warring characters, thus permitting more emotional distance than that of their *Second Life* counterparts.

From a sociological perspective, virtual worlds are creating a new context in which young people are socialized to group norms, learn intellectual skills, and express their individuality. Not only are these games entertaining, but they are also used for escape and to explore opportunities not found in everyday life. Players may use their avatars to express their ideal selves, or aspects thereof, thus augmenting their sense of personal power. Gamers are connected to their online personas psychologically, socially, and emotionally. They can use the anonymity of the Internet to manifest wish-fulfilling fantasies and to explore aspects of themselves not available in the real world.

Fascination and enthusiasm for online activity morph into abuse and dependence when the medium becomes a vehicle for harmful consequences. Online players may skip basic needs such as sleep and eating, or ignore work and school so that they can keep playing. Nearly 6% of Internet users show patterns of dependence, while many more fit the category of abuse. Symptoms of Internet addiction include, but are not limited to, preoccupation with the Internet, increasing periods of activity, lack of success at cutting back, and continuation despite harmful consequences.

Internet addiction is particularly damaging when virtual relationships substitute for real-life intimacy. Another area of concern is the toll it takes on students who compromise their academic standing as the Internet becomes a pervasive element in their lives. A third crisis involves employees who abuse the Internet while at work.

Has online communication made teenagers more isolated and emotionally damaged, or has it actually strengthened their social connections? The authors agree with the research concluding that, although we are still in the early days of this type of study, "the positives outweigh the negatives." At its worst, the Internet can have negative effects on social development and self-esteem as well as contribute to social inadequacy and increased levels of social anxiety. On balance, Internet activity reflects the universal drive toward survival and self-realization. It has enormous potential as an "engine of creativity," a tool for enhanced learning. It is conceivable that natural selection and mutation may ultimately favor individuals with neural networking designed to thrive in the computer age.

Note

1. A collaboration of the Woodrow Wilson School of Public and International Affairs at Princeton University and the Brookings Institution.

10

Fantasy and the Drug Experience

Figure 10.1　　**Fantasy and the drug experience.**

Were it not for the motion and color play of the soul, man would suffocate and rot away in his great passion, idleness.

—Carl G. Jung

Introduction: The "Trip" Begins

When Hernán Cortés entered Mexico in the early 16th century, he found the inhabitants involved in religious ceremonies that included use of psychedelic plants such as magic mushrooms. The Aztecs were especially known for using magic mushrooms (Psilocybe mexicana). The Nahuatl (language of the

Aztecs) name for the mushrooms was *teonanactl,* which means "flesh of the gods." The inhabitants of Mexico as well as the southwest United States also used the peyote cactus in their religious ceremonies. Mescaline, the active ingredient of the peyote cactus buttons, was named after the Mescalero Apaches who ingested the buttons as part of their religious ceremonies.

Psychedelic research began in 1897 when the German chemist Arthur Heffter isolated mescaline, the primary psychoactive compound of the peyote cactus. As noted in Chapter 1, in 1938 the Swiss chemist Albert Hofmann isolated the active ingredient in LSD (lysergic acid diethylamide) from compounds that he derived from ergot, a fungus that grows on rye grass. Five years after Hofmann created the drug, he accidentally ingested a small amount of the compound and experienced the first recorded "trip" with LSD:

> My surroundings . . . transformed themselves in more terrifying ways. Everything in the room spun around, and the familiar objects and pieces of furniture assumed grotesque, threatening forms. They were in continuous motion, animated, as if driven by an inner restlessness. . . . Even worse than these demonic transformations of the outer world were the alterations that I perceived in myself, in my inner being. Every exertion of my will, every attempt to put an end to the disintegration of the outer world and the dissolution of my ego, seemed to be wasted effort. A demon had invaded me, had taken possession of my body, mind, and soul. (Hofmann, 1980, p. 12)

In 1958, fifteen years after his fateful "trip," Hofmann was the first to isolate psilocybin and psilocin—the psychoactive components of the Mexican "magic mushroom," *Psilocybe mexicana* (D. J. Brown, 2007).

The modern drug epidemic is thought to have begun when a small group of antiestablishment intellectuals called for a consciousness revolution through the use of what they referred to as "mind expanding" drugs. The natural hallucinogenic compounds derived from mushrooms and cacti were soon displaced by LSD, a synthetic hallucinogen, free of the uncomfortable side effects associated with peyote and magic mushrooms (nausea, discomfort, and dizziness). Beginning in the mid-60s, Timothy Leary became the iconic high priest of LSD, long remembered by his signature phrase, "Turn on, tune in, and drop out."

Hallucinogens and the Brain

Hallucinogens are a complex and diverse class of drugs, generally consumed orally. Scientifically they are divided into two basic chemical groups, *tryptamines* (e.g., LSD, DMT, and psilocybin) and *phenethylamines* (e.g., mescaline and MDMA). In terms of chemical structure, tryptamines have more than one carbon ring, whereas phenethylamines have only one (DuPont & Ford, 2000). In addition, some researchers consider the so-called dissociative anesthetics (e.g., ketamine and PCP) to be psychedelic even though their actions in the brain are quite different from the traditional hallucinogens (D. J. Brown, 2007). The chemical makeup of mescaline, psilocybin, and LSD is similar in structure to our brain's own neurotransmitter, serotonin (Figure 10.2)—which all hallucinogenic drugs share a common capacity to inhibit (DuPont & Ford, 2000).

Because of the structural similarity between LSD and serotonin, it is not surprising that scientists believe that LSD as well as the other plant-derived hallucinogens act on serotonin receptors in two brain regions (Sanders-Bush, 1994). One is the *cerebral cortex,* which is involved in cognition, perception, and mood. The other is the *locus coeruleus,* an area that becomes activated during panic attacks, agoraphobia, and other anxiety disorders (DuPont & Ford, 2000). Consciousness is understood as a complex interaction among the cortex, thalamus, and striatum. The most prevalent theory of the mind-altering effects of tryptamine and phenethylamine psychedelics involves disruption of this network by activation of the serotonin 2A receptors (D. J. Brown, 2007).

MDMA (Ecstasy) is also chemically classified as a phenethylamine; however, its action in the brain is substantially different from the other drugs discussed in this section. In contrast to most psychedelics, MDMA does not directly affect the serotonin 2A receptors; rather, it causes dopamine, serotonin, and norepinephrine to be released from their storage sites in neuron endings (D. J. Brown, 2007; Nichols, 1997).

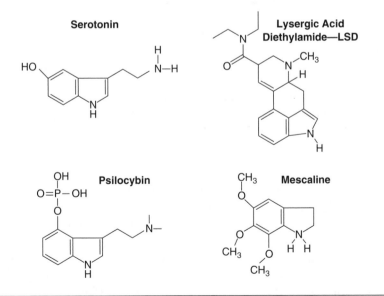

Figure 10.2	**Structure of serotonin and selected hallucinogens.**
	Hallucinogenic drugs are much like the neurotransmitter serotonin in their molecular structure as well as where and how they act on the brain.

LSD

LSD is a clear or white, odorless, water-soluble material synthesized from lysergic acid, a compound derived from the rye fungus. LSD is initially produced in crystalline form. The pure crystal can be crushed to powder and mixed with binding agents to produce tablets known as microdots or tiny squares of gelatin called "window panes." More commonly, it is dissolved, diluted, and applied to paper or other material (NIDA, 2001). LSD is the most potent mood- and perception-altering drug known: oral doses as small as 30 micrograms can produce effects that last 6 to 12 hours. The effects of hallucinogenic drugs vary greatly from one person to another and within any person, from one episode to another. The most common effects of LSD are perceptual distortions (Figure 10.3).

Figure 10.3   **Perceptual distortions.** The effects of hallucinogenic drugs vary greatly from one person to another and within any person, from one episode to another. The most common effects of LSD are perceptual distortions.

Objects may lose their boundaries and merge, faces become distorted, and perceptions become more salient. Users may attach great significance to previously unattended-to objects or events. The sense of time and normal relatedness is dramatically altered and personal identity seems to become fragmented or lost, thus giving way to mystical experiences or frightening delusions. The overall effects of LSD are unpredictable, ranging from euphoria to panic and depression (DuPont & Ford, 2000).

The experience of LSD is sometimes compared to "watching a theater in the mind." The user may experience being in two mental worlds simultaneously, where bizarre perceptual distortions are witnessed by another part of the psyche that remains anchored in the "real" world. LSD commonly produces such novel perceptional distortions as this one: "My cheeks became gills and suddenly a dorsal fin formed from my spine while my fingers became webbed for surviving in water." Trips commonly include perceptions of floating in a void, moving between planets or clouds, or somehow being able to travel within one's own body (DuPont & Ford, 2000). Figure 10.4 represents the common LSD experience of witnessing two worlds simultaneously. In other words, the man viewing himself in the mirror knows he is "tripping."

Long-term effects include tolerance, including tolerance to psilocybin and mescaline, but not to marijuana and amphetamine, as they do not target serotonin receptors. Other long-term effects are persistent psychosis and occasional "flashbacks." The psychosis is characterized by distortion of reality as well as the ability to think rationally. Some users experience long-lasting psychotic states including dramatic mood shifts, visual disturbances, and hallucinations.

Dissociative Drugs

Two other mind-altering drugs, PCP (phencyclidine) and ketamine, were originally developed in the 1950s and 1960s to be used in surgery as general anesthetics. They are often referred to as hallucinogenic because they bring about feelings of detachment from reality and distortions of space, sounds, sight, and body image. Because of these effects, which are not true hallucinations, PCP and ketamine are known as "dissociative" rather than hallucinogenic drugs.

Figure 10.4   **Experiencing two worlds.** The experience of LSD is sometimes compared to "watching a theater in the mind."

PCP—"Zombie" an Accurate Description

Known by such street names as *zombie, dummy dust, angel dust, boat,* or *peace,* PCP acts on the brain by altering the receptor sites for the neurotransmitter glutamate. These receptors are involved with the way we perceive pain, as well as in emotion and cognition, which affects our ability to learn and to remember. The rush from PCP is caused by the increase in the release of the neurotransmitter dopamine into the nucleus accumbens. Generally, these effects are felt within minutes and last several hours or even days. Even after a year of abstinence, the user may experience memory loss and depression. PCP also has effects on other parts of the body besides the brain. These include elevated body temperature, increased heart rate, and dangerous increases in blood pressure.

Ketamine: Let Me Fix You a Drink

A less violent chemical cousin of PCP is ketamine, known on the street as *K, Special K,* and even *cat valium.* It was developed in 1963 to replace PCP in surgery and is used in human anesthesia as well as in veterinary medicine (hence the nickname, cat valium). Although its effects are similar to PCP, the effects of ketamine are milder and of shorter duration. It has been used as a "date rape drug." Since it is tasteless and odorless, it can be slipped into drinks to bring about amnesia in its victims. The victim may not remember the resulting sexual assault.

Dextromethorphan: Cough Syrup Anyone?

The amount of dextromethorphan found in most cough syrups is not harmful. However, abuse can occur using the "extra strength" variety. If the dosage exceeds 4 ounces of dextromethorphan, dissociative effects similar to PCP and ketamine may result. However, the chance of this amount of the drug being ingested with the normal cough suppressant is very unlikely.

Can Hallucinogens Heal?

Before 1972, there were close to 700 studies that focused on the psychiatric healing properties of psychedelic drugs. The research suggested that the psychedelics could be of significant value in helping alcoholics abstain, soothing anxiety in terminal cancer patients, and reducing symptoms for some difficult-to-treat psychiatric illnesses like obsessive-compulsive disorder (OCD). Grof (e.g., 1975, 1980), for example, in his work with terminal cancer patients, showed that LSD combined with psychotherapy could be of great benefit in fostering peace of mind and inspiring spiritual beliefs.

The individual comes to realize, through these [perinatal] experiences, that no matter what he does in his life, he cannot escape the inevitable; he will have to leave this world bereft of everything that he has accumulated and achieved and to which he has been emotionally attached. The similarity between birth and death—the startling realization that the beginning of life is the same as its end—is the major philosophical issue that accompanies the perinatal experiences. The other important consequence of the shocking emotional and physical encounter with the phenomenon of death is the opening up of areas of spiritual and religious experiences that appear to be an intrinsic part of the human personality and are independent of the individual's cultural and religious background and programming. In my experience, everyone who has reached these levels develops convincing insights into the utmost relevance of the spiritual and religious dimensions in the universal scheme of things. Even hard-core materialists, positively oriented scientists, skeptics and cynics, and uncompromising Marxist philosophers suddenly became interested in a spiritual search after they confronted these levels in themselves. (Grof, 1975, pp. 95–96)

Between 1972 and 1990, however, due to the legal backlash against the psychedelic subculture, there were no human studies on the use of psychedelic drugs (D.J. Brown, 2007).

In 1990, things started to change as the FDA began to reopen the doors to psychedelic drug and medical marijuana research. Current studies are under way in the United States, Switzerland, Israel, and Spain that focus on psychedelic treatments for cluster headaches, OCD, severe anxiety in terminal cancer patients, and posttraumatic stress disorder (D. J. Brown, 2007). The beneficial therapeutic effects of the psychedelics are thought to result from activation of the 2A serotonin receptors, causing the number of these receptors expressed on the surface of neurons to decrease (downregulation). The neurochemical effects of psychedelics somehow change the way subjects perceive pain and distress, thereby producing cognitive changes that evoke new insight—the ability to see the world differently—and thus reducing anxiety and raising the threshold for pain (D. J. Brown, 2007). According to Strassman (2001), who investigated the effects of DMT (dimethyltryptamine) on 60 human subjects, psychedelics may be therapeutic insofar as they elicit mental processes known to be useful in the therapeutic context, including transference, enhanced symbolism, heightened suggestibility, controlled regression, and increased contact between thoughts and emotions.

Chapter Summary

Plant-derived hallucinogenic drugs have been used by ancient societies for centuries. Many of these societies, such as the Aztecs of Mexico as well as

Native American tribes, used mushrooms and peyote cactus buttons in their religious ceremonies to create visions, which they believed enabled them to communicate with their gods.

LSD was synthesized by Albert Hofmann, a Swiss chemist who experienced the first "acid trip." In 1958, fifteen years after his fateful discovery, Hofmann isolated psilocybin and psilocin—the psychoactive components of the Mexican "magic mushroom." Beginning in the mid-60s, Timothy Leary became the iconic high priest of LSD, long remembered by his signature phrase, "Turn on, tune in, and drop out."

The chemical makeup of mescaline, psilocybin, and LSD is similar in structure to our brain's own neurotransmitter, serotonin, which all hallucinogenic drugs share a common capacity to inhibit. LSD affects the cerebral cortex and the locus coeruleus, resulting in short-term effects such as rapid mood changes and overstimulation of sights, sounds, and smells. The most prevalent theory of the mind-altering effects of psychedelics involves disruption of brain networks by activation of the serotonin 2A receptors.

The experience of LSD is sometimes compared to "watching a theater in the mind." The user may experience being in two mental worlds simultaneously where bizarre perceptual distortions are witnessed by another part of the psyche that remains anchored in the "real" world. Other mind-altering drugs are PCP (phencyclidine) and ketamine. Even the cough syrup ingredient dextromethorphan can be abused to produce dissociative effects.

Current studies are being conducted in the United States, Switzerland, Israel, and Spain that focus on psychedelic drug treatments for cluster headaches, OCD, severe anxiety in terminal cancer patients, and posttraumatic stress disorder. Psychedelics may be therapeutic to the extent that they elicit mental processes known to be useful in the therapeutic context.

11 Compelled by Fantasy

Our normal waking consciousness, rational consciousness as we call it, is but one special type of consciousness, whilst all about it, parted from it by the filmiest of screens, there lie potential forms of consciousness entirely different.

—William James

Introduction

When imagination is more satisfactory than direct action, we find ourselves on a slippery slope. With each experience of pleasure or removal from pain, the probability of seeking out an imaginary solution increases. Our work, love, and play may progressively falter as the result of an increasing reliance on imaginary pleasures. Hence, those who compulsively fantasize may suffer the same perils as their "rushing" (arousal) or "laid back" (satiation) counterparts: compulsion, loss of control, and continuation despite adverse consequences.

This chapter explores how fantasy is often an integral part of extremely harmful behavior, for the individual, the community, or even human survival. The Heaven's Gate cult is examined in terms of how a shared delusional system can lead to mass suicide. The Columbine massacre demonstrates how innocent lives were sacrificed at the hands of the fantasy-driven behavior of two high school misfits. Sadomasochistic sexual fantasy is explored through a glimpse into the world of a male homosexual prostitute. A woman's struggle with paranoid schizophrenia is viewed through exploration of her remarkable delusional system. Finally, terrorism is examined as a state of mind, grounded in the mind's capacity to utilize fantasy as a means to allay the devastating anxiety resulting from juxtaposition of the will to survive and the immutable fact of death.

Shared Delusions

Excessive use of fantasy does not always remain a private affair. Fantasy may become integrated with the lives of those around us and form a symbiotic system in which the parties involved reap mutual benefit from a shared alteration of reality. The French term *folie à deux* (a madness shared by two) describes a rare psychiatric syndrome in which a symptom of psychosis (particularly a paranoid or delusional belief) is transmitted from one individual to another. The same syndrome shared by more than two people may be called *folie à trois, folie à quatre, folie à famille,* or even *folie à plusieurs* (madness of many). Recent psychiatric classifications refer to the syndrome as a "shared psychotic disorder" (American Psychiatric Association, 2000). Although psychiatric nomenclature recognizes the existence of this pattern, the following example of Heaven's Gate shows how idiosyncratic, bizarre, and compelling group fantasies can become (Bearak, 1997).

Case Example: Shared Delusion Guides Group Suicide

Heaven's Gate, a religious group begun in the 1970s, believed that the earth was about to be "recycled" (wiped clean) and that the only hope for survival was to leave immediately via suicide. The group's structure was similar to that of a medieval monastic order. The tightly knit members lived an ascetic lifestyle and their possessions were communally shared. Six of the males—including the group's leader, Marshall Applewhite—voluntarily underwent castration as an extreme means of maintaining the ascetic lifestyle. The group funded itself by offering professional Web site development for paying clients under the business name Higher Source. The mass suicide occurred after the group updated its Heaven's Gate Web site with a statement saying the comet Hale-Bopp's appearance revealed that their time had come. "Hale-Bopp's approach is the 'marker' we've been looking for. . . . We are happily prepared to leave this world."

The group believed that one of the paths to survival before "recycling" was through extreme hatred of this world and by using their "human" bodies as "vessels" designed to help them on their journey. The death scene included corpses of 21 women and 18 men. Most were found with small pieces of paper containing the suicide recipe: "Take pudding or applesauce and mix it with phenobarbital, drink it down and relax." In preparing to kill themselves, members drank citrus juices to ritually cleanse their bodies of impurities. In accordance with their "prescription," the suicide was accomplished by ingestion of phenobarbital mixed with vodka. Plastic bags were secured around their heads to induce asphyxiation. Members were found lying neatly in their bunks, their faces and torsos covered by a square, purple cloth. Each carried a $5 bill and three quarters in his or her pocket. All 39 were found with their hair closely cropped, dressed in identical black shirts and sweat pants, brand new black-and-white Nike "Cortez" athletic shoes, and armband patches reading "Heaven's Gate Away Team." The suicides were conducted in shifts, and the remaining members of the group cleaned up after each prior group's death.

Unfortunately, suicide is but one violent outcome of collaborative fantasy. The infamous *Trenchcoat Mafia* team of Eric Harris and Dylan Klebold unveiled the horrendous power of fantasy to affect innocent lives. Together they annihilated 12 classmates and a teacher as well as killing themselves. In the aftermath of the Columbine shootings, investigators put together a retrospective formulation of how and why the event occurred.

Duggan, Shear, and Fisher (1999) described the boys as "bright young men who became social outcasts at their suburban Denver high school, and then built their own internal society by plucking strands from the pop whirlwind of cyberspace and fantasy games, the sound track of American youth and the netherworld that glamorizes Nazi symbols and terrorist violence" (p. A1). Harris was a fan of the video game *Doom*, and using special software he created new levels filled with monsters to be killed, which he distributed on the Internet using an AOL Web site.

Klebold and Harris left behind a trail of fantasy productions that in hindsight were solid clues to the horrific event. These included writing death poetry for their English class, making a video about their new guns for a school class, and shouting murderous slogans that were posted on the AOL Web site. Harris's ramblings on his AOL member profile provide a glimpse into the mind-set of the killers: "Man has ruled this world as a stumbling, demented child king long enough. . . . As his empire crumbles, my precious black widow shall rise as his most fitting successor" (Duggan et al., 1999, p. A1).

In the days before the shooting, they were seen marching down the school halls, wearing berets, dark glasses, and boots; making military turns; and knocking into anyone in their way. They spoke broken German and often referred to "4/20," Hitler's birthday and the day they chose for the assault.

From a psychological perspective, wish-fulfilling fantasies of ultimate power and "sweet" revenge were strengthened through ongoing validation and approval from each other. Their friendship was so close and insular that they linked their home computers into a mini network. Mutual support for the virtue of violence, admiration of Hitler, and use of technology to broadcast dark intensions (e.g., how to build pipe bombs) were repeatedly played out in fantasy scripts. These mental "intoxicants" served to compensate for profound feelings of insecurity, lack of intimacy, and intense anger.

Facilitator-Assisted Fantasy

Case material from a self-referred client whom we shall call Bill illustrates how sadomasochistic sexual fantasies can be facilitator assisted. At the age of 30, Bill made a living as a male prostitute whose clientele mostly included middle-aged homosexual men. Bill was often contracted to act out various sexual fantasies. Most of the staged scenarios involved some form of make-believe domination of the client. Bill describes his relationship with his primary repeat client, followed by his overall perspective on the type of relationships he has had with other customers.

Case Example: Facilitator-Assisted Fantasy

The primary repeat client with whom I deal has a very interesting fantasy in which he is symbolically powerful and powerless, super-stud and super-slut, lady of great refinement, and common slut. The evening starts out with him in a supra-masculine, Nazi, black leather motorcycle type outfit. He is a physically imposing and very handsome man and one would expect him to be quite dominant in sex (inserter) or play (master, whipper, etc.). However, this is only a preliminary posturing . . . [W]hen he makes contact, visual, verbal, or physical, with a potential playmate, he immediately switches to a very feminine role. He becomes a refined lady who wants to be used and abused; to be whipped on his "pussy" (his anus) . . . to have clamps put on his shaved "titties."

He has done this frequently, while being restrained in stocks or slings in front of a large public audience (30–100 people) or at an S&M bar. In the privacy of my bedroom he likes to change into full female undergarments and beg me to fuck his "pussy." I find myself unable to be aroused by either his fantasy or his submission and so I talk dirty, make up fantasies for him and bring him to a climax with my hand on his "clitoris" (penis) and a vibrator in his anus.

Other typical fantasies also center on sexual domination. The clients almost always (more than 90%) want to feel as though I want to "use" them to get off (climax or not, but I have to be apparently desirous of the contact and the "use" of them). They may want me to be the hot young stud in which case I "talk high school" and dominate or they may want me to be 25–30, in which case I develop scenes with older men for them to visualize while I dominate them sexually. Some also want me to be the helpless boy-stud that they take advantage of. So they are the oppressor; but even when they are the aggressor and nominally dominant, they give me the control almost always because the whole point for them is to succeed in giving *me* pleasure.

In addition to prostitution, Bill conducted a lucrative "phone sex" business where he received credit card payments for acting out sexual fantasies. Phone sex is commonly advertised on late-night TV and in local newspapers. Internet porn sites feature webcam access to interactive sexual fantasy. Similar to how drug dealers cater to the pharmaceutical needs and whims of a steady drug-using clientele, phone and Internet sex dealers dispense fantasy. Interestingly, a popular fantasy script for Bill and other operators is usually a run of sexy verbiage with a general theme of the caller being dominated. One man, for example, enjoys having his operator describe a scenario where he is diapered and repeatedly spanked. Like drugs, phone sex can provide temporary relief from loneliness, anxiety, and fear.

The fantasy of being punished for one's wrongdoing, while at the same time being attended to and sexually desired, is wish-fulfilling for the consumer. For Bill, the short-term psychological payoff of acting out his own sexual and interpersonal wishes, while earning money for self-maintenance, outweighed considerations of personal risk or legal culpability. In the years that followed, Bill was diagnosed as HIV positive.

Schizophrenic Fantasy

When a person's belief system challenges mainstream cultural precepts, he or she is often called crazy or mentally ill. It is not uncommon for people with a diagnosis of "schizophrenia" to hear voices that seem to come from other worlds or to believe that they are Napoleon or Christ. To be sure, some of those burdened by this disease (particularly the paranoid subtype) are among the most fantasy-oriented people in our midst. Disorders of the schizophrenic syndrome affect nearly 1 in every 100 people.

Contrary to the view of most psychiatric researchers and practitioners, Szasz (1960) has argued that the entire concept of schizophrenia as a disease is erroneous. In *The Myth of Mental Illness,* he reasons that without definitive evidence of organic dysfunction, people should not be labeled as sick because of their beliefs. In fact, people frequently experience problems in living, and they may develop eccentric beliefs (i.e., fantasies) as highly personal and specialized coping devices.

Clearly, biochemical imbalances are involved in much of the personality disorganization that we describe as severe mental illness. Yet the ability of many who have psychotic thoughts to function at times with apparent rationality stimulates a fascinating question. Are some clinically "crazy" people compulsively dependent on fantasy, as drug addicts may be dependent on heroin or alcohol? Certainly there are some intriguing parallels, as revealed in the following list of elements of schizophrenia and drug addiction.

Denial: Unwillingness to recognize that there is anything wrong or that one's perceptions are inaccurate

Compulsion: Refusing antipsychotic medicines, which when properly administered reduce the prevalence and impact of dysfunctional fantasy

Loss of Control: Suffering great damage to social, economic, and health functions as a result of the person's uncompromising belief in the importance and authenticity of his or her delusions or hallucinations

Relapse Rates: For schizophrenia, drug addiction, and alcoholism, recidivism is roughly the same: about 60% to 80% after 6 to 12 months of "abstinence."

In Lindner's (1954) now-classic psychiatric tale, "The Jet-Propelled Couch," he takes the position that Kirk Allen's psychosis, which involves his belief that he can transport himself back and forth, to and from different galaxies, is actually an addiction to fantasy. Kirk was brought up by a series of governesses as the only white child on a remote island. One of the governesses, whom he called Sterile Sally, imbued him with a dread of contamination from his surroundings. She considered the native children to be "filthy niggers," and forbade Kirk to converse with his friends.

As a consequence of this added isolation, his fantasy life—until then of a fashion and degree usual among lonely children—increased sharply. Daydreaming now came to occupy much of his time, and there appeared those lavish, imaginative reconstructions of the world which were to be so significant for him and so characteristic of his life up to the day we met. The details of the initial fantasy that Kirk toyed with during Sterile Sally's residence and for some while thereafter need not concern us here. It was a childish hodge-podge, constructed from odd remnants of reading. He identified himself with characters from the Oz books, for example, and mentally played out a cordial existence in a friendlier, more exciting world. This primary experience unfolded the imaginative facility and the technique of mental detachment which he developed to astonishing proportions in adulthood. (Lindner, 1999, pp. 236–237)

The case of Beverly Delores Dark presented below reveals the intense and relentless fantasy preoccupation of a 67-year-old woman who has suffered from paranoid schizophrenia since the age of 21.

Case Example: Attachment to Fantasy in Paranoid Schizophrenia

Beverly Delores Dark is the pen name of a 67-year-old woman who was first diagnosed as paranoid schizophrenic at the age of 21. Her self-proclaimed identity is "the writer." Prior to her first psychiatric diagnosis and subsequent hospitalization, she was an aspiring college student engaged in the study of English literature. "Pierre Blake" is one of her early writings, exemplary of her creativity, logic, and humor.

Pierre Blake

There once lived a man, Pierre Blake

Who constantly craved milk and cake

His baker named Glum

One day couldn't come

Said Blake, "My own cake I shall bake."

Quite often he'd watched how Glum fussed

So he started right off but got mussed

Though he used enough dough

And the flame wasn't low

'Stead of cake he got stuck with the crust.

Pierre Blake though was quite a shrewd guy

"Throw it out!" he exclaimed, "No, not I!"

Fruit filling he found

Shaped it out to be round

And short for Pierre

Called it "pie."

After a series of late-adolescent disillusionments with friends, teachers, and writing, Beverly became absorbed in the idea that her destiny was to bring a universal language to earth. She began to "see" movies of her life projected on her bedroom wall. Shortly after the onset of these bizarre experiences, at the age of 21, Beverly was diagnosed as paranoid schizophrenic. She was given shock treatment and drug therapy, and began a prolonged series of psychiatric hospitalizations.

Episodically, Beverly returned to college, where she completed a baccalaureate degree in English literature. In her junior year, she began to develop the notion that Shakespeare had written much of his poetry about herself and her college friends. She increasingly believed that Shakespeare had used his famed sonnets as a secret device to communicate his inner feelings about their relationship. The fact that their physical lives were chronologically quite separate had nothing to do with their communication and romance on a spiritual plane.

The comparative writing samples shown in Table 11.1 are excerpted from one of Beverly's academic papers entitled "Six Sic Sonnets." In the left panel, she describes Shakespeare's "hidden motive" for composing his poetry. The discussion centers on her belief that Shakespeare is actually a sensitive, young, bisexual poet, reincarnated in the twentieth century. His love sonnets contain cryptic messages about his relationships with Beverly and two of her close friends.

According to Beverly, only she can decipher the secret sonnet code. The right panel shows how "decomposition" unveils the "true meaning" of the sonnets. The "writer's" pen name, Beverly Delores Dark, is combined with a particular sonnet number, for example, Sonnet Sixteen Beverly Delores Dark. Then "using each letter once only and rearranging the order," Beverly reveals the secret meaning.

Table 11.1   Six Sic Sonnets

My thesis cites that, at least on one level, Shakespeare—in his sonnets—sees himself as a beautiful, sensitive, young, bi-sexual poet reincarnated in the 20th Century; and that he is writing about three women with whom this young Poet is involved: The Dr., Elaine, who graduated from College in '61; the Psychologist, Arlene, in '62; and the Artist, Beverly (Beverly Delores Dark) in '63. Sonnet 61 is a companion piece to Sonnet 16, because upon graduation the woman involved (rival Elaine) is like a 16 yr. old girl; Sonnet 62 is a companion piece to Sonnet 26 because after graduation, the woman involved (rival Arlene) marries a 26 year old young man, is therefore parallel to him chronologically (as is later to be revealed in the 26th Sonnet); and Sonnet 63 is a love-sonnet which is to be coupled with Sonnet 36—because the Dark Lady (Who is always addressed as one with the Homosexual Friend) possesses the faculties of a 36 yr. old woman upon termination of her early education.	*Decomposition*
	(using each letter once only and re-arranging the order)
	SONNET SIXTY DASH ONE BEVERLY DELORES DARK
	N.Y. Broken Dr. Elaine tt (tooties) (to tease) loves hard sex. Dos(e)s Yo(u) (her)
	(e) (u)
	knee u
	SONNET SIXTEEN BEVERLY DELORES DARK
	RT Elaine loves sex . . . body reeks
	N-O n(u)t(s)
	(u) (s)
	SONNET SIXTY DASH TWO BEVERLY DELORES DARK
	vd hr sub dodo ns
	(vide-French) (whore) (substitute) (anus)
	Arlene seeks trix to lay you
	(tricks)
	SONNET TWENTY DASH SIX BEVERLY DELORES DARK
	iu tt Arlene looks bad here
	Dry sex u donut
	(a "dough" nut)
	SONNET SIXTY DASH THREE BEVERLY DELORES DARK
	Rx:
	Love her dark say yy notes.
	(too wise)
	N-O sleet bed . . . H(u)rts
	(u)
	SONNET THIRTY DASH SIX BEVERLY DELORES DARK
	Dislikes hard sex. Lover her rays
	Don't toy . . . B(u)rnt (u)
	(u) (us) (e) (uu)
	You use'd e to use
	a U.S. e to use
	(knee)

According to Beverly, she and Shakespeare are carrying on a love affair through the sonnets. She is Shakespeare's mistress (or Dark Lady), and her friends are jealous of the relationship. Shakespeare's outrage at his lover's friends is revealed when the sonnets are "de-composed." The writing samples included represent only a small segment of "Six Sic Sonnets," which is a thesis of approximately 30 pages in length. Another paper by the same author is entitled "Space Travel During the Renaissance." In recent years, the "writer" has concluded that she is "The Messiah of all the Messiahs."

As is clear from the case example, Beverly's unusual thought process involves more than simply a chemical imbalance, resulting in mental illness. She shows a tenacious clinging to her highly personalized relationship with Shakespeare and lives a fantasy identity as Shakespeare's mistress. As stated in *The Divided Self* by Laing (1959),

> The self, in order to develop and sustain its identity and autonomy, and in order to be safe from the persistent threat and danger from the world, has cut itself off from direct relatedness with others and has endeavored to become its own object (of interest): to become, in fact, related directly only to itself. Its cardinal functions become fantasy and observation. (p. 147)

Laing (1973), who set up an experimental project for working with mental patients at Kingsley Hall in England, believes that the "returned schizophrenic" is the most effective therapist since only such a person can fully comprehend the dimensions of another's schizophrenic experience. This model has long been appreciated in the treatment of addictive disorders. In the end, there is no benefit in forming negative judgments about those who are compelled to seek out the fantasy state. "If we cease to degrade those who may truly 'see' the world in a grain of sand . . . and eternity in an hour, they may stop responding with confusion and fear to their perceptions" (p. 11).

The Terrorist Mind-Set

> Man's socio-genetic evolution is about to reach a crisis in the full sense of the word, a crossroads offering one path to fatality, and one to recovery and further growth. Artful perverter of joy and keen exploiter of strength, man is the animal that has learned to survive "in a fashion," to multiply without food for the multitudes, to grow up healthy without reaching personal maturity, to live well but without purpose, to invent ingeniously without aim, and to kill grandiosely without need. (Erikson, 1964, p. 227)

As discussed in Chapter 9, Internet access allows for widespread availability of fantasy experiences that may be shared by two, three, or even hundreds of people. In this section, we discuss the use of fantasy by terrorists as a primary means to cope with harsh realities of abject poverty and social inequity. In fact, by providing scripted images of the martyr's glory, in heaven and on earth, the Internet has become a major recruitment tool for terrorists around the globe. The World Trade Center and Pentagon attacks of 2001, the Madrid bombings of 2004, and the London suicide bombings of 2005—all of these incidents were carried out by individuals considered to be terrorists. What is their psychological makeup?

Thoughts of genocide by suicide provide comfort to those who subjectively experience inexorable psychological pain. Ideas of death leading to martyrdom are strengthened by images of glory and reprieve from misery. When wish-fulfilling suicidal fantasy (religious piety, defeat of the enemy, and reward in the afterlife) becomes primary for a particular ethnic group, violence can occur on an enormous scale.

Is terrorism a kind of *folie à plusieurs*, where legions of mentally disordered people are attracted by the magnetic effect of a "war of terror"? Not likely. Unlike schizophrenia, the majority of terrorists do not suffer from biological aberrations characteristic of severe mental disorder. According to Goertzel (2002), "Terrorists think rationally, but they think within the limits of belief systems that may be irrational" (p. 98). They have strongly held beliefs that they defend with great emotional fervor. Terrorists do not see their actions as a means of war against a particular nation or ethnic group; rather, they see themselves as fighters of freedom who are protecting their religion (Goertzel, 2002; Harris, 2002).

Ferracuti (1982) highlights the importance of fantasy in the terrorist mind:

Terrorism . . . is fantasy war, real only in the mind of the terrorist. Fantasy war, of course, is only partial war, real for only one of the contestants who then adopts war values, norms, and behaviors against another, generally larger group, trying to solve through strength a conflict based on legitimate or illegitimate grievances. (p. 137)

Some of the hypocrisies of these fantasy wars include claiming the power of life and death over noncombat citizens and engaging in criminal activities while declaring their lawfulness.

Terrorists perceive themselves as different from and superior to others because they belong to a group with intense ideological, cultural, and political beliefs. They view terrorist actions as a revolutionary struggle of the oppressed (Harris, 2002). Their enemies are dehumanized as mere props, in that they are perceived as not having independent wills and thoughts. According to Harris (2002), rehabilitation from terrorist ideology would require an immense mental adjustment. The objects of attack need to be transformed back into real people with real feelings and wills. When surrounded with others that hold similar views, fanatical ideas become validated and more likely to become firmly held beliefs. Harris claims that history abounds with people unable to see themselves as others see them, unable to recognize the horror they are causing others.

In the mind of the terrorist, martyrdom is the ultimate reward for acting on fanatical beliefs. Harris (2002) states that, by attacking the World Trade Center, the collective fantasy of radical Islam was brought to life. There could be no better proof that God was on the side of radical Islam and that the end of the reign of the Great Satan (America) was at hand. A small group of devout Muslims, men whose wills were absolutely pure, as proven by their martyrdom, brought down the mighty towers created by the Great Satan. Suicide to the radical Islamist is not a means to an end but an end in itself, as it leads to martyrdom. Martyrdom for the terrorist consists of transcendent glory, magical powers, and the infamous 72 virgins who will greet them when they arrive in heaven.

Sociocultural Origins of Terrorism

How are the radical viewpoints of fundamentalist religion propagated? Fundamentalist beliefs (based upon religious scriptures that reveal the supernatural as the literal truth of God's message) can be described (as can other human traits, e.g., intelligence) by a distribution ranging from least rigid and open-minded to the most exclusionary and dogmatic. Through religious schools, terrorist media, and even conversation on the street, the absolute ideologies of radical Islam are spread to children who would otherwise lack opportunities for schooling, jobs, or obvious future direction (Harris, 2002). In some quarters, religious training promotes an institutionalized view that suicide and mass murder followed by paradise is a plausible solution, fulfilling the need for escape from earthly hopelessness and ego annihilation.

> In the many circles of hell that exist for young men in Pakistan, the lowest is found at Dabaray Ghara, on the outskirts of Peshawar. It is an expanse of pits, dug out of the sunbaked earth, in which several thousand men, mostly refugees from Afghanistan, make bricks. It is the hardest of labor because it takes place outdoors, no matter how hot or cold, pays next to nothing and is literally backbreaking.

> You see children as young as 4 or 5 in the pits, except they are not playing. They are making bricks. . . . Bakhtiar Kahn began working in the pits when he was 10. He is now 25 or 26. He isn't sure, because nobody keeps close track; time passes, that is all. He works from 5 in the morning until 5 in the afternoon, making 1000 bricks a day, six days a week, earning a few dollars a week. He is thin, he wears no shirt or shoes and he cannot believe that a foreigner is asking about his life. . . . "Life is cruel," he says [w]hich is not unusual and helps explain why Peshawar's youth are tinder for Islamic extremism. (Maass, 2001, p. 48)

Based on interviews with scores of religious zealots including the Bajrang Dal in India, the Jewish Underground in Israel, Hamas in Palestine, and violent fundamentalist Christians in the United States, Stern (2004) describes the sociocultural roots of terrorism:

> My interviews suggest that people join religious terrorist groups partly to transform themselves and to simplify life. They start out feeling

humiliated, enraged that they are viewed by some Other as second class. They take on new identities as martyrs on behalf of a purported spiritual cause. . . . What seems to happen is that they enter a kind of trance, where the world is divided neatly between good and evil, victim and oppressor. . . . [A] sense of transcendence is one of many attractions of religious violence for terrorists, beyond the appeal of achieving their goals. (pp. 281–282)

The ecstasy is very much of a sexual character: "call out in joy . . . a wedding to 'the black-eyed' awaits your son in paradise," proclaims the last will of a Hamas suicide bomber to his mother. (p. 54)

In Silke's (1998) exploration of the relationship between terrorism and mental illness, he found no evidence for increased levels of mental disorder within the terrorist population. This validates older research in which terrorists on average are found to be psychologically healthier than violent criminals in prisons for non-terrorism-related crimes (Rasch, 1979). If psychopathology can't adequately explain the psychological foundation of a terrorist, what mechanism is responsible for driving a seemingly normal person to extreme acts of violence toward others?

The segue into terrorism appears to be more social than psychological. In his paper "Terrorism, Suicide Bombing, Fear, and Mental Health," Palmer (2007) uses a social learning model to explain how madmen are created from average people. The terrorist's environment may include individuals, groups, and even larger entities like his or her nation or religion that reinforce extremist and violent beliefs. Observations of praise for martyrdom or dedication to the terrorist organization become reinforcing to the outsider. Upon joining a radical group, the bonds and pressures from fellow terrorists become key factors in the continuation and escalation of violent activity. Close-knit connections and strong levels of commitment are accomplished through a focus on developing and maintaining small groups (replicating the family unit) with a central leader who delivers orders from the top. Fellow members replace each other's real family and relationships outside the group. Members will do and act in accordance with what the "family" wants or values. Thus, the terrorist organization can influence its members to take their own lives, willingly for the cause of their supposed brethren.

Armageddon: The Ultimate Fantasy

Occasionally, a completely irrational precept is embraced as gospel by a powerful constituency of society. In such cases, the adverse consequences of fantasy dependence may reach catastrophic proportions. For example, the history of the Aztec people of Mexico reveals the destruction of an entire civilization in relation to a bizarre and destructive belief. The Aztecs believed that the sun needed to be nourished by human hearts. They felt compelled to feed the sun with thousands upon thousands of human hearts ripped from the bodies of sacrificial victims. What started as a well-contained ritual sacrifice degenerated into compulsive genocide when 75,000 humans were sacrificed in a 15th-century ceremony at El Templo Mayor (the Great Temple). The necessity of purging neighboring cultures in order to obtain sacrificial victims led to a state of war with victimized groups. When Cortés began the conquest of Mexico, surrounding civilizations were thus eager to join him in the destruction of Tenochtitlan, the Aztec capital.

A fundamentalist belief within Western culture has the earmarks of a devastating social intoxicant. The theology of Armageddon is described in Revelation, the last book in the New Testament, traditionally attributed to John. According to contemporary fundamentalist interpretations, Revelation predicts that before Christ returns to earth to establish his second kingdom, a last great battle between the forces of good and evil will occur. As told in Revelation 9:2–6,

He opened the shaft of the bottomless pit, and from the shaft rose smoke like the smoke of a great furnace, and the sun and the air were darkened with the smoke from the shaft.

Then from the smoke came locusts on the earth, and they were given power like the power of scorpions on the earth;

They were told not to harm the grass of the earth or any green growth or any tree, but only those of mankind who have not the seal of God upon their foreheads; they were allowed to torture them for five months, but not to kill them, and their torture was like the torture of a scorpion, when it stings a man.

And in those days men will seek death and will not find it; they will long to die, and death will fly from them.

Armageddon, the worst time on earth, will be preceded by an exceedingly troubled period referred to as the Tribulation. Believers explain current world unrest as evidence that we have entered this period. Those who have accepted Christ into their hearts will "in the wink of an eye" experience Rapture. During the Rapture, those who are aligned with the forces of good, namely fundamentalist Christians, will be brought to heaven and protected from the destruction below. There is a fundamentalist bumper sticker that reads, "Caution, in case of Rapture this vehicle will be unmanned." Armageddon theology is explained in *Late Great Planet Earth* (Lindsey, 1970), which is reported to have sold more than 10 million copies.

Some have used Armageddon theology as a defense for the use of nuclear weapons. They believe that the Bible identifies such entities as the Soviet

Union, China, or Iran with the Antichrist or Evil Empire and the precipitator of the final battle between good and evil—Armageddon. Of course, those who are on the side of good need not fear a nuclear holocaust (Armageddon) because it is God's will that the Evil Empire be destroyed.

One of the signs of the imminence of Armageddon is that people will wear the "mark of the beast," which is said to be the number 666. Revelation 13:16–17 explains, "Also it causes all, both small and great, both rich and poor, both free and slave, to be marked on the right hand or the forehead, so that no one can buy or sell unless he has the mark, that is the name of the beast or the number of its name."

The "mark of the beast" is interpreted by some as the symbolic representation of our credit card culture. When the Antichrist gains control of the earth, no one will be able to participate in any commerce without the "mark" on his or her American Express, Carte Blanche, MasterCard, or other "beastly" credit-charging device.

The apocalyptic fantasy in which "nuclear winter" is attributed to the will of God may be psychologically construed as a denial of nuclear addiction. Like the hopeless alcohol addict who insists that he can control his drinking, militant leaders insist that we can control the world's most devastating intoxicant. Part of the report rushed to President Truman in 1945, after the earliest nuclear test explosion, reads as follows: "It lighted every peak, crevasse and ridge of the nearby mountain range with a clarity and beauty that cannot be described but must be seen to be imagined. It was the beauty the great poets dream about but described most poorly and inadequately. . . . Then came the strong, sustained, awesome roar which warned of doomsday and made us feel that we puny things were blasphemous to dare tamper with the forces heretofore reserved to the Almighty" (General Thomas Farrell, 1945, quoted in "The Manhattan Project: An Enduring Legacy," 1999).

"Heretofore reserved to the Almighty" and today reserved for the leaders of nuclear-armed countries—no wonder there is so much inclination to attribute this awesome power to a superior being. Yet the fantasy that it is God's plan to arrange for Armageddon permits a mystical rationalization for the continued development of nuclear armaments. Armageddon theology serves as a denial mechanism for those who will not take responsibility for the fact that, like lemmings, we are rushing headlong toward the precipice of world destruction. Indeed, we have far exceeded the thresholds of compulsion and loss of control when a war between the nuclear powers could mean a Third World War every second.

Terror Management

A group of social scientists has undertaken the noble task of examining the root causes of terrorism, perhaps shedding light on a possible corridor to peace. *Terror management theory* (TMT; J. T. Greenberg, Pyszczynski, & Solomon, 1986; Pyszczynski, 2004; Solomon, Greenberg, & Pyszczynski, 1991) takes the position that the two common elements of human consciousness are fear of death and will to survive (Pyszczynski, 2004). In terms of evolutionary psychology, humans, early on, developed intellectual means to manage the potentially terrifying knowledge of death by developing worldviews that provide means for attaining immortality in either a literal or symbolic sense. Beliefs in literal immortality, which are nearly universal, pertain to the notion that death is not the end of existence; rather, some part of us will live on, in heaven, through reincarnation, merging our consciousness with God, or the attainment of enlightenment. Cultures also provide us with symbolic immortality, which pertains to the belief that by being part of something more important and enduring than ourselves (i.e., families, nations, ethnic groups, and nations), we can access immortality.

We need others to agree with and validate our cultural worldview (CWV) in order to develop our self-concepts and to maintain faith in our immortality. When we encounter others who view the world differently, this threatens our faith and ignites existential anxiety (i.e., fear of death). Historically, people have vanquished opposing worldviews by ignoring their proponents as savages, converting them to their own ideologies, or simply exterminating them (Pyszczynski, 2004).

More than 250 TMT studies conducted in more than 13 countries (including the United States, Israel, Iran, and Japan) provide support for the TMT hypothesis that when the exsistence of a cultural group is threatened—such as during the 9/11 attacks on the World Trade Center or due to nuclear development in Iran—people become more fervently invested in their cultural worldview (Pyszczynski, 2004). Increasing faith in one's CWV tends to reduce death anxiety. Correspondingly, reminding people of death's inevitability leads to a broad range of attempts to maintain faith in their means for immortality. Convincing "evidence" of some form of an afterlife reduces the effects of "mortality salience" and provides a boost to self-esteem. According to Pyszczynski (2004), TMT studies show that reminders of mortality trigger a yearning for structure, thus evoking acceptance of quick and easy answers to complex problems. By controlling the political agendas of "fearmongering," people become more amenable to open-minded thinking, which can lead to growth, change, and improvement.

The challenge for humanity is to demonstrate that there are, in fact, options to rigid adherence to a CWV designed to protect immortality. A cognitive shift along the lines of this basic question should be the target of a worldwide sociological intervention.

Chapter Summary

This chapter explores how fantasy is often an integral part of extremely harmful behavior, for the individual, the community, or even human survival. Fantasy may become integrated with the lives of those around us and form a symbiotic system in which the parties involved reap mutual benefit from a shared alteration of reality. The Heaven's Gate cult is examined in terms of how a shared delusional system can lead to mass suicide. The Columbine massacre demonstrates how innocent lives may be sacrificed at the hands of fantasy-driven behavior.

Case material from a man that earned money as a male prostitute illustrates how sadomasochistic sexual fantasies can be facilitator assisted. The theme of most of his paid sexual encounters was the acting out of various sexual acts that involved some form of make-believe domination of the client. The fantasy of being punished for one's wrongdoing, while at the same time being attended to and sexually desired, was a wish-fulfilling fantasy for many of his homosexual male customers.

In another case example, a woman's struggle with paranoid schizophrenia is viewed through exploration of her remarkable delusional system. She increasingly believed that Shakespeare had used his famed sonnets as a secret device to communicate his inner feelings about their relationship. The fact that they lived at completely different times had nothing to do with their communication and romance on a spiritual plane.

Finally, terrorism is examined as a state of mind, grounded in the mind's capacity to utilize fantasy as a means to allay the terrifying anxiety resulting from juxtaposition of the will to survive and the immutable fact of death. The theology of Armageddon is explored as a fundamentalist belief within Western culture that has the earmarks of a devastating social intoxicant. Last, terror management theory is used to explore the root causes of terrorism, perhaps shedding light on how to improve human chances for survival.

SECTION V

Craving for Intimacy

To love is to receive a glimpse of heaven.

—Karen Sunde

Overview: The Importance
of Human Connection

Never Once

India is filled

with many

exceptionally beautiful women

who don't desire me

I verify this

every single day

as I walk around the city of Bombay

I look into face after face

and never once

have I been wrong

—Leonard Cohen

Loneliness is not a healthy human condition. The brain needs connections with other people in order to maintain health of mind and body. Maslow (1954/1970), in his renowned hierarchy of human needs, recognized love and belonging as essential to developing positive self-esteem en route to realizing our full potential.

Inadequate bonding affects blood pressure and the incidence of heart disease (Hawkley, Masi, Berry, & Cacioppo, 2006). It has also been shown that quality time spent in meaningful relationships is a factor that enhances the brain's healing process, which leads to a greater life expectancy (Ornstein & Sobel, 1987).

Today, the importance of attachment, the strong emotional bond that forms between children and their caregivers, is perhaps the most rigorously studied area of developmental psychology. It is widely believed that the nature of the evolving relationship between the child and his or her caregivers is a critical feature of personality and social development, one that has a lifelong influence on the child's mental and emotional growth (e.g., Ainsworth & Bowlby, 1991). "Parenting practices have been found to have an effect on children's substance abuse, school problems, academic success, behavioral problems, social competency, ego resiliency, ego control, depression, and employment in adulthood" (Schwartz, Thigpen, & Montgomery, 2006, p. 41). Satir (1972) describes the impact of the family:

Any infant coming in[to] the world has no past, no experience in handling himself, no skill by which to judge his own worth. He must rely on the experiences he has with people around him and the messages they give him about his worth as a person. For the first five or six years the child's self-esteem is formed by the family almost exclusively. After he starts school other influences come into play, but the family effect remains throughout his adolescence. Outside forces tend to reinforce the feelings of self-worth or worthlessness that he learned at home. The high self-esteem child can weather many failures in school among peers. The low self-esteem child can experience many successes and yet feel a gnawing doubt about his own value. (p. 24)

Children need the knowledge that their feelings and emotions are valid. Satir found that families and their constituent members thrive when provided with what she referred to as the *Five Freedoms:* (1) the freedom to see and hear what is here and now, rather than what was, what will be, or should be; (2) the freedom to think and know what one thinks and knows, rather than what one should think and know; (3) the freedom to think and express what one feels, rather than what one should feel and express; (4) the freedom to want and to choose what one wants, rather than what one should want; and (5) the freedom to imagine one's own self-actualization, rather than playing a rigid role or always playing it safe (Satir & Baldwin, 1983, p. 163).

While supervising a child's behavior with appropriate limit setting promotes strength and resiliency, manipulation and psychological control may increase drug use and delinquent behaviors (de Kemp, Scholte, Overbeek, & Engels, 2006). Lack of parental support is directly related to depression in early adolescence. Parental disinterest and lack of support are correlated with a child's self-perception as unworthy and a quest for other means of finding support and comfort. De Kemp et al. (2006) confirmed earlier studies, finding that many facets of mental health and psychological well-being are adversely affected by inappropriate parental controls:

> Parenting is directly related to the intensified delinquent behavior of early adolescents. . . . Psychological control appeared to be related to an increased frequency of delinquent behavior. Controlling an adolescent's behavior by manipulation and guilt induction may contribute to feelings of insecurity and frustration. The use of psychological control is especially detrimental in early adolescence, during which young people firmly define themselves as connected to—yet separate from—their significant others. Repeated exposure to psychological intrusion increases the risk for developing internalizing as well as externalizing problems. As a means of relieving the negative atmosphere created by guilt induction, a youth might act out aggressively. (p. 505)

This section explores the basic struggle for human relatedness, which, when mismanaged in childhood or unsatisfied later in life, can result in internal distress and dysfunctional relationships. Disruption of the fundamental needs for love and belonging is closely aligned with seeking wholeness and connection through drugs, promiscuity, and other forms of unhealthy attachment.

Chapter 12, Love or Addiction? examines the agony and ecstasy of romance in terms of the neurochemical underpinnings of infatuation, desire, and loss of control. The psychology of love is revealed as a dynamic interplay of arousal, relaxation, and fantasy. Obsessive and tormenting love is seen as a miscarriage of our natural attraction toward people who evoke feelings of safety, pleasure, and the possibility to procreate. In Chapter 13, Marijuana—Reefer Madness Revisited, marijuana is examined as prototypical of various drug involvements whereby powerful cultural influences combine with innate longings for closeness and belonging. Chapter 14, Romantic Sex Fantasy, examines the monumental demand for novel, no-strings-attached sexual stimulation through fantasy and paid companionship.

Together, these chapters are designed to provide readers with an expanded view of a broad spectrum of activities that deliver partial satisfaction, often at great cost, of life's greatest challenge and most precious gift—intimacy.

> For one human being to love another, that is perhaps the most difficult of all our tasks, the ultimate, the last test and proof, the work for which all other work is preparation.
>
> —Rainer Maria Rilke

12 Love or Addiction?

S ome dyed-in-the-wool romantics describe the insatiable craving for an elusive, unattainable, yet tantalizing lover as a "jones." A jones means that you've got a habit—a bad habit. Eventually, it might even do you in. As with uncontrolled dependence on heroin, no matter how much you get, you always want more. Like an infant who has been abandoned by its mother, you fall to pieces when "mamma" won't give you a "fix."

We can all catch a glimpse of ourselves in this grim, shadow side of romance. In proper proportion, the majestic clockwork of love—a synchronized blend of arousal, satiation, and fantasy—gives rise to life's most fulfilling experiences. By nature, we become impassioned by elements that create or sustain life. But all too often the delicate process goes amiss: angels transform into devils, joy becomes jealousy, and heaven changes to hell. The nightmare of tormenting love is nothing but a miscarriage of our natural attraction toward people who evoke feelings of safety and pleasure. And so it is with all addictions; they are self-destructive outgrowths of adaptive, life-enhancing behaviors.

Infatuation and the Legend of St. Valentine

According to Slater (2006), romantic love is panhuman: It proliferates in almost every culture on earth and has been embedded in our brains since Pleistocene times. In a study of 166 cultures, evidence of romantic love was found in 147 of them. Indeed, the phenomenon of infatuation is so powerful that some people compulsively attempt to re-create the experience, time and time again. In fact, some researchers hypothesize that romantic love is rooted in our quest to recapture our earliest infantile experiences with intimacy, that is, the feeling at mother's breast, the look of her face, the caring and gentle touch (Slater, 2006). The usual failure of such pursuit leads some people toward a repetitive and seemingly compulsive search for intimacy.

In simplest terms, falling in love means thinking about another person all the time. In *Love and Limerence: The Experience of Being in Love,* Tennov (1979) describes the symptoms of romantic love, which she collectively calls *limerence.* In limerence, there is constant thought about one person, to the exclusion of all others, usually as a possible sex partner. When for some reason the prospective lover is not readily taken, romantic sentiments are further intensified. Obsessed suitors are able to achieve some degree of solace through rich and elaborate fantasies of lovemaking and courtship. If the "chosen" shows even the slightest inclination toward amorous reciprocation, feelings of elation are likely to follow. For a state of true limerence, at least the potential for mating must exist, tinged with an umbra of uncertainty or doubt about the future of the relationship. Therefore, the answer to the age-old question is, yes—do play "hard to get."

A brief excursion into the legend of St. Valentine, the unofficial patron saint of romance, illuminates Tennov's portrait of limerence. During his reign, the Roman Emperor Claudius Gothicus (Claudius II) issued a decree that all Roman citizens must worship and pay homage to the 12 Roman gods. The monk Valentinus is said to have been a man of learning and a devout Christian. He refused to forsake his religion and was arrested for secretly marrying Roman soldiers when Claudius had forbidden it. Disobedience of this sort was considered a crime analogous to treason and punishable by death. Valentinus was kept in prison until the date of his scheduled execution.

During his captivity, Valentinus met a beautiful young woman named Julia, who, like love itself, was completely blind. She was the daughter of the jailer, who recognized Valentinus as a learned man. The jailer appealed to Valentinus to provide Julia with an education. She was delighted by Valentinus's teachings and cherished his accounts of nature and God. Julia confessed to Valentinus that each day she prayed for sight so that she could discover all the beauty that he had described. Valentinus is said to have assured her, "God does what is best for us only if we believe in Him." As the story goes, they sat quietly in prayer when suddenly the prison cell was enveloped by a brilliant white light. Julia's shrill voice pierced the air. "Valentinus, I can see," she shrieked, "I can see!"

On the eve of his death, Valentinus wrote a note to Julia urging her to remain close to God, even in his absence. He signed it, "From Your Valentine." His death sentence was carried out the next day, February 14, 270 AD, near a gate that was later named Porta Valentia, in his honor. He was buried at what is now the Church of Praxedes in Rome. According to the legend, Julia planted a pink-blossomed almond tree near his grave, which has endured as a symbol of abiding love and affection.

Undoubtedly, if Tennov (1979) could have observed the legendary courtship, she would have concluded that indeed a strong state of limerence had occurred. Julia, the blind child of a watchful father, presumably had little opportunity for intimate male contact. Valentinus, even though he was a prisoner, was as close as she might ever come to an attainable lover.

Admittedly, the probability of actualizing a sexual relationship was quite remote, but Julia's blindness might have intensified her romantic fantasies. Valentinus, knowing that he was to die, might well have telegraphed his natural desires to be wanted and loved. Of course, the slightest hint from Valentinus that Julia's affection might be reciprocal would fuel her desire even more. Finally, the impending execution—particularly when we consider that Julia must have prayed for Valentinus's life, and on some level must have believed that God would spare him—most definitely meets Tennov's criterion of uncertainty regarding the future.

In some sense, the abrupt curtailment of Julia's short-lived romance was a blessing in disguise. Had Valentinus's sentence been commuted to life imprisonment, Julia might have encountered an even more difficult predicament. She would have continuously longed for the love of her life: the unattainable soul mate that helped her to see beauty in nature and affirmed her faith in God. The limitations of her childhood, coupled with the incomparable joy that she experienced with Valentinus, would etch a permanent imprint on her psyche. The fleeting moments of pleasure that she could extract from periodic visits to his cell would only enlarge her desire and prolong her suffering. Indiscretion would surface, as rationality would eventually dwindle to a mere silent observer. The folly of love would progressively erode her happiness, and eventually she would reach the same tortured state that many of us have endured—feeling desperately entrapped in love's crushing grip. Her behavior might well have been characterized by compulsion, loss of control, and continuation despite harmful consequences.

We can all identify with Julia's hypothetical plight. The combination of psychological need and social pressure "to be in love" is so great that we compulsively hang on, even after the game is over. In the short run, having a lover, no matter how problematic the relationship, serves to deflect the ubiquitous existential concern, "I am afraid to face my life and death alone." Objectively, it is not whether two people stay together, but *how* they stay together, that separates genuine intimacy from love addiction. In a healthy love relationship, both members strive to enrich and fulfill their lives through intense, mutual involvement. The love addict, despite a multitude of protestations to the contrary, cares little about the well-being of his or her partner. Romance junkies demand or beg for approval and affection in an escalating cycle of disappointment and reprisal. Eventually, harmful consequences result, including deterioration of work, social, or health functions. Alcohol, for example, may be used as a temporary stopgap for feelings of anger and despair. Unfortunately, most demoralized lovers who take refuge in the womb of spirits cannot honestly echo the famous boast attributed to W. C. Fields, "It was a woman who drove me to drink and I haven't had the decency to thank her."

Those who become addicted usually lack confidence in their ability to cope without some form of support, either real or imagined, from a love object. Klein and Liebowitz (1979) of the New York State Psychiatric Institute have proposed the term *hysteroid dysphoria*—a chronic and intense form of lovesickness—as a category of mental disturbance. The disorder, which they have observed with surprising frequency in the course of their psychiatric practice, is characterized by depression, depletion of energy, and increased appetite in response to feelings of rejection. Conversely, when a romantic figure shows even minimal signs of approval, hysteroids react with increased energy and euphoria. People who suffer from this disturbance seem to fall in love more easily than others, and with less discretion. Their moods are marked by great sensitivity to even the slightest sign of disapproval, particularly from people in whom they have made romantic investments.

If you seem to have more than an academic interest in this syndrome, then perhaps you may be questioning your own propensity as a love addict. Fear not; nearly everyone has a similar reaction: "Is that me?" Don't forget, however, that you can have mild, moderate, or severe degrees of love dependence, as with addiction to food, drugs, or alcohol, and the symptoms are remarkably the same. If your relationship meets three or more of the criteria listed below, then love may be your Achilles' heel.

- *Denial.* Your friends and family say you're in a bad relationship, but you don't agree.
- *Immediacy.* You require frequent emergency "pow-wows" with your lover in social and business situations.
- *Compulsion.* You've broken up (seriously) at least twice, yet you always make up.
- *Loss of control.* You often feel powerless to control your feelings or behavior with regard to your lover.
- *Progression.* Over time you suspect that your relationship has been on a downward spiral.
- *Withdrawal.* You become depressed and experience physical disturbance (loss of sleep or altered eating and drinking patterns) when distanced from your lover.

Neurochemistry of Romance

While the language of love is undoubtedly poetry, the language of the brain where love abides is chemistry. We respond chemically to other human beings. In fact, romantic attachment has been attributed in part to *oxytocin,* a hormone first released when the baby is nursing and in subsequent love connections throughout life. It has been postulated that those suffering from autistic spectrum disorders may have an oxytocin deficiency (Slater, 2006).

At the level of the neuron, our synapses are stirred by a lover's furtive glance. Love itself has become a legitimate target for neurochemical analysis. And why not? Through the use of positron-emission tomography (PET) and magnetic resonance imaging (MRI), scientists can now take pictures of the brain at work. It has been shown that emotion-laden events trigger the release of neurotransmitters that affect particular regions of the brain. In anxious people, for example, neurochemical activity increases in the right brain hemisphere. Altered neurotransmission in people with severe depression or schizophrenia has been the focus of intensive brain research for the past three decades. Some neuroscientists have now turned their attention to the study of positive feeling states. Anthropologists at Rutgers University recruited subjects who claimed to be "madly in love" for an average of 7 months (Fisher, Aron, & Brown, 2005). Each was shown a neutral photo and one of his or her beloved. MRI data showed that love lights up the *caudate nucleus*, which is home to a rich network of dopamine receptors.

> What excited Fisher most was not so much finding a location, an address for love, as tracing its specific chemical pathways. . . . [Fisher came to think of] dopamine as part of our own endogenous love potion. In the right proportions, dopamine creates intense energy, exhilaration, focused attention, and motivation to win rewards. It is why, when you are newly in love, you can stay up all night, watch the sun rise, run a race, ski fast down a slope ordinarily too steep for your skill. Love makes you bold, makes you bright, makes you run real risks, which you sometimes survive and sometimes . . . don't. (Slater, 2006, p. 35)

Writing for *Scientific American Mind,* in an article entitled "Affairs of the Lips," Walter (2008) unravels the neurochemistry of kissing. We all know that a "good" kiss can enhance a relationship and that a "bad" kiss can destroy what may have initially been perceived as a possible long-term commitment. A "good" kiss should produce an increase in oxytocin, which is involved in social bonding, and a decrease in cortisol, which should decrease stress. Hill and Wilson (2007, cited in Walter, 2008) compared the levels of oxytocin and cortisol in college male–female couples before and after kissing and while talking and holding hands. The researchers were surprised to find that only the males in the study experienced a rise in oxytocin after kissing. The females experienced a decrease in oxytocin after kissing or talking while holding hands. Perhaps females need more than a kiss to feel emotionally connected. As expected, the level of cortisol dropped in both sexes no matter the level of intimacy. Kissing also boosts blood pressure and increases pulse rate. Unfortunately, rationality decreases as emotional intensity increases—a classic example of the amygdala dominating the cortex.

According to Liebowitz, author of *The Chemistry of Love* (1983), a substance known to biochemists as phenethylamine (recall Chapter 2) or PEA is released in the brain when we fall in love. The PEA molecule, which is considered an excitatory amine, bears striking structural similarity to the pharmaceutically manufactured stimulant amphetamine. Liebowitz regards the accelerated use of PEA, which occurs during infatuation, as the key to feelings of excitation, exhilaration, and euphoria.

An important similarity between PEA and amphetamine is that the benzene ring is basic to each of their molecular structures. The nineteenth-century German chemist Kekulé, who dreamed about the chemical composition of benzene, may have been even more of a seer than anyone has yet realized. Kekulé had spent many hours trying to discover the structure of the benzene molecule. One evening, while dozing in front of a fire in a half-dream state, he imagined the leaping flames to be snakes that twisted and turned. Suddenly, the snakes curled around and held onto their tails with their mouths. At this moment, Kekulé awoke and realized that he had visualized the structure of benzene, which is a closed carbon ring, as he had imagined the snakes to be. He is currently credited with having discovered the chemical structure of benzene. Until now, however, Kekulé's snake has evaded recognition as the same cunning serpent that tempted Eve to eat from the Tree of Knowledge. Indeed, there is the sense of having violated our own innocence as we trespass on the heretofore unspoiled *Garden of Romance*. There is a tinge of shame as we reduce one of life's most exalted experiences to more mundane fluctuations in brain chemistry.

Yet rapidly advancing brain science will not be slowed by the sentimental reins of romance. No matter how mystical we perceive love to be, we are now aware of its neurochemical aspects. Indeed, remarkable biological parallels exist between pathological drug use and the unhealthy need for affection. Becoming dependent on love may be described as a dynamic process with two distinct biochemical phases: infatuation and attachment.

Infatuation is usually an experience of heightened energy and feelings of euphoria. According to Liebowitz (1983), the initial period of psychosexual attraction produces increased concentrations of the neurotransmitter-like substance phenethylamine. The brain responds to this chemical in much the same fashion as it would to amphetamine or cocaine; infatuated lovers seem to experience boundless energy, elation, and a remarkable sense of well-being. They have no problem in "painting the town red," then going to work, then going out the following night and doing it all over again.

After a short time, however, the speedy feeling appears to reach a maximum level, and lovers begin to recognize that their relationship is on a plateau. The romance remains exciting, yet the remarkable sensations of invigoration and euphoria appear to be dwindling. In chemical terms, the pleasure of falling in love is derived not from increased production of PEA, but rather from steady increases in the rate of PEA production. When PEA acceleration reaches zero, that is, when increments in the rate of chemical reward have stopped, the honeymoon is over.

At this juncture, one of two possible biochemical processes becomes operative: amphetamine-like withdrawal, or a shift to an endorphin-mediated relationship. In the attachment phase, long-term lovers are able to make the transition from zooming around in the fast lane to enjoying cuddles and quiet evenings at home. But recall the chemistry of contentment. The prolonged love-swoon is, after all, an opiate-mediated experience. If one member of the relationship is a "dyed-in-the-wool" arousal type, he or she may seek excitement from people and places outside the relationship. The pair bond may dissolve as one or the other partner subjectively experiences boredom, stagnation, and depression.

Love and Death

It is love's unequaled capacity to profoundly influence each of the three pleasure planes—arousal, satiation, and fantasy—that qualifies it as the pièce de résistance of the addictions. While the human inclination toward intimate pairing affixes a territory within which mating can occur, it also holds the trigger to the most primitive impulses on earth. An instant of reflection on love's hearty contribution to homicide and suicide reminds us of the horrifying consequences of uncontrolled passion.

Poetry, the language of love, is often used to express the agony and ecstasy of life's most exalted emotion. In "Porphyria's Lover," Robert Browning (1888) encapsulates a man's compulsion to murder his sweetheart, aspiring to preserve forever his moment of ecstasy.

Be sure I look'd up at her eyes

Happy and proud; at last I knew

Porphyria worshipp'd me; surprise

Made my heart swell, and still it grew

While I debated what to do.

That moment she was mine, mine, fair,

Perfectly pure and good: I found

A thing to do, and all her hair

In one long yellow string I wound

Three times her little throat around,

And strangled her. No pain felt she;

I am quite sure she felt no pain.

Edgar Allen Poe writes of his morbid obsession upon the death of his wife, in "Annabel Lee":

For the moon never beams without bringing me dreams

Of the beautiful Annabel Lee,

And the stars never rise but I feel the bright eyes

Of the beautiful Annabel Lee.

And so, all the night-tide I lie down by the side

Of my darling, my darling, my life, and my bride,

In her sepulcher there by the sea,

In her tomb by the sounding sea.

"Annabel Lee" follows Poe's favorite theme: the death of a beautiful woman (J. Meyers, 1992), which Poe (1849) has called "the most poetical topic in the world."

The addictive quality of romantic attachment becomes painfully obvious during periods of actual or anticipated separation. As in the examples of Browning's "Porphyria's Lover" and Poe's "Annabel Lee" above, sudden or prolonged absence can cause paranoid thoughts and deranged conduct. Forlorn satiation types may become as pathetic as any heroin junkie who suddenly finds himself without a fix. Love addicts may survive for years, completely undetected, so long as there is a constant drug supply. However, they may cheat, lie, steal, or kill—even for a minimal dose—to avoid the dreaded pain of withdrawal.

Some people become so dependent on the rush of increased concentrations of PEA that they encounter severe depression, fatigue, and lethargy as their rate of excitatory neurotransmission begins to level off. Marazziti and Dell'osso (2008), at the University of Pisa, Italy, found neurochemical similarities between love and obsessive-compulsive disorder (OCD). They measured serotonin levels in the blood of people who had fallen in love in the last 6 months and admitted to obsessing about this love object for at least 4 hours per day. When compared with people suffering from OCD, they found the levels of serotonin in both groups were 40% lower than normal. Serotonin-enhancing drugs like Prozac may alleviate some of the negative feelings associated with obsession, but one's ability to fall in love and stay in love may be jeopardized.

Prozac might have been a godsend in the highly publicized and extremely bizarre love affair of Burton Pugach and Linda Riss. Upon learning that Riss, his ex-lover, had recently become engaged, Pugach hired a thug who threw acid in her face, disfiguring and eventually blinding her. Interestingly, low levels of serotonin are also associated with impulsivity and violence. We speculate that Pugach's depression was related to low levels of serotonin (Krakowski, 2003). Pugach was released after serving 14 years in prison for the assault, and then the couple married. The story of their twisted romance, detailed in the case study that follows, was recorded in newspapers and magazines throughout the United States and was also made into a documentary film (*Crazy Love*, 2007).

Case Example: Mr. and Mrs. Pugach

> On the morning of Monday, June 15, 1959, as 22-year-old Linda Riss prepared to leave her apartment . . . the doorbell rang. "Package for Miss Linda Riss," a man behind the door called out. The young woman, who had celebrated her engagement to a Brooklyn man named Larry Schwartz the previous afternoon, ran to the door, hoping to find a gift from her new fiancé. As the door was opening, she saw a flash of cardboard, then felt burning liquid spray across her face. At first she thought it was hot water. The scorching liquid was lye. It instantly left her blind in one eye and, despite years of subsequent surgery, would [eventually] leave her totally blind; it also left scars across her scalp and on her right cheekbone. Though she did not recognize the attacker, she immediately knew who was responsible: the powerful, smooth-talking Bronx lawyer named Burton Pugach who was her ex-boyfriend. (Fass, 2004, p. 4)

Pugach had tried to convince Linda Riss that he would soon be divorced. After about a year of waiting, she concluded that it would never happen and had tried to break off contact. Pugach, by his own admission, was "obsessed" and in the 6 months that followed he became increasingly violent. Carrying a gun, he would wait for her after work, hiding in the bushes near her apartment. He once hired someone to throw a rock through her apartment window, and he developed a pattern of calling and threatening to kill her if she continued to reject him. When she called the police, they typically responded that because he was a lawyer, nothing could be done. At this point, she decided to marry Larry Schwartz, an upbeat 23-year-old who worked in the uniform rental business. Because of his apparent calmness and pleasant demeanor, Ms. Riss thought of Schwartz as a perfect antidote to Pugach's vicious intensity (Fass, 2004).

At the engagement party, she received what would be the last of the threatening phone calls. "If I can't have you," Mr. Pugach told her, "no one else will have you. And when I get through with you, no one else will want you." At 8 the next morning, a man named Heard (Joe Louis) Harden appeared at her door, hiding a container of lye in a cardboard box. To this day, Mr. Pugach denies that he hired anyone to do such a thing. . . . "I didn't even know what it was. I just asked him to beat her up. They say love is a form of insanity, that you lose all rationality" (Fass, 2004, p. 4).

> After being imprisoned for 14 years, Pugach was granted parole on March 21, 1974. Upon his release, he was interviewed by two local TV stations. According to the conditions of his parole, he was forbidden from speaking directly to his victim, so he proposed to her over the nightly news. A few months later, one of her friends arranged a double date, and so in August 1974, the couple had their first meeting since the trial. (Fass, 2004, p. 4)

Pugach credited several factors, in the years that followed his imprisonment, which might account for Riss's striking decision to marry him: a Christian sense of forgiveness; the advice of a fortune-teller; and an increasing conviction that the police were to blame because of their failure to act. She also feared that Pugach might be such a good catch that someone else would quickly grab him (Fass, 2004).

> "After we were married," said Mr. Pugach, who was disbarred after his conviction and now has a lucrative practice as a paralegal, "believe it, she loved me." "Well, 'love' might be a little strong," his wife replied with a laugh. After 30 years of marriage, the two don't seem that different from many other long-married couples, although there have been blips in their relationship, like Mr. Pugach's conviction several years ago on of a (*sic*) violation after harassing a woman with whom he was having an affair. They have even developed their own dark jokes on the subject. Mrs. Pugach, whose skin looks remarkable for her 67 years, responds to compliments by saying, "Lye is good for the skin but bad for the vision." When asked if his wife holds a grudge, Mr. Pugach, now 76, replied with a smile, "She doesn't throw it in my face" (Fass, 2004, p. 4).

MDMA: Synthetic Love

Mr. and Mrs. Pugach's craziness may be an extreme version of the prototypic "whirlwind romance" where the couple enacts wildly fluctuating changes in brain chemistry. Yet describing love in terms of its properties of arousal, relaxation, and fantasy doesn't capture what many regard as a "spiritual quality." When you gaze into your lover's eyes and all of infinity opens before you, you are one with your partner and at one with the world around you, as if time itself has stopped. Aesthetics explode—art, nature, theater, and music become backdrops for your courtship.

It would seem that there must be yet another chemical mediator, even more potent than dopamine, PEA, oxytocin, or endorphin, to account for these transcendent experiences. In fact, Liebowitz (1983) postulates that there is an additional, albeit not yet discovered, neurochemical factor, shorter in duration than the psychedelic drugs, yet similar in effect, that is responsible for the spiritual wonders of love. Liebowitz suspects that there is a psychedelic version of PEA that endows transcendent love with its mystical quality. As William Shakespeare wrote in his Sonnet 29,

> Haply I think on thee, and then my state,
>
> Like to the lark at break of day arising
>
> From sullen earth, sings hymns at heaven's gate;
>
> For thy sweet love remember'd such wealth brings
>
> That then I scorn to change my state with kings.

If Liebowitz is correct, then perhaps there is a synthetic drug that mimics the action of the suspected neurochemical Aphrodite. It has long been recognized, and particularly underscored by the discovery of endorphins, that addictive drugs are structurally quite similar to naturally occurring brain chemicals. Is there a manmade drug that possesses the combination to the vault of mystical love? On the street, they call it Ecstasy (a.k.a. Disco biscuit, Go, XTC, or the Hug Drug). In the laboratory, it is properly referred to as 3,4-methylenedioxymethamphetamine, or MDMA (see Chapter 8).

MDMA is less potent and differs only slightly in chemical structure from the psychedelic MDA, known in the 1960s as the "love drug." In *The Marriage of the Sun and Moon*, Weil (2004) describes his observations of how people react to MDA.

> Such experiences confirm in a powerful way the sense of well-being. It feels as if nothing is threatening, and, in fact, things in the external world behave differently. This theme carries through to interpersonal relations. When people feel well, centered, unthreatened, and aware of their own strength and loveliness, they are able to drop many of the

usual barriers that develop in groups. It is common in group MDA experiences for people to explore mutual touching and the pleasures of physical closeness. Participants may feel very loving toward one another, but the feelings are not explicitly sexual because MDA tends to decrease the desire for orgasm. For many people the experience of enjoying physical contact and feeling love with others in the absence of a specific hunger for sex is unique and welcome. (Some people do use MDA to heighten sexual experience.) (p. 178)

Ecstasy seems to combine some of the hallucinogenic effects of mescaline with the stimulant effects of amphetamine. Those who endorse Ecstasy cite case histories where MDMA was used as a tool in psychotherapy, triggering insight and releasing patients from emotional injury.

> Inside the gerbil treadmill that is my brain, I stopped and blinked, exhaled and looked around. My mind was clear. "I am so happy," I thought. . . . I didn't feel stoned or daydreamy. Unlike classic psychedelics, MDMA—or as it is known to scientists, methylenedioxymethamphetamine—doesn't disrupt your basic sense of who you are. You barely even feel weird. Also it doesn't scramble your external perceptions, except that soft things feel softer, music sounds better. It was in no way hallucinogenic. With Ecstasy, I had simply stepped outside the worn paths in by brain and in the process, gained some perspective on my life. It was an amazing feeling. (Klam, 2001, p. 69)

Should I Try Ecstasy?

Many advocates for MDMA believe, "Nothing that can make you feel so good could be bad." There is an abundance of anecdotal evidence for the drug's capacity to bring out beauty and love. And then there is the scientific perspective. As discussed in Chapter 8, research has shown that MDMA may cause irreversible and long-term damage to dopaminergic neurons and damage to serotonergic nerve endings. There is also a decrease in the gray matter in several parts of the brains of users. Therefore, it is not surprising that there is evidence for long-term memory and other cognitive deficits. However, some of this research has been disproven by other scientists. So what are we to believe?

The conflicting data does show damage to serotonin-releasing neurons, although the extent of this damage is controversial. However, other effects on health that seem to be substantiated are dehydration, hypertension, brain swelling, hyperthermia, and heart and kidney failure. Considering the potential damage to the brain and the rest of the body, use of Ecstasy appears to present considerable risk. R. K. Siegel (1986), a psychopharmacologist at UCLA, finds that under high doses people may become insane rather than ecstatic. The case of Legba provides a vivid example of the inane and irrational quality of one user's Ecstasy experience.

The Case of Legba

Legba grew up in a small, lovely red house surrounded by trees, beside a church. Now after being buffeted for hours by hurricanes of throbbing techno bass, shuddering astral hisses, a monsoon of sound amid a deluge of bodies, kids grinning into their shoes that they'd found it, the nirvana that Tim Leary dangled in front of another generation—now, after a long night on the cusp of revelation, 5 in the morning, the house was awfully quiet in comparison. Legba didn't need to go to bed yet, and like any good evangelist at sunrise, he kept reaching out, this time to the only living thing that would let him near—the family bird. He tried to talk to the cockatiel, Chippie. Dr. Doolittle opened the cage door and tried to grab it. He felt that love, undeniable, universal, and blind. Legba tried to hug Chippie, more gently now, so as not to scare it. The bird screamed. It thrashed at him, it tried to bite and claw him. There was nothing left, nothing else to swallow or smoke or love, there was nowhere to go now. He gave up, there in Mom's kitchen, and went to bed. (Klam, 2001, p. 69)

Chapter Summary

Romantic love is panhuman: It proliferates in almost every culture on earth, embedded in our brains since Pleistocene times. The nightmare of tormenting love is nothing but a miscarriage of our natural attraction toward people who evoke feelings of safety and pleasure.

Tennov (1979) describes the romantic love people seek as *limerence*. Limerence occurs when thoughts are dramatically focused on one person and there is uncertainty about the future of the relationship. Love is a psychological and social need of humans, and a healthy love is one in which both members are mutually involved in the relationship. Love junkies, on the other hand, demand attention and hang on even when harmful consequences follow. They tend to follow a repeating pattern of finding support from one love object, then moving on to the next. Some characteristics of love addiction include denial, immediacy, compulsion, loss of control, progressive problems, and withdrawal. The compulsion to find and be in love can become unmanageable, painful, and insatiable.

Using MRI data from people who were "madly in love," Fisher et al. showed that love lights up the caudate nucleus, which is home to a rich network of dopamine receptors. According to Fisher et al., the increased availability of dopamine is the neurochemical basis for why, "when you are newly in love, you can stay up all night, watch the sun rise, run a race," and so forth. Hill and Wilson found that after kissing, males had increased levels of the hormone oxytocin, which is important in the formation of secure bonding and attachment; however, females showed a decrease in the same hormone. Both males and females showed a decrease in the stress hormone, cortisol, after kissing or talking while holding hands.

The neurochemical phenethylamine (PEA) is released in the brain while one is falling in love. PEA closely resembles the molecular structure of the stimulant amphetamine, perhaps a reason for the intense feelings of excitement, exhilaration, and euphoria when love is in the air. The roller-coaster tide of heightened energy and euphoria one experiences when falling in love will reach a maximum level after some time, and love can either go to an endorphin-mediated relationship or an amphetamine-like withdrawal, which at some point will need to be replaced with a new experience of falling in love. Love addicts experience severe depression, fatigue, and lethargy when their PEA increases level off. Love addicts share neurologic similarities with those who suffer from obsessive-compulsive disorder—low levels of serotonin in their brains.

Some seek to experience love-like sensations by tinkering with their brain chemistry. Ecstasy has been referred to as the "hug drug" because of its euphoric, anxiety-dissolving, communication-enhancing, and insight-amplifying properties. The hallucinogenic and stimulant effects of the drug have encouraged some research into using the drug for psychotherapeutic purposes. Regarding harmful effects, scientific data does show damage to serotonin-releasing neurons, although the extent of this damage is controversial. Other effects on health that seem to be substantiated are dehydration, hypertension, brain swelling, hyperthermia, and heart and kidney failure. Considering the potential damage to the brain and the rest of the body, use of Ecstasy appears to present considerable risk.

13 Marijuana—Reefer Madness Revisited

> But I would not feel so all alone
>
> Everybody must get stoned
>
> —Bob Dylan, "Rainy Day Woman," 1966

Marijuana is the most widely used illicit drug in the United States. It can be taken orally, mixed with food, smoked in concentrated form as hashish (more common in Europe), smoked in rolled cigarettes (i.e., "joints," the form of nearly all consumption in the United States), or smoked in pipes and occasionally hollowed-out cigars ("blunts"). In 2007, an estimated 14.4 million Americans age 12 and older had used marijuana at least once in the month prior to being surveyed (SAMHSA, 2008). The NIDA-funded 2008 Monitoring the Future Study (cited in Johnston, O'Malley, Bachman, & Schulenberg, 2008) showed that 10.9% of eighth graders, 23.9% of tenth graders, and 32.4% of twelfth graders had used marijuana at least once in the year prior to being surveyed. Table 13.1 summarizes some of the potential adverse health effects of this widely used drug. Given the well-known threat potential as shown, why do so many people—some brilliant and well established, even some health professionals— throw caution to the wind?

"Benefits" of Pot: Why Do So Many People Smoke?

Those who are pro-legalization assert that the beneficial uses of marijuana have been documented for thousands of years (Nadelmann, 2004). Consider this testimonial by the late Carl Sagan, world famous for writing popular science books and for cowriting *Cosmos: A Personal Voyage*, seen by more than 600 million people in over 60 countries, making it one of the most widely watched PBS programs in history (Svetkey, 1997). The following

Table 13.1   Adverse Health Effects of Marijuana

Acute (present during intoxication)

- Impairs short-term memory
- Impairs attention, judgment, and other cognitive functions
- Impairs coordination and balance
- Increases heart rate

Persistent (lasting longer than intoxication, but may not be permanent)

- Impairs memory and learning skills

Long-term (cumulative, potentially permanent effects of chronic abuse)

- Can lead to addiction
- Increases risk of chronic cough, bronchitis, and emphysema
- Increases risk of cancer of the head, neck, and lungs

SOURCE: National Institute on Drug Abuse (2005b).

account was written for publication in *Marihuana Reconsidered* (Grinspoon & Sagan, 1971). Sagan was in his mid-thirties at that time. He continued to use cannabis for the rest of his life.

> There is a very nice self-titrating aspect to cannabis. Each puff is a very small dose; the time lag between inhaling a puff and sensing its effect is small; and there is no desire for more after the high is there. I think the ratio, R, of the time to sense the dose taken to the time required to take an excessive dose is an important quantity. R is very large for LSD (which I've never taken) and reasonably short for cannabis. Small values of R should be one measure of the safety of psychedelic drugs. When cannabis is legalized, I hope to see this ratio as one of the parameters printed on the pack. I hope that time isn't too distant; the illegality of cannabis is outrageous, an impediment to full utilization of a drug which helps produce the serenity and insight, sensitivity and fellowship so desperately needed in this increasingly mad and dangerous world.

Marijuana remains illegal in the United States, and it seems that the consequences of getting caught should deter novice users, yet they do not (Amonini & Donovan, 2006). Why does pot retain its status as the most popular illicit drug? Essentially, marijuana aficionados expect positive effects and have a less negative view of possible problems. Gaher and Simons (2007) investigated users' and nonusers' appraisals of the "benefits" of relaxation and tension reduction, facilitation of social and sexual contexts, and enhancements of mind and perception. They found that cannabis users anticipated positive outcomes in each of these domains while forecasting fewer and less frequent problems (i.e., less harmful consequences as the result of use) than nonusers. Johnston, O'Malley, Bachman, and Schulenberg (2007) have shown that since 1975 there has been an inverse relationship between the percentage of high school students who smoke pot and their perception of risk. The period from 1990 to 1991 in which the lowest percentage of high school students reported marijuana use in the past 12 months (about 20%) corresponds to the period where the highest percentage (about 80%) reported seeing "great risk" in regular use. Further, users find pot to be more morally acceptable than other drugs (Amonini & Donovan, 2006), and a primary reason that adolescents initiate use is peer approval. When peers discourage use, chances of abstinence increase significantly. Of course, the opposite is true as well (Henry & Kobus, 2007).

Tidal social forces appear to be far more powerful determinants of contemporary pot culture than an individual's attitudes about the benefits or risks of using marijuana. In Zinberg's classic work, *Drug, Set, and Setting: The Basis for Controlled Intoxicant Use* (1984), the author presented compelling evidence that social setting is a primary (perhaps the major) determinant of an individual's choice to use an intoxicant. Drug use is intimately related to large social influences such as media, war, and massive environmental change (Halperin & Bloom, 2007; Zinberg, 1984). As the Beatles cheerfully sang, "I get by with a little help from my friends / I get high with a little help from my friends / Gonna try with a little help from my friends." From the jazz "vipers" of the 1930s to the hippies of the 1960s to the stoners of the 21st century, marijuana has been used as a unifying element within subsets of the larger society (Halperin & Bloom, 2007). From "stoner slogans" such as "Puff, puff, pass," to "Can't we all just get a bong?" the media consistently refers to cannabis as a formidable social influence (Halperin & Bloom, 2007). Major movies such as *Dazed and Confused* (1993), *Half-Baked* (1998), *Easy Rider* (1969), *Fast Times at Ridgemont High* (1982), and the collection of films by Cheech and Chong (1978, 1980, 1981, 1983) often portray friendship and love as promoted by pot (Halperin & Bloom, 2007). The growth and success of many marijuana festivals and marijuana rallies give some insight into the steadfast and growing popularity of mass social gatherings tied to marijuana. Events such as the Fourth of July Smoke-In, which was founded in 1970; Hash Bash, founded in 1971; and the Marijuana March, established in 1971 still "toke" on today. Newer rallies including the Boston Freedom Rally and the Seattle Hempfest hold crowds of between 15,000 and 50,000 marijuana-loving individuals per day (Halperin & Bloom, 2007). Music festivals have been popular since Woodstock, and some of the largest music festivals of today promote the peaceful gathering of potheads, including the Bonnaroo Music and Arts Festival, which holds up to 80,000 people, and the New Orleans Jazz and Heritage Festival, which takes in up to 100,000 people per day (Halperin & Bloom, 2007).

Osborne and Fogel (2008) found that participants used marijuana in what they considered to be appropriate social contexts for two purposes: either to become more relaxed to enjoy the activity or to become more focused on the activity so that they could better enjoy it. This study found that especially for adult users, marijuana had predominantly a social function. Almost half of the participants reported that a primary motive for using the drug was enhancing social contact. Many of the participants said that the drug "brings people closer together" and creates camaraderie between users. It appears that facilitation of a sense of intimacy along with relaxation and pleasurable cognitive and perceptual shifts are alluring aspects of this powerful plant. Given all the positive propaganda for the "pot scene" and testimonials from the drug users themselves, why would someone not want to use marijuana?

Effects on the Brain

According to the Drug Abuse Warning Network (SAMHSA, 2003), the most frequent drug-related visits to hospital emergency rooms for youths 12 to 19 are for marijuana abuse. In 2001, there were over 26,000 emergency room visits by youths in this age-group for problems related to marijuana or marijuana in combination with other drugs.

Cabral (1996) summarizes the effects of chronic marijuana abuse on the brain, the endocrine system, and the immune system. Since marijuana in sufficient doses is hallucinogenic, we would expect that the main ingredient (tetrahydrocannabinol, or THC) responsible for this effect would have receptors in the brain. Such receptors have been found in the hippocampus, the cortex, and the cerebellum. These are the areas of the brain involved in memory, cognition, and coordination. Our brains are programmed to react to THC by conveniently providing receptors for a naturally occurring cousin of THC, *anandamide,* named after the Sanskrit word for "bliss."

These naturally occurring neurotransmitters are referred to as *endo-cannabinoids* (endogenous cannabinoids). As shown in Figure 13.1, THC receptors have not only been found in the cerebellum, hippocampus, and neocortex but also in the nucleus accumbens (reward), basal ganglia (movement), hypothalamus (temperature regulation), amygdala (emotion), spinal cord (pain), central gray (analgesia), brain stem (sleep, arousal), and the nucleus of the solitary tract (nausea, vomiting) (Nicoll & Alger, 2004).

In addition, marijuana also has a negative effect on psychomotor speed and manual dexterity. It is obvious from the effects listed above that driving while under the influence is very hazardous.

The 1939 film *Reefer Madness* became a cult classic in the 1960s and 1970s because of its outlandish claims of the harmful effects of marijuana. This type of ridiculous treatment of a serious drug problem does a disservice to law enforcement besides taking lightly the actual negative health effects of marijuana.

Withdrawal

One of the hallmarks of addiction is the presence of negative physiological and psychological effects upon removal of the drug. The occasionally

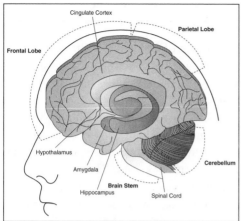

When marijuana is smoked, its active ingredient, THC, travels throughout the body, including the brain. To produce its many effects, THC attaches to sites called cannabinoid receptors on nerve cells in the brain, affecting the way those cells work. Cannabinoid receptors are abundant in parts of the brain that regulate movement, coordination, learning and memory, higher cognitive functions such as judgment, and pleasure.

Brain Region	Functions Associated With Region
Brain regions in which cannabinoid receptors are abundant	
Cerebellum	Body movement coordination
Hippocampus	Learning and memory
Cerebral cortex, especially cingulated, frontal, and parietal regions	Higher cognitive functions
Nucleus accumbens	Reward
Basal ganglia	Movement control
Substantia nigra pars reticulata	
Entopeduncular nucleus	
Globus pallidus	
Putamen	
Brain regions in which cannabinoid receptors are moderately concentrated	
Hypothalamus	Body housekeeping functions (body temperature regulation, salt and water balance, reproductive function)
Amygdala	Emotional response, fear
Spinal cord	Peripheral sensation, including pain
Brain stem	Sleep and arousal, temperature regulation, motor control
Central gray	Analgesia
Nucleus of the solitary tract	Visceral sensation, nausea and vomiting

Figure 13.1   Marijuana's effect on the brain.

SOURCE: National Institute on Drug Abuse. (2005, July). *Marijuana abuse* (Research Report Series, NIH Publication Number 05-3859). Washington, DC: Author.

proclaimed view that marijuana in nonaddicting is contradicted by observed withdrawal effects. Kouri, Pope, and Lukas (1999) found that long-term marijuana users who were unsuccessful at quitting became more aggressive during withdrawal than did former users who managed to stop using without much difficulty. Haney, Ward, Comer, Foltin, and Fischman (1999) found that chronic users experience other withdrawal symptoms such as anxiety, stomach pain, and irritability. Budney, Hughes, Moore, and Novy (2001) showed that during abstinence and while living at home, marijuana smokers experienced sleep difficulties; decreased appetite; and increased anger, aggression, and irritability. These studies on withdrawal effects clearly indicate that contrary to earlier opinions, marijuana use can be associated with drug dependence.

Effects on Cognition

One area in which there is little difference of opinion is that of the effect of marijuana on the brain with accompanying deficits in cognition. This observed impairment is not surprising since animal studies have shown that marijuana causes structural damage to the hippocampus, a brain region involved in memory and learning. Bolla, Brown, Eldreth, Tate, and Cadet (2002) found that heavy abusers, compared with light abusers of marijuana, suffered deficits in verbal and visual memory, executive functioning, visual perception, psychomotor speed, and manual dexterity. These impairments lasted for at least 28 days and possibly longer after discontinuing use. An interesting observation by Bolla and coworkers was that *cognitive impairment* from smoking marijuana was greater among those with lower IQ scores than those with higher scores. Bolla believes that those with higher IQs have more cognitive reserves, and the impairment from marijuana will not be as obvious as among those with lower cognitive reserves, that is, lower IQs. Earlier research by Pope, Gruber, Hudson, Huestis, and Yurgelun-Todd (2001) indicated that cognitive impairment from heavy marijuana use seemed to *disappear after one month*.

According to Pope and Yurgelun-Todd (1996), it is very clear that heavy marijuana use decreases the ability to learn and remember while under the influence of the drug. The problem is not so much getting the abusers to remember a previously learned item; the basic problem is "getting them to learn in the first place." Therefore, students who smoke marijuana might be expected to get lower grades in school than those who abstain.

Serious Mental Disorder

Perhaps the most devastating insult to cognition, excluding Alzheimer's disease, is the development of delusions and hallucinations, the most salient symptoms of psychosis and the chronic brain disease, schizophrenia. Studies conducted in Holland, New Zealand, and the United States have examined links between cannabis use, psychosis, and schizophrenia. Although it has not been proven that there is a causal link between excessive marijuana use and severe mental disorder, the following conclusions have been drawn:

- There is a strong association between use of cannabis and age at first psychotic episode in male schizophrenic patients (Veen et al., 2004).
- There is either a common vulnerability with cannabis and psychosis or a two-way causal relationship between the two (Ferdinand et al., 2005).
- Cannabis is the trigger for psychosis in genetically predisposed frequent marijuana users (Fergusson, Horwood, & Ridder, 2005).

- Cannabis psychosis cases are arguable misdiagnoses of extreme cases of acute cannabis intoxication and harmful cannabis use or mental-behavioral disorders stemming from other or multiple drug use (Newcombe, 2004).
- Cannabis use is not a sufficient cause for psychosis, but rather a component cause (i.e., part of a complex mix of factors that lead to psychosis) (Arseneault, Cannon, Witton, & Murray, 2004).

Marijuana and the Endocrine System

Murphy, Muñoz, Adrian, and Villanúa (1998) indicated that several studies have shown that the *reproductive system* of marijuana users may be affected by alteration of the secretion of hormones from the *pituitary gland*. This gland secretes a number of hormones that control reproductive function in humans. These include follicle stimulating hormone (FSH), luteinizing hormone (LH), and prolactin, all of which play a role in the secretion of both the female hormone estrogen and the male hormone testosterone. Clearly, tinkering with Mother Nature at this basic level is a prescription for disaster.

Marijuana and the Immune System

The human immune system is a complicated one that enables the body to resist the invasion of bacteria, viruses, and other microbes. This system also offers protection against tumors by inhibiting cancer growth. Cabral, speaking at the National Conference on Marijuana Use: Prevention, Treatment, and Research (1996), presented evidence that the ingredient in marijuana that is responsible for the negative effects observed in the immune system is our familiar hallucinogenic compound THC. This is not exactly a surprise. The scavenger cells of the immune system, which are responsible for ridding the body of pathogens, are subject to damage by exposure to THC. Marijuana has also been shown to have a negative effect on T- and B-lymphocytes, which are important in fighting bacterial and viral infections. Because marijuana use is often associated with sexual promiscuity, impairment of the immune system creates an additional risk factor that may be associated with the spread of herpes, type B hepatitis, and AIDS.

Long-Term Effects on Health

Although there may be some conflicting evidence on long-term brain damage from smoking marijuana, there is no difference of opinion on the damage to the lungs. These effects from long-term abuse are similar to and in many cases worse than in the case of cigarette smoking. Marijuana smokers experience frequent respiratory illnesses, daily coughing with phlegm production, obstructed breathing pathways, and frequent lung infections. Other effects on the lungs of marijuana smokers may include acute pneumonia, inflammation of airways, chronic bronchitis, acute chest illnesses, and possibly emphysema. The carcinogenic molecules and tars in marijuana smoke make smokers especially vulnerable to lung cancer, as well as head and neck cancers.

Medical Marijuana

There has been recent interest in using marijuana for medical purposes, especially relief from pain. In 2005, Canada became the first country in the world to approve a *cannabis-based* painkiller derived from marijuana for those suffering from multiple sclerosis. Several states in the United States have laws legalizing the use of marijuana for medical purposes. These laws run contrary to the federal ban on such usage. The U.S. Supreme Court (B. Mears, 2005) ruled that the federal law supersedes the state laws and that users of medical marijuana could be arrested.

Chapter Summary

Marijuana is the most controversial of the illegal drugs and is the most widely used illicit drug in the United States. The NIDA-funded 2007 Monitoring the Future Study showed that a surprising number of school-age kids had used marijuana at least once in the year prior to being surveyed. Zinberg presented compelling evidence that social setting is a primary determinant of an individual's choice to use an intoxicant. Drug use is intimately related to large social influences such as media, war, and major environmental change. Tidal social forces seem to be greater determinants of pot culture than one's attitude regarding the benefits or risks of using marijuana.

Those in favor of unrestricted use claim that marijuana is beneficial in appropriate social contexts for two primary purposes: (1) It helps users become more relaxed to enjoy the activity; and (2) it enhances their enjoyment by making them more focused on the activity. Many adult users report that a primary motive is to enhance social contact. They believe that it "brings people closer together" and creates camaraderie between users. Facilitation of a sense of intimacy along with relaxation and pleasurable perceptual shifts are alluring aspects of this drug.

Despite the enjoyable aspects of marijuana use and widespread endorsement of looser government controls, there is substantial evidence that chronic marijuana usage has negative effects on memory, learning, and cognition. There is some dispute regarding how long these effects last. However, with animal studies showing destruction of cells in the hippocampus, there can be little doubt that long-term marijuana smoking impacts the ability to remember and especially to learn new information. One of the most deleterious effects of marijuana smoking is permanent damage to the lungs. Although it has not been proven that there is a causal link between excessive marijuana use and severe mental disorder, the correlation is important to consider.

14

Romantic
Sex Fantasy

Of the delights of this world, man cares most for sexual inter-course. He will go to any length for it—risk fortune, character, reputation, life itself.

—Mark Twain

The euphemistic "Gentlemen's Club" is by far the most prevalent type of sex bar facility. Needs for sensation seeking, sexual arousal, and intimacy are routinely handled by a cadre of fantasy lovers. In terms of money, the exchange between dancers and patrons occurs on three levels: selling of drinks, table dances, and private performances (Brewster, 2003). Sexual interaction occurs in three distinct spaces: the stage, the floor, and the private room (Forsyth & Deshotels, 1997). The club's public performance areas are usually the dancer's first encounter with "paying clients" and her opportunity to size up future economic gains. Performances are time-framed around a set of musical songs. Dancers use "impression management" techniques (Goffman, 1959) by dressing in various costumes and performing certain erotic movements to arouse a particular client's sexual fantasy (Brewster, 2003).

Although some venues may occasionally provide access to male strippers, sex bars primarily cater to a heterosexual male clientele. Emboldened by the club's explicit license for sexual pursuit, patrons may indulge in any manner of erotic fantasy. At center stage, stimulation is primarily visual, with interludes of close-up, one-on-one interaction, as strippers make special maneuvers for attentive customers. Stage-side customers usually tip when they are personally addressed, by conveying rolled-up dollar bills to the forbidden ecstasy beneath a dancer's G-string.

If attraction is consummated, the provocative female may be invited to perform more private and intimate dances at café-style tables. "Lap dances" are often the prelude to more isolated settings where the level of touch and intimacy is further advanced. Activities such as these allow for limited sexual pleasure; they conjure feelings of intimacy and romance, without the interpersonal demands, anxiety, guilt, and fear that often accompany sexual encounters.

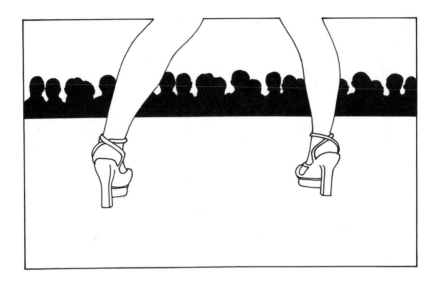

Figure 14.1   Arousing sexual fantasies. Dancers use "impression management" techniques, dressing in various costumes and performing certain erotic movements to arouse a particular client's sexual fantasy.

Who Attends and Why

Erickson and Tewksbury (2000) have described the following six types of strip club patrons:

- *Lonely:* Motivated to establish companionship, attention, and conversation
- *Socially impotent:* Unable to maintain normal interaction within other public settings
- *Bold lookers:* Found mostly at the large stage, openly objectifying dancers, rarely attempting conversation, attending strictly for visual stimulation
- *Detached lookers:* Not interested in companionship or conversation, they attend for visual stimuli, but not to "look" as intensely as the bold lookers
- *Players:* Seek conversation and companionship and use their social personalities to obtain these goals; regular but small tippers, rarely willing to spend the money for a private couch dance
- *Sugar daddies:* Older compared to other patrons and appearing more affluent, the sugar daddy often establishes a long-term relationship with a dancer and while in the club relates exclusively with "his girl" (p. 281)

The predominant motive for infrequent or intermittent attendees at a strip club may be the sexual "turn-on" with the underlying idea of having a sexual encounter outside the club (Ronai & Ellis, 1989). This type of motivation is particularly relevant to the group identified above as "players" who may obtain bragging rites by dating a stripper. But sexual arousal and having sex outside the club are not the underlying motivating factors for those with more stable bonds to the sex club atmosphere. For many, the need to be intimate, to be seen close up, to feel recognized, to feel attracted by and attracted to another human being, are the driving human forces.

Four lines from John Lennon and Paul McCartney connote society's challenge to provide positive means to meet the needs of the lonely and forlorn.

All the lonely people

Where do they all come from?

All the lonely people

Where do they all belong?

—John Lennon and Paul McCartney, "Eleanor Rigby," 1966

In fact the predominant source of income for women who sometimes earn nightly pay in excess of $1,000 at the Gentleman's Club is simply providing conversation to a mostly male clientele who seek comfort, closeness, friendship, and companionship. Intimacy-for-pay seems a fair price to those who struggle with profound loneliness and lack of belonging. In Chapter 17, Maintaining Close and Intimate Relationships, we offer concrete examples of how needs for intimacy can be met by consciously orchestrating more fulfilling and meaningful relationships within the contexts of marriage, family, and friendship. The answers to the questions posed in the lyrics above are self-evident. Loneliness is a condition brought about by a lack of intimacy in our lives. The solution is to promote healthy alternatives to the purchase of closeness at erotic dance clubs. Table 14.1 summarizes a broad spectrum of motives for strip club attendance.

Several researchers have recognized the importance of intimacy and companionship among club "regulars" (e.g., Erickson & Tewksbury, 2000; Forsyth & Deshotels, 1998). Enck and Preston (1988) characterize the dancer–patron relationship as "counterfeit intimacy" where the posturing of words, facial expressions, and body movements mimic genuine romance. Price (2000) describes "monetary regulars" (sugar daddies) as patrons who appear to have a very strong commitment to "their girl," and Ronai and Ellis (1989) noted that "some regular customers acted as if they were involved in a long-term serious relationship with a dancer . . . forgetting the businesslike nature of the bar setting" (p. 287). Egan (2003) comments further that

regular customers . . . form both emotional and erotic bonds with their dancers, viewing themselves as "more than costumers." These men view themselves as "lovers" and/or "boyfriends" of the dancer they come to see on a regular basis and on whom they spend large amounts of money (up to $50,000) on services and gifts (ranging from roses to breast implant surgery and cars). (p. 109)

Table 14.1   Motives for Strip Club Attendance

- Most men, especially regulars, recognize that sexual activity is available at other venues of the sex industry and state that they go to clubs to "relax."
- Strip clubs provide a different atmosphere from work and home where male sexuality is accepted by women and sexual experiences are offered without pressure, with some degree of safety.
- There is a permissive sexualized atmosphere compared with other spaces where sexual disinhibition may cause difficulty.
- The presence of nudity and the opportunity to talk allow for the creation of fantasies that are stimulating to customers.
- Clubs provide safe opportunities for interactions with women without the risk of rejection.
- Clubs serve as a site for the return of adolescent fantasy; dancers become the high school girl that got away.
- Visits are intertwined with men's concerns about losing a youthful body; reinvigorating the sexual response allays concerns over loss of masculinity.
- The fantasies of sexual possibility and interpersonal intimacy are alluring.
- One can be rid of his everyday persona, with its many demands and frustrations, and given a new script from which to play a different part. There is a fetishization* of the new role, that is, a fantasy self, as well as a fetishization of the dancer.
- Patrons do not desire a real physical relationship (that they could easily obtain by paying sex workers at other venues) but rather a realistic fantasy of such a relationship.
- Many men claim to be committed to monogamy and choose strip clubs because they would neither be expected nor tempted to have sexual contact with the dancers.
- Encounters are secret and interactive, sexualized but not sexual, seen as guilt-free romantic encounters, outside of committed relationships.
- Nonsexual liaisons and relationship building with strippers provide opportunity for newness and excitement as committed relationships evolve from passionate to affectionate.
- Visiting the club, even when undetected, is a means of enacting vengeful fantasies toward the spouse or significant other. The partner would be hurt by being excluded from a sexualized relationship.

*. Fetish: an object, idea, or activity that a person is irrationally obsessed with or attached to (Encarta Online Dictionary).

Men who find continued club refuge usually experience varying degrees of conflict in their external pursuit of sexual and emotional intimacy. Disinhibited by alcohol (and sometimes other drugs), patrons interact with nude (or nearly nude) women without concerns of commitment, need to perform, or rejection. Based on her experience as both a dancer and an ethnographic researcher, Egan (2003) offers a psychoanalytic perspective on the symbolic nature of the stripper–patron relationship:

Sex workers in general and exotic dancers in particular occupy a more complex site than do most women in the matrix of desire, fantasy and power. Like other women, they become objects in the symbolic in order to sustain the male ego and his position within the phallic function. However, exotic dancers also occupy a unique position in that their bodies are sought out in the market as objects of desire and as such it is their job to recognize men and make them feel desired and desirable. Moreover it is their job to become screens for male fantasy, quelling male anxiety of the unknowability of the feminine. (p. 112)

Sex bar recreation bears similarity to a widely used sex therapy treatment technique known as sensate focus. The basic premise is that apprehension during sexual interaction interferes with sexual excitement and pleasure. In females, anxiety blocks the lubrication and swelling phase; in the male, it suppresses erection. The goal of treatment is to reduce tension and to restore confidence. This may be achieved by promoting sexual enjoyment while minimizing the demands associated with arousal and intercourse. Couples are instructed to avoid having intercourse or orgasm, while actively appreciating the erotic sensations of non-demand sexuality.

Hartley (1997), a self-proclaimed "hard core" stripper, explains how being an effective "sex therapist" is an important dimension of her self-identity:

Through my experiences stripping, I learned many valuable lessons. I learned that my body was attractive to many different men, even though I am many inches and pounds way from any magazine model. I found that the majority of heterosexual men will follow sexually if the woman will only lead, and that men feel victimized around sex just as women do, only in different aspects of the sexual dance. I realized that, as a committed feminist, I had to be open to men's pain and see it [as] equally valid to women's. I discovered that a woman who is willing to talk about sex honestly and show her body can get men to listen, learn, and be better lovers with their partners. Finally, I learned that to be eternally mad at men's sexual "nature" was as useful as being mad that water is wet. Anger inhibits intimacy and shared pleasure, to the detriment of all involved. I seek in my work to defuse anger so that the pleasure I invoke can work its healing magic. (p. 61)

On the basis of interviews with 22 female strippers, Barton (2002) found that these women initially derive feelings of empowerment from being sexually liberated, generating substantial income, and being told they are beautiful. Toward the latter stages of the stripper's career, however, these "benefits" are eventually countered by feelings of being emotionally drained and feeling worse about their bodies, their sexuality, their intelligence, and ultimately their identity in the social world. This liability is highlighted by radical feminists who emphatically condemn the sex service industry. No matter where they are in the continuum from empowerment to degradation, many strippers claim they derive a positive sense of purpose from their therapeutic role:

Vivienne happily described herself as the resident therapist at the Velvet Lounge. She, like other dancers, felt that an important part of her job was talking to customers about their wives, girlfriends, and families and being supportive and caring. For the most part, dancers expressed enjoyment of this aspect of the job as long as the customer treated them with respect. Indeed, Vivienne feels that this part of the job is not really "work."

As Vivienne herself put it, "You strive toward being able to go in there and not have to dance and make as much money as you possibly can. To dance the least and make the most, I think that's the goal. To get paid strictly for talking, strictly for being a companion because there's no real work in that." (p. 596)

Case Example: "Intimacy" at the Gentlemen's Club

Nicky, a master's degree candidate in counseling psychology (by day) and a popular stripper (by night), describes how the need for intimacy is the major driving force for many of her paying customers:

I have personally experienced the phenomenon of men seeking intimacy without sexuality. Dean is an excellent example. I met him during a convention in Denver. All he wished [for] was companionship and a dinner partner. He explicitly expressed that he had no desire to have me dance or disrobe for him. Dean is not alone; many men I have met are seeking intimacy beyond physical sexuality. Initially, the erotic component may be what draws them in, being that it is socially acceptable in a patriarchal society, where masculinity is valued. However, the men I have encountered, who return to the same club and the same woman for years, are not ultimately interested in the sexual aspect of the environment. They seek companionship and intimacy. I know of numerous men who have developed long-term relationships with entertainers that transcend the immediate suggestion of the environment. These men come to talk to the entertainers. They ask the women about their lives and families. They ask for advice and express concerns. They want someone who will listen to their triumphs and disappointments. They want someone who will empathize and connect with them.

Often, these men want a woman to whom they can give gifts and celebrate holidays. It is an interesting situation which can be interpreted in many ways. Perhaps this woman is similar to a wife without strings attached or commitments or pressures. Maybe some of these men want to do something good for someone else, take care of someone. Maybe they want to be important in someone's life. I believe the motives are complex, fluid, and derived from numerous sources. They may change day to day within the context of each individual man's experience. However complex the motives are for engaging in such behavior, it is clear to me that these patrons seek something much different from the surface content.

Another phenomenon I have noticed with other entertainers and myself is that of patrons taking entertainers to the private dance area and paying the usual price for each song ($20–$30), except wanting to sit and talk to the women instead of having them disrobe and dance.

They may desire other non-erotic activities as well, such as giving or receiving a backrub or engaging in prolonged eye-contact. A regular client of mine, Adam, has prolonged eye-contact as his favorite activity. He enjoys receiving some dances and some conversation, but frequently desires that we gaze silently into each other's eyes for at least 5 minutes at a time.

Another interesting point to note is the concept of "skin hunger," the idea that people who are deprived of appropriate physical contact with others crave any sort of physical contact. This need may be misinterpreted as sexual desire. I believe that this may be especially true for males in our culture. It is not socially acceptable for most men to receive nurturing touch and care. I have found examples of this phenomenon with men who continually attempt inappropriate physical contact with me.

For some men, having their primary intimate relationship with an entertainer in an adult establishment can be a negative or damaging experience. I have known many men who become obsessed with an entertainer, putting unhealthy amounts of time, energy, and money into this largely one-way relationship. Conversely, I have also known many men who have benefited from such one-way relationships.

Henry is a man who has been married for 20 years. He loves his wife, yet he has not been able to achieve the level of intimacy with his wife to share certain personal aspects of himself. Henry has several entertainers to whom he has become appropriately close. With the women, he is safe to share ideas, fears, and thoughts that he is not comfortable doing with his wife. Rarely does Henry allow an entertainer to dance for him. When one does, it is almost never one of those he sees regularly. Henry's relationship with myself and his other favorite entertainers reminds me in some ways of counseling relationships. The entertainers self-disclose appropriately, but do not return the same openness displayed by Henry. The relationships between Henry and each of these women [are] characterized by warmth and respect from both parties. These relationships differ, of course, from psychotherapy in numerous ways, the most salient being the fact that Henry also likes to be entertained with alcoholic beverages, light and humorous conversation, and watching the on-stage entertainment taking place in the room.

Frederick is another example of how intimacy in a gentlemen's club can be beneficial. Frederick desired a relationship with a woman, but had gone through a bad marriage and in general, lacked social skills and confidence related to dating. He also felt cynical about women and relationships due to his divorce. He met an entertainer in a club who was warm, accepting, kind, and patient. He began coming to the club to see her once every one or two weeks. He paid her to dance for him, but mostly to spend time talking with him. After awhile, Frederick quit visiting the club. Several months later, he sent "his" entertainer a letter (at the club). He thanked her for spending time with him, making him feel good, being genuine, and giving him the courage and hope to begin dating.

The Allure of Prostitution

Some men go beyond the wish-fulfilling fantasies of the strip club, seeking pleasure, intimacy, and physical contact with prostitutes. By promoting themselves as the "sugar daddies," they cull favors from sex surrogates who rely on steady cash to fulfill their economic agenda. Prostitution exists at all levels of society, from back-alley slums to upscale escort services. Some consumers travel to known sex-service destinations such as Costa Rica or Thailand for full-blown "case management." Women at various sex venues are readily solicited as surrogate lovers; they may be available for minutes or hours; a given evening as weekend partners; or even as long-term, live-in companions. A number of entrepreneurial travel agents have built surrogate lovers into special vacation packages.

Prostitution is one of the world's oldest professions (Ramirez, 2008) and has existed in just about every culture. Today, it is a lucrative business, with the state of Nevada alone bringing in around $50 million in revenue each year. Brothels are legal in Nevada in counties with fewer than 400,000 residents. Cities such as Las Vegas attract the gamblers, but often vacations include a trip north or south to brothel businesses. Nevada has become more lenient with their laws regarding prostitution, as brothels can now advertise in areas outside of the county where they are based. The old-fashioned word-of-mouth advertising has been surpassed by bill-boards, Internet ads, telephone book listings, and radio and television commercials.

Different kinds of prostitution rings have been uncovered, ranging from the high-end "D.C. Madam" operation to a "brothel on wheels" in South Beach, Florida (Skipp & Campo-Flores, 2008). This limousine bus was a custom conversion with leather benches and a full-service bar, with prices ranging from $10 for a "stand-up" dance to over $100 for access to a special curtained-off VIP area. Then, of course, there are the women who are termed "street workers." These girls and women, as their title implies, work the streets in seedy areas of cities across the world.

Deborah Palfrey was the backbone of an elite, sophisticated, alleged prostitution ring (Hosenball & Conant, 2007). Her escort service catered to a wealthy, upper-class, male clientele by hiring powerful elite women. This business ran under the name Pamela Martin & Associates and employed women who worked white-collar jobs as paralegals, lawyers, college pro-fessors, and even military professionals. These were not just young women, new to the world of prostitution; rather, they ranged in age from 23 to 55. Another high-end escort service, the Emperor's Club VIP, was busted with New York governor Eliot Spitzer's fall from grace. This type of elite escort service caters to a wealthy clientele and operates in cities all over the world. Clients shell out anywhere from $5,500 an hour to $31,000 a day (Campo-Flores & Smalley, 2008).

There are some important lifestyle differences between high-end escorts, indoor sex workers, and women who operate from the street. The "com-mercial sex" of indoor workers (i.e., those who work in spas or massage parlors, or for escort services) allows for the service providers to set some psychological boundaries between their job and their personal lives (Sanders, 2005). These women are more likely to be aware of the dangers in selling their bodies. Escort service workers tend to have some control over selection of their customers and the settings in which prostitution occurs (Sanders, 2005).

In contrast, street-working prostitutes tend to have polydrug-using habits, experience more violence in their work and home lives, and are usually under the thumb of a pimp or partner. Street workers are exposed to far more violence, from verbal abuse to assault, rape, and murder. Their mortality rates are up to 40 times the national average. Studies have found that these women are more likely to have experienced sexual and physical abuse as children. The average age of introduction into prostitution in the United States is around 13 to 14 years old.

Why is paying for sex so widespread? Plumridge, Chetwynd, Reed, and Gifford (1997) studied the motives of men who frequented massage parlors. Subjects were from 23 to 78 years old. Many were married or in serious relationships. Their professions ranged from white collar, to blue collar, to self-employed. Although a small percentage acknowledged looking for "kinky" sex, most claimed they just wanted "normal" services such as vaginal intercourse, fellatio, and masturbation. The men taking part in the study had been purchasing sex for some time; that is, none of them were first-timers. All asserted that the main reason behind purchasing sex was pleasure. Many viewed prostitution as an exciting step out of the monotonous sex they had with their wives or lovers. While there was almost universal appreciation of having sex with no strings attached, "the men argued that paid sex was not just a social contact, it was represented as emotional" (Plumridge et al., 1997, p. 174). It was not the same as love to these men, but they experienced some emotional attachment. Perhaps the most interesting finding of this study was that these men all truly believed in reciprocal and mutual feelings on the part of the prostitutes with whom they had sex. In fact, research shows that most prostitutes do not get enjoyment from their work and do not experience romantic feelings toward the men they service. As street solicitation is more common and is different in character from "indoor" prostitution, these results may not be generalizable to men obtaining services from street workers.

There has been a recent shift in law enforcement's response to prostitution. Police around the United States focus on the demand for services, rather than on the sellers (Ohtake, 2008). Programs such as the First Offender Prostitution Program (FOPP), or the "School for Johns," have been implemented in many states. These programs use former street workers to get the johns arrested for soliciting sex, then dispel their fantasies of mutual enjoyment and provide them with a dose of reality. Many street prostitutes have HIV, other STDs, or Hepatitis C, thanks to unsafe sex, rapes, and drug use, and they only make around $20,000 a year. Police are hoping with a reduction in the rate of demand will come a reduction in the rate of service. Demand reduction is predicated on educating men to see that *they* are the ones in the business for the company and what they experience as intimacy. The woman is there to make ends meet, to get another fix, or because she just does not realize that she deserves more in life than selling her body.

Chapter Summary

The "Gentlemen's Club" is by far the most common sex bar facility. Clients' needs for excitement, closeness, and intimacy are satisfied to some degree by fantasy lovers. While male strippers have an increasing role in the strip club industry, gentlemen's clubs primarily cater to a heterosexual male clientele. Six types of strip club patrons have been identified: lonely, socially impotent, bold lookers, detached lookers, players, and sugar daddies.

Several researchers have recognized the importance of intimacy and companionship to club "regulars." The dancer–patron relationship functions as a sort of "counterfeit intimacy" where words, facial expressions, and body movements imitate genuine romance. Sex bar recreation resembles a widely used sex therapy treatment technique known as sensate focus, the basic premise being that apprehension during sexual interaction gets in the way of sexual excitement and pleasure. The goal of treatment is to reduce tension and restore confidence. The sex club atmosphere is free of performance expectations and associated anxiety.

Sex club dancers initially experience feelings of empowerment from being sexually liberated, generating a good income, and being told they are beautiful. However, in the latter stages of their career, these "benefits" are eventually countered by negative feelings about their bodies, their sexuality, their intelligence, and ultimately their identity. Even so, many strippers say they get a positive sense of purpose from what they see as their therapeutic role in helping men feel better about themselves.

Some men go beyond the wish-fulfilling fantasies of the strip club, seeking excitement and intimacy by having sex with prostitutes. There are some important lifestyle differences among high-end escorts, indoor sex workers, and women who operate from the street. The "commercial sex" of indoor workers allows them to set some psychological boundaries between their job and their personal lives. In contrast, street-working prostitutes tend to have multiple drug-use habits, experience more violence in their work and home lives, and are usually under the thumb of a pimp or partner.

Only a small percentage of sex customers in massage parlors or other indoor commercial venues acknowledge looking for "kinky" sex. Most claim interest in "normal" services such as vaginal intercourse, fellatio, and masturbation. Many view prostitution as an exciting alternative to boring sex with their wives and lovers. Repeat customers believe reciprocal and mutual feelings are felt by their paid sex partners. In fact, most prostitutes do not enjoy their work and do not experience romantic feelings toward the men they service.

Finally, the chapter noted a recent shift in law enforcement's response to prostitution in that U.S. police programs are focusing more on reducing demand for services, rather than reducing the supply of sellers. Former street workers are sometimes employed to set up johns who are then arrested for soliciting sex, and their fantasies of mutual enjoyment are actively dispelled.

Many street prostitutes have STDs or Hepatitis C, because of unsafe sex, rapes, and drug use, and they only make around $20,000 a year. Demand reduction is brought about by educating men to see that *they* are the ones who think they are experiencing closeness or intimacy with the sex worker. The woman is merely there to earn a buck, to get another fix, or because of low self-esteem or low expectations for her life.

SECTION VI

Journey to Oblivion

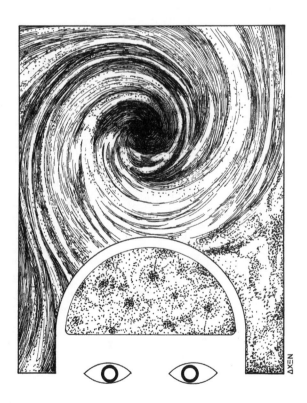

Obsessed by a fairy tale, we spend our lives searching for a magic door and a lost kingdom of peace.

—Eugene O'Neill

15

The Voyage of Hardship and Suffering

Drugs are a waste of time. They destroy your memory and your self-respect and everything that goes along with your self-esteem.

—Kurt Cobain

Introduction: The Disease Concept of Addiction

The concept of addiction as a progressively incapacitating disease (i.e., a "journey to oblivion") originates from a series of lectures presented by Jellinek (1952) at the Yale Summer School of Alcohol Studies in 1951 and 1952. On the basis of a questionnaire study of more than 2,000 male alcoholics, Jellinek formulated his four-phase concept of alcohol addiction. He distinguished between two categories of alcoholics: "alcohol addicts" and "habitual symptomatic excessive drinkers." The disease concept applies only to alcohol addicts who, after a variable period of problem drinking, lose control over their alcohol intake. Excessive drinkers, on the other hand, may pathologically use alcohol to relieve conflict for many years, yet the phenomenon of loss of control never becomes part of their drinking history.

In the first phase of alcohol addiction, which Jellinek (1952) called the "pre-alcoholic symptomatic phase," the prospective alcoholic begins to experience an inordinate amount of tension reduction through drinking and drinking-related activities. Generally, within a period of 6 months to 2 years, Jellinek's typical subject begins to use alcohol nearly every day to relieve stress. Although his tolerance for alcohol exceeds that of his peers—that is, he can drink a good deal more than they before reaching a desired level of intoxication—his excessive drinking remains relatively inconspicuous and undetected.

The sudden emergence of alcohol-related blackouts marks the second, "prodromal phase" of alcohol addiction. A blackout may be understood as a period of intermediate memory loss, whereby a person who imbibes as few as 2 ounces of absolute alcohol may carry on a reasonable conversation or complex pattern of activity without a trace of memory of it the following day. The blackout period is indeed intermediate in that the drinker experiences normal memory functions before and after the lost interval.

Soon after the onset of blackouts, the drinker begins to understand, in some very vague manner, that his pattern of drinking is different from that of others. He begins to sneak drinks at social gatherings and becomes preoccupied with when and how to get high. At this point, the prodromal drinker may be observed to gulp drinks while increasing guilt leads to more obvious signs of covering up. The incipient alcohol addict may, for example, conspicuously avoid any reference to alcohol, pro or con, during conversation. Depending on the drinker's physical and psychological condition, as well as the nature of his social network, the prodromal period may persist for anywhere from 6 months to 4 or 5 years.

The next stage of alcohol addiction, which Jellinek (1952) referred to as the "crucial phase," is marked by loss-of-control drinking. The addict appears to lose the faculty of making rational choices about how much to consume. Any level of consumption, even the taste of one drink, seems to trigger an irresistible demand for alcohol that continues until he is either too drunk or too ill to consume any more.

Loss of control comes into play only when people respond to conflict or stress by succumbing to drink. Before drinking, the alcoholic may appear sensible, affable, and emotionally intact. During this phase, he begins to rationalize his unseemly drinking by creating easily detected alibis (i.e., transparent excuses for drinking), attempting to convince himself that he has good reason to become intoxicated. He minimizes the extent of his disturbance by drawing attention to irresponsible actions among friends and associates.

At this point, alcoholism begins to bring about warnings and reprisals from family, friends, and business associates. The drinker, now thoroughly entrenched in the crucial phase of alcohol addiction, progressively withdraws from his usual social environment. He becomes noticeably more aggressive, with more frequent and penetrating feelings of desperation and remorse. He loses contact with most of his "straight" friends. Flurries of overcontrol (going on the wagon) alternate with episodes of alcoholic debauchery. The addict attempts to regain control by altering specific aspects of his behavior: He may change the times, beverages, or locations that have characterized his past drinking. His entire behavioral repertoire becomes markedly alcohol-centered, as drinking becomes his most salient need. Support from family and friends dwindles to a pittance, while sexual drive and nutritional prudence are negligible when compared with the need to consume alcohol. The drinker may now experience the first of a series of alcohol-related hospitalizations resulting from accidents or physical illness.

The crucial phase begins to terminate when the addict becomes so demoralized and confused by the conflict among outside pressures, inner needs, and his growing dependence on alcohol that he begins each day by steadying himself with a drink. Intoxication, however, usually remains restricted to the evening hours. The crucial-phase alcoholic may succeed in retaining his employment through many years of compulsive, loss-of-control drinking, although family life usually deteriorates dramatically.

The final or "chronic phase" is marked by prolonged periods of intoxication, colloquially referred to as *binges*. At this stage, the alcohol addict may drink with characters who are morally and intellectually inferior to his customary clique. His thinking and physical functioning begin to show dramatic signs of impairment. A relatively small percentage (approximately 10%) of alcoholics experience full-blown psychotic symptoms, such as hallucinations, delusions, or both. Tolerance for alcohol is diminished (half the amount previously required may be sufficient for intoxication and stupor), while indefinable fears and physical tremors begin to emerge. These symptoms of withdrawal appear as soon as alcohol is no longer present in the body. Consequently, the drinker "controls" them through continuous consumption.

Finally, the need for alcohol looms so large that the addict can no longer maintain any pretense that he has control over his drinking. According to Jellinek (1952), many alcohol addicts (approximately 60%) develop vague spiritual desires as they begin to call upon a higher power to rescue them from the alcoholic abyss. At this point, the addict has spontaneously become amenable to treatment for the disease (Figure 15.1).

The case example of John, a former addict, now a licensed alcohol and drug counselor, provides a personal account of one man's progression through Jellinek's (1952) phases of addictive disease. As illustrated by John's story, the disease model describes a general pattern, a progression of addictive behavior. The specific events of each person's journey, however, are unique to his or her genetics, sociocultural background, and current life situation.

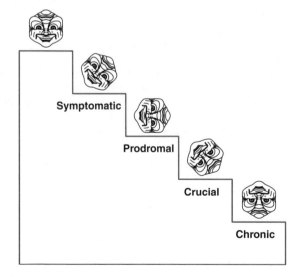

Figure 15.1   **Jellinek's disease model of alcoholism.** The disease concept applies to "alcohol addicts" who, after a variable period of problem drinking, progressively lose control over their alcohol intake.

Case Example: Journey to Oblivion and Back

Raised by both parents, I remember having a great early childhood of security, serenity, and happiness. At the age of 12, my life slowly began to change as I became aggressive and progressed to become the bully of bullies.

Pre-alcoholic Symptomatic

At the start of high school, I was introduced to drugs and alcohol and I really liked them. I began by sneaking drinks because I was underage and still living with my parents who did not approve. I did not have to get angry, sad, or frustrated anymore. I didn't have to feel anything. It started out with sneaking some here and there, then quickly progressed to a weekend thing, pretty much every weekend, then my use went to three or four times a week—plus the weekend. Most of the time I was relying on alcohol to soothe those feelings I didn't want to be feeling. I saw my tolerance was well above my peers, as I would be finishing off my second beer when they were just getting through their first.

Prodromal

During my sophomore year in high school, the blackouts started. I didn't try to hide my excessive drinking because I was always a jerk so I never cared who saw me. I was aware of the difference in my drinking from others, but I didn't think much of it. I isolated from anyone who was straight, turning to the streets, hanging around gangs and experimenting with more and bigger types of drugs, which triggered a lot of warnings from the judicial system.

Crucial/Chronic

Life took a drastic turn as my family was falling apart. My parents divorced, and I was overwhelmed with sadness and anger from seeing my mom suffer. I drank and used even more because the pain and anger were so extreme. Looking back, the first real experience that the game began was when I was drunk and found my dad and beat him pretty badly. I got a juvenile domestic violence charge, which I tried to fight. I claimed I was not in a relationship with my dad, but because it was family, the courts considered it a relationship and so the charge stuck.

I would say I was going to quit and not drink for a month or two, but then I would flip around and drink and use cocaine for weeks at a time. I was never officially in a gang, but members of my family were involved in the north side gangs and I was good pals with many members of a south side gang. The more we drank, the more eager we were to stir up some drama in the streets. One time we were real intoxicated and we went and shot at some guys from a gang on the west side. They found out pretty damn quick who we were, and about 3 hours later we were kicking it at my friends' and the members from the other gang came by and did a drive-by. A few of my pals got injured, shot in the leg, what have you, and I was sitting next to my partner Louie and my cousin was on the other side of him. Louie was shot in the neck, my partner, my friend, he died.

There were lots of drunken fights, [and] almost every single one ended in gunfire. At this time I was selling lots of drugs and always had guns on me. If we were shot at, we had to retaliate, and sometimes we were the aggressors. There were a couple times that I blacked out, only to wake up to hear that I had beaten up some good friends so badly that the damage in the friendships was irreparable. It felt horrible, and still to this day it feels that way, to not even remember doing something so brutal to people that I was so close with.

When I was incarcerated, I drank even more than I had been. My kidneys would be in so much pain if I didn't drink that no matter what I took, aspirin, whatever, it didn't help the pain. Only alcohol would relieve the intensity of it, but this helped me justify my drinking at the same time. I witnessed many stabbings, both in prison and on the streets. In prison, hooch (slang for alcohol made in prison) often goes hand-in-hand with power. The more *items* (a.k.a. drugs and alcohol) you could trade or swap for the more power you would get, the more comfortable you could live, and the more options you could have. I was in the hole multiple times, but luckily never for being caught with hooch. The hole is a small cell that you sit in 23 to 23½ hours a day locked down in nothing but your underwear, and the showers are brought to you. You have to wash your hair while handcuffed; it's basically jail inside of jail.

Recovery

I was put in the south end of Buena Vista, known for its nickname as Gladiator Camp because everybody in there is in there for a gang charge or a murder charge. There is lots of politics in prison and it's a dog-eat-dog world. There are lots of perpetrators preying on others to survive. One time I observed a little Chicano kid, 18 or 19 years old, come in and mouth off to a big African American guy. The African American guy was drunk and horny and raped the little Chicano in the shower. A couple days later, after the boy got out of the infirmary, the African American tried to say he had only done it because he was drunk but the Chicano went up to this huge guy and started pounding him in the face. [H]e ended up stabbing the big guy to death, stabbed him over 40-some times, but the whole situation was blamed on the alcohol. I started to hate everything that alcohol stood for.

At that point, I became truly aware that my life had become unmanageable and I started to ask God for help. It may not seem like a big thing to others, but by denying myself my second parole I gave myself the life I am living today. I knew if I was released at that time that once I got out, I would be right back in . . . back in the alcohol, the drugs, the violence. It means a lot to me that I stayed in jail almost another 6 months until a bed in a rehabilitation center opened up because at that point I was able to start living. When I got out of the horrible clutch of that alcohol and drug addiction, I was able to get on the path I am now.

I entered into rehab complemented with Alcoholics Anonymous. I completed the rehab program and have maintained my sobriety since. I still go to AA meetings and I am fond of the group I found. I am now happily married, and have two beautiful daughters. I am grateful to say that the trials and tribulations I have been through made me the man I am now, motivated and determined to stay away from the life I once led. But that experience provided me with a path to help others, and I've been counseling adults and adolescents for the last 6 years.

Since Jellinek's (1952) early formulation more than half a century ago, the disease model for alcoholism has been embraced by Alcoholics Anonymous, the National Council on Alcoholism, the National Institute on Alcohol Abuse and Alcoholism, and the American Medical Association. Alcoholism is now widely accepted as a disease when loss of voluntary control over alcohol consumption is the cause of an individual's social, psychological, and physical dysfunction. In short, an alcoholic may be thought of as a person who cannot always control when he or she starts or stops drinking. His or her life becomes unmanageable, with or without the bottle. Recent evidence for genetic and biochemical influences on alcohol abuse and dependence is covered in Chapter 3 (e.g., Crabbe, 2002; Heinz, 2006).

In the past two decades, the disease concept, originally formulated for addiction to alcohol, has been enlarged by treatment practitioners to include a slew of potentially addictive agents such as gambling, sex, and eating, as well as a plethora of addictive substances including cocaine, amphetamines, and opiates (e.g., Donovan, 2005; Lesieur & Blume, 1993; Schneider & Irons, 2001). Like cancer, addiction is viewed as a potentially fatal disease that may be triggered by a variety of causes. Among the many substances associated with addictive disease are (1) alcohol; (2) the sedative hypnotics, including the barbiturates (e.g., Seconal and Tuinal) and the benzodiazepines (e.g., Valium and Librium); (3) the opiates and opioids (e.g., heroin, morphine, codeine, Percodan, Demerol, and methadone); (4) the central nervous system stimulants, including methamphetamine and cocaine; and (5) the hallucinogens, including LSD, PCP, and marijuana. Addictive substances may be used separately or in various combinations. Alcoholism has a high rate of co-occurrence with cigarette addiction as well as addiction to various other drugs (Crabbe, 2002). The process behind this comorbidity has proven to be heavily influenced by genetics (Edenberg & Foroud, 2006).

Michael's escalating struggle with cocaine exemplifies how the disease model for alcoholism may be applied to millions of cocaine addicts in the United States today.

Case Example: Cocaine and Addictive Disease

Michael began to enjoy "recreational" use of cocaine nearly 4 years ago. Although he seemed to enjoy coke somewhat more than his friends, he limited his use to parties and what he considered to be weekend treats. After several years, he began to rely on cocaine as a source of energy for business and school obligations. About 2 years ago, he found himself working on three separate, yet highly demanding projects: completing course requirements for a college degree in creative writing, editing the advertising section of a commercial newsletter, and devising a business plan to open and operate a video store with several of his friends. He rationalized that he needed cocaine daily in order to muster sufficient energy to complete each task. Michael realized that his drug problem was becoming severe when he found that he was using more cocaine even after his school obligations were completed. In what may be described as the prodromal phase of cocaine addiction, he began to make up excuses for why he needed to get high. Each time there was any sort of business or advertising deadline, he would rationalize that he needed cocaine to help him get through.

Michael agreed with his therapist that he was in the loss-of-control or crucial phase of cocaine addiction when he spent $10,000 in 3 months solely to purchase the drug. He repeatedly experienced an irresistible urge to buy just a moderate amount, allegedly to help him cope with some temporary business stress. When the coke was gone, he would purchase more and more, until he either ran out of money or could find no more coke. Like the crucial-phase alcoholic, Michael would alternate between flurries of complete abstinence and cocaine debauchery.

As in other disease processes (e.g., diabetes), a person may have a genetic predisposition for a particular disorder, yet may circumvent most of its complications by avoiding the substances or activities that trigger its symptoms. For example, a person who has a genetic predisposition to skin cancer may be able to dodge most of its harmful consequences by avoiding undue exposure to the sun. Similarly, a person who is predisposed to drug addiction may avoid the disease by abstaining from all mind-altering drugs.

Addiction and the Adolescent Brain

Although the addictive journey can begin "anywhere in time and space," adolescence is particularly ripe for sowing the seeds of compulsive pleasure seeking. Youth face the challenge of daily exposure to electronic media, which seem obsessed with explicit reference to drugs, sex, and violence (e.g., hip hop music, Internet chat rooms, and pornographic Web sites). Concurrently, there is widespread exposure to a panoply of drugs and thrill-seeking activities, coupled with teenage propensities for sensation, risk, and experimentation. There is a major problem, however, with the adolescent's discovery of his or her capacity to "ramp up" dopamine in the brain's pleasure center—the immature neurobiological system required to interpret and manage intense pleasure.

Although the overall size of the brain changes very little after childhood, there are important changes in neuronal connections occurring between childhood and adulthood. These changes are especially noticeable in the frontal lobes of the neocortex. There are other dramatic changes occurring in the brains of adolescents. For example, Giedd et al. (1999) found that the *corpus callosum,* which relays information between the two hemispheres of the brain, also undergoes growth during adolescence. The *cerebellum,* which is involved in motor coordination, also undergoes changes during adolescence. Using animal studies, Teicher, Andersen, and Hostetter (1995) showed that dopamine receptors increase in the nucleus accumbens at an age that corresponds to adolescence in humans.

Changes in the architecture of the brain have a great impact on behavior during adolescence. Using functional magnetic resonance imaging (fMRI), researchers have shown that the prefrontal cortex have begins growing just before puberty (Giedd et al., 1999). This part of the brain controls higher functions such as rational thinking, planning, organization, working memory, and behavioral inhibition, and also assists in modulating emotions. The continuing maturation of the prefrontal cortex enables older adolescents to exert more control over emotional impulses and make more rational decisions as they mature. This is good news for parents. Since development of the frontal lobes, which are involved in rational decision making, continue into the twenties, the more emotionally driven teenager will likely mature into a more focused and logical adult. As the cortex begins to control the amygdala (the part of the brain involved in emotions), impulsive and mood-driven behaviors are expected to give way to cortically dominated rationality.

A teenager's ability to make sound judgments may be compromised by the relative immaturity of his or her frontal cortex (Giedd et al., 1999). This concept is supported by the use of fMRI, which records activity in the working brain. When processing emotional decisions, adults have a higher level of activity in their frontal lobes than adolescents processing the same decisions. Adults also have lower activity in their amygdala than teenagers when confronted with the same emotional decision. The data imply that the immaturity of the frontal lobes of the adolescent's brain prevents him or her from reliably making rational decisions. Instead, the decisions are processed in the amygdala, the emotional part of the brain (Giedd et al., 1999).

As an example, when pressured by peers to engage in a harmful activity such as drug use, committing a crime, or taking a potentially lethal risk, an adult has the ability to weigh the desire to conform against the perceived harmful effects and arrive at a rational decision. However, because of immature frontal lobes, the adolescent may not have the same capacity to moderate his or her response. In this case, the more developed amygdala is likely to be the region of the brain that processes the decision, and the emotional desire to conform overcomes the weak response from the frontal cortex. In other words, "the amygdala has hijacked the cortex" and the adolescent takes poorly calculated risks as in delinquent actions, drug abuse, lapses in self-care, and lack of concern for the welfare of others. Further, because of the relative dominance of the amygdala, cues that remind the adolescent of the drug-taking experience may trigger urges and cravings, which he or she experiences as almost impossible to overcome.

Consistent with the above, Childress (2006) discusses the likelihood that genetic vulnerabilities (e.g., low number of dopamine [D2] receptors in the striatum) may interact with adolescent brain development. Childress uses a "GO!" and "STOP!" framework to explain an emerging corpus of data showing that individual differences in impulse control may lie in the function and dysfunction of two vital brain systems: (1) the ancient "GO!" system, which is related to seeking out rewards for behaviors that enhance survival such as sex and eating; and (2) the brain's "STOP!" system, which is responsible for "putting on the brakes" when an activity is perceived as dangerous or harmful in the long run (p. 51).

In normal adolescence, changes in the GO! system are self-evident in that hormonal signals prepare the organism for being "ready, willing, and able" when the potential for reproduction arises. Contrastingly, the brain's STOP! system is not yet fully developed, as evidenced by brain imaging studies (described above), which show a more gradual development of the frontal lobes. The "developmental imbalance" of the STOP! and GO! mechanisms (i.e., frontal cortex vs. amygdala) during adolescence may account for why teenagers are especially vulnerable to psychoactive drugs. Despite this imbalance, most adolescents who smoke, drink, or use illicit drugs can put them aside and continue their normal developmental trajectory. However, given the GO/STOP imbalance, the "right" environmental configuration (e.g., drug-using peers, poor parental controls) and genetically loaded neurological template (e.g., low number of D2 receptors) may "tip the scales" toward addiction (Childress, 2006, p. 49).

The Downward Spiral of Addiction

As previously discussed in Chapter 2, there is a huge array of drugs or activities that can increase dopamine in the pleasure centers of the brain. The allegorical story of a "Journey to Oblivion" captures the essence of the addictive process.

Journey to Oblivion

What are the conditions of a trip to oblivion? The voyage is destined for hardship and suffering. It can begin anywhere in time and space. The universe abounds with capsules for transport. One blurs the senses with lightning velocity. Another creeps slowly, leaving trails of combustion. The passenger sleeps through much of the way, while observers mark progress via symbols of change. A robot pilot is strong at the helm. Only mutiny can adjust the ship's scattered course. A guard must be posted or the android returns. The traveler remains altered by this sojourn in hell.

Capsules for Transport: Licit and Illicit Drugs

Cigarettes and alcohol, both legal drugs, continue to be of primary concern. According to the 2007 Monitoring the Future Survey (Johnston et al., 2008), approximately half (46%) of twelfth-grade students have tried alcohol and nearly a quarter (22%) are current smokers. If inhalant use is included in the definition of illicit drug use, almost a third (28%) have used an illicit drug as early as the eighth grade. Marijuana is the most prevalent of the illicit drugs. In 2007, the annual prevalence of marijuana use among twelfth graders was 31.7% (Johnston et al., 2008). Although the use of many drugs, including cigarettes, alcohol, methamphetamine, and marijuana, has declined during the past few years, Ecstasy has shown an increase in use (annual prevalence rate for twelfth graders, 4.1%). In the category of "club drugs," 0.7% of students in the eighth grade reported past-year use of GHB, as did 0.6% and 0.9% of students in Grades 10 and 12, respectively. Past-year use of ketamine was reported by 1.3% of twelfth graders, and annual prevalence of Rohypnol use

Figure 15.2   **Journey to oblivion.** "What's up! Gym candy, roofies, easy lay, hug drug, snappers, skank, embalming fluid, shrooms, blotter, snow, crank, oxy, skag . . . whatever you need" (21st-century drug dealer).

was about 0.5% in all three grades surveyed (eighth, tenth, twelfth). Almost 4% of twelfth graders reported having used Ritalin without medical instruction. Abuse of inhalants and over-the-counter cough and cold medicines are additional areas of threat. Cough medicines used for "getting high" usually contain dextromethorphan, a cough suppressant that can cause alterations in consciousness and mood when taken in high doses. Street names for these drugs include DXM, Dex, and skittles. In 2006, the proportions of students abusing cough and cold medications were 4%, 5%, and 7% in Grades 8, 10, and 12, respectively (Johnston et al., 2008).

Consequences of Adolescent Drug Abuse

A major consequence of high exposure during adolescence is continuation into adulthood, resulting in life-course persistent patterns of abuse and dependence. Based on face-to-face interviews with a representative sample of the U.S. adult population (N = 43,093), the National Epidemiologic Survey on Alcohol and Related Conditions (Hasin, Stinson, Ogburn, & Grant, 2007) reports that the prevalence of lifetime and 12-month alcohol abuse were 17.8% and 4.7%, and the prevalence of lifetime and 12-month alcohol dependence were 12.5% and 3.8%, respectively.

Figure 15.3 shows the number in thousands of Americans who abuse or are dependent on the various categories of legal and illegal drugs.

Table 15.1 describes some of the emotional, behavioral, and physical consequences associated with a wide spectrum of contemporary drugs.

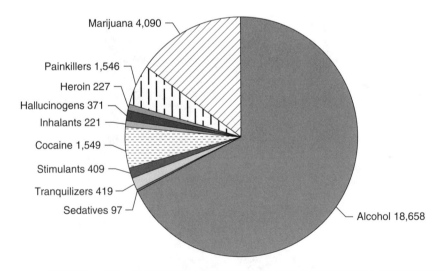

Figure 15.3   **Addiction in America: The substance of abuse (numbers shown in thousands).** An estimated 22 million Americans age 12 and over suffer from dependence or abuse of drugs or alcohol. Of this total, more than 18 million abuse or are dependent on alcohol and more than 4 million abuse or are dependent on marijuana.

SOURCE: Adapted from Hoffman, J., & Froemke, S. (2007). *Addiction.* New York: Rodale, p. 44.

(Text continued on page 284)

Table 15.1   Contemporary Drugs and Their Effects

Drug	Street Names	Possible Effects	Withdrawal Symptoms	Adverse/Overdose Reactions
Narcotics				
Heroin	H, smack, dope, junk, ska, skag, Mexican black tar	Euphoria, alternating wakeful and drowsy states, dry mouth, heavy extremities, itching, clouded mental functioning	Drug craving, restlessness, muscle and bone pain, insomnia, diarrhea and vomiting, cold flashes with goose bumps ("cold turkey"), kicking movements ("kicking the habit")	Low blood pressure, rapid heart rate, shallow breathing, convulsions, coma, possible death, collapsed veins, infection of the heart lining and valves, abscesses, cellulitis, and liver disease
OxyContin Darvon Vicodin Dilaudid Demerol Percodan	Perks, perkies, oxy, vic, dem	Analgesic, pain relief, euphoria, drowsiness, constipation, depressed breathing	Restlessness, muscle and bone pain, insomnia, diarrhea, vomiting, cold flashes with goose bumps, involuntary leg movements	Severe respiratory depression or death, vomiting, convulsions, coma
Depressants				
Xanax Valium Nembutal	Xanies, vals, Vs, downers, nerve pills, tranks	Calming effect, slows normal brain functioning, psychomotor slowing, drowsiness, poor concentration, ataxia, dysarthria, motor incoordination, diplopia (double vision), muscle weakness, vertigo, and mental confusion	Seizures, increased heart rate and blood pressure level, tremulousness, insomnia and sensory hypersensitivity, delirium, depression	Slow breathing, slowing of the heart, death
Alcohol	Booze, liquor, juice, sauce, brew, brewski, vino, forty, hooch	Difficulty walking, blurred vision, slurred speech, slowed reaction times, impaired memory, disturbed sleep, nausea	Feeling jumpy and nervous, shakiness, anxiety, irritability, emotional volatility, depression, fatigue, headache, sweating, nausea, vomiting, loss of appetite, insomnia, paleness, rapid heart rate, dilated pupils, clammy skin, tremor of the hands, delirium tremens, agitation, fever, convulsions	Vomiting, dizziness, blackouts, death

(Continued)

279

Table 15.1 (Continued)

Drug	Street Names	Possible Effects	Withdrawal Symptoms	Adverse/Overdose Reactions
Stimulants				
Methamphetamine	Meth, speed, crank, ice, glass, chalk, crystal	Euphoria, wakefulness, increased energy, decrease in appetite, increased respiration, rapid heart rate, irregular heartbeat, increased blood pressure, hyperthermia	Fatigue, disturbed sleep, irritability, intense hunger, moderate to severe depression, hallucinations and delusions (psychotic reactions), anxiety	Tremors, muscle twitches, rapid breathing, confusion, hallucinations, panic, aggressiveness, fever or flu symptoms, nausea, vomiting, diarrhea, stomach pain, uneven heartbeats, feeling light-headed, fainting, convulsions, coma, or death
Cocaine	Coke, blow, snow, flake, yay-yo	Euphoria; increased energy and alertness; reduced fatigue and appetite; constricted blood vessels; dilated pupils; increased temperature, heart rate, and blood pressure	Fatigue, lack of pleasure, anxiety, irritability, sleepiness, agitation or extreme suspicion, cravings, depression	Paranoid psychosis, auditory hallucinations, heart attacks, chest pain and respiratory failure, strokes, seizures, headaches, gastrointestinal complications such as abdominal pain and nausea
Dexedrine Ritalin Adderall	Bennies, speed, uppers, beans, dexies, black beauties, go pills, LA turnarounds	Increased alertness, attention, and energy; euphoria; increased blood pressure and heart rate; constricted blood vessels; increased breathing	Fatigue, depression, insomnia, hostility, paranoia	Irregular heartbeat, dangerously high body temperatures, potential for cardiovascular failure or seizures, paranoia, hallucinations
Nicotine				
Cigarettes	Butts, stogies, squares, coffin nails, fags, snuff, chew, cig, chaw, skag, gasper	Increased heart rate and respiration, relaxation, calmness, alertness	Anger, hostility, aggression, headache, anxiety, nausea, cravings, tingling in hands and feet, nausea, cramps	Nausea, vomiting, cancer, stroke, coronary heart disease, emphysema, aneurysm

Drug	Street Names	Possible Effects	Withdrawal Symptoms	Adverse/Overdose Reactions
Hallucinogens				
LSD	Acid, blotter, microdot	Dilated pupils; increased heart rate, body temperature, and blood pressure; sweating; loss of appetite; sleeplessness; dry mouth; magnified emotions; fascination with ordinary objects; heightened aesthetic responses to color and texture	No withdrawal symptoms reported	Delusions, visual hallucinations, panic, severe and terrifying thoughts and feelings, fear of losing control, fear of insanity, despair, sometimes death
Psilocybin	Mushrooms, shrooms, boomers, God's flesh, little smoke, Mexican mushrooms, musk, sacred mushroom, silly putty, simple simon	Euphoria, disorientation, lethargy, enhancement of colors and sensations, confusion, hilarity, general feeling of connection to nature and the universe	No reported withdrawal symptoms	Nausea, vomiting, muscle weakness, drowsiness, lack of coordination, hallucinations, inability to discern fantasy from reality, panic, psychosis
PCP	Angel dust, wack, rocket fuel, ozone, hog, shermans, embalming fluid	Distorts perceptions of sight and sound; produces feelings of detachment from the environment and self; increased breathing, blood pressure, and pulse; flushing; profuse sweating; numbness of extremities; loss of muscular coordination	No withdrawal symptoms reported	Blood pressure, pulse rate, and respiration drop; nausea; vomiting; blurred vision; flicking up and down of the eyes; drooling; loss of balance; dizziness; seizures; coma; death; delusions; hallucinations; paranoia; disordered thinking; sparse and garbled speech

(Continued)

281

Table 15.1 (Continued)

Drug	Street Names	Possible Effects	Withdrawal Symptoms	Adverse/Overdose Reactions
Cannabis				
Marijuana	Pot, herb, weed, grass, Mary Jane, reefer, Aunt Mary, skunk, boom, gangster, kif, ganja	Euphoria, relaxed inhibitions, distorted perceptions, impaired coordination, difficulty in thinking and problem solving, problems with learning and memory	Irritability; sleeplessness; decreased appetite, anxiety, and drug craving	Rare but include paranoia, fatigue, panic, psychosis
Inhalants				
Inhalants	Whippets, poppers, snappers	Slurred speech, lack of coordination, euphoria, dizziness, light-headedness, hallucinations, delusions	Not common but can include anxiety, depression, loss of appetite, irritation, aggressive behavior, dizziness, tremors, nausea	Heart failure and death, hearing loss, peripheral neuropathies or limb spasms, central nervous system or brain damage, bone marrow damage
Club Drugs				
MDMA	Ecstasy, X, XTC, Adam, hug, beans, love drug	Mental stimulation, emotional warmth, enhanced sensory perception, increased physical energy, increased blood pressure and body temperature	Fatigue, loss of appetite, depressed feelings, trouble concentrating, confusion, sleep disturbances, drug craving, severe anxiety	Muscle tension; involuntary teeth clenching; nausea; blurred vision; faintness; chills; sweating; liver, kidney, and cardiovascular system failure; death
Ketamine	K, Special K, Vitamin K	Dry mouth, euphoria, sedation, dreamlike states, hallucinations	No withdrawal symptoms reported	Hallucinations, nightmares, delirium, amnesia, impaired motor function, nausea, vomiting, double vision, high blood pressure, depression, potentially fatal respiratory problems

Drug	Street Names	Possible Effects	Withdrawal Symptoms	Adverse/Overdose Reactions
GHB	Liquid ecstasy, soap, easy-lay, vita-G, Georgia home boy	Euphoria, sedation	Insomnia, anxiety, tremors, sweating	Coma and seizures, nausea, vomiting, breathing difficulties, poisonings, overdoses, date rapes, death
Rohypnol	Roofies, rophies, roach, rope	Sleepy, relaxed, drunk feelings	Insomnia, anxiety, tremors and sweating	Blackouts, loss of memory, dizziness, disorientation, nausea, difficulty with motor movements and speaking, vomiting, headache, rapid mood changes and violent outbursts
Steroids				
Steroids	Juice, roids, gym candy, pumpers, stackers, balls, bulls, weight trainers, Arnies, As, anabolics	Rapid weight gain, rapid muscle development, increased endurance	Mood swings, fatigue, restlessness, loss of appetite, insomnia, reduced sex drive, steroid cravings	Acne flare-up, fluid retention, jaundice, mood swings, depression, aggressive behavior, premature balding, high blood pressure, paranoid jealousy, manic episodes, extreme irritability, delusions, stunted growth, shrinking testicles, growth of body and facial hair

SOURCES: Longo & Johnson (2000); U.S. Department of Health and Human Services (2004); Web sites for the following: American Council for Drug Education; MedIndia.com; National Institutes of Health; National Drug Intelligence Center; National Institute on Drug Abuse; Partnership for a Drug-Free America; Smack Foundation.

Behavioral Addictions _____

After a moment of reflection, it becomes obvious that any stress-reducing activity—whether ingesting a psychoactive substance, eating junk food, or gambling excessively—may be subject to compulsive overuse and the escalating consequences of loss of control. In fact, the disease concept may be applied to the entire spectrum of compulsive problem behaviors. As we have shown throughout this book, the distinction between internally and externally induced alterations of mood, thought, or behavior is arbitrary and misleading. Activities that evoke sensations of arousal, satiation, or fantasy bring about alterations in brain chemistry and patterns of compulsive behavior that are similar to the symptoms traditionally associated with psychoactive substances. Arousal, satiation, and fantasy may be regarded as psychological systems, vulnerable to attack by multiple agents of addiction. As in viral and bacterial infections, the specific disease carriers may differ widely in origin and structure, and yet the consequences of foreign invasion may be virtually identical in terms of symptoms, prognosis, and treatment. Each of the behaviors shown in Table 15.2 may become an agent of addiction, subject to compulsion, loss of control, and continuation despite harmful consequences.

The dimension of *religious extremism and cults* transverses all levels and may be used to short-circuit the usual course of an addictive process. We have observed a multitude of recovering addicts who seem to strengthen their resolve by leaning on the pillars of religion or spiritual practice. Members of Alcoholics Anonymous (AA), for example, usually proclaim a renewed faith in a higher power, who aids them in maintaining sobriety. Yet religion may be a double-edged sword. In the tragic examples of Jonestown (November 18,

---

Table 15.2   List of Behavioral Addictions

- Drug ingestion—Includes major psychoactive drugs and marijuana, alcohol, and nicotine
- Eating—Includes overuse of particular foods, for example, sugar
- Sex—Includes autoeroticism, pornography, and varieties of sadomasochistic activities
- Gambling—Includes numbers, horses, dogs, cards, and roulette
- Activity—Includes work, exercise, and sports
- Pursuit of power—Includes spiritual, physical, and material power
- Media fascination—Includes TV, Internet, and other electronic media devices
- Isolation—Includes sleep, fantasy, and dreams
- Risk taking—Includes excitement related to danger
- Religious extremism and cults—Includes groups using brainwashing or other techniques of psychological restructuring
- Crime and violence—Includes crimes against people and property
- Bonding-socializing—Includes excessive dependence on relationships or social gatherings
- Institutionalization—Includes excessive need for environmental structure, such as prisons, mental hospitals, and religious sanctuaries, and institutional use of psychoactive medication

---

1978: more than 900 people involved in mass suicide) and Waco, Texas (April 19, 1993: 76 people died along with Branch Davidian leader David Koresh), blind devotion to a religious cult burned a path straight to the suicidal vortex. To be sure, the widespread belief in Armageddon (the site of the final battle between God and Satan) across many religious faiths supplies a context through which fanatic, contemporary religious beliefs may result in untold hardship and suffering. The phenomenon of fantasy addiction was examined in detail in Section IV of this book.

The Passenger Sleeps

When children are asked if they would like to be addicts when they grow up, invariably they respond with a combination of disdain and perplexity. There is no way that they want to be hooked on anything, and besides, how could you have ever come up with such a goofy question? Yet statistically, 5% to 10% of all grade-school children will eventually become dependent on alcohol or drugs; if we include food and other behavioral compulsions such as gambling or sex, the figure easily exceeds 20% (see Table I.1, p. 5, Prevalence and Severity of Common Hedonic Dependencies). Nobody wants to be dependent on anything, yet the number of people who develop pathological habits is huge. How do people reconcile the difference between what they value in the morning of their life and what they actually do in the afternoon and twilight hours?

Those who suffer from hedonic dependencies insulate themselves from the glaring discrepancy between their natural inclination toward well-mindedness and the depraved lifestyle of addiction. As if they have fallen into a deep sleep, space trippers become oblivious to a multitude of observers imploring them to take heed of their compulsion and loss of control. In the face of massive evidence to the contrary, they continue to believe in their capacity to maintain adequate functioning. Reverend Joseph L. Kellermann (1970) describes alcoholism as "a merry-go-round named denial," in which the alcoholic, together with a regular cast of supporting actors, enacts a predictable scenario: There is a group composed of family or friends that unwittingly protects the afflicted from the harsh reality of his or her desperate plight. Whatever the vehicle for transport, the addict's support system usually includes three unintentional contributors to the avalanching predicament: an *enabler,* a *victim,* and a *provoker.*

The *enabler* is a character who is available to bail the addicted darling out of any crisis that might ensue from the demanding journey. This support person might be a professional, such as a physician or counselor, who helps the addict to "get by" with irresponsible behavior. He or she may also be a friend who fills in, on the job or at home, when the journey to oblivion takes a wild turn.

The part of the *victim* is played by the boss, employer, or supervisor who saves the addict's job when he or she cannot perform the expected duties.

The victim picks up the tab for irresponsible conduct because love or concern for the addict prevents the him or her from initiating proper consequences or disciplinary action at home or in the workplace.

Finally, the *provoker*—usually the girlfriend or wife of a male addict—is the person who seeks to control the alcoholic's life by crying, nagging, bargaining, blackmailing, and so on. She alternates among the roles of counselor, physician, mother, and wife as the addict vacillates among needing to be forgiven, taken care of, and reprimanded, on a cyclical basis. Although the provoker is deeply troubled by the addict's lifestyle, he or she is always there to compensate for any action that might threaten to dissolve the tenuous family unit.

According to Reverend Kellermann (1970), if recovery from addiction is to occur, it must start with the people who unwittingly maintain the addict's system of denial. The victim and enabler should find a source of information and insight if they are to change their characteristic roles. The provoker should enter some form of ongoing group program, such as Al-Anon, to receive the support that this person will need to make a substantial change in his or her life. Finally, parents are asked to consider that they may be unintentionally playing support roles on the "merry-go-round of denial" for addicted teenagers. "Denial"—disbelief that a member of their family actually suffers from an addictive disorder—is perhaps the most elemental concept that parents, other family members, and close friends need to understand.

We suggest that the concept of denial is better understood and communicated to those affected by addiction when replaced by the word *defensiveness*. The concept of denial is often perceived as implying poor character (i.e., deliberate lying and deception) and lack of awareness about "what's really going on." Defensiveness, on the other hand, communicates a degree of concern, dissatisfaction with the status quo, and a desire for something different (personal communication with Kenneth Wanberg, January 20, 2009).

Symbols of Change

It is virtually impossible for a friend or family member to accurately gauge the extent to which an addict depends on a neurochemical prop. After tolerance has developed, the addict may appear completely normal during an extended voyage in his or her capsule for transport. By far the most reliable indication of continuing addiction is the person's apparent inability to integrate his or her goals and behaviors. The allegedly recovering person is exposed by an obvious inability to coordinate stated objectives and actual performance. He or she may miss appointments with intimate friends or fail to appear for critical work assignments. These inconsistencies, which might be dismissed among nonaddicts as faux pas, are the telltale signs of a flourishing hedonic dependency.

Figure 15.4 shows the deterioration of a person's values as the journey to oblivion progresses over time. The values closest to the center represent guiding principles in the addict's life. In the pre-addiction (symptomatic) phase, a person's behavior may reflect the entire spectrum of moral precepts that he or she has internalized from well-minded people in society. However, as addiction progresses through prodromal, crucial, and chronic phases, the person's ability to function in accord with his or her own values dwindles to near zero.

With the onset of recovery, the principles that guide one's behavior may become reorganized. Those which formerly occupied positions of highest priority, such as the experience of excitement, may become peripheral and of minimal importance during the recovery phase of an addict's career. When a person assumes the commitment to get well, the preliminary and possibly the most superficial aspect of the task is to stop the self-defeating behavior, whatever that may be. The greater challenge, which may take years of self-discipline and support from treatment personnel, is to regain the full capacity to operate in accord with the values that the individual has chosen as guiding principles for his or her life.

The Robot Pilot

If you have never been enslaved by an irresistible impulse, it is difficult for you to appreciate a person's apparent inability to captain his or her own ship.

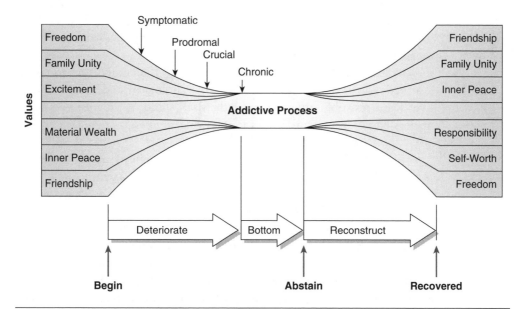

Figure 15.4   **Deterioration of values.** As addiction progresses through prodromal, crucial, and chronic phases, the addict's ability to function in accord with his or her own values dwindles to near zero.

Whatever the seductive agent—substances, actions, or sweets—addicts repeat time and time again, "Whenever it's right there in front of me, I have no choice. I've never been able to turn down a . . ." This subordination of rational thought and value-based decision making to the lure of momentary pleasure is at once the most mystifying and destructive aspect of the addictive process. In the case of recovering alcoholics, higher cue sensitivity (increased cravings elicited by alcohol stimuli) was found to be highly predictive of later relapse (Drummond, 2000).

In order to understand the compulsion to be at craving's beck and call, we must again consider the multifactorial basis of addiction. From the standpoint of biology, our formulation rests on the position that we can become physically dependent on the experiences of arousal, satiation, or fantasy, independent of whether the capsule for transport is a substance or an activity. Behavior in each sphere may be related to a particular kind of neurotransmission, possibly involving specific neural pathways and neurotransmitter combinations. Arousal dependence may be compared to biochemical alterations related to excessive amphetamine use, while satiation effects may be compared to those related to opiate use. Fantasy behaviors can be related to such neurotransmitters as dopamine, norepinephrine, or serotonin, all of which are chemically similar to the main psychedelic drugs, LSD, mescaline, or psilocybin. Repetition of each type of activity sets up a compensatory biochemical reaction that restores neurochemical balance in the central nervous system. The individual must increase the level of addictive behavior—for example, risk taking—to continue to achieve a subjective experience of pleasure. Addicts are also motivated by increasing discomfort from withdrawal effects when they stop or reduce the need-satisfying activity. The tendency toward reinstatement (doing it again) is encouraged by a substratum of neurochemical instability.

Witkiewitz and Marlatt (2007) have studied the compulsion to repeat destructive behaviors from a combined psychological and social perspective. The irresistible urge to reenter the drab spiral of progressive impairment is based on pressure from the following sources:

- The addict's expectation that some positive effects might be experienced through a brief interlude with the seductive agent
- The initial rush of pleasure produced by the object of craving
- Social pressures to be one of the group

The seasoned addict engages in a fierce battle for control over the object of his or her craving. Episodes of abstinence typically alternate with nearly complete submission and loss of control. The likelihood that an addict will repeat the characteristic pattern of excess and moral depravity is increased by an identified series of psychological reactions. The combined influence from a predictable set of internal messages convinces the addict to abandon control.

This process begins just after the first tastes of forbidden fruit. When a person who tries to be straight, sober, controlled, or clean experiences a slip, he or she becomes confused in self-concept: "I thought I had control over . . . but now it appears that I don't." Most often, the individual attributes his or her failure or slip to personal weakness. These two psychological factors—identity conflict and self-blame—are cumulative in effect. The internal discord produced by the discrepant self-concept of "I am in control" versus "I have failed" results in a regressive shift in self-image from responsible person to out of control addict. By attributing the slip to personal weakness, the addict unwittingly creates the expectation for continued failure in the future. The cumulative effect of role confusion and loss of confidence makes submission to the robot pilot an easier posture to maintain than abstinence or self-regulation. The intensity of this reaction depends on several factors:

- The degree of personal commitment to maintain abstinence
- The period of sustained abstinence—the longer the duration, the greater the effect
- The importance of the behavior to the individual involved (Witkiewitz & Marlatt, 2007)

The Mutiny

The course of addiction is remarkably resistant to change. Hunt, Barnett, and Branch (1971) found that approximately 75% of all addicts who attempted abstinence from heroin, alcohol, or cigarettes resumed their habits between 3 and 6 months after beginning a program for recovery. The statistics for attempted weight control are equally grim (Kolata, 2007). In other outcome studies, approximately 65% to 70% of patients treated for alcoholism were found to relapse within 1 year of treatment, with the majority relapsing within less than 3 months (Emrick, 1974; W. R. Miller & Hester, 1986). In studies of drug- or polysubstance-dependent patients, relapse rates following treatment are similar to, if not higher than, those found for patients solely dependent on alcohol (McKay, Alterman, Rutherford, Cacciola, & McLellan, 1999). Recidivism rates for juvenile and adult crime range from 70% to 80%, depending on how recidivism is defined (Wanberg & Milkman, 2006).

In consideration of the powerful influences from biological, psychological, and social sources, a continuing pattern of struggle and failure seems inevitable. To be sure, the traveler who survives must organize a powerful mutiny, to overthrow the tyrannical "commander." The rebellious survival force must battle a slew of weapons, massively deployed by a malevolent robot whose sophisticated armament includes habitual psychological responses, biochemically based emotional and physical disturbances, intense social pressure, and the random stress of unavoidable negative circumstance.

A successful rebellion must effectively counteract all of these forces. Each mutiny must be tailor-made to fit the special requirements of each journey.

In the realm of substance abuse, for example, the initial tactics for recovery are determined by the specific needs of the user and the unique qualities of his or her drug. Withdrawal from a single drug, drugs from the same group, or a combination of drugs from different groups requires diverse detoxification procedures. Withdrawal from opiate dependence, for example, produces a well-defined abstinence syndrome, characterized by gastrointestinal distress, muscle aches, anxiety, insomnia, and narcotics hunger—none of which is life threatening. In contrast, withdrawal from barbiturates, or a barbiturate-alcohol combination, may produce potentially fatal seizures, requiring vigorous medical intervention, often hospital-based care.

Withdrawal from cocaine, amphetamine, or meth usually involves depression and lethargy. For these drugs, the symptoms of high-dose intoxication may become life threatening. Cocaine toxicity may result in brain seizures, heart failure, delusions, hallucinations, and potentially violent behavior. In addition, mixed addiction may result from the alternating use of antagonistic substances as observed in the upper-downer cycle. Some addicts use high doses of stimulants such as amphetamines or cocaine and then use a secondary drug such as alcohol, a short-acting barbiturate, or an opiate to calm the side effects of excessive stimulation. Dependence and tolerance may develop to the secondary depressant drug as well. Dependence on drugs such as opiates, cocaine, phencyclidines, and cannabinoids has been shown to be comorbid with alcohol dependence in 64% of individuals (Compton, Cottler, Phelps, Abdallah, & Spitznagel, 2000). During detoxification, those dependent on more than one drug may experience a complex of symptoms associated with the withdrawal from drugs of different classes.

For non-substance addictions, the primary strategy for recovery usually involves either completely stopping the compulsive activity (as in gambling) or dramatically reducing the pattern of abuse (as in eating disorders). Although addicts take the first steps to recovery for a variety of reasons, including family pressure, the threat of being fired, health concerns, or legal problems, the ensuing battle for control is always decided according to one fundamental principle: The addict must discover alternative means to satisfy the needs that were previously resolved through the addictive activity.

An innovative client, whom we shall refer to as Max, developed a set of nonchemical alternatives that he successfully used to overcome his dependence on alcohol. With assistance from his therapist, Max realized that he used alcohol to cope with an identifiable set of psychological and physical needs. He and his therapist devised a program of behavioral alternatives, specifically designed to cope with the emotions and conflicts previously managed through drinking. The program involved the use of sensory isolation, video movies, massage, and weekly psychotherapy sessions. After one year, Max was able to successfully terminate psychotherapy and continue to enjoy a comfortable and responsible life without using drugs or alcohol. Table 15.3 outlines the cognitive (insights gained from psychotherapy) and behavioral (alternative behavior) techniques that Max used to regain control over his own life.

Table 15.3 Cognitive-Behavioral Alternatives to Alcohol Dependence

	Isolation Tank	Massage	Fantasy	Psychotherapy
Device	Float in water to alleviate the effects of gravity. As much as possible, eliminate all temperature difference while shutting out light and sound.	Soothing sensations to the skin and musculature are delivered by a qualified practitioner.	Video movies are selected from the complete range of fantasy productions available in the contemporary retail video market.	Individual psychotherapy is delivered by a qualified professional with a cognitive-behavioral orientation.
Rationale	Reduce external stimulation to trigger fantasies of power and immortality. Results in altered state of consciousness.	Reduce tension through internal chemicals released by touch. Diminish unresolved dependency needs.	Movies allow for passive means to achieve relaxation without the unwanted effects of intoxication and hangovers.	Therapist helps client understand the emotional, sensory, and intellectual needs that were previously met through alcohol.
Goals	Fantasies of power help to compensate for feelings of helplessness and lack of self-worth. These are examined during psychotherapy and replaced by self-actualizing behaviors.	Vigorous massage is used to dampen anxiety and aggressive drive. The client gradually learns to subdue emotional discomfort through positive interpersonal relationships.	Provide gratification for aesthetic, intellectual, and emotional needs that have been mismanaged at home or at the bar. Gain insight into origins of anxiety and fear.	The client learns to separate himself from infantile needs previously resolved in a self-destructive fashion. Through a safe, caring, insight-oriented relationship, client enlarges the scope of his coping skills.

SOURCE: From "An innovative approach to methadone detoxification," H. Milkman, D. Metcalf, & P. D. Reed, 1980, *International Journal of the Addictions, 15*(9), 1199–1211.

A Guard Must Be Posted

Co-occurring disorder is an almost ubiquitous problem in treatment for addiction. Among drug-dependent clients (not including alcoholics), the co-occurrence of some other form of mental disorder is as high as 84% (Compton et al., 2000). These include a range of mood, anxiety, and personality disorders. In alcohol-dependent subjects, comorbid depression, bipolar I and II disorders, and personality disorders have also been found at elevated rates (Frye & Salloum, 2006; Lowe & Kranzler, 1999). From these findings, the case is clear that abstaining from one's drug(s) of choice is likely the first step toward wellness. To that end, not treating an underlying mental disorder can be as detrimental as not treating the substance-dependent individual at all!

The recovering addict must gain the upper hand over negative social or peer influences, internal and external states of conflict, and sometimes excruciating physical discomfort. Often the challenge is too great, and the mindless robot returns. Those who avoid subjugation to the addictive process need to develop a mature set of emotional, intellectual, and behavioral skills that promote attainment of pleasure through internal rewards and life-enhancing activities. This may be accomplished through delivery of an individually tailored treatment program combined with strong environmental support. We will more fully explore evidence-based tools for the treatment of hedonic dependency in Section VII.

The vast majority of recovery programs—with the obvious exception of those designed for eating disorders—stress the need for abstinence, although it is recognized by some distinguished health professionals that some individuals may benefit from initiating their treatment with the aim of moderating their use of, rather than abstaining from drinking, alcohol (Marlatt, 1998). George Vaillant (1995) summarized the effective ingredients of programs for the treatment of alcohol dependence, all of which are embodied by the tenets of AA. The same principles apply to the broad range of addictive behaviors:

- Offer the client or patient a non-harmful substitute dependency for the addictive agent.
- Remind him or her ritually that even one encounter with the addictive agent can lead to pain and relapse.
- Support recovery through the formation of new relationships in which addictive behavior is neither encouraged nor tolerated.
- Repair the social and medical damage that has already occurred.
- Promote participation in an inspirational group.
- Restore self-esteem (p. 367).

Depending on the personality and situation of the client, a recovery-oriented self-help group, such as AA or an AA derivative such as Narcotics Anonymous or Sexaholics Anonymous, is often indicated.

The relief effect from participating in a group that offers empathy and belonging while continuously rewarding sobriety may be essential to the recovery process (Litt, Kadden, Kabela-Cormier, & Petry, 2007). A change in social support is often stressed for alcoholics (Litt et al., 2007), rather than trying to white-knuckle the addiction away in isolation (Interlandi, 2008). AA is an existing social network that does all of the things listed above. In many cases, group support can be bolstered by individual counseling. In other cases, the only form of treatment that the addict will accept is one-to-one psychotherapy. Most addiction experts agree that addicts attempting to terminate their use will almost always need some sort of psychological support (Interlandi, 2008). Whether individual or group, effective treatment requires a readiness on both sides (client and therapist) for intensive work.

Community residential programs often incorporate the social models of AA, including "frequent on-site presence of alumni and community Alcoholics Anonymous (AA) and Narcotics Anonymous (NA) members, an emphasis on building clean and sober networks, and an ethic of volunteerism which incorporates program upkeep and service" (Witbrodt et al., 2007, p. 948). Currently, most residential rehabilitation centers follow a fairly similar program of a 28-day typical stay, a 12-step program paradigm, and supplemental cognitive-behavioral therapy and motivational interviewing (J. Adler, 2007). There are exceptions to this model—including hermetic designs that ban all cell phones, magazines, and other distractions; pragmatic models that attempt to integrate sobriety into everyday life; and lush, resort-like centers, complete with an ocean view, that cost up to $100,000 per stay. Around 90% of treatment programs in the United States are at least partially founded on AA principles (Kingree et al., 2006).

As the disease of addiction has moved from being explained by a lack of willpower to the more recent explanation as a "bio-psycho-social-spiritual disorder" (Interlandi, 2008), most AA groups are attempting to keep up with the times (Summers, 2007). With the American Medical Association's recognition of addiction as a disease in 1956 and all of the neurological and biochemical evidence that supports the belief in the malfunctioning of the brain in addicted individuals, society is now accepting addiction as a legitimate illness (Interlandi, 2008).

Recent research has shown that an effective way to fight addiction may be to find therapies that work on the affected areas of the brain, implying benefits from using a pill or vaccine (Swaminathan, 2008). The medical model asserts that a disease needs to be treated with medicine, a thought not always held in high regard among AA groups (Interlandi, 2008). After opium and cocaine were first introduced as cures for alcoholism, 12-step programs traditionally discouraged use of any psychoactive substances because of the fear that the addict would be trading one addiction for another. However, the evidence of dual diagnosis (addiction plus a mental disorder) and the need for treatment for the disorders is becoming more evident. As the research on medicine to reduce withdrawal symptoms and cravings as well as the much-needed medications for any underlying mental disorders has offered mounting evidence, AA programs have needed to stay with the times so as to help as many addicts as possible. While some AA groups still discourage the talk or use of any medication, most groups accept it, and AA does not endorse advice to ignore doctors' prescriptions (Summers, 2007).

Improving the Odds

According to Kingree et al. (2006), "the dropout rate from AA is high and some persons do not participate at sufficient levels to benefit" (p. 453). Although recovery-oriented treatment has helped millions of addicts to reclaim their freedom, by far the most humane solution to addiction problems would be to prevent the life-corroding process from gaining even a foothold in the human psyche. As evidenced time and time again by the failure of our legal system to effectively bind the crippling hands of addiction, education—not legislation—is the key to preserving our cherished values of life, liberty, and the pursuit of happiness. Parents-as-educators are obliged to ensure that their children are successfully inoculated against the false promise of external charms.

The cognitive-behavioral strategy that we suggest is based on flexible use of a three-phase, addiction-inoculation approach that involves the following:

- Mental preparation
- Skill development
- Rehearsal

The procedure can be modified to accommodate the specific needs of children, students, patients, or other high-risk community groups. The technique is based on Meichenbaum's (1985) cognitive-behavioral method for managing anxiety, depression, and pain, and has been adapted for the long-term treatment of juvenile and adult criminal justice clients (Milkman & Wanberg, 2005; Wanberg & Milkman, 2006, 2008).

Mental Preparation

In the mental preparation phase, high-risk people are taught basic principles that explain addiction in terms of biochemistry, psychology, and sociology. In terms of biochemistry, students learn the neurological and physiological origins and consequences of dangerous pleasure-seeking behaviors. When a child vividly understands the deleterious effects of tampering with his or her own brain chemistry, he or she is less likely to later be duped by claims such as "LSD brings you closer to God," or "Cocaine will make you a better lover."

Psychologically, children are helped to form positive values and sound judgment and to empathize with others. We communicate our expectation that they will grow up as caring people who will make special contributions to a great society. In this phase, subjects learn how unconscious perceptions of low self-esteem can lead to increasing personal failure and reliance on the "quick fix." On the sociological plane, children learn to appreciate how society itself may promote a deviant career: from a child who perceives him- or herself to be of little self-worth; to a marked or stigmatized adolescent; and then finally to a person who loses all self-respect as a sorrowful, depraved, and incapacitated adult. Young people are taught the effects of peer influence, parental role models, and learning through observation. Children are imbued with a firm understanding of how advertising and street rumor may entice youngsters to experiment with short-term pleasure that results in long-term harm. As parents, educators, and community members, we can insist on responsible advertising while we develop our own slogans and symbols in the war against compulsive pleasure seeking.

Skill Development

The process of skill acquisition involves learning to cope adaptively with stress, through behaviors that provide internal satisfaction resulting in heightened perceptions of self-worth. On the interpersonal level, children learn to experience a sense of well-being when they master the ability to withstand negative peer pressure. This can be accomplished through programmatic exposure to positive role models. At the level of emotional control, subjects are taught how to use relaxation techniques to gain mastery over their own internal states. Muscle relaxation, guided fantasy, and breathing exercises have all been shown to reduce tension and promote feelings of well-being. An exemplary program would accommodate individual differences in the attainment of pleasure through the channels of arousal, satiation, or fantasy. Ideally, students could develop a large repertoire of coping skills, including wholesome activities from each plane of pleasurable experience—arousal, relaxation, and fantasy.

Rehearsal

In the rehearsal phase, which can overlap with mental preparation and skill development, the learner is encouraged to role-play appropriate mental and behavioral responses to potentially harmful seductions. Simulated encounters with addictive agents are created in family, classroom, or group counseling situations. All phases of the inoculation procedure should be conducted by addiction-free adults who command respect and admiration from the student population. Effective inoculators not only have the skills to cope with obstinacy and defensiveness from vulnerable clients, but also communicate a sense that he or she can "walk the talk" of an addiction-free lifestyle. The rehearsal stage should signify to every parent, therapist, and educator that one talk, one picture, or one story about addiction is not enough. We must go over and over this message in a variety of ways to overcome the enormous temptation to find quick and powerful means to feelings of empowerment and euphoria.

Finally, through the family, the school, and the culture, children should be inoculated to develop a healthy resistance to the seduction of a false paradise. To achieve this outcome, we must successfully promote the values of commitment, control, and challenge (Kobasa, Maddi, & Kahn, 1982). These three Cs may be thought of as the antidote for the three Cs of compulsion, loss of control, and continuation despite harmful consequences. We must demonstrate *commitment* to self, family, and community; believe in our individual strengths and abilities to exert a significant measure of *control* over personal destiny; and view life as a *challenge*, a grand adventure, a mystery to be explored with the benefit of our full mental capacity, rather than as a riddle to be solved through artificial means.

In the final section of this book, Natural Highs: The Cutting Edge of Mood Alteration, we provide an in-depth view of how to use the tools of cognitive-behavioral psychology to find and achieve prolonged pleasure without harmful consequences, to experience meaning and fulfillment in work, love, and play.

Chapter Summary

Addiction is regarded by some addiction scientists as a chronic and relapsing brain disease. On the basis of a questionnaire study of more than 2,000 male alcoholics, Jellinek formulated his four-phase concept of alcohol addiction: the pre-alcoholic symptomatic phase, the prodromal phase, the crucial phase, and the chronic phase. This final stage of alcoholism is characterized by prolonged periods of intoxication, known as binges. Withdrawal symptoms appear as soon as alcohol is no longer present in the body. Finally, the need for alcohol is so great that the addict can no longer pretend that he has control over his drinking.

Since the formulation of Jellinek's phases of alcoholism, the disease model has been embraced by Alcoholics Anonymous, the American Medical Association, and many others. More recently, the disease concept has widened to include many other potentially addictive agents such as gambling, sex, and eating, as well as a host of other addictive substances such as cocaine, amphetamines, and opiates.

Adolescence is a time particularly ripe for sowing the seeds of compulsive pleasure seeking. Along with a propensity for thrill seeking and risk, and widespread availability of many mind-altering drugs, youth face the challenge of daily exposure to electronic media, which seem obsessed with explicit reference to drugs, sex, and violence. A major problem with readiness and opportunity to experience extreme pleasure is the adolescent's relatively immature neurobiological system. A teenager's ability to make sound judgments may be compromised by the relative immaturity of his or her frontal cortex. Because of the relative dominance of the amygdala, cues that remind the adolescent of drug-induced euphoria and associated "benefits" may trigger urges and cravings that he or she finds almost impossible to control.

There is a huge array of drugs and activities that can increase dopamine in the nucleus accumbens. Cigarettes and alcohol, both legal, continue to be of primary concern. Approximately half (46%) of twelfth-grade students have tried alcohol and nearly a quarter (22%) are current smokers. Marijuana is the most prevalent of the illicit drugs. In 2007, the annual prevalence of marijuana use among twelfth graders was 31.7%. Along with "club drugs" such as GHB, Ecstasy, ketamine, and Rohypnol, inhalants and over-the-counter cough and cold medicines are additional areas of threat. A survey of more than 3,000 college students showed that about 20% used mind-altering prescription drugs without a prescription, for the purpose of getting high.

A major consequence of extensive exposure during adolescence is continuation into adulthood, resulting in life-course persistent patterns of abuse and dependence. In fact, according to recent SAMHSA statistics, 22.2 million Americans age 12 and older currently suffer from dependence on or abuse of drugs and alcohol.

Any stress-reducing activity—whether ingestion of a psychoactive substance or masturbation—may be subject to compulsive overuse and the escalating consequences of loss of control. In fact, the disease concept may be applied to the entire spectrum of compulsive problem behaviors. As in viral and bacterial infections, the origin and structure of specific disease carriers may be very different, and yet the consequences of foreign invasion may be the same as far as symptoms, prognosis, and treatment.

Reverend Joseph L. Kellermann describes alcoholism as "a merry-go-round named denial," in which the alcoholic, together with supporting actors, acts out a predictable scenario. Without professional guidance, the addict and supporting actors find it hard to face the realities of emptiness and destruction exacerbated by addictive lifestyles. We suggest that the concept of denial is better understood and communicated to those affected by addiction when replaced by the word *defensiveness*.

A person loses touch with his or her core values as the journey to oblivion progresses over time. In the pre-addiction (symptomatic) phase, where drinking has not caused any major problems, the individual may maintain functioning with an intact and positive system of morals and values (i.e., progressing toward life goals as a contributing member of society). However, as addiction progresses through prodromal, crucial, and chronic phases, the person's ability to function in accord with his or her own values greatly diminishes. With the onset of recovery, positive principles that guide one's behavior may reemerge or become reorganized. This type of prosocial reorientation, however, requires ample support from family and friends, personal commitment, and ample time to become ingrained as a new pattern of thoughts, feelings and actions.

In consideration of the powerful influences from biological, psychological, and social sources, a continuing pattern of struggle and failure seems inevitable. Relapse may occur when the individual experiences pressure from one or more of the following sources: negative emotional states, interpersonal alliances that promote substance use, or stimulus cues that reinstate memories of powerful sensations of pleasure associated with the drug. The intensity of an individual's reaction to a lapse in abstinence or commitment to moderation is dependent upon (1) the degree of personal commitment to abstinence; (2) the importance of the behavior to the individual involved; and (3) the period of sustained abstinence—the longer the duration, the greater the effect (i.e., increased probability to relapse).

Although addicts take the first steps to recovery for a variety of reasons, the battle for control is always decided according to one fundamental principle: The addict must find alternative means to satisfy the needs that were previously met through the addictive activity. George Vaillant summarized the effective ingredients of programs for the treatment of alcohol dependence, all of which are embodied in the tenets of AA. The same principles apply to the broad range of addictive behaviors.

The relief experienced by participating in a group that offers empathy and belonging while rewarding sobriety may be crucial to the recovery process. In addition to 12-step rehabilitation and other psychosocial treatment models, most AA groups accept that some hedonically dependent people benefit from taking medication to deal with a withdrawal or co-occurring mental disorder. AA does not endorse advice to ignore doctors' prescriptions.

In summary, although recovery-oriented treatment has helped many to reclaim their dignity and freedom, by far the most humane solution to substance dependence or behavioral addictions is to prevent the process from occurring in the first place. Parents and other educators must ensure that their children are successfully inoculated against the false promise of such activities and behaviors. The strategy that we suggest is based on flexible use of a three-phase, addiction-inoculation approach that involves mental preparation, skill development, and rehearsal. This cognitive-behavioral approach is fully explained in the next section.

SECTION VII

Natural Highs

*The Cutting Edge
of Mood Alteration*

But we should be mindful of the fact that the maps of joy can be falsified by a host of drugs and thus fail to reflect the actual state of the organism.

—Antonio Damasio

Overview: The Era of Self-Regulation and Natural Highs

We have explored hedonic pursuit from multiple perspectives. Culture, social learning, brain chemistry, and genetics all conspire toward the relentless quest for exalted delight. Zest for life is a virtue. Pleasure and relief from suffering, however, easily morph into hardship and despair.

Upon the first goblet he read the inscription: Monkey wine; upon the second: lion wine; upon the third: sheep wine; upon the fourth: swine wine. These four inscriptions expressed the four descending degrees of drunkenness: the first, that which enlivens; the second, that which irritates; the third, that which stupefies; the fourth, that which brutalizes.

—Victor Hugo, *Les Misérables*

It can be excruciatingly difficult to overcome renegade biological processes that are further encouraged by powerful social and psychological influences. Yet, it can be done.

Biologically, the question is, can the human brain gain control over inherited impulses that were appropriate for prehistoric man but are inappropriate in the 20th century? We know that compulsive pleasure seeking lifestyles are self-induced and are under both cortical and limbic system control. We also know that the cerebral cortex, the center of thought and memory, is much larger in humans than in other animals. With this great reasoning capacity, we should be able to exercise more control over the basic emotions directed by the lower brain centers. In fact, there are rational and healthy means to regulate the universal drive to experience pleasure.

We are in the midst of a revolution in how humans manage stress. The old standbys of being angry, depressed, anxious, drunk, or otherwise misbehaving are no longer acceptable. We have reached an evolutionary junction in self-regulation. Culture now calls upon humans to take charge of their emotions and actions by changing or managing dysfunctional thoughts from which negative feelings and problem behaviors arise. We refer to this perspective as the *cognitive-behavioral revolution*. Cognitive-behavioral therapy, as we have noted previously, has become the predominant treatment modality for the three pillars of maladaptive functioning: addiction, crime, and mental disorder. More than 300 controlled studies of CBT have been completed for a variety of psychiatric and psychological disorders (Butler & Beck, 2000).

However, the value of CBT extends far beyond treating the broad spectrum of social problem behaviors. It has also become the predominant means for better managing the ups and downs of everyday life. By learning the principles and skill sets of cognitive-behavioral restructuring (CBR), readers will take a quantum leap toward improving their overall quality of life. Increased control and flexibility in how we interpret and respond to both crisis and everyday events increase the chances for success and happiness throughout one's life span. As educators, counselors, parents, and friends, we can influence others to take on the mantle of self-discovery and positive change.

A critical step toward positive mood alteration (i.e., natural highs) and enduring happiness is to develop a state of mindfulness or focused awareness on our present thoughts. As William James has said, "The greatest weapon against stress is our ability to choose one thought over another." *Acceptance and commitment therapy* (ACT) (Hayes, Follette, & Linehan, 2004; Hayes & Smith, 2005) and *dialectical behavioral therapy* (DBT) (Linehan, 1993a, 1993b; Robins, Schmidt, & Linehan, 2004) have improved our understanding of mindfulness in prevention, intervention, treatment, and everyday life. The concept of mindfulness generally includes awareness and attention, focusing on the present, sensitivity to surrounding stimuli, awareness of the connections between self and the outside world, and a lack of desire or urge to escape the current situation (Fruzzetti & Iverson, 2004). It is a practice that has to do with being aware of and taking part in everyday living. "It is a way of living awake, with one's eyes wide open" (Robins et al., 2004, p. 37). Rooted in the thoughtful approaches common to Eastern and Western spiritual disciplines, it "allows" experiences rather than suppressing or avoiding them (Robins et al., 2004, p. 37). It is a conscious process of observing, describing, and taking part in the reality of the moment, putting aside judgment, conclusions, and opinions. According to Robins et al., it is looking at thoughts as thoughts, rather than looking *from* thoughts or looking at the world *through* thoughts. We not only have the capacity to diffuse and disengage from risky or harm-directing thoughts; we can also select and focus on those that are in our own and others' best interest.

Linehan (1993a, 1993b) sees mindfulness as involving "what to do" and "how to do" skills. Wanberg and Milkman (2008) summarize these as follows: The "what to do" skills in being mindful are

- Observing, noticing, awareness of the present.
- Verbally describing what has been observed or experienced.
- Taking part fully in the behavior and letting go without a lot of conscious activity.

The "how to do" skills involve

- Not being judgmental or evaluative or focusing on the "good" or "bad" of the thoughts or experiences.
- Focusing on the present, here and now, and on one thing at a time.
- Engaging in actions that are congruent with one's life goals, purpose, or values.

Another facet of being in the here and now is accepting the reality of the situation at hand. Robins et al. (2004) describe "radical acceptance" as a process of "focusing on the current moment, seeking reality as it is without 'delusions' and accepting reality without judgment" (p. 39). In DBT, "clients are taught and encouraged to use skills for accepting life completely and radically as well as for changing it" (p. 39). Fruzzetti and Iverson (2004) identify several components or defining features of acceptance:

- The person is fully aware of what is being accepted.
- Regardless of whether the experience is pleasant or unpleasant, wanted or not wanted, the focus is on accepting, rather than mobilizing resources to change the situation or experience.
- The person has some understanding of how the experience is related to stimuli that preceded it.

Acceptance is seen at two levels: pure acceptance with no efforts to change, and acceptance in balance with change. The almost universal appreciation of AA's Serenity Prayer is evidence for the sensibility of this approach.

God grant me the serenity to accept the things I cannot change

Courage to change the things I can

And the wisdom to know the difference

Get out of Your Mind and Into Your Life (Hayes & Smith, 2005) is a self-help workbook designed to teach mindfulness and acceptance as a means to overcome depression and emotional pain. The manual provides exercises on how to *understand and choose*, rather than blindly follow, the positive or negative thoughts that constitute ordinary human consciousness. A poignant example from this book of a mindfulness and acceptance exercise is presented below.

Exercise: Floating Leaves on a Moving Stream

This will be an eyes-closed exercise. First, read the instructions and then when you are sure you understand them, close your eyes and do the exercise.

Imagine a beautiful slow-moving stream. The water flows over rocks, around trees, descends downhill, and travels through a valley. Once in a while, a big leaf drops into the stream and floats away down the river. Imagine you are sitting beside the stream on a warm, sunny day, watching the leaves float by.

Now become conscious of your thoughts. Each time a thought pops into your head, imagine that it is written on one of those leaves. If you think in words, put them on the leaf in words. If you think in images, put them on the leaf as an image. The goal is to stay beside the stream and allow the leaves on the stream to keep flowing by. Don't try to make the stream go faster or slower; don't try to change what shows up on the leaves in any way. If the leaves disappear, or if you mentally go somewhere else, or if you find that you are into the stream or on a leaf, just stop and notice that this happened. File that knowledge away, and then once again return to the stream, watch a thought come into your mind, write it on a leaf, and let the leaf float away down the stream.

Continue doing this for at least 5 minutes. Keep a watch or clock close by and note when you start the exercise. This will be useful in answering some of the questions below. If the instructions are clear to you now, go ahead and close your eyes and do the exercise.

- How long did you go until you got caught by one of your thoughts?
- If you got the stream flowing and then it stopped, or if you went somewhere else in your mind, write down what happened just before that occurred.
- If you never got the mental image of the stream started, write down what you were thinking while it wasn't starting.

SOURCE: Hayes, S. C., & Smith, S. (2005). *Get out of your mind and into your life: The new Acceptance and Commitment Therapy.* Oakland, CA: New Harbinger, pp. 76–77.

Hayes and Smith (2005) recommend that you do this exercise regularly to see if you can do better in allowing the stream to flow.

According to the World Values Survey, an ongoing study conducted by a global network of social scientists, Denmark was found to be the "world's happiest country." Political scientist Ronald Inglehart's (quoted in "Denmark World's Happiest Country," 2008) analysis of this finding is that the most important determinant of happiness is the extent to which people have free choice in how to manage their lives. The premise of this book is that through self-regulation of thoughts, feelings, and actions, we can orchestrate our natural brain chemistry to evoke positive feeling states and lasting happiness. Hence, the final chapters explore the six basic tenets of the natural highs perspective:

Chapter 16: The Cognitive-Behavioral Revolution: How to Manage Thoughts, Feelings, and Behaviors

Chapter 17: Maintaining Close and Intimate Relationships

Chapter 18: Relaxation, Mindfulness, and Meditation

Chapter 19: Eating Yourself Fit

Chapter 20: Exercise: The Magic Bullet

Chapter 21: Meaningful Engagement of Talents

16

The Cognitive-Behavioral Revolution

How to Manage Thoughts, Feelings, and Behaviors

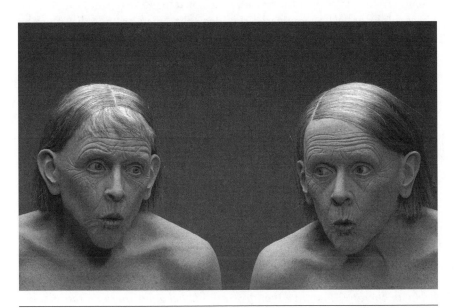

Figure 16.1   **Thinking makes it so.** The greatest weapon against stress is our ability to choose one thought over another.—William James

SOURCE: Used with permission of Tip Toland from the collection of Doug and Dale Anderson.

Introduction: Evolution of the Cognitive-Behavioral Model

The goal of this chapter is to capture the essence of cognitive-behavioral restructuring and to show how it can be incorporated in everyday life. We begin with a discussion of how the CBR model ascended to its current role as the preeminent tool for self-discovery and change. The basic principles of the cognitive-behavioral model are discussed, with case examples illustrative of how thinking is intimately related to feelings and actions. Readers are encouraged to utilize these principles to improve their overall quality of life.

The perspective that developing a healthy style of thinking can reduce distress or enhance well-being is a common theme across many generations and cultures. The *cognitive-behavioral revolution* is predicated upon fundamental principles from ancient Persian, Buddhist, Roman, and Greek philosophies. According to the Persian prophet and religious poet Zoroaster (estimated to have lived in the 6th century BC), "your good thoughts, good words, and good deeds alone will be your intercessors. Nothing more will be wanted. They alone will serve you as a safe pilot to the harbor of Heaven, as a safe guide to the gates of paradise" (quoted in Barrows, 1893, p. 904). Buddha (563–483 BC) is quoted as saying, "We are what we think. . . . All that we are arises with our thoughts. . . . With our thoughts, we make the world" (quoted in Kornfield, 1993, p. 222). Plato (428–347 BC) (De Cuypere, 2008) described "ideal forms" as existing within the mind and representing what is real in the world, and Epictetus (55–135 AD), an ancient Greek philosopher, promulgated the idea that "men are not disturbed by things which happen but by their opinions about things" (Templeton, 1998, p. 114). Marcus Aurelius, who presided as emperor of Rome from 161 to his death in 180 AD, is reputed to have stated, "Our life is what our thoughts make it" (Goodman & Goodman, 1997, p. 831).

Philosophers of the 17th and 18th centuries also built their view of the world around the idea that the mind determines reality. This is particularly found in René Descartes' concept, "I think, therefore I am," and Immanuel Kant's idea that the mind makes nature (Collingwood, 1949). According to William James (1842–1910), regarded by many as the father of American psychology, "The greatest discovery of my generation is that a man can alter his life simply by altering his attitude of mind" (quoted in Hamilton, 2008, p. 117).

The National Association of Cognitive-Behavioral Therapists (2008) describes cognitive-behavioral therapy as a general classification of psychotherapy, including several intervention approaches: *rational emotive behavior therapy, cognitive therapy, rational behavior therapy, rational living therapy, schema focused therapy,* and *dialectical behavior therapy.* Each approach has its own developmental history.

Albert Ellis, Grandfather of Cognitive Therapy

Although there are many approaches covered by the rubric of cognitive therapy, Ellis is generally regarded as the grandfather of the cognitive approach. In reaction to his perception of psychoanalysis as "in-efficient and in-directive," Ellis developed *rational emotive therapy* (RET) (Ellis, 1962; Ellis & Harper, 1961). He was influenced by Alfred Adler (1956), a neo-Freudian, who stated, "I am convinced that a person's behavior springs from his ideas" (p. 172).

Having been trained in psychoanalysis, Ellis searched for a more rapid way to facilitate change. He discovered that he was often quicker than his clients at discovering the source of their problems. Furthermore, their difficulties usually stemmed from a common pattern of distorted thinking. He developed *rational therapy* (RT) to enable clients to not only recognize distortions in their thinking but also to "vigorously dispute" them. Ellis soon expanded RT to rational emotive therapy (Ellis, 1962), and more recently to *rational-emotive behavioral therapy* (REBT) (Ellis, 2004). Although his theories have evolved over the past five decades, some common themes emerge from his writings.

1. There is an important distinction between rational and irrational beliefs (Dryden & Ellis, 1986). Whereas rational beliefs are useful in helping individuals get what they want, irrational beliefs are more closed-minded and inflexible and usually interfere with satisfaction of needs and desires. People become disturbed by a self-imposed prison of *shoulds* (e.g., I should do that) and *musts* (e.g., I must do this) leading to self-condemnation and negative emotions as they try to satisfy a litany of impossible self-imposed demands.

2. ABC: The **A** (activating event)–**B** (belief)–**C** (consequence) method of cognitive and behavioral analysis and change. It is one's *belief* (B) about the *activating event* (A) that leads to the emotional or behavioral *consequence* (C). From this perspective, clients can change C by changing B, even if the activating events in their lives don't change. REBT typically involves an active and directive therapist who helps the client first identify and then vigorously confront, challenge, and dispute his or her irrational thoughts. Although Ellis uses homework assignments as means for behavioral rehearsal, the primary targets for change are an individual's thoughts and beliefs about certain aspects of life. Like behavioral therapy, REBT is present focused. Inquiry into past events, thoughts, or feelings is deemed unnecessary; rather, it is important to identify and dispute current irrational beliefs (Ellis, 1962).

Contemporary Cognitive Therapy

The preeminent authority on cognitive therapy is Aaron Beck. In the 1960s, Beck (1963, 1964) developed a theory called *thinking and depression*, which set the stage for Beck being recognized as the foremost expert on using cognitive therapy for a spectrum of emotional disorders (Leahy, 1996). The perspectives of several post-Freudian analysts, such as Adler, Honey, and Sullivan, influenced his work, particularly their focus on distorted self-images, which paved the way to more systematized cognitive-behavioral formulations of psychiatric disorders and personality structure. Kelly's (1955) theory of personal constructs (core beliefs or self-schemas) and Ellis's rational emotive therapy (1962) also contributed to the development of Beck's cognitive theories.

Beck's early work considered the role of maladaptive information processing in depression and anxiety disorders. He posited a cognitive conceptualization of depression by relating problems in mood, motivation, and physical malaise to characteristically negative thoughts about the self, world, and future. This became known as the "negative cognitive triad" (A. T. Beck, 1963, 1964). Beck theorized that there are characteristic errors in logic in the automatic thoughts (expectations, appraisals, attributions, and decisions) and other cognitions of persons with emotional disorders. Subsequent research has confirmed the importance of cognitive errors in pathological styles of information processing. As shown in Table 16.1, Beck described six categories of cognitive errors.

In implementing CBT methods for reducing cognitive errors, therapists typically teach clients that the most important aim is to recognize that one is making cognitive errors—not to identify each and every error in logic that is occurring.

Table 16.2 shows Beck's formulation of *schemas*, the core mental structures that guide automatic thinking. Schemas are enduring principles of thinking that start to take shape in early childhood and are influenced by a multitude of life experiences, including parental teaching and modeling, formal and informal educational activities, peer experiences, traumas, and successes (Wright, Fasco, & Thase, 2006). The relationship between schemas and automatic thinking is understood according to the diathesis-stress hypothesis. Beck and others have explained that in depression and other conditions of mental disturbance, maladaptive schemas (diathesis, i.e., mental predisposition) may remain dormant until a condition of stress arises that activates the core beliefs (A. T. Beck, Rush, Shaw, & Emery, 1979; Clark, Beck, & Alford, 1999; Miranda, 1992).

In summary, according to the cognitive approach (Wright et al., 2006), the highest level of functioning is consciousness—therapists encourage the development and application of rational thinking and problem solving. In terms of irrational or maladaptive thinking, CBT teaches clients to recognize and change their response to pathological thinking on two levels:

Automatic Thoughts—cognitions that stream rapidly through our minds when we are in the midst of situations (or recalling events): "This talk is boring; get me out; I can't take it anymore."

Schemas—core beliefs that give meaning to information from the environment: "Academics know nothing about the real world."

There is an emphasis on techniques designed to help clients *detect and modify* their inner thoughts, especially those that are associated with emotional symptoms such as depression, anxiety, or anger. One of the most important clues that automatic thoughts might be occurring is the *presence of strong emotions*. In depression and other conditions, maladaptive schemas may remain dormant until a stressful life event occurs that activates the core belief (A. T. Beck et al., 1979). The maladaptive schema is then strengthened

Table 16.1   Cognitive Errors

Selective Abstraction

Sometimes called the mental filter. A conclusion is drawn after looking only at a small portion of the available information.

- A depressed man with low self-esteem doesn't receive a holiday card from an old friend. "I'm losing all my old friends. Nobody cares about me anymore."

Arbitrary Inference

Coming to a conclusion in the face of contradictory evidence or in the absence of evidence.

- A woman with a fear of elevators is asked to predict the chance of the elevator falling if she rides in it. She replies, "The chances are 10% or more that the elevator will crash if I ride in it."

Overgeneralization

A conclusion is made about one or more isolated incidents and then extended illogically to cover broad areas of functioning.

- A depressed college student gets a B on a test. He considers this unsatisfactory and overgeneralizes when he has these automatic thoughts. "I'm in trouble in this class. . . . I'm falling short everywhere in my life. . . . I can't do anything right."

Magnification and Minimization

The significance of an attribute, event, or sensation is exaggerated or minimized.

- A woman with a panic disorder starts to feel light-headed during the onset of a panic attack. She thinks, "I'll faint. . . . I might have a heart attack or a stroke."

Personalization

External events are related to oneself when there is no evidence for doing so. Excessive responsibility or blame is taken for negative events.

- In an economic downturn, a previously successful businessman struggles to meet the annual budget. Layoffs are being considered. Although many factors have contributed to the financial crisis, the manager thinks, "It's my fault. . . . I should have seen this coming and done something about it. . . . I've failed everybody in the company."

Dichotomous Thinking

Also called absolutist or all-or-none thinking. Judgments about oneself, personal experiences, or others are placed into one of two categories (e.g., all bad or all good, total failure or total success).

- "Ted has everything and I have nothing."

SOURCE: Adapted from Wright, J., Fasco, M., & Thase, M. (2006). *Learning cognitive-behavioral therapy: An illustrated guide.* Arlington, VA: American Psychiatric Publishing, pp. 11–12.

to the point that it stimulates and drives the more superficial stream of negative automatic thoughts.

This formulation may be used to explain the breakdown of logic and civility in emotionally charged situations. Consider the example of a celebrity actor/director spewing anti-Semitic remarks upon learning of his DUI arrest.

Table 16.2   Three Main Groups of Schemas

1. Simple schemas

Rules about the physical nature of the environment, practical management of everyday activities, or laws of nature that may have little or no effect on psychopathology.

- e.g., "Be a defensive driver"; "A good education pays off"; Take shelter during a storm."

2. Intermediary beliefs and assumptions

Conditional rules such as if-then statements that influence self-esteem and emotional regulation.

- e.g., "I must be perfect to be accepted"; "If I don't please others all the time, they will reject me"; "If I work hard, I can succeed."

3. Core beliefs about the self

Global and absolute rules for interpreting environmental information related to self-esteem.

- e.g., "I'm unlovable"; "I'm stupid"; "I'm a failure"; "I'm a good friend"; "I can trust others."

SOURCE: From "Learning cognitive-behavioral therapy: An illustrated guide" by J. Wright, M. Fasco, & M. Thase, 2006, Arlington, VA: American Psychiatric Publishing, pp. 11–12.

Case Example: Mel Gibson's Anti-Semitic Tirade

According to a series of widely publicized media reports (see "Gibson's Anti-Semitic Tirade," 2006; Marquez, 2006), on July 28, 2006, at 2:36 AM PDT, Mel Gibson was arrested on suspicion of driving under the influence (DUI) of alcohol after being stopped for speeding (84 mph in a 45 mph zone). He was apprehended in his 2006 Lexus LS 430 on the Pacific Coast Highway in Malibu, California. Gibson's blood-alcohol level was measured at 0.12 (the legal limit in California is 0.08). A three-quarters-full bottle of Cazadores Tequila was found next to him.

The arresting officer, James Mee, described Gibson as cooperative until the time of his arrest when, while handcuffed in the police car, he became belligerent and made anti-Semitic remarks to Mee, who is of Jewish decent. The entertainment Web site TMZ.com reported that Gibson said, "The Jews are responsible for all the wars in the world," and asked the arresting officer, "Are you a Jew?" Citing an unnamed law enforcement source, TMZ further alleged that Gibson asked a female sergeant at the station, "What are you looking at, sugar tits?" Gibson was released on bail at 9 AM PDT. The next day, he confessed to driving under the influence and to "despicable" behavior during his arrest. He made several public apologies. A frenzy of media coverage followed (e.g., Chris Suellentrop's article "Mel Gibson's Moment" in the *New York Times,* August 1, 2006).

As shown in Figure 16.2, the cognitive view of the mind shows that under stress, deep-seated beliefs, which under ordinary conditions may remain dormant, become energized and activate automatic thinking (Wanberg & Milkman, 2008).

As discussed in the section overview, mindfulness training (Hayes et al., 2004; Hayes & Smith, 2005) can serve as a powerful antidote to the usual knee-jerk stress response of blindly activating maladaptive beliefs, energizing automatic thoughts that fall prey to distortion by errors in logic. Of course, consuming six alcoholic beverages (as is likely in the case of Mr. Gibson, based on the bottle found in his car and his blood-alcohol level) is likely to exacerbate any proclivity toward the above.

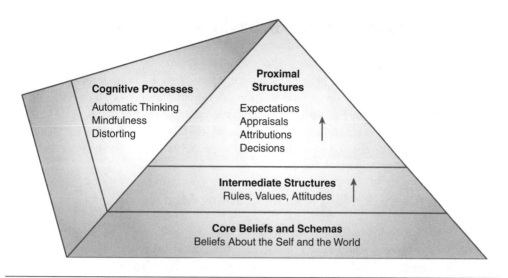

Figure 16.2   Model of cognitive structures and processes. Stress may activate dysfunctional core beliefs that energize automatic thoughts, which are filtered through characteristic errors in logic.

SOURCE: From Wanberg and Milkman, 2008.

Behaviorist Contributions

The development of behavioral theory in the late 1950s and 1960s provided the foundation for the behavioral component of cognitive-behavioral therapy, but behaviorism itself has a longer history. It dates back to John B. Watson's groundbreaking 1913 publication "Psychology as the Behaviorist Views It" (often referred to as "The Behaviorist Manifesto").

> Give me a dozen healthy infants, well-formed and my own specified world to bring them up in and I'll guarantee to take any one at random and train him to become any type of specialist I might select—doctor, lawyer, artist, merchant, chief and yes even beggar man and thief, regardless of the talents, penchants, tendencies, abilities, vocations, and race of his ancestors. (J. B. Watson, 1924, p. 104)

Other contributions to the behavioral component are drawn from Ivan Pavlov's (1927) work in "classical conditioning" (involuntary behavior triggered by a stimulus) and the "operant conditioning" models (voluntary behavior encouraged or discouraged by consequences) of B. F. Skinner (1938). Behaviorism, as such, focuses on observable, external behaviors and disregards internal mental processes.

Combining Cognitive and Behavioral Theories

In modern psychology, the cognitive approach was a reaction to the narrower view of behavioral psychology, which did not attend to—and even rejected—the importance of internal thought processes. Bandura's (1969, 1977) pioneering work on *social learning* and Meichenbaum's (1977) focus on an individual's *internal dialogue or self-talk* paved the way for the blending of the cognitive and behavioral approaches to self-discovery and change.

Albert Bandura's Social Learning Model

Bandura's classic work, *Principles of Behavior Modification* (1969), showed the limitations of a strictly behavioral approach to therapy. Bandura disagreed with traditional behaviorists about there being a direct link between stimulus and response or between behavior and reinforcement. Instead, cognitive processing mediates between stimulus and response. Human functioning is a product of the interaction of environment, behavior, and thinking. Bandura conducted research on the concept of *self-efficacy,* an individual's sense of self-esteem and competence in dealing with life's problems. People with high self-efficacy believe they are capable of dealing effectively with the diverse events in their lives. Conversely, when confronted with a challenge or significant life problem, those with low self-efficacy are likely to give up if their initial problem-solving attempts fail (Schultz & Schultz, 2004).

Bandura (1977) stressed the influence of external reinforcement schedules on such thought processes as beliefs, expectations, and instructions. People are not merely machines that automatically respond to external stimuli. Instead, reactions to stimuli are self-activated, initiated by the person. Bandura's principle of *reciprocal determinism* posits that not only do environmental contingencies influence human behavior, but humans in turn influence themselves and their environment. Bandura showed that a perceived reinforcer was more reinforcing than an actual reinforcer not perceived as such. What happens in the "black box" (the mind) is of crucial importance.

Bandura's work on *modeling* is also of great significance to modern CBT approaches. He discovered that individuals did not have to be reinforced directly for performing a behavior in order for that behavior to increase in probability. If fact, it is sufficient to observe another person (a model) having been reinforced for performing that behavior. Hyperaggressive adolescents model the aggressive hostile attitudes of their parents (Bandura, 1973; Bandura & Walters, 1959). In his experiments where children were exposed to models demonstrating either violent or nonviolent behaviors toward a "Bobo doll," he contradicted standard learning theory. Simply observing a model without being personally reinforced resulted in aggression. Thus, behavior can be learned without direct reinforcement. In *Social Learning and Personality Development,* Bandura and Walters (1963) demonstrated the principle of vicarious reinforcement: Learning occurs through the observation of other people's behavior and seeing the consequences of such behavior. Social learning can affect behavior by teaching new behaviors, increasing the frequency with which already learned behaviors are carried out, encouraging previously forbidden behaviors, and increasing or decreasing similar behaviors (e.g., a child observing his or her parents using alcohol may increase the probability of that child using marijuana or other drugs; Wanberg & Milkman, 2008).

Bandura (1977) identified four component processes that influence whether an observer will effectively model a particular behavior:

- *Attention:* The learner must pay attention to the person engaging in a particular behavior (the model).
- *Retention:* The observer must have the capacity to remember what the model has demonstrated.
- *Motor Reproduction:* The observer must have the ability to replicate the behavior being introduced (e.g., if one is to learn juggling, he or she must have the capability to throw, track, and catch a ball).
- *Motivation and Opportunity:* The observer must be motivated to carry out the behavior he or she has observed and remembered and have opportunities to do so. For example, if a person is to reproduce the social bonding, giddiness, and imaginative use of language characteristic of gatherings where marijuana use is a primary focus, he or she must be motivated to attend and have ample opportunities to do so.

Meichenbaum's Stress Inoculation Model

As research in behavioral techniques for managing various forms of behavioral dysfunction (e.g., conduct disorder, phobias, anxiety disorders) expanded in the 1960s and 1970s, a number of prominent researchers such as Meichenbaum (1977) and Lewinsohn, Hoberman, Teri, and Hautzinger (1985) found that the cognitive perspective added *context depth and understanding* to behavioral interventions. Drawing on the work of Soviet psychologists Luria (1973) and Vygotsky (1978), Meichenbaum found that when faced with a task, children talk to themselves about how to perform that task. Private speech serves as an important regulator of behavior. Developmentally, these self-verbalizations are initially overt, but as the child grows older, they become increasingly covert to form the internal dialogue.

Meichenbaum (1977) developed a training program for impulsive children who showed deficits in the ability to regulate their behavior by self-instructions. He set up situations where adult models, while performing a task, would talk out loud about how to perform the task. This training program sequentially facilitated (1) the child performing the task while talking out loud; and (2) the child performing the task while talking covertly. Based on the success of this technique, Meichenbaum formulated a three-stage "stress inoculation" model for improved coping with critical life events. It consisted of (1) an educational phase (mental preparation), (2) modeling and rehearsing the new skills (skills development), and (3) practicing the new skills in the environment (rehearsal). These programs became the blueprint for Meichenbaum's theory of cognitive-behavioral modification (recall the discussion in Chapter 15).

Clients are first instructed on how to become aware of their behaviors and of the internal dialogues that sustain their behavior. Then they are trained in emitting incompatible behavior and internal dialogue (i.e., talking to themselves differently), and finally they are taught to exhibit this new behavior in the environment and to think differently about this new behavior (Meichenbaum, 1977). The therapist's threefold job is to teach or coach clients to (1) notice the behavior, (2) think about and change the behavior, and (3) reconstruct the internal dialogue about the behavior. Meichenbaum's model assumes that various therapeutic systems simply provide different explanatory constructs to help clients think about their problems differently—in other words, to change the nature and content of their internal dialogue. A refreshing thought is that whether one chooses a 12-step recovery program, RET, Buddhism, or to join a political party, if the new alliance provides a basis for an improved internal dialogue that features optimism and purpose, the participant will experience a process of positive growth and change.

> [A]s a result of therapy a translation process talks place . . . the translation is from the internal dialogue the client engaged in prior to therapy to a new language system that emerges over the course of treatment. (Meichenbaum, 1977, p. 217)

Examination of the principles outlined by Bandura (social learning), Meichenbaum (internal dialogue), and Beck (cognitive errors) leads to the conclusion that "self-reinforcement" is the combination of cognitive and behavioral approaches (Wanberg & Milkman, 2008). Cognitive and behavioral changes reinforce each other. When cognitive change leads to changes in action and behavior, there occurs a sense of well-being that strengthens (reinforces) the change in thought and in turn further strengthens the behavioral changes. This self-reinforcing feedback process is a key element of the cognitive-behavioral approach and is the basis for understanding the cognitive-behavioral process.

The self-reinforcing mechanism of CBR is illustrated in Figure 16.3. This graphic device provides a visual anchor for cognitive-behavioral restructuring. The map is of benefit to people at all stages of emotional and behavioral unrest, including mild irritability, moderate anxiety, severe depression, and violent anger. Clients, students, and psychologically minded readers can learn to recognize high-risk situations, consider and rehearse lifestyle modifications, and learn a variety of strategies for identifying and changing distorted thinking processes.

The figure shows how stressful life events trigger a cascade of automatic thoughts (shaped by underlying beliefs), which are then translated into emotions that lead to behaviors. If an individual chooses a positive (adaptive) course of action (through rational thought and emotional control) or opts against a negative one (distorted thought and emotional dysregulation), the outcome will likely be good. This in turn strengthens the recurrence of positive behavior and encourages positive thought processes. Conversely, if the individual chooses a negative (maladaptive) course of action, the outcome will likely be bad, strengthening more negative thought processes (Milkman & Wanberg, 2007).

The main idea of this model is to learn skills for self-regulation of emotions and behavior by making conscious choices regarding the thoughts that one selects to explain the events in his or her life. Recall William James's sage remark, "The greatest weapon against stress is our ability to choose one thought over another."

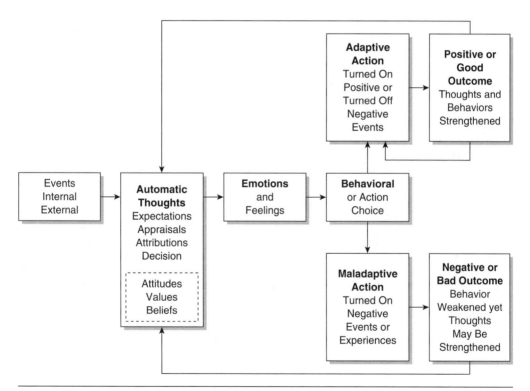

Figure 16.3   The cognitive-behavioral map for learning and change. Events trigger automatic thoughts (activated by underlying beliefs), which energize emotions that lead to behaviors.

SOURCE: From "Criminal conduct and substance abuse treatment: Strategies for self-improvement and change. The provider's guide (2nd ed.)" by K. W. Wanberg & H. B. Milkman, 2008, Thousand Oaks, CA: Sage Publications.

Working With Automatic Thoughts and Core Beliefs

Cognitive-behavioral therapy is effective in the treatment of a wide array of conditions including anxiety disorders, eating disorders, schizophrenia, bipolar disorder, chronic pain, personality disorders, and substance abuse (Butler & Beck, 2000; Dobson, 1989; Wright et al., 2006). The case of Rick, below, illustrates how the cognitive model is used as a tool to improve resiliency and decrease vulnerability to stress.

Case Example: Cognitive Restructuring for Relapse Prevention

Rick had a past history of alcohol dependence. During his first years in high school, he felt insecure among his peers, especially with the opposite sex. When he started drinking at the age of 16, Rick found that he could outdrink and outlast his peers, and could overcome his shyness with girls. After about 4 years of abusive drinking, he started to drink every day. During his freshman year, he dropped out of college and his parents signed him into a 30-day, AA-oriented residential treatment center.

Upon discharge, he continued to attend AA meetings where he met his first wife, who was also recovering from alcohol dependence. They soon became engaged and after a year of courtship they decided to marry. After going back to school, Rick graduated from college and was hired as a manager in a large advertising firm. The couple had their first child after Rick's promotion to an executive position during his third year with the company.

Upon receiving the news that he was being dismissed from his "dream job" because the company needed to downsize in an unstable economic climate, Rick began to have recurrent thoughts of returning to drink. He became overwhelmed by self-blame (i.e., getting fired was all his fault) and the belief that his life would be permanently ruined. Soon after his relapse, Rick and his wife agreed to have him admitted to a cognitively oriented outpatient treatment program. Through a trusting relationship with his counselor, Rick became mindful of the dysfunctional mental processes that culminated in relapse.

Beginning with the powerful stressor (loss of employment), Rick's deep-seated distal structures (beliefs)—"I fall apart under pressure"; "I'm damaged"; "Life isn't fair"—become activated. The intermediate structures (attitudes, values, rules) that determine the quality of his automatic thoughts are set into motion: "Who cares, anyway? Life sucks." (attitude) . . . "I need peace of mind." (value) . . . "I'll do whatever it takes to get over it" (rule). These energized an onslaught of automatic thoughts: "It's all my fault." (attribution) . . . "It will affect everything that I do." . . . "Getting fired is the worst thing that can happen." (appraisal) . . . "I can't cope; if I have a drink, I'll feel better" (expectation). These proximal cognitive structures triggered what Rick experienced as unbearable emotional states (fear, anxiety, and depression). His decision was to get drunk.

In treatment, Rick was able to successfully challenge the deep-seated belief structures that led to his undoing. In fact, he could recount many times when he did not fall apart under pressure: when his child was born prematurely and Rick had to take care of both his child and wife who became bedridden after a fall; when he got a promotion and turned in some of his best work at a time when he had some of the most difficult clients; when his mother passed away and he made all the proper funeral arrangements and gave a heartwarming eulogy to relatives and friends about her life.

After thoroughly challenging and modifying the underlying beliefs, intermediate structures, and automatic thoughts that characteristically led him back to the bottle, Rick was successfully discharged from the 3-month course of outpatient treatment. He and his counselor were confident of Rick's commitment and capacity to live a comfortable and responsible life without alcohol. To date, Rick and his wife have raised four healthy children and neither one has had a slip or relapse in the past 30 years.

The purpose of cognitive-behavioral counseling is to facilitate the discovery of alternative ways of appraising a given situation, and then identify any barriers to thinking and acting in this more adaptive and satisfying way. Table 16.3 maps Rick's relapse process and the protective cognitive restructuring that led to a healthy and productive lifestyle.

The Trans-ideological Power of Cognitive-Behavioral Restructuring

In June of 2005, Aaron Beck, who had long been intrigued by the apparent similarities between Buddhist philosophy and cognitive therapy (CT), engaged in a dialogue with the Dalai Lama, the spiritual leader of Tibetan Buddhism. Their meeting took place at the International Congress of Cognitive Psychotherapy in Göteborg, Sweden. In Beck's (2005) "Reflections on My Public Dialogue With the Dalai Lama," he discusses commonalities between Buddhism and CT.

According to Beck (2005), "Buddhism is the philosophy and psychology closest to cognitive therapy and vice versa" (p. 4). Perhaps the most elemental similarity is that both approaches use the mind to understand and cure the mind. The two share common goals of serenity, peace of mind, and relief of suffering. Both adhere to common values that stress the importance of acceptance, compassion, knowledge, and understanding, with a clear focus on altruism (vs. egoism) and universalism (vs. groupism). Personal responsibility for one's actions and science taking precedent over superstition are core principles.

Regarding the causes of distress, there is a common view of the intrinsic goodness of people, which is overlaid by layer after layer of "negative thoughts." In the Buddhist tradition, these can be neutralized by positive thinking (focusing on positive and good things), whereas CT stresses pinpointing thinking errors and facilitating their correction. Both share common methods of focusing on the immediate (here and now), targeting biased thinking through reflectiveness, perspective taking, use of imagery, identifying toxic beliefs, distancing, and nurturing constructive experiences and positive thoughts.

According to the Dalai Lama in his work *Ethics for the New Millennium* (1999), "If we can reorient our thoughts and emotions, and reorder our behavior, not only can we learn to cope with suffering more easily, but we can prevent a great deal of it from starting in the first place" (p. xii).

At the core of the philosophies embraced by both CBR and the Dalai Lama is *secular ethics*, whereby people of different faiths and cultural backgrounds can accept the importance of positive thought, without necessarily invoking the instrument of religion. These trans-ideological and common-sense aspects of CBR are major factors in its enormous success around the globe. At the time of this writing, a Google search for *cognitive-behavioral therapy* yielded 2,010,000 citations. One of the authors (Milkman), during

Table 16.3   Relapse Thoughts and Protective Cognitive Restructuring

Proximal Structures
(Automatic Thoughts)

Decision—GET DRUNK   *Decision—HANG TOUGH*

Expectation

If I have a drink, I'll feel better; I can't cope.   I don't need a drink; I have a lot to lose.

Appraisal

Getting fired is the worst thing that can happen.   I can manage tough times; I've done it before.

Attribution

It's entirely my fault; it will affect everything   Bad circumstances, but I've still got a lot going for me.
that I do.

Intermediate Structures

Rules

Do whatever you can to get over it.   I won't go back to the old crutch.

Values

Peace of mind   Life is often stressful; I can accept challenges.

Attitudes

Who cares, anyway? Life sucks.   I care about my life and family.

Distal Structures
Core Beliefs; Schemas

I'm damaged; life isn't fair.   A lot of things have gone my way.

I fall apart under pressure.   I can be pretty tough when it comes down to it.

Stress

Loss of employment

a Fulbright lectureship at the Psychology Department of the University of Kebangsaang in Malaysia (1985–1986), discovered that CBT was the preferred treatment approach, equally endorsed by ethnic Malay students who were predominantly Muslim, ethnic Chinese students who were Christian and Buddhist, and ethnic Indian students who were raised primarily in the Hindu tradition. As strange as it may seem, a recent approach to combating terrorism in Saudi Arabia is consistent with the cognitive-behavioral psychology described above.

> At a government detention camp an hour outside Riyadh, jihadis are asked to rethink their radicalism. . . . Welcome to the Care Rehabilitation Center, a three-year-old experiment to reform malleable minds who have fallen under the sway of Osama bin Laden's radical brand of Islam. To get here, jihadis have to demonstrate during a prison interview a readiness to rethink their extremist views. . . . The program, developed by a team of Saudi scholars, psychiatrists and sociologists, tries to convince these men of their mistakes and make them productive members of Saudi society which has been rocked by terrorism. (MacLeod, 2007, p. 8)

Cognitive-Behavioral Restructuring in Everyday Life

It is our hope and expectation that readers will extrapolate the principles above to improve the quality of their lives. CBR methodologies, which have become preeminent across the spectrum of counseling domains (i.e., mental health, substance abuse, and criminal conduct), are applicable in everyday life. By practicing the techniques of mindfulness, acceptance, and cognitive restructuring, readers can improve their relationships, not only with themselves (dealing more effectively with emotions and behavioral choices), but with others across the board. A parent can better relate to his or her children, employees can increase cooperation and positive feelings among coworkers, project managers can improve relationships with their supervisees, and all of us can achieve improved affective states stemming from our interactions with significant others. It might be of particular benefit to reflect on the cognitive restructuring schema (Table 16.3) and cognitive-behavioral map (Figure 16.3) above as personal checkpoints during an episode of stress or interpersonal conflict. Improved self-regulation and positive outcomes are likely to follow. Anyone struggling with hedonic dependencies is likely to benefit from this approach.

Much of our everyday thinking involves a stream of cognitive processing just below the surface of our conscious awareness. This type of automatic thinking may be regarded as preconscious, because thoughts of this nature can be recognized if attention is brought to them (Clark et al., 1999). Perhaps the most important clue that automatic thoughts are taking place is the presence of *strong feelings* (Wright et al., 2006). People who struggle with depression or anxiety often experience automatic thoughts that, through the errors in logic described above, become maladaptive and distorted. When these thoughts (guided by underlying schemas or core beliefs) are activated by stress, they can generate strong emotional reactions and dysfunctional behavior. Alcohol misuse or maladaptive reliance on any tension-relieving behavior may be the behavioral outcome of maladaptive cognitive processing.

The relationship between events, automatic thinking, and emotions in everyday life is illustrated by the example of Susan, a woman who successfully turned her thoughts around after realizing that they were formative to her depressed feelings.

Case Example: Susan's Automatic Thought

Event	Automatic Thoughts	Emotions
My father calls and asks why I forgot to call him about going to lunch.	There I go again. There's no way that I will ever please him. I can't do anything right; I might as well give up.	Sadness Anger
Thinking about a term paper that is due at school.	I can't handle it. I'll never meet the deadline. I won't be able to face my teacher. I'll get a low grade and screw things up like I do everything else.	Anxiety
My husband complains that I'm cranky every time he sees me.	He's really on my case. I'm not being a good wife. I don't enjoy life. Nobody would like to spend time with me.	Sadness Anxiety

Susan's automatic thoughts are consistent with the common finding of negatively based cognitions in anxiety and depression. Themes of hopelessness, low self-esteem, and failure are common in depressive feeling states. People who find themselves riddled with anxiety usually have automatic thoughts that include prediction of danger, harm, uncontrollability, and inability to manage threats (Wright et al., 2006).

Everyone has automatic thoughts; they do not just occur in people who seek treatment for depression, anxiety, or other emotional disorders. By recognizing our personal automatic thoughts and underlying beliefs and by deploying alternative cognitive-behavioral processes, we can strengthen our empathy for others, enhance our counseling skills, and step up the overall quality of our lives.

Automatic Thoughts Exercise: Write down an example of automatic thoughts. Try this for a situation from your own life. If a personal example does not come to mind, you can use an example from someone you know.

1. Draw three columns on a sheet of paper and label them *Event, Automatic Thoughts,* and *Emotions*.

2. Recall a recent situation or memory of an event that seemed to stir up emotions such as anxiety, anger, sadness, physical tension, or happiness.

3. Try to imagine being back in this situation, just as it happened.

4. What automatic thoughts were occurring in this situation? Write down the event, the automatic thoughts, and the emotions in each column of your record.

5. Try to identify the underlying beliefs that energize these thoughts.

6. What kind of errors in logic might you be using?

7. What alternative cognitive process can you use to alter your emotional states?

Chapter Summary

The perspective that developing a healthy style of thinking can reduce distress or enhance well-being is a common theme across many generations and cultures. The cognitive-behavioral revolution is based on fundamental principles from ancient Persian, Buddhist, Roman, and Greek philosophies.

Albert Ellis is generally regarded as the grandfather of the cognitive approach to therapy. Today, the preeminent authority on cognitive therapy is Aaron Beck. Beck put forth a cognitive conceptualization of depression that relates problems in mood, motivation, and physical malaise to typically negative thoughts about the self, world, and future. This became known as the "negative cognitive triad." Beck theorized that there are characteristic errors in logic in the automatic thoughts (expectations, appraisals, attributions, and decisions) and other cognitions of those with emotional disorders. Subsequent research has confirmed the importance of cognitive errors in pathological styles of information processing.

There is an emphasis on techniques designed to help clients detect and modify their inner thoughts, especially those that are associated with emotional symptoms such as depression, anxiety, or anger. The presence of strong emotions is a prime indicator that automatic thoughts might be occurring. In depression and other conditions, maladaptive schemas may remain dormant until a stressful life event occurs and activates the core belief. The schema is then strengthened to the degree that it stimulates and drives the more superficial negative, automatic thoughts. Emotional discomfort, substance abuse, interpersonal conflict, and other harmful patterns of behavior are seen as sequels to dysfunctional patterns of thought.

The development of behavioral theory in the late 1950s and 1960s provided the foundation for the behavioral component of cognitive-behavioral therapy. Examination of the principles outlined by Bandura (social learning), Meichenbaum (internal dialogue), and Beck (cognitive errors) leads to the conclusion that "self-reinforcement" is the combining element of cognitive and behavioral approaches. Changes in thinking and behavior strengthen one another. When a change in cognition leads to a change in action, which is followed by a positive outcome, the resultant sense of well-being reinforces (strengthens) both the initiating thought and subsequent behavior. This self-reinforcing aspect of the cognitive-behavioral approach facilitates the transition from an effortful form of cognitive-behavioral self-management to a relatively effortless pattern of thinking and acting in a new and more adaptive manner.

People of different faiths and cultural backgrounds can accept the importance of positive thought without necessarily invoking a particular religion or philosophy of life. These trans-ideological and commonsense aspects of CBR are great contributors to its tremendous success around the world. By practicing the techniques of mindfulness, acceptance, and cognitive restructuring, readers can improve how they think and feel about themselves, the world, and their relationships with others.

17 Maintaining Close and Intimate Relationships

Your soul is your relationship with other people. What you say and do does not die.

—Tom Wolfe

Introduction: The Three Faces of Love

"Love represents a cognitive, behavioral and emotional stance toward others that takes three prototypical forms" (Peterson & Seligman, 2004, p. 304). The first and perhaps the foundation for all future attachments is the love that we feel for our first caregivers. We trust them to make our welfare a priority and to be at our side in times of need. They comfort and reassure us when we are disquieted by long periods of separation. The prototype for this form is a child's love for a parent.

Another kind of love is for those who depend on us to make them feel safe and looked after. We provide them with comfort and safety, assistance and support when they are in need and put their welfare above our own. We feel uplifted when they are happy and sad when things don't go their way. The prototype of this form is a parent's love for a child.

The third form of love is one that involves passionate desire for sexual, physical, and emotional closeness with another person. We consider this person special, and being with him or her makes us feel special. The prototype here is romantic love.

Freud (1905/1962) was among the first to describe the commonalities between love for a child and romantic love. He noted striking similarities between lovers and mother–infant pairs. Both spend a good deal of time in mutual gazing, cuddling, kissing, and having skin-to-skin contact, along with touching body parts that are considered "private." Today, there is biological evidence for a similar neurochemical underpinning between the two types. Oxytocin, released during suckling/nursing, is thought to induce feelings of bonding and attachment between mother and child. The same chemical is released at sexual climax and is believed to play a role in the cuddling and feelings of closeness that follow intercourse (Carter, 1992; Slater, 2006; Walter, 2008).

This chapter is designed to provide readers with an understanding of the importance of flourishing human relationships to our overall happiness and well-being. In the context of natural highs, the thrust of our discussion is on developing improved ways of satisfying basic needs for love and belonging, for ourselves and those whom we cherish and admire. We begin our discussion of maintaining close and intimate relationships with infant–caretaker attachment. Healthy bonding at this vital stage of development is a critical model for trust and safety in future relationships (Erikson, 1982). The derivative of healthy bonding and security—through infancy, childhood, and adolescence—is secure adult attachment, which is closely linked to healthy relationships. Our discussion of secure attachment sets the stage for examining the qualities of mature love and the importance of consciously engaging in behaviors that sustain interpersonal connections over time and contribute to flourishing relationships (Snyder & Lopez, 2007).

The Universal Need for Love

Maslow (1954/1970) posited that human motives are hierarchically arranged. Ascending in order from a base of *biological* needs, hunger and thirst, next the needs for *safety* (i.e., to become free from threats of danger, both psychological and physical) come into play. Next in the hierarchy is the need for attachment, which leads to our quest for connection to others, to love and to be loved. When these are satisfied, our motives turn toward the need to feel valued or *esteemed* by ourselves and others. The drives toward knowledge, understanding, and novelty are grouped together as *cognitive* needs. We then experience *aesthetic* needs, which become manifest in our desires for order and beauty. At the upper tier of the hierarchy is the need for *self-actualization:* "the full use and exploitation of talents, capacities, and potentialities" (Maslow, 1954/1970, p. 150). The self-actualized individual is characterized by such traits as spontaneity, autonomy, sense of humor, and *deep interpersonal relationships.* At the apex of the hierarchy is the need for *transcendence,* pertaining to spiritual or religious needs.

In their classic work called *Character Strengths and Virtues,* Peterson and Seligman (2004) classify six broad virtues that consistently emerge across history and culture: wisdom, courage, humanity, justice, temperance, and transcendence. From both Peterson and Seligman's and Maslow's perspective, the capacity to establish and maintain deep interpersonal relationships is germane to the experience of happiness and fulfilling one's potential. This view of the intimate connection between optimal life experience and the capacity to form close interpersonal bonds is also a vital component of our view of natural highs as "self-induced changes in brain chemistry that result in positive feeling states, health, and well-being for the individual and society," as noted in Chapter 1.

The characteristics of Peterson and Seligman's (2004) core virtue of "humanity" are helpful in conceptualizing ideal human connections.

Humanity: Interpersonal strengths
that involve tending and befriending others

- *Capacity to Love and Be Loved:* Valuing close relations with others, in particular those in which sharing and caring are reciprocated; being close to other people
- *Kindness [generosity, nurturance, care, compassion, altruistic love, "niceness"]:* Doing favors and good deeds for others; helping them; taking care of them
- *Social Intelligence [emotional intelligence, personal intelligence]:* Being aware of the motives and feelings of other people and oneself; knowing what to do to fit into different social situations; knowing what makes other people tick. (p. 29)

Secure Attachment: A Prototype for Successful Relationships

Studies of human attachment shed light on how people remain "on track" with their needs for love and belonging and how others may become "derailed." As discussed in Section V, "craving for intimacy" can override our sense of right or wrong and judgment concerning harm to the self or others. We may use drugs, join cults, or purchase sexual favors to find relief from loneliness and despair.

The roots of scholarly work in the area of human connectedness are found in the study of traumatic separation (e.g., Bowlby, 1969) and failed relationships (e.g., Carrere & Gottman, 1999). With the recent turn toward "positive psychology," theorists and researchers have undertaken the study of developmental precursors to successful relationships (e.g., Gable, Reis, & Elliot, 2003; Harvey, Pauwels, & Zickmund, 2001; Peterson & Seligman, 2004; Snyder & Lopez, 2007).

Attachment is a process that may begin in utero and continue throughout one's life span. It is the emotional link that forms between an infant and a caregiver, and it physically bonds people together over time (Ainsworth, Bell, & Stayton, 1992). Bowlby (1969), a clinician who worked with delinquent and orphaned children, identified certain styles of caregiving that resulted in secure or insecure patterns of attachment. Maladaptive parental behaviors include chaotic and unplanned attempts to meet the child's needs. Contrastingly, adaptive parenting centers on responsiveness to the child's behavioral cues such as smiling when happy or crying when upset.

Inconsistency in responding is associated with anxiety and frustration later in life, whereas consistency is associated with later development of contentment and trust. Lopez (2003) describes the two-way connection between infant and caregiver as "a unique, evolutionary-based motivational system (i.e., independent of gratification of the libidinal needs and drives) whose primary function is the provision of protection and emotional security" (p. 286).

By studying children that became disconnected from their caregivers, Bowlby (1969) realized that insecure attachment sets the stage for a host of developmental struggles. The growing child may have difficulty in mood regulation or in cooperating with others. On the other hand, those children who were raised under conditions of secure attachment became more appealing to their caregivers and those around them. In time, mutually beneficial patterns of interaction allow for positive growth and development in children as well as their caregivers. Ainsworth, Blehar, Waters, and Wall (1978) developed the "Strange Situation" technique, which is regarded as the classic assessment strategy to explore the attachment system in infants and toddlers. A child is exposed to a novel situation (new room) in the company of his or her caregiver. Then the caregiver leaves and is reintroduced into the situation twice. A stranger first enters the room in the presence of the caregiver and tries to engage the child in play. Then the caregiver leaves the child alone with the stranger. Then the caregiver returns for the first reunion and the stranger leaves unobtrusively. The caregiver then leaves and the child is alone. Then the stranger returns and tries to settle the child. The caregiver returns for the second time and the stranger leaves unobtrusively. During this time, the child's responses are coded by trained observers.

Table 17.1 shows the categorization of the quality of the child's attachment in the Strange Situation (Ainsworth, 1979).

Table 17.1   Qualities of Attachment in the Strange Situation

Secure Attachment	Balance between exploration of the environment and contact with the caregiver;
	As the situation unfolds, the child seeks more proximity to and contact with the caregiver;
	He or she explores the environment only to return for comfort as necessary.
Insecure Attachment	Increasing tension between child and parent.
Insecure-Avoidant	Child avoids the caregiver when he or she returns.
Insecure-Resistant/Ambivalent	Child passively or actively demonstrates hostility toward the caregiver while simultaneously wanting to be held or comforted.

SOURCE: Based on "Infant-mother attachment," by M. D. S. Ainsworth, 1979, *American Psychologist, 34,* 932–937.

As measured by the Strange Situation, quality of attachment is predictive of a child's behavior many years later. Bretherton and Walters (1985) found that among preschoolers, insecurely attached children had difficulty in relating to adults and their caregivers and they were less able to cope with their parents' absence. Belsky and Nezworski (1988) found that long-term consequences of insecure attachment include relationship problems, emotional disorders, and conduct problems.

Conversely, infants and toddlers with secure attachment were more likely to manifest healthy personalities through late childhood and into adolescence (Bowlby, 1988; Shaver, Hazan, & Bradshaw, 1988). These findings may be understood as the result of children being able to form an internal model of themselves and others. Children with secure attachment develop positive perceptions of themselves as competent, appealing, and loveable, and internal constructs for caregivers as accessible, responsive, and consistent. These models remain relatively stable during development because they are self-reinforcing (i.e., when the child responds with affection to the caregiver, he or she receives more consistent attention and love from caregivers).

> If people carry forward a secure mindful state, they see the world as safe and others as reliable. Unfortunately, negative or insecure schema also may be perpetuated. For example, people who see the world as unpredictable and other people as unreliable have difficulty overcoming their desires to keep others at a distance. (Snyder & Lopez, 2007, p. 303)

Of course, having achieved a state of secure attachment as an infant or toddler does not guarantee healthy adjustment later in life. However, of all the predictors of overall adjustment, the quality of social functioning is among the strongest. "Being securely attached to a caregiver in the first year of life provides a solid foundation for affect regulation and exploration as well as the expectation of future responsiveness from and the tendency to turn to and rely on others during times of need" (Peterson & Seligman, 2004, p. 314).

Attachment theory has been extended across the life span in an attempt to understand how adolescents relate to their peers and how adults relate to each other and to the children for whom they are caregivers. Hazan and Shaver (1987) found that Ainsworth's (1979) three categories of attachment— secure, avoidant, and anxious—accurately described adult attachments to a significant other. Secure adult attachment involves comfort and emotional closeness and a general lack of anxiety about being abandoned. The most important benefit of having secure adult attachment is that it provides avenues to healthy development and even enhanced survival. By cultivating support from significant others, children and adults become more adept at managing threats. Furthermore, by being open to exploring individual growth experiences without fear of rejection or abandonment, we can pursue self-actualization, or optimal human functioning. Kobak and Hazan (1991) found that secure attachment in adolescence and adulthood is related to more supportiveness and less rejection toward partners in tasks that require joint problem solving. Brennan and Shaver (1995) showed secure attachment to be related to safer sex practices.

> In sum, secure adolescents and adults cope more effectively with the stresses of life and are more skilled at forming social ties that are enduring, satisfying and characterized by trust and intimacy. Both of these skills predict better psychological adjustment and physical health. (Peterson & Seligman, 2004, p. 315)

Healthy Love

Four constructs, denoted by Greek terms, are highlighted by Singer (1984a, 1984b, 1987) in what many refer to as the definitive history of love: (1) eros—search for the beautiful; (2) philia—affection in friendship; (3) nomos—submission and obedience to the divine; and (4) agape—bestowal of love by the divine. Hendrick and Hendrick (1992) asserted that although it has only been in the last 300 years that people have been able to develop a sense of self, capable of loving and caring for a romantic partner, "Life without love would be for many people like a black-and-white movie—full of events and activities but without the color that gives vibrancy and provides a sense of celebration" (p. 117).

Aron and Aron's "self-expansion theory of love" (A. Aron & Aron, 1986; E. N. Aron & Aron, 1996), which was influenced by Eastern conceptualizations, posits that humans have a basic drive to expand the self, which strives to include everyone and everything. The emotions, thoughts, and actions of love energize self-development. According to this model, satisfying relationships are the natural by-products of self-expansion. Being in a love relationship brings on positive feeling states, which in turn reinforce or strengthen the commitment to the relationship.

Triangular Theory of Love

Sternberg's (1986) prominent "triangular theory of love" explains various dimensions of the love experience. He posits that love is a mix of three primary factors: (1) passion, or physical attractiveness and romantic drives; (2) intimacy, or feelings of closeness or connectedness; and (3) commitment, involving the decision to initiate and sustain a relationship. Various combinations of these components result in eight forms of love. For example, when intimacy and passion are combined, they form the basis of romantic love. The combination of intimacy and commitment result in companionate love. According to Sternberg, consummate love, the most durable (long-lasting) form, is manifested when all three components are present in high levels and in balance across both partners. Silberman (1995), in a study of 104 couples who were married an average of 13 years, found that marital satisfaction was highest for couples who were high on intimacy, followed by passion.

Intimacy and Sexuality

Intimacy helps to satisfy our needs to feel connected, to give and receive affection, and to develop self-esteem. Intimate relationships provide our support system when life gets difficult. Intimacy can best be described as a caring and trusting relationship in which thoughts, needs, and feelings can be openly expressed and unconditionally accepted. Therefore, freedom in communication is an essential aspect of an intimate relationship. Developing true intimacy requires taking risks. It means exposing some of our most guarded emotions and vulnerable areas to another person. It is through this kind of risk taking that genuine trust can develop. If partners are unaccustomed to heartfelt emotional communication, the thought of revealing one's feelings can seem quite threatening. Many relationships must learn to allow intimacy to develop.

When emotional intimacy fails to develop or is purposely avoided, sex often becomes a goal-oriented performance. That is, sex is perceived as a single, instantly gratifying act that blocks emotional awareness to the point of diminished interest in sex or one's partner. Sexual responsiveness declines, and any sense of intimacy may be lost (Masters & Johnson, 1974).

Negotiating differences in a sexual relationship requires commitment and practice. Conflict doesn't have to be viewed as a negative situation; it can instead be considered a stimulus for growth, provided both partners are working toward resolution. In *The Pleasure Bond*, Masters and Johnson (1974) explain that couples can achieve resolution of conflict using two principles: neutrality and mutuality.

Neutrality means that each partner respects the good intentions of the other and trusts that those intentions are genuine and sincere. Each partner takes personal responsibility for his or her actions and sexual responses. If a couple is to enjoy a positive physical relationship, each must strive to be responsive to the other, not responsible for the other.

The principle of mutuality defines the sexual interaction between two persons. Whether by speech or by actions, all sexual exchanges should occur in the spirit of working toward a mutual cause. The common goal of partners in a healthy sexual relationship is to discover and accept what pleases each other; to be sensitive to individual needs and differences; and to be committed to working together toward mutual satisfaction, knowing that their sexual preferences will not always match perfectly.

The key is a commitment to full communication of our honest feelings in order to remain attuned to our partner's needs as well as our own. We have a responsibility to accept each other as unique individuals and to honor each other's wants or desires in a way that enables us to satisfy our sexual needs. This is the mutually cooperative effort that will sustain a healthy and successful sexual relationship.

Some fundamentally important aspects are involved in developing and maintaining a healthy sexual relationship. First, honesty and direct communication form the cornerstone to building trust and intimacy. When problems arise, it is important to find resolution rather than solution. That is, both partners must be committed to openly expressing their feelings in a caring way and to accepting those ideas with concern and respect for individual likes and differences. Freedom of expression and effective communication are essential elements of an intimate relationship and are the key to conflict resolution (Peterson & Seligman, 2004). We are not automatic interpreters of body language or semi-audible verbal cues. It takes effort and assertiveness for partners to discover what is best for each other. Both partners are responsible for expressing thoughts and feelings as clearly as possible. If clear communication is lacking, neither partner will be able to respond effectively and satisfaction will slip into frustration.

Second, partners should strive to not bring "old garbage" into a new relationship. If, for instance, one person has been betrayed in a previous relationship, it is crucial to future relationships to work on feelings of hurt and trust so that this sort of unfinished business is not brought into the current relationship. Expecting that a previously negative experience is going to repeat itself is harmful to the relationship. When a partner brings remnants of the past, it invalidates the other individual's uniqueness. It puts a new person in an old scenario, which is destructive.

Third, it is important to the success of the relationship that both parties remain individuals with their own interests. Maintaining independence within a relationship gives us the capacity to set goals, pursue new interests, and function well as an individual and partner. The self-actualization and personal satisfaction that are enjoyed enhance the quality of the relationship and make each partner more interesting to the other. Pursuing outside interests not only encourages self-awareness, but also promotes personal autonomy, preventing partners from becoming overly dependent on each other. When autonomy fails to develop (insecure attachment) before a serious relationship is formed, dependencies are simply transferred from parents to partners (Masters & Johnson, 1974).

Last, sexual commitment involves sexual responsibility. That is, each of us takes responsibility for clearly expressing our sexual wants and needs and for remaining attuned to our partner's wants and needs. The responsibility, however, does not end with the mutual satisfaction of the sexual encounter; rather, it includes the obligation of full commitment of both partners to the responsibility of pregnancy and birth control as well as protecting against sexually transmitted diseases. Every potential outcome of sexual interaction is the mutual responsibility of both partners.

Intimacy Versus Individuality

Whether sexual or platonic, healthy intimacy is predicated upon reconciliation of two fundamental human needs: belonging and individuality. Needs for intimacy and closeness and needs for individuality and separateness are often in conflict. A healthy balance of closeness and separateness is key to developing mature and healthy relationships, predicated on a foundation of secure attachment. Figure 17.1 depicts healthy and unhealthy balances between closeness and individuality (Wanberg & Milkman, 2006, p. 223).

Table 17.2 provides a set of guidelines for keeping a healthy closeness with one's friends or significant other.

Circle One: Enmeshed
Relationship dominates
individuals, little separation or
individuality

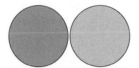

Circle Two: Detached
Individual needs dominate,
little giving to the relationship

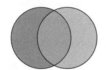

Circle Three: Balanced
Healthy balance between closeness and
separateness, between
individuality and relationship

Figure 17.1   **Relational balance between closeness and separateness.** Ideal relationships maintain a healthy balance between individuality and closeness.

SOURCE: Wanberg, K. W., & Milkman, H. B. (2006). *Criminal conduct and substance abuse treatment: Strategies for self-improvement and change. The participant's workbook* (2nd ed.). Thousand Oaks, CA: Sage Publications, p. 223.

Optimizing Relationships

Positive psychologists have focused on identifying elements of highly successful relationships and what skills partners can learn to optimize their interpersonal connections. Three interrelated constructs have emerged from this area of study: (1) minding relationships, (2) creating a culture of appreciation, and (3) capitalizing on positive events (Snyder & Lopez, 2007).

Table 17.2   Guidelines for Intimacy and Uniqueness

Be proactive and active.	Put energy into the relationship. Make things happen. Do your share of planning activities.
Let your partner be proactive and active.	Respect and support your partner's effort to energize the relationship.
Interact rather than react to what your partner does.	Use active listening and active sharing to interact. When you react, you make your partner responsible rather than taking responsibility.
Keep a balance between closeness and separateness.	Be okay even when your partner is not. When you are not okay, let your partner be okay. Each safeguards the self and the relationship.
Always work for a win–win when settling problems.	Keep the focus on the problem, not on the other conflicts. Restate the other person's side to make sure you understand it. Talk about yourself, not the other person. Use "I" messages, not "you" messages. After a conflict is resolved, be sure that each of you is better off.
Help the other person to be successful and celebrate that success.	Show enthusiasm, appreciation, and respect for the other's achievements.
Combine strengths for the good of each other.	Be proud of and profit from the other person's strengths. What attracted you to each other was the strength of your differences.
Don't let things build up between you.	Tell your partner what bothers you. Don't expect your partner to read your mind, to know what you want or feel or think.
Keep your relationship fresh and romantic.	Take trips, go to different places, have fun. Keep up the romance. See physical and sexual intimacy as more than having sex. Take part in healthy play—to move freely in space together.
Give and receive compliments and praise.	Show that you appreciate the other person. Make the positives outweigh the negatives. All parts of the relationship improve when there are positive expressions. Sexual intimacy occurs when there are positive feelings between people.

SOURCE: Wanberg, K. W., & Milkman, H. B. (2006). *Criminal conduct and substance abuse treatment: Strategies for self-improvement and change. The participant's workbook* (2nd ed.). Thousand Oaks, CA: Sage Publications, p. 222.

Minding Relationships

Harvey et al. (2001) developed a five-component model of what they refer to as *minding relationships*. Minding is the "reciprocal knowing process involving the nonstop interrelated thoughts, feelings and behaviors of people in a relationship" (p. 424). Minding is a conscious knowing process that involves a moment-to-moment awareness of the workings of our conscious mind. Couples seeking to optimize their relationship are encouraged to develop skills according to the following guidelines:

- Through an in-depth knowing process, both partners are united by a common purpose of knowing the other and being known by the other.
- Both members of the partnership are invested in using the information gained through "knowing" to enhance their relationship.
- There is mutual acceptance concerning what is learned and respect for the person they learn about.
- Both partners agree to continue this process (minding relationships) indefinitely until a synchrony of thought, feeling, and behavior arises.
- In time, both partners develop a deep sense of being unique and appreciated in the relationship.

Creating a Culture of Appreciation

Using what was learned from observing couples, Gottman, with the assistance of a group of mathematicians (Gottman, Murray, Swanson, Tyson, & Swanson, 2003), developed the "magic ratio" for successful marriages—five positive interactions to one negative (5:1) is formulaic for a flourishing relationship. As the ratio approaches 1:1, divorce is likely. Adhering to a positive ratio does not mean avoiding all arguments. Rather, by infusing warmth, humor, respect, and good listening skills into difficult conversations, couples are able to thrive. A lack of positive interactions during emotionally charged situations can lead to contempt and the ultimate breakdown of the relationship.

Crystallizing decades of research on his "sound marital house" theory, Gottman and his colleagues (Gottman, Driver, & Tabares, 2002) developed a marital counseling strategy designed to move partners from conflict to comfortable interactions. Therapeutic goals include enhancing *communication and social skills* and *mindfulness* of the downsides of negative communication messages (i.e., criticism, contempt, defensiveness, and stonewalling). By creating a culture of appreciation, regardless of marital status or sexual involvement, partners experience more rewarding and fulfilling relationships. Expressing gratitude for the small behaviors that often go unnoticed is the primary vehicle for infusing a relationship with positive energy. Saying thanks to a spouse for tidying up the house, making a fellow student aware that you value his or her comments in class, thanking a friend for taking the time to listen—all of these contribute to the sense of mutual appreciation that then becomes normative for the relationship.

Capitalizing on Positive Events

Gable, Reis, Impett, and Asher (2004) found that the process of *capitalization* (i.e., telling partners about the good things in your life) reaps many benefits. When a partner responds enthusiastically to your good fortune, you experience personal gain by reliving the experience. *Active/constructive* responses are most beneficial for capitalizing (i.e., amplifying the pleasure) on a good event or situation. Those in flourishing relationships were apt to characterize their partner's response to hearing good news in the following ways:

- My friend/relative/partner reacts enthusiastically.
- My friend/relative/partner appears to be even more happy than I am about the event.
- My friend/relative/partner typically asks many questions and shows genuine interest in the positive event.

The strategy for achieving capitalization on positive events simply involves making a point of telling trusted friends about the daily events that bolster your sprit. If there are people in your life who tend to undermine your communication of happiness (e.g., "That promotion at work will probably mean you'll have to bust your butt with long hours . . ."), then they probably shouldn't remain privy to news of your good fortune. The skill of offering positive responses (mirroring happiness and asking meaningful questions) about the good fortune of others is relatively easy to attain and well worth pursuing. It will not only enhance the quality of the relationship for your partner; through your example, it will also most likely encourage reciprocal responses to your disclosures as well.

Chapter Summary

This chapter deals with the concept of intimacy from the perspective of natural highs. Caring and close relationships are viewed as instrumental in orchestrating thoughts, feelings, and behaviors toward happiness and fulfillment for the individual, for his or her partner, and for society at large. Three forms of love are articulated: love for our caregivers, love for those who depend on us, and passionate desire.

Maslow (1954/1970) posited that human motives are hierarchically arranged. Near the top of the hierarchy is the need for *self-actualization*. The self-actualized individual is characterized by spontaneity, autonomy, sense of humor, and deep interpersonal relationships. Peterson and Seligman's core virtue of "humanity" is helpful in conceptualizing ideal human connections. Humanity is defined as "interpersonal strengths that involve tending and befriending others." Love is seen as the valuing of close relationships with others, especially those where sharing and caring are reciprocal, and being close to people.

Studies of human attachment show how people stay "on track" with their needs for love and belonging. Attachment is a process that may begin in utero and continue throughout one's life. It is the emotional link between an infant and a caregiver and it physically bonds people together over time. Bowlby identified certain styles of caregiving that resulted in secure or insecure patterns of attachment. Maladaptive parental behaviors include inconsistent attempts to meet the child's needs. Adaptive parenting is focused on responsiveness to the child's behavioral cues. Inconsistency in responding is associated with anxiety and frustration later in life, whereas consistency is associated with later development of contentment and trust.

Attachment theory has been extended to explore how adolescents relate to their peers and how adults relate to each other and to the children for whom they are caregivers. Kobak and Hazan found that secure attachment in adolescence and adulthood is related to more supportiveness and less rejection toward partners in tasks that require joint problem solving. Peterson and Seligman discovered that secure adolescents and adults handle life stresses better and are more able to develop lasting social ties that are characterized by trust and intimacy. These particular skills were found to be the best predictors of good psychological adjustment and physical health.

Sternberg's triangular theory of love explains love as a mix of three primary factors: (1) passion, (2) intimacy, and (3) commitment. Consummate love, the most durable type, occurs when all three of the above components are highly present and are balanced across both partners.

Regarding the relationship between intimacy and sexuality, when emotional intimacy fails to develop or is purposely avoided, sex often becomes merely goal-oriented. Masters and Johnson state that couples can achieve intimacy and conflict resolution by using the principles of neutrality and mutuality. Neutrality means that each partner respects the good intentions of the other and trusts that those intentions are genuine and sincere. The principle of mutuality defines the sexual interaction between two persons. All words and actions should occur in the spirit of working toward mutual well-being.

Whether sexual or platonic, healthy intimacy is based on reconciliation of two fundamental human needs: belonging and individuality. Needs for intimacy and closeness and needs for individuality and separateness are often in conflict. A healthy balance of closeness and separateness in relationships is central to forming mature and healthy relationships, predicated on a foundation of secure attachment.

Finally, positive psychologists have focused on identifying elements of highly successful relationships and what skills can be taught to partners to optimize their interpersonal connections. Three interrelated constructs have emerged: (1) minding relationships, (2) creating a culture of appreciation, and (3) capitalizing on positive events. Those who learn and practice these relationship skills have been shown to experience increased intimacy and overall satisfaction from their most cherished relationships.

18

Relaxation, Mindfulness, and Meditation

Now, there are about 20,000 moments of 3 seconds in a 16-hour day, so this is what life consists of; it consists of a sequence of moments. Each of these moments is actually very rich in experience, so if you could stop somebody and ask, "What is happening to you right now?" a great deal is happening to us at any one of these moments. There is a goal, there is a mental content, there is a physical state, there is a mood, there might be some emotional arousal. Many things are happening. And then you might ask, "What happens to these moments?"

—Daniel Kahneman, Nobel Laureate

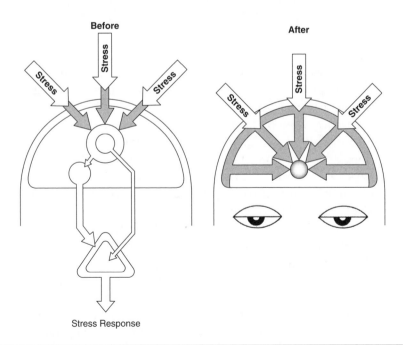

Figure 18.1 **Mindfulness and stress management.** The premise of this chapter is that through learning skills to develop a nonjudgmental attention to stimuli in the internal and external environments, the human stress response is diminished, resulting in improved mental and physical health and a more positive state of mind.

Introduction: Meditation Comes of Age _____

By learning techniques for being "in the present," we gain the invaluable opportunity to live life more fully and with increased novelty; diminished stress; greater empathy; fewer value judgments; and a deeper sense of beauty, contentment, and meaning. Today there is an abundance of scientific research on how meditative, self-calming skills can improve physical and mental health (e.g., Oman, Hedberg, & Thoresen, 2006; G. A. Parks & Marlatt, 2006; Perez-De-Albeniz & Holmes, 2000; Rausch, Gramling, & Auerbach, 2006; Shigaki, Glass, & Schopp, 2006). In addition, meditation has become a common practice throughout Western culture.

Our chapter begins with Herbert Benson's (1975, 1984, 1989, 2000) pioneering work on bringing meditative practice, formerly regarded by Western health practitioners as "new age" or religiously based, into the domain of respected medical, psychiatric, and psychological interventions.

Increasing Personal Calm

After completing medical training in cardiology, Benson, now director emeritus of the Benson-Henry Institute for Mind Body Medicine, became interested in how the mind affects the body, and particularly how high blood pressure might be influenced by emotional states. Benson was trying to gather scientific evidence for what had long been assumed in medical circles: that there is a positive correlation between stress and cardiovascular disease, and, further, that relaxation training could diminish the harmful effects of environmental threat. Colloquial expressions supporting his notion were commonplace: "Keep your cool—your blood pressure will go up"; "Don't get excited—you'll develop hypertension." In the late 1960s, Benson and his colleagues (Benson, 1975; Benson, Greenwood, & Klemchuk, 1975) were able to show that certain environmental influences could, in fact, raise or lower blood pressure in a group of laboratory monkeys. Further, the monkeys could be trained to increase or decrease their blood pressure on cue. One day, a group of young people came in to see Benson with a soft-spoken challenge: "Why are you fooling around with monkeys? Why don't you study us? We practice Transcendental Meditation."

Benson, acting in his role as Harvard scientist, tried to dissuade the group. But they persisted. Finally, he decided that little would be lost by seeing whether or not there might be physiological changes attendant to the practice of Transcendental Meditation (TM). He and his colleagues brought healthy volunteers to the laboratory and had them sit for an entire hour, getting used to the instruments that would measure oxygen consumption (an index of the body's total metabolism) and carbon dioxide elimination (the amount of waste product that parallels oxygen usage). Measurements were taken in three

20-minute intervals corresponding to (1) premeditation; (2) meditation—during which the subjects changed neither their posture nor their activity, only what they were thinking about; and (3) post meditation—wherein subjects were instructed to go back to their regular mode of thinking (Benson, 1975, 2000).

Benson (1975, 2000) found a 16% to 17% decrease in oxygen consumption, with a parallel decrease in the amount of carbon dioxide elimination. This meant that by simply changing their thoughts, meditators could induce a significant change in their body's overall metabolism (i.e., they self-induced a hypometabolic state). The fact that the ratio of oxygen to carbon dioxide remained constant between the premeditation and meditation conditions showed that the meditators were nether breathing rapidly nor holding their breath to bring about the observed physiological changes. There was a true decrease in the overall amount of oxygen being used by the body. Correspondingly, during the meditation interval, there was a decrease of about 2 or 3 breaths per minute in rate of breathing (dropping from 13 or 14 breaths per minute to about 11 breaths). Subsequently, while studying advanced meditators in India, Benson and his colleagues (1982) were able to document respiratory rates as low as zero to one breath per minute for 3 to 4 minutes on end; the advanced meditators could so quiet their overall metabolism that they could, in effect, stop breathing. Further, there was no change in the arterial concentration of oxygen. The cells were getting enough oxygen; they were simply using less. There was also a precipitous fall in arterial blood lactate, high levels of which are associated with stress, anxiety, or disquietude and low levels with peace and tranquility (Benson, 1975, 2000; Benson, Steinert, Greenwood, Klemchuk, & Peterson, 1975).

To his amazement, Benson (2000; Benson et al., 1982) documented some of the lowest levels of human metabolic activity ever recorded. At the time, there were only two physiological states known to cause these kinds of changes: sleep and hibernation.

A hibernating animal shows a decrease in rectal temperature of 2 to 3 degrees, whereas a sleeping animal shows a change of only 0.2 to 0.3 degrees. According to Benson (1989), after sneaking into the den of some Alaskan grizzly bears and finding the animals sleeping while sitting up, two intrepid physiologists placed several quarts of maraschino cherries in front of one bear, which naturally, because of its love of sweet fruit, leaned forward. The investigators, taking advantage of the postural tilt, proceeded to make their measurements. The bear awoke, was understandably irate, and chased the investigators, who miraculously escaped unharmed, data in hand (so to speak). In fact, bears do not hibernate—they sleep.

Under much less hazardous conditions, Benson and his colleagues were able to show that meditation was not a hibernatory state. But the data could not be explained as a sleep state, either (Benson, Steinert, et al., 1975). The observed increase in alpha and theta wave frequencies of meditating subjects was distinctly different from frequency rates measured during ordinary sleep. Benson suspected that the changes brought about through TM were the opposite of what had been described nearly three-quarters of a century earlier by Cannon (1915, 1929) as the *fight-or-flight* response. Cannon showed that stimulation of a region of the hypothalamus leads to a series of physiological changes resulting in a 300% to 400% increase in blood flowing to the muscles. But it made no sense to Benson to say that TM was the *only* way to bring about this reversed, anti-stress response. So he and his colleagues (Benson, 1975, 2000) dissected the TM instructions into two basic components: (1) the repetition of a word, sound, prayer, or muscular activity; and (2) the passive disregard of everyday thoughts when they come to mind.

By examining the religious and secular literatures of the world, Benson found that the same steps existed in virtually every culture (Benson, 1975, 1987). The earliest examples come from the Hindu scriptures—the Upanishads—dating back to the 7th and 8th centuries BC. It was written that to achieve a union with God, one should sit quietly, pay attention to one's breathing, and on each out-breath, repeat a word or phrase from the scriptures, the Vedas, or the Bhagavad Gita. When other thoughts came to mind, one should passively disregard them and come back to the repetition. In a similar manner today, Hindu worshippers can be heard chanting the words "Ohm, shanti, shanty," (God, peace, peace) while sitting in a meditative position.

The next examples come from Judaism, dating back to the Second Temple, which was roughly from the 2nd century BC to the 1st century AD. In a particular school of thought, people were told to squat in a fetal-like posture, pay attention to their breathing, and on each out-breath, repeat over and over again the name of God or a formula containing such a divine name. When other thoughts came to mind, they were to passively disregard them and come back to the repetition.

Regarding early, middle, and late Christianity, one can trace the evolution of meditative techniques through prayers back to the time of Christ. These were practiced by the Desert Fathers—4th-century Christian monks who lived as hermits in the most remote part of the Egyptian desert—and ultimately codified in the 14th century on Mount Athos in Greece. To this day, there are hallowed Greek Byzantine monasteries espousing that people twice daily kneel quietly by themselves, pay attention to their breathing, and on each out-breath, say quietly to themselves, "Lord Jesus, have mercy" or "Lord Jesus, have mercy on us sinners." When other thoughts come to mind, the meditator is to passively disregard them and come back to the repetition.

The method of this whole process is called Hesychasm, traced back to Hesychius of Jerusalem, a 5th-century teacher of the uses of the Jesus prayer. According to Goleman (1988), in his classic work, *The Meditative Mind,* Hesychius describes prayer as "a spiritual art that releases one completely from passionate thoughts, words and evil deeds, and gives a 'sure knowledge of God the Incomprehensible'" (p. 55). Hesychius describes thoughts as "enemies who are bodiless and invisible, malicious and clever at harming us, skillful, nimble and practiced in warfare" (p. 55), who enter through the five senses. The idea is that a mind preoccupied with the senses or thought is distant from Jesus; one can be with him only by overcoming the lure of sensations and by attaining a silent mind. Followers are instructed to find a teacher who carries the spirit within him or her and to devote themselves to the master, obeying all commands.

Virtually the same instructions were given in 14th-century Judaism, where the mystical Kabbalistic tradition was evolving. Rabbi Abraham Abulafia, in one of the most detailed elaborations of Kabbalistic medita-tion, described a safe approach to the inner paradise (Goleman, 1988):

> According to Kabbalist lore, the entry into the inner Paradise by one who has not properly prepared a foundation through self-purification can be dangerous. The Talmud tells the story of four rabbis who entered Paradise: one went mad, one died, and another lost faith; only one, Rabbi Akiba, came back in peace. (p. 51)

Abulafia's method calls for paying attention to one's breathing and, on each out-breath, repeating the components that make up God's name, Adonis. When thoughts come to mind, they should be passively disregarded, returning to the aforementioned repetition. A similar pathway is described in Sufism, where the way to purity is the constant remembrance of God. The main meditation among Sufis is Zikr, which means "remembrance"— La ilaha illa' llah: "There is no god but God." According to the prophet Muhammad, "There is a polish for everything that taketh away rust; and the polish of the Heart is the invocation of Allah" (Goleman, 1988, p. 59). Remarkably parallel traditions are found in Zen Buddhism, Shintoism, Taoism, and Confucianism—only the words are different. In the so-called primitive or shamanistic religions, people achieve similar states by chanting in time to the stamping of feet or the beating of drums—an echo of their heartbeats.

Benson (1987, 2000) has shown that the *relaxation response* can be viewed as an extraordinary tool for behavior change that can be used in any desired fashion. The method of elicitation, however, is critical. Practitioners select a personally meaningful word, sound, prayer, phrase, or muscular activity for repetition. When given a choice, most people will prefer prayer (e.g., the 23rd Psalm; Lord's Prayer; Hail Mary; or repetition of the Hebrew word for peace, "shalom"). Regular practitioners often report they have made contact with their Higher Power through this process. In effect, the relaxation response is a tailor-made method of complementing each indi-vidual's belief system.

As a matter of fact, many patients say to me, "Thank you, doctor, for telling me to pray again. It's something that I've always wanted to do, but felt funny about. But now that you as a doctor tell me about it, it's something that I'll do." You can then utilize that mind-opening effect brought about by the elicitation of the *Relaxation Response* to change behavior. If you wish the person to be more positive, simply have that individual read affirmations afterwards. It can be anything from Norman Vincent Peale to Robert Schuller, to statements of truth. If the person desires better health, have them think healthy thoughts about themselves. And this isn't just a thought, but these thoughts translate, insofar as mind can affect body, into physiologic change. This is what has been proposed, for example, by the Symingtons as a way of treating cancer. They first elicit the *Relaxation Response* through meditation, and then they visualize white cells in Pac-man fashion sort of chewing up cancer cells. Does that work? We don't know, but it is the same basic mind/body technology that they are utilizing. (Benson, 1989)

Benson (1987, 2000) recommends a series of steps for increasing calm and optimizing life experiences. The steps can be used to promote the development of an array of artistic and recreational skills consistent with one's sense of purpose and meaning. Readers are encouraged to explore how the relaxation response can serve as a physiological bridge to natural highs. By participating in these steps readers may not only develop a sense of inner peace, but also experience enhanced feelings of pleasure, because they are more attuned to dormant proclivities, interests, and abilities that may have been suppressed by inattention, anxiety, or stress. Table 18.1 presents the generic technique taught at the Benson-Henry Institute for eliciting the relaxation response.

Regular elicitation of the relaxation response has been scientifically proven to be an effective treatment for a wide range of stress-related disorders. In fact, to the extent that any disease is caused or made worse by stress, the relaxation response can help.

Mindfulness

Benson's work on the relaxation response paved the way for exploration of a range of techniques designed to facilitate the attainment of positive emotional and behavioral experiences. The general practice of learning how to live positively in the moment, with a flexible awareness of what is and what can be, may be subsumed under the construct of *mindfulness*. Langer (2002) defines this construct in general terms:

It is a flexible state of mind, openness to novelty, a process of actively drawing novel distinctions. When we are mindful we become sensitive

Table 18.1   Steps to Your Maximum Mind

The following is the generic technique taught at the Benson-Henry Institute:

1. Pick a focus word, short phrase, or prayer that is firmly rooted in your belief system, such as "one," "peace," "The Lord is my shepherd," "Hail Mary, full of grace," or "shalom."

2. Sit quietly in a comfortable position.

3. Close your eyes.

4. Relax your muscles, progressing from your feet to your calves, thighs, abdomen, shoulders, head, and neck.

5. Breathe slowly and naturally, and as you do, say your focus word, sound, phrase, or prayer silently to yourself as you exhale.

6. Assume a passive attitude. Don't worry about how well you're doing. When other thoughts come to mind, simply say to yourself, "Oh well," and gently return to your repetition.

7. Continue for 10 to 20 minutes.

8. Do not stand immediately. Continue sitting quietly for a minute or so, allowing other thoughts to return. Then open your eyes and sit for another minute before rising.

9. Practice the technique once or twice daily. Good times to do so are before breakfast and before dinner.

SOURCE: Reprinted with permission of the Benson-Henry Institute for Mind Body Medicine (2006), http://www .mbmi.org/basics/whatis_rresponse_elicitation.asp (retrieved February 7, 2009).

to context and perspective; we are situated in the present. When we are mindless, we are trapped in rigid mindsets, oblivious to context or perspective. When we are mindless, our behavior is rule and routine governed. In contrast, when mindful, our behavior may be guided rather than governed by rules and routines. Mindfulness is not vigilance or attention when what is meant by those concepts is a stable focus on an object or an idea. When mindful, we are actively varying the stimulus field. (p. 214)

Snyder and Lopez (2007) offer what they refer to as a "nuts and bolts" definition of mindfulness, one that is used by the practicing community: "attending non-judgmentally to all stimuli in the internal and external environments" (p. 249). In moments of mindfulness, "positive psychological processes" are reported to enter consciousness (Snyder & Lopez, 2007). These include acceptance, patience, generosity, empathy, trust, gratitude, nonattachment, and gentleness (S. L. Shapiro, Schwartz, & Santerre, 2002).

From the definitions above, Benson's relaxation response and the cognitive-behavioral restructuring techniques detailed in Chapter 16 may be considered tools for the attainment of mindfulness. In addition, the principle strategy presented in Chapter 17 is referred to as "minding relationships" (i.e., being attuned to the ongoing stream of thoughts in a close or intimate relationship). In fact, a broad spectrum of meditative and relaxation techniques provides segues to a nonevaluative and present-centered state of consciousness.

We shall now consider *insight meditation* as another tool for the attainment of mindfulness. In *Insight Meditation: The Practice of Freedom*, J. Goldstein (1993) presents a commonsense rationale for the Buddhist approach to meditation and offers specific instructions for its incorporation into everyday life:

> The Buddha's teaching inspires the journey because he articulates so clearly where the path of practice [meditation] leads: to deeper levels of insight and freedom, to that purity and happiness of a mind-heart free from grasping, free from hatred, and free from ignorance. (p. 29)

When we consider the nature of our experience, it is clear that everything we do—whether related to work, family, relationships, or creativity—has some mental representation. Since much, if not all, human endeavor has its origins in our thoughts and feelings, then it would seem exceedingly worthwhile to understand the nature of our mind. The commitment to comprehend more about our own mental processes is at the core of Buddhist meditation.

One of the most obvious facts about the human psyche is that it is not static or fixed. Rather, our ideas, feelings, and fantasies are in a continuous state of evolution and flux. Also, our perceptions—the interpretations we assign to the objects and events in our midst—are colored by emotions. When we feel anger, our consciousness or awareness is tainted by hostility. When we feel love or compassion, there is increased likelihood of benevolence toward others and a positive explanation concerning events in our lives. Meditation aims to clarify the mental conditions that are associated with increased tightness, suffering, or pain, versus the qualities that lead to greater openness, ease, and well-being. But how should one choose from the array of meditative traditions and relaxation practices in the self-help marketplace (e.g., Benson's relaxation response vs. Goldstein's insight meditation)? An ancient Persian story helps to resolve this dilemma.

Ancient Parable: Finding Truth

The Mullah Nasrudin is a mythical Sufi teaching figure about whom there are hundreds of legends. Nasrudin is half crazy, half saint; half wise man, half fool. One day, a friend came to borrow a donkey and Nasrudin said, "I'm sorry, the donkey isn't here; I don't have it; I can't lend it to you." Just at that moment, when Nasrudin was speaking about not having the donkey, the donkey, which was outside the window, began to bray. The friend became increasingly angry and said, "How can you tell me you don't have the donkey? I hear it outside the window!" And Nasrudin, in turn, became very offended and said, "Well, who are you going to believe—me or the donkey?"

Buddha gave a very definitive answer to this question. "Don't believe anybody," he said. "Don't believe the books or the teachers and don't believe me." He advocated looking into our own mind and investigating the factors that seem conducive to greed, hatred, and delusion. These things are to be abandoned. Buddha taught that we should attend to and develop whatever actions of mind, body, and speech cultivate greater understanding and compassion.

Thus, according to J. Goldstein (1993), the practice of insight meditation is a matter of taking on personal responsibility for understanding the basis or purpose of our actions—for having insight. It has little or nothing to do with dogma, ritual, or religious conviction.

As a prerequisite for gaining insight—deeper understanding and a sense of purpose—one should cultivate "mindfulness," the skill of being able to attend to what is happening in each moment. Although the directive seems quite simple—to pay attention to what is happening in each instant (like now)—it's actually quite difficult to do. A cornerstone of Buddhist teaching is the delineation of succinct practice techniques to develop the quality of awareness. Practitioners are instructed to begin with the most tangible way of cultivating a strong, well-focused attention: "Be mindful of the body." What aspect of ourselves could be more accessible than the sensations that emanate from our own physical processes, particularly the act of breathing?

Concentration on breathing develops the skill to recognize when the mind is wandering or going off—that is, losing the quality of attentiveness. It also promotes a sense of relaxation. As described earlier in the discussion of Benson's relaxation response, Buddhist meditators also report increased calm and feelings of well-being. As a matter of fact, breathing awareness is also used as a means for stress reduction or relaxation, quite apart from any meditative practice. Yet whether the technique is introduced by a mental health counselor, medical adviser, or spiritual leader, the benefits of observing our breathing while detaching ourselves from everyday thoughts are quite similar.

Beginning meditators may, however, quickly lose interest in just attending to routine activities such as breathing. However, when we consider the consequences of not being able to breathe—someone holding our head under water, for example—breathing quickly becomes our number one priority. Practitioners are reminded that in a very literal way, every breath we take is vital to sustaining our life. Not all environmentalists may be Buddhists, but Buddha would have had no objections to their campaign for clean air.

Another aspect of mindfulness of the body is paying attention to every little thing we do: standing up, sitting down, making tea, opening the door, working at our job. A tremendous conservation of energy occurs when we develop the skill to bring our attention back to the simple movements we make throughout the day. How often do we become needlessly lost in thinking, fantasizing, or planning about some event that never takes place? As Mark Twain quipped, "I've had a lot of problems in my life, but most of them never happened." Much of our worrisome rumination is not useful—the mind, by habit, just seems to go on and on. By coming back to the simple movements of the body, we can resume concentration on the moment.

Here is a popular Zen story that illustrates this point:

It seems this one person had been practicing meditation for a very long time, and he had some great insight. He was sitting in meditation and this cosmic insight unfolded, and he thought he understood the truth of things. Very excited, he went running up to his teacher, who lived in another hut in the forest. It was raining out. Before he went in to visit his teacher, he left his shoes and umbrella outside. He went in and he bowed down to his teacher, all excited about his insight. And his Zen master simply asked him, "On which side of your shoes did you leave your umbrella?" He couldn't remember. And the Master sent him back for 10 more years of practice.

The first half of meditation practice is learning to be aware. Few of us have the opportunity to devote our lives to pure meditation. How can we Westerners daily incorporate meditation into our busy lives? We have to commit to applying the practice to our everyday activities—by noting on which side of our shoes we left our umbrella. One important benefit of increasing mindfulness of our bodies, particularly while sitting, is that we become keenly aware of the tension we carry. We usually remain unaware of this stress and therefore don't release it. By increasing the awareness of our breathing, we take greater notice of the body's condition. When we become aware of the tension, rather than fighting it, we begin to release it. We let go, and stress-related illness begins to reverse its course. There is an abundance of stories from meditation centers in Thailand and Burma about very severe organic diseases actually being cured through the practice of meditation.

Perception of one's mind—thoughts, emotions, feelings—is also increased. While the brain is constantly engaged in thinking—judging, remembering, planning, evaluating, processing sensory input—we spend very little time cognizant of our thoughts; that is, we leave our brain on "automatic pilot." Like a high-flying kite, our mind is often carried astray by random gusts of thought. How often in a day do we get distracted by a thought and get lost in a daydream? Many times these so-called stray thoughts are a learned pattern or reaction to past experiences and cause us to react reflexively, not purposefully. How often do we get carried away by thoughts about our mother, father, lover, or children that have absolutely no basis in reality? *The thought of your mother is not your mother.*

Meditation allows us to explore the nature of thought and how it drives us. By increasing awareness of our thoughts, we can more easily recognize the motivation for the thought, and we can choose to act—rather than react—accordingly. Similarly, we can become more attuned to our emotions. As with thought, it is possible to observe emotions as they arise. We become more accepting and experience them on a more cognitive plane. Because we are able to filter out the "white noise" of our emotions, we can bring about increased personal calm and balance behavior, thoughts, and feelings.

The second half of meditative practice is observing the nature of all these insights, emotions, thoughts, and breaths. The one constant that binds all of these elements together is change. Life is not static or fixed, and neither are we. The greater our understanding of the nature of change, the greater our ability to let go and adapt. One of Buddha's teachings is that we cause suffering in our lives when there's attachment in the mind, because all things change. Buddhists teach their children, before they even enter grade school, that all people at some time must get old, get sick, and die. A familiar metaphor for teaching the value of detachment describes a monkey trap widely used in Asia.

> A hollowed-out coconut with a small hole in the bottom is attached to a tree. A sweet is placed inside the coconut. A monkey comes along, slips its hand in, and grasps the sweet. The hole is big enough for the monkey to slip its hand in when the monkey's hand is open, but not large enough to allow the monkey to withdraw its hand when the hand is closed. Thus, the monkey is ensnared by its own greed and attachment. It is an extremely rare monkey that will open its hand, release the sweet, and thus extricate itself.

We humans place ourselves in the same predicament. We are trapped by our own attachments. We refuse to acknowledge that we are the cause of our suffering, and we place the blame on external causes. It takes a great deal of sensitivity and openness to accept our responsibility and learn how to release it. When we are successful, our bodies, minds, and lives become more harmonious and free.

> For twenty-five hundred years the practices and teachings of Buddhism have offered a systematic way to see clearly and live wisely. They have offered a way to discover liberation within our own bodies and minds, in the midst of this very world. (Kornfield, 2004, p. x)

As shown in Table 18.2, J. Goldstein (1993) provides the instructions for insight meditation.

Process Meditation

Another, perhaps more active and deliberate, approach to accessing critical aspects of the mind is Progoff's (1975, 1980) *Process Meditation*. His technique of "intensive journal writing" is designed for becoming actively involved in discovering the movement and meaning of your life. Distinctly different from a diary, Progoff's method provides a multilevel feedback system that integrates conscious and unconscious fantasies, gently unfolding the meaning and purpose of one's life. As Progoff (1975) puts it,

Table 18.2   Goldstein's Instructions for Insight Meditation

- Sit fairly still and stable. Frequent changes of position break the concentration. If you become very uncomfortable and painful, shift, but for the most part try to sit as still as possible. Arrange your hands in any comfortable position, either on your knees or in your lap.

- Let your eyes close gently and softly. Take a few deep breaths to connect yourself with the breathing. Begin to feel the rise and fall of the abdomen that happens with each breath. When you breathe in, there's a rising moving of the abdomen, an expansion. When you breathe out there's a natural falling or contraction. Focus your awareness on that movement, feeling the sensations of the rising movement, and the falling movement. Be aware of the movement—from the very beginning, to the middle, and end of the falling movement.

- Don't rush or force the breathing in any way. Let the rising and falling happen in its own time. See how subtle and careful your awareness and attention can be.

- Make a soft mental note of rising at the beginning of the rising movement, and a soft mental note of falling at the beginning of the falling movement. Just a soft whisper in the mind. The words "rising" . . . "falling . . . ."

- If sounds become distracting and call your attention away from the rising and falling, make a note of hearing, focusing your attention just on the vibration of the sound. Make the note "hearing," "hearing," without thinking of the cause of the sounds, just experiencing the actual phenomenon of hearing, and then return again to the rising and falling.

- Let the sounds simply arise and pass away, noting "hearing" when they are distracting and calling your attention, and returning in a very careful and subtle way to the rising and falling of the abdomen.

- If any sensations in the body become predominant—tightness, pressure, aching, vibration, tingling, itching—make a note of the particular sensation, observing it carefully. Observe what happens to it as you notice. Does it get stronger? Does it get weaker? Does it disappear?

- And again, return to the rising and falling. See how carefully you can feel each breath, making the soft note of "rising" and "falling," and if sounds distract you, calling your attention away, make a note of "hearing." And return to the rising and falling.

- If there are any strong sensations in the body that are more predominant than the breath, make a note of the sensation, feeling it, observing it, and noticing what happens as you note it. Does it get stronger? Does it get weaker? How does it change? And return to the rising and falling.

- Whenever you become aware of a thought in the mind, make a note of "thinking," trying to notice as close to the beginning as possible. Observe what happens to the thought as you note it. Does it continue? Does it disappear?

- Keep the mind alert and wakeful, noting in each moment the rise and fall of the breath, or hearing, or sensations in the body, or thinking—aware in each moment of the predominant object.

- See how carefully you can feel each breath: the entire movement of the rising, the entire movement of the falling.

- As soon as you are aware that the mind is wandering, make a note of "thinking," observe what happens to the thought as you note it, come back to the breathing.

- And if there is any strong mind state or emotion—of boredom, of interest, happiness, sadness, anger, fear, compassion—if any strong emotion should arise, that also should be noted. Feel it, be aware of it, and return again to the breath.

- Feel each rising and falling carefully and accurately, making the soft mental note.

- Make a note of any strong, predominant sensation in the body that may call your attention away from the breathing.

- If there are any images or pictures in the mind, make a note of "seeing"; observe what happens to the picture or image as you note it; then return to the rise and fall.

- Keep your attention on the breath, on any sounds which may become predominant, or any sensations, noting also images as they may come to mind, keeping the mind wakeful and alert in each moment, seeing all phenomena arising and passing away.

SOURCE: Adapted from Goldstein, J. (1993). *Insight meditation: The practice of freedom.* Boston: Shambhala Publications, p. 34.

Process Meditation enables us to work actively and systematically at this inner level, reaching toward an experience both of personal meaning and of a meaning in life that is more than personal. . . . The practice of Process Meditation makes it possible to work tangibly with the dimension of spiritual meaning in the specifics of our individual life history. (p. 9)

Readers are invited to adopt the guidelines, as shown in Table 18.3, for utilizing the amazing gift of fantasy to improve self-understanding and personal intimacy—in Progoff's (1975) words,

Our workbook becomes a place where a person's private intimations of meaning can be articulated, respected, and explored. More important even than the basic fact of acknowledging our spiritual feelings and treating them as realities, our method gives us a means of working with them in tangible ways so that their intimations of truth can be nurtured, can be considered, altered, or brought to further development. (p. 273)

According to Anaïs Nin (quoted in Kaiser, 2001), a diarist who logged more than 150,000 pages, "The lack of intimacy with one's self and consequently with others is what created the loneliest and most alienated people in the world." In recognition of intimacy as a basic human need, we have dedicated an entire section of this book (Section V) to the topic of "Craving for Intimacy."

Table 18.3   The Way of the Journal

- Where are you right now in your life? Form an image.
- Recapitulations and Remembering—Quick, significant scenes in our lives.
- Stepping Stones—Note important events or people captured in a word or two or an image.
- Intersections—Describe roads taken and not taken.
- Twilight Imagery—Turn your attention inward and wait in stillness, letting yourself observe the various forms of imagery that present themselves.
- Dialogue Dimension—Engage in imaginary conversations with some of the significant people already listed in the Stepping Stones section. Go through a short Stepping Stone exercise for the "other." After the exercise, reread what you have written and write down how you feel.

SOURCE: Adapted from "The way of the journal," by B. Kaiser, 1981, March, *Psychology Today*.

Does Meditation Work?

In 1974, the late Tibetan teacher Chögyam Trungpa predicted that "Buddhism will come to the West as a psychology." And indeed it has! Perez-De-Albeniz and Holmes (2000) found that meditation can do the following:

- Improve memory
- Provide acceptance and tolerance of affect
- Increase happiness, joy, and positive thinking

- Increase confidence and productivity
- Improve problem-solving skills
- Enhance the acceptance of, compassion for, and tolerance of self and others
- Improve relaxation, resilience, and the ability to control feelings

Shigaki et al. (2006) consider mindfulness as a form of cognitive therapy in that both techniques focus on directing the client's attention toward improvements in managing harm-generating thoughts and reducing autonomic responses. While traditional cognitive therapy teaches the replacement of maladaptive thoughts with more adaptive ones, mindfulness focuses on one's *approach to thinking,* that is, "emphasizing the awareness of thoughts, appreciation for the transient nature of thoughts, and developing tolerance for observing one's own thoughts and feelings" (Segal et al., 2002, quoted in Shigaki et al., 2006, p. 210). Shigaki et al. report on the likening of "mindfulness" to exposure and desensitization techniques. Through mindfulness, one is given the opportunity to observe thoughts, emotions, and the physical sensations as they occur and without catastrophic consequences. Meditation may allow for exposure and desensitization to "catastrophizing," which may improve adaptive coping styles with issues such as chronic pain and substance abuse.

Oman et al. (2006) evaluated an 8-week, 2-hr per week training for physicians, nurses, chaplains, and other health professionals using nonsectarian, spiritually based self-management tools based on passage meditation. Their Eight-Point Program (EPP) for stress management is outlined below:

- Passage meditation for 30 minutes each morning, which includes the silent repetition in one's mind of memorized inspirational passages (23rd Psalm, Prayer of St. Francis, or Discourse on Goodwill of the Buddha's *Sutta Nipata*)
- Repetition of a holy word or mantra
- Slowing down, setting priorities, and reducing stress and friction caused by rushing
- Focused attention to the matter at hand
- Training the senses to overcome conditioned habits and learning to enjoy what is beneficial
- Putting others first and gaining freedom from selfishness and separateness; finding joy in helping others
- Spiritual association with others who follow the same program for mutual inspiration and support
- Inspirational reading from scriptures of all religions to draw upon the writings by and about great spiritual figures

Beneficial treatment effects were observed on stress and mental health. When subjects adhered to the study's meditative practices, stress reductions remained large at 19 weeks. The authors concluded that this program reduces stress and may enhance mental health.

Not only has meditation been shown to improve one's sense of psychological well-being; it has proven effective in medical practice as well. Perez-De-Albeniz and Holmes (2000) claim that the physiological effects of meditation include the following:

- Increased cardiac output
- Slower heart rate
- Muscle relaxation
- Decreased renal and hepatic blood flow
- Increased cerebral flow
- Decreased respiratory frequency
- Significantly decreased sensitivity to ambient carbon dioxide
- Less oxygen consumption
- Increased skin galvanic resistance
- Decreased spontaneous electrodermal response
- EEG synchrony with increased intensity of slow alpha in central and frontal regions, and increased theta waves in frontal areas of the brain
- Enhancement of brain stem auditory evoked response, increased alpha and beta coherence
- A shift in hemispheral dominance with greater activation of the centers in the right hemisphere

Critical Study: Does Meditation Improve Mental and Physical Health?

In what appears to be a breakthrough validation of the capacity of meditation to improve mental and physical health, Davidson et al. (2003) explored underlying changes in biological processes that are associated with meditation. The authors performed a randomized, controlled study on the effects of meditation on brain and immune function with healthy employees. Brain electrical activity was studied before and immediately after an 8-week training program in mindfulness meditation, and then again 4 months later. "Twenty-five subjects were tested in the meditation group. A wait-list control group (N = 16) was tested at the same points in time as the meditators. At the end of the 8-week period, subjects in both groups were vaccinated with influenza vaccine" (p. 564).

Davidson et al. (2003) reported for the first time "significant increases in left-sided anterior activation, a pattern previously associated with positive affect [positive affect = happiness], in the meditators compared with the nonmeditators" (p. 564). The researchers also found that meditators, when compared with the control group, had significant increases in antibody titers (substance concentration) to influenza vaccine. Interestingly, the magnitude of increase in left-sided activation predicted the strength of the antibody challenge to the influenza vaccine. According to the study's authors, "these findings demonstrate that a short program in mindfulness meditation produces demonstrable effects on brain and immune function. . . . meditation may change brain and immune function in positive ways and underscore the need for additional research" (p. 264).

The research above illustrates the promise of mindfulness as an important component for prevention, intervention, and treatment of a multitude of health issues. Carey (2008), writing for the *New York Times,* captures some of the enthusiasm about this therapeutic technique from academia, health science, and clinical practice.

> At workshops and conferences across the country, students, counselors and psychologists in private practice throng to lectures on mindfulness. The National Institutes of Health is financing more than 50 studies testing mindfulness techniques, up from 3 in 2000, to help relieve stress, soothe addictive cravings, improve attention, lift despair and reduce hot flashes. . . . [Mindfulness] has become perhaps the most popular new psychotherapy technique of the past decade. (n.p.)

Meditation and Hedonic Dependencies

Marlatt (2002), an iconic figure in psychological research and treatment for substance abuse, finds meditation an invaluable tool for improving treatment outcomes. Marlatt explains how Buddhist philosophy provides a useful framework for addiction treatment. From the Buddhist perspective, "addiction represents 'a false refuge' from the pain and suffering of life" (p. 49). According to Marlatt, the Four Noble Truths of Buddha can be used to gain insight into the addict's experience and potential course of recovery.

First Noble Truth: "Suffering is ubiquitous" and is experienced in multiple ways including anxiety, pain, and misery in association with life changes or existence in general (Kumar, 2002). Engaging in drug use (or other forms of hedonic escape) constitutes a "false refuge," motivated by a desire or "craving" to avoid suffering. The pleasure addict is ignorant of the fact that, in the long run, continuation of addictive behavior prolongs and intensifies suffering rather than reducing pain.

Second Noble Truth: Suffering and pain, essential to all life experience, are caused by craving and attachment. Rather than viewing addiction as a physical disease, the affliction may be conceived as a "disease of the mind," characterized by an intense form of the attachment process, perpetuated by ignorance of the fact that addictive behavior is only a temporary or "false" refuge (Marlatt, 2002).

Third Noble Truth: Cessation of suffering is based on "the complete fading and extinction of this craving, its forsaking and abandonment, liberation from it, detachment from it" (Groves & Farmer, 1994, p. 186).

Fourth Noble Truth: This describes the Noble Eightfold Path leading toward enlightenment: right vision, conception, speech, conduct, livelihood, effort, mindfulness, and concentration (Kumar, 2002).

Meditation is viewed as

a pathway from the heavy burden of addiction to the freedom of enlightenment. Ignorance can be replaced by a combination of "right conception or understanding" as to the true nature of addiction and the development of new coping skills (right conduct, or "skillful means"). As such the practice of meditation and following the *Eightfold Path* offers a clearer and distinctive alternative to the 12-steps approach and the disease model of addiction. (Marlatt, 2002, p. 46)

G. A. Parks and Marlatt (2006) discuss the use of Vipassana meditation (VM), a widely practiced Buddhist form of mindful meditation, as an alternative for individuals who have not succeeded with traditional addiction treatment. They assert that VM allows for an environment that is tolerant of a variety of religious beliefs, has flexible treatment goals, and involves less stigma than traditional treatment programs.

VM courses teach "mindfulness through objective, detached self-observation without reaction" (G. A. Parks & Marlatt, 2006, p. 343). G. A. Parks and Marlatt studied the effectiveness of VM courses at the North Rehabilitation Facility (Seattle, Washington), a minimum-security jail with adult male and female inmates. Participants showed decreased alcohol-related problems and psychiatric problems and an increase in positive psychosocial outcomes. Three months after release, there was significantly less use of alcohol, marijuana, and crack cocaine as well as fewer alcohol-related negative consequences. In addition, the former inmates reported lower levels of psychiatric symptoms, more internal alcohol-related locus of control, and higher levels of optimism.

Obviously, there are many similarities between mindfulness and cognitive-behavioral treatment. In evidence-based practice, CBT is the most widely utilized treatment modality for the sometimes independent, but usually intersecting, problems of substance abuse, mental disorder, and criminal conduct. Teasdale et al. (2002) draw some interesting distinctions between traditional CBT and CBT combined with a mindfulness training approach. Unlike CBT, where there is great emphasis on changing the contents of thoughts, mindfulness-based cognitive therapy (MBCT) teaches individuals to be more aware of thoughts and feelings and to relate to them with a more detached, broader perspective, as "mental events" that can be observed and not necessarily associated with accurate reflections of reality. The CBT model for growth and change, as discussed in Chapter 16, integrated with the mindfulness perspective, as presented here, are the mental underpinnings of our natural highs approach.

A Word of Caution

Some researchers have addressed the phenomenon of meditation-related problems (Lukoff, Lu, & Turner, 1998; Perez-De-Albeniz & Holmes, 2000). Several negative side effects have been reported: uncomfortable kinesthetic sensations, mild dissociation, and psychosis-like symptoms (Craven, 1989). D. H. Shapiro's (1992) study of 27 long-term meditators reported such adverse effects as depression, relaxation-induced anxiety and panic, paradoxical increases in tension, impaired reality testing, confusion, disorientation, and feeling "spaced out." Kutz, Borysenko, and Benson (1985) note the possibility that meditation might trigger strong emotional reactions. The following quotation by Perez-De-Albeniz and Holmes (2000) highlights the need for caution and guidance in managing some of the mental contents that may arise in relation to the meditative experience.

> Sobbing and hidden memories and themes from the past, such as incest, rejection, and abandonment appeared in intense, vivid forms. . . . [However,] it is not uncommon to encounter a meditator who claims to have found "the answers" when in fact he has been actively engaged in a subtle [maneuver] of avoiding his basic questions. (p. 52)

There is some evidence that meditation has the potential to bring about serious side effects, even among long-term practitioners. The tendency of meditation to release unconscious material (e.g., Perez-De-Albeniz & Holmes, 2000) implies that the beginning meditator should approach the practice with moderation. Meditation, as with other need-gratifying activities discussed throughout this book, can slip over the line into hedonic dependency (see Chapter 1). However, by approaching time-proven and research-validated meditative techniques with respect and professional guidance, the odds are certainly in favor of positive mental and physical health outcomes.

Science-Based Relaxation Techniques

While the specific meditative techniques described above (i.e., relaxation response and insight meditation) have been of enormous value, a related and overlapping set of relaxation skills also have the potential to diminish stress and elicit some qualities of mindfulness. *Progressive muscle relaxation* (PMR), the most widely studied relaxation method, has been shown to reduce anxiety, decrease cortisol levels, reduce pain, and re-regulate physiological processes, thereby increasing the general quality of life (Rausch et al., 2006). Table 18.4 provides a summary of prominent science-based techniques for relaxation. In each case, there is an instruction to repetitiously focus on something outside the realm of ordinary thought, with passive disregard for intruding ideas or stimuli.

Managing Stress in the Here and Now

We have developed the acronym BRAIN to highlight five essential skills to diffuse stress in a myriad of provocative situations (e.g., problems at work, at home, in the community). The BRAIN formula integrates many of the techniques germane to the relaxation and meditative strategies discussed throughout this chapter.

B—*Breathing:* Concentrate on focusing your attention on the area of your body near your heart. Inhale deeply for about 5 seconds, imagining the breath flowing in through your heart. Then exhale for about 5 seconds, visualizing the breath flowing out from your solar plexus (the area in the center of your body just below the middle of your rib cage).

R—*Recognize and disengage:* Notice your mood and the physical signs of distress (e.g., knot in the stomach, raising the level of your voice, tenseness of muscles, flushing of face). Make a decision to "freeze the frame" of this discomfort, almost like pressing the pause button on your VCR, and then move on to a different experience—a bit like skipping over an e-mail that holds no interest for you.

A—*Ask yourself, "Is there a better alternative?"* Is there a different way of managing the situation without feeling angry, depressed, or guilty? What other thoughts might we use to replace those that are leading to uncomfortable emotions? Use self-talk skills: "Why am I angry? What can I do about it positively?" Discover what thoughts are causing the feelings, and then replace them with some of your positive thoughts.

I—*Invoke a positive feeling:* Focus on images that make you feel good. An example might be a walk in the woods, or laughing with some childhood friends on the playground, or being on top of your game in some sport that you have enjoyed.

N—*Note the change in perspective:* In a very quiet manner, notice any change in your mood, physical sensations, or negative thoughts. Maintain these positive changes as long as you can.

SOURCE: Adapted from Cryer, B., McCraty, R., & Childre, D. (2003). Managing yourself: Pull the plug on stress. *Harvard Business Review, 81*(7), 102–107.

Table 18.4   Prominent Relaxation Techniques

Technique	Instruction
Progressive Muscle Relaxation (PMR)	The most extensive relaxation technique used today, this method involves the systematic focus of attention on the gross muscle groups throughout the body: "Actively tense each muscle group for a few seconds and then release the muscles and relax; for example, I want you to stop tensing, and simply concentrate on what these muscles feel like as you learn to relax." The sequence of tension release and attention is sequentially applied to the dominant hand and forearm; dominant upper arm; nondominant hand and forearm, forehead; eyes, nose, cheeks, and mouth; neck and throat; chest; back and respiratory muscles; abdomen; dominant upper leg, calf, and foot; nondominant upper leg, calf, and foot. Progression to each muscle group is predicated upon successful and complete relaxation of the prior group.
Calm Scene and Breathing	Imagine a personally calming scene: for example, peacefully walking on a beach with a toddler; watching a sunset; relaxing near a cool stream on a summer day. Breathe from your diaphragm, slow and steady, in and out for several minutes, focusing on the rising of the abdomen on the in-breath and the falling of the abdomen on the out-breath.
Deep Breathing	Beginning with normal breathing, slowly start to make each breath deeper until you have inhaled deeply five times. Inhale through the nose and exhale through the mouth, making a small opening through the lips and breathing out slowly. Return to normal breathing after five deep breaths.
Active Relaxation	Walk or jog 15 minutes each day. Vary your body posture; for example, swing your arms, and then put them behind your back, while reflecting on your positive state of mind. Work out a few times a week by playing a sport, swimming, or going to the gym.
Grounding	Turn attention to the outside world and focus on the here and now, not the past or future. Describe what is around you at this moment in time: for example, the chair is wood, the sky is blue, the breeze is cool.
Massage	Via the manipulation of soft tissues and muscles with massage, relaxation is produced, thereby relieving muscle aches and pain. Various massage techniques have developed based on cultural idioms. Examples include Swedish, reflexology, Rolfing, Hellerwork, Alexander technique, and Feldenkrais. Evidence shows that massage reduces anxiety scores in short-term care settings.
Freeze-Frame Technique	Conscious perception is like watching a movie, and we perceive each moment as an individual frame. When the so-called scene becomes stressful, the freeze-frame technique allows one to "freeze," or isolate, the perceptual frame so that one can observe it from a detached and objective view. • Recognize and disengage, taking time out to temporarily retreat from thoughts and feelings, particularly stressful ones. • Breathe through your heart, focusing breaths through the area of your solar plexus. • Invoke positive feelings by making a sincere effort to be positive. • Ask yourself if there is a better alternative and what would be an efficient, effective attitude or action in order to reduce stress. • Note how your perspective has changed; sense your change in perception or feelings and sustain it as long as possible.

SOURCES: Derived from Cryer, McCraty, & Childre (2003); Davidson & Schwartz (1976); Mamtani & Cimino (2002); Najavits (2006); Wanberg & Milkman (2006).

Chapter Summary

Meditation and other calming techniques are evidence-based means for stress reduction and improved quality of life. Using principles derived from ancient meditative practice, Benson's relaxation response is discussed as a Western prototype for the use of meditation as a technique to reduce stress and achieve a positive state of mind. By examining the religious and secular literatures of the world, Benson found that the same steps exist in virtually every culture.

1. The repetition of a word, sound, prayer, or muscular activity

2. The passive disregard of everyday thoughts when they come to mind

Those who practice Benson's relaxation response are instructed to select a personally meaningful focus word or phrase, followed by muscle relaxation and attention to their breathing. The focus word or phrase is repeated upon exhaling. The steps are used to promote the development of an array of artistic and recreational skills consistent with one's sense of purpose and meaning.

Based on Buddhist tradition, insight meditation presents an alternative pathway to peace of mind. By increasing awareness of our thoughts, we can more easily recognize the motivation for the thought, and we can *choose to act*—rather than react—accordingly. Similarly, we can become more attuned to our emotions. As with thought, it is possible to observe emotions as they arise. We become more accepting and experience them on a more cognitive plane, gaining freedom from actions based on transient feelings.

The chapter further explains how Buddhist philosophy provides a useful framework for addiction treatment. From the Buddhist perspective, addiction represents a "false refuge" from the pain and suffering of life.

Another approach to accessing critical aspects of the mind is Progoff's process meditation technique of intensive journal writing. This technique provides a multilevel feedback system that integrates conscious and unconscious fantasies, gently stimulating insight into the meaning and purpose of one's life. Instructions are given for utilizing fantasy to improve self-understanding and personal intimacy.

Related forms of instruction are germane to other techniques for achieving relaxation or peace of mind. Progressive muscle relaxation (PMR), the most widely studied relaxation method, has been shown to reduce anxiety, decrease cortisol levels, reduce pain, and re-regulate physiological processes, thereby increasing the general quality of life. A summary of prominent science-based techniques for relaxation shows that in each case there is an instruction to repetitiously focus on something outside the realm of ordinary thought, with passive disregard for intruding ideas or stimuli.

Research data from psychology and medicine support the use of meditation and relaxation exercises as important tools for improving health and one's overall sense of well-being. Meditation has been shown to improve memory; provide acceptance and tolerance of affect; increase happiness, joy, and positive thinking; increase confidence and productivity; improve problem-solving skills; enhance the acceptance of, compassion for, and tolerance of self and others; and improve relaxation, resilience, and the ability to control feelings. Davidson and colleagues showed that a short program in mindfulness meditation produces positive effects on brain and immune function.

Meditation, like other need-gratifying activities, can cross the line into hedonic dependency. However, by approaching the discipline with preparation, respect, and professional guidance when needed, there is great likelihood that these time-honored strategies will result in improved states of physical and mental well-being, not only for the individual, but for society at large. We conclude this section with advice from the Dalai Lama.

> We are visitors on this planet. We are here for ninety, a hundred years at the very most. During that period we must try to do something good, something useful with our lives. Try to be at peace with yourself and help others share that peace. If you contribute to other people's happiness, you will find the true goal, the true meaning of life. (quoted in J. Goldstein, 1993, p. 160)

19

Eating Yourself Fit

Introduction: Does Dieting Work?

In *Rethinking Thin,* Kolata (2007), a science writer for the *New York Times,* argues that scientists have a far better understanding of factors that lead to obesity than of how to lose weight permanently. Paradis and Cabanac (2008) find that people have "set points," and their bodies will slow down or speed up metabolic activity in order to keep their weight constant. Given that biological influences are important determinants of a person's weight, is there any recourse for the huge proportion of American adults who qualify as being obese?

> C. D. Gardner et al. (2007) published the results of one of the longest and most persuasive comparisons of weight-loss programs ever conducted. Three of the four diets in the study are heavily promoted regimens that have made their originators famous: the Atkins diet and the Zone diet, which both emphasized high-protein foods and the Ornish diet, a plan that prohibits most fatty foods. The fourth was the no-frills, low-fat diet that most nutrition experts recommend. (Raeburn, 2007, quoted in Nestle, 2007, p. 66)

A year after starting their diets, people on the Atkins plan had dropped an average of 10 pounds. Subjects on the other diets lost between 3 and 6 pounds, and members of the Atkins group showed no jump in cholesterol levels, despite the high levels of cholesterol in their diet. All groups showed modest weight loss and improvement in individuals' levels of cholesterol, blood pressure, and insulin (see Figure 19.1). "Contrary to expectations, the high-fat Atkins diet produced greater weight losses than three other popular weight-reduction plans" (Raeburn, 2007, quoted in Nestle, 2007, p. 67).

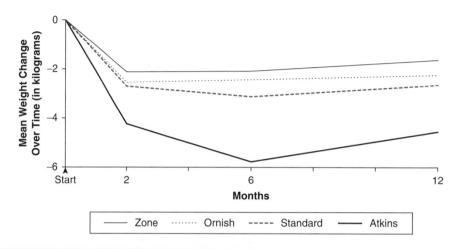

Figure 19.1   Battle of the diet plans.

SOURCE: Adapted from P. Raeburn, and appeared in Nestle, M. (2007, August). Eating made simple: How do you cope with a mountain of conflicting advice? *Scientific American.*

However, Mann et al. (2007) analyzed 31 long-term studies and found that although most participants lost about 5% to 10% of their total body mass, using all kinds of diets, most also regained all that weight over the long term and some put on even more than they had lost. Gorman (2004) reported on long-term weight loss among people who'd dropped at least 30 pounds and kept them off for a year, with an average 70-pound weight loss maintained for 6 years. Although there appears to be no commonality regarding how people in the study lost the weight, there is a striking similarity in how they succeeded in keeping it off—*exercise,* with an average of about an hour of physical activity a day!

The Natural Highs Alternative: Think Thin, Moderate, Work Out!

Although there are a plethora of regimens designed to encourage exercise and restrained caloric intake, *state of mind* is a critical ingredient regarding one's ability to follow through. People who desire to lose weight permanently while remaining healthy and productive must take a serious inventory of their behavioral budget. They must become converts to "thin thinking" and be prepared for a degree of persistent discomfort from relentless dieting. They must first recognize that they eat too much and exercise too little.

A few commonsense recommendations set the stage for a health approach to weight control. Crash dieting is not helpful, as the diet is almost always broken, resulting in rapid weight gain (and the consequent erosion of the individual's confidence that he or she can succeed). Eating when emotionally aroused is another hazard, as food serves as a means to reduce stress, with calorie consumption far outpacing nutritional need. Weight loss should be planned as a gradual process taking place over a period of several months (as opposed to a few weeks as in crash dieting) with a usual goal of about a pound per week. Moderation and portion control are the rules of thumb, with the inclusion of regular (planned and incidental) exercise as a part of the overall weight management scheme. A small excess of calories, even as little as a handful of peanuts or one alcoholic beverage, consumed on a regular basis, can add one pound per month, and in as little as one year can advance the dieter from petite to plump without the person ever appearing to lose control.

Developing the Right State of Mind

In *The Beck Diet Solution,* Dr. Judith Beck (2007) applies the principles of cognitive-behavioral therapy to include goals, values, and rational thinking in any program for weight loss. The basic ideas of her approach are summarized in Table 19.1.

Table 19.1   Thinking Like a Thin Person

Create Your Advantages Response Card: Write down all the reasons you want to lose weight and rate how important these are to you. Then read the card 2x daily plus whenever you are threatened by cravings.

Pick Two Reasonable Diets: Pick any reasonable and healthy one that seems appealing to you and a second one in case the first doesn't work out.

Eat Sitting Down: Unplanned eating is much more likely if you eat while standing up.

Give Yourself Credit: Recognize all the positive things you are doing each day so when you make a mistake you don't magnify it out of proportion.

Eat Slowly and Mindfully: Concentrate on what you are eating in order to derive satisfaction from smaller portions; i.e., savor each bite.

Get a Diet Support Coach: The coach helps with motivation, accountability, keeping perspective, and giving yourself credit.

Prevent Unplanned Eating: Establish the rule that there is "no choice" about giving in to unplanned eating.

End Overeating: Remember that excess food will go to waste in your body; it is better to go to waste in the garbage.

Change Your Definition of Full: Think about how easily you could take a moderately brisk walk before eating. If you can't imagine keeping the same pace after a meal, you have overeaten.

Stop Fooling Yourself: Beck lists examples of fake excuses, such as "I'll eat less later," or "It's not that fattening," or "I'm so upset and I just don't care."

Get Back on Track: Acknowledge the mistake and recommit to the diet instead of giving in to relapse.

Get Ready to Weigh In: The advantages of weekly weigh-ins are that they celebrate success, build confidence, keep us honest if we've gained weight, and help us stay committed.

(Continued)

Table 19.1 (Continued)

Arrange Your Environment: Eliminate foods at home and work that trigger your cravings.

Make Time and Energy for Dieting: Devote time to shopping, preparing meals, exercising, etc.

Select an Exercise Plan: Exercise should be both incidental and planned.

Pick a Reasonable Goal: An attainable short-term goal might be to lose 5 pounds.

Differentiate Between Hunger, and Desire and Cravings: If the time elapsed after a reasonable sized meal is less than 3 hrs., the probability is that you are dealing with the urge to eat, not hunger.

Practice Hunger Tolerance: Hunger comes and goes; as you attend to other things, hunger diminishes.

Overcome Cravings: The more you wait out your cravings, the less frequently and intensely they will occur.

Plan for Tomorrow: Prepare a food plan that each day describes what you will eat tomorrow.

Monitor Your Eating: By keeping a written record of what you are eating and following your daily food plan, you increase the chances of losing weight and keeping it off.

Say, "Oh Well" to Disappointment: Accept your cravings and hardships around not eating what you want, acknowledging that although you might not like dieting, it is necessary to achieve your goals.

Countering the Unfairness Syndrome: "Everyone has some unfairness in life; having to regulate my food intake is mine and I can handle it."

Deal With Discouragement: When faced with thoughts of giving up, it's important to challenge those by focusing on the here and now, reminding ourselves that we can do what we need to do.

Identify Sabotaging Thoughts: It is important to learn how to spot thoughts that undermine your resolve, e.g., "Dieting is too hard" or "I'm treating myself."

Recognize Thinking Mistakes: Thoughts are transient; just because you're thinking something doesn't mean it's true or that you have to act on the thought.

Master the Seven Questions Technique:

1. What kind of thinking error could I be making? 2. What's the evidence that this thought might not be true? 3. Is there an alternative explanation or another way of viewing this? 4. What is the most realistic outcome of this situation? 5. What is the effect of my believing this thought, and what could be the effect of changing my thinking? 6. What should I tell a close friend/family member if he or she were in this situation and had this thought? 7. What should I do now?

Resist Food Pushers: Be direct; do not communicate any wiggle room or ambiguity in your refusal to indulge.

Decide About Drinking: Know how many calories are in an alcoholic beverage and plan accordingly, making sure that any loss of judgment does not provoke unplanned eating.

SOURCE: Reprinted with permission from *The Beck Diet Solution: Train Your Brain to Think Like a Thin Person.* Published by Oxmoor House, © Judith S. Beck, PhD, 2007.

The immediate benefits of maintaining a healthy lifestyle are looking good, feeling good, and being a positive role model. In the long term, a balanced program of exercise and nutrition can help prevent chronic diseases such as heart disease, diabetes, and some cancers.

Partial Fasting

The Bible says that Moses and Jesus fasted for 40 days for spiritual renewal. Hippocrates, Socrates, and Plato recommended fasting for health reasons. According to Neufeld (quoted in Neighmond, 2007), an endocrinologist at UCLA, by studying newborns we can gain a clearer picture of how the body reacts to a lack of food. Babies may need to feed every few hours because their bodies cannot produce enough glycogen, the body's form of stored sugar required to make energy. Glycogen is needed for basic functions of the brain and body: thinking, muscle action, and cell survival. According to Neufeld, adults require about 2,000 calories a day to make energy or glycogen and it might help the body to fast, that is, to stop eating for short periods of time (24 hours once a week) while still consuming water. "You re-tune the body, suppress insulin secretion, reduce the taste for sugar, so sugar becomes something you're less fond of taking" (n.p.).

Mattson (2007), of the National Institute on Aging, says that when we convert food into energy, our bodies create a lot of unnecessary by-products including free radicals, which attack proteins, DNA, the nucleus of cells, and cell membranes. Mattson cites studies where rats and mice were fed every other day. The finding of reduced disease in comparison to regularly fed rats suggests that humans could also benefit from partial fasting. From Mattson's perspective, partial-fasting benefits range from improving glucose regulation, which can protect against diabetes, to lowering blood pressure. Some animal studies have also shown that partial fasting has very beneficial effects on the brain, protecting against Alzheimer's, Parkinson's, and stroke. Partial fasting may even extend the life span because eating less sends a message to the cells of the body that they should conserve and use energy more efficiently. "When they're exposed to a mild stress, [the body's cells] sort of expect that maybe this is going to happen again. . . . So maybe next time I may have to go longer without food, so I'd better be able to deal with that when it comes on" (Mattson, 2007, p. 337).

Fasting may work in a similar fashion to the way muscles get built up when they're stressed by exercise. Although advocates claim that short-term studies have found complete fasting lowers blood pressure and reduces cancer risk, Neufeld (quoted in Neighmond, 2007) is concerned that after the first few days of liquid only, the body uses up all its stored glucose to make energy. Then it turns to other sources, including fat and muscle. "The main tissue that's the target in long-term fasting is muscle, because muscle has readily available amino acids which can be converted to glucose right away. . . . In that way, your brain is never deprived of needed glucose" (n.p.). The problem, according to Neufeld, is that when muscle breaks down, potentially toxic proteins are released. These proteins are partly composed of nitrogen, which can be toxic to the kidneys and liver. This is when starvation officially begins.

What Is a Healthy Diet?

Willett and Stampfer (2006), professors of epidemiology and nutrition at the Harvard School of Public Health, strongly emphasize weight control through exercising daily and avoiding excessive caloric intake. The majority of our diet should contain healthy fats (liquid vegetable oils, e.g., olive, canola, soy, corn, sunflower, and peanut) and healthy carbohydrates (whole grain foods such as whole wheat bread, oatmeal, and brown rice). Fruits and vegetables should be eaten liberally with encouragement for moderate amounts of healthy proteins, that is, nuts, legumes, fish, poultry, and eggs, with everyday consumption limited to two servings per day. Willett and Stampfer recommend minimizing the consumption of red meat, butter, refined grains (e.g., white bread, white rice, and white pasta), potatoes, and sugar. Trans fats should be avoided entirely, and a multivitamin is suggested for most people. If not contraindicated by medical conditions or medication, moderate consumption of alcohol of any kind (wine, beer, or spirits) can be a healthy option. Their recommendations for a healthy diet are shown in Figure 19.2.

The Bottom Line

Excluding not smoking, the World Cancer Research Fund (cited in "To Avoid the Big C, Stay Small," 2007) makes the recommendations shown in Table 19.2 (p. 366) concerning nutrition and reducing the risk of cancer and other health problems:

Finally, "the simplest message may be the best: do not overeat, exercise more, consume mostly fruits, vegetables and whole grains, and avoid junk foods" (Nestle, 2007).

People gain weight when intake exceeds expenditure and lose weight when expenditure exceeds intake. Energy intake (right side of scale in Figure 19.3) is determined by the sum of the calories contained in the carbohydrate (hexagons, 4 kcal/g), fat (circles, 9 kcal/g), and protein (ovals, 4 kcal/g) components of the diet. Total daily energy expenditure (left side of scale) is the sum of the energy needed to sustain vital functions at rest (RMR, the resting metabolic rate), the energy expended during exercise (TEE, the thermic effect of exercise), and the energy used to digest and absorb food (TEF, the thermic effect of feeding).

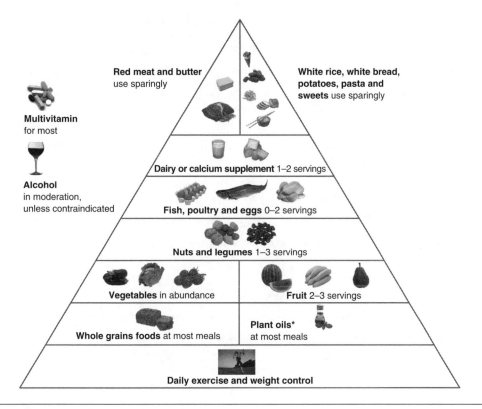

Figure 19.2   A better food pyramid.

SOURCE: Adapted from *Scientific American,* Volume 16, Number 4, 2006: Eating to Live, Rebuilding the Food Pyramid, by Walter C. Willett and Meir J. Stampfer, p. 18.

Chapter Summary

Given that biological influences are important determinants of a person's weight, is dieting a viable option for the huge proportion of American adults who qualify as overweight or obese?

It appears that many diets will facilitate short-term weight loss; however, those who manage to sustain control over their weight include a healthy quantum of exercise in their daily and weekly schedules. Successful dieters realize that they eat too much and exercise too little. Crash dieting is ill-advised as it results in nothing more than a setup for failure and lowered self-esteem. The diet is almost always broken, and whatever weight has been lost is rapidly regained. Dr. Judith Beck's work is described, as she applies the principles of cognitive-behavioral therapy to weight loss programs.

Table 19.2   Nutrition Recommendations to Reduce Risk of Cancer

Body fatness	Be as lean as possible within the normal range of body weight, BMI 21–23.
Physical activity	Be physically active; for example, walk briskly at least 30 minutes a day.
Foods and drinks that promote weight gain	Limit consumption of energy foods. Average energy intake should be 125kcal/100g of food. Avoid sugary drinks.
Plant foods	Eat mostly foods of plant origin; fruits and nonstarchy vegetables at least 600g a day.
Animal foods	Limit intake of red meat, no more than 300g a week. Avoid processed meat including bacon and ham.
Alcoholic drinks	Limit alcoholic drinks, two a day for men and one a day for women.
Preservation, processing, and preparation	Limit consumption of salt to less than 5g per day.
Dietary supplements	Aim to meet nutritional needs through diet alone.
Breastfeeding	Mothers should breastfeed; children should be breastfed.
Cancer survivors	Follow the recommendations for cancer prevention.

SOURCE: World Cancer Research Fund, cited in Nestle, 2004.

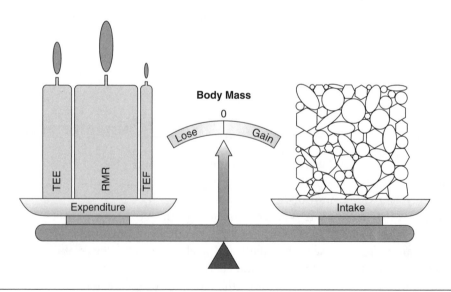

Figure 19.3   Energy balance. Body mass depends on the balance between energy intake and energy expenditure.

RMR = Resting Metabolic Rate; TEE = Thermic Effect of Exercise; TEF = Thermic Effect of Feeding.

Some researchers are extolling the advantages of partial fasting. Possible benefits range from improving glucose regulation to lowering blood pressure. Some animal studies have also shown that partial fasting has beneficial effects on the brain, protecting against Alzheimer's disease, Parkinson's, and stroke. Partial fasting may even prolong life because eating less sends a message to the cells of the body that they should conserve and use energy more efficiently.

With respect to healthy dieting, Willet and Stampfer strongly emphasize weight control through exercising daily and avoiding excessive caloric intake. They recommend minimizing the consumption of red meat, butter, refined grains, potatoes, and sugar. Trans fats should be eliminated, and multivitamins are suggested for most people. Moderate consumption of alcohol is okay if not contraindicated by medical conditions or medication. Perhaps the most succinct and coherent statement about food and fitness is: Consume moderate portions; make exercise a priority; avoid junk foods; and eat plenty of fruits, vegetables, and whole grains.

20

Exercise

The Magic Bullet

No drug in current or prospective use holds as much promise for sustained health as a lifetime program of physical exercise.

—Walter Bortz, Stanford University Medical School

The purpose of this chapter is to develop a better understanding of the whole-life benefits of a sensible exercise program. Physical fitness is not just for those who wish to lose weight. It is also a prescription for participating in the fullness of life. Exercise can enhance self-esteem, social interaction, motivation, and self-image as well as decreasing stress levels, anxiety, and depression (Perham & Accordino, 2007). Another benefit of regular exercise is enhanced energy and decreased fatigue (Puetz, O'Connor, & Dishman, 2006). It is clearly associated with improved physical and mental health. For those with a bent toward sensation seeking and excitement, exercise (and competitive sports) can supply a natural high alternative to such risk-taking behaviors as gambling, promiscuity, and the abuse of stimulant drugs. Health and psychological benefits have been shown to accrue when exercise is used as an adjunct to treatment in complex mental health problems such as alcohol and drug rehabilitation (Donaghy, 2007). To put icing on the cake, regular exercisers have been found to be 10 years younger physiologically than their sedentary counterparts (Cherkas et al., 2008)!

There is an abundance of research that shows exercise as conducive to improved intellectual functioning (Hillman, Erickson, & Kramer, 2008), mood adjustment (Donaghy, 2007), and physical health (Cherkas et al., 2008). According to Hillman et al., "research strongly supports the positive effects of exercise on cognition: aerobic activity improves learning and task acquisition, increases the secretion of key neurochemicals associated with synaptic plasticity and promotes the development of new neuronal architecture" (p. 63). These findings are supported by neuroimaging studies that show positive changes in brain structure from exercise.

In terms of mental health, exercise increases blood flow to the brain, stimulating the release of "those wonderful endorphins" (Donaghy, 2007). Animal studies have shown increases in serotonin, dopamine, and norepinephrine during exercise (Chaouloff, 1997). As graduates of Neurochemistry 101, we know that these neurotransmitters allow for elevated moods and good feelings.

So not only can exercise help your intellectual capacity and your mental and physical health; it also slows aging. If you don't want to be spending all your money on beauty creams and potentially carcinogenic tanning salons (International Agency for Research on Cancer [IARC], 2007), go outside for a jog and keep your body moving.

Exercise of Choice

So, what is "sensible" exercise? Doesn't this word *sensible* sound a little wimpy? Isn't the old marathoner adage, "No pain, no gain," the real way to exercise for good health as well as muscular fitness? Absolutely not! Health benefits are not directly proportional to the total amount of energy expended. If your exercise of choice is running and you run more than 20 miles a week, you are most likely running for more than reasons of health. Although this level of commitment is not necessarily harmful, don't expect to achieve greater health benefits than those who run 12 to 15 miles a week. The operative concept here is health, not "Olympian Superstar." Cherkas et al. (2008) found that people who participate in moderate exercise for 30 minutes at least 5 days a week are effectively reducing their vulnerability to a host of illnesses. Regular workouts have been linked to lower rates of cardiovascular disease, type 2 diabetes, cancer, high blood pressure, obesity, and osteoporosis (Stein, 2008b).

To be effective, exercise must suit your lifestyle, including your personal and professional life. Finding an exercise that you enjoy should not be difficult, since hundreds of different options are available. All of these alternatives can be broken down into five categories: isometric, isotonic, isokinetic, anaerobic, and aerobic. Figure 20.1 represents the four dimensions of an exercise plan set to meet a given individual's needs and preferences.

Isometric exercise: Bodybuilder Charles Atlas popularized this form of exercise (97-pound weakling punches out beach bully), which he termed *dynamic tension.* In isometric exercise, muscles push hard against each other. While this does produce a gain in strength, isometrics do not lead to overall body conditioning. The advantage is that these exercises can be performed anywhere, anytime. This is beneficial for those who must sit for long periods or who are immobilized, however insufficient such exercise may be for improving cardiovascular health.

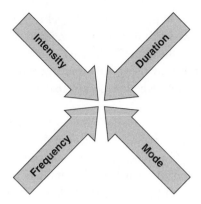

Figure 20.1 **Exercise prescription.** The four components of an exercise prescription are intensity (how hard), duration (how long), frequency (how many times per week), and mode (type of exercise, e.g., swimming or running). For example, an exercise prescription to increase cardiopulmonary endurance could be to run (mode) at a heart rate of 150 beats/min (intensity) for 20 minutes per day (duration) three times per week (frequency) (Axen & Axen, 2001, p. 232).

Isotonic exercise (pumping iron): The difference between isometric and isotonic exercise is that in isotonic exercise (e.g., weightlifting and push-ups), muscles contract with the accompanying movement of the joints. Generally speaking, weight-training programs oriented toward bodybuilding are based on isotonic exercises. A number of popular magazines are devoted entirely to isotonic workouts (e.g., *Muscle and Fitness*). While pumping iron might lead to a cover-page physique, it is woefully insufficient as the sole source of exercise for individuals seeking improved overall conditioning or who have a history of heart disease.

For those not wishing to join an exercise gym, a weight bench with an attached knee exerciser and accompanying weight set can be purchased for less than $100 at discount stores. Obviously, the bench must be sturdy; this is much more important than having a number of costly attachments that may never be used. Individuals attempting weight training should either do it under the guidance of a trained instructor or very carefully follow the instructions given with the exercise equipment. It is possible to do both muscle and structural damage to the body by attempting to move too quickly from a sedentary lifestyle to an Arnold Schwarzenegger–type workout.

Isokinetic exercise (work those pecs!): Isokinetic exercises are very much like isotonic ones, except that exertion is required both going from the starting position and then returning to it. This form of exercise usually requires special equipment, such as a Nautilus machine, in which the individual can adjust the tension according to his or her level of training. Isokinetic exercise is not only expensive, but also inconvenient, in that it requires the individual to belong to a health club in order to use its equipment. This may be a plus for those who enjoy the social atmosphere of a gym. Unfortunately, taken by itself, it does not provide a complete exercise program.

Anaerobic exercise (no sweat): As the name implies, anaerobic exercise does not require an overall increase in the consumption of oxygen. Many everyday activities fall into this category. Exercises such as calisthenics, playing Frisbee, bounding up stairs two at a time, running to the copy machine, hailing a cab in New York City, playing softball, and other activities requiring short but rather intensive bursts of energy are considered anaerobic. Clearly, this is not a complete exercise program, in that it does nothing to increase overall cardiovascular and respiratory fitness. The benefit of such exercises is that they are often fun, which is a major reason to engage in them.

Aerobic exercise (gasp): As the name implies, aerobic exercise requires an increase in the amount of oxygen used by the body. For aerobic exercise to be effective, it must be performed over a prolonged length of time, preferably 20 to 30 minutes at submaximal effort. The most common forms of this exercise are running, jogging, and formal aerobic workouts. Other forms of aerobic exercise can, however, be equally beneficial. Rapid walking and bicycling are other examples of aerobic exercise that can be performed by nearly everyone. For walking, all that's needed is a good pair of comfortable walking shoes, which cost around $80 and are good for up to 2,000 miles. For people living in congested areas such as cities, walking, as well as running during rush hour, can be quite harmful due to the pollution from traffic. It is recommended that any exercise in which oxygen consumption is significantly increased be performed away from polluted areas.

The Chemistry of Working Out

Many undertake exercise programs to lose weight (or to maintain their weight loss after dieting) rather than to enhance their overall health or to achieve euphoria. Happily, unless the desire to lose weight is pathological, these benefits are closely related. A loss of excess body fat will nearly always lead to better health and an improved sense of well-being. Obviously, the body's repository of excess fat (rather than muscle) is the appropriate target of weight-loss programs. To discover how different kinds of exercise can lead to the maximum loss of body fat, we need to learn some basic truths about the physiology of exercise.

Exercise requires energy in order to propel the muscles of the body. This comes from a molecule known as adenosine triphosphate (ATP), which releases energy as it breaks down during exercise. After breaking down, ATP must then be regenerated in order for the muscles to continue working. The fuel that the body uses to regenerate ATP is either fats or carbohydrates. This fuel is burned in the body by using oxygen, just as a stove uses oxygen to burn coal or wood. Fats and carbohydrates are completely consumed under aerobic (oxygen-rich) conditions to produce carbon dioxide and water. Fat, however, has more than twice the fuel capacity (9 calories per gram) of carbohydrates (4 calories per gram). Although fat has more calories, it burns more slowly than carbohydrates during exercise, just as coal burns more slowly than wood, but releases more total energy. When you are simply puttering around the house or garden, you do not have a high-energy demand. During these activities, fat is the primary source of energy consumed to regenerate ATP. But if you start jogging or running, you suddenly need more energy and more oxygen to supply your muscles with ATP. Because you need more energy immediately, the body quickly shifts from burning fat to burning carbohydrates, such as glucose or glucose from glycogen (a starch-like substance stored in the liver). Carbohydrates produce ATP faster but less efficiently than fat in terms of the calories contained per gram (Axen & Axen, 2001).

Figure 20.2 shows how glucose (fuel) is broken down to provide energy needed to perform exercise. After this glycogen is gone, or even before it is completely gone, the exerciser will begin to falter and be unable to continue the pace. Marathoners and long-distance cyclists call this experience of

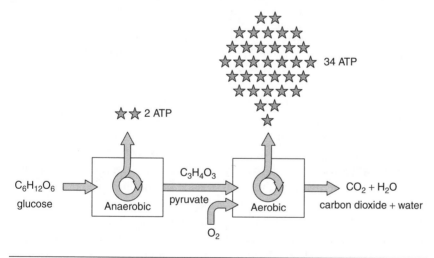

Figure 20.2   **ATP production.** A 6-carbon molecule of glucose is broken down to two 3-carbon molecules of pyruvic acid (pyruvate) in the anaerobic pathway of glycolysis (no oxygen is required). The energy released during this process is sufficient to synthesize two molecules of ATP, a stored form of energy. The 3-carbon molecules of pyruvate can then enter aerobic pathways (which require a continuous supply of oxygen) where they get broken down to carbon dioxide and water with a net yield of 34 ATP molecules per molecule of glucose (Axen & Axen, 2001).

glycogen deficiency "hitting the wall." The individual has pushed him- or herself until all of the stored glycogen in the muscles and the liver is nearly exhausted. At this time, the primary fuel available to continue is fat. As indicated, fat burns very slowly, and an individual is unable to continue vigorous running or cycling by burning fat alone.

Individuals who hit the wall will stagger about and sometimes collapse. Running to this level of carbohydrate depletion is extremely dangerous, since the brain itself needs glucose (a carbohydrate) in order to function. To avert depletion of glycogen during the race, marathoners may load up with pasta and other forms of carbohydrates for several days before running. The goal is to build up a supply of glycogen in the muscles and in the liver in order to minimize the chances of hitting the wall.

Case Example: Hitting the Wall

Sandy had not run a marathon for some time when she first began to train for an upcoming race. The night before the marathon, she was at a dinner party where considerable amounts of protein, in the form of fish, and carbohydrates, in the form of rice, were served. Her friend, thinking of the upcoming marathon, urged Sandy to eat more rice and less fish. Yet, as the fish was exceedingly good, Sandy proceeded to ignore the rice, which is rich in carbohydrates, and ate primarily fish. Her friend later described the race:

> The next day, during the race, I went back to a point about 4 or 5 miles from the finish line to cheer Sandy on as she ran past. I saw her about 300 yards away and I knew immediately that something was wrong. She was not running with her usual confident and strong stride. I quickly hurried back to the finish and arrived just as she crossed the line and collapsed. Fortunately, because she was in superb physical condition, she was soon revived.

Can we use present knowledge of physiology to achieve our optimum physical state? Let's imagine that you went for a vigorous run after some hours of light exercise in the garden or around the house. As you began to run, fat consumption dropped dramatically, because it is slow to furnish energy. Carbohydrate consumption increased dramatically, as it burns faster than fats and can immediately furnish the energy needed for the larger demand from the muscles. At this point in the aerobic process, the body, by necessity, is consuming carbohydrates much more rapidly than fat. In fact, the consumption of carbohydrates will increase to about 85% of total energy consumed almost immediately after one begins to run, and use of fat will fall dramatically. After a short period of time (20 to 30 minutes), however, if the initial pace is not too fast (slow jogging or fast walking), the consumption of fat now begins to rise slowly. As you continue exercising, the body will attempt to conserve carbohydrates (glycogen) and begin to burn fat more efficiently. Provided the intensity of the exercise is below maximal, consumption of fat exceeds carbohydrate consumption after about 30 to 40 minutes. At the end of an hour, fat consumption will be much more prevalent than carbohydrate consumption. This is the typical pattern of energy supplied during an aerobics class or a 5- to 10-mile jog. Another added benefit, and a bona fide motivator for strenuous exercise, is that you will continue burning both fat and carbohydrates even after you have stopped exercising. The longer you exercise, the longer you will continue to burn calories after you have quit the exercise.

It should be very clear that longer periods of submaximal aerobic exercise are more productive for weight loss than shorter bursts of intense anaerobic exercise. During the more intense, short-term maximal exercise, the body's demand for energy is so great that it cannot be furnished by fat and the body will utilize primarily carbohydrates. On the other hand, with exercise less intense than fast running, such as rapid (but not power) walking, the body soon converts from carbohydrate consumption to fat consumption. In other words, if your exercise intensity is somewhat below maximum, the efficiency of oxygen use is high, and this permits the body to utilize fat for fuel as opposed to using carbohydrates. Conversely, if your workout is extremely intense, as you approach your maximum oxygen uptake, your consumption of fats will decrease and the consumption of glycogen will increase. Therefore, three workouts of an hour or so at lower intensity will burn more fat than six workouts of 30 minutes or so at a higher intensity. In addition, high-intensity exercises are more likely to result in muscular or skeletal injury.

The bottom line is that not everyone needs to be a marathon runner in order to be physically fit. The myth that one must "go for the burn" and that with "no pain, no gain" is just not true and keeps what may otherwise be motivated people on the couch. Now that we know how we need carbohydrates as well as fats to fuel our aerobic body, how can we use this information to devise a suitable exercise program and help us achieve a better physique as well as a healthier mind and body?

Exercise for Body Trimming

O, that this too, too solid flesh would melt, thaw and resolve itself into a dew!

—William Shakespeare, *Hamlet*

It is certainly true that not everyone is, nor should everyone be, satisfied with his or her present body weight or condition. For these individuals, exercise offers a mechanism but certainly not a guarantee of success; tenacity and dedication do. It is sad but true that the body gives up its pound (or even ounce) of fat very grudgingly. The body's conservation of fat is an evolutionary survival mechanism, resulting from its experience with periods of food deprivation. For early humans, it was equally important for survival that the stored body fat not be depleted too rapidly, even when normal activity was maintained. The fact that you are here today is due in great measure to the large amount of energy (9 calories per gram) stored in fat. The bad news is that to reduce your weight by 1 gram (454 grams are equal to 1 pound), you need to burn at least this amount (1 gram) of fat.

Table 20.1 shows the estimated amount of calories expended during various activities for a 160-pound person (people with more body weight will burn more calories per hour; e.g., a 160-pound person will burn an estimated 183 calories after walking at the rate of 2 mph for an hour, whereas a 200-pound person will burn an estimated 228 calories and a 240-pound person will burn around 273 calories). Calorie expenditure varies widely depending on the type of exercise, the level of intensity, and the individual's unique physical characteristics.

Table 20.1   Calories Expended per Hour of Activity

Activity	Calories
Walking, 2 mph	183
Dancing, ballroom	219
Walking, 3.5 mph	277
Bicycling, 10 mph	292
Golf, carrying clubs	329
Skiing, downhill	365
Swimming laps	511
Tennis, singles	584
Stair treadmill	657
Rope jumping	730
Rollerblading	913
Running, 8 mph	986

SOURCE: Selected activities derived from Mayo Foundation for Medical Education and Research (MFMER). (2007). *Weight loss.* Retrieved February 11, 2009, from http://www.mayoclinic .com/health/exercise/SM00109.

The information presented in Table 20.1 is discouraging for anyone trying to lose weight by exercise alone. Exercise, even hard exercise, does not burn that many calories. If your sole purpose is to lose body fat, the facts are even worse than the table indicates. Unfortunately, as we have seen, the aerobically active body needs to burn carbohydrates as well as fat. Remember that, for about 30 minutes into your exercise workout, you are burning more calories in the form of carbohydrates than fat. It is only after this time that fat calories are being consumed in greater amounts. Even more discouraging is the fact that even if you are burning equal calories from fat and carbohydrates, you must expend more than twice as many calories to consume 1 pound of fat as those needed to consume 1 pound of carbohydrates.

Assuming that your exercise program consumes 50% of total calories as fat and 50% as carbohydrates, walking for 1 hour at 3.75 miles per hour would burn off 150 calories of fat at 9 calories per gram, or less than 0.04 pounds. (For reference, there are 100–120 calories in a slice of many kinds of bread.) Put in practical terms, you would need to walk 25 miles at this speed to burn off 1 pound of fat. Very depressing, isn't it? And they say exercise helps depression!

Clearly, the most effective way to shape up our bodies, including enhancing muscle tone and reducing fat, is to combine a sensible exercise program with an equally sensible diet (see Chapter 19, Eating Yourself Fit). In fact, dieting programs to lose weight nearly always fail unless they are combined with a regular exercise program. It is critical for each person to choose an exercise program and diet that fits into his or her lifestyle and is consistent with his or her personal preferences. If the exercise is not enjoyable and the diet barely palatable, this is a recipe for failure. The Personal Pleasure Inventory (see Appendix) should be useful in helping you to select an exercise program that is both enjoyable and beneficial. If spending time outdoors and enjoying nature is a natural high for you, why not consider running, walking, hiking, cycling, cross-country skiing, or playing tennis, rather than an aerobics class or swimming in an indoor pool?

Training for Physical Health

It has been said that the human body is the only machine that wears out when not used. Probably no single factor is as important to your health as a sensible program of exercise. People with active lifestyles are far less likely to die from cancer and heart disease than their physically out-of-shape contemporaries.

Over the course of almost five decades, Paffenbarger and Lee (1996) of Stanford University conducted large epidemiologic studies proving that increased exercise lowers the chance of death from heart disease. Paffenbarger used periodic questionnaires to chronicle the personal characteristics, physical activity levels, illnesses, and deaths of over 50,000 college alumni. He examined the role of multiple factors in coronary heart disease: blood pressure, body mass, physical activity, cigarette smoking, history of hypertension, and family history of hypertension and heart attacks. Of all these factors, physical inactivity ranked ahead of all except hypertension as a predictor of coronary heart disease (CHD). The health benefits of physical activity were found to be independent of all the other variables tested. For example, inactive men who had a history of hypertension and smoked ("suicide in the fast lane") had a rate of CHD more than twice that of physically active smokers.

According to the American College of Sports Medicine (Pescatello et al., 2004),

Exercise remains a cornerstone therapy for the primary prevention, treatment, and control of hypertension. The optimal training frequency, intensity, time, and type (FITT) need to be better defined to optimize the BP [blood pressure] lowering capacities of exercise, particularly in children, women, older adults, and for certain ethnic groups. Based upon the current evidence, the following exercise prescription is recommended for those with high blood pressure:

Frequency: on most, preferably all, days of the week

Intensity: moderate intensity

Time: ≥ 30 min of continuous or accumulated physical activity per day

Type: primarily endurance physical activity supplemented by resistance exercise (p. 533)

Besides the well-established relationship between exercise and reduced cardiovascular disease, working out has been shown to have benefits in preventing a host of other life-threatening ailments including obesity, type 2 diabetes, osteoporosis, and cancer (Stein, 2008b). By examining blood samples of some 2,400 twins, Cherkas and her colleagues (2008) at Kings College London determined that telomeres (repeated DNA sequences) on the ends of chromosomes in white blood cells (leukocytes) were longer in subjects who exercised the most (an average of 199 minutes weekly) compared with more sedentary subjects who exercised an average of 16 minutes or less per week. Telomeres are believed to be markers of aging because they shrink over time. Individuals who exercised regularly were found to have telomeres equal in length to sedentary types who were on average 10 years younger. The researchers speculate that stress, inflammation, and oxidative stress (damage to cells caused by exposure to oxygen) may have caused the shortening of telomeres in sedentary types.

Another spectacular finding has been reported by Dean Ornish (2008), founder and president of the Preventive Medicine Research Institute at the University of California, San Francisco. Ornish and his colleagues found that the activity of more than 500 genes in the normal tissue of 30 men with low-risk prostate cancer changed after the patients began to exercise regularly; practice yoga stretching; and eat diets that were low in red meats and fat, and heavy in fruit, vegetables, and whole grain (supplemented by soy, fish oil, selenium, and vitamins C and E). According to the research team, the study shows that lifestyle changes of stress management, regular exercise, and sound nutrition may prompt swift and profound differences in the behavior of tumor-suppressing genes (turning them on) whereas certain disease-promoting ones (including oncogenes implicated in both prostate and breast cancer) were down-regulated or switched off. The study challenges the widely held belief that "it's all in my genes and there is nothing I can do." Ornish refers to this type of reasoning as "genetic nihilism," arguing that "genes may be our disposition but not our fate" (quoted in Stein, 2008a).

Running Away From Depression

Opposite to Exercise is Idleness or want of exercise, the bane of body and mind . . . and a sole cause of Melancholy.

—Robert Burton, 1632

As earlier stated, exercise can be beneficial to a person's everyday functioning by enhancing self-esteem as well as decreasing stress levels, anxiety, and depression (Perham & Accordino, 2007; Donaghy, 2007). In a pioneering study of the relationship between exercise and mental health, Griest and colleagues (1978) at the University of Wisconsin found that a program of regular jogging reduced symptoms in a group of depressed outpatients more than a regimen of psychotherapy. Even more encouraging was the one-year follow-up, which found that most of the members of the running group had become regular runners and remained symptom free. Since that time, dozens of studies (Donaghy, 2007) have been conducted on the effect of both acute (usually single aerobic events) and chronic (long-term physical fitness) exercise. In nearly all cases, exercise—even anaerobic exercise—was found to be beneficial in reducing symptoms of depression, although moderate aerobic training seems to be most beneficial (Netz, Wu, Becker, & Tenenbaum, 2005).

As encouraging as these results may be, they do not necessarily relate to most of us, who are not clinically depressed but do have occasional episodes of mild depression that rob us of some of life's joys. Most research indicates that exercise can help rid us of the often too frequent "blahs." I. L. McCann and Holmes (1984) at the University of Kansas randomly assigned a group of mildly depressed females into three groups: (1) an aerobic exercise group, (2) a group that practiced muscle relaxation, and (3) a no-treatment group. At the end of 10 weeks, only those in the aerobic group showed dramatic decreases in depression. Nearly every study since has confirmed that exercise provides excellent protection against depression. According to Donaghy (2007), "Fifteen randomized controlled trials (RCTs) and three meta-analyses provide evidence that exercise can reduce depression and that it can be as effective as cognitive therapy" (p. 76).

Healthy Body, Healthy Mind

The natural healing force within us is the greatest force in getting well.

—Hippocrates

We know that a healthy mind free from stress promotes good bodily health, but can a healthy body produce a healthy mind? Can there actually be a connection between bodily fitness and mental health? Clearly, this concept is not new. Holistic medicine, which regards the mind and body as a single entity, has been a tenet of Hindu philosophy for centuries. As we have seen, modern research clearly indicates a correlation between mind and body. But how does it work? In order to understand this relationship, we shall review and look more closely at the mind-body connection, discussed earlier in Chapter 2 (Figure 2.4) and Chapter 8 (Figure 8.4) as the hypothalamus-pituitary-adrenal (HPA) axis.

Figure 20.3 shows the HPA axis, including beta-endorphins, which are thought to play a role in the runner's high and general feelings of well-being after vigorous exercise. The release of endorphins during exercise may step down the body's response to stress.

In reaction to outside stimuli, including stress, higher centers in the brain, such as the hippocampus, relay messages to the hypothalamus, the portion of the brain that regulates emotion as well as many other basic processes of life, such as eating and body temperature. The hypothalamus then relays the stress signals by sending certain chemicals (corticotropin-releasing hormone) to the pituitary gland, which lies at the base of the brain. This gland then releases other molecules, including endorphins (in the brain and in the blood) and ACTH, which in turn alert the outer layer (cortex) of the adrenal

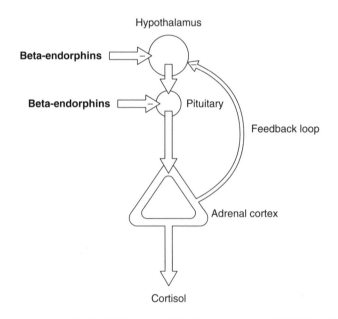

Figure 20.3   Regulation of the HPA axis. The activity of the HPA axis is inhibited by beta-endorphins, which act on the hypothalamus and pituitary gland, as well as by negative feedback from the adrenal cortex. These effects reduce the amount of cortisol released during stress (see Fig. 2.4).

glands, which are situated on top of the kidneys. The adrenal cortex secretes other molecules, known as corticosteroids such as cortisol, which control a number of body functions. These include preparing the body for an emergency by releasing adrenaline and norepinephrine. As seen in Figure 20.3, in our HPA system, one of the regulating mechanisms is a negative feedback loop to the hypothalamus that is activated by corticosteroids from the adrenal glands. This in turn inhibits sending the molecular message from the hypothalamus to the pituitary gland. There are other molecular organizations that regulate the HPA system, including the now familiar neurotransmitters dopamine, norepinephrine, and serotonin (Donaghy, 2007), as well as the equally familiar endorphins (Mutrie & Faulkner, 2003).

Once again, it seems that molecules of the mind literally have the power to control our lives both physically and mentally. It is well-known that stress can upset the HPA system and that continued, unrelenting stress can lead to depression. Nemeroff (1998) argues that in depressed people, the homeostasis of the HPA axis is upset. Since stress can upset HPA homeostasis and possibly lead to depression, it would seem logical that exercise, which we have shown to relieve stress, would at least reduce depression by reestablishing homeostasis in the HPA system.

Runner's High: Fact or Fiction?

How does exercise, which has such a positive effect on mental attitude, restore homeostasis to a disregulated HPA system? There are a number of theories, many of which are not completely proved or accepted by the scientific community. Since depression is a disease of the mind, it seems logical that we should look to that part of the HPA axis that lies within the brain, that is, the hypothalamus and the pituitary. These regions of the brain, like most others, use the language of chemistry in communication. The words of this language are neurotransmitters and hormones, which we now see are involved in regulation of the HPA axis. Depletion of norepinephrine (NE) in the hypothalamus may bring about disruption of the HPA system and lead to depression (Sherman, 2001). Studies with humans and animals support this hypothesis, although other neurotransmitters as well as other hormones are involved. If exercise is to have any effect on mood, including depression, we should look to an increase in the level of NE as a result of the exercise.

In fact, this has been shown to be true. Studies have shown an increase in the levels of NE in the brains of chronically exercising mice. Other studies suggest that exercise promotes entry of the amino acid tryptophan into the brain, where, as we have seen in Chapter 2 (see "The Joy of Dopamine and the Reward Cascade"), it forms the neurotransmitter serotonin. Enhanced levels of NE and serotonin are important in that low levels of NE and serotonin have been implicated in depression, commonly treated with antidepressant medication (e.g., Effexor). Equally fascinating is the fact that serotonin seems to be the neurotransmitter that activates the reward cascade (Figure 2.5). Therefore, release of serotonin would also be expected to enhance overall feelings of well-being and self-esteem.

Fortunately, we don't need to be depressed to experience the positive mental benefits of exercise. Also, if exercise does increase levels of NE, we would expect to experience a mild case of mania while running. But hypo-mania is not the only feeling experienced by vigorous prolonged exercise such as running. There is a sense of serenity and euphoria that pervades our entire being. It is as if somehow our body is releasing those "keys to paradise," endorphins, which are the crucial molecules needed as final regulators of our reward cascade, our internal antidepressant mechanism.

Most of the early work on the relationship between exercise and endor-phins was done by studying the increase in blood levels of endorphins following acute exercise. Every study to date has shown that prolonged vig-orous exercise produces peripheral increases in the level of endorphins. This would account for decreased pain perception following exercise; however, because endorphins do not easily pass from the blood to the brain, scientists have puzzled over the role of exercise-generated endorphins in reducing depression (Donaghy, 2007). Since it is considered "bad form" to surgically examine the brains of athletes following exercise, research has turned to ani-mals. Blake, Stein, and Vomachka (1984), at Marquette University, have shown that prolonged submaximal exercise (not brief and strenuous) increases the level of endorphins in the brains of rats. Other studies have basi-cally shown the same results.

The interesting feature of research findings on exercise and mood is that prolonged, submaximal exercise produces endorphins, the euphoric and analgesic chemical, whereas short bouts of acute exercise produce NE, the excitatory neurochemical. Interviews with runners suggest that running has two phases: the NE phase, followed by the endorphin phase. The first phase produces a manic state, presumably due to the release of NE in the locus coeruleus. Only after prolonged exertion does the effect of endorphins become noticeable. Consider the possible roles of NE and endorphin-mediated experience in the following descriptions of runners' states of mind.

Case Examples: Runner A

Thirty minutes out and something lifts. Legs and arms become light and rhythmic. My snake brain is making the best of it. The fatigue goes away, and feelings of power begin. I think I'll run 25 miles today. I'll double the size of the research grant request. I'll have that talk with the dean. . . .

Then, sometime into the second hour comes the spooky time. Colors are bright and beautiful, water sparkles, clouds breathe, and my body, swimming, detaches from the earth. A loving contentment invades the basement of my mind, and thoughts bubble up without trails. I find the place I need to live.

Runner B

All of a sudden, my throat opens up, [and] the air flows back into my lungs. All the tension in my body is released, and at that moment, a rush of power surges through my body. I can feel the tautness of every muscle in my being. I hear and feel my breath billowing out through my mouth, and I feel a moment of exhilaration. It's as if I'm looking through the eyes of a new and baptized person. And at that moment, I feel like I could run forever.

These vignettes are but minute examples of the powerful impact exercise has on our mental health and attitude. Regardless of the neurochemical mechanism involved, the indisputable evidence is that exercise does have a positive effect on mood. Clearly, if you want to improve your attitude, your health, and your life, get off the couch and get going. If you don't follow this advice, you should at least increase your health insurance.

Take care of your body. There's not a spare in the trunk.

—Bumper sticker

Make Life a Moving Experience

Table 20.2 presents a few simple ways to increase our everyday physical movement. These "incidental" activities may not burn many calories but are likely to increase your odds of having a longer, healthier, and happier life.

Table 20.2   Incidental Exercise

- Use the stairs (up and down) instead of the elevator. Start with one flight and gradually build up to more.
- Park a few blocks from your destination and walk the rest of the way. If you ride on public transportation, get off a few stops early.
- Take an exercise break—get up from your computer, stretch, walk around, and give your muscles and mind a chance to relax.
- Instead of snacking, take a walk.
- When traveling, choose a hotel with a good exercise facility or near a walking trail and make use of it.
- Instead of using the cell phone while driving, try phoning while walking.
- Some physical activity can save you money: Mow the lawn or do your own housework.
- When you walk the dog, try walking a little faster and a little longer. If you don't have a pet, adopt one.
- Try "aerobic shopping": Wear track shoes and take a few extra laps around the mall. Stretch to reach items in high places and squat or bend to look at items at floor level. Trying this in the supermarket will extricate you from the "impulse buying" zone at eye level that's easy to reach.
- Add any moving activity that you find to be enjoyable and stress free.

Chapter Summary

The focus of this chapter is on developing a better understanding of the whole-life benefits of regular exercise. Exercise can build self-esteem, provide social interaction, increase motivation, and improve self-image as well as decreasing stress levels, anxiety, and depression.

For those who like sensation seeking and excitement, exercise can offer a natural high alternative to riskier activities such as gambling, promiscuity, and the abuse of stimulant drugs. It can also be useful as an adjunct treatment for complex mental health problems such as alcohol and drug addiction.

People who exercise moderately for 30 minutes at least 5 days a week are effectively reducing their vulnerability to a range of illnesses from cardiovascular disease to cancer. It is important to develop an exercise regimen that is consistent with one's lifestyle and personal preferences. All of the different exercise modalities can be grouped into five categories: isometric, isotonic, isokinetic, anaerobic, and aerobic. For aerobic exercise to be effective, it must be performed over a prolonged length of time, preferably 20 to 30 minutes at submaximal effort.

Exercise may be used for body trimming, but most successful weight reduction programs involve significant attention to diet as well. During less vigorous activities (e.g., gardening), fat is the primary source of energy consumed. But if you start jogging or running, you suddenly need more energy and more oxygen to supply your muscles with ATP. Because you need more energy immediately, the body quickly shifts from burning fat to burning carbohydrates such as glucose or glycogen (a starch-like substance stored in the liver). Carbohydrates produce ATP faster but less efficiently than fat in terms of the calories contained per gram. Provided the intensity of the exercise is below maximal, consumption of fat exceeds carbohydrate consumption after about 30 or 40 minutes. At the end of an hour, fat consumption will be much more prevalent than carbohydrate consumption. Longer periods of submaximal aerobic exercise are more productive for weight loss than shorter bursts of intense anaerobic exercise.

In addition to the well-established relationship between exercise and protection against a host of life-threatening ailments, exercise preserves youth. Individuals who exercised regularly were found to have cells marked by the aging process to a degree consistent with those found in sedentary types who were on average 10 years younger. Another spectacular finding is that regular exercise and sound nutrition may prompt tumor-suppressing genes to "turn on," and certain disease-promoting genes are down-regulated or switched off. In short, genes may be our predisposition but not our destiny.

Studies examining the relationship between exercise and mental health confirm that exercise offers excellent protection against depression. Such studies show that exercise can reduce depression and that it can be as effective as cognitive therapy. Stress can upset HPA homeostasis and possibly lead to depression; therefore exercise, which is known to relieve stress, is likely to reduce depression by reestablishing homeostasis in the HPA system.

Does exercise produce a runner's high? Research findings on exercise and mood show that prolonged, submaximal exercise produces endorphins, whereas short bouts of acute exercise produce norepinephrine. Prolonged vigorous exercise causes peripheral increases in the level of endorphins; however, more research is necessary to determine how endorphins, which are known to exist in the blood, may affect the brain. Interviews with runners suggest that running has two phases: the NE phase, followed by the endorphin phase.

Finally, the health benefits of exercise are more attainable when integrated into one's daily routine. Such minor lifestyle modifications as using the stairs, walking the dog longer, vigorous mall shopping, and getting away from your computer can result in longer life and improved happiness.

21

Meaningful Engagement of Talents

The artist, at the moment of creating, does not experience grati-
fication or satisfaction. . . . Rather it is a joy, joy defined as the
emotion that goes with heightened consciousness, the mood that
comes with the experience of actualizing one's own potentialities.

—Rollo May, *The Courage to Create*

Introduction: Capitalizing on Abilities and Strengths

Howard Gardner (1983, 1993; Hatch & Gardner, 1993) points our attention to children who, at a very early age, evidence great talent in such domains
as music, art, mathematics, language, and athletics. Since prodigies appear
only in certain areas of endeavor, these proclivities seem to tap biological
abilities inherent in the human species. Gardner views intelligence as a plural
characteristic, that is, a set of distinct and specific abilities.

Gardner (1983) initially formulated a provisional list of seven intelligences.
As described below, linguistic and logical-mathematical abilities are traditionally valued in schools; musical, bodily-kinesthetic, and spatial abilities are usually associated with the arts; intrapersonal and interpersonal capacities are
referred to as "personal intelligences" (Gardner, 1999). M. K. Smith (2008) outlined the components of Gardner's pluralistic model of intelligence as follows:

Linguistic intelligence involves sensitivity to spoken and written language, the ability to learn languages, and the capacity to use language to
accomplish certain goals. This intelligence includes the ability to effectively use language to express oneself rhetorically or poetically, and as a
means to remember information. Writers, poets, lawyers, and speakers
are among those that Gardner (1983, 1993) sees as having high linguistic intelligence.

Logical-mathematical intelligence consists of the capacity to analyze problems logically, carry out mathematical operations, and investigate issues

scientifically. It encompasses the ability to detect patterns, reason deductively, and think logically. This intelligence is most often associated with scientific and mathematical thinking.

Musical intelligence involves skill in the performance, composition, and appreciation of musical patterns. It encompasses the capacity to recognize and compose musical pitches, tones, and rhythms. According to Gardner (1983, 1993), musical intelligence runs in an almost structural parallel to linguistic intelligence.

Bodily-kinesthetic intelligence entails the potential of using one's whole body or parts of one's body to solve problems. It is the ability to use mental abilities to coordinate bodily movements. Gardner (1983, 1993) sees mental and physical activity as related.

Spatial intelligence involves the potential to recognize and use the patterns of wide space and confined areas.

Interpersonal intelligence is concerned with the capacity to understand the intentions, motivations, and desires of other people. It allows people to work effectively with others. Educators, salespeople, religious and political leaders, and counselors all need a well-developed interpersonal intelligence.

Intrapersonal intelligence entails the capacity to understand oneself and to appreciate one's feelings, fears, and motivations. In Gardner's (1983, 1993) view, it involves having an effective working model of ourselves, and being able to use such information to regulate our lives.

Since Gardner's (1983) original formulation of multiple intelligences, he and his colleagues have examined the possibility of additional constructs for intelligence: naturalistic, spiritual, existential, and moral (Gardner, 1999). After much research and scholarly discussion of the four proposed contructs, *naturalist intelligence*—one that permits humans to recognize, categorize, and draw upon certain features of the environment—has been added to the list. Gardner (1983) believes that the challenge of effectively utilizing human capital is "how to best take advantage of the uniqueness conferred on us as a species exhibiting several intelligences" (p. 45).

The manifestation of any intellectual trait is most likely the result of the combination of innate propensity and environmental support. While intelligence is traditionally considered as the "ability to solve problems," psychologists posit a "group of 'hot' intelligences, so called because they process 'hot' information: signals concerning motives, feelings, and other domains of direct relevance to an individual's well-being and survival" (Peterson & Seligman, 2004, p. 338). When intelligence is considered in the context of evolution, the brain would be expected to provide reward (neurochemically mediated pleasure) upon realization of one's intellectual capacity. There is an abundance of corroborative evidence to support this view.

Csikszentmihalyi was intrigued by the stories of artists who lost themselves in the passion for their work. Over the past 30 years, he has interviewed and observed thousands of people who described the experience as being in a state of "flow." Nakamura and Csikszentmihalyi (2002) characterize flow as follows:

- Intense and focused concentration on what one is doing in that present moment
- Merging of action and awareness
- Loss of reflective self-consciousness (i.e., loss of awareness of oneself as a social actor)
- A sense that one can control one's actions—that is, a sense that one can, in principle, deal with the situation because one knows how to respond to whatever happens next
- Distorting of temporal experience, typically a sense that time has passed faster than normal
- Experience of the activity as intrinsically rewarding such that often the end goal is just an excuse for the process

Csikszentmihalyi (1975, 2000) graphically depicted the necessary elements and trajectory of flow experiences by comparing relationships between perceived challenges and skills. As shown in Figure 21.1, three domains of momentary experience were identified: (1) *flow*—when an individual is profoundly engaged in a task, feeling competent and fulfilled; (2) *boredom*—a lack of interest and a sense of discomfort when opportunities to perform are

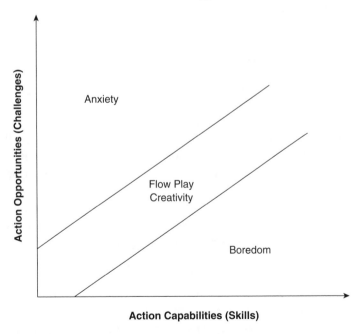

Figure 21.1   **The original model of the flow state.** Flow is experienced when perceived opportunities for action are in balance with the actor's perceived skills.

SOURCE: Adapted from *Flow: The psychology of optimal experience* by M. Csikszentmihalyi, 1990, New York: HarperCollins, p. 74.

too easy relative to one's skills; and (3) *anxiety*—a sense of discomfort when demands of the task at hand exceed one's ability to perform.

The likelihood of achieving a state of flow increases as challenges and skills move beyond an individual's average level. Whatever the type of intelligence (e.g., music, art, mathematics, sports), the desired state of "flow" requires pushing the envelope beyond one's comfort zone (e.g., in sports, your opponent may have a bit more skill; in mathematics, the answers are not so easy to come by; in art, the task requires heightened attention and deep concentration).

Longitudinal studies provide evidence of the positive relationship between flow and long-term success. Csikszentmihalyi, Rathunde, and Whalen (1993) followed the development of teenagers throughout high school. Students who, at the age of 17, were committed to a talent (academics, work, or sports) reported having experienced their talent as a source of flow 4 years earlier during the initial data gathering when they were 13 years old. Similarly, Heine (1996) showed that students who excelled in the second half of a math class (controlling for initial abilities and grade point average) were the ones who experienced flow in the first half. Extrapolating from these findings, attributes such as commitment and perseverance—factors necessary for lasting satisfaction and success—are related and are possible offshoots from the experience of flow. "The experience of absorption provides intrinsic rewards that encourage persistence and return to the activity" (Snyder & Lopez, 2007, p. 258).

Integrating Models for Self-Discovery and Change

The implication of flow research is that pleasure, achievement, satisfaction, and productivity are enhanced by access to states of flow. Csikszentmihalyi (1990, 1996) and his colleagues (Csikszentmihalyi & Robinson, 1990; Jackson & Csikszentmihalyi, 1999) and Perry (1999) describe two paths to becoming meaningfully engaged in one's talents or abilities: (1) identifying and shaping environments that are conducive to flow experiences, and (2) identifying personal characteristics and attentional skills that can be honed to make the experience of flow more likely.

With the goal of facilitating natural highs for at-risk youth as healthy alternatives to drugs, crime, and emotional distress, Milkman and colleagues (Milkman, 2001; Milkman, Wanberg, & Robinson, 1996) integrated Gardner's theory of multiple intelligences and Csikszentmihalyi's conceptualization of flow. Youth were recruited from three at-risk populations: (1) criminal justice referrals from probation and parole, (2) mental health referrals from the department of social services, and (3) students at risk for suspension or expulsion from high school. They were encouraged to join Project Self-Discovery (PSD) to discover and expand their abilities and talents.

The results of offering art in students' preferred area of interest (music, dance, or visual art), adventure-based counseling (beyond the comfort zone), and cognitive-behavioral psychology (interpersonal and intrapersonal intelligences) to transform the lives of this "covert" treatment population are striking. Milkman et al. (1996, 2001) were able to show that PSD had a positive impact on participants by increasing their ability to use artistic involvement to replace drugs and crime.

The spirit of this unique program is captured through the case example, "Better Than Dope," presented below.

Case Example: Better Than Dope[1]

"Living" is a word David never understood. To him, living meant running for his life from gangs and guns. It meant trying to avoid drugs and drinking. It meant being afraid. When he was growing up, he lived in a bad neighborhood. Down the street from him was a group of the worst people you would ever wish to avoid. He had to walk past them every day. In his neighborhood, death was an everyday occurrence; he fell asleep to the sound of gunshots.

At home, his mother had men visiting at all hours. She would ignore David and his sisters. She loved to drink with her men friends. When she let one of them move in, he thought he was king of the world. He would beat David and his sisters. David missed his dad because his dad didn't beat him. His dad didn't treat him like dirt. Still, he wasn't a stable father figure, either. In fact, David didn't have an adult male figure he could talk with.

At school, he didn't think he would fit in. At lunch hour, he would sit by himself. Later, he figured the only way to fit in was by using drugs and drinking. When he joined the Junior Reserves Officers Training Corps, he found the common link was doing drugs. The more he hung out with this crowd, the more he used drugs. Because of his habits, he was failing most of his classes. During his sophomore year, he went to class only 9 days. Soon, he didn't go at all. His life fueled his self-loathing. He hated himself so much, he even attempted suicide. He tried a number of methods—hanging himself, overdosing on aspirin, and drinking way beyond any safe amount.

At about that time, he started to eat a lot. In less than a year, he had gained over 100 pounds. He was so alienated from his family that he barely spoke to his mom. Whenever she asked to talk, he would tell her to go to hell. Sadly, she also began abusing drugs, which made their relationship even worse. She had her drug addiction and David had his. Then, at age 16, David had a mild heart attack. The drugs were the reason behind his heart problems. Right then, he decided to quit.

After that summer, he enrolled in school. His guidance counselor told David about Project Self-Discovery. PSD is a community-based, after-school program that provides artistic alternatives to teenagers who have problems with school, their family, or the community. Participants use music, art, and dance to reach their goals. Students also receive school credit for attending. David signed up for the music program.

Although David's story is unique, his needs are similar to the majority of youth who participate in the project. Artistic activities have proven to be powerful antidotes to emotional distress, drug abuse, crime, and violence. In fact, PSD evolved into a model for treating a broad spectrum of teenage problems.

At PSD, one could find youths with varied backgrounds and behaviors.

Betty Jo, a 15-year-old African American, lives at Daybreak, a community corrections residential placement. She describes her mother as "a bitch" and "evil," and she (Betty Jo) has attempted suicide twice by overdosing on Tylenol. Betty Jo's art teacher says she is interacting nicely with other students and "demonstrates an orderly, precise, and methodical way of working on projects."

(Continued)

(Continued)

Peter, age 16, is diagnosed as schizoaffective. Since the age of 8, he bounced around foster homes, some of which were sexually abusive. Now in custody of the Department of Social Services, he is excited about learning to act at PSD so he will be "noticed" and begin his career in theater arts. His dance teacher reports that he is interacting well with his peers while benefiting from her coaching and her advice.

Rosa, a 15-year-old Latina, has decided to never again "bang" with her sect of the gang, Gangster Disciples. Five of her close friends have died or have been murdered during the past year. She is considered highly motivated by her music teacher and is getting along well with her fellow students and staff.

The usual outcome for these kids is enormous frustration and failure. These teenagers have a variety of mental disorders and behavioral problems and come from radically diverse backgrounds. Why does participation in a community arts program engender hope and dramatic improvements? In the United States, 10% to 20% of the 30 million youth between the ages of 10 and 17 experience emotional or behavioral problems (Costello & Angold, 1999; D. Shaffer et al., 1996). Forty percent of their waking time is "discretionary." In fact, the majority of teenage crimes are committed between 3 in the afternoon and midnight (Felson & Poulsen, 2003). During these hours, there is little structure or guidance from the community. For these teenagers, a forum for positive self-expression is vital.

The inspiration for PSD came from viewing substance abuse as just one of many forms of dangerous pleasure-seeking behaviors (Jessor, 1998; Milkman & Sunderwirth, 1983, 1987, 1993, 1998; H. J. Shaffer, LaPlante, et al., 2004). Any action that deposits a hearty dose of dopamine in the brain's reward center—be it drink, money, sex, calories, crime, or cocaine—can trigger addiction. Yet rather than using drugs, people can actually bring about self-induced changes in brain chemistry through natural highs.

Drugs and alcohol are seen as "chemical prostitutes," or counterfeit molecules that compromise the clockwork of nature's most complex and delicate entity: the brain. According to the Monitoring the Future Survey, 29% of high school twelfth graders reported having "been drunk" sometime in the past month. The prevalence rates for marijuana use in the past year are 10%, 25%, and 32% for Grades 8, 10, and 12, respectively. The annual prevalence rate for the use of Ecstasy by twelfth graders was 4.1% in 2007 (Johnston et al., 2008; refer to Chapter 15 for additional statistics).

PSD began serving teenagers in January 1993 as the result of a 4-year national grant through the Center for Substance Abuse Prevention. The project was designed to show that natural highs could serve as viable alternatives to drug abuse and associated high-risk lifestyles. Teenagers were targeted because of their extreme vulnerability to substance abuse, crime, and violence. The most common causes of death among young adults between ages 15 and 24 are alcohol-related accidents at 46%, homicide at 15%, and suicide at 13% (Stibich, 2007). Juan talks about his brush with death in the description that follows.

The Hood

They came up the dirt hill. There were eight or nine of them and there was just six of us. My homeboy gave me a .25. It was already loaded, cocked, and ready to bust some caps. So I went up to them and said, "I know you, the punk motherfucker who just tagged up my locker. You disrespected my hood. Just kill me motherfucker. Get it over with." So he pulls out this crowbar. And I pulled out the .25. I put it to his head and said, "What hood you from?' He said "CMG Blood." And I said "WHAT FUCKIN' HOOD YOU FROM?" And he said, "CMG Blood." Then he said, "Crip." I made that fool cry and shit. When you gotta strap [gun], you feel like you got the power to do anything in the world. You can make anybody scared of you with a strap.

—Juan

While dance connects one to sensuality, music provides a safe vehicle for the expression of emotional unrest. Painting and drawing provide an opportunity to visualize topics that may be too difficult for words. In this excerpt from Paula's script, it is evident that through writing and drama, she is discovering important means to transcend the wounds of her childhood.

The Family

He's my father. I don't even know what that means. I don't even know what a father is. I don't even know what a father is supposed to be. I used to think it was someone who took me fishing, or maybe camping. Someone who I could talk to, who protected me, took care of me. But if you ask me, I'd say a father is someone who beats up his family. A father is someone who screams, yells, and cusses out his family. A father is someone who breaks things, smashes things, ruins things. I HATE HIM! I HATE THIS HOUSE WHEN HE'S IN IT! It's like a war zone and he is the enemy. Every second, I'm looking over my shoulder to see if he's coming after me. He didn't tear up my drawings. He tore up my dreams. I HATE HIM! I hate it when he beats on my mom. I hate seeing my mother on the floor; I hate feeling like I have to protect her from the enemy and I HATE THAT THE ENEMY IS HIM. WHY AM I PROTECTING THE ENEMY? He's my father. I love him.

—Paula

At-risk teens experience traditional talking therapies as invasive and persecutory. We have discovered that adventure-based counseling, using hands-on games and physical challenges—like using stilts to "feel 10 feet tall"—are far more engaging than standard lecture presentations. A kid who has a strong drive for thrill seeking and novelty can avoid gang violence by satisfying his needs through the performance of poetry, hip hop, or rap. Almost magically, the conga, paintbrush, or guitar can become formidable substitutes for pistols or joints.

It is no secret that people who are hopelessly dependent on drugs can still participate in the creative process. The necessary complement to artistic skill development is learning to restructure habitual patterns of thought (e.g., "I can't cope") and feelings (e.g., fear, anger, sadness) that trigger destructive actions (e.g., drugs, crime, violence). We raise the question, "What else is possible?" To this end, PSD youth participated in a 32-session life-skills curriculum entitled Pathways to Self-Discovery and Change (PSD-C): A Guide for Responsible Living (Milkman & Wanberg, 2005). The Pathways curriculum, now widely used in youth correctional and substance abuse treatment settings in the United States and abroad, is predicated upon the use of modeling, role-plays, skits, comic strips, and interactive exercises to groove in neuropsychological pathways for prosocial thought and behavior.

The client's workbook (PSD-C) is geared toward a range of reading and conceptual abilities and uses comic strip illustrations (e.g., Figure 21.2) and interesting stories that are presented through the narrative voice of adolescents who experience a broad spectrum of problems with substance abuse, criminal conduct, and mental health issues. This allows the clients to engage in active discussion about the situations, thoughts, emotions, and behaviors that have become embroidered in life problems. An excerpt from Jeb's Story is shown below.

I started smoking weed when I was 12. I didn't really listen to my mom when she gave me her anti-drug lecture. After all, what did she know? She was always at work anyway. So I started hanging out with the people around my block, and realized that there was a potential job scene. People wanted drugs, but they couldn't get them on a regular basis. That is when I became a drug pusher. I could make money, they could get their drugs, and I wasn't hurting anyone by doing it. After all, these people already chose their path in life.

(Continued)

(Continued)

CHAPTER 1

Building Trust and Motivation to Change

JEB'S STORY

GOAL OF THIS CHAPTER

To discuss the progam

Getting to know each other

To learn how thoughts affect feeling and actions

To recognize the importance of change

Figure 21.2   **Jeb's story.** Comic strip illustrations are used to engage client interest in cognitive-behavioral restructuring.

SOURCE: From *Criminal Conduct and Substance Abuse Treatment for Adolescents: Pathways to Self-Discovery and Change* by H. Milkman & K. Wanberg, 2005, Thousand Oaks, CA: Sage Publications, Inc.

Things were going good until some other dealers moved into the neighborhood. They were selling cheaper drugs, and I had to struggle to keep up with my old customers. I started pushing on the streets instead of just quitting the game. Ended up trying to sell to an undercover, and now I'm here in jail, waiting to be tried as an adult.

Figure 21.3 shows the visual model used throughout the curriculum for restructuring thoughts, emotions, and actions. Events experienced by an individual trigger automatic thoughts (shaped by underlying beliefs), which are then translated into emotions that lead to behaviors. As presented in Chapter 16, if an individual chooses a positive (adaptive) course of action (through rational thought and emotional control), or opts against a negative one (distorted thought and emotional dysregulation), the outcome will likely be good, which strengthens the recurrence of positive behavior and encourages positive thought processes. Conversely, if the individual chooses a negative (maladaptive) course of action, the outcome will likely be bad, strengthening more negative thought processes (Milkman & Wanberg, 2007).

David describes his experience in the Pathways course:

We gathered in a theater and talked about our past experiences with gangs, drugs, and all the other things that teens face. We also talked about ways we could avoid these situations. I tried to be quiet, but my mouth would just shoot open. When it came to bad situations, I thought that I had a lot to offer the group.

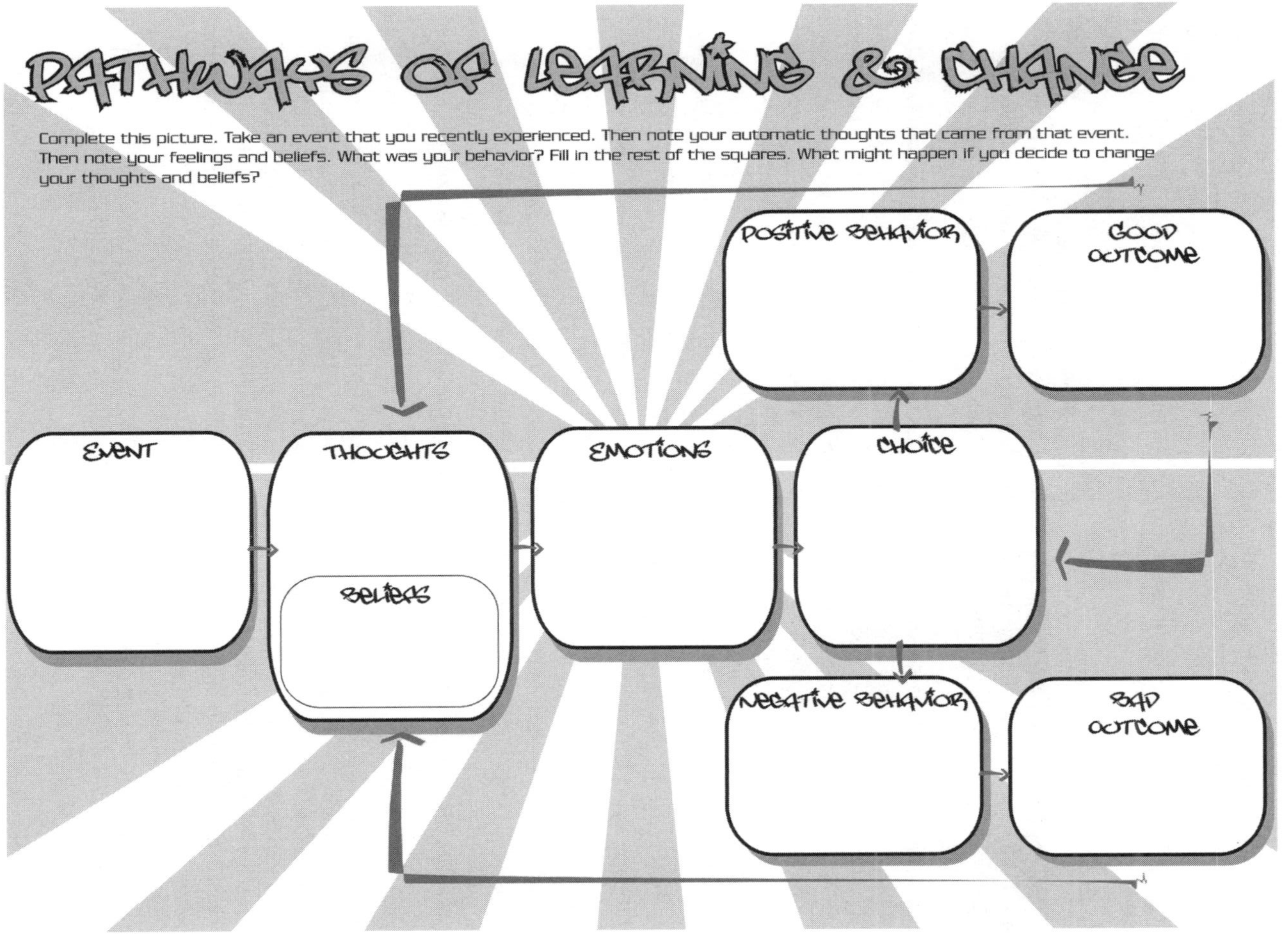

Figure 21.3 **Pathways to learning and change.** The cognitive-behavioral map for change is artistically enhanced to appeal to the teenage mind-set.

(Continued)

David was making great progress. He had successfully embarked on the first stage of our three-tiered program, each phase providing the foundation for the next level of growth and change. Level I, called the Intervention Program, lasted 12 weeks and the youth met after school for 3 hours, 2 days a week. Level II, the Graduate Program, was on an ongoing, scheduled meeting one afternoon a week. Level III, the Mentorship Program, allowed graduate students who had demonstrated leadership skills to serve as facilitators and mentors to youth in the initial, 12-week Intervention Program.

The Rites of Passage is another component designed to transform the participants. Here is David's description:

> We went up to the mountains and froze our butts off for the sake of getting to know each other and ourselves. There was a ropes course that scared me beyond belief. I had always thought that I was afraid of nothing. But we were hooked up to a rope that was connected to a wire between two large poles. I kept thinking, I am going to die.

When David hooked up his harness, everyone in the group started to cheer for him. Suddenly, his face took on a funny expression, like the Grinch learning the meaning of Christmas. "I got the strength to hurry through the course and when I got down, it felt as though a huge weight had been lifted off my shoulders." Later that night, the kids and staff sat in the cabin and talked about the course, and all the students wrote in their journals about their day. The thing that David remembers most was "the acceptance between everyone."

Around the campfire, all participants shared their thoughts. David, for example, spoke about his drug abuse and his plans for the future: "When we returned from the mountains, I felt a change in me."

David stayed with the program for 2 additional years. He learned the guitar and the drums, performed on stage, acted in a video film, and became a mentor for others who were new to the program. He felt wanted and he helped others realize they were wanted, too.

The results of PSD have been impressive. During 10 years of program operation (1992–2002), PSD received 1,700 referrals from Denver-area youth advocates. Short- and long-term outcome data show that artistic endeavor and adventure-based counseling are effective antidotes to drugs and other high-risk behaviors (Milkman, 2001; Milkman et al., 1996). Not only do participants show test scores reflecting improved mental health and family functioning, but they also reveal decreased reliance on negative peer influences and decreased drug and alcohol use. These positive outcomes are sustained long after graduation.

As David puts it, because of PSD he has "become a better person." He has learned how to care for others and himself. "Without this experience, I don't know what I would be doing. I would probably be living on the streets using drugs, and not having any direction," he says.

Today, David shares a house with an old friend from school, has a full-time job, and visits his mother once a week. He has also started boxing to relieve stress and lose weight. And for the last 4 years, he has been completely drug free. He plans to go to college and major in business and computer science. In David's words,

> PSD showed me that the world is full of possibilities. The program also showed me that when a door is closed a window is open. What does living mean to me now? Living is knowing that you are not alone.

Project Self-Discovery demonstrated that so-called at-risk youth are amenable to positive growth and development, providing that the means for engagement are perceived as nonjudgmental, adventurous, and creatively rewarding. Those who completed the program showed significant improvements on scores that measure mental health, resistance to negative peers, sustained drug or alcohol use, criminal conduct, and family functioning.

Self-Discovery in Everyday Life

The positive outcomes derived from participation in PSD show that many types of dysfunctional patterns of thinking, feeling, and acting are improved though artistic engagement, adventure-based counseling, and cognitive-behavioral restructuring. These results seem almost too good to be true. How could a single program be restorative for so many different types of problems?

Certainly the common malaise of depression underlies many faces of emotional and behavioral disorder. In *Listening to Prozac*, Kramer (1997) convincingly argues that there are many manifestations of mood disorders with a common biological underpinning—low levels of the neurotransmitter serotonin. Prozac seems to have beneficial effects on a range of personality problems, including shyness; sensitivity to rejection; obsessive traits; and of course, depression. From our discussion of the reward cascade in Chapter 2, we learned that by increasing the availability of serotonin (common to Prozac and other SSRIs), the flow of dopamine is increased in the nucleus accumbens. But the jury is still out on the wisdom of relying so heavily on antidepressant medications. Recent discoveries in brain science point to the conclusion that a broad array of mood disturbances and problem behaviors can be effectively reduced through behavioral means (Lambert, 2008). The data suggest that the flow of dopamine can be enhanced through anticipating and engaging in complex and challenging tasks, that is, meaningful engagement of talents.

Lambert (2008) was intrigued by research reports of dramatically increased rates of depression among those born in the middle third of the 20th century compared with those who were born in the first third. In fact, one study showed that the rate of depression was 10 times greater for people born in the latter part of the 20th century than it was for those born earlier. Lambert reasoned that since the anatomy of the human brain probably has not changed much in the last few decades, the answer to the question of increased rates of depression probably resides in lifestyle changes. We have dramatically decreased our reliance on physical effort to enhance survival. Microwave ovens eliminate the complex tasks of food preparation, computers save us from retyping our manuscripts, and online games save us from scuffing our knees playing schoolyard sports.

Our brains are programmed to receive rewards when we carry out tasks that enhance our survival. When our physical effort produces something tangible, that is, visible and meaningful toward survival, we are hardwired to derive a deep sense of satisfaction and pleasure. Lambert (2008) refers to this emotional payoff as "effort-driven rewards" (p. 33). These rewards are rooted in the chemical messages and neural infrastructure of our brain.

As shown in Figure 21.4, the nucleus accumbens, which we have discussed throughout this book as the brain's primary pleasure center, is positioned in close proximity to the motor system, or striatum, and the

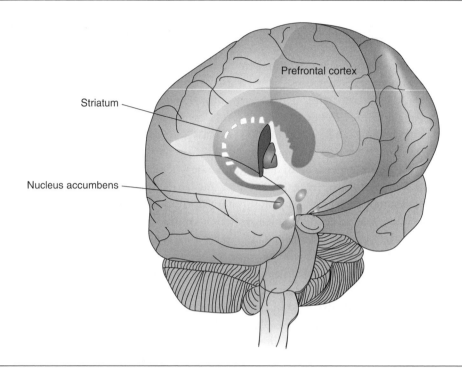

Figure 21.4   Accumbens-striatal-cortical network. The nucleus accumbens forms a critical interface between the motor system (striatum) and the prefrontal cortex that controls thought.

SOURCE: Adapted from Lambert, K. (2008, August/September). Depressingly Easy. *Scientific American Mind,* 33.

limbic system, a series of structures that control emotions and learning. The closely linked motor and emotional systems also extend to our frontal cortex, which is a vast assembly of neurons responsible for problem solving, planning, and judgment. "Essentially the accumbens is a critical interface between our emotions and our actions. . . . It is the proposed neuroanatomical network underlying the symptoms of depression" (Lambert, 2008, p. 35). In fact, according to Lambert, all of the major symptoms of depression can be correlated to a brain part on the accumbens-striatal-cortical network. "Loss of pleasure? The nucleus accumbens. Sluggishness and slow motor responses? The striatum. Negative feelings? The limbic system. Poor concentration? The prefrontal cortex" (p. 35).

The upshot of this analysis is that "effort-driven rewards" derived from the accumbens-striatal-cortical network are seen as behavioral antidotes to depression. By engaging in complex tasks that engage our innate capacities for multiple intelligences (e.g., kinesthetic, spatial, musical), we can achieve a state of neurochemical balance conducive to happiness and well-being. Engaging one's talents such as playing a favorite sport, sketching a waterfall, hip hop dancing, or campaigning for political office—especially if the activities are perceived as meaningful—is likely to charge up the reward cascade. Through meaningful engagement of talents, we can orchestrate the natural release of serotonin, endorphins, and dopamine, thereby reducing our reliance on alcohol, drugs, or other false props to improve mental and physical well-being.

The Personal Pleasure Inventory

A secret to deriving happiness and meaning in life is to integrate an array of enjoyable activities with the values that guide our existence. Too often we remain largely unaware of not only our value priorities, but also the very activities we find enjoyable. By bringing our pleasure orientations to the forefront of our awareness, we increase the likelihood of achieving a balance between what we deem important and the things we actually do. Wanberg and Milkman (2008) have classified the kinds of activities from which human beings derive pleasure. After having administered the *Personal Pleasure Inventory* (PPI) to a diverse population of adults, four broad pleasure dimensions have been identified: (1) Physical Expression, (2) Self-Focus, (3) Aesthetic Discovery, and (4) Collective Harmony.

Each dimension is defined by a specific group of related activities. The dimension of *Physical Expression* includes sports, challenging nature, and physical fitness. Within the dimension of *Self-Focus* are the factors for romance, calming sensations, and material comforts. The dimension of *Aesthetic Discovery* includes seeking adventure, enjoying nature, home involvement, mental relaxation, and artistic stimulation. *Collective Harmony* combines the factors of mental exercise, people closeness, spiritual involvement, and helping others. Pleasure orientations are not mutually exclusive; that is, aesthetic appreciation of music and art may coincide with pleasurable stimulation derived from learning to play a musical instrument, combined with joy from playing with others.

Readers are invited to complete the Personal Pleasure Inventory as presented in the Appendix. The scoring system allows respondents to measure themselves on the 15 aforementioned pleasure orientations. By focusing on the activities from which you derive pleasure, not only will you become more mindful of your needs and desires, but you will also begin to pursue more goal-directed pathways to pleasure. By challenging yourself to engage more deeply in your identified pleasure preferences, you will most likely orchestrate natural highs.

Chapter Summary

At a very early age, some children show tremendous talent in such areas as music, art, mathematics, language, and athletics. These talents appear to tap biological abilities inherent in the human species. Howard Gardner views intelligence as a plural characteristic, that is, a set of distinct and specific abilities. Gardner initially formulated a provisional list of seven intelligences. Linguistic and logical-mathematical abilities; musical, bodily-kinesthetic, and spatial abilities; and intrapersonal and interpersonal capacities ("personal intelligences"). After much research and scholarly discussion, naturalist intelligence has been added to the list. Gardner believes that the challenge of the future is to effectively capitalize on our species' unique capacity for multiple intelligences.

Csikszentmihalyi was intrigued by the stories of artists who lost themselves in the passion for their work. Over 30 years, he and his colleagues developed the concept of "flow": intense and focused concentration on what one is doing, merging of action and awareness, loss of reflective self-consciousness, a sense that one can control one's actions, distorting of temporal experience, and experience of the activity as intrinsically rewarding.

The likelihood of achieving a state of flow increases as challenges and skills move beyond an individual's average level. Whatever the type of intelligence (e.g., music, art, writing, mathematics, sports), the desired state of flow requires pushing the envelope beyond one's comfort zone. Longitudinal studies provide evidence of the positive relationship between flow and long-term success. Extrapolating from these research studies, such attributes as commitment and perseverance—factors necessary for lasting satisfaction and success—are related and possible offshoots from the experience of flow. The experience of absorption provides intrinsic rewards that encourage persistence and return to the activity.

The implication of flow research is that pleasure, achievement, satisfaction, and productivity are enhanced by access to states of flow. Csikszentmihalyi and his colleagues describe two paths to becoming fully absorbed in one's talents or abilities: (1) identifying and shaping environments conducive to flow experiences, and (2) identifying personal characteristics and attentional skills that can be honed to make the experience of flow more likely.

With the goal of facilitating natural highs as healthy alternatives to drugs, crime, and emotional distress, Milkman and colleagues integrated Gardner's theory of multiple intelligences and Csikszentmihalyi's conceptualization of flow, resulting in a program for at-risk high school students called Project Self-Discovery. Program participants showed evidence of improved mental health and family functioning, and they also experienced decreased reliance on negative peer influences and decreased drug and alcohol use. These positive outcomes were sustained long after graduation.

Results of the PSD program show that many types of dysfunctional patterns of thinking, feeling, and acting are improved though artistic engagement, adventure-based counseling, and cognitive-behavioral restructuring. Recent discoveries in brain science point to the conclusion that a broad array of mood disturbances and problem behaviors can be effectively reduced through behavioral means. The data suggest that the flow of dopamine,

which leads to absorption, commitment, and success in personally meaningful tasks, can be enhanced through anticipating and engaging in complex
and challenging multisensory activities. Readers are invited to complete
the Personal Pleasure Inventory in the Appendix to become more mindful of
the activities and experiences that are likely to promote natural highs.

Note

1. Project Self-Discovery: Artistic Alternatives to Teenage Drug Abuse, Crime,
and Violence received the 2000 Coming Up Taller Award from the National
Endowments for the Arts and Humanities and the President's Committee on the Arts
and the Humanities—one of 10 programs nationwide to receive this honor.

Appendix_____

The Personal Pleasure Inventory

Personal Pleasure Inventory: Using one of the five choices below, rate the degree of pleasure you get from each activity. Place the number (0 through 4) of your choice on the blank line by the activity.

0 = Never engaged in activity or no pleasure derived from activity

1 = Low degree of pleasure derived

2 = Moderate degree of pleasure derived

3 = High degree of pleasure derived

4 = Very high degree of pleasure derived

WORKSHEET

1. SPORTS

____ Playing basketball
____ Tennis
____ Watching sports
____ Softball
____ Going to sporting events
____ Playing golf
____ Playing team sports
____ Playing volleyball

Total Score___

2. CHALLENGING NATURE

____ Climbing
____ Canoeing
____ White water rafting
____ Camping out
____ Hiking
____ Skiing/snowboarding

Total Score___

3. PHYSICAL FITNESS

____ Eating healthy foods
____ Exercising/stretching
____ Biking/rollerblading
____ Swimming
____ Walking/running

Total Score___

4. ROMANCE

____ Making love
____ Kissing and cuddling
____ Giving gifts to your lover
____ Sharing intimate moments
____ Being together in nature

Total Score___

5. CALMING SENSATIONS

____ Listening to soft music
____ Warming self by fire
____ Soaking in hot tub
____ Having back rubbed
____ Massage
____ Eating in nice restaurant

Total Score___

Personal Pleasure Inventory, (Continued)

6. MATERIAL COMFORTS

____ Making money
____ Shopping/spending money
____ Taking a luxury vacation
____ Having a nice car
____ Improving outward appearance

Total Score___

7. SEEKING ADVENTURE

____ Driving to new places
____ Visiting different cities
____ Experiencing new places
____ Experiencing new things
____ Traveling to foreign cities
____ Visiting different cultures

Total Score___

8. ENJOYING NATURE

____ Being in nature
____ Being in the woods/mountains/ seashore
____ Watching wildlife
____ Watching the stars/moon
____ Watching the sunrise/sunset

Total Score___

9. HOME INVOLVEMENT

____ Redecorating your home
____ Remodeling your home
____ Working on home projects
____ Painting your house
____ Working in the yard and gardening

Total Score___

10. MENTAL RELAXATION

____ Meditation
____ Relaxation exercises
____ Yoga
____ Self-reflection
____ Journal writing

Total Score___

11. ARTISTIC STIMULATION

____ Going to movies/theater/concerts
____ Going to museums/art galleries
____ Creating art work
____ Reading books/poetry/fiction
____ Writing poetry/fiction

____ Playing musical instrument
Total Score___

12. MENTAL EXERCISE

____ Word games
____ Playing cards/board games
____ Crossword or other puzzles
____ Solving mystery games
____ Playing computer games

Total Score___

13. PEOPLE CLOSENESS

____ Helping family members
____ Playing with children
____ Being with family
____ Time with friends
____ Hugging
____ Being with your partner

Total Score___

14. RELIGIOUS INVOLVEMENT

____ Spiritual thinking
____ Worship
____ Religious study
____ Church work
____ Going to services
____ Praying/meditation

Total Score___

15. HELPING OTHERS

____ Counseling others
____ Helping others
____ Teaching others
____ Volunteering services
____ Supporting friends or family

Total Score___

END OF INVENTORY

When you have finished, put the total score for each group of activities on the Total Score line. Then, put that score on the PPI Profile. Find your score on the row for each activity and mark it with an X. Find your percentile rank for that activity. The percentile score shows how you compare with a sample of adult men and women. For example, if your raw score for SPORTS is 15, you enjoy this pleasure activity more than 65% of the people in that sample.

NAME: _____ DATE: _____ GENDER: _____ ☐ MALE ☐ FEMALE AGE: _____

	RAW SCORE	LOW		LOW-MEDIUM			HIGH-MEDIUM			HIGH	
DECILE RANK		1	2	3	4	5	6	7	8	9	10
PHYSICAL — 1. SPORTS		0 2 3 4	5 6 7	8 9 10	11 12	13	14 15	16 17	18 19 20	21 22 23	24 26 32
2. CHALLENGING NATURE		0 2 3 5	6 7	8	9 10	11 12	13	14 15	16 17	18 19	20 21 24
3. PHYSICAL FITNESS		2 5 6 7	8	10	11		12	13	14	15	16 18 20
SELF FOCUS — 4. ROMANCE		1 6 8 9	10 11 12	13	14	15	16	17	18		19 20
5. CALMING SENSATIONS		4 10 11	12 13 14	15	16	17	18	19	20	21 22	23 24
6. MATERIAL COMFORTS		4 7 8 9	10 11	12	13	14	15	16	17	18	19 20
AESTHETIC DISCOVERY — 7. SEEKING ADVENTURE		4 7 8 9	10 11 12	13	14 15	16	17 18	19	20 21	22	23 24
8. ENJOYING NATURE		1 6 7 8	9 10	11	12	13	14	15	16 17	18	19 20
9. HOME INVOLVEMENT		0 1 2	3	4	5 6	7	8	9	10	11 12 13	14 15 20
10. MENTAL RELAXATION		0 1 2	3	4	5	6	7	8	9 10	11 12	13 15 20
11. ARTISTIC STIMULATION		0 2 3	4 5 6	7	8	9	10 11	12	13 14	15 16 17	18 20 24
HARMONY — 12. MENTAL EXERCISE		0 1 2	3 4	5	6	7		8	9	10 11	12 14 20
13. PEOPLE CLOSENESS		4 11 12	13 14	15 16	17	18	19	20	21	22	23 24
14. RELIGIOUS INVOLVEMENT		0	1 2	3	4 5	6	7 8	9 10	11 12	13 14 15	16 19 24
15. HELPING OTHERS		1 6 7	8	9	10	11	12	13	14	15	16 17 20
PERCENTILE	0	10	20	30	40	50	60	70	80	90	99

SOURCE: *The personal pleasure inventory*, Wanberg, Milkman and Harrison.
Copyright 2009 © K.W. Wanberg and H.B. Milkman

405

References _____

Acohido, B., & Swartz, J. (2005). Meth addicts' other habit: Online theft. In H. T. Wilson (Ed.), *Annual editions: Drugs, society, and behavior 2007/2008* (pp. 117–121). Dubuque, IA: McGraw-Hill. (Originally published in *USA Today,* December 15, 2005)

Adler, A. (1956). *The individual psychology of Alfred Adler* (H. Rowena & R. Ansbacher, Eds.). New York: Basic Books.

Adler, J. (2007, November 5). Rehab reality check. *Newsweek.* Retrieved July 9, 2008, from http://www.newsweek.com/id/68441

Ainsworth, M. D. S. (1979). Infant-mother attachment. *American Psychologist, 34,* 932–937.

Ainsworth, M. D. S., Bell, S. M., & Stayton, D. J. (1992). Infant-mother attachment and social development: "Socialization" as a product of reciprocal responsiveness to signals. In M. Woodhead, R. Carr, & P. Light (Eds.), *Becoming a person* (pp. 30–55). London: Routledge.

Ainsworth, M. D. S., Blehar, M. C., Waters, E., & Wall, S. (1978). *Patterns of attachment: Assessed in the strange situation and at home.* Hillsdale, NJ: Lawrence Erlbaum.

Ainsworth, M. D. S., & Bowlby, J. (1991). An ethological approach to personality development. *American Psychologist, 46,* 333–341.

Allison, S. E., von Wahlde, L., Shockley, T., & Gabbard, O. (2006). The development of the self in the era of the Internet and role-playing fantasy games. *American Journal of Psychiatry, 163,* 381–385.

American Council for Drug Education. (2002). *Basic facts about drugs: Steroids.* Retrieved July 15, 2008, from http://www.acde.org/common/Steroids.htm.

American Heart Association. (2008). Cigarette smoking and cardiovascular disease. Retrieved June 5, 2008, from http://www.americanheart.org/presenter.jhtml?identifier=4545

American Psychiatric Association. (1994). *Diagnostic and statistical manual of mental disorders* (4th ed.). Washington, DC: Author.

American Psychiatric Association. (2000). *Diagnostic and statistical manual of mental disorders* (4th ed., text revision). Washington, DC: Author.

Amonini, C., & Donovan, R. J. (2006). The relationship between youth's moral and legal perceptions of alcohol, tobacco and marijuana and use of these substances. *Health Education Research: Theory & Practice, 21*(2), 276–286.

Anderson, C., & Horne, J. A. (2006). A high sugar content, low caffeine drink does not alleviate sleepiness but may worsen it. *Human Psychopharmacology: Clinical and Experimental, 21*(5), 299–303.

Anderson, K. (1999, August). *Internet use among college students: Should we be concerned?* Paper presented at the American Psychological Association, Boston.

Anderson, R. N. (2002). *Deaths attributable to obesity: Making sense of the numbers.* Washington, DC: National Center for Health Statistics. Retrieved January 6, 2009, from http://www.cdc.gov/nchs/ppt/bsc/anderson.ppt.

Aron, A., & Aron, E. N. (1986). *Love and the expansion of self: Understanding attraction and satisfaction.* New York: Hemisphere.

Aron, E. N., & Aron, A. (1996). Love and expansion of the self: The state of the model. *Personal Relationships, 3,* 45–58.

Arseneault, L., Cannon, M., Witton, J., & Murray, R. M. (2004). Causal association between cannabis and psychosis: Examination of the evidence. *British Journal of Psychiatry, 184,* 110–117.

Atran, S. (2002). *In gods we trust: The evolutionary landscape of religion.* New York: Oxford University Press.

Axen, K., & Axen, K. V. (2001). *Illustrated principles of exercise physiology.* Englewood Cliffs, NJ: Prentice Hall.

Baan, R., Straif, K., Grosse, Y., Secretan, B., El Ghissassi, F., Bouvard, V., et al. (2007, April). Carcinogenicity of alcoholic beverages. *Lancet Oncology, 8*(4), 292–293.

Back, S. E., Brady, K. T., Jaanimagi, U., & Jackson, J. L. (2006). Cocaine dependence and PTSD: A pilot study of symptom interplay and treatment preferences. *Addictive Behavior, 31,* 351–354.

Bainbridge, S. W. (2007). The scientific research potential of virtual worlds. *Science, 317,* 472–476.

Baker, H. S., & Baker, M. N. (1987). Heinz Kohut's self psychology: An overview. *American Journal of Psychiatry,* 1–9.

Ball, D. (2008). Addiction science and its genetics. *Addiction, 103*(3), 360–367.

Bandura, A. (1969). *Principles of behavior modification.* Oxford, UK: Holt, Reinhart & Winston.

Bandura, A. (1973). *Aggression: A social learning analysis.* Englewood Cliffs, NJ: Prentice Hall.

Bandura, A. (1977). *Social learning theory.* Oxford, UK: Prentice Hall.

Bandura, A., & Walters, R. H. (1959). *Adolescent aggression.* New York: Ronald Press.

Bandura, A., & Walters, R. H. (1963). *Social learning and personality development.* New York: Holt, Rinehart & Winston.

Barrows, J. (1893). *The world's parliament of religions.* Chicago: The Parliament Publishing Company.

Bartlett, T. (2004, February 27). Ecstasy agonists: A retracted study on a controversial substance raises questions about the reliability of government-sponsored research on drugs. *Research & Publishing.* Retrieved August 8, 2008, from http://chronicle.com/free/v50/i25/25a01401.htm

Barton, B. (2002). Dancing on the Mobius strip: Challenging the sex war paradigm. *Gender & Society, 16*(5), 585–602.

Bassuk, S., Glass, T., & Berkman, L. F. (1999). Social disengagement and incident cognitive decline in community-dwelling elderly persons. *Annals of Internal Medicine, 131,* 165–173.

Bayse, G. (1998). *Introduction to PTSD*. Retrieved April 8, 2006, from http://campus.houghton.edu/orgs/psychology/ptsd/Introduction.htm

Beall, L. S. (1997). Post-traumatic stress disorder: A bibliographic essay. *Choice, 34*(6), 917–930. Retrieved February 20, 2007, from http://www.lib.auburn.edu/socsci/docs/ptsd.html

Beck, A. T. (1963). Thinking and depression: I. Idiosyncratic content and cognitive distortions. *Archives of General Psychiatry, 9*(4), 324–333.

Beck, A. T. (1964). Thinking and depression: II. Theory and therapy. *Archives of General Psychiatry, 10*(6), 561–571.

Beck, A. T. (1970). Cognitive therapy: Nature and relation to behavior therapy. *Behavior Therapy, 1*(2), 184–200.

Beck, A. T. (1972). *Depression: Causes and treatment*. Philadelphia: University of Pennsylvania Press.

Beck, A. T. (1976). *Cognitive therapy and the emotional disorders*. Oxford, UK: International Universities Press.

Beck, A. T. (1987). Cognitive models of depression. *Journal of Cognitive Psychotherapy, 1*, 5–37.

Beck, A. T. (1993). Cognitive approaches to stress. In P. M. Lehrer & R. L. Woolfolk (Eds.), *Principles and practice of stress management* (2nd ed.). New York: Guilford.

Beck, A. T. (1996). Beyond belief: A theory of modes, personality, and psychopathology. In P. M. Salkovskis (Ed.), *Frontiers of cognitive therapy* (pp. 1–25). New York: Guilford.

Beck, A T. (1999). *Prisoners of hate: The cognitive basis of anger, hostility, and violence*. New York: HarperCollins.

Beck, A. T. (2005). Reflections on my public dialogue with the Dalai Lama. *Cognitive Therapy Today, 10*(2), 4.

Beck, A. T. (2006). *Beck Depression Inventory—BDI*. San Antonio, TX: Psychological Corporation.

Beck, A. T., Rush, A. J., Shaw, B. F., & Emery, G. (1979). *Cognitive therapy of depression*. New York: Guilford.

Beck, J. S. (2007). *The Beck diet solution: Train your brain to think like a thin person*. Des Moines, IA: Oxmoor House.

Begley, D. J. (2007). Structure and function of the blood-brain barrier. In E. Touitou & B. Barry (Eds.), *Enhancement in drug delivery* (pp. 571–590). Boca Raton, FL: CRC Press.

Belsky, J., & Nezworski, T. (Eds.). (1988). *Clinical implications of attachment*. Hillsdale, NJ: Lawrence Erlbaum.

Bender, E. (2004). Chronic health problems often accompany PTSD in women. *Psychiatric News, 39*(17), 36.

Benson, H. (1975). *The relaxation response*. New York: Morrow.

Benson, H. (1984). *Beyond the relaxation response*. New York: Berkley Press.

Benson, H. (1987). *Your maximum mind*. New York: Random House.

Benson, H. (1989, August). *Meditation: A physiological bridge to natural highs*. Keynote address, Natural Highs Conference, Boulder, CO.

Benson, H. (2000). *The relaxation response—updated and expanded (25th anniversary edition)*. New York: Avon.

Benson, H., Greenwood, M., & Klemchuk, H. (1975). The relaxation response: Psychophysiologic aspects and clinical applications. *International Journal of Psychiatric Medicine, 6*(1–2), 87–98.

Benson, H., Lehmann, J., Malhotra, M., Goldman, R., Hopkins, J., & Epstein, M. (1982, January 21). Body temperature changes during the practice of g Tum-mo yoga. *Nature, 295,* 234–236.

Benson, H., & Proctor, W. (1984). *Beyond the relaxation response.* New York: Putnam/Berkeley.

Benson, H., Steinert, R. F., Greenwood, M. M., Klemchuk, H. M., & Peterson, N. H. (1975). Continuous measurement of O_2 consumption and CO_2 elimination during a wakeful hypometabolic state. *Journal of Human Stress, 1,* 37–44.

Bessiere, K., Seay, A. F., & Kiesler, S. (2007). The ideal elf: Identity exploration in World of Warcraft. *CyberPsychology & Behavior, 10*(4), 530–535.

Bettelheim, B. (1976). *The uses of enchantment: The meaning and importance of fairy tales.* New York: Knopf.

Betz, C., Milhalic, D., Pinto, M. E., & Raffa, R. B. (2000). Could a common biochemical mechanism underlie addictions? *Journal of Clinical Pharmacy and Therapeutics, 25,* 11–20.

Black S. (1819). *Clinical and pathological reports.* Newry, UK: Alex Wilkinson.

Blake, M. J., Stein, E. A., & Vomachka, A. J. (1984). Effects of exercise training on brain opioid peptides and serum LH in female rats. *Peptides, 5,* 220–226.

Blonigen, D. M., Hicks, B. M., Patrick, C. J., Krueger, R. F., Iacono, W. G., & McGue, M. (2005). Psychopathic personality traits: Heritability and genetic overlap with internalizing and externalizing pathology. *Psychological Medicine, 35,* 637–648.

Blum, K. (1991). *Alcohol and the addictive brain: New hope for alcoholics from biogenetic research.* New York: Free Press.

Boellstorff, T. (2008). *Coming of age in Second Life: An anthropologist explores the virtually human.* Princeton, NJ: Princeton University Press.

Boeringer, S. B. (1999). Associations of rape-supportive attitudes with fraternal and athletic participation. *Violence Against Women, 5*(1), 81–90.

Bolla, K. I., Brown, K., Eldreth, D., Tate, K., & Cadet, J. L. (2002). Dose-related neurocognitive effects of marijuana use. *Neurology, 59,* 1337–1343.

Bowlby, J. (1969). *Attachment and loss: Vol. 1. Attachment.* London: Tavistock.

Bowlby, J. (1988). *A secure base: Parent-child attachment and healthy human development.* New York: Basic Books.

Brady, K. T., Grice, D. E., Dustan, L., & Randall, C. (1993). Gender differences in substance use disorders. *American Journal of Psychiatry, 150,* 1707–1711.

Bremner, J. D. (2002). *Does stress damage the brain?* New York: Norton.

Bren, L. (2006). Some cold medicines move behind counter. *FDA Consumer.* In H. T. Wilson (Ed.), *Annual editions: Drugs, society, and behavior 2007/2008* (pp. 109–110). Boston: McGraw-Hill.

Brenhouse, H. C., & Anderson, S. L. (2008). Delayed extinction and stronger reinstatement of cocaine conditioned place preference in adolescent rats, compared to adults. *Behavioral Neuroscience, 122*(2), 460–465.

Brennan, K. A., & Shaver, P. R. (1995). Dimensions of adult attachment, affect regulation, and romantic relationship functioning. *Personality and Social Psychology Bulletin, 23,* 23–31.

Breslau, N., Johnson, E., Hiripi, E., & Kessler, R. (2001). Nicotine dependence in the United States: Prevalence, trends, and smoking persistence. *Archives of General Psychiatry, 58,* 810–816.

Bretherton, I., & Waters, E. (Eds.). (1985). Growing points of attachment theory and research. *Monograph of the Society for Research in Child Development, 50*(209).

Brewster, Z. W. (2003). Behavioral and interactional patterns of strip club patrons: Tipping techniques and club attendance. *Deviant Behavior, 24*(3), 221–243.

Briere, J., & Rickards, S. (2007). Self-awareness, affect regulation, and relatedness: Differential sequels of childhood versus adult victimization experiences. *Journal of Nervous and Mental Disease, 195,* 497–503.

Broening, H. W., Morford, L. L., Inman-Wood, S. L., Fukumura, M., & Vorhees, C. (2001). 3,4-methylenedioxymethamphetamine (Ecstasy)-induced learning and memory impairments depend on the age of exposure during early development. *Journal of Neuroscience, 21*(9), 3228–3235.

Brooks-Gunn, J., & Donahue, E. H. (2008). Introducing the issue: Children and electronic media. *Future of Children, 18*(1), 3–10.

Brown, D. J. (2007, December 28). Psychedelic healing? Hallucinogenic drugs which blew minds in the 1960s soon may be used to treat mental ailments. *Scientific American,* 66–71. Available at http://www.sciam.com/article.cfm?id=psychedelic-healing

Brown, P. J. (2000). Outcome in female patients with both substance use and posttraumatic stress disorder. *Alcoholism Treatment Quarterly, 18*(3), 127.

Browning, R. (1888). *The poetical works of Robert Browning.* London: Smith, Elder & Co.

Brown University Health Education. (2008, December 15). *Caffeine and energy boosting drugs: Energy drinks.* Retrieved December 20, 2008, from http://www.brown.edu/Student_Services/Health_Services/Health_Education/atod/energydrinks.htm

Bruch, H. (1961). Transformation of oral impulses in eating disorders: A conceptual approach. *Psychiatric Quarterly, 35,* 458–481.

Buddie, A. M., & Parks, K. A. (2003). The role of the bar context and social behaviors on women's risk for aggression. *Journal of Interpersonal Violence, 18*(12), 1378–1393.

Budney, A. J., Hughes, J. R., Moore, B. A., & Novy, P. L. (2001). Marijuana abstinence effects in marijuana smokers maintained in their home environment. *Archives of General Psychiatry, 58,* 917–924.

Bulik, C. M., Reba, L., Siega-Riz, A. M., & Reichborn-Kjennerud, T. (2005). Anorexia nervosa: Definition, epidemiology, and cycle of risk. *International Journal of Eating Disorders, 37,* S2–S9.

Burt, S. A., McGue, M., Krueger, R. F., & Iacono, W. G. (2005). Sources of covariation among the child-externalizing disorders: Informant effects and the shared environment. *Psychological Medicine, 35*(8), 1133–1144.

Burton, R. (1632). *The anatomy of melancholy.* Oxford, UK: Henry Cripps.

Butler, A. C., & Beck, J. S. (2000). Cognitive therapy outcomes: A review of meta-analyses. *Journal of the Norwegian Psychological Association, 37,* 1–9.

Butterfield, F. (2005, January 30). States may restrict cold pills with ingredient in meth. *New York Times.* Retrieved October 15, 2008, from http://www.nytimes.com/2005/01/30/national/30meth.html?pagewanted=1&n=Top/Reference/Times%20Topics/People/B/Butterfield,%20Fox

Cabral, G. (1996). Effects of marijuana on the brain, endocrine system and immune system. In *Conference highlights: National Conference on Marijuana Use: Prevention, Treatment, and Research.* Rockville, MD: National Institute on Drug Abuse, National Institute of Health. NIH Publication 96-4106, 21–24.

Cadet, J., Ordonez, S., & Ordonez, J. (1997). Methamphetamine induces apoptosis in immortalized neural cells: Protection by the proto-oncogene, bcl-2. *Synapse, 25*(2), 176–184.

Calleja, G. (2007, July). Digital game involvement. *Games and Culture, 2*(3), 236–260.

Camargo, C. A., Hennekens, C. H., Gaziano, J. M., Glynn, R. J., Manson, J. E., & Stampfer, M. J. (1997). Prospective study of moderate alcohol consumption and mortality in U.S. male physicians. *Archives of Internal Medicine, 157,* 79–85.

Campo-Flores, A., & Smalley, S. (2008, March 15). On top of the world? *Newsweek.* Retrieved January 20, 2009, from http://www.newsweek.com/id/123566

Cannon, W. B. (1915). *Bodily changes in pain, hunger, fear, and rage: An account of recent researches into the function of emotional excitement.* New York: Appleton.

Cannon, W. B. (1929). *Bodily changes in pain, hunger, fear, and rage.* New York: Appleton.

Caraballo, R. S., Yee, S. L., Gfroerer, J., & Mirza, S. A. (2008). Adult tobacco use among racial and ethnic groups living in the United States, 2002–2005. *Preventing Chronic Disease, 5*(3), A78.

Carelli, R. M. (2002). The nucleus accumbens and reward: Neurophysiological investigations in behaving animals. *Behavioral and Cognitive Neuroscience Reviews, 1*(4), 281–296.

Carey, B. (2008, May 27). Lotus therapy. *New York Times* [online]. Retrieved July 1, 2008, from http://www.nytimes.com/2008/05/27/health/research/27budd.html

Carrere, S., & Gottman, J. (1999). Predicting divorce among newlyweds from the first three minutes of a marital conflict discussion. *Family Process, 38,* 293–301.

Carroll, J. S., Padilla-Walker, L. M., Nelson, L. J., Olson, C. D., Barry, C. M., & Madsen, S. (2008). Generation XXX: Pornography acceptance and use among emerging adults. *Journal of Adolescent Research, 23*(1), 6–30.

Carter, C. S. (1992). Oxytocin and sexual behavior. *Neuroscience and Biobehavioral Review, 16,* 131–144.

Carter, R. (1998). *Mapping the mind.* Berkeley: University of California Press.

Centers for Disease Control and Prevention. (2005, July 1). Annual smoking-attributable mortality, years of potential life lost, and productivity losses—United States, 1997–2001. *Morbidity and Mortality Weekly Report* [online serial], *54*(25), 625–628. Available from http://www.cdc.gov/mmwr/preview/mmwrhtml/mm5425a1.htm

Chang, L., Ernst, T., Speck, O., Patel, H., DeSilva, M., Leonido-Yee, M., et al. (2002). Perfusion MRI and computerized cognitive test abnormalities in abstinent methamphetamine users. *Psychiatry Research, 114,* 65–79.

Chaouloff, F. (1997). Effects of acute physical exercise on central serotonergic systems. *Medicine and Science in Sports Exercise, 29,* 58–62.

Chasnoff, I. J. (1997). Prenatal exposure to cocaine and other drugs: Is there a profile? In P. J. Accardo, B. K. Shapiro, & A. J. Capute (Eds.), *Behavior belongs in the brain: Neurobehavioral syndromes* (pp. 147–163). Timonium, MD: York Press.

Chein, I., Gerard, D. L., Lee, R. S., & Rosenfeld, E. (1981). The road to H: Narcotics, delinquency, and social policy. In H. Shaffer & M. Burglass (Eds.), *Classic contributions in the addictions* (pp. 95–116). New York: Brunner/Mazel.

Cherkas, L. F., Hunkin, J. L., Kato, B. S., Richards, J. B., Gardner, J. P., Surdulescu, G. L., et al. (2008). The association between physical activity in leisure time and leukocyte telomere length. *Archives of Internal Medicine, 168*(2), 154–185.

Childress, A. (2006). What can human brain imaging tell us about vulnerability to addiction and to relapse? In W. Miller & K. Carroll (Eds.), *Rethinking substance abuse*. New York: Guilford.

Christenson, G. A., Faber, R. J., de Zwaan, M., Raymond, N. C., Specker, S. M., Ekern, M. D., et al. (1994). Compulsive buying: Descriptive characteristics and psychiatric comorbidity. *Journal of Clinical Psychiatry, 55*(1), 5–11.

Christy, M. M., (1994). *Your own perfect medicine*. Scottsdale, AZ: Future Medicine.

Ciccocioppo, R., Economidou, D., Fedeli, A., Angeletti, S., Weiss, F., Heilig, M., et al. (2004). Attenuation of ethanol self-administration and of conditioned reinstatement of alcohol-seeking behaviour by the antiopioid peptide nociceptin/orphanin FQ in alcohol-preferring rats. *Psychopharmacology (Berlin), 172*, 170–178.

Clapp, J. D. (2008, January 6). College drinking games lead to higher blood alcohol levels. *HealthDay News*. Retrieved June 30, 2008, from http://www.washington post.com/wp-dyn/content/article/2008/01/06/AR2008010600771.html

Clark, D. A., Beck, A., & Alford, B. A. (1999). *Scientific foundations of cognitive theory and therapy of depression*. New York: Wiley.

Clark, D. M., Ehler, A., McManus, F., Hackmann, A., Fennel, M., Campbell, H., et al. (2003). Cognitive therapy versus fluoxetine in generalized social phobia: A randomized placebo-controlled trial. *Journal of Consulting & Clinical Psychology, 71*(6), 1058–1067.

Cleckley, H. M. (1941). *The mask of sanity: An attempt to reinterpret the so-called psychopathic*. Oxford, UK: Mosby.

Cloninger, C. R. (2004). *Feeling good: The science of well-being*. New York: Oxford University Press.

Cloninger, C. R. (2007). Spirituality and the science of feeling good. *Southern Medical Journal, 100*(7), 740–743.

Cloninger, C. R., Svrakic, D., & Przybeck, R. (1993). A psychobiological model of temperament and character. *Archives of General Psychiatry, 50*, 975–990.

Cloyd, J. W. (1976). The market-place bar: The interrelation between sex, situation, and strategies in the pairing ritual of Homo Ludens. *Journal of Contemporary Ethnography, 5*, 293–312.

Cohen, L. (2006). *Book of longing*. New York: HarperCollins.

Cohen, M. R., Cohen, R. M., Pickar, D., & Murphy, D. L. (1985). Naloxone reduces food intake in humans. *Psychosomatic Medicine, 47*(2), 132–138.

Colado, M. I., & Green, A. R. (1995). The spin trap reagent alpha-phenyl-N-tert-butyl nitrone prevents "ecstasy"-induced neurodegeneration of 5-hydroxytrypt amine neurons. *European Journal of Pharmacology, 280*, 343–346.

Colado, M. I., O'Shea, E., & Green, A. R. (2004). Acute and long-term effects of MDMA on cerebral dopamine biochemistry and function. *Psychopharmacology (Berlin), 173*, 249–263.

Cole, H., & Griffiths, M. D. (2007). Social interactions in massively multiplayer online role-playing gamers. *CyberPsychology and Behavior, 10*(4), 575–583.

Collingwood, R. G. (1949). *The idea of nature*. London: Oxford University Press.

Compton, W. M., Cottler, L. B., Phelps, D. L., Abdallah, A. B., & Spitznagel, E. L. (2000). Psychiatric disorders among drug-dependent subjects: Are they primary or secondary. *American Journal of Addiction, 9*(2), 126–134.

Connors, G. J., Carroll, K. M., DiClemente, C. C., Longabaugh, R., & Donovan, D. M. (1997). The therapeutic alliance and its relationship to alcoholism treatment participation and outcome. *Journal of Consulting and Clinical Psychology, 41,* 588–598.

Conway, K. P., Compton, W., Stinson, F. S., & Grant, B. F. (2006). Lifetime comorbidity of DSM-IV mood and anxiety disorders and specific drug use disorders: Results from the National Epidemiologic Survey on Alcohol and Related Conditions. *Journal of Clinical Psychiatry, 67,* 247–257.

Cooper, A., Delmonico, D. L., & Burg, R. (2000). Cybersex users, abusers, and compulsives: New findings and implications. *Sexual Addiction & Compulsivity, 7,* 5–29.

Cooper, M. J. (2005). Cognitive theory in anorexia nervosa and bulimia nervosa: Progress, development, and future directions. *Clinical Psychology Review, 25*(4), 511–531.

Costello, E. J. (1999). Commentary on "Prevalence and impact of parent-reported disabling mental health conditions among U.S. children." *Journal of the American Academy of Child and Adolescent Psychiatry, 38,* 610–613.

Costello, E. J., & Angold, A. (1999). Adolescent outcomes of childhood disorders: The consequences of severity and impairment. *Journal of the American Academy of Child and Adolescent Psychiatry* [Special section], *38,* 121–128.

Covington, S. S. (2000). Helping women to recover: Creating gender-specific treatment for substance-abusing women and girls in community corrections. In M. McMahon (Ed.), *Assessment to assistance: Programs for women in community corrections* (pp. 171–234). Lanham, MD: American Correctional Association.

Cowan, R. L., Lyoo, I. K., Kong, S. W., Sung, S. M., Haga, E., Lukas, S. W., et al. (2003). Reduced focal cortical gray matter density in human MDMA (Ecstasy) users: A voxel-based morphometry study. *Drug and Alcohol Dependence, 72,* 225–235.

Crabbe, J. C. (2002). Alcohol and genetics: New models. *American Journal of Medical Genetics (Neuropsychiatric Genetics), 114,* 969–974.

Craig, A. H. (1897). A temperance address—The nickel behind the bar. In *Pros and cons: Complete debates.* New York: Hinds & Noble.

Craven, J. L. (1989). Meditation and psychotherapy. *Canadian Journal of Psychiatry, 34*(7), 648–653.

Crawford, M., & Unger, R. (2000). *Women and gender: A feminist psychology* (3rd ed.). Boston: McGraw-Hill.

Crick, F. H. C. (1995). *The astonishing hypothesis: The scientific search for the soul.* New York: Scribner.

Cryer, B., McCraty, R., & Childre, D. (2003). Pull the plug on stress. *Harvard Business Review, 81*(7), 102–107.

Csikszentmihalyi, M. (1975). *Beyond boredom and anxiety.* San Francisco: Jossey-Bass.

Csikszentmihalyi, M. (1990). *Flow: The psychology of optimal experience.* New York: Harper & Row.

Csikszentmihalyi, M. (1996). *Creativity: Flow and the psychology of discovery and invention.* New York: HarperCollins.

Csikszentmihalyi, M. (2000). *Beyond boredom and anxiety* (25th anniversary ed.). San Francisco: Jossey-Bass.

Csikszentmihalyi, M., Rathunde, K., & Whalen, S. (1993). *Talented teenagers.* Cambridge, UK: Cambridge University Press.

Csikszentmihalyi, M., & Robinson, R. (1990). *The art of seeing*. Malibu, CA: J. Paul Getty Museum/Getty Center for Education in the Arts.

Dalai Lama. (1999). *Ethics for the new millennium*. New York: Riverhead.

Davidson, R. J., Kabat-Zinn, J., Schumacher, J., Rosenkranz, M., Muller, D., Santorelli, S. F., et al. (2003). Alterations in brain and immune function produced by mindfulness meditation. *Psychosomatic Medicine, 65*, 564–570.

Davidson, R. J., & Schwartz, G. E. (1976). The psychobiology of relaxation and related states: A multiprocess theory. In D. I. Mostofsky (Ed.), *Behavior control and the modification of physiological activity* (pp. 399–442). Englewood Cliffs, NJ: Prentice Hall.

De Bellis, M. D., Clark, D. B., Beers, S. R., Soloff, P. H., Boring, A. M., Hall, J., et al. (2000). Hippocampal volume in adolescent-onset alcohol use disorders. *American Journal of Psychiatry, 157*, 737–744.

De Cuypere, L. (2008). *Limiting the iconic: From the metatheoretical foundations to the creative possibilities of iconicity in language*. Amsterdam: John Benjamins.

De Kemp, R. A. T., Scholte, R. H. J., Overbeek, G., & Engels, R. C. (2006, August). Early adolescent delinquency: The role of parents and best friends. *Criminal Justice and Behavior, 33*(4), 488–510.

Delgado, M. R. (2007). Reward-related responses in the human striatum. *Annals of the New York Academy of Sciences, 1104*, 70–88.

Demasio, A. (2003). *Looking for Spinoza: Joy, sorrow, and the feeling brain*. New York: Harcourt.

Denmark world's happiest country, survey finds. (2008, June 30). *Reuters.* Retrieved October 15, 2008, from http://www.reuters.com/article/africaCrisis/IdUSN30454695

Dennis, T., Bendersky, M., Ramsay, D., & Lewis, M. (2006). Reactivity and regulation in children prenatally exposed to cocaine. *Developmental Psychology, 42*(4), 688–697.

Diamond, S., Bermudez, R., & Schensul, J. (2006, May). What's the rap about ecstasy? Popular music lyrics and drug trends among American youth. *Journal of Adolescent Research, 21*(3), 269–298.

Di Chiara, G., & Imperto, A. (1988). Drugs abused by humans preferentially increase synaptic dopamine concentrations in the mesolimbic system of freely moving rats. *Proceedings of the National Academy of Sciences, 85*, 5274–5278.

Dietz, P. E. (1983). Recurrent discovery of autoerotic asphyxia. In R. R. Hazelwood, P. E. Dietz, & A. W. Burgess (Eds.), *Autoerotic fatalities* (pp. 13–44). Lexington, MA: Lexington.

DiFranza, J. R. (2008, May 3). Hooked from the first cigarette. *Scientific American,* 84–87.

DiFranza, J. R., Savageau, J. A., Fletcher, K., Ockene, J. K., Rigotti, N. A., McNeill, A. D., et al. (2002). Measuring the loss of autonomy over nicotine use in adolescents: The Development and Assessment of Nicotine Dependence in Youths (DANDY) study. *Archives of Pediatric Adolescent Medicine, 156*, 397–403.

Dobson, K. A. (1989). A meta-analysis of the efficacy of cognitive therapy for depression. *Journal of Consulting and Clinical Psychology, 57*(3), 414–419.

Donaghy, M. (2007). Exercise can seriously improve your mental health: Fact or fiction? *Advances in Physiotherapy, 9*(2), 76–89.

Donato, A., & Stanton, M. (2004). Toward a syndrome model of addiction: Multiple expressions, common etiology. *Harvard Review of Psychiatry, 12*(6), 367–374.

Donovan, D. M. (2005). Assessment of addictive behaviors for relapse prevention. In D. M. Donovan & G. A. Marlatt (Eds.), *Assessment of addictive behaviors* (2nd ed., pp. 1–48). New York: Guilford.

Drummond, D. C. (2000). What does cue-reactivity have to offer clinical research? *Addiction, 95,* S129–S144.

Dryden, W., & Ellis, A. (1986). Rational-emotive therapy. In W. Dryden & W. Golden (Eds.), *Cognitive-behavioral approaches to psychotherapy* (pp. 129–168). London: Harper & Row.

Dryden-Edwards, R., & Stopler, M. C. (2007). Post-traumatic stress disorder (PTSD). *MedicineNet.com.* Retrieved March 4, 2008, from http://www.Medicinenet.com/posttraumatic_stress_disorder/article.htm

Dufour, M. C. (1999). What is moderate drinking? Defining "drinks" and drinking levels. *Alcohol Research & Health, 23*(1), 5–14.

Duggan, P., Shear, M. D., & Fisher, M. (1999, April 22). Shooter pair mixed fantasy, reality. *Washington Post,* p. A1.

DuPont, R. L., & Ford, B. (2000). *The selfish brain: Learning from addiction.* New York: Hazelden.

Edenberg, H. J., & Foroud, T. (2006). The genetics of alcoholism: Identifying specific genes through family studies. *Addiction Biology, 11*(3/4), 386–396.

Egan, R. D. (2003). I'll be your fantasy girl if you'll be my money man: Mapping desire, fantasy, and power in an exotic dance club. *Journal of Psychoanalysis, Culture and Society, 8*(1), 109–120.

Einstein, A. (1956). Moral decay. In A. Einstein, *The Einstein Reader.* New York: Kensington. (Original work published 1937)

Elkind, D. (1970). Origins of religion in the child. *Review of Religions Research, 12,* 35–42.

Ellis, A. (1962). *Reason and emotion in psychotherapy.* Oxford, UK: Lyle Stuart.

Ellis, A. (2004). *The road to tolerance: The philosophy of rational emotive behavior therapy.* Amherst, NY: Prometheus Books.

Ellis, A., & Harper, R. A. (1961). *A guide to rational living.* Oxford, UK: Prentice Hall.

Emrick, C. (1974). A review of psychologically oriented treatment of alcoholism. *Journal of Studies on Alcohol, 35,* 523–549.

Enck, G. E., & Preston, J. D. (1988). Counterfeit intimacy: A dramaturgical analysis of an erotic performance. *Deviant Behavior, 9,* 369–381.

Englert, H. (2003). Sussing out stress. *Scientific American Mind, 14*(1), 56–61.

Erickson, D., & Tewksbury, R. (2000). The gentlemen in the club: A typology of strip club patrons. *Deviant Behavior, 21*(4), 271–293.

Erikson, E. H. (1964). *Insight and responsibility.* New York: Norton.

Erikson, E. H. (1982). *The life cycle completed.* New York: Norton.

Eron, L. D. (1982). Parent-child interaction, television violence, and aggression of children. *American Psychologist, 42,* 435–442.

Escobedo, I., O'Shea, E., Orio, L., Sanchez, V., Segura, M., De la Torre, R., et al. (2005). A comparative study on the acute and long-term effects of MDMA and 3,4-dihydroxymethamphetamine (HHMA) on brain monoamine levels after I. P. or striatal administration in mice. *British Journal of Pharmacology, 144,* 231–241.

Evans, S. M., & Foltin, R. W. (2006). Exogenous progesterone attenuates the subjective effects of smoked cocaine in women, but not in men. *Neuropsychopharmacology, 31, 659–674.*

Falkowski, C. L. (2003). Methamphetamine across America: Misconceptions, realities, and solutions. *State Government News.* In H. T. Wilson (Ed.), *Annual editions: Drugs, society, and behavior 2007/2008* (pp. 9–12). Dubuque, IA: McGraw-Hill.

Farley, F. (1986, May). The big T in personality. *Psychology Today,* 45–52.

Fass, M. (2004, March 21). A sort of love story. *New York Times,* sec. 14, p. 4.

Felson, M., & Poulsen, E. (2003). Simple indicators of crime by time of day. *International Journal of Forecasting, 19*(4), 595–601.

Ferdinand, R. F., Sondeijker, F., van der Ende, J., Selten, J. P., Huizink, A., & Verhulst, V. C. (2005). Cannabis use predicts future psychotic symptoms, and vice versa. *Addiction, 100*(5), 612–618.

Ferguson, R. A., & Goldberg, D. M. (1997). Genetic markers of alcohol abuse. *Clinica Chimica Acta, 257*(2), 199–250.

Fergusson, D., Horwood, L., & Ridder, E. (2005). Tests of causal linkages between cannabis use and psychotic symptoms. *Addiction, 100*(3), 354–366.

Ferracuti, F. (1982). A sociopsychiatric interpretation of terrorism. *Annals of the American Academy of Political and Social Science, 463*(1), 129–140.

Fisher, H., Aron, A., & Brown, L. L. (2005). Romantic love: An fMRI study of a neural mechanism for mate choice. *Journal of Comparative Neurology, 493*(1), 58–62.

Flack, W. F., Daubman, K. A., Caron, M. L., Asadorian, J. A., D'Aurelli, N. R., Gigliotti, S. N., et al. (2007). Risk factors and consequences of unwanted sex among university students: Hooking up, alcohol, and stress response. *Journal of Interpersonal Violence, 22,* 139–157.

Floresco, S. B. (2007). Dopaminergic regulation of limbic-striatal interplay. *Journal of Psychiatry & Neuroscience, 32*(6), 400–411.

Forsyth, C. J., & Deshotels, T. H. (1997). The occupational milieu of the nude dancer. *Deviant Behavior: An Interdisciplinary Journal, 18*(2), 125–142.

Forsyth, C. J., & Deshotels, T. H. (1998). A deviant process: The sojourn of the stripper. *Sociological Spectrum, 18,* 77–82.

Fort, J. (1969). *The pleasure seekers: The drug crisis, youth, and society.* New York: Grove Press.

Freud, S. (1962). *Three essays on the theory of sexuality* (J. Strachey, Trans.). New York: Basic Books. (Original work published 1905)

Freud, S. (2005). *Civilization and its discontents* (J. Strachey, Ed., Trans.). New York: Norton. (Original work published 1929)

Fruzzetti, A. E., & Iverson, K. M. (2004). Mindfulness, acceptance, validation, and "individual" psychopathology in couples. In S. C. Hayes, V. M. Follette, & M. M. Linehan (Eds.), *Mindfulness and acceptance: Expanding the cognitive-behavioral tradition* (pp. 168–191). New York: Guilford.

Frye, M. A., & Salloum, I. M. (2006). Bipolar disorder and comorbid alcoholism: Prevalence rate and treatment considerations. *Bipolar Disorders, 8*(6), 677–685.

Gable, S. L., Reis, H. T., & Elliot, A. J. (2003). Evidence for bivariate systems: An empirical test of appetition and aversion across domains. *Journal of Research in Personality, 37*(5), 349–372.

Gable, S. L., Reis, H. T., Impett, E. A., & Asher, E. R. (2004). What do you do when things go right? The intrapersonal and interpersonal benefits of sharing positive events. *Journal of Personality and Social Psychology, 87,* 228–245.

Gaher, R. M., & Simons, J. S. (2007). Expectancies and evaluations of alcohol and marijuana problems. *Psychology of Addictive Behaviors, 21*, 545–554.

Gardner, C. D., Kiazand, A., Alhassan, S., Kim, S., Stafford, R. S., Balise, R. R., et al. (2007). Comparison of the Atkins, Zone, Ornish, and LEARN diets for change in weight and related risk factors among overweight premenopausal women: The A to Z weight loss study: A randomized trial. *Journal of the American Medical Association, 297*, 969–977.

Gardner, H. (1983). *Frames of mind: The theory of multiple intelligences.* New York: Basic Books.

Gardner, H. (1993). *Frames of mind: The theory of multiple intelligences* (10th ed.). New York: Basic Books.

Gardner, H. (1999). *Intelligence reframed: Multiple intelligences for the 21st century.* New York: Basic Books.

Garland, T. S., Hughes, M. F., & Marquart, J. W. (2004). Alcohol, sexual innuendos, and bad behavior: An analysis of a small town bar. *Southwest Journal of Criminal Justice, 1*(2), 11–29.

Gergen, M. M., & Davis, S. N. (Eds.). (1997). *Toward a new psychology of gender: A reader.* New York: Routledge.

Gibson's anti-Semitic tirade—alleged cover up. (2006, July 28). *TMZ.com.* Retrieved October 21, 2008, from http://tmz.com/2006/07/28/gibsons-anti-semitic-tirade-alleged-cover-up

Giedd, J., Blumenthal, J., Jeffries, N., Castellanos, F., Liu, H., Zijdenbos, A., et al. (1999). Brain development during childhood and adolescence: A longitudinal MRI study. *Nature Neuroscience, 2*, 861–863.

Gilman, S. E., & Abraham, H. D. (2001). A longitudinal study of the order of onset of alcohol dependence and major depression. *Drug and Alcohol Dependence, 63*, 277–286.

Gips, M. A. (2006, February). High on the job: Security management. In H. T. Wilson (Ed.), *Annual editions: Drugs, society, and behavior 2007/2008* (pp. 147–151). Dubuque, IA: McGraw-Hill.

Glassman, A. H., Jackson, W. K., Walsh, B. T., Roose, S. P., & Rosenfeld, B. (1984). Cigarette craving, smoking withdrawal, and clonidine. *Science, 226*(4676), 864–866.

Glenn, N., & Marquardt, E. (2001). *Hooking up, hanging out, and hoping for Mr. Right: College women on mating and dating today. An Institute for American Values Report to the Independent Women's Forum.* New York: Institute for American Values.

Goertzel, T. (2002). Terrorist beliefs and terrorist lives. In C. Stout (Ed.), *The psychology of terrorism* (Vol. 1, pp. 97–111). Westport, CT: Praeger.

Goffman, E. (1959). *The presentation of self in everyday life.* Garden City, NY: Doubleday.

Goffman, E. (1963). *Stigma: Notes on the management of spoiled identity.* Englewood Cliffs, NJ: Prentice Hall.

Goffman, E. (1967). *Interaction ritual.* Garden City, NY: Doubleday.

Goldin, R. (2006). Hyping Internet addiction. *STATS.* Retrieved February 6, 2008, from http://stats.org/stories/hype_web_addiction_nov16_06.htm

Goldstein, A. (1994). *Addiction: From biology to drug policy.* New York: W. H. Freeman.

Goldstein, J. (1993). *Insight meditation: The practice of freedom.* Boston: Shambhala.

Goleman, D. (1988). *The meditative mind.* Los Angeles: Tarcher.

Goodman, C., & Goodman, T. (1997). *The Forbes book of business quotations: 14,266 thoughts on the business of life.* New York: Black Dog & Leventhal.

Gorman, C. (2004, June 28). Dieting: The secrets of their success. *Time.*

Gosline, A. (2007, December). Bored? *Scientific American.* Retrieved February 1, 2009, from http://www.sciam.com/article.cfm?id=bored—find-something-to-live-for

Gottman, J. M., Driver, J., & Tabares, A. (2002). Building the sound marital house: An empirically derived couple therapy. In A. S. Gurman & N. S. Jacobson (Eds.), *Clinical handbook of couple therapy* (pp. 373–399). New York: Guilford.

Gottman, J. M., Murray, J. D., Swanson, C., Tyson, R., & Swanson, K. R. (2003). *The mathematics of marriage: Dynamic nonlinear models.* Cambridge: MIT Press.

Gould, S. J. (1997). The adaptive excellence of spandrels as a term and prototype. *Proceedings of the National Academy of Sciences USA (94),* 10750–10755.

Gould, S. J. (2002). *The structure of evolutionary theory.* Cambridge, MA: Belknap.

Graham, A., & Glickauf-Hughes, C. (1992). Object relations and addiction: The role of "transmuting externalizations." *Journal of Contemporary Psychotherapy, 22,* 1.

Grant, B. F., Dawson, D. A., Stinson, F. S., Chou, S. P., Dufour, M. C., & Pickering, R. P. (2004). The 12-month prevalence and trends in DSM-IV alcohol abuse and dependence: United States, 1991–1992 and 2001–2002. *Drug and Alcohol Dependence, 74,* 223–234.

Grant, B. F., & Harford, T. C. (1995). Comorbidity between DSM-IV alcohol use disorders and major depression: Results of a national survey. *Drug and Alcohol Dependence, 39,* 197–206.

Grant, B. F., Stinson, F. S., Dawson, D. A., Chou, S. P., Dufour, M. C., Compton, W., et al. (2004). Prevalence and co-occurrence of substance use disorders and independent mood and anxiety disorders: Results from the National Epidemiologic Survey on Alcohol and Related Conditions. *Archives of General Psychiatry, 61,* 807–816.

Greenberg, H. R. (1975). *The movies on your mind.* New York: Dutton.

Greenberg, J. T., Pyszczynski, T., & Solomon, S. (1986). The causes and consequences of a need for self-esteem: A terror management theory. In R. F. Baumeister (Ed.), *Public self and private self.* New York: Springer-Verlag.

Greenemeier, L. (2007, December 28). For the holidays: Good things come in virtual packages. *Scientific American.* Retrieved October 15, 2008, from http://www.sciam.com/article.cfm?id=2007-year-in-robots

Greenspan, S. I. (1985). Research strategies to identify developmental vulnerabilities for drug abuse. Etiology of Drug Abuse: Implications for Prevention. *NIDA Research Monograph Series, 56,* 136–154.

Griest, H., Klein, M. H., Eischens, R. R., Paris, J., Gurman, A. S., & Morgan, W. P. (1978). Running through your mind. *Journal of Psychosomatic Research, 22,* 259–264.

Grimm, O. (2007, April/May). Addicted to food. *Scientific American Mind,* 36–39.

Grinspoon, L., & Sagan, C. (1971). *Marihuana reconsidered.* New York: Bantam.

Grof, S. (1975). *Realms of the human unconscious: Observations from LSD research.* New York: Viking.

Grof, S. (1980). *LSD psychotherapy.* Pomona, CA: Hunter House.

Groves, I., & Farmer, R. (1994). Buddhism and addictions. *Addiction Research, 2,* 183–194.

Gupta, R., Derevensky, J. L., & Ellenbogen, S. (2006). Personality characteristics and risk-taking tendencies among adolescent gamblers. *Canadian Journal of Behavioural Science, 38*(3), 201–213.

Hakim, D., & Rashbaum, W. K. (2008, March 11). Spitzer is linked to prostitution ring. *New York Times*, p. 1.

Halliburton, R. (2005). HIV/1: Crystal clear danger. *New Statesman, 10*(1).

Halperin, S., & Bloom, S. (2007). *Pot culture*. New York: Abrams Image.

Hamajima, N., Hirose, K., Tajima, K., Rohan, T., Calle, E. E., Heath, C. W., et al. (2002). Alcohol, tobacco and breast cancer—collaborative reanalysis of individual data from 53 epidemiological studies, including 58,515 women with breast cancer and 95,067 women without the disease. *British Journal of Cancer, 87,* 1234–1245.

Hamilton, A. (2008). *The cure within: A history of mind-body medicine*. Norton.

Haney, M., Ward, A. S., Comer, S. D., Foltin, R. W., & Fischman, M. W. (1999). Abstinence symptoms following smoked marijuana in humans. *Psychopharmacology, 14,* 395–404.

Hanna, J. L. (2005). Exotic dance adult entertainment: A guide for planners and policy makers. *Journal of Planning Literature, 20*(2), 116–134.

Harris, L. (2002, August/September). Al Qaeda's fantasy ideology: War without Clausewitz. *Policy Review*. Retrieved January 27, 2008, from http://www.hoover.org/publications/policyreview/3459646.html

Hartley, N. (1997). In the flesh. In J. Nagle (Ed.), *Whores and other feminists* (pp. 57–65). New York: Routledge.

Harvard School of Public Health. (2008). *The nutrition source: Alcohol and heart disease*. Retrieved October 21, 2008, from http://www.hsph.harvard.edu/nutritionsource/what-should-you-eat/alcohol-and-heart-disease/index.html

Harvey, J. H., Pauwels, B. G., & Zickmund, S. (2001). Relationship connection: The role of minding in the enhancement of closeness. In C. R. Snyder & S. J. Lopez (Eds.), *The handbook of positive psychology* (pp. 423–433). New York: Oxford University Press.

Hasin, D. S., Stinson, F. S., Ogburn, E., & Grant, B. F. (2007). Prevalence, correlates, disability, and comorbidity of DSM-IV alcohol abuse and dependence in the United States: Results from the National Epidemiologic Survey on Alcohol and Related Conditions. *Archives of General Psychiatry, 64*(7), 830–842.

Hatch, T., & Gardner, H. (1993). Finding cognition in the classroom: An expanded view of human intelligence. In G. Salomon (Ed.), *Distributed cognitions. Psychological and educational considerations* (pp. 164–187). New York: Cambridge University Press.

Hawkley, L. C., Masi, C. M., Berry, J. D., & Cacioppo, J. T. (2006). Loneliness is a unique predictor of age-related differences in systolic blood pressure. *Psychology and Aging, 21*(1), 140–151.

Hayes, S. C., Follette, V. M., & Linehan, M. M. (Eds.). (2004). *Mindfulness and acceptance: Expanding the cognitive-behavioral tradition*. New York: Guilford.

Hayes, S. C., & Smith, S. (2005). *Get out of your mind and into your life: The new acceptance and commitment therapy*. Oakland, CA: New Harbinger.

Hazan, C., & Shaver, P. (1987). Romantic love conceptualized as an attachment process. *Journal of Personality and Social Psychology, 52,* 511–524.

Heath, A. C., Bucholz, K. K., Madden, P. A. F., Dinwiddie, S. H., Slutske, W. S., Dinwiddie, S., et al. (1997). Genetic and environmental contributions to alcohol dependence risk in a national twin sample: Consistency of findings in women and men. *Psychological Medicine, 27,* 1381–1396.

Heath, A. C., & Martin, N. G. (1994). Genetic influences on alcohol consumption patterns and problem drinking: Results from the Australian NH&MRC twin panel follow-up survey. *Annals of the New York Academy of Sciences, 708,* 72–85.

Heine, C. (1996). *Flow and achievement in mathematics.* Unpublished doctoral dissertation, University of Chicago.

Heinz, A. (2006, April/May). Staying sober. *Scientific American Mind,* 57–61.

Hendrick, S. S., & Hendrick, C. (1992). *Romantic love.* Newbury Park, CA: Sage Publications.

Henig, R. M. (2007, March 4). Darwin's God. *New York Times.* Retrieved July 29, 2008, from http://www.nytimes.com/2007/03/04/magazine/04evolution.t.html?n=Top/Reference/Times%20Topics/People/D/Dawkins,%20Richard

Henry, D. B., & Kobus, K. (2007). Early adolescent social networks and substance use. *Journal of Early Adolescence, 27*(3), 346–362.

Herbert, J. D., & Sageman, M. (2004). First do no harm: Emerging guidelines for the treatment of posttraumatic reactions. In G. M. Rosen (Ed.), *Psychotraumatic stress disorder: Issues and controversies* (pp. 213–232). Chichester, UK: Wiley.

Herman, J. (1997). *Trauma and recovery: The aftermath of violence—from domestic abuse to political terror.* New York: Basic Books.

Hickey, T. J. (Ed.). (2008). *Taking sides: Clashing views in crime and criminology* (8th ed.). Boston: McGraw-Hill.

Hicks, B. M., Bernat, E., Malone, S. M., Iacono, W. G., Patrick, C. J., Krueger, R. F., et al. (2007). Genes mediate the association between P3 amplitude and externalizing disorders. *Psychophysiology, 44,* 98–105.

Hillman, C. H., Erickson, K. I., & Kramer, A. F. (2008). Be smart, exercise your heart: Exercise effects on brain and cognition. *Nature Reviews Neuroscience, 9,* 58–65.

The history of rave culture. (n.d.). *Thesite.org.* Retrieved September 18, 2008, from http://www.thesite.org/drinkanddrugs/drugculture/drugstrade/thehistoryofrave

Hoek, H. W. (2006). Incidence, prevalence, and mortality of anorexia nervosa and other eating disorders. *Current Opinions in Psychiatry, 19,* 389–394.

Hoffman, J., & Froemke, S. (2007). *Addiction.* New York: Rodale.

Hofmann, A. (1980). *LSD, my problem child: Reflections on sacred drugs, mysticism, and science* (J. Ott, Trans.). Mt. View, CA: Wiretap.

Holden, S. (2008, January 2). John Lennon's death revisited through the words of his killer. *New York Times.*

Hopwood, C. J., Baker, K. L., & Morey, L. C. (2008). Personality and drugs of choice. *Personality and Individual Differences, 44,* 1413–1421.

Hosenball, M., & Conant, E. (2007, July 23). An elite escort service. *Newsweek.* Retrieved January 20, 2009, from http://www.newsweek.com/id/35004/output/print

Hu, J., & Quick, M. W. (2008). Substrate-mediated regulation of aminobutyric acid transporter 1 in rat brain. *Neuropharmacology, 54,* 309–318.

Hudson, J. I., Hiripi, E., Pope, H. G., & Kessler, R. C. (2007). The prevalence and correlates of eating disorders in the National Comorbidity Survey Replication. *Biological Psychiatry, 61,* 348–358.

Hughes, J. (1975). Isolation of an endogenous compound from the brain with pharmacological properties similar to morphine. *Brain Research, 88,* 295–308.

Hunt, W., Barnett, L., & Branch, L. (1971). Relapse rates in addiction programs. *Journal of Clinical Psychology, 27,* 455–456.

Iacono, W. G., Malone, S. M., & McGue, M. (2003). Substance use disorders, externalizing psychopathology, and P300 event-related potential amplitude. *International Journal of Psychophysiology, 48,* 147–178.

Ikegami, A., Olsen, C. M., D'Souza, M. S., & Duvauchelle, C. L. (2007). Experience-dependent effects of cocaine self-administration/conditioning on prefrontal and accumbens dopamine responses. *Behavioral Neuroscience, 121*(2), 389–400.

Interlandi, J. (2008, February 23). What addicts need. *Newsweek.* Retrieved July 9, 2008, from http://www.newsweek.com/id/114716

International Agency for Research on Cancer. (2007). Working group on ultraviolet (UV) light and skin cancer: The association of use of sunbeds with cutaneous malignant melanoma and other skin cancers: A systematic review. *International Journal of Cancer, 120*(5), 1116–1122.

International Food Information Council. (2008, August 4). *2008 Food and Health Survey: Consumer attitudes toward food, nutrition, and health.* Retrieved October 21, 2008, from http://www.ific.org/research/foodandhealthsurvey.cfm.

Is overweight okay? (2006). *Harvard Health Letter.* Cambridge, MA: Harvard Health Publications.

Jackson, S., & Csikszentmihalyi, M. (1999). *Flow in sports.* Champaign, IL: Human Kinetics.

Jacobsen, L. K., Southwick, S. M., & Kosten, T. B. (2001, August). Substance use disorders in patients with posttraumatic stress disorder: A review of the literature. *American Journal of Psychiatry, 158,* 1184–1190.

James, W. (1890). *Principles of psychology.* New York: Henry Holt.

James, W. (1902). *The varieties of religious experience: A study in human nature.* Cambridge, MA: Riverside Press.

Jarvis, T. J. (1992). Implications of gender for alcohol treatment research: A quantitative and qualitative review. *British Journal of Addiction, 87,* 1249–1261.

Jefferson, D. J. (2005). America's most dangerous drug. *Newsweek.* In H. T. Wilson (Ed.), *Annual editions: Drugs, society, and behavior 2007/2008* (pp. 16–19). Dubuque, IA: McGraw-Hill.

Jellinek, E. M. (1952). The phases of alcohol addiction. *Quarterly Journal of Studies on Alcohol, 13,* 672–684.

Jessor, R. (1998). *New perspectives on adolescent risk behavior.* New York: Cambridge University Press.

Jha, P., Chaloupka, F. J., Moore, J., Gajalakshmi, V., Gupta, P. C., Peck, R., et al. (2006). Tobacco addiction. In D. T. Jamison et al. (Eds.), *Disease control priorities in developing countries* (2nd ed., pp. 869–886). New York: Oxford University Press.

Johnston, L. D., O'Malley, P. M., Bachman, J. G., & Schulenberg, J. E. (2007). *Monitoring the Future national survey results on drug use, 1975–2006: Vol. 1. Secondary school students* (NIH Publication No. 07-6205). Bethesda, MD: National Institute on Drug Abuse.

Johnston, L. D., O'Malley, P. M., Bachman, J. G., & Schulenberg, J. E. (2008). *Monitoring the Future national results on adolescent drug use: Overview of key findings, 2007* (NIH Publication No. 08-6418). Bethesda, MD: National Institute on Drug Abuse.

Jones, D. C., Duvauchelle, C., Ikegami, A., Olsen, C. M., Lau, S. S., de La Torre, R., et al. (2005). Serotonergic neurotoxic metabolites of ecstasy identified in rat brain. *Journal of Phamacological Experimental Therapy, 313,* 422–431.

Jones, S. R., Gainetdinov, R. R., Jaber, M., Giros, B., Wightman, R. M., & Caron, M. G. (1998). Profound neuronal plasticity in response to inactivation of the dopamine transporter. *Proceedings of the National Academy of Sciences USA, 95,* 4029–4034.

Jones, S. R., Gainetdinov, R. R., Wightman, R. M., & Caron, M. G. (1998). Mechanisms of amphetamine action revealed in mice lacking the dopamine transporter. *Journal of Neuroscience, 18,* 1979–1986.

Joseph, M. H., Young, A. M. J., & Gray, J. A. (1998, December 4). Are neurochemistry and reinforcement enough? Can the abuse potential of drugs be explained by common actions on a dopamine reward system in the brain? *Human Psychopharmacology: Clinical and Experimental, 11*(Suppl. 1), S55–S63.

Kahneman, D. (2003, August 17). Toward a science of wellbeing. Transcript of interview with Nobel Laureate Daniel Kahneman, interviewed by Natasha Mitchell on ABC Radio National program *All in the Mind.* Retrieved October 11, 2008, from http://www.abc.net.au/rn/allinthemind/stories/2003/923773.htm.

Kahr, B. (2008). *Who's been sleeping in your head.* Cambridge, MA: Perseus.

Kaiser, R. B. (2001, March). The way of the journal. *Psychology Today.*

Kandel, D. B., & Maloff, D. R. (1983). Commonalities in drug use: A sociological perspective. In P. K. Levison, D. R. Gerstein, & D. R. Maloff (Eds.), *Commonalities in substance abuse and habitual behavior* (pp. 3–28). Lexington, MA: Lexington Books.

Kassebaum, P. (1999). *Substance abuse treatment for women offenders: Guide to promising practices* (DHHS Publication No. SMA 99-3303). Washington, DC: U.S. Government Printing Office.

Kellermann, J. L. (1970). *Alcoholism: A merry-go-round named denial* [Pamphlet]. New York: Hazelden.

Kelly, G. A. (1955). *The psychology of personal constructs: Vol. 1. A theory of personality; Vol. 2. Clinical diagnosis and psychotherapy.* Oxford, UK: Norton.

Kendler, K. S., Bulik, C. M., Silberg, J., Hettema, J. M., Myers, J., & Prescott, C. A. (2000). Childhood sexual abuse and adult psychiatric and substance use disorders in women: An epidemiological and cotwin control analysis. *Archives of General Psychiatry, 57,* 953–959.

Kendler, K. S., Neal, M. C., Heath, A. C., Kessler, R. C., & Eaves, L. J. (1994). A twin-family study of alcoholism in women. *American Journal of Psychiatry, 151,* 707–715.

Kendler, K. S., Prescott, C. A., Myers, J., & Neale, M. C. (2003). The structure of genetic and environmental risk factors for common psychiatric and substance use disorders in men and women. *Archives of General Psychiatry, 60,* 929–937.

Kesey, K. (1962). *One flew over the cuckoo's nest.* Boston: Twayne.

Kessler, R. C. (2004). The epidemiology of dual diagnosis. *Biological Psychiatry, 56,* 730–737.

Kessler, R. C., Berglund, P., Demler, O., Jin, R., & Walters, E. E. (2005). Lifetime prevalence and age-of-onset distributions of DSM-IV disorders in the National Comorbidity Survey Replication. *Archives of General Psychiatry, 62*(6), 593–602.

Kessler, R. C., Crum, R. M., Warner, L. A., Nelson, C. B., Schulenberg, J., & Anthony, J. C. (1997). Lifetime co-occurrence of DSM-III-R alcohol abuse and dependence with other psychiatric disorders in the National Comorbidity Survey. *Archives of General Psychiatry, 54,* 313–321.

Kessler, R. C., McGonagle, K. A., Zhao, S., Nelson, D. B., Hughes, M., Eshleman, S. W., et al. (1994). Lifetime and 12-month prevalence of DSM-III-R psychiatric disorders in the United States: Results from the National Comorbidity Survey. *Archives of General Psychiatry, 51*(1), 8–19.

Khantzian, E. J. (1997). The self-medication hypothesis of substance use disorders: A reconsideration and recent applications. *Harvard Review of Psychiatry, 4*(5), 231–244.

Khantzian, E. J. (2001). *Understanding addiction as self medication: Finding hope behind the pain.* Keynote Address, 2000 American Academy of Addiction Psychiatry Annual Meeting Proceedings.

Kilpatrick, D. G., Resnick, H. S., Saunder, B. E., & Best, C. L. (1998). Victimization, posttraumatic stress disorder, and substance use and abuse among women. In C. L. Wetherington & A. B. Roman (Eds.), *Drug addiction research and the health of women* (pp. 285–307) (NIH Publication No. 98-4290). Rockville, MD: U.S. Department of Health and Human Services.

Kimerling, R., Prins, A., Westrup, D., & Lee, T. (2004). Gender issues in the assessment of PTSD. In J. P. Wilson & T. M. Keane (Eds.), *Assessing psychological trauma and PTSD* (2nd ed., pp. 565–602). New York: Guilford.

Kinchin, D. (2005). *Post-traumatic stress disorder: The invisible injury.* Oxfordshire, UK: Success Unlimited.

King, S. M., Iacono, W. G., & McGue, M. (2004). Childhood externalizing and internalizing psychopathology in prediction of early substance use. *Addiction, 99,* 1548–1559.

King County Bar Association Drug Policy Project. (2005). *Drugs and the drug laws: Historical and cultural contexts.* Seattle, WA: Author.

Kingree, J. B., Simpson, A., Thompson, M., Tonigan, J. S., McCrady, B., & Lautenschlager, G. (2006). The development and initial evaluation of the Survey of Readiness for Alcoholics Anonymous Participation. *Psychology of Addictive Behaviors, 20*(4), 453–462.

Klam, M. (2001, January 21). Experiencing ecstasy. *New York Times Magazine,* p. 69.

Klatsky, A. L. (2006, December 23–29). Drink to your health? *Scientific American Reports, 288,* 74–81.

Klatsky, A. L., Armstrong, M. A., & Friedman, G. D. (1990). Risk of cardiovascular mortality in alcohol drinkers, ex-drinkers, and nondrinkers. *American Journal of Cardiology, 66*(17), 1237–1242.

Klein, D., & Liebowitz, M. (1979). Hysteroid disphoria. *Psychiatric Clinics of North America, 2,* 555–575.

Klump, K. L., Kaye, W. H., & Strober, M. (2001). The evolving genetic foundations of eating disorders. *Psychiatric Clinics of North America, 24*(2), 215–225.

Kobak, R. R., & Hazan, C. (1991). Attachment in marriage: Effect of security and accuracy of working models. *Journal of Personality and Social Psychology, 60,* 861–869.

Kobasa, S. C., Maddi, S. R., & Kahn, S. (1982). Hardiness and health: A prospective study. *Journal of Personality and Social Psychology, 42*(1), 168–177.

Kohut, H. (1977). *The restoration of the self.* New York: International Universities Press.

Kolata, G. (2007). *Rethinking thin: The new science of weight loss—and the myths and realities of dieting.* New York: Farrar, Straus & Giroux.

Kornfield, J. (1993). *A path with Heart: A guide through the perils and promises of spiritual life.* Bantam Books.

Kornfield, J. (Ed.). (2004). *Teachings of the Buddha.* Boston: Shambhala Publications.

Kosterlitz, H. W., & Hughes, J. (1975). Some thoughts on the significance of enkephalin, the endogenous ligand. *Life Science, 17*(1), 91–96.

Kouri, E. M., Pope, H. G., Jr., & Lukas, S. E. (1999). Changes in aggressive behavior during withdrawal from long-term marijuana use. *Psychopharmacology, 143*(3), 302–308.

Krakowski, M. (2003). Violence and serotonin: Influence of impulse control, affect regulation, and social functioning. *Journal of Neuropsychiatry and Clinical Neuroscience, 15*, 294–305.

Kramer, P. D. (1997). *Listening to Prozac: The landmark book about antidepressants and the remaking of the self* (Rev. ed.). New York: Penguin.

Kroon, C. van der. (1996). *The golden fountain: The complete guide to urine therapy.* Scottsdale, AZ: Wishland.

Krueger, R. F., Hicks, B. M., Patrick, C. J., Carlson, S. R., Iacono, W. G., & McGue, M. (2002). Etiologic connections among substance dependence, antisocial behavior, and personality: Modeling the externalizing spectrum. *Journal of Abnormal Psychology, 111*, 411–424.

Kumar, S. M. S. (2002). An introduction to Buddhism for the cognitive behavioral therapist. *Cognitive and Behavioral Practice, 9*(1), 40–43.

Kutz, I., Borysenko, J. Z., & Benson, H. (1985). Meditation and psychotherapy: A rationale for the integration of dynamic psychotherapy, the relaxation response, and mindfulness meditation. *American Journal of Psychiatry, 142*(1), 1–8.

Ladika, S. (2005). Meth madness. In H. T. Wilson (Ed.), *Annual editions: Drugs, society, and behavior* (pp. 166–169). Dubuque, IA: McGraw-Hill.

Laing, R. D. (1959). *The divided self: An existential study in sanity and madness.* New York: Tavistock.

Laing, R. D. (1973). The reality of madness. In J. Fadiman & D. Kewman (Eds.), *Exploring madness: Experience, theory, and research.* Monterey, CA: Brooks/Cole.

Laing, R. D. (1999). *The divided self: An existential study in sanity and madness.* New York: Taylor & Francis.

Lambert, K. (2008, August/September). Depressingly easy. *Scientific American Mind,* 31–37.

Lampert, T. A., Kahn, A. S., & Apple, K. J. (2003). Pluralistic ignorance and hooking up. *Journal of Sex Research, 40*, 129–133.

Langer, E. J. (2002). Well-being: Mindfulness versus positive evaluation. In C. R. Snyder & S. J. Lopez (Eds.), *Handbook of positive psychology* (pp. 214–230). New York: Oxford University Press.

LaPlante, D. A., & Shaffer, H. J. (2007). Understanding the influence of gambling opportunities: Expanding exposure models to include adaptation. *American Journal of Orthopsychiatry, 77*, 616–623.

Lask, B., & Bryant-Waugh, R. (Eds.). (2000). *Anorexia nervosa and related eating disorders in childhood and adolescence.* Hove, UK: Psychology Press.

Leahy, R. L. (1996). *Cognitive therapy: Basic principles and applications.* Northvale, NJ: Jason Aronson.

Legrand, L. N., Iacono, W. G., & McGue, M. (2005). Predicting addiction. *American Scientist, 93*, 140–147.

Lejuez, C. W., Bornovalova, M. A., Reynolds, E. K., Daughters, S. B., & Curtin, J. J. (2007). Risk factors in the relationship between gender and crack/cocaine. *Experimental and Clinical Psychopharmacology, 15*(2), 165–175.

Leonard, K. E., Quigley, B. M., & Collins, R. L. (2002). Physical aggression in the lives of young adults: Prevalence, location, and severity among college and community samples. *Journal of Interpersonal Violence, 17,* 533–550.

Leshner, A. (2007). Addiction is a brain disease. *Issues in Science and Technology.* University of Texas at Dallas. Retrieved February 11, 2009, from http://www.issues .org/17.3/leshner.htm

Lesieur, H. R., & Blume, S. B. (1993). Pathological gambling, eating disorders, and the psychoactive substance use disorders. *Journal of Addictive Diseases, 12*(3), 89–102.

Leutwyler, K. (2006, December). Dying to be thin. *Scientific American Reports.*

Levitt, P., Harvey, J. A., Friedman, E., Simansky, K., & Murphy, E. H. (1997). New evidence for neurotransmitter influences in brain development. *Trends in Neuroscience, 20,* 269–274.

Lewinsohn, P. M., Hoberman, H. M., Teri, L., & Hautzinger, M. (1985). An integrated theory of depression. In S. Reiss & R. Bootzin (Eds.), *Theoretical issues in behavior therapy* (pp. 331–359). New York: Academic Press.

Li, M. D. (2006). The genetics of nicotine dependence. *Current Psychiatry Reports, 8*(2), 158.

Lieber, C. S. (2001). Alcohol and hepatitis C. *Alcohol Research and Health, 25*(4), 245–254.

Liebowitz, M. R. (1983). *The chemistry of love.* Boston: Little, Brown.

Liechti, M. E., Saur, M. R., Gamma, A., Hell, D., & Vollenweider, F. X. (2000). Psychological and physiological effects of MDMA ("Ecstasy") after pretreatment with the 5-HT(2) antagonist ketanserin in healthy humans. *Neuropsychopharmacology, 23,* 396–404.

Liechti, M. E., & Vollenweider, G. A. (2001). Gender differences in the subjective effects of MDMA. *Psychopharmacology, 154,* 161–168.

Lin, Y., Kikuchi, S., Tamakoshi, A., Wakai, K., Kawamura, T., Iso, H., et al. (2005). Alcohol consumption and mortality among middle-aged and elderly Japanese men and women. *Annals of Epidemiology, 15,* 590–597.

Lindner, R. M. (1954, December). The jet-propelled couch: Part I. *Harper's,* 49–57.

Lindner, R. M. (1999). *The fifty-minute hour: A collection of true psychoanalytic tales.* New York: Other Press.

Lindsey, H. (1970). *Late great planet earth.* Grand Rapids, MI: Zondervan.

Linehan, M. M. (1993a). *Cognitive-behavioral treatment of borderline personality disorder.* New York: Guilford.

Linehan, M. M. (1993b). *Skills training manual for treating borderline personality disorder.* New York: Guilford.

Litt, M. D., Kadden, R. M., Kabela-Cormier, E., & Petry, N. (2007). Changing network support for drinking: Initial findings from the Network Support Project. *Journal of Consulting and Clinical Psychology, 75*(4), 542–555.

Littleton, J., (1998). Neurochemical mechanisms underlying alcohol withdrawal. *Alcohol Health & Research World, 22*(1), 13–24.

Longo, L. P., & Johnson, B. (2000, April 1). *Addiction: Part I. Benzodiazepines— Side effects, abuse risk, and alternatives.* Retrieved February 1, 2009, from http://www.aafp.org/afp/20000401/2121.html

Lopez, F. G. (2003). The assessment of adult attachment security. In S. J. Lopez & C. R. Snyder (Eds.), *Positive psychological assessment: A handbook of models and measures* (pp. 285–299). Washington, DC: American Psychological Association.

Lowe, V. D., & Kranzler, H. R. (1999). Diagnosis and treatment of alcohol-dependent patients with comorbid psychiatric disorders. *Alcohol Research and Health, 23*(2), 144–149.

Lukoff, D., Lu, F. G., & Turner, R. P. (1998). From spiritual emergency to spiritual problem: The transpersonal roots of the new DSM-IV category. *Journal of Humanistic Psychology, 38*(2), 21–50.

Luria, A. R. (1973). *The working brain.* New York: Basic Books.

Lutfullah. (1985). *Autobiography of Lutfullah.* New Delhi, India: International Writers Emporium. (Original work published 1857)

Lynch, W. J., Roth, M. E., & Carroll, M. E. (2002). Biological basis of sex differences in drug abuse: Preclinical and clinical studies. *Psychopharmacology, 164,* 121–137.

Maass, P. (2001, October). Emroz Khan is having a bad day. *New York Times,* pp. 48–51.

MacLeod, S. (2007, October 29). Postcard: Saudi Arabia. *Time,* p. 8.

Madden-Fuentes, L. (2007, Summer). Methamphetamine, nicotine, cocaine vaccine. *Solutions, 3*(2).

Mahler, M. (1967). On human symbiosis and the vicissitudes of individuation. *Journal of the American Psychoanalytic Association, 15,* 740–763.

Mahler, M. S., Pine, F., & Bergman, A. *The psychological birth of the human infant: Symbiosis and individuation.* New York: Basic Books.

Mamtani, R., & Cimino, A. (2002). A primer of complementary and alternative medicine and its relevance in the treatment of mental health problems. *Psychiatric Quarterly, 73*(4), 367–381.

Mander, J. (1978). *Four arguments for the elimination of television.* New York: Harper Perennial.

Manhart, K. (2005, September 22). Lust for danger. *Scientific American Mind.* Retrieved June 18, 2008, from http://www.sciam.com/article.cfm?id=lust-for-danger&print=true

The Manhattan Project: An enduring legacy. (1999, December 6). *PhysicsWorld.com.* Retrieved January 30, 2009, from http://physicsworld.com/cws/article/print/855

Mann, T., Tomijama, A. J., Westling, E., Lew, A. M., Samuels, B., & Chatman, J. (2007). Medicare's search for effective obesity treatments: Diets are not the answer. *American Psychologist, 62*(3), 220–233.

Mansvelder, H. D., & McGehee, D. S. (2002). Synaptic mechanisms underlie nicotine-induced excitability of brain reward systems. *Neuron, 33*(6), 905–919.

Marazziti, D., & Dell'osso, M. C. (2008). The role of oxytocin in neuropsychiatric disorders. *Current Medical Chemicals, 15*(7), 698–704.

Marlatt, G. A. (1985). Relapse prevention: Theoretical rationale and overview. In G. A. Marlatt & J. R. Gordon (Eds.), *Relapse prevention: Maintenance strategies in the treatment of addictive behaviors* (p. 38). New York: Guilford.

Marlatt, G. A. (Ed.). (1998). *Harm reduction: Pragmatic strategies for managing high-risk behaviors.* New York: Guilford.

Marlatt, G. A. (2002). Buddhist philosophy and the treatment of addictive behavior. *Cognitive and Behavioral Practice, 9,* 44–49.

Marlatt, G. A., & Gordon, J. R. (Eds.). (1985). *Relapse prevention: Maintenance strategies in the treatment of addictive behaviors.* New York: Guilford.

Marlatt, G. A., Parks, G. A., & Witkiewitz, K. (2002, December). *Clinical guidelines for implementing relapse prevention therapy.* Available at http://www.bhrm.org/guidelines/RPT%20guideline.pdf

Marlatt, G. A., & Roberts, L. J. (1998). Introduction to special issue on treatment of comorbid addictive behaviors: Harm reduction as an alternative to abstinence. *In Session: Psychotherapy in Practice, 4,* 1–8.

Marlatt, G. A., & Witkiewitz, K. (2005). Relapse prevention for alcohol and drug problems. In G. A. Marlatt & D. M. Donovan (Eds.), *Relapse prevention: Maintenance strategies in the treatment of addictive behavior* (pp. 1–44). New York: Guilford.

Marquez, J. (2006, July 31). Mel Gibson's anti-Semitic remarks cited in official police report. *San Francisco Chronicle.* Retrieved January 26, 2009, from http://www .sfgate.com/cgi-bin/article.cgi?f=/n/a/2006/07/31/entertainment/e143903D69 .DTL&type=politics

Maslow, A. (1970). *Motivation and personality.* New York: Harper. (Original work published 1954)

Masters, W. H., & Johnson, V. E. (1974). *The pleasure bond.* New York: Bantam.

Mathias, R., & Zickler, P. (2001). NIDA conference highlights scientific findings on MDMA/Ecstasy. *NIDA Notes, 16,* 5.

Matlin, N. W. (1996). *The psychology of women.* Fort Worth, TX: Harcourt Brace.

Mattson, M. (2007). Calcium and neurodegeneration. *Aging Cell, 6,* 337–350.

Mayes, L. C. (1995). Substance abuse and parenting. In M. H. Bornstein (Ed.), *The handbook of parenting* (pp. 101–125). Hillsdale, NJ: Lawrence Erlbaum.

Mayo Foundation for Medical Education and Research. (2007). *Weight loss.* Retrieved February 11, 2009, from http://www.mayoclinic.com/health/exercise/SM00109

McCabe, S. E. (2008). Screening for drug abuse among medical and nonmedical users of prescription drugs in a probability sample of college students. *Archives of Pediatrics and Adolescent Medicine, 162*(3), 225–231.

McCann, I. L., & Holmes, D. S. (1984). Influence of aerobic exercise on depression. *Journal of Personality and Social Psychology, 46*(5), 1142–1147.

McCann, U. D., Szabo, K., Scheffel, U., Dannals, R. F., & Ricaurte, G. A. (1998). Positron emission tomographic evidence of toxic effects of MDMA (Ecstasy) on brain serotonin neurons in human beings. *Lancet, 352,* 1433–1437.

McCaughan, J. A., Carlson, R. G., Falck, R. S., & Siegal, H. A. (2005). From "Candy-kids" to "Chemikids": A typology of young adults who attend raves in the Midwestern United States. *Substance Use and Misuse, 40*(9–10), 1503–1523.

McGinnis, J., & Foege, W. H. (1993). Actual causes of death in the United States. *Journal of the American Medical Association, 270,* 2207–2212.

McKay, J. R., Alterman, A. I., Rutherford, M. J., Cacciola, J. S., & McLellan, A. T. (1999). The relationship of alcohol use to cocaine relapse in cocaine dependent patients in an aftercare study. *Journal of Studies on Alcohol, 60,* 176–180.

McMahon, M. (Ed.). (2000). *Assessment to assistance: Programs for women in community corrections.* Lanham, MD: American Correctional Association.

Mears, B. (2005, June 7). Law center: Supreme Court allows prosecution of medical marijuana. *CNN.com.* Retrieved January 19, 2009, from http://www.cnn .com/2005/LAW/06/06/scotus.medical.marijuana/index.html

Mears, C. (2007). Computer gaming: When virtual violence becomes real. *Psychiatric Times, 24*(13), 1–3.

Meichenbaum, D. (1977). Dr. Ellis, please stand up. *Counseling Psychologist, 7*(1), 43–44.

Meichenbaum, D. (1985). *Stress inoculation training.* New York: Pergamon.

Melby, T. (2008). How Second Life seeps into real life. *Contemporary Sexuality, 41*(12), 3–5.

Meyers, J. (1992). *Edgar Allan Poe: His life and legacy.* New York: Cooper Square.

Meyers, R. D. (1989, May). Isoquinolines, beta-carbolines and alcohol drinking: Involvement of opioid and dopaminergic mechanisms. *Cellular and Molecular Life Sciences, 45*(5), 436–443.

Milkman, H. (1981). Trip to China. Unpublished notes.

Milkman, H. (1987). Interview with Detective Daril Cinquanta. In H. Milkman & S. Sunderwirth, *Craving for ecstasy: The consciousness and chemistry of escape* (p. 115). Lexington, MA: Lexington Books.

Milkman, H. (2001, April/May). Better than dope. *Psychology Today.*

Milkman, H., & Frosch, W. (1973). On the preferential abuse of heroin and amphetamines. *Journal of Nervous and Mental Disease, 156*(4), 242–248.

Milkman, H., & Frosch, W. (1977). The drug of choice. *Journal of Psychedelic Drugs, 9*(1), 11–24.

Milkman, H., & Hunter, A. (1987, October 3–5). *Say Yes to Natural Highs: A Conference on New Directions* [conference brochure]. Sponsored by the Colorado Alcohol and Drug Abuse Division, Clarion Hotel, Boulder.

Milkman, H., & Hunter, A. (1988, September 16–18). *Natural Highs: New Directions for Individual, Family, and Community Well-Being* [conference brochure]. Sponsored by the Colorado Alcohol and Drug Abuse Division, in association with the Colorado Department of Education, Clarion Hotel, Boulder.

Milkman, H., Metcalf, D., & Reed, P. D. (1980). An innovative approach to methadone detoxification. *International Journal of the Addictions, 15*(9), 1199–1211.

Milkman, H., & Sederer, L. (Eds.). (1990). *Treatment choices for alcoholism and substance abuse.* Lexington, MA: Lexington Books.

Milkman, H., & Sunderwirth, S. (1982). Addictive processes. *Journal of Psychoactive Drugs, 14,* 177–192.

Milkman, H., & Sunderwirth, S. (1983, October). The chemistry of craving. *Psychology Today,* 36–44.

Milkman, H., & Sunderwirth, S. (1987). *Craving for ecstasy: How our passions become addictions and what we can do about them.* San Francisco: Jossey-Bass.

Milkman, H., & Sunderwirth, S. (1993). *Pathways to pleasure: The consciousness and chemistry of optimal living.* Lexington, MA: Lexington Books.

Milkman, H., & Sunderwirth, S. (1998). *Craving for ecstasy: How our passions become addictions and what we can do about them* (paperback reissue of 1987 ed.). San Francisco: Jossey-Bass.

Milkman, H., & Wanberg, K. (2005). *Criminal conduct and substance abuse treatment for adolescents: Pathways to self-discovery and change.* Thousand Oaks, CA: Sage Publications.

Milkman, H., & Wanberg, K. (2007). *Cognitive-behavioral treatment: A review and discussion for corrections professionals.* Washington, DC: National Institute of Corrections. (NIC Accession No. 021657)

Milkman, H., Wanberg, K., & Gagliardi, B. (2008). *Criminal conduct and substance abuse treatment for women in correctional settings: Adjunct provider's guide.* Thousand Oaks, CA: Sage Publications.

Milkman, H., Wanberg, K., & Robinson, C. (1996). *Project Self-Discovery: Artistic alternatives for high-risk youth.* Hoboken, NJ: Wiley.

Miller, H. (1987). *Tropic of cancer.* New York: Grove.

Miller, W. (1990). Alcohol treatment alternatives: What works? In H. B. Milkman & L. I. Sederer (Eds.), *Treatment choices for alcoholism and substance abuse* (pp. 253–264). Lexington, MA: Lexington Books.

Miller, W. R., & Hester, R. K. (1986). The effectiveness of treatment for substance abuse treatment: What research reveals. In W. R. Miller & N. Heather (Eds.), *Treating addictive behaviors: Processes of change* (pp. 121–174). New York: Plenum.

Miranda, J. (1992). Dysfunctional thinking is activated by stressful life events. *Cognitive Therapy and Research, 16,* 473–483.

Moore, K., & Miller, S. (2005, August). Living the high life: The role of drug taking in young people's lives. In H. T. Wilson (Ed.), *Annual editions: Drugs, society, and behavior 2007/2008* (pp. 5–8). Dubuque, IA: McGraw-Hill. (Originally published in *Drugs and Alcohol Today*)

Morahan-Martin, J. (2001). Impact of Internet abuse for college students. In C. Wolfe (Ed.), *Learning and teaching on the World Wide Web* (pp. 191–219). San Diego: Academic Press.

Morasco, B. J., Pietrzak, R. H., Blanco, C., Grant, B. F., Hasin, D., & Petry, N. M. (2006). Health problems and medical utilization associated with gambling disorders: Results from the National Epidemiologic Survey on Alcohol and Related Conditions. *Psychosomatic Medicine, 68,* 976–984.

Mukamal, K. J., Conigrave, K. M., Mittleman, M. A., Camargo, C., Stampfer, M., Willett, W., et al. (2003). Roles of drinking pattern and type of alcohol consumed in coronary heart disease in men. *New England Journal of Medicine, 348,* 109–118.

Murphy, L. L., Muñoz, R. M., Adrian, B. A., & Villanúa, M. A. (1998, December). Function of cannabinoid receptors in the neuroendocrine regulation of hormone secretion. *Neurobiology of Disease, 5*(6), 432–446.

Mutrie, N., & Faulkner, G. (2003). Physiotherapy and occupational therapy in mental health: An evidence-based approach. In T. Everett, M. Donaghy, & S. Fever (Eds.), *Physical activity and mental health* (pp. 211–215). Oxford, UK: Butterworth Heinemann.

Nadelmann, E. A. (2004, July 12). An end to marijuana prohibition: The drive to legalize picks up. *National Review,* pp. 28–33.

Najavits, L. M. (2006). Present- versus past-focused therapy for PTSD/substance abuse: A study of clinician preferences. *Brief Treatment and Crisis Intervention, 6*(3), 248–254.

Nakamura, J., & Csikszentmihalyi, M. (2002). The concept of flow. In C. R. Snyder & S. J. Lopez (Eds.), *The handbook of positive psychology* (pp. 89–105). New York: Oxford University Press.

Nash, M. (1997, May 5). Addicted. *Time.*

National Association of Cognitive-Behavioral Therapists. (2008). *History of cognitive-behavioral therapy.* Weirton, WV: Author. Retrieved August 7, 2008, from http://www.nacbt.org/historyofcbt.htm

National Center for Posttraumatic Stress Disorder. (2007). *How common is PTSD?* [fact sheet]. Washington, DC: U.S. Department of Veterans Affairs. Retrieved August 29, 2007, from http://www.ncptsd.va.gov/ncmain/ncdocs/fact_shts/fs_how_common_is_ptsd.html

National Comorbidity Survey. (n.d.). National Comorbidity Survey Publications. Retrieved June 10, 2008, from http://www.hcp.med.harvard.edu/ncs/publications.php

National Drug Intelligence Center. (2003, August). *Psilocybin Fast Facts.* Retrieved July 15, 2008, from http://www.usdoj.gov/ndic/pubs6/6038/index.htm

National Institute on Alcohol Abuse and Alcoholism of the National Institutes of Health. (2005). *Helping patients who drink too much: A clinician's guide.* Bethesda, MD: Author.

National Institute on Drug Abuse. (2001). *Hallucinogens and dissociative drugs.* Washington, DC: U.S. Department of Health and Human Services: Author.

National Institute on Drug Abuse. (2005a). *Inhalant abuse.* Research report series (Publication No. 05-3818). Washington, DC: Author.

National Institute on Drug Abuse. (2005b). *Marijuana abuse.* Research report series (Publication No. 05-3859). Washington, DC: Author.

National Institute on Drug Abuse. (2007a, April). *Drugs, brains, and behavior: The science of addiction.* Retrieved January 5, 2009, from http://www.drugabuse.gov/ScienceofAddiction/sciofaddiction.pdf

National Institute on Drug Abuse. (2007b, June). *Heroin.* Retrieved July 14, 2008, from http://www.nida.nih.gov/drugpages/heroin.html

National Institute on Drug Abuse. (2007c, June). *Marijuana: Facts parents need to know.* Retrieved July 14, 2008, from http://www.nida.nih.gov/marijbroch/MarijparentsN.html

National Institute on Drug Abuse. (2007d, June). *NIDA for Teens: Nicotine.* Retrieved July 14, 2008, from http://teens.drugabuse.gov/facts/facts_nicotine1.asp.

National Institute on Drug Abuse. (2007e, June). *NIDA Info Facts: Club drugs (GHB, ketamine, and Rohypnol).* Retrieved July 14, 2008, from http://www.nida.nih.gov/infofacts/Clubdrugs.html

National Institute on Drug Abuse. (2007f, June). *NIDA Info Facts: Cocaine and crack.* Retrieved July 14, 2008, from http://ww.nida.nih.gov/infofacts/cocaine.html

National Institute on Drug Abuse. (2007g, June). *NIDA Info Facts: Inhalants.* Retrieved July 14, 2008, from http://www.nida.nih.gov/infofacts/inhalants.html

National Institute on Drug Abuse. (2007h, June). *NIDA Info Facts: LSD.* Retrieved July 14, 2008, from http://www.nida.nih.gov/infofacts/lsd.html

National Institute on Drug Abuse. (2007i, June). *NIDA Info Facts: Marijuana.* Retrieved July 14, 2008, from http://www.nida.nih.gov/infofacts/marijuana.html

National Institute on Drug Abuse. (2007j, June). *NIDA Info Facts: Methamphetamine.* Retrieved July 14, 2008, from http://www.nida.nih.gov/infofacts/methamphetamine.html

National Institute on Drug Abuse. (2007k, June). *NIDA Info Facts: PCP (phencyclidine).* Retrieved July 14, 2008, from http://www.nida.nih.gov/infofacts/pcp.html

National Institute on Drug Abuse. (2007l, June). *NIDA Info Facts: Prescription and over-the-counter medications.* Retrieved July 14, 2008, from http://www.nida.nih.gov/infofacts/PainMed.html

National Institute on Drug Abuse. (2007m, June). *NIDA Info Facts: Steroids (anabolic-androgenic).* Retrieved July 14, 2008, from http://www.nida.nih.gov/infofacts/steroids.html

National Institute on Drug Abuse. (2008, August). *NIDA InfoFacts: Crack and cocaine.* Retrieved February 1, 2009, from http://www.nida.nih.gov/Infofacts/cocaine.html

National Institutes of Health. (2008, January 1). *Cocaine withdrawal.* Retrieved July 14, 2008, from http://www.nlm.nih.gov/medlineplus/ency/article/000947.htm

National Survey on Drug Use and Health. (2005). *Alcohol: A women's health issue.* Washington, DC: U.S. Department of Health and Human Services. (NIH Publication No. 04-4956, revised)

National Survey on Drug Use and Health. (2006). *SAMHSA's latest National Survey on Drug Use and Health.* Washington, DC: U.S. Department of Health and Human Services. Retrieved April 6, 2009 from http://www.oas.samhsa.gov/NSDUHlatest.htm

Neighmond, P. (2007, November 21). Retune the body with a partial fast [transcript of radio broadcast]. National Public Radio, *All Things Considered.* Retrieved July 1, 2008, from http://www.npr.org/templates/story/story.php?storyId=16513299

Nelson, K. G., & Oehlert, M. E. (2008). Evaluation of a shortened South Oaks Gambling Screen in veterans with addictions. *Psychology of Addictive Behaviors, 22*(2), 309–312.

Nemeroff, C. B. (1998, June). The neurobiology of depression. *Scientific American,* 42–49.

Nestle, M. (2007, August). Eating made simple: How do you cope with a mountain of conflicting advice? *Scientific American,* 60–69. Retrieved July 1, 2008, from http://www.sciam.com/article.cfm?id=eating-made-simple

Netz, Y., Wu, M., Becker, B. J., & Tenenbaum, G. (2005). Physical activity and psychological well-being in advanced age: A meta-analysis of intervention studies. *Psychology and Aging, 20*(2), 272–284.

Newcombe, R. (2004). *Cannabis psychosis: Mental disorder or myth?* Unpublished paper, John Moores University, Liverpool, UK.

Nichols, D. E. (1997). Role of serotonergic neurons and 5-HT receptors in the action of hallucinogens. In H. G. Baumgarten & M. Gothert (Eds.), *Handbook of experimental pharmacology: Serotoninergic neurons and 5-HT receptors in the CNS* (pp. 563–585). Heidelberg, Germany: Springer-Verlag.

Nicoll, R. A., & Alger, B. E. (2004). The brain's own marijuana. *Scientific American, 291*(3), 67–75.

Nikoshkov, A., Drakenberg, K., Wang, X., Horvath, M., Keller, E., & Hurd, Y. L. (2008). Opioid neuropeptide genotypes in relation to heroin abuse: Dopamine tone contributes to reversed mesolimbic proenkephalin expression. *Proceedings of the National Academy of Sciences of the United States of America, 105*(2), 786–791.

Nizza, M. (2007, November 7). A deadly school shooting, this time in Finland. *New York Times.*

Obituary: Albert Hofmann. (2008, May 8). *Economist,* p. 90.

Odegaard, S., Peller, A., & Shaffer, H. J. (2005). Addiction as syndrome. *Paradigm, 9*(3), 12–13, 22.

Office of National Drug Control Policy. (2008). *Club drugs facts & figures.* Retrieved January 13, 2009, from http://www.ondcp.gov/drugfact/club/club_drug_ff.html

Ohtake, M. (2008, July 24). A school for johns. *Newsweek.* Retrieved January 20, 2009, from http://www.newsweek.com/id/148531

Olds, J., & Milner, P. (1954). Positive reinforcement produced by electrical stimulation of septal area and other regions of the rat brain. *Journal of Comparative Physiology & Psychology, 47,* 419.

Oman, D., Hedberg, J., & Thoresen, C. E. (2006). Passage meditation reduces perceived stress in health professionals: A randomized, controlled trial. *Journal of Consulting and Clinical Psychology, 74,* 714–719.

Oncken, C., Cooney, J., Feinn, R., Lando, H., & Kranzler, H. (2007). Transdermal nicotine for smoking cessation in postmenopausal women. *Addict Behaviors, 32,* 296–309.

Ornish, D. (1998). *Love and survival: The scientific basis for the healing power of intimacy.* New York: HarperCollins.

Ornish, D. (2008). Dean Ornish shows how to reverse prostate cancer with nutrigenomics. Retrieved July 27, 2008, from http://articles.directorym.net/Dean_Ornish_Shows_How_to_Reverse_Prostate_Cancer_with_Nutrigenomics_Sacramento_CA-r861391-Sacramento_CA.html

Ornstein, R., & Sobel, D. (1987). *The healing brain: Breakthrough discoveries about how the brain keeps us healthy.* New York: Simon & Schuster.

Osborne, G., & Fogel, G. (2008). Understanding the motivations for recreational marijuana use among adult Canadians. *Substance Use and Misuse, 43*(3–4), 539–572.

Ott, A., Andersen, K., Dewey, M. E., Letenneur, L., Brayne, C., Copeland, J. R. M., et al. (2004). Effect of smoking on global cognitive function in nondemented elderly. *Neurology, 62,* 920–924.

Ouimette, P. C., Wolfe, J., & Chrestman, K. R. (1996). Characteristics of posttraumatic stress disorder—alcohol abuse comorbidity in women. *Journal of Substance Abuse, 8*(3), 335–346.

Owen, F. (2007). *No speed limit: Meth across America.* New York: St. Martin's Press.

Ozelli, K. L. (2007). This is your brain on food. *Scientific American, 297*(3), 84.

Paffenbarger, R. S., & Lee, I. M. (1996). Physical activity and fitness for health and longevity. *Research Quarterly for Exercise and Sport, 67*(3), S11–S28.

Palmer, I. (2007). Terrorism, suicide bombing, fear, and mental health. *International Review of Psychiatry, 19*(3), 289–296.

Paradis, S., & Cabanac, M. (2008). Dieting and food choice in grocery shopping. *Physiological Behavior, 93*(4–5), 1030–1032.

Parascandola, R. (2006, June 26). "Crack is Wack" mural now icon. *AM New York/Newsday.* Available at http://www.newsday.com/news/local/wire/newyork/am-crack0626,0,200232.story

Parker, G., Parker, J., & Brotchie, H. (2006). Mood state effects of chocolate. *Journal of Affective Disorders, 92,* 149–159.

Parks, G. A. (2005). Use relapse prevention techniques. In S. Sacks & R. K. Ries (Eds.), *Substance abuse treatment for persons with co-occurring disorders: Treatment Improvement Protocol (TIP) 42* (pp. 127–133). Rockville, MD: U.S. Department of Health and Human Services, Substance Abuse and Mental Health Services Administration, Center for Substance Abuse Treatment.

Parks, G. A., & Marlatt, G. A. (2006). Mindfulness meditation and substance use in an incarcerated population. *Psychology of Addictive Behaviors, 20*(3), 343–347.

Parks, K. A., Miller, B. A., Collins, R. I., & Zetes-Zanatta, L. (1998). Women's descriptions of drinking in bars: Reasons and risks. *Sex Roles, 38,* 701–717.

Partnership for a Drug-Free America. (2008). *Rohypnol.* Retrieved July 15, 2008, from http://www.drugfree.org/Portal/Drug_guide/Rohypnol

Patrick, C. J., Bernat, E., Malonel, S. M., Iacono, W. G., Krueger R. F., & McGue, M. K. (2006). P300 amplitude as an indicator of externalizing in adolescent males. *Psychophysiology, 43,* 84–92.

Paul, E. L., & Hayes, K. A. (2002). The casualties of "casual" sex: A qualitative exploration of the phenomenology of college students' hookups. *Journal of Social and Personal Relationships, 19*(5), 639–661.

Pavlov, I. (1927). *Conditioned reflexes.* New York: Oxford University Press.

Perez-De-Albeniz, A., & Holmes, J. (2000). Meditation: Concepts, effects, and uses in therapy. *International Journal of Psychotherapy, 5*(1), 49–59.

Perham, A. S., & Accordino, M. P. (2007). Exercise and functioning level of individuals with severe mental illness: A comparison of two groups. *Journal of Mental Health Counseling, 29*(4), 350–362.

Perry, S. K. (1999). *Writing in flow.* Cincinnati, OH: Writer's Digest Books.

Pescatello, L. S., Franklin, B. A., Fagard, R., Farquhar, W. B., Kelley, G. A., & Ray, C. A. (2004, March). American College of Sports Medicine position stand: Exercise and hypertension. *Medicine & Science in Sports & Exercise, 36*(3), 533–553.

Peterson, C., & Seligman, M. E. P. (2004). *Character strengths and virtues: A handbook and classification.* New York: Oxford University Press.

Phillips, P., Stuber, G., Heien, M., Wightman, R., & Carelli, R. (2003). Subsecond dopamine release promotes cocaine seeking. *Nature, 422,* 614–618.

Pink, D. H. (2005). *A whole new mind.* New York: Riverhead Books.

Plumridge, E. W., Chetwynd, J. W., Reed, A., & Gifford, S. J. (1997). Discourses of emotionality in commercial sex: The missing client voice. *Feminism and Psychology, 7,* 165–181.

Poe, E. A. (1849). Annabel Lee. *Sartain's Union Magazine.*

Pollock, M. J. (1998). *Counseling women in prison.* Thousand Oaks, CA: Sage Publications.

Pope, H. G., Gruber, A. J., Hudson, J. I., Huestis, M. A., & Yurgelun-Todd, D. (2001). Neuropsychological performance in long-term cannabis users. *Archives of General Psychiatry, 58*(10), 909–915.

Pope, H. G., Jr., & Yurgelun-Todd, D. (1996). The residual cognitive effects of heavy marijuana use in college students. *Journal of the American Medical Association, 275*(7), 521–527.

Popkin, B. M. (2007). Understanding global nutrition dynamics as a step towards controlling cancer incidence. *Nature Reviews Cancer, 7*(1), 61–67.

Potenza, M. N. (2001). The neurobiology of pathological gambling. *Seminars in Clinical Neuropsychiatry, 6,* 217–226.

Potter, B. (1991). *The tale of Peter Rabbit.* New York: Penguin. (Original work published 1902)

Prescott, C. A., & Kendler, K. S. (1999). Genetic and environmental contributions to alcohol abuse and dependence in a population-based sample of male twins. *American Journal of Psychiatry, 156,* 34–40.

Price, K. (2000). Stripping women: Workers control in strip clubs. *Current Research on Occupations and Professions, 11,* 3–33.

Professor, 49, died from anorexia. (2008). *BBC News.* Retrieved April 23, 2008, from http://news.bbc.co.uk/1/hi/england/dorset/7360470.stm

Progoff, I. (1975). *At a journal workshop: The basic text and guide for using the intensive journal process.* New York: Dialogue House.

Progoff, I. (1980). *The practice of process meditation: The intensive journal way to spiritual experience.* New York: Dialogue House.

Puetz, T. W., O'Connor, P. J., & Dishman, R. K. (2006). The effect of chronic exercise on feelings of energy and fatigue: A quantitative synthesis. *Psychological Bulletin, 132,* 866–876.

Pyszczynski, T. (2004). What are we so afraid of? A terror management theory perspective on the politics of fear. *Social Research, 71*(4), 827–848.

Quit Smoking Hub. (n.d.). *Smoking statistics in the United States.* Retrieved January 6, 2009, from http://www.quitsmokinghub.com/smoking_statistics.shtml

Raeburn, P. (2007). Can fat be fit? *Scientific American, 297*(3), 70–71.

Ramirez, J. (2008, June 16). Feeling the pinch: Nevada's brothels hit hard times. *Newsweek*. Retrieved January 20, 2009, from http://www.newsweek.com/id/141848

Rasch, W. (1979). Psychological dimensions of political terrorism in the Federal Republic of Germany. *International Journal of Law and Psychiatry, 2,* 79–85.

Rausch, S. M., Gramling, S. E., & Auerbach, S. M. (2006). Effects of a single session of large-group meditation and progressive muscle relaxation training on stress reduction, creativity, and recovery. *International Journal of Stress Management, 13*(3), 273–290.

Regier, D. A., Farmer, M. E., Rae, D. S., Locke, B. Z., Keith, S. J., Judd, L. L., et al. (1990). Comorbidity of mental disorders with alcohol and other drug abuse: Results from the Epidemiologic Catchment Area (ECA) study. *Journal of the American Medical Association, 264,* 247–257.

Rehm, J., Patra, J., & Popova, S. (2007). Alcohol drinking cessation and its effect on esophageal and head and neck cancers: A pooled analysis. *International Journal of Cancer, 121*(5), 1132–1137.

Reich, A. (1960). Pathologic forms of self-esteem regulation. *Psychoanalytic Study of the Child, 15,* 215–232.

Reissig, C., Strain, E., & Griffiths, R. (2008). Caffeinated energy drinks—a growing problem. *Drug Alcohol Dependency, 165*(10), 1256–1260.

Reith, G. (2007). Gambling and the contradictions of consumption: A genealogy of the "pathological" subject. *American Behavioral Scientist, 51*(1), 33–56.

Renaud, S. C., Gueguen, R., Schenker, J., & d'Houtaud, A. (1998). Alcohol and mortality in middle-aged men from eastern France. *Epidemiology, 9,* 184–188.

Renaud, S. C., Gueguen, R., Siest, G., & Salamon, R. (1999). Wine, beer, and mortality in middle-aged men from eastern France. *Archives of Internal Medicine, 159,* 1865–1870.

Renik, O. (2002). Defining the goals of clinical psychoanalysis. *Psychoanalytic Quarterly, 71,* 117–123.

Reuter, J., Raedler, T., Rose, M., Hand, I., Glascher, J., & Buchel, C. (2005). Pathological gambling is linked to reduced activation of the mesolimbic reward system. *Nature Neuroscience, 8,* 147–148.

Ricaurte, G. A., Yuan, J., Hatzidimitriou, G., Cord, B. J., & McCann, U. D. (2002). Severe dopaminergic neurotoxicity in primates after common recreational dose regimen of MDMA ("Ecstasy"). *Science, 297,* 2260–2263.

Rilke, R. M. (1954). *Letters to a young poet.* New York: Norton.

Rimm, E. B., Klatsky, A., Grobbee, D., & Stampfer, M. J. (1996). Review of moderate alcohol consumption and reduced risk of coronary heart disease: Is the effect due to beer, wine, or spirits. *British Medical Journal, 312,* 731–736.

Rivas-Vasquez, R. A., & Delgado, L. (2002). Clinical and toxic effects of MDMA ("Ecstasy"). *Professional Psychology: Research and Practice, 33*(4), 422–425.

Robbins, S. J., Ehrman, R. N., Childress, A. R., & O'Brien, C. P. (1999). Comparing levels of cocaine cue reactivity in male and female outpatients. *Drug and Alcohol Dependence, 53,* 223–230.

Roberts, D. F., & Foehr, U. G. (2008). Trends in media use. *Future of Children, 18*(1), 1–37.

Roberts, D. F., Foehr, U. G., & Rideout, V. (2005). *Generation M: Media in the lives of 8- to 18-year-olds.* Menlo Park, CA: Kaiser Family Foundation.

Robins, C. J., Schmidt, H., III, & Linehan, M. M. (2004). Dialectical behavior therapy: Synthesizing radical acceptance with skillful means. In S. C. Hayes,

V. M. Follette, & M. M. Linehan (Eds.), *Mindfulness and acceptance: Expanding the cognitive-behavioral tradition* (pp. 30–44). New York: Guilford.

Rodgers, J., Buchanan, T., Scholey, A. B., Heffernan, T. M., Ling, J., & Parrott, A. C. (2001). Ecstasy and cannabis: Differential effects on aspects of prospective memory. *Human Psychopharmacology, 16,* 621–627.

Ronai, C. R., & Ellis, C. (1989). Turn-ons for money: Interactional strategies of the table dancer. *Journal of Contemporary Ethnography, 18*(3), 271–298.

Ropelato, J. (2007). *Internet pornography statistics.* Retrieved March 27, 2007, from http://internet-filter-review.toptenreviews.com/internet-pornography-statistics.html

Rosenberg, N. L., Grigsby, J., Dreisbach, J., Busenbark, D., & Grigsby, P. (2002). Neuropsychologic impairment and MRI abnormalities associated with chronic solvent abuse. *Journal of Clinical Toxicology, 40,* 21–34.

Rossel Waugh, E.-J. (2006, August 25). A short history of electronic arts. *Business News.* Retrieved January 29, 2009, from http://www.businessweek.com/print/innovate/content/aug2006/id20060828_268977.htm

Routtenberg, A. (1978). The reward system of the brain. *Scientific American, 239*(5), 154–164.

Rouvalis, C. (2006, June 14). Risk-taking can be a two-faced monster. *Pittsburg Post-Gazette.* Available at http://www.post-gazette.com/pg/06165/698069-66.stm

Rowland, C. V. (1980). Hyperobesity as indirect self-destructive behavior. In N. L. Farberor (Ed.), *The many faces of suicide: Indirect self-destructive behavior* (pp. 232–242). Boston: McGraw-Hill.

Rupp, J. C. (1973). The love bug. *Journal of Forensic Sciences, 18,* 259–262.

Saldaña, S. H., & Barker, E. L. (2004). Temperature and 3,4-methylene-dioxymethamphetamine alter human serotonin transporter-mediated dopamine uptake. *Neuroscience Letters, 354*(3), 209–212.

Sanders, T. (2005) *Sex work: A risky business.* Cullompton, Devon, UK: Willan.

Sanders-Bush, E. (1994). Neurochemical evidence that hallucinogenic drugs are 5-HT1c receptor agonists: What next? *NIDA Research Monograph,* 146203–14613.

Santucci, A. C. (2008). Adolescent cocaine residually impairs working memory and enhances fear memory in rats. *Experimental and Clinical Psychopharmacology, 16*(1), 77–85.

Sapolsky, R. M. (1994). *Why zebras don't get ulcers.* New York: Henry Holt.

Satir, V. (1972). *People making.* Palo Alto, CA: Science and Behavior Books.

Satir, V., & Baldwin, M. (1983). *Satir step by step: A guide to creating change in families.* Palo Alto, CA: Science and Behavior Books.

Satran, A., Bart, B. A., Henry, C. R., Murad, B., Talukdar, S., Satran, D., et al. (2005). Increased prevalence of coronary artery aneurysms among cocaine users. *Circulation, 111,* 2424–2429.

Schaefer-Jones, J. (2007). *Preparing for the worst: A comprehensive guide to protecting your family from terrorist attacks, natural disasters, and other catastrophes.* Westport, CT: Greenwood.

Schlosser, E. (1997, February 10). The business of pornography: Most of the outsized profits being generated today are by business not traditionally associated with the sex industry. *U.S. News & World Report, 122,* 42.

Schneider, J. P., & Irons, R. R. (2001). Assessment and treatment of addictive sexual disorders: Relevance for chemical dependency relapse. *Substance Use and Misuse, 36*(13), 1795–1820.

Scholey, A., & Kennedy, D. (2004, November). Cognitive and physiological effects of an "energy drink": An evaluation of the whole drink and of glucose, caffeine and herbal flavouring fractions. *Psychopharmacology, 176*(3–4).

Schuckit, M. A. (1984). Acetaldehyde and alcoholism: Methodology. In V. Hesselbrock, E. Shaskan, & R. Meyer (Eds.), *Biological and genetic markers of alcoholism* (pp. 23–48). Washington, DC: National Institute on Alcohol Abuse and Alcoholism.

Schultz, D. P., & Schultz, S. E. (2004). *A history of modern psychology* (8th ed.). Belmont, CA: Wadsworth/Thompson.

Schwartz, J. P., Thigpen, S. E., & Montgomery, J. K. (2006). Examination of parenting styles of processing emotions and differentiation of self. *Family Journal: Counseling and Therapy for Couples and Families, 14*(1), 41–48.

Seligman, M. E. P. (2002). *Authentic happiness: Using the new positive psychology to realize your potential for lasting fulfillment.* New York: Free Press.

Selye, H. (1956). *The stress of life.* Boston: McGraw-Hill.

Selye, H. (1971). *Hormones and resistance.* New York: Springer-Verlag.

Selye, H. (1974). *Stress without distress.* Philadelphia: Lippincott.

Shaffer, D., Wilcox, H., Lucas, C., Hicks, R., Busner, C., & Parides, M. (1996). *The development of a screening instrument for teens at risk for suicide.* Poster presented at a meeting of the Academy of Child and Adolescent Psychiatry, New York.

Shaffer, H. J. (2004). *Internet gambling and addiction.* Boston: Harvard Medical School Division on Addictions.

Shaffer, H. J., Hall, M. N., & Vander Bilt, J. (1999). Estimating the prevalence of disordered gambling behavior in the United States and Canada: A research synthesis. *American Journal of Public Health, 89,* 1369–1376.

Shaffer, H. J., & Korn, D. A. (2002). Gambling and related mental disorders: A public health analysis. *Annual Review of Public Health, 23,* 171–212.

Shaffer, H. J., LaBrie, R., LaPlante, D., Nelson, S., & Stanton, B. (2004, August). The road less traveled: Moving from distribution to determinants in the study of gambling epidemiology. *Canadian Journal of Psychiatry, 49*(8), 504–516.

Shaffer, H. J., LaPlante, D. A., La Brie, R. A., Kidman, R. C., Donato, A., & Stanton, M. V. (2004). Toward a syndrome model of addiction: Multiple manifestations, common etiology. *Harvard Review of Psychiatry, 12*(6), 367–374.

Shapiro, D. H. (1992). Adverse effects of meditation: A preliminary investigation of long-term meditators. *International Journal of Psychosomatics, 39*(1–4), 62–67.

Shapiro, S. L., Schwartz, G. E. R., & Santerre, C. (2002). Meditation and positive psychology. In C. R. Snyder & S. J. Lopez (Eds.), *The handbook of positive psychology* (pp. 632–645). New York: Oxford University Press.

Sharp, S. (2003). *The incarcerated woman: Rehabilitative programming in women's prisons.* Englewood Cliffs, NJ: Prentice Hall.

Shaver, P., Hazan, C., & Bradshaw, D. (1988). Love as attachment. In R. J. Sternberg & M. L. Barnes (Eds.), *The psychology of love* (pp. 68–99). New Haven, CT: Yale University Press.

Sheehan, W., & Garfinkel, B. D. (1987). Adolescent autoerotic deaths. *Journal of the American Academy of Child and Adolescent Psychiatry, 27,* 367–370.

Sherman, C. (2001, September 1). Depression may lurk in stress-response system. *Clinical Psychiatry News, 29,* 14.

Shigaki, C. L., Glass, B., & Schopp, L. H. (2006). Mindfulness-based stress reduction in medical settings. *Journal of Clinical Psychology in Medical Settings, 13*(3), 209–216.

Siegel, A. J., Sholar, M. B., Mendelson, J. H., Lukas, S. E., Kaurman, M. J., Renshaw, P. F., et al. (1999). Cocaine-induced erythrocytosis and increase in von Willebrand factor. *Archives of Internal Medicine, 159,* 1925–1930.

Siegel, R. K. (1986). MDMA: Nonmedical use and intoxication. *Journal of Psychoactive Drugs, 18,* 349–354.

Silberman, S. W. (1995). The relationship among love, marital satisfaction, and duration of marriage. *Dissertation Abstracts, 56,* 2341.

Silke, A. (1998). Cheshire-cat logic: The recurring theme of terrorist abnormality in psychological research. *Psychology, Crime, and Law, 4,* 51–69.

Singer, I. (1984a). *The nature of love: Vol. 1. Plato to Luther* (2nd ed.). Chicago: University of Chicago Press.

Singer, I. (1984b). *The nature of love: Vol. 2. Courtly and romantic.* Chicago: University of Chicago Press.

Singer, I. (1987). *The nature of love: Vol. 3. The modern world.* Chicago: University of Chicago Press.

Singer, J. L. (1976). Towards the scientific study of imagination. *Imaginations, Cognition, and Personality, 1*(1), 5–28.

Singer, J. L., & Kolligian, J. (1987, January). Personality: Developments in the study of private experience. *Annual Review of Psychology, 38,* 533–574.

Sinha, R., & Rounsaville, B. J. (2002). Sex differences in depressed substance abusers. *Journal of Clinical Psychiatry, 63,* 616–627.

Skinner, B. F. (1938). *The behavior of organisms: An experimental analysis.* Oxford, UK: Appleton-Century.

Skipp, C., & Campo-Flores, A. (2008, June 30). Rough ride above the South Beach "brothel bus." *Newsweek.* Retrieved January 20, 2009, from http://www.newsweek.com/id/144102/output/comments

Slater, L. (2006, February). Love. *National Geographic Magazine,* 32–49.

Smack Foundation, Inc. (2001, September 7). *Benzodiazepines.* Retrieved July 14, 2008, from http://www.smackfoundation.com/Benzodiazepines.htm

Smith, M., Jaffe, J., & Segal, J. (2008). *Post-traumatic stress disorder: Symptoms, types, and treatment. Helpguide.org.* Retrieved March 3, 2008, from http://www.Helpguide.org/mental/post-traumatic-stress-disorder-symptoms-treatment.htm

Smith, M. K. (2008). *Howard Gardner, multiple intelligences and education.* Retrieved July 10, 2008, from http://www.infed.org/thinkers/gardner.htm.

Snyder, C. R., & Lopez, S. J. (2007). *Positive psychology: The scientific and practical explorations of human strengths.* Thousand Oaks, CA: Sage Publications.

Society for Neuroscience. (2003, October). Sugar addiction. *Brain Briefings.* Washington, DC: Author. Retrieved January 5, 2009, from http://www.sfn.org/skins/main/pdf/BrainBriefings/BrainBriefings_Oct2003.pdf

Solomon, R. L. (1980). The opponent-process theory of acquired motivation: The costs of pleasure and the benefits of pain. *American Psychologist, 35*(8), 691–712.

Solomon, R. L., & Corbit, J. D. (1974). An opponent-process theory of motivation. I. Temporal dynamics of affect. *Psychological Review, 81*(2), 119–145.

Solomon, S., Greenberg, J., & Pyszczynski, T. (1991). Terror management theory of self-esteem. In C. R. Snyder & D. Forsyth (Eds.), *Handbook of social and clinical psychology: The health perspective* (pp. 21–40). New York: Pergamon.

Spencer, A. (2005). *The erotic economy.* Unpublished manuscript. Available from http://www.woodhullfoundation.org

Stampfer, M. J., Colditz, G. A., Willett, W. C., Speizer, F. E., & Hennekens, C. H. (1988). A prospective study of moderate alcohol consumption and the risk of coronary disease and stroke in women. *New England Journal of Medicine, 319*, 267–273.

Stanford University School of Medicine. (2006, October 17). *News release: Internet addiction: Stanford study seeks to define whether it's a problem.* Retrieved February 12, 2009, from http://med.stanford.edu/news_releases/2006/october/internet.html

Stein, L. (2008a). Can lifestyle changes bring out the best in genes? *Scientific American.* Retrieved July 27, 2008, from http://www.sciam.com/article.cfm?id=can-lifestyle-changes-bring-out-the-best-in-genes

Stein, L. (2008b). Work it out: More activity equals slower aging. *Scientific American.* Retrieved June 18, 2008, from http://www.sciam.com/article.cfm?id=new-study-links-exercise-to-longevity

Steinberg, M. B., Akincigil, A., Delnevo, C. D., Crystal, S., & Carson, J. L. (2006). Gender and age disparities for smoking-cessation treatment. *American Journal of Preventative Medicine, 30*(5), 405–412.

Stern, J. (2004). *Terror in the name of God: Why religious militants kill.* New York: HarperCollins.

Sternberg, R. J. (1986). A triangular theory of love. *Psychological Review, 93*, 119–135.

Stewart, J. (2000). Pathways to relapse: The neurobiology of drug- and stress-induced relapse to drug-taking. *Journal of Psychiatry Neuroscience, 25*, 125–146.

Stibich, M. (2007, June 21). Top 10 causes of death for ages 15–24. *About.com.* Retrieved February 11, 2009, from http://longevity.about.com/od/longevity101/tp/mortalityyoung.htm

St. Leger, A. S., Cochrane, A. L., & Moore, F. (1979). Factors associated with cardiac mortality in developed countries with particular reference to the consumption of wine. *Lancet, 1*, 1017–1020.

Strassman, R. (2001). *The spirit molecule: A doctor's revolutionary research into the biology of near-death and mystical experiences.* Rochester, VT: Park Street Press.

Stratton, V. N., & Zalanowski, A. H. (1999). The relationship between characteristic moods and most commonly listened to types of music. *Journal of Music Therapy, 36*, 145–152.

Subrahmanyam, K., & Greenfield, P. (2008). Online communications and adolescent relationships. *Future of Children, 18*(1), 119–146.

Substance Abuse and Mental Health Services Administration. (2005). *National Surveys on Drug Use and Health. Patterns and trends in nonmedical use of prescription pain reliever use: 2000–2005.* Washington, DC: U.S. Department of Health and Human Services.

Substance Abuse and Mental Health Services Administration. (2007a). Drug Abuse Warning Network, 2006: National estimates of drug-related emergency department visits (DAWN Series D-30, DHHS Publication No. SMA 08-4339). Rockville, MD: Author. Retrieved January 13, 2009, from http://dawninfo.samhsa.gov/files/ED2006/DAWN2k6ED.pdf

Substance Abuse and Mental Health Services Administration. (2007b, September/October). *Substance Abuse and Mental Health Services Administration News, 15*, 5.

Substance Abuse and Mental Health Services Administration. (2008). *Results from the 2007 National Survey on Drug Use and Health: National findings* (NSDUH Series H-34, DHHS Publication No. SMA 08-4343). Rockville, MD: Author.

Suellentrop, C. (2006, August 1). Mel Gibson's moment. *New York Times.*

Summers, N. (2007, August 21). A struggle inside AA. *Newsweek*. Retrieved July 9, 2008, from http://www.newsweek.com/id/35018

Sumnall, H. R., Woolfall, K., Edwards, S., Cole, J. C., & Beynon, C. M. (2008). Use, function, and subjective experiences of gamma-hydroxybutyrate (GHB). *Drug and Alcohol Dependence, 92*, 286–290.

Sun, A. P. (2006). Program factors related to women's substance abuse treatment retention and other outcomes: A review and critique. *Journal of Substance Abuse Treatment, 30*, 1–20.

Svetkey, B. (1997, July 18). Making contact. *Entertainment Weekly*. Retrieved February 6, 2007, from http://www.ew.com/ew/article/0,,288672,00.html.

Swaminathan, N. (2008, April). Can the brain be rebooted to stop drug addiction? *Scientific American*. Retrieved July 6, 2008, from http://www.sciam.com/article.cfm?id=can-the-brain-be-rebooted-to&print=true

Szasz, T. S. (1960). The myth of mental illness. *American Psychologist, 15*, 113–118.

Tanda, G., Pontieri, F. E., & Di Chiara, G. (1997). Cannabinoid and heroin activation of mesolimbic dopamine transmission by a common opioid receptor mechanism. *Science, 276*, 2048–2050.

Teasdale, J. D., Moore, R. G., Hayhurst, H., Pope, M., Williams, S., & Segal, Z. V. (2002). Metacognitive awareness and prevention of relapse in depression: Empirical evidence. *Journal of Consulting and Clinical Psychology, 70*, 275–287.

Teicher, M. H., Andersen, S. L., & Hostetter, J. C., Jr. (1995). Evidence for dopamine receptor pruning between adolescence and adulthood in striatum but not nucleus accumbens. *Brain Research. Developmental Brain Research, 89*(2), 167–172.

Templeton, J. (1998). *Worldwide laws of life: 200 eternal spiritual principles*. West Conshohocken, PA: Templeton Foundation Press.

Tennov, D. (1979). *Love and limerence: The experience of being in love*. New York: Stein and Day.

Ter Bogt, T. F. M., & Engels, R. C. M. E. (2005). "Partying" hard: Party style, motives for, and effects of MDMA use at rave parties. *Substance Use and Misuse, 40*(9–10), 1479–1502.

Thayer, A. M. (2006). Drugs to fight addiction. *Chemical & Engineering News, 84*(39), 21–44.

Thun, M. J., Peto, R., Lopez, A. D., Monaco, J. H., Henley, S. J., Heath, C. W., et al. (1997). Alcohol consumption and mortality among middle-aged and elderly U.S. adults. *New England Journal of Medicine, 337*, 1705–1714.

Timko, C., Moos, R. H., Finney, J. W., & Connell, E. G. (2002). Gender differences in help-utilization and the 8-year course of alcohol abuse. *Addiction, 97*, 877–889.

To avoid the Big C, stay small. (2007, November 3). *Economist*.

Tyre, P. (2005). Fighting anorexia: No one to blame. *Newsweek*. Retrieved July 1, 2008, from http://www.msnbc.msn.com/id/10219756/site/newsweek/print/1/displaymode/1098

Uhl, G. R., Liu, Q.-R., & Naiman, D. (2002, August). Substance abuse vulnerability loci: Converging genome scanning data. *Trends in Genetics, 18*, 420–425.

U.S. Department of Health and Human Services. (2004, October). *Alcohol alert: Alcohol's damaging effects on the brain*. Retrieved July 14, 2008, from http://pubs.niaaa.nih.gov/publications/aa63/aa63.htm

U.S. Weight Loss & Diet Control Market. (2005). Tampa, FL: Marketdata Enterprises.

Uva, J. L. (1995). Review: Autoerotic asphyxiation in the United States. *Journal of Forensic Sciences, 40*, 574–581.

Vaillant, G. (1983). *The natural history of alcoholism.* Cambridge, MA: Harvard University Press.

Vaillant, G. E. (1995). *The natural history of alcoholism revisited.* Cambridge, MA: Harvard University Press.

Veen, N., Selten, J. P., van der Tweel, W., Feller, H. W., Hoek, H., & Kahn, R. S. (2004). Cannabis use and age at onset of schizophrenia. *American Journal of Psychiatry, 161,* 501–506.

Velez, M. L., Montoya, I. D., Schwietzer, W., Golden, A., Jansson, L. M., Walters, V., et al. (2006). Exposure to violence among substance-dependent pregnant women and their children. *Journal of Substance Abuse Treatment, 30,* 31–38.

Virtual online worlds. (2006, September 28). *Economist.*

Vogt, D. (2007). *Women, trauma, and PTSD. National Center for Posttraumatic Stress Disorder Fact Sheet.* Washington, DC: U.S. Department of Veterans Affairs.

Vygotsky, L. S. (1978). *Mind in society: The development of higher psychological processes.* Cambridge, MA: Harvard University Press.

Wade, T. D., Bulik, C. M., Neale, M., & Kendler, K. S. (2000). Anorexia nervosa and major depression: Shared genetic and environmental risk factors. *American Journal of Psychiatry, 157*(3), 469–471.

Walter, C. (2008, January 31). Affairs of the lips: Why we kiss. *Scientific American.* Retrieved October 21, 2008, from http://www.freerepublic.com/focus/f-chat/1967046/posts

Wanberg, K. W., & Milkman, H. B. (2006). *Criminal conduct and substance abuse treatment: Strategies for self-improvement and change: The participant's workbook* (2nd ed.). Thousand Oaks, CA: Sage Publications.

Wanberg, K. W., & Milkman, H. B. (2008). *Criminal conduct and substance abuse treatment: Strategies for self-improvement and change: The provider's guide* (2nd ed). Thousand Oaks, CA: Sage Publications.

Watson, H., Khachaturian, H., Akil, H., Coy, D. H., & Goldstein, A. (1982). Comparison of the distribution of dynorphin systems and enkephalin systems in brain. *Science, 218*(4577), 1134–1136.

Watson, J. B. (1913). Psychology as the behaviorist views it. *Psychological Review, 20,* 158–177.

Watson, J. B. (1924). *Behaviorism.* New York: Norton.

Weil, A. (2004). *The marriage of the sun and moon: Dispatches from the frontiers of consciousness.* Boston: Houghton Mifflin Harcourt.

Weisner, C. (2005). Substance misuse: What place for women-only treatment programs? *Addiction, 100,* 7–8.

Werner, E. (1989, April). Children of the Garden Island. *Scientific American,* p. 106.

Wexler, A., & Wexler, S. (1992). *Facts on compulsive gambling and addiction.* Trenton: Council on Compulsive Gambling of New Jersey. (ERIC Document Reproduction Service No. ED372337)

White, T. L., Lejuez, C. W., & de Wit, H. (2007). Personality and gender differences in effects of d-amphetamine on risk taking. *Experimental and Clinical Psychopharmacology, 15*(6), 599–609.

Wikler, A. (1973). Dynamics of drug dependence: Implications of a conditioning theory for research and treatment. *Archives of General Psychiatry, 28,* 611–616.

Will, G. F. (2002). Electronic morphine. *Newsweek, 140*(22), 92.

Willett, W. C., & Stampfer, M. J. (2006). Eating to live: Rebuilding the food pyramid. *Scientific American, 16,* 18.

Williams-Quinlan, S. L. (2004). Guidelines for treatment of women in psychotherapy. In G. Koocher, J. Norcross, & S. Hill (Eds.), *Psychologists' Desk Reference* (2nd ed.). New York: Oxford University Press.

Will Wright on creating "The Sims" and "SimCity." (2000, November 30). [Chat transcript]. *CNN.com*. Retrieved from http://www.cnn.com/chat/transcripts/2000/12/1/wright.chat.

Winton, R., Blankstein, A., & Garvey, M. (2006, August 1). Sheriff's office debated Gibson's arrest report. *Los Angeles Times,* Edition A-1. Retrieved October 21, 2008, from http://articles.latimes.com/2006/aug/01/local/me-gibson1

Wise, R. A. (1996). Addictive drugs and brain stimulation reward. *Annual Review of Neuroscience, 19,* 319–340.

Witbrodt, J., Bond, J., Kaskutas, L. A., Weisner, C., Pating, D., & Moore, C. (2007). Day hospital and residential addiction treatment: Randomized and nonrandomized managed care clients. *Journal of Consulting and Clinical Psychology, 75*(6), 947–959.

Witkiewitz, K. A., & Marlatt, G. A. (2007). High-risk situations: Relapse as a dynamic process. In K. A. Witkiewitz & G. A. Marlatt (Eds.), *Therapist's guide to evidence-based relapse prevention* (pp. 19–33). London: Academic Press.

Wolfe, T. (1980). *The right stuff.* New York: Bantam.

Woods, S. C., West, D. B., Stein, L. J., McKay, L. D., Lotter, E. C., Porte, S. G., et al. (1981, March). Peptides and the control of meal size. *Diabetologia, 20*(1), 305–313.

World Health Organization. (1948). *Preamble to the Constitution of the World Health Organization as adopted by the International Health Conference,* New York, 19 June–22 July 1946 (Official Records of the World Health Organization, no. 2, p. 100) and entered into force on April 7, 1948.

World Health Organization. (2007, December). *Third meeting on influenza vaccines that induce broad spectrum and long-lasting immune responses.* Geneva, Switzerland: Author. Retrieved October 21, 2008, from http://www.who.int/vaccine_research/diseases/influenza/meeting_071203/en/print.html

Wright, J., Fasco, M., & Thase, M. (2006). *Learning cognitive-behavioral therapy: An illustrated guide.* Arlington, VA: American Psychiatric Publishing.

Wurtman, J. J., & Marquis, N. F. (2006). *The serotonin power diet: Use your brain's natural chemistry to cut cravings, curb emotional overeating, and lose weight.* Emmaus, PA: Rodale Books.

Wurtman, R. J., & Wurtman, J. J. (1989). Carbohydrates and depression. *Scientific American,* January, 68–75.

Wurtman, R. J., & Wurtman, J. J. (1995). Brain serotonin, carbohydrate craving, obesity, and depression. *Obesity Research, 4,* 477S–480S.

Young, K. S. (2004). Internet addiction: A new clinical phenomenon and its consequences. *American Behavioral Scientist, 48*(4), 402–415.

Zernike, K. (2006). A more addictive meth emerges as states curb homemade type. In H. T. Wilson (Ed.), *Annual editions: Drugs, society and behavior 2007/2008* (pp. 71–72). Dubuque, IA: McGraw-Hill.

Zimmer, C. (2008, September 1). Spore: When games and science collide. *Discover.* Retrieved January 15, 2009, from http://blogs.discovermagazine.com/loom/2008/09/01/spore-when-games-and-science-collide

Zinberg, N. E. (1984). *Drug, set, and setting: The basis for controlled intoxicant use.* New Haven, CT: Yale University Press.

Zuckerman, M. (1994). *Behavioral expressions and biosocial bases of sensation seeking.* New York: Cambridge University Press.

Zuckerman, M. (2007). *Sensation seeking and risky behavior.* Washington, DC: American Psychological Association.

Index _____

About the Authors _____

Harvey B. Milkman, PhD, received his baccalaureate degree from City College of New York and his doctorate from Michigan State University. He is currently professor of psychology at Metropolitan State College of Denver.

His doctoral research was conducted with William Frosch, MD, at Bellevue Psychiatric Hospital in New York City, on the "User's Drug of Choice." From 1980 to 1981, he completed a sabbatical exploration of addictive behavior in Africa, India, and Southeast Asia; in the year 1985–1986, he was recipient of a Fulbright-Hays lectureship award at the National University of Malaysia. He has represented the United States Information Agency as a consultant and featured speaker in Australia, Brazil, Iceland, the Netherlands, Peru, Turkey, and the former Yugoslavia. In March of 1998, Dr. Milkman was the keynote speaker at the 21st Annual Treating the Addictions Conference, hosted by the Cambridge Hospital, in affiliation with Harvard Medical School. He is principal author with Stanley Sunderwirth of "The Chemistry of Craving," and author of "Better Than Dope," featured articles in *Psychology Today,* October 1983 and April 2001, respectively. From September 1992 to June 2002, he was author, principal investigator, and director of Project Self-Discovery: Artistic Alternatives for At-Risk Youth, a national demonstration model funded by the Center for Substance Abuse Prevention and the Edward Byrne Foundation.

In addition to having authored numerous articles on the personality characteristics of drug abusers and behavioral addiction, Dr. Milkman is principal author of a number of titles including *Craving for Ecstasy: The Consciousness and Chemistry of Escape* (with Stanley Sunderwirth, 1987, 1998, in press), *Pathways to Self-Discovery and Change: Criminal Conduct and Substance Abuse Treatment for Adolescents* (with Kenneth Wanberg, 2005), and *Criminal Conduct and Substance Abuse Treatment for Women in Correctional Settings: Adjunct Provider's Guide* (with Kenneth Wanberg and Barbara Gagliardi, 2008). He is also principal author, with Kenneth Wanberg, of *Cognitive-Behavioral Treatment: A Review and Discussion for Corrections Professionals* (National Institute of Corrections, May 2007; available at http://www.nationalinstituteofcorrections.gov/Library/021657 www.nicic.org).

Dr. Milkman is coauthor of the following works: *Criminal Conduct and Substance Abuse Treatment: Strategies for Self-Improvement and Change: The Participant's Workbook* (with Wanberg, 1998, 2006), *Criminal Conduct and Substance Abuse Treatment: Strategies for Self-Improvement and Change: The Provider's Guide* (with Wanberg, 1998, 2008), and *Driving With CARE: Education and Treatment of the Alcohol or Other Drug Driving Offender* (with Wanberg and David Timkin, 2006).

In addition, Dr. Milkman is coeditor of *Addictions: Multidisciplinary Perspectives and Treatments* (with Howard Shaffer, 1983), winner of the Choice Award for outstanding academic books, and *Treatment Choices for Alcoholism and Substance Abuse* (with Lloyd Sederer, 1990).

Stanley G. Sunderwirth, PhD, is Professor Emeritus at Indiana University–Purdue University Columbus. Dr. Sunderwirth received his doctorate in organic chemistry from The Ohio State University in 1955 and has held teaching positions at Colorado State University and at Pittsburg State University in Kansas. He has been the chairman of the Chemistry Department of Pittsburg State University, Dean and Vice President at Metropolitan State College, and Vice President at Community College of Philadelphia. Dr. Sunderwirth has received five Fulbright Awards, four to Uruguay and one to India.

Dr. Sunderwirth has authored many scientific publications on brain chemistry and its effect on mind, mood, and behavior. These include "Harnessing Brain Chemicals: The Influence of Molecules on Mind, Mood, and Behavior," in *Treatment Choices for Alcoholism and Substance Abuse* (edited by H. Milkman and L. Sederer, 1990), and "Addiction and Neurotransmission," in *The Addictions: Multidisciplinary Perspectives and Treatments* (edited by H. Milkman and H. Shaffer, 1985). He is coauthor with Dr. Milkman of "The Chemistry of Craving" (*Psychology Today,* October 1983); *Craving for Ecstasy: The Consciousness and Chemistry of Escape* (1987, 1998); and *Pathways to Pleasure: The Consciousness and Chemistry of Optimal Living* (1993).

About the Illustrator

Kenneth Axen, PhD, is a biomedical research scientist who has written and illustrated books and journal articles on physiology, exercise physiology, and pulmonary disease. He is currently a clinical associate professor at the School of Medicine at New York University. He is also an adjunct full professor at Brooklyn College, CUNY, where he teaches human physiology and conducts research based on the relationship between obesity and diabetes.

Supporting researchers for more than 40 years

Research methods have always been at the core of SAGE's publishing program. Founder Sara Miller McCune published SAGE's first methods book, *Public Policy Evaluation*, in 1970. Soon after, she launched the *Quantitative Applications in the Social Sciences* series—affectionately known as the "little green books."

Always at the forefront of developing and supporting new approaches in methods, SAGE published early groundbreaking texts and journals in the fields of qualitative methods and evaluation.

Today, more than 40 years and two million little green books later, SAGE continues to push the boundaries with a growing list of more than 1,200 research methods books, journals, and reference works across the social, behavioral, and health sciences. Its imprints—Pine Forge Press, home of innovative textbooks in sociology, and Corwin, publisher of PreK–12 resources for teachers and administrators—broaden SAGE's range of offerings in methods. SAGE further extended its impact in 2008 when it acquired CQ Press and its best-selling and highly respected political science research methods list.

From qualitative, quantitative, and mixed methods to evaluation, SAGE is the essential resource for academics and practitioners looking for the latest methods by leading scholars.

For more information, visit **www.sagepub.com**.